palgrave macmillan law masters

# constitutional and administrative law

## john alder

Professor of Law, University of Newcastle-upon-Tyne

### Fifth edition

**Series editor:** Marise Cremona

*Professor of European Commercial Law,*
*Centre for Commercial Law Studies*
*Queen Mary University of London*

This edition first published 2005 by
PALGRAVE MACMILLAN
Houndmills, Basingstoke, Hampshire RG21 6XS and
175 Fifth Avenue, New York, N.Y. 10010
Companies and representatives throughout the world

PALGRAVE MACMILLAN is the global academic imprint of the Palgrave Macmillan division of St. Martin's Press, LLC and of Palgrave Macmillan Ltd. Macmillan® is a registered trademark in the United States, United Kingdom and other countries. Palgrave is a registered trademark in the European Union and other countries.

ISBN-13: 978–1–4039–3392–8
ISBN-10: 1–4039–3392–8

This book is printed on paper suitable for recycling and made from fully managed and sustained forest sources.

A catalogue record for this book is available from the British Library.

10  9  8  7  6  5  4  3  2
14  13  12  11  10  09  08  07  06  05

Printed and bound in Great Britain by
Creative Print & Design (Wales), Ebbw Vale

palgrave macmillan law masters

# constitutional and administrative law

O rk

£4-50 arezon

2-75 del.

*Series editor:* Marise Cremona

*Business Law* (2nd edn)   Stephen Judge

*Company Law* (5th edn)   Janet Dine

*Constitutional and Administrative Law* (5th edn)   John Alder

*Contract Law* (6th edn)   Ewan McKendrick

*Conveyancing* (3rd edn)   Priscilla Sarton

*Criminal Law* (4th edn)   Jonathan Herring

*Employment Law* (4th edn)   Deborah J. Lockton

*Evidence* (2nd edn)   Raymond Emson

*Family Law* (4th edn)   Kate Standley

*Housing Law and Policy*   David Cowan

*Intellectual Property Law* (3rd edn)   Tina Hart and Linda Fazzani

*Land Law* (5th edn)   Kate Green and Joe Cursley

*Landlord and Tenant Law* (5th edn)   Margaret Wilkie and Godfrey Cole

*Law of the European Union* (3rd edn)   Jo Shaw

*Law of Succession*   Catherine Rendell

*Legal Method* (5th edn)   Ian McLeod

*Legal Theory* (3rd edn)   Ian McLeod

*Social Security Law*   Robert East

*Torts* (3rd edn)   Alastair Mullis and Ken Oliphant

# Contents

# Preface

As in previous editions my aims are firstly to identify the main principles of United Kingdom constitutional law in the context of the political and legal values that influence their development and secondly to provide the main competing arguments. This edition has been restructured so as to focus upon contemporary topics that are common to most constitutional law or public law syllabuses and to bring out important underlying themes, and to emphasise difficult and controversial issues.

The advent of the Human Rights Act, the increasing informal powers of the executive and the government's recent forays into constitutional reform have drawn attention to the general principles and values underlying the constitution. I have therefore devoted more space than in previous editions to the topics of the rule of law, the separation of powers, the accountability of the executive, judicial review and human rights. To make room I have removed some specialised chapters including those on local government, the police and the armed forces. Important principles relating to these are of course discussed in more general contexts. I have also reorganised some parts, particularly those on devolution, to bring out general principles more clearly and, in the case of devolution, to encourage comparisons between the different regimes.

The most important development since the last edition has been the introduction of the Constitutional Reform Bill, which attempts to restructure the formal relationship between the judiciary and the executive and which has not on the whole been well received. There has also been substantial legislation increasing executive and police powers – ostensibly to combat terrorism – and considerable development in the case law relating to human rights. The Freedom of Information Act is now in force. Attempts to reform the House of Lords and to rationalise the incoherent mix of laws and practices that governs the civil service and its relationship with politicians are in progress. In the case of the House of Lords there remains little agreement as to the direction of reform. Electoral reform also remains in the doldrums despite claims that the parliamentary electoral system may be biased in favour of the ruling party.

Three main themes underlie this book. First, there is the tradition that the unwritten constitution of the UK relies heavily on informal practices generated by a circle of 'insiders' selected by the government of the day and which can therefore easily be manipulated for short-term reasons. This can be set against the claim that a constitution should provide an external framework that constrains the power of temporary administrations. The topics of control of government spending (expanded in this edition) and the relationships between ministers and civil servants particularly illustrate this theme. The second theme is the tension between 'legal' (in the sense of decisions made by the courts) and 'democratic' controls over government. The Human Rights Act 1998 has become a platform from which judges sometimes make grand pronouncements about such matters as democracy, freedom, equality and liberalism. All these notions are highly uncertain and controversial. Therefore the third theme is the importance in a free society of keeping alive different points of view and not attempting to impose any particular orthodoxy on the people. Chapter 1 therefore attempts a broad account of the main different moral and political points of view that have influenced the constitution.

Part I discusses general principles. These include political values (Chapter 1), the sources of the constitution (Chapter 2), how powers are divided up and controlled (Chapters 3, 4 and 8) and pervasive legal values and doctrines (Chapters 5, 6 and 7). Chapter 3 offers an overview of the structure of the constitution and a guide to the more detailed discussion of the main institutions in Part II. Part III deals with conflict between the state and the individual. It includes the powers of the courts to review government action (expanded in this edition), the Human Rights Act and selected topics which particularly relate to the political freedoms that underpin democracy. These include freedom of expression and assembly, access to information, and national security. In this area, selection is exceptionally difficult. In view of the burgeoning of specialist courses on human rights and civil liberties, I have reluctantly excluded discussions of moral freedoms, obscenity and so on, and of routine police powers.

I am extremely grateful to those who directly and indirectly helped me to produce this edition. These include, pre-eminently, Barry Hough of Bournemouth University, who made substantial contributions to the topics of conventions and the royal prerogative and who contributed the sections on ministerial responsibility, Richard Mullender of Newcastle Law School, who contributed to the section on freedom of expression, Ann Sinclair of Newcastle Law School, who revised the tables, and Rhiannon Talbot of Newcastle Law School, who contributed the section on anti-terrorist law. I am of course wholly responsible for all errors and omissions.

JOHN ALDER (alder@netbreeze.co.uk)

## Note on further reading

The references to books and articles in the text are to more detailed or advanced reading related to points of particular controversy, obscurity or difficulty. They are not meant to be essential to understanding the text itself. The Further Reading at the end of each chapter is more general and emphasises fundamental and controversial issues for those who require greater depth or more ideas, arguments and points of view. Some of the journal articles cited, particularly in relation to judicial review and human rights, overlap but I have tried to balance the main points of view.

Unless otherwise stated, the main classical works cited throughout are as follows:

Bagehot, W., *The English Constitution*, 2nd edn, 1902 (London, Kegan Paul).

Dicey, A.V., *An Introduction to the Law of the Constitution*, 8th edn, 1915 (London, Macmillan).

Hobbes, T., *Leviathan*, Minogue, K. (ed.) 1973 (London, Dent).

Locke, J., *Two Treatises of Government*, Laslett, P., (ed.), 1960 (Cambridge, CUP).

Mill, J.S., *Utilitarianism, On Liberty and Considerations of Representative Government*, Acton, H.B. (ed.), 1972 (London, Dent).

Montesquieu, *'L'Esprit de Lois'* extracted in Stirk, P.M.R. and Weigall, D.W., *An Introduction to Political Ideas*, 1995 (London, Cassell).

Paine, T., *The Thomas Paine Reader*, Foot, M. and Kramnick, I. (eds), 1987 (London, Penguin).

Rousseau, J.J., *The Social Contract*, Cranston, M. (ed.), 1968 (London, Penguin).

The law is stated on the basis of sources available on 7th January 2005.

# Table of cases

# Table of statutes

# Part I

# General principles

# Chapter I

# Introduction: constitutional issues and structures

> Government, even in its best state, is but a necessary evil; in its worst state, an intolerable one. Government, like dress is the badge of lost innocence; the palaces of kings are built upon the ruins of the bowers of paradise. (Thomas Paine, *Common Sense* 1776, Chapter 1)

## Key words

- Written and unwritten constitutions
- Custom and reason
- The informal constitution
- Positive and negative freedom
- Accountability
- Different kinds of liberalism
- Republicanism
- Different kinds of democracy: parliamentary government; party government
- Limitations on democracy
- Disagreement: incommensurable values

Constitutional law concerns the struggle between rival claimants to govern us, how our rulers are chosen, called to account and removed, and the rights of the individual against the rulers. In this chapter I shall introduce some general ideas, themes and perspectives. It should be borne in mind that there is no single 'correct' recipe for a good constitution. A constitution is the result of historical events and personalities. The political and legal concepts that appear in this book have filtered into our culture, thereby influencing people to make and accept particular arrangements – all of which are temporary and changeable.

## 1.1 What is a Constitution?

A constitution provides a framework of rules that creates the structure and functions of a human organisation. Any organisation might have a constitution, although an organisation that depends on close personal bonds such as a family is unlikely to do so. We are concerned with the organisation of a country comprising millions of people with few common purposes capable of giving shape to a constitution.

Thus constitutional law is concerned with conflicts both between different groups struggling for power and between those in power and individuals. Some constitutions make grandiose and sometimes perplexing claims to shared ideals and values. For example, the Canadian *Charter of Rights and Freedoms* announces that 'Canada is founded upon principles that recognise the supremacy of God and the rule of law', and the proposed European Constitution assures us of 'the central role of the human person' and 'social and territorial cohesion'.

The legal and political aspects of a constitution are interrelated. Indeed law is a manifestation of politics, a term that broadly means the organisation of a community and particularly the management of disagreement within it. Both are therefore concerned with ideals of fairness and justice. Law can be distinguished from other aspects of politics in at least the following respects. It relies on impersonal and usually written sources of authority in the form of binding general rules. It emphasises certainty, coherence and formal procedures for settling disputes. Most fundamentally, law authorises violence against individuals in the name of the community. By contrast, politics is concerned primarily with outcomes, for which law is only one among several instruments, and is more willing than law to use, for example, personal relationships, rewards and compromises in order to achieve those outcomes.

Many writers have tried to capture the essence of a constitution. Professor A.V. Dicey (Dicey, 1915, p. 22) gives a bland definition:

all rules which directly or indirectly affect the distribution and exercise of the sovereign power in the state.

Sir John Laws (1996), a contemporary Court of Appeal judge, described a constitution as:

that set of legal rules which governs the relationship in a state between the ruler and the ruled.

He takes a narrow approach focusing on law and the individual. This ignores the fact that much of the UK constitution comprises understandings and practices that are not legally binding and also concerns the internal relationships of government. By contrast Anthony King, a political scientist, asserts that:

[a] constitution is the set of the most important rules that regulate the relations among the different parts of the government of a given country and also the relations between the different parts of the government and the people of the country. (*Does the United Kingdom Still Have a Constitution?* 2001, London: Sweet & Maxwell) 2001)

Freidrich exemplifies another politically orientated approach which stresses the consent of the community:

a constitution is the ordering and dividing of the exercise of political power by that group in an existent community who are able to secure the consent of the community and who thereby make manifest the power of the community itself. (*Limited Government: A Comparison*, 1974, p. 21)

Tully (2002) offers a legally orientated definition capturing the notion that the constitution has a special status:

the cluster of 'supreme' or 'essential' principles, rules and procedures to which other laws, institutions and governing authorities within the association are subject.

Marshall (2003), a political theorist, identifies four possible meanings of constitution:

(a) the combination of legal and non-legal ... rules that currently provide the framework of government and regulate the behaviour of the major political actors;
(b) a single instrument promulgated at a particular point in time and adopted by some generally agreed authorisation procedure under the title 'constitution' or equivalent rubric such as 'basic law;'
(c) the totality of legal rules ... (wherever contained) that affect the working of government;
(d) a list of statutes or instruments that have an entrenched status and can be amended or repealed only by a special procedure.

Nothing much seems to link these four. Senses (b) and (d) say nothing about the purpose or content of the rules in question, which could relate for example to the running of a golf club. The United Kingdom, in common with every state, has a constitution certainly in sense (c) and possibly in sense (a), if there is sufficient coherence in it to be called a framework. The UK does not have a constitution in senses (b) or (d).

### 1.1.1 Written Constitutions

The most important source of disagreement relates to Marshall's sense (b). This identifies what is usually called a 'written constitution' containing in a single document the main constitutional principles governing the state. The idea of a written constitution is a legacy of the revolutionary period in eighteenth- and early nineteenth-century Europe when, with mixed success, widespread uprisings challenged traditional aristocratic, colonial and religious regimes. Since the French Revolution (1789) almost every nation has adopted a written constitution, sometimes as a reaction against a hated previous regime and sometimes to mark a new event such as independence from colonial status.

Alone among the major nations of the world the UK has no written constitution in this sense, although some of our constitution – in Marshall's sense (a) – is written down in the form of particular pieces of legislation or case law dealing with constitutional matters. The historical reasons for this concern the fact that our revolution in 1688 sought to assert traditional customs and practices favoured by the aristocracy and gentry against, what was then, modernistic claims to absolute rule of the king. A wholesale redesign of the constitution was not therefore politically opportune. During the following centuries the aristocracy gradually conceded power without reaching the point of revolution (Chapter 3). We also have a cultural tendency to trust in the personalities that claim to rule us rather than in formal rules. For example, the office of Prime Minister has developed gradually during the last three centuries by virtue of practices known as 'conventions' (Chapter 2) but has no legal basis.

Those familiar with 'written' constitutions sometimes suggest that the UK does not have a constitution. However, such an argument is, at least historically, wrong in that the term 'constitution', although originally meaning a government enactment, was in use in its modern sense in 1610 (see McIlwain, C.H., *Constitutionalism Ancient and Modern*, 1947, London, Cornell University Press, Chapter 1). More importantly, the substantive content of a constitution can be the same whether or not it is written. The matter could be regarded essentially one of convenience in selecting and storing the information. Dicey (1915) pointed out a written constitution can be torn up whereas the unwritten constitution of the UK is embedded in the structure of the law as a whole (Chapter 5). One might revere a written constitution, as is the case in the USA, but the same is true of any convenient symbol. For example, Walter Bagehot (1826–77) thought that mystical reverence for royalty was essential to the authority of the UK constitution (or, as he considered it, the 'English' constitution).

Moreover, it cannot reasonably be believed that a written constitution can be self-contained, self-applying and comprehensive. As in the case of any organisation, unwritten standards, rules and practices are used to fill gaps in the written document, to adjust to new circumstances and provide background to interpret the document (Chapter 2). It is sometimes said that a written constitution encourages the use of abstract linguistic legalistic techniques at the expense of the underlying political realities. However, courts have often emphasised the need for a broad and flexible approach to constitutional interpretation that stresses the underlying moral and political context (see e.g. *Robinson* v *Secretary of State for Northern Ireland* (2002); Chapter 4). Indeed the language of a written constitution may be very vague leaving plenty of room for disagreement. For example, the US constitution has been interpreted at different times as both justifying and outlawing slavery.

Even without a written constitution judges give special weight to rights, principles or statutes that they consider to be 'constitutional rights'. To this end they require Parliament, the lawmaker, to use express words or necessary implication in order to exclude such a right (Chapters 5, 7). Compensation can also be awarded for 'misfeasance in public office' against a public official who violates a constitutional right even where no loss or damage has occurred (*Ashby* v *White* (1703): right to vote; *Watkins* v *Secretary of State* (2004): interference with prisoner's access to lawyer). In *R* v *Secretary of State ex parte Simms* [1999] 3 All ER 400, 412 (right of a prisoner to freedom of speech), Lord Hoffmann stated that we apply 'principles of constitutionality little different from those which exist in countries where the power of the legislature is expressly limited by a constitutional document.' (See also Laws LJ in *Thoburn* v *Sunderland City Council* (2002): European Community law, and *R* v *Lord Chancellor ex parte Witham* (1997): right of access to the courts; Lord Browne-Wilkinson in *R* v *Secretary of State ex parte Pierson* [1998] AC 539, 575. Moreover, proposed legislation that Parliament regards as 'of first class constitutional importance' is examined by a committee of the whole House rather than the normal 'standing committee' (Chapter 11).

On the other hand, without an authoritative written document we might reasonably disagree as to what counts as a constitutional right or constitutional legislation. The above are merely examples of what the courts consider important in a 'liberal democracy' (see Brooke LJ in *Watkins* above). More fundamentally, if subject to a special procedure, a written constitution provides some assurance that important rules have the consent of the people outside the control of temporary ruling regimes. In *Cullen Chief Constable of the RUC* (2004) (prisoner denied right to access to a solicitor), Lord Hutton (at [46]) said that a written constitution does have a special significance. He referred to a right:

> which a democratic assembly representing the people has enshrined in a written constitution. In the latter case a person who has suffered harm can recover damages the written constitution being 'clear testimony that an added value is attached to the protection of that right'. (see *Mohammed* v *State* [1999] 2 AC 111 at 123)

### 1.1.2  The Informal Constitution

A written constitution encourages a rationalistic process of constitutional design whereas an unwritten constitution tends to develop pragmatically in response to short-term factors. It can be argued that, in a matter as large and open to disagreement as a constitution, human beings are not capable of sensible grand designs and that the trial and error approach is preferable. Edmund Burke (1729–97), a prominent parliamentarian and conservative thinker, claimed that the constitution has special status by virtue of its being rooted in long-standing custom and tradition of which the aristocracy were the guardians. Burke regarded attempts to engineer constitutions on the basis of abstract reason as ultimately leading to tyranny. This is because he believed that humans with their limited understanding and knowledge are inevitably at the mercy of unforeseen events and that reasoning based on abstract general principles, by trying to squeeze us into rigid templates, is a potential instrument of oppression:

> the age of chivalry is gone … That of sophisters, economists and calculators has succeeded; and the glory of Europe is extinguished for ever. (*Reflections on the Revolution in France*, 1790)

On the other hand, an unwritten constitution invites those in power to invent or manipulate 'customs' or 'conventions' to suit their own interests. The claim that the informal constitution can easily adjust to changing politics exemplifies this. Thus Burke's adversary, the democratic activist Thomas Paine (1737–1809) labelled the British government as 'power without right'. In 'The Rights of Man', Paine asserted that, without a written constitution authorised directly by the people there was no solid constitution (*The Thomas Paine Reader*, 1987, 220–1, 285–96). Moreover the European Court of Human Rights has recently emphasised the need to justify restrictions on individual rights on the basis of 'considered debate', rather than on 'unquestioning and passive obedience to a historic tradition' (*Hirst v UK* (2004); Chapter 10).

Many of the rules concerning the workings of government are derived from no more than the practices of those involved expressed in an uncoordinated profusion of: 'concordats', 'memoranda', 'codes of practice' and the like which act as a barrier against outsiders. This is particularly true in the area of financial controls over government and where government holds inquiries into its own activities (Chapters 10, 13).

Daintith and Page (*The Executive in the Constitution*, 1999, Chapter 1) classify those who attempt to understand the unwritten constitution as 'foxes', 'hedgehogs', 'rude little boys' and 'Humpty Dumpties'. A fox regards the constitution as no more than a collection of working practices developed by those who join the government enterprise. A hedgehog looks for a single grand overarching principle such as parliamentary supremacy (this volume, Chapter 7) or the power of the Prime Minister (this volume, Chapter 13). It is unlikely that in a matter as complex as government any such principle is credible. A rude little boy therefore asserts that the emperor has no clothes; the constitution being a fiction disguising a power struggle between control freaks. Humpty Dumpties, who probably represent most academic commentators, seek to explain the constitution on the basis of vague theories of their own such as liberalism, fairness social welfare etc., sometimes claiming that these ideals are inherent in the rules. We shall meet examples of each approach throughout the book.

## 1.2 Forms of Government

In a tradition dating back at least to Aristotle, three fundamental types of government can be identified. These are monarchy, or rule by one person; aristocracy: literally rule by a group of the 'best' people; and democracy: rule by the many or the people as a whole. According to Aristotle each form of constitution has its virtues but also corresponding vices or deviations. The virtues exist when the ruler rules for the benefit of others, the vices when the ruler rules for the benefit of itself.

The main merit of monarchy is its authority since monarchs have a quasi-godlike status. The corresponding defect is despotism. The merit of aristocracy is wisdom, its defects are oligarchy (rule by a selfish group). The merit of democracy is consent of the community, its defect is factionalism and, ultimately, mob tyranny. Aristotle postulated a vicious cycle in which a monarch becomes a despot, is deposed by an aristocracy which turns into oligarchy and is overthrown by a popular rebellion. The ensuing democracy degenerates into chaos that is resolved by the emergence of a dictator who takes on the characteristics of a monarch and so on.

Aristotle therefore favoured what he called polity, a 'mixed government' combining all three (but loaded in favour of the middle classes) and with 'checks and balances' between different branches of government. This strategy remains at the heart of modern constitutional design. However a cynical view, 'the iron law of oligarchy', claims that, whatever form the constitution takes, power will inevitably accumulate in the hands of a group of selfish cronies – a King by whatever name and his courtiers. In contemporary conditions this might well be a political party:

> who says organisation says oligarchy ... the oligarchical structure of the building suffocates the basic democratic principle. (Robert Michels, 1966, in Lipset (ed.), *Political Parties, New York: Free Press*)

Western European constitutions have also been influenced by three broad and overlapping perspectives or ideals of political thought. They are loosely termed liberalism, republicanism and communitarianism. They share overlapping ingredients albeit for different purposes and with different outcomes. Each of them has played a part in influencing the UK constitution.

Liberalism is based on the idea of individual freedom. It assumes that the individual is valuable for its own sake, emphasises private life and regards each as responsible for deciding his or her own way of life ('autonomy'). Republicanism favours the notion of equal citizens participating actively in public life for the common good, the Aristotelian notion of the 'virtuous citizen'. There has been a recent revival of interest in republican ideas stimulated by evidence of widespread apathy among voters and disenchantment with political processes remote from popular experience. Republicanism shades into communitarianism which stresses the social nature of human beings, regarding the individual primarily as a component of the community.

In the following sections we shall discuss these ideals and indicate their main constitutional implications. We should not expect any constitution to correspond to any one model. Each model represents a partial truth about human nature so that a given constitution is likely to be a mixture of all of them in different combinations changing with the dominant personalities and circumstances of the time.

## 1.3 Hobbes: The Impersonal State and Individualism

A fundamental change in political thinking emerged in the sixteenth century when the church and the state became separated. The idea of the state as an impersonal organisation intended to serve everyone was revived from classical antiquity by republican thinkers such as Machiavelli (1469–1527). Thomas Hobbes (1588–1679) was one of the earliest English exponents of this approach and, although not a liberal, generated ideas that are basic to liberalism.

Hobbes published his most influential work, *Leviathan*, in 1651 following a time of widespread political unrest when England was in the grip of religious turmoil and civil war between king and Parliament. He tried to explain the existence of the state without drawing upon religion. Hobbes doubted whether it was possible to discover objective truth about anything although, confusingly, he thought that reason was objective. He had a strongly individualistic approach and believed that human affairs involve endless disagreement and, therefore, that a constitution has solid foundations only in the minimum on which it is possible rationally to agree. This is the preservation of life and, therefore, a need for someone to settle disputes and keep order.

Hobbes did not believe that humans are inherently wicked but thought that our different ideas of good inevitably set us in conflict with each other: a war of 'all against all' so that, without government, we would destroy each other. According to Hobbes, outside the private sphere of family and personal relationships we are motivated by three impulses: competition, fear and the desire for power over others. We constantly strive to fulfil new desires in a never-ending and ultimately doomed search for what he called 'felicity'. Hobbes therefore argued that any government is better than none.

Hobbes's most famous passage encapsulates both his basic principle and the beauty of his language:

Hereby it is manifest, that during the time men live without a common Power to keep them all in awe, they are in that condition which is called Warre; and such a warre, as is of every man against every man ... In such condition, there is no place for Industry: because the fruit thereof is uncertain; and consequently no Culture of the Earth, no Navigation, nor use of the commodities that may be imported by Sea; no commodious Building; no Instruments of moving and removing such things as require much force; no knowledge of the face of the Earth; no account of Time; no Arts; no Letters; no Society; and which is worst of all, continuall feare, and danger of violent death; And the life of man, solitary, poore, nasty, brutish and short. (*Leviathan*, p. 65)

Hobbes provided an early example of the 'social contract' device which some theorists even today (e.g Rawls, below) employ as a hypothetical basis of a constitution. The social contract is an imaginary mechanism for deciding what kind of constitution rational beings in a 'state of nature' would hypothetically agree upon. It asserts that government depends on the consent of the governed which Hobbes thought to be the only rational possibility, hence his relevance to contemporary democratic ideas.

Hobbes believed that humans have certain 'natural' rights based on keeping promises, respect for individual freedom and equality: 'Do not that to another, which thou wouldest not have done to thyself' (*Leviathan*, pp. 14, 15). However he regarded these as meaningless without laws. Hobbes's hypothetical contract is made between the people, who agree with each other to surrender their natural freedom to a sovereign: the 'Leviathan', who makes and enforces the laws. The sovereign is not itself a party to the social contract which produces a 'covenant', a one-sided promise, to obey. In order to minimise disagreement, the sovereign must be a single unitary body, an 'artificial man'. This could be either a monarch or an assembly. Hobbes's sovereign has no special qualifications for ruling but is merely the representative of the community.

Hobbes's government has two crucial features. Firstly, because of the uncertainty of human affairs, Leviathan must have unlimited power since otherwise there would be the very disagreement that the sovereign exists to resolve. Hobbes thought that by definition the sovereign can never act unjustly to a subject because the subject has agreed to accept every decision of the sovereign. He recognised however that some methods of government might be better than others and, in the later part of his work, *The Dialogues*, made many suggestions such as that the sovereign should act through general laws and should consult Parliament. However, Hobbes rejected the view of the judges that law is 'artificial reason' that resides in the learning of an elite group (i.e. themselves) with which the king is not qualified to interfere.

Secondly, Hobbes's sovereign exists for one purpose only, that of preserving life by keeping order and has no authority to act for any other purpose. 'When the realm is at peace Leviathan sleeps.' According to Hobbes, the obligation of the sovereign derives from its gratitude to the people for the free gift of power. Thus the sovereign should act 'so that the giver shall have no just occasion to repent him of his gift' and 'all the duties of the rulers are contained in this one sentence, the safety of the people is the supreme law.' Therefore we have an inalienable right of self-defence even against the sovereign. However, Hobbes was clear that it is for the ruler alone to decide whether it needs to exercise its powers and provided no legal remedy against a ruler that exceeded its power.

Hobbes's ideas have an important influence on the modern constitution in that they identify recurring themes:

- They emphasise scientific rationality at the expense of custom and tradition.
- They promote the ideas that the ruler is the representative of the community and that government depends on the consent of the people.
- They emphasise what is perhaps the most pervasive dilemma in a constitution, that between security and justice.
- They embody the principle that all citizens are equal. No one should have powers, or rights or be subject to special obligations based on factors such as birth, custom, social status, or religion.
- Hobbes encourages change and frees the individual from commitments to the past. This challenges the tradition in English constitutional thought that custom is an indication of success and should not be lightly changed.
- Freedom is the natural state of affairs as opposed to a gift bestowed by authority. It is true that the sovereign can make any law but, unless it positively does so, the individual is free to do what he or she likes: 'freedom lies in the silence of the laws' (*Entick* v *Carrington* (1765)).
- The distinction between the public and the private sphere. In relation to areas of life not controlled by the state, namely those where public order and safety are not at risk, what I do is not the state's business.
- Hobbes's insistence on an absolute sovereign has influenced what many believe to be the central doctrine of the UK constitution, that of unlimited parliamentary sovereignty (Chapter 7).

Hobbes did not tackle the problem of how to make government accountable. Nor did he deal with the problem that, in all but the simplest societies, power must be divided up, thereby generating the possibility of disagreement between the ruler's advisers. Much constitutional debate therefore concerns the question of what checks and balances are desirable to restrain the abuse of power. It has often been asserted that there is a risk that all persons in power will misuse it.

Now it is a universally observed fact, that the two evil dispositions in question, the disposition to prefer a man's selfish interests to those he shares with other people, and his immediate and direct interests to those which are indirect and remote, are characterised most especially called forth and fostered by the possession of power ... this is the meaning of the universal tradition, grounded on universal experience, of men's being corrupted by power. (J.S. Mill, *Representative Government*, p. 242)

Similar sentiments have been expressed by Montesquieu (Chapter 5), Pitt the Elder (1708–78), Lord Acton (1834–1902), Lord Hailsham (1907–2001) and recently by Lord Hope: 'institutions tend to protect their own and to resist criticism from wherever it may come', *R* v *Shaylor* [2002] 2 All ER 477, [70].

## 1.4 Liberalism

It will be recalled that liberalism broadly centres on individual freedom. Liberalism coupled with democracy is currently part of the orthodoxy of the courts. For example, according to Lord Steyn in *R* v *Secretary of State ex parte Pierson* [1997] 3 All ER 577 at 603:

> Parliament does not legislate in a vacuum. Parliament legislates for a European liberal democracy founded on the principles and traditions of the common law. And the courts approach legislation on this initial assumption.

Indeed the practice of UK courts reflects a strongly liberal tradition in which judges present their judgments as individuals rather than as part of a collective group and there is full freedom to dissent.

Emerging out of the religious wars of the sixteenth century as a method of preserving peace, liberalism stresses limited government. It seeks a constitution that free and equal people would support. Typical of liberalism is the following assertion of Rawls (1921–2000):

> Our exercise of political power is proper and hence justifiable only when it is exercised in accordance with a constitution the essentials of which all citizens may be reasonably expected to endorse in the light of principles and ideas acceptable to them as reasonable and rational. This is the liberal principle of legitimacy. (*Political Liberalism*, NY, Columbia, 1993, p. 217)

The problem with this is its reliance on the word 'reasonably' since we may disagree as to what is reasonable. Who decides what is 'reasonably expected' in a society made up of people with many different beliefs?

Liberalism also implies the following not necessarily consistent ideas making Lord Steyn's guidance (above) somewhat vague.

- *Neutrality:* the state should be 'neutral' between different ways of life (but often impossible where different ways of life conflict).
- *Public and private distinction:* the private sphere should be outside state interference and that state should not carry out functions regarded as private. But who decides what counts as the private sphere? For

example, problems concerned with religious discrimination can be fudged by claiming that religion is a private matter.

▶ *Equality:* John Stuart Mill (1806–73) for example said:

> The true virtue of human beings is fitness to live together as equals; claiming nothing for themselves but what they would freely concede to everyone else; regarding command of any kind as an exceptional necessity, and in all cases a temporary one. (*The Subjection of Women*, 1869, Chapter 2)

However this depends on a wide measure of agreement. I might be happy to have things done to me to which someone from a different culture would seriously object. Mill's 'harm' principle requires that all be equally free unless they harm others. However, we might disagree as to what counts as harm so that the notion of equality begs the question, for example the case of abortion.

▶ *Optimism:* many liberals (e.g. Mill) place faith in progress generated by the freedom of individuals to develop their own lives.

John Locke (1632–1704) is widely regarded as a founder of modern liberalism. Locke's writings (*Second Treatise of Government,* 1690) supported the 1688 revolution, which founded our present constitution, against the claims of absolute monarchy. His approach was grounded in the Protestant religion, which stressed individual conscience and self-improvement by hard work. Unlike Hobbes, Locke proposed a social contract in which governmental power is limited in favour of individual rights and subject to democratic principles in the form of majority voting. Locke believed that individuals had certain natural rights existing, as he saw it, to serve God, these being life, health, freedom and property. For him, the purpose of government was to protect these rights in the exceptional cases where conflicts arise. To this extent Locke's government serves the same function as that of Hobbes's except that Locke's government has limited powers.

According to Locke, the people first hypothetically contract with each other unanimously to establish a government and then choose an actual government by majority vote. The government as such does not enter into a contract but takes on a trust, a one-sided promise, whereby it undertakes to perform its functions of protecting natural rights and advancing well-being. Thus government has duties but no rights of its own.

Locke's basic principles can be found in modern liberal constitutions, albeit without their religious underpinning. Firstly there is the idea (shared with Hobbes) that government depends on the consent of the people. According to Locke, government should be appointed and dismissed periodically by a majority vote representing those with a stake in the community, which to him meant non-Catholic property owners. He justified majority voting on the basis that the majority commands most force but recognised that there is no reason why a majority should be 'right' in relation to any particular issue.

Secondly, Locke was concerned to limit the power of government in order to protect the rights and freedoms of the individual. This is perhaps the most distinctive feature of liberalism, although liberals do not agree how this should be done, whether for example by courts or by democratic mechanisms (Chapter 17). Locke did not favour detailed legal constraints on government regarding the contribution of lawyers as 'the Phansies and intricate contrivances of men, following contrary and hidden interests put into words' (*Two Treatises of Government*, para. 12). He relied on dividing up government power so that no one branch can be dominant: the separation of powers (Chapter 6). He also insisted that governments should be periodically held to account by means of elections and upheld as a last resort a right to rebel against a government that broke its trust.

Thirdly, Locke promoted 'toleration' of different ways of life provided that they did not upset the basic liberal framework. For example, he did not favour toleration of Catholics who he regarded as subversive. He also favoured intensive agriculture, regarding humans as having a God given duty to exploit nature. This double standard is one of the alleged contradictions of liberalism.

Locke directly influenced the American revolution. Indeed a modified passage from Locke (*Essay on Human Understanding*) famously prefaced the United States Declaration of Independence (1776).

> Civil interests I call life, liberty, health and indolency of the body [substituted in the Declaration by 'the pursuit of happiness']. It is the duty of the Civil Magistrate, by the impartial execution of equal laws, to secure unto all the people ... the just possession of these things belonging to this life.

Liberalism is not universally admired, being condemned by communitarians (below) as selfish and uncaring. A modest defence of liberalism is the claim that at least it tries to make room for other beliefs, recognising the 'lurking doubt' in all human affairs. Liberal societies have been relatively stable and peaceful. Even if there is some objective truth as to how to live, it has so far eluded the human race which is in a state of permanent instability: 'where ignorant armies clash by night', (Matthew Arnold, *Dover Beach*). Indeed the desire for peace was the historical origin of liberalism as a response to the religious conflicts that disrupted Europe during the sixteenth and seventeenth centuries. Once the bond supplied by a dominant religion had been dissolved, it became impossible to govern people of widely different beliefs without either conferring a large amount of individual freedom or resorting to oppression which would ultimately destroy the community.

### 1.4.1    Positive and Negative Freedom

The idea of individual freedom is central to liberalism but has different, vague, and sometimes conflicting meanings. Some regard freedom as an end in itself: 'he who desires in liberty anything other than itself is born to be a servant' (de Tocqueville, *L'Ancien Regime*, 1856). However, it is difficult to regard freedom as an end in itself, let alone the highest end. Do we for example regard Hitler's freedom to pursue his interests as something good in itself, although offset by the harm he did? Moreover some freedoms are more important than others. Do we compare for example freedom to smoke in a restaurant with freedom to go to church? Arguably it is the content of the freedom that matters. Moreover freedom of this kind may conflict with 'equality' since the strong are free to exploit the weak. However, 'equality' is also a vague notion. Despite featuring in the rhetoric of the courts (e.g. *Ghaidan* v *Mendoza* (2004) [132]), equality is merely a measure, the real question always being 'equality of what?'

These problems have generated a distinction between 'negative freedom' and 'positive freedom'. Negative freedom is what most of us understand by freedom. A person is free if he is not controlled by others: 'By Liberty, is understood ... the absence of external impediments' (Hobbes, *Leviathan*, Chapter 14, para.1). Positive freedom, a more ancient idea, is freedom not to do what we want as such, but to do what is good for us by exercising the power of reason to make choices. In one sense the two freedoms support each other since negative freedom enables us to exercise choices. However, proponents of positive freedom change Hobbes's notion of the absence of impediments to the absence of arbitrary or unreasonable impediments, thereby introducing the merits of different choices. They justify this on the ground that, without reason, we would be unable to exercise the choices available to us but would be prisoners of our animal instincts. Positive freedom is therefore an expression of our 'higher' rational selves. Thus Plato (c.428–c.348 BC) insisted:

> you are not free when you are slave to your desires. Freedom is mastery by the rational self, mastery by knowledge of what is really good. (Gorman, 2003, *Rights and Reason*, p. 33 Chesham: Acumen)

The attitudes towards law of negative and positive freedom are very different. Negative freedom regards law as a restriction and points towards the most limited kind of state possible. Positive freedom allows us to claim, paradoxically, that obeying the law is 'freedom' in that law gives us rational choice by providing stability which enables us to plan our lives. Locke seems to endorse this:

> Law in its true notion is not so much the limitation as the direction of a free and intelligent agent to his proper interest and prescribes no further than is for the general good of those under that law. (*Second Treatise of Government* VI: 57)

Positive freedom therefore may support a constitution that stresses state interference in favour, for example, of economic equality in order to enhance choices in life (see e.g. Tawney, in Stirk and Weighall, 1995, *An Introduction to Political Ideas*, p. 157 London: Cassell). Positive freedom also links with democracy since it is connected with the idea that we control our own lives if we participate in collective decision making: what Constant (1767–1830) called 'the freedom of the ancients'. In this sense, by obeying rational laws we are apparently exercising freedom since we are 'obeying laws that we have made ourselves' (Kant, 1724–1804). In contemporary society there is little direct participation of this kind. Our form of democracy normally requires only that people can vote periodically for alternative ruling groups (below, and see Tully, 2002). In this context, positive freedom might for example favour compulsory voting.

The distinction between positive and negative freedom sometimes underlies disagreements in the courts. For example in *Tomlinson* v *Congleton District Council* (2003) the claimant had, despite warning notices, jumped into a pool owned by a local authority and broken his neck. The question was whether a local authority was obliged to do more to protect against this risk. Lord Hoffmann from the negative-freedom perspective remarked that our liberal individualistic system meant that the nanny state should not be encouraged and, given that there was a clear warning notice, the claimant should be responsible for his own safety. By contrast, Sedley LJ in the Court of Appeal had taken the view characteristic of positive freedom, that the local authority should have taken precautions to guard people against their own irrationality.

Positive freedom has a sinister aspect. The link between law and reason is one way in which people are persuaded to respect bad laws since it is easy to shift from the truth that the idea of law as such is rational to the untruth that particular laws are rational. Human affairs are prone to disagreement and there are different ideas of what is rational. Who decides what is rational? As Isiaah Berlin famously argued, positive freedom might justify the state claiming that one way of life, for example one based on a religious cult or on an economic theory or on belonging to the EU, is 'rationally' better than others and is therefore what the people would 'really' want if they could think properly, just as we say that someone who is drunk is not 'himself'. Thus a person detained in a hospital for 'his own good' could be claimed to be not 'detained' at all but freely submitting.

> Once I take this view I am in a position to ignore the actual wishes of men or societies, to bully, oppress, torture them in the name, and on behalf, of their real selves, in the secure knowledge that whatever is the true goal of man (happiness, performance of duty, wisdom, a just society, self-fulfillment) must be identical with his freedom – the free choice of his 'true', albeit often submerged and inarticulate self. (Berlin, 2002, p. 180)

Berlin therefore insists that freedom means negative freedom, the right to do what we like however irrational, and that other good things are what we do with our freedom not freedom itself:

Liberty is liberty, not equality or fairness or justice or human happiness or a quiet conscience. (*ibid*.)

Berlin of course recognises that that the state might sometimes have good reason for interfering with freedom. His point is that by lumping together freedom and other goods we are disguising hard choices and encouraging tyranny.

### 1.4.2 The Liberal Constitution: Different Forms of Liberalism

Different notions of freedom and equality lead to different conceptions of liberalism. By itself therefore liberalism as proclaimed by Lord Steyn (above) may be an unreliable guide to the shape of the constitution. However liberal constitutions have some broad features in common. They are likely to rely on some notion of individual rights and to support mechanisms designed to limit government power. These include the rule of law (Chapter 5), a separation of powers between different branches of government (Chapter 6), and perhaps independent local government (a feature not present in the UK). Beyond that there is a conflict between liberalism as such and democracy (below). This manifests itself particularly in the role of the courts. A liberal constitution might favour entrusting the protection of the constitution to independent courts with power to check even the lawmaker whereas a democrat might insist that the lawmaker elected by the people should have the last word. The main forms of liberalisms that affect a constitution are discussed below.

#### 1.4.2.1 'Libertarian' (Political or Classical) Liberalism

This stresses individual negative freedom from state interference. It regards the state as at best an unfortunate necessity to be limited and controlled. Its most extreme advocates (e.g. Hayek, 1991; Nozick, *Anarchy, State and Utopia*, 1974 Oxford: Blackwell) argue that the constitution should confine government to the smallest possible role: 'red light' theory (*Law and Administration*, Harlow and Rawlings, 2nd edn, 1997, Chapter 2. London: Butterworth). The role of the state should be minimal: defence, policing, enforcing agreements, settling disputes and punishing wrongdoers. The state should not advance any preferences as to how people should live. Hayek (1991) seems to assume that shared understandings will emerge on which enough people agree for life to be harmonious, what he called the 'spontaneous order'. There is no particular historical evidence in support of this. Moderate versions of political liberalism follow Mill in asserting that the state should interfere with individual freedom only to prevent harm to others.

### 1.4.2.2 *Welfare Liberalism (Social Democracy)*

This is the sense in which liberalism is understood in US politics. It is linked to positive freedom (above) and regards the state primarily as benevolent. It claims that the state should provide people with resources to enable them to flourish. It shares the concerns of individualists with rights such as freedom of speech but would also favour social and economic rights such as health and education. Welfare liberalism favours democratic mechanisms rather than the courts: 'green light' theory (Harlow and Rawlings above; Chapter 3). From this perspective, the law is one among several levers of government, the others being persuasion and payment. The courts might be presented as in 'partnership' with government to secure good administration (see *R* v *Lancashire County Council ex parte Huddleston* [1986] 2 All ER 941, 945 and the recent 'ill tempered outburst' by former Home Secretary David Blunkett asserting that the courts' role was to 'help' the government deliver its policies (2003, *Public Law* 397).

The most influential version of welfare liberalism is utilitarianism. Utilitarianism seeks the greatest good of the community and regards this as the accumulation of the preferences of individuals, giving effect to the wishes of the majority. David Hume (1711–76) was a founder of utilitarianism. He thought that government is a matter of practical compromise driven by habit, and our psychological need to cooperate with each other. He rejected the social contract as a fiction and regarded ideas of abstract justice and natural rights as myths useful for persuading people to conform.

Hume advocated a pragmatic society based on coordinating individual interests. He believed that our limited knowledge, strength and altruism provided the moral basis for a legal system. He thought that self-interest and our natural feelings for others would generate principles of cooperation such as respect for private property, voluntary dealings and fulfilling expectations. Hume favoured the common law as a vehicle for this which he described as a happy combination of circumstances, according to which the law is developed pragmatically in the light of changing social practices and values.

Jeremy Bentham (1748–1832) is the most celebrated exponent of utilitarianism. He thought that the notion of the interests of the 'community' was a fiction masking the competing interests of individuals. Using the slogan 'the greatest happiness of the greatest number', Bentham measured utility by counting people's actual demands, giving each demand equal weight ('each counts for one and none for more than one') and refusing to treat any preference as better than any other: 'pushpin is as good as poetry'. He favoured strong centralised government accountable democratically to the people, its main instrument being legislation. Bentham regarded laws and courts as subordinate to utilitarian considerations. In particular he regarded legal certainty, and judicial independence, what we call the 'rule of law,' as a sham (Chapter 5) and thought that the idea of natural rights was 'nonsense on stilts', claiming that rights were simply legal mechanisms, that law is merely a tool of government and that public opinion is the ultimate authority.

Utilitarianism does not in itself tell us what sort of constitution to adopt. For example, Hayek argues that government by central directive is doomed to failure in that no government has the knowledge to identify and coordinate the many competing interests of individuals even if this were desirable in principle. He favours the maximum possible individual freedom. By contrast Bentham's version permits unlimited state interference but subject to strong democratic controls to ensure that the majority are overall benefited (see Craig, P.P. 'Bentham, Public Law and Democracy', [1989] *Public Law* 407). Although, as a crude instrument of policy, utilitarianism is much favoured by officials, it is replete with problems particularly in relation to justice and fairness. For example utilitarianism is consistent with slavery in that the standard of living of a majority might be held to outweigh the loss of freedom of a minority. A utilitarian could reasonably think that wrongly convicted people should be kept in jail or even executed in order to preserve public confidence in the police (see *McIlkenny v Chief Constable of the West Midlands* [1980] 2 All ER 227, 239–40 per Lord Denning). Utilitarianism also finds difficulty with the notion of rights and obligations. Why should I pay you what I have agreed to, if I now discover a use for the money which benefits more people, for example by giving it to a disaster fund? Can utilitarianism really give equal weight to all preferences without some non-utilitarian filter to exclude 'irrational' or 'immoral' preferences such as those of paedophiles? These and other problems have been widely discussed without a conclusion.

Mill and Hayek (above) tried to reconcile utilitarianism with liberal individualism by claiming that maximising individual freedom is the best way to advance the general welfare. This includes Mill's famous 'harm' principle that the only ground on which the state should interfere with freedom is to prevent harm to others. Interference cannot be justified for a person's own good. However, distortions creep in. For example Mill was less egalitarian than Bentham, since for Mill preferences were not equal. Mill favoured the 'higher' and more, intellectual and artistic capacities of the human mind (positive freedom above). He was also a romantic reminding us that ideas such as justice may not be purely rational in the sense of being possible to pin down as legal rules but have an emotional and spiritual dimension (see

Ward, 'The Echo of a Sentimental Jurisprudence', 2002, *Law and Critique*, **15**, 107). One implication of this is to avoid the constitution being dominated by lawyers.

### 1.4.2.3 *Liberal Pluralism: Group Liberalism*

Liberal pluralism, sometimes called 'identity politics' or 'the politics of recognition', requires the state to respect the identities and way of life of different groups such as national religious, ethnic or sexual minorities as well as political associations, trade unions, vocational groups and the like. It departs from Hobbes in not necessarily regarding the state as the supreme body and, as with other liberal genres, requires the state to be a neutral umpire. These groups might be disadvantaged because of the stereotype of the 'normal' person represented by the ruling group, in our case the white, able bodied, heterosexual, culturally Christian male. Liberal pluralism requires active steps to ensure that all such groups have the leverage to participate fully in the life of the community, and to express their own identity, for example by being represented in public institutions, using their own language and giving effect to their own law and courts as in the case of Islamic Sharia law and Rabbinical law. It is not enough merely to tolerate or attempt to integrate such groups into the mainstream since this implies disapproval. To liberal pluralists the 'public interest' is the result of negotiating accommodations between the interests of the different groups. There is a danger of 'corporatism' in liberal pluralism in that the government will favour the groups with the loudest voices. There must also of course be sufficient common ground to enable the community to function efficiently and in this respect the values of a dominant group are likely to prevail (eg. the official language).

Liberal pluralism might therefore conflict with other kinds of liberalism particularly where the values of the group conflict with the values of other groups, for example disputes concerning blasphemy and freedom of speech (Chapter 18). A group might claim that its way of life should be supported by the state, for example religious schools, or should have special treatment to compensate for past injustices. Most fundamental is the problem of a group whose values are authoritarian: the famous liberal dilemma of 'tolerating intolerance'. Some liberals believe that liberalism contains universal truths derived from reason and therefore suggest, for example, that a liberal law should not permit any group to prevent its members from leaving it voluntarily (see e.g. Barry, 1995). Indeed, Article 9 of the European Convention on Human Rights (freedom of religion) includes 'freedom to change his religion or belief'. However, such freedom might be unacceptable to a religion which teaches that compulsion is in a person's best interests. Some liberals suggest the proper approach is that the members of any group must accept that the state, in order to protect itself, can override their interests provided that the decision process used is fair to all interests. However, there may not be agreement as to what fairness means. (See Galston, 2002; Raz, 'Multiculturalism', 1998, *Ratio Juris* 11/3 193.)

In terms of constitutional arrangements we would expect liberal pluralists to emphasise open and dispersed government, local government and the representation of minority groups in public institutions such as the judiciary. The devolved arrangements in Scotland, Northern Ireland and Wales (Chapter 4) exemplify this approach to different extents. A suggestion that is often canvassed is that one part of the legislature, the House of Lords, might comprise representatives of important interest groups. At present the only such groups represented in Parliament are Church of England bishops (Chapter 10). Liberal pluralism would also favour voluntary mechanisms to enable individuals to participate in society, for example tax breaks for charities and other voluntary bodies ('civil society').

### 1.4.2.4 *Market Liberalism*

Based on the writings of Adam Smith – (*The Theory of Moral Sentiments* (1759), *The Wealth of Nations* (1776) – this asserts that welfare is maximised if people are free to buy and sell goods and services through open competition with the minimum of government interference since the market provides incentives to meet needs efficiently. Supporters of the market claim that it enhances civilisation and culture by providing for peaceful interaction and encouraging creativity and the provision of things to enjoy. However, Adam Smith also recognised bad effects of market forces in encouraging selfishness and ruthlessness and believed in the need for a strong overarching morality.

Market liberals such as Hayek (above) may also support political freedom although there is no necessary connection between the two ideas. Indeed market liberalism might distort elections by enabling the wealthy to finance political campaigns. Market liberalism might also require the sacrifice of political freedom in order to secure fairness and the equality of access to markets that is needed for competition and to ensure that people conform sufficiently to require the goods and services on offer, particularly as standardised production is a driver of the market. Moreover, the smooth operation of the market might require restraints over those who lose out from competition.

## 1.5 Civic Republicanism: Equality and Citizenship

The term 'republic' means the absence of monarchy. However republicanism is more than this. Aristotle's approach (above) is the source of the 'civic republican' tradition. Revived in the Renaissance and developed in the seventeenth and eighteenth centuries (Machiavelli (above), Harrington (1611–77), Montesquieu (1689–1755)), its key notions are the 'virtuous', politically active citizen, the authority of a general lawmaker and political equality. It emphasises positive freedom (above) in the sense of 'the freedom of the ancients' to participate in public life. A republican constitution is therefore one in which equal citizens govern themselves. It relies upon law to ensure that no single group can become dominant, and upon the notion of 'mixed government' combining all the interests of the community (Chapter 6). It is somewhat ill at ease with a contemporary society dominated by powerful commercial interests.

Republicanism and liberalism both emphasise the rule of law (Chapter 5) and share some aspirations, particularly towards limited, open and accountable government. Thus there is a notion of 'liberal republicanism' focusing on the rule of law. However, their reasons for doing so are different and in the end the two perspectives are irreconcilable. Republicanism assumes there is a common 'public interest' that benefits all, which can be discovered by reasoned discussion between equals and which is more than just an accommodation of individual interests. In a republic, equal citizens must be protected by law against interference at the will of others as a matter of human dignity. In common with liberalism, republicanism rejects the notion that we should put our trust in a ruler, even a democratic majority, since we would then be in the position of slaves with a kind master (arguably the nature of the UK constitution).

Republicanism also favours a particular way of life: that of the active citizen (Aristotle's notion of the virtuous man). Thus republicanism contains the idea that citizens have a duty to participate actively in public affairs and would favour constitutional devices that would reduce or at least disperse the element of self-interest, for example two chambers of the legislature chosen on a different basis and a federal structure (Chapter 4). Republicanism favours private property as a means of ensuring the independence of the citizen (a notion that makes sense only if property is equally distributed). Republicanism therefore has sinister overtones for those who value individual freedom. Liberalism regards it as the main function of the state to protect the rights of the individual, believing that the individual is entitled to live for private pleasures and, according to some versions of liberalism, that the state should not favour any particular way of life. By contrast, republicanism may regard rights as conditional upon being a virtuous citizen and so might for example deny the right to opt out into private life by making voting compulsory.

## 1.6  Communitarianism

Communitarians overlap with republicans and with group liberalism (above) but go further away from the individual. They believe that the most important feature of the human condition is that we are social animals and depend on each other. They reject individualistic forms of liberalism as aggressive and uncaring, treating people as isolated from the community. They aspire to reconcile the individual with the community by denying the separateness of the individual whom they regard as essentially the creation of the community. Their ideas of justice focus on sympathy and affection rather than on rights.

> None of these so-called rights of man go beyond the egoistic man … as man separated from life in the community and withdrawn into himself, into his private interest and his private arbitrary will. These rights are far from conceiving man as a species being. (Marx 'On the Jewish Question', 1846, in Waldron (ed.) *Nonsense on Stilts: Bentham, Burke and Marx on the Rights of Man*, London, 1987, p. 147)

A liberal might respond by pointing out that liberalism does not prevent people from caring for each other but does not wish to compel them to conform by force. Moreover human nature comprises both individualistic and social instincts in irreconcilable tension with each other (see Note: below). Some communitarians such as Marx rely on versions of scientific reason claiming to identify objective forces shaping communities. This version has little impact on the UK constitution. Other communitarians deny that abstract reason is capable of forging sufficiently strong links to hold a community together preferring the customs and practices of the community, sometimes arguing that individual freedom is an illusion. From this perspective law is essential as a means of storing common values and understandings. Such communitarians, including Burke (1739–97) and Bagehot (1826–77) have strongly influenced English constitutional thought. The common law, based as it is on an appeal to precedent and practice, is a communitarian element in the UK constitution (Chapter 2). Thus Burke famously defended our customary common law constitution against the abstract reason that attempted to justify the French Revolution (1789) as 'a cord of sentiment that binds past, present and future'. He claimed that abstract reason is unreliable, politics being susceptible to uncertain events and to emotional forces. In common with liberal pluralists, Burke favoured the traditional institutions of 'civil society', families, neighbourhoods, clubs, companies and political parties as defences against centralising governments that claim the authority of 'reason'. He thought that the notion of individual rights leads to instability, letting in tyranny. Bagehot similarly favoured unelected institutions such as the monarchy and the House of Lords as methods of preserving respect for authority, continuity and tradition.

Communitarianism therefore has an authoritarian and conformist element; and it might threaten minorities as 'outsiders'. It is sometimes argued that Human Rights Law is communitarian in that it requires a balance between the individual and the public interest and gives particular importance to democratic processes (Chapter 17). However, few liberals would disagree with either of these features and the rights embodied in the Human Rights Act are primarily individual rights.

Despite or perhaps because of his personal life as a pathological loner, the views of Jean Jacques Rousseau (1712–78) reveal the strengths and the problems of both republicanism and communitarianism (*The Social Contract*, 1762). Rousseau was a precursor of the romantic movement of the nineteenth century which reacted against the scientific reason and individualism of the Enlightenment and stressed the spiritual and emotional sides of human nature. Rousseau thought that, far from being the solution as suggested by Hobbes and Locke, the state was part of the problem. He believed that man was by nature good, but had been corrupted by authoritarian government ('man is born free but everywhere he is in chains'). He believed that there is no conflict between the needs of the individual and the interests of the community provided that the government of the community includes everyone. Rousseau thought that the public are united by shared values and that decisions made by 'experts' are likely to be corrupt and self-seeking.

Rousseau's version of the social contract requires all to combine their individual separate wills in what he called the 'general will'. This meant that all should participate in government on equal terms by voting and accepting the verdict of the majority. The general will is our 'higher' unselfish or rational will. It is what an assembly of equals ought to decide as being best overall for the community as opposed to what Rousseau called the 'will of all', where each votes for his or her own selfish interest. Rousseau notoriously invoked the idea of 'positive freedom' (above) when he asserted that by being 'forced' to obey the general will, we become 'free' in that our thinking is not distorted by selfishness nor slave to our animal instincts nor dominated by the vested interests of others.

> Therefore, in order for the social compact not to be an ineffectual formula, it tacitly includes the following engagement, which alone can give force to the others: that whoever refuses to obey the general will shall be constrained to do so by the entire body; which means only that he will be forced to be free. (*The Social Contract*, I, 7: 55)

The general will depends on the whole community participating in lawmaking so that each can be said to be bound by a law which he 'freely' makes himself. Rousseau was disparaging of the English system in which, to make laws, the people elect representatives in Parliament who are not bound by the views of those who have elected them.

> The English People believes itself to be free; it is gravely mistaken; it is free only during the election of members of Parliament; as soon as the Members are elected, the people is enslaved; it is nothing. (*The Social Contract*, 141)

In order to encourage the uniform thinking that supports the general will, Rousseau favoured state censorship and rejected 'mini-general wills' such as trade unions within the state and wanted to restrict freedom of expression and association in order to promote the 'right' way of thinking on which the general will depends. He also favoured compulsory state education and a state religion. He thought that people must be roughly equal in terms of wealth in order for the general will to operate effectively. Rousseau also said that the general will could never be wrong:

> When the contrary opinion to mine prevails, that proves nothing except that I was mistaken, and what I thought to be the general will was not. If my private will had prevailed, I would have done something other than what I wanted. It is then that I would not have been free. (*The Social Contract*, IV, 2:111)

However, there is no logical reason why a majority should be 'right' on any issue. (Rousseau might however have meant the ideal rather than the fallible application of it in the real world.) The general will is therefore not a convincing idea in a modern society composed of people with many different beliefs and interests. Rousseau's general will can be contrasted with the liberal perspective which denies that there is any overarching ideal of the public good and which uses democracy as a method of achieving a compromise between competing interests. It illustrates the fears of Berlin (above) in his insistence that freedom means the right not to interfered with (negative freedom).

## 1.7 Democracy

Liberalism, republicanism and communitarianism may share ideals of democracy in a general sense but there are different versions of democracy. Democracy has been defined as:

> the people of a country deciding for themselves the contents of the laws that organise and regulate their political association. (Michaelman, 1998, *Californian Law Review* 86, 399, 400, quoted by Harlow in Beaumont, Lyons, Walker (eds) *Convergence and Divergence in European Public Law*)

According to this definition there is unlikely to be much democracy in the modern world and yet most states label themselves democracies. Michaelman's aspiration is the republican one of citizen self-government by active participation, sometimes called deliberative democracy. This might be practicable in a village where everyone knows each other, but in contemporary nation states comprising millions of strangers with conflicting goals and interests, it is unrealistic. Democracy has therefore become government with the 'consent' of the people, a more slippery notion. The people cannot decide anything until there are rules determining who counts as 'the people' and how they express their wishes. For example, different voting formulae produce very different outcomes (Chapter 10).

From the earliest times democracy has meant decisions made by a majority. The proposed European Constitution, quoting Thucydides (*c*.460–*c*.400 BC), claims that:

> our constitution is called a democracy because power is in the hands not of a minority but of the greatest number.

The justification for majoritarianism is not that a majority is likely to be 'right' since this is clearly untrue, but that majority voting is fair since it treats everyone equally. However, it has well known problems. Firstly, unless there is a simple choice between only two options, the mathematics of majority voting will not necessarily produce a majority preference. Secondly, a majority may oppress unpopular minorities or introduce repressive laws as a panic response to an emergency or become the passive tool of a selfish ruling group.

Thus John Adams, one of the founders of the United States Constitution, feared 'elective despotism', and de Tocqueville (1805–59), commenting on the newly formed United States Constitution, referred to the 'tyranny of the majority':

> I am trying to imagine under what novel features despotism may appear in the world. In the first place, I see an innumerable multitude of men, alike and equal, constantly circling around in pursuit of the petty and banal pleasures with which they glut their souls ... Over this kind of men stands an immense, protective power which is alone responsible for securing their enjoyment and watching over their fate. (*Democracy in America* (trans. Lawrence), London, Fontana, 1968, Vol. 2, p. 898)

### 1.7.1 Representative Democracy

The characteristic form of modern democracy is 'representative democracy'. The ideal of representative democracy is that of government which the people can call to account and replace. The primary role of the people is to choose representatives, leaving it to them to carry out government, choosing others to assist them with a clear chain of responsibility. A famous early statement is that of Chief Justice Sir John Fortescue (*On the Governance of the Kingdom of England*, 1537), who distinguished between '*dominium regale*', the rule of the king alone, necessary in certain cases for example to deal with an emergency and '*dominium politicum et regale*', the rule of the king with the assent of representatives of the community after discussion collectively in Parliament. More recently in *R* (*Alconbury*) v *Secretary of State* [2001] 2 All ER 929 at 980, Lord Hoffmann informed us that in the UK:

> decisions as to what the general interest requires are made by democratically elected bodies or by persons accountable to them.

Representative democracy favours the individualistic varieties of liberalism since the citizen's only power is to vote as a private solitary act without any requirement for discussion. Representative democracy relies upon a passive population, provided that enough people vote to give those chosen some legitimacy. As Mill argued (*Representative Government*), representative democracy is also closely linked with utilitarianism (above) which favours government by experts subject to their delivering what is best for the majority. Republicans and communitarians who favour the active participation of citizens are less comfortable with representative democracy.

Typically the people choose a lawmaking assembly as the highest branch of government. In some cases the people also vote for the head of state (below). Bentham and his utilitarian followers (above) recommended that even judges be removable by the people since to them the people are the final court but this is not the case in the UK. Mill (above) especially favoured representative democracy. However, like many contemporary public officials, Mill distrusted the 'people'. He recommended slewing the voting system so that the highly educated had greater voting power. He also suggested that Parliament should include a quota chosen from a list of people with a 'national reputation' and that people on welfare benefits should be disqualified from voting on the ground they might be biased. Although Mill believed active democratic participation to be an important aspect of freedom, he confined this to local government as a means of improving the character of the people. Fear of democracy remains a significant theme of the constitutional debate in the UK.

The term 'representative', is ambiguous. A representative assembly could be 'a portrait' or microcosm of those it represents, being for example representative in terms of the political balance of opinion or ethnic and racial groupings.

Alternatively, a representative could be an *agent* of the people not having any specified composition but chosen by a majority for his or her personal qualities. The mathematics of different voting systems produces different outcomes (Chapter 10). The UK Parliament operates the agency model but the devolved regimes in Scotland, Wales and Northern Ireland have moved in the direction of the portrait model.

Another basic issue is whether representatives on either model are bound by the views of those who voted for them or should vote according to their own consciences. The UK constitution has traditionally taken the attitude that representatives must not be bound by any outside commitments. For example, elected local authorities must not bind themselves in law to carry out any political mandate on which they are elected (see e.g. *Bromley LBC* v *GLC* (1983)).

Representative democracy provides mechanisms for ensuring that the government is accountable to the electorate. Accountability is an ambiguous idea (Chapter 13), but basically means that decisions must be explained and justified. The main accountability devices employed by representative democracies are as follows:

- Right to question legislature and executive (Chapter 13)
- Policing financial limits on government spending (Chapter 11)
- Internal control mechanisms within government (Chapter 13)
- Judicial review (Chapters 14, 15, 16)
- Public consultation and access to information (Chapter 18).

### 1.7.2 Participatory Democracy

Sometimes called 'deliberative democracy', participatory democracy promotes direct participation by individuals and groups in decisions which affect them. Its supporters claim that it can harness 'reason' from a wide range of perspectives. However, participants are voiceless without rules which stage-manage their involvement. Such rules may privilege some groups over others, notably the more articulate and those who benefit the rule makers. It is not clear how deliberative democracy can be organised. Notions such as town meetings have been proposed although it is unclear what matters might be appropriate to their remit. Recognising that in a complex society full participation might be impracticable, many have argued (e.g. the feminist theorist Carol Pateman and Hannah Ahrendt, 1906–75, a republican advocate of active citizenship) that participation should apply primarily to the smaller units (civil society) that contribute to the political system such as local government, charities and the workplace. However, liberals, notably Mill, have objected that deliberative democracy is likely to attract busybodies, the self-promoting, the ignorant and cranks. It also invades the personal freedom to opt out.

UK law provides for participation only in a limited and piecemeal way. For example there is provision for public inquiries into many decisions relating to land development and transport infrastructure but the outcome is not normally binding on the government. There is also provision for referendums (see Political Parties, Elections and Referendums Act 2000). However, these are rarely held and are triggered by the government which can therefore use the device for its own political ends. Referendums have been held in 1976, concerning continued membership of what is now the European Union, in the late 1990s, concerning devolution for Scotland, Wales and Northern Ireland (Chapter 4) and in 2004 in relation to a proposal for a regional assembly in the North East of England. In recent years the courts seem to have adopted a more sympathetic approach to direct participation (compare *Berkeley* v *Secretary of State* (2000) with *Bushell* v *Secretary of State* (1981)).

The jury systems of the UK and the USA are sometimes promoted as examples of deliberative democracy where a randomly chosen panel of citizens deliberates as to the guilt or innocence of those accused of serious offences (Juries Act 1974). This seems a little fanciful since a jury is faced with a predetermined question defined by law and within the rigid institutional framework of the courtroom. There is also some participation in the provision for 'Parish Meetings' at local government level in very small rural villages. However, these have little power other than in relation to local amenities such as playgrounds.

### 1.7.3    Political Parties: Market Democracy

In practice, democratic constitutions are dominated by political parties. Political parties publicise and coordinate different opinions and, as Burke somewhat idealistically asserted, make it possible to achieve by discussion a notion of the common good (*On the Present Discontents*, 1770, II). Without them an elected assembly would be a rabble. However, when Burke wrote, MPs were usually of independent means as opposed to the salaried functionaries of the present day, and party structures were relatively loose. A modern political party can ensure that people who are subservient to its leaders are selected as candidates for election and that once elected they vote in accordance with the party line (Chapter 9).

Liberalism regards political parties as private, self-governing organisations even though they are central to government. In the interests of freedom there is therefore resistance to legal controls over political parties, for example in respect of how they raise funds or control their members. On the other hand, fair elections require certain controls – a tension characteristic of liberal democracy (Chapter 10).

'Market democracy' recognises the role of parties but provides a limited choice. According to Weber (1864–1920) and Schumpter (1883–1950), this is the only version appropriate to contemporary society, the voter's only role being to choose between products offered by competing party leaders who present themselves for election every few years. Market democracy has significant implications for the constitution. No longer is the state the neutral umpire of Hobbes and Locke but is a player in the game. In particular there is the danger that political parties will be captured by the vested interests of those who fund them. However, supporters of market democracy argue that our contemporary, individualistic and mobile society means that one party is unlikely to stay in control permanently. People have many different views and backgrounds and mass communications make opinions volatile. Thus, groups sharing enough common ground to secure themselves in power are unlikely to be in place for long provided that the electoral system properly reflects the range of opinion – a matter which is questionable in the UK (Chapter 10).

It could be argued that contemporary society is too fragmented and diverse to fit into the mold of large-scale contesting parties and is represented more accurately by single issue or special interest pressure groups. Modern governments may therefore be chosen not on the basis of broad ideological or class differences but on the basis of the managerial competences of the individuals standing for election. Moreover, market democracy encourages government polices to be expressed in terms of outcomes, targets and 'value for money' rather than in terms of 'process' values of fairness and justice. The emphasis on outputs also blurs the traditional divide between the public and the private sectors. For example, over the last 20 years governments have 'privatised' many functions by transferring them, sometimes on a competitive basis, to private bodies including, for example, the running of prisons, the construction of schools and hospitals, and the provision of social housing. Privatisation raises concerns relating to conflicts of interest, democratic accountability and whether the law should control privatised activities in the same way that it does those of government proper.

## 1.8 Liberalism, the Courts and Democracy

European states including the UK claim to be 'liberal democracies'. However, while these good things can support each other there is no necessary connection between them. Liberals, republicans and communitarians may all regard democracy as the best way of achieving their goals. In a democracy the people can choose any kind of government. Conversely, a constitution could require a king to run a liberal system. Liberal values such as freedom of expression might also sometimes conflict with democracy as in the US case of *Buckley* v *Valeo* (1976) where restrictions on expenses for election advertising designed to ensure equal competition were held to violate the right to freedom of expression.

Liberals fear the 'tyranny of the majority' (above) but usually prefer a democratic constitution as a compromise between individual freedom and the public good. On the one hand, this accepts that an elected government can restrict freedom by promoting policies that favour one way of life over another, for example protecting the environment. On the other hand, a liberal constitution must not rule out change or claim universal truth for any policy. The liberal constitution therefore must not attempt to tie the hands of the future and must include machinery for removing any regime and repealing any law (hence anxieties about the European Union, Chapter 8).

Liberals also however favour partial checks on democracy by dividing up power. A device favoured by lawyers to link democracy with liberalism and both with law is to claim firstly that independent courts must ensure that government keeps within the powers given to it by the people (see Lord Hoffmann in *Alconbury* (above), at 980). It is also claimed that if democracy is not to be a sham, certain rights and freedoms on which democracy itself depends should be protected against the majority (ibid.), the paternalistic assumption being that the majority might be tricked, panicked or seduced into mistaken measures and therefore should be protected against itself. These include equality of participation in public life, open and accessible government, remedies against abuse of power, and freedom of speech and association (Chapter 17). This is coupled with the claim, promoted as 'the rule of law' (Chapter 5), that the courts should be the custodian of these values since with their lawyerly training they can take a rational, impartial look at the matter.

On the other hand 'reason' of this kind is capable of reinforcing the interests of an established elite.

Thus John Adams (above) expressed a widely held belief when he asserted that 'despotism, or unlimited sovereignty or absolute power, is the same in a majority of a popular assembly, an aristocratic council, an oligarchical junta, and a single emperor' (letter to Thomas Jefferson, 13 November, 1815 in *Oxford Dictionary of Quotations*, OUP, 2001).

## 1.9 Parliamentary and Presidential Systems

Within representative democracy the main distinction is between 'parliamentary' and 'presidential' forms of government. The influential nineteenth-century commentator Walter Bagehot remarked:

> The practical choice of first rate nations is between the Presidential government and the Parliamentary: no state can be first rate that has not had a government by discussion, and those are the only two existing species of that government. (*The English Constitution*, 2nd edn, 1902, Introduction)

In a parliamentary system such as that of the UK and most western European countries (although some countries, for example France, have a mixture of the two), the people choose representatives who form the legislature, Parliament. The main functions of Parliament are to choose and remove the executive government, scrutinise it through a process of debate, consent to laws, and provide the government with finance. In the UK the leader of the majority party in Parliament is automatically Prime Minister although there is no law to this effect. The Prime Minister in turn appoints other ministers to form the executive. In the UK these are invariably members of parliament but again there is no law to this effect. The legislature can ultimately dismiss the executive by withdrawing its support.

In a presidential system such as that of the USA the leader of the executive, the President, is elected independently of the legislature and holds office for a fixed period subject in some countries to dismissal by the legislature. The President appoints the rest of the executive who need not and sometimes cannot be members of the legislature. The President is also the head of state thus removing a constitutional safeguard. In a parliamentary system there is usually a separate head of state who formally and ceremonially represents the state and is the source of its authority but has little political power except perhaps as a safety mechanism in the event of a serious political breakdown (Chapter 12). Sometimes the ceremonial head of state might confusingly be called a president (e.g. Ireland).

The presidential system produces competition between the legislature and the executive since each is elected separately. Thus, only where there is strong popular support for a particular policy can the law be easily changed, and where the people are divided the government cannot easily impose partisan laws. The courts may be stronger in a presidential system. In a parliamentary system the same party controls both legislature and executive. This encourages cooperation and accountability. However in practice the executive is likely to be dominant.

In a parliamentary system the device of a separate head of state has the advantages of separating the *authority* of the state, in the head of state, from its functional powers. In a parliamentary system the Prime Minister and other members of the executive are merely government employees who cannot claim to identify themselves with the state as such and so claim reflected glory and immunity from criticism. The head of state has a symbolic role and also ensures continuity in the constitution. If the governmental system were to collapse, for example if no leader emerged from the political process, it would be the responsibility of the head of state, to ensure that government continued. Apart from this exceptional situation, the Queen has little power, so that any respect due to her as representing the state does not carry the risk of tyranny.

In the UK's parliamentary system it is important that the leading members of the executive are themselves elected and so directly responsible to Parliament. In recent years however there has been substantial reliance on informal groups of 'advisors', many being unelected and selected by the Prime Minister on the basis of personal acquaintance or political affiliation and without direct democratic accountability (Chapters 3, 13).

## 1.10   Note: Incommensurability

Much debate in constitutional law concerns disagreement on fundamental issues underlying government although we do at least share some broad ideas about what counts as valid reasoning and to a certain extent common feelings as to what is fair and just. However, these are often too vague to be easily applied. In other words, as Hobbes perceived, disagreement is an inescapable feature of human life. The concept of incommensurability expresses this. Incommensurability means that there is no objective measure or standard against which the interests or values at issue can be compared and therefore no 'higher' principle to which we can appeal when they conflict. On an everyday level we cannot compare, for example, the relative value of breaking a promise to take a friend to the airport for an important business trip and saving a cat's life by taking it to the vet. Incommensurability reflects the fact that human nature is contradictory. We are simultaneously (although each of us in different proportions) liberals as individuals who want to be left alone and communitarians as social animals who could not survive without the help of others.

Sometimes one good cannot be achieved without sacrificing another: a 'tragic choice'. In such cases, at best we can seek an accommodation that is widely accepted and be open as to what we are doing. For example in *Airedale NHS Trust v Bland* (1993) the courts had to decide whether doctors should withdraw medical support from a man who had been so severely injured that he would never recover consciousness. The judges unanimously held that the patient should be allowed to die on the grounds that continuing treatment could not benefit the patient. Hoffmann LJ in the Court of Appeal identified the tragic choice between the sanctity of life and 'the principle that the individual should be free to choose what should happen to him and, if he is unable to choose, we should try our honest best to choose as we think he would have chosen'. He rejected the government's argument that these values could be harmonised, as empty rhetoric, 'intended to dull the pain of having to choose.'

Incommensurability does not mean that all choices of incommensurable goods are irrational. Indeed the role of the constitution is to provide a means of making rational choices in the interests of stability. There may be no master principle but there is usually a range of reasons that can support any given decision. It is the *choice between* alternative lines of reason that in the end defies reason. The constitution must therefore provide an ultimate decision maker as suggested by Hobbes but required to justify its decision in a fair and public procedure. For example in *Campbell v MGN Ltd* (2004) the House of Lords disagreed as to whether intrusive newspaper reports and photos of a famous model undergoing treatment for drug addiction were unlawful. On the one hand there is the interest of freedom of the press, on the other a legitimate concern with privacy, both being liberal values. Either outcome could be rationally defended but a three to two majority favoured the privacy interest. On a future occasion the accommodation may be different which is desirable as keeping healthy disagreement alive.

# Summary

▶ I introduced some general ideas and suggested their application to constitutional law. I pointed out that constitutions deal with the fundamental framework of government and its powers reflect the political interests of those who design and operate them.

▶ I discussed different meanings of a constitution and examined the distinction between written and unwritten constitutions pointing out that the distinction is of some but not fundamental importance. I described the UK constitution as an untidy mixture of different kinds of law practices and customs and pointed out that we might disagree as to what is a constitutional matter.

▶ I introduced fundamental ideas about possible forms of government, the purpose of a constitution and its underlying values, pointing out that while none of them provides comprehensive perspective each has influenced the shape of the UK constitution. I distinguished between liberal and communitarian perspectives and identified civic republicanism as overlapping with both. In particular I set out the different approaches of Hobbes, Locke, and Rousseau. Hobbes favours government with unlimited powers as a necessary evil but only for the purpose of protecting individual life. Locke's liberal version uses government to protect natural rights, would limit the powers of government and make government accountable to the people. Rousseau (communitarian and republican) believed that humans were only fully free if acting democratically for the general good.

▶ In the light of claims that the United Kingdom constitution is based on liberalism, I discussed different kinds of liberalism with a view to suggesting that there are irreconcilably different beliefs. I used the distinction between positive and negative freedom in order to expose the kinds of disagreement that arise. I distinguished between those who advocate a minimum state, such as Hayek, those who rely on respecting individual rights ( Locke) and those who favour majoritarian democracy (Bentham) or a skewed version in favour of an educated elite ( Mill).

▶ I identified different kinds of democracy including deliberative/participatory democracy, representative democracy and market democracy and emphasised the difference between a parliamentary and a presidential system. I pointed out that democracy and liberalism are not necessarily connected and discussed some relationships between them, emphasising the debate concerning whether the courts or an elected body should have the last word.

▶ I introduced the idea of incommensurability as a tool of analysis. This suggests that democratic constitutions cannot work without sacrificing valuable goods, so that a constitution should manage but welcome disagreement.

▶ Having read this chapter you should be equipped with some general ideas and perspectives which you can use to assess the United Kingdom constitution.

# Exercises

**1.1** You are discussing constitutional law with an American who claims that the UK has no constitution. What does she mean and how would you respond?

**1.2** 'It is both a strength and a potential weakness of the British constitution, that almost uniquely for an advanced democracy it is not all set down in writing' (*Wakeham Report*, on reform of the House of Lords, 2000 cm 4534. Discuss.

**1.3** Think of some examples where different versions of liberalism might conflict. What would be the main principles of a liberal constitution?

**1.4** The government is considering a proposal to make decisions of Islamic Sharia courts – to be established in the UK to decide matters of divorce and inheritance among the Muslim community – binding in English law. What would be your advice?

**1.5** Sedley (*London Review of Books*, 15 Nov. 2001) describes a case where a French court upheld a ban on local funfairs where revellers had been permitted to shoot a dwarf from a cannon. The decision was made in the name of public morals and human dignity even though the dwarfs made their living from the spectacle and were among the chief opponents of the ban. Discuss.

**1.6** 'A democratic constitution is in the end undemocratic if it gives all power to its elected government' (Sir John Laws, 'Law and Democracy', 1995, *Public Law*, **73**). Explain and discuss.

**1.7** Compare the merits of the parliamentary and presidential systems of government.

## Further reading

Alexander, L. (ed.) (1998) *Constitutionalism, Philosophical Foundations*, Cambridge, Cambridge University Press.

Barendt, E. (1997) 'Is There a United Kingdom Constitution?', *Oxford Journal of Legal Studies*, **17**(1): 137.

Barry (1995) *Justice as Impartiality*, Oxford, Oxford University Press.

Bellamy, R. (2002) in Campbell, T., Ewings, K.D. and Tomkins, A. (eds) *Sceptical Essays on Human Rights*, Oxford, Oxford University Press.

Berlin, I. (2002) 'Two Concepts of Liberty', in *Liberty* (ed. Hardy, H.), Oxford, Oxford University Press.

Ewing, K. (2000) 'The Politics of the British Constitution', *Public Law*, 405.

Finer, S.E., Bogdanor, V. and Rudden, B. (1995) *Comparing Constitutions*, Oxford, Oxford University Press, Chapter 1.

Galston, W.A. (2002) *Liberal Pluralism*, Cambridge, Cambridge University Press.

Hayek (1991) 'Freedom and Coercion' in Miller, D. (ed.) *Liberty*, Oxford, Oxford University Press.

## Further reading cont'd

Laws, J. (1996) 'The Constitution: Morals and Right', *Public Law* 622.

Marshall, G. (2003) in Bogdanor, V. (ed.), *The British Constitution in the Twentieth Century*, London, the British Academy.

Munro, C.R. (1999) *Studies in Constitutional Law*, 2nd edn, London, Butterworth, Chapter 1.

Pettit, P. (1997) *Republicanism: A Theory of Freedom and Government*, Oxford, Oxford University Press, Chapters 1–3, 5, 6.

Skinner, Q. (1991) 'The Paradoxes of Political Liberty', in Miller, D. (ed.) *Liberty*, Oxford, Oxford University Press.

Taylor, C. (1991) 'What's Wrong with Negative Freedom', in Miller, D. (ed.) *Liberty*, Oxford, Oxford University Press.

Tomkins, A. (2002) 'In Defence of the Political Constitution', *Oxford Journal of Legal Studies*, **22**: 157.

Tully, J. (2002) 'The Unfreedom of the Moderns', *Modern Law Review*, **65**: 204.

Walker, D. (2002) 'The Idea of Constitutional Pluralism', *Modern Law Review*, **65**: 317.

Wolff, J. (1996) *An Introduction to Political Philosophy*, Oxford, Oxford University Press, Chapters 1–4.

# Chapter 2

# The sources of the constitution

An insider's constitution. (Peter Hennessy)

## Key words

▶ Authority and reason
▶ Power and authority
▶ Obligation and practice
▶ Insider self-interest
▶ Law and politics
▶ Constitutional 'silences'

## 2.1 Introduction

As we saw in Chapter 1 the UK is unique among the major nations in not having a written constitution. A written constitution in the form of 'articles of government' was introduced in England by the revolutionary regime of Oliver Cromwell in 1653 but after a year was superseded by a military dictatorship. Apart from that our constitution has developed pragmatically, usually out of accommodations struck between different sectional interests and we value the appearance of continuity and tradition as a means of social cohesion (or social control). For example, our most recent revolution in 1688 was presented to the public as a return to ancient values, which the Stuart monarchs were supposed to have subverted, rather than the establishment of a new regime. In this respect, contemporary attempts to modernise the constitution (Chapter 3) might be said to strike a discordant note.

During the eighteenth century the ruling elite continued to promote the constitution as resting upon widely accepted traditions and Britain's unwritten constitution was widely admired as a source of stability and justice. For example, Lord Chesterfield remarked that 'England is now the only monarchy in the world that can properly be said to have a constitution' (OED). However, historians disagree as to how impartial that justice was in practice, and eighteenth- and early nineteenth-century politics is sometimes characterised as aristocratic oligarchy oiled by patronage and bribery with a ruthless enforcement of public order and property rights (see e.g. Roy Porter, 1990). Latterly our constitution, with its restricted voting system and its concentration of power in the hands of the executive, has become less admired and is sometimes regarded as the least democratic constitution in western Europe.

Our unwritten constitution is constructed partly out of the general sources of law. These are Acts of Parliament, the common law in the form of decisions of the higher courts, and the 'laws and customs of Parliament' made by each House in order to control its affairs. The conventional view is that, as an expression of democracy, statute law is the highest form of law in our constitution.

The UK constitution also relies heavily upon unwritten rules known as constitutional conventions. These are not strictly speaking law at all because they are not directly enforceable through the courts and have no authoritative sources other than recognition and obedience by those affected by them. They are nevertheless very important and would certainly feature in a written constitution if we had one. Examples include the rules that the Queen must appoint as Prime Minister the person who commands a majority in the House of Commons, and must act on the advice of ministers, and the rule that the government must resign if it loses the confidence of the House. The combination of these conventions creates what are perhaps the central political tensions in our constitution, namely the concentration of power in the executive and the responsibility of Parliament both to sustain the executive, in the sense of providing the resources to keep the government functioning, and to hold the executive to account.

There are also 'practices' which are of constitutional significance even though they are not in any sense binding. The most obvious of these is of course political parties through which contenders for power organise themselves. There is no legal or conventional requirement that there be political parties and strictly speaking a political party is a private voluntary organisation. However, in a large and complex society containing many different points of view, the existence of parties as means of coordinating and organising competing claims is inevitable and no one would doubt that political parties are in fact a central feature of the constitution. Because the majority party in Parliament also forms the executive, party leaders can control both the legislature and the executive. Indeed it has been said that:

> parties have substituted for a constitution in Britain. They have filled all the vast empty spaces in the political system where a constitution should be and made the system in their own image. (Wright, quoted in Nolan and Sedley (eds) 1997, p. 83)

The importance of political parties has been recently recognised by legislation which attempts to ensure that the funding of political parties is fair and transparent (Political Parties, Elections and Referendums Act 2000).

Some writers argue that the dependence of the UK constitution upon conventions and practices makes it no more than the wishes of those in power: hence Griffith's much quoted aphorism 'the constitution is no more and no less than what happens' ('The Political Constitution', 1979, *Modern Law Review*, **42**(1): 19). Similarly Hennessy (1995, and see Chapter 1) describes the UK constitution as an 'insider's constitution' which is under the control of the government of the day and in particular the unelected officials who secure the continuity of the system at times of political crisis or change. He recounts the Victorian conceit that conventions embody 'the general agreement of public men' about 'the rules of the game' (ibid, p. 37), a proposition that remains significant today. Thus Bogdanor described the UK constitution as 'a very peculiar constitution which no one intended whereby the government of the day decides what the constitution is' (ibid., p. 165).

We often rely upon informal non-legally binding mechanisms on the grounds that they can be implemented quickly and cooperation may be secured more easily where there is no legal threat. This blurring of the distinction between law proper and conventions may be one factor contributing towards the stoical deference to authority that is a prominent cultural characteristic in the UK. For example, under the auspices of the Committee on Standards in Public Life various non-statutory codes of conduct have been made in respect of ministers, civil servants and MPs. In the case of the *Ministerial Code* it is not clear who is responsible for enforcement although, according to the Committee (6th Report Cm 4557-1), it should be the Prime Minister.

## 2.2 Statute Law

From the sixteenth century it became increasingly established that Parliament, in the sense of the Queen, the House of Lords and the House of Commons combining to enact statutes (Acts of Parliament), is the supreme lawmaker although some argue even today that the courts can overturn laws made by Parliament (Chapter 7). Some of the most radical constitutional changes have been made by statute. These include for example the Bill of Rights 1688 which, following the 1688 revolution, defined the relationship between the Crown and Parliament, The Act of Settlement 1700 which regulated succession to the Crown and gave the senior judges security of tenure, The Parliament Acts 1911 and 1949 which made the House of Lords subordinate to the House of Commons within the legislature and fixed the maximum duration of a Parliament as five years, the European Communities Act 1972 which made European law part of the law of the United Kingdom, and the Human Rights Act 1998 which incorporated parts of the European Convention on Human Rights into UK law.

Two things might be noted about these statutes. Firstly, they do not add up to a general constitutional code. They deal with specific issues and are usually responses to particular problems facing the government at the time. Any general principles in our constitution must be found elsewhere.

However, some statutes might have a special status. In *Thoburn* v *Sunderland City Council* (2002) Laws J, in the context of the European Communities Act 1972, spoke of a 'constitutional' statute, meaning a statute which the courts will not read as overridden by other statutes unless very clear language is used (Chapters 5, 7; see also *Robinson* v *Secretary of State for Northern Ireland* (2002): devolution legislation). The problem here is that we may not agree as to what counts as a constitutional statute. The above examples may be fundamental on any view but what, for example, of a statute that regulates local government?

Secondly, what statutes are enacted depends mainly on the government of the day. For example, there are no statutes (other than some dealing with incidental matters such as pensions and salaries) concerning important officials such as the Prime Minister, the internal organisation of the government, the nature of the executive and the regulation of the civil service nor the accountability of the government to Parliament. This is because these matters have evolved gradually from the eighteenth century, almost entirely by means of unwritten practices and conventions. Another gap which opens up the risk of abuse of power is that there are no statutes concerning the terms on which the government may hand over public functions and assets to the private sector.

## 2.3 The Common Law

The common law, developed by the judges on a case-by-case basis from disputes focusing on individual rights, claims legitimacy as the embodiment of the values of the community mediated by reason and given order and certainty by precedent. Liberals, republicans and communitarians might each find it congenial (Chapter 1). Historically, the common law predates Parliament as lawmaker since it emerged from customary laws which are sometimes claimed to go back to the ancient Britons. Indeed the idea of an ancient common law constitution is part of the rhetoric of English constitutional debate, designed to instil reverence for existing arrangements. The common law was strengthened from the thirteenth century by the practice of the King's judges touring the country on his behalf as 'the fount of justice' settling disputes, with the main courts later gravitating to London. Although the judges are in theory Crown servants, from the seventeenth century it was established that the King cannot act as a judge himself but is bound by the law as made by the judges (see *Prohibitions Del Roy* (1607), *M* v *Home Office* (1993)).

There is a tension between the classical common law view of the constitution – advocated with varying degrees of emphasis in the seventeenth century by judges such as Chief Justice Coke (1552–1634) and Hale (1609–76) – and the modern political notion of the constitution initiated, as we have seen, by Hobbes as the application of sovereign power, in our case vested in Parliament, able to make whatever laws it wishes. Coke, who became a leader of the parliamentary opposition to the King claimed that the common law, which he assumed to originate with the ancient Britons, was the supreme arbiter of the constitution – an argument that is pursued today (Chapter 7). According to Coke the common law is a matter of reason, but:

> the artificial perfection of reason … gotten by long study and experience … No man (out of his private reason) ought to be wiser than the law, which is the perfection of reason. (*Institutes*, 1(21))

Artificial reason is apparently the collective wisdom of the judges refined over long periods of time and organised through precedents. The classical view envisages the common law constitution as the product of the evolutionary development of community practices adapting the law to meet changing circumstances and, importantly, recognising that disagreement requires practical judgements rather than general principles. Hale's famous metaphor of the Argonauts' ship has often been used with the same ship returning that had set sail but having been so often mended, no piece of the original remains (Hale, *A History of the Common Law*, (1713), p. 40).

Hobbes (Chapter 1) roundly condemned Coke's claims. He denied that there is anything special about lawyers' reasoning and refused to accept that custom and tradition in themselves carry any legal authority. According to Hobbes the rule of law derives from authority, subject to 'natural reason' which is available to everyone. He objected to the common law on the ground that disagreement between judges picking over conflicting precedents creates the very uncertainty that the law exists to prevent. Jeremy Bentham (Chapter 1) also objected to the common law on the ground that relying on precedent was contrary to reason. We might therefore be cynical about the notion that the common law represents community values and, at the extreme, may view the common law as the creation of a professional elite of lawyers, concerned to protect the traditional status quo, and filtering experience through their own self-interest even if unintentionally.

An Act of Parliament outranks the common law so that democracy has the last word. However, some liberals argue that the courts are the guardians of fundamental freedoms and in extreme cases should have the power to override an Act of Parliament (Chapter 7). A compromise position is a 'twin' or 'bi-polar' sovereignty between Parliament and the courts according to which Parliament makes legislation and the courts interpret it in the light of basic values of justice and respect for individual rights, each respecting the autonomy of the other in its own sphere (*X v Morgan Grampian Publishers Ltd* [1991] 1 AC 1 at 48.) Such an accommodation gives the courts considerable scope to interpret the law in the light of their moral and political beliefs but requires them to give way to a clear expression of democratic will. The conventional approach characteristic of the UK's approach to uncertainty ('constitutional abeyance', below) is that there is an 'understanding' between the institutions of government as to their respective roles and limits.

## 2.4 Constitutional Conventions

Much of the UK constitution comprises understandings and practices that are not legally binding. These are conveniently known as 'constitutional conventions'. Their primary concern is the internal relationships of government. Their existence is an important example of how the UK constitution must be pieced together without a blueprint other than tradition and the opinions of 'important' people. They also show how there has been a reluctance to develop the constitution according to principles of abstract reason. Conventions express the contemporary political morality of the constitution, and one argument for their existence is their achievement in continually modernising the constitution. Among the problems conventions pose is the extent to which our constitution is uncertain. They also raise the question of who decides what our constitution is and how it should be changed. Is it acceptable that the government of the day is able freely to change the constitution by means of its use of conventions?

Conventions are generally considered to be binding principles or rules, often derived from the practices of politicians. For example, convention (and not law) requires that the Queen must grant her assent to a bill passed by both Houses of Parliament, and that Parliament must meet annually. Many conventions relate to the exercise of the prerogative powers that survive as vestiges of the legal powers of the Crown. These powers, if exercised, could have profound political consequences, determining who, for example, might be Prime Minister. There would be no legal impediment if the Queen chose to dismiss all her ministers. These powers are, however, required to be exercised according to conventions. Thus a fundamental shift of power, which has largely been achieved by conventions, has significantly reduced the role of the sovereign since the eighteenth century without the controversy which might have been associated with a series of statutory reforms.

However, the very existence of conventions generates controversy. If the purpose of a constitution is to impose external limits on government, then conventions that are generated *within* government are highly suspect. Horwitz, has argued, for instance, that conventions were developed as undemocratic devices to reassure the ruling class that constitutional fundamentals would continue to be developed within government largely beyond the influence of the rising middle classes following rapid extension of the franchise after the Reform Act 1867 (1997, *OJLS*, 551). This echoes

Mill's utilitarianism in so far as he preferred to leave government to an elite of professionals. If conventions exist as a matter of politics and not law does it mean that the constitution is merely what the government of the day claims it to be?

Further, the absence of formal parliamentary debate, or indeed any public and systematic discussion, exposes an important concern about the democratic legitimacy of conventions. Who determines the timing, and nature of reforms? Are the voices of persons selected by those in power as likely to conform to their wishes given particular weight (for example academics anxious for recognition)? Why should not the fundamentals of the constitution such as responsible and accountable government be protected against those they are intended to police? For example, the government refused to allow either Parliament or the public access to the text of the Attorney-General's legal opinion concerning the legality of the invasion of Iraq in 2003. By convention such advice is normally confidential (although there are precedents for disclosing the advice) but the refusal to disclose could be seen to screen government from uncomfortable questions regarding the legality of the use of force.

### 2.4.1 Definitions

It is important to distinguish constitutional conventions from other forms of constitutional behaviour such as practices, traditions and legal principles. However, commentators disagree as to the tests used to identify conventions. Most fundamentally, this signals doubt about the very nature of conventions and, indeed, the nature of law. At a practical level, there is inevitable uncertainty as to whether some practices really are conventions (and so become obligatory). There is no consensus as to which practices have constitutional status: for example doubt surrounds the rules for electing the leaders of political parties or the codes of public morality that have recently been promulgated by bodies such as the Nolan Commission. Moreover, like some laws, those rules that are acknowledged as conventional rules often lack precise scope, which means that even if a convention can be stated in general terms there can be difficulties surrounding its application.

Sir Kenneth Wheare (*Modern Constitutions*, (2nd edn 1966, p. 102) defined conventions as 'a rule of behaviour accepted as obligatory by those concerned in the working of the constitution'. This emphasises that the crucial matter is the belief of the politicians to whom a convention applies that there is an obligation to act in a particular manner. A convention exists if, as a matter of fact, the belief is present. But it is arguable that a convention ought to engage what politicians *should* consider themselves bound to do and not merely what they actually consider their obligations to be.

A further issue concerns the extent to which a practice must be accepted as binding before it is recognised as a convention. Does *any* disagreement about the status of the practice prevent the practice from being a convention? This seems unsatisfactory because, if unanimity (rather than consensus) is required, it suggests that a person whose actions ought to be governed by an existing conventional obligation can apparently destroy that obligation by disputing its existence. An alternative approach might be to identify a convention where there was a *consensus* as to the binding nature of a constitutional practice. A consensus may be said to arise informally provided there is substantial support for the proposed convention. But who consensus is to be among raises republican worries (Chapter 1). Evidence might be found through the collective memory of senior officials or persons recognized as constitutional 'experts', possibly selected on the basis that they are congenial to those in power. Reliance may be placed upon the views of important non-elected officials who represent the continuity of power, such as Peter Hennessy's 'golden triangle' of Cabinet Secretary, the Queen's advisors and the Prime Minister's Principal Private Secretary (ibid.). Hennessy (1995) describes how private secretaries, the Sovereign's advisers at Buckingham Palace and officials of the Cabinet Office monitor and record practice in a 'Precedent Book', which, characteristically of the UK constitution, is not open to public inspection. Officials and politicians refer to the records contained within this collection to guide future behaviour, and this may eventually lead to a consensus that the practice is obligatory.

Dicey famously defined conventions negatively. He stated that apart from laws, '(t)he other set of rules consist of conventions, understandings, habits, or practices which, though they may regulate the conduct of several members of the sovereign power, of the Ministry, or of other officials, are not in reality laws at all since they are not enforced by the courts' (*An Introduction to the Study of the Law of the Constitution*, 10th edn, 1959, p. 24). Thus, for Dicey, it is the absence of judicial enforcement which fundamentally characterises conventions. Dicey's approach ventures a clear distinction between law and politics; but it does not clearly explain how conventions evolve. Dicey seemed to have envisaged an inferior class of usages and customs which would not be binding on those to whom they applied. Since neither conventions nor non-binding practices are enforced by the courts, Dicey's test does not identify that which is a convention as opposed to non-binding practice (c.f. Munro, 1999, p. 81 arguing that non-legal rules are best viewed as of one type provided we accept that conventions vary in stringency).

Jennings offered three tests to identify a convention (*The Law and the Constitution*, 5th edn, 1959, London, University of London Press, p. 136).

First, are there any precedents? Second, do those operating the constitution believe that they are bound by a rule? Third, is there a constitutional reason for the convention? This has been accepted by the Canadian courts (*Reference re Amendment of the Constitution of Canada (Nos 1, 2 and 3)* (1982) 105 DLR (3d) 1).

In the absence of an authoritative decision maker such as a court, there are plainly difficulties with precedents because there may be many occasions on which politicians disagree about the precedents they are supposed to follow. This uncertainty clouds even established conventional rules, making fundamentally important conventions difficult to apply. An example is the preference expressed by the King and Chamberlain that Chamberlain should be succeeded as Prime Minister by Lord Halifax (and not Churchill) at a crucial moment for the nation in the conduct of the Second World War. This was so notwithstanding the established convention that a Prime Minister should have a seat in the Commons. More recently, it is unclear whether the practice of not creating new hereditary peers that was universally applied for almost twenty years ever hardened into a binding convention. If it did, the convention disappeared as a result of its breach in 1983 when William Whitelaw was elevated to the peerage.

Sometimes precedent is unnecessary because a convention can be created by agreement, for example by the Cabinet, or even laid down unilaterally by the Prime Minister. For example, by the Balfour Declaration, made at an Imperial Conference in 1926, a convention was created that no legislation affecting the dominions would be passed by the Westminster Parliament unless the government of the country affected by it had requested that legislation and consented to it. This convention was substantially placed on a statutory footing by the Statute of Westminster 1931.

The important principles contained in the *Ministerial Code* (Cabinet Office, July 2001) may well furnish an example of conventions laid down by Prime Ministerial edict (Hennessy, 1995, pp. 36–7). However, Lord Nolan thought that the Code's predecessor, known as *Questions of Procedure for Ministers*, lacked constitutional status (see *First Report of the Committee on Standards in Public Life*, Cm 2850, 1995).

Jennings also suggested that a convention exists if those subject to it regard themselves as bound by the rule. It seems odd to say that a rule is binding only as long as it is obeyed, a principle that would undoubtedly be welcomed by armed robbers. However, whilst conventions are obligatory they do not all have the same degree of binding force. Some are vague (e.g. ministerial responsibility), some may have exceptions (e.g. the personal powers of the monarch), some may not be regarded as important. It may be difficult to decide whether a particular pattern of behaviour amounts to a convention. For example, is the Cabinet merely a working practice?

It is necessary to distinguish between conventions and practices because practices, however important, are not binding at all. The party system provides an example of a practice which is fundamental to the workings of the constitution but which has no binding force. There is a logical gulf between practice – what is – and rule – what 'ought' to be – although it must be conceded that well-established practices carry at least a presumption that they ought to be continued. This seems to be a basic psychological fact about human motivation. Furthermore a practice ceases to exist if it is broken. If a convention is broken it ceases to exist only if no criticism follows. To this extent conventions are at the mercy of raw politics.

Jenning's requirement of a reason for the convention is also problematic. Who decides whether such a reason exists? In the absence of an independent judge, the reason for a practice depends upon contested political views as to what the constitution should be like. These are vulnerable to the self-interest of the government in power. Indeed, a fundamental distinction between convention and law is that there is no authoritative mechanism for settling disputes as to the meaning and application of a convention.

### 2.4.2　The Purposes of Conventions

Conventions perform a number of roles. They deal mainly with the relationship between the different branches of central government, the Crown, the executive and Parliament, ministers and the civil service, the Prime Minister and the Cabinet. There are, for example, no legal rules requiring there to be either a Prime Minister or a Cabinet; indeed the powers of the Prime Minister are largely conventional. It is sometimes argued that fundamental principles relating to the structure of the constitution such as parliamentary supremacy and the separation of powers are conventions (*R v H.M. Treasury ex parte Smedley* (1985)).

Conventions relating to the monarch ensure that vestigial prerogative powers are normally exercised only in accordance with advice received from ministers who are themselves accountable to Parliament. For example, as we have seen, it is a convention that the sovereign should assent to bills passed by both Houses of Parliament. The Royal Assent would seem to be automatic, although Marshall has suggested that the assent might be refused if, for example, a bill purporting to repeal an earlier 'entrenched' enactment had not gone through all the special processes required in the earlier enactment (1984, 22). Related to the convention governing assent is the sovereign's obligation in almost all matters to act on the advice of ministers (whether collective advice or that offered by an individual minister) although even here there are ill-defined circumstances in which such advice need not be followed. For example, the sovereign might be able to refuse a Prime Minister's advice to dissolve Parliament if a general election would be harmful to the interests of the country, such as might be the case in a national emergency, and an alternative viable government could be formed (Chapter 12). There is considerable debate about the extent to which, and on whose advice, the monarch can exercise personal powers.

By convention the sovereign should choose as Prime Minister the person who can command a majority in the House of Commons. This usually means the leader of the largest party. This apparently straightforward rule is designed to keep the sovereign out of politics. Lord Salisbury, who resigned in 1902, was the last Prime Minister to sit in the Lords. When the Earl of Hume was chosen to be the leader of the Conservative Party in 1963 he renounced his title and won a Commons seat at a by-election, which reveals that the convention was almost certainly established by that date. However, it can be argued that an obligation had been recognised by 1923 when the King passed over Lord Curzon in favour of Stanley Baldwin, although this was disputed by Jennings. By 1923 the House of Lords had already lost many of its powers and was clearly subordinate to the Commons so there was clearly a purpose in appointing the Prime Minister from the Commons.

The chain of conventions embodied in the doctrine of ministerial responsibility to Parliament is of fundamental importance, being intended to ensure that the legal powers of the crown are subject to democratic control (Chapter 13). Dicey (1915) for example suggested that these conventions reconcile legal sovereignty and political sovereignty. T.R.S. Allan (*Law Liberty & Justice*, 1993, p. 253) concludes that conventions 'give effect to the principle of governmental accountability that constitutes the structure of responsible government'. However, the supposed chain of accountability is not satisfactory. Dicey had not anticipated the dominance of the executive in Parliament nor the dispersal of executive power to miscellaneous bodies, including private companies outside the central government structure. Moreover, if ministerial accountability is to be effective it assumes that members of Parliament will act as parliamentarians and not through party loyalty. Accountability to Parliament is often accountability to the minister's own party against the background of the adversarial nature of party politics and the government's desire to avoid political embarrassment. Politics is the final arbiter.

Other conventions concern the relationship between the two Houses and Parliament and the judiciary. Prior to the Parliament Acts of 1911 and 1949 the House of Lords had a legal power to veto bills passed by the Commons, although there was an important convention that, in the event of a conflict between them, the House of Lords would defer. Breach of that convention, resulting from the Lords' initial refusal to pass the Liberal government's reforms promulgated in the Finance Bill 1909, resulted in the Parliament Act

1911 replacing the Lords' veto with a power to suspend. Conventions are also likely to evolve concerning the relationship between the UK government and the devolved governments (Chapter 4).

### 2.4.3 Conventions and Constitutional Change

An unwritten constitution such as the UK constitution assumes that change and flux are permanent. This insists that constitutional fundamentals can be modified or even abandoned according to their contemporary context. As we have seen, conventions have discreetly achieved such major changes as the transfer of power from sovereign to Parliament. But if politicians are required to follow conventions, how can evolution be possible? One solution to this is that the conventions cannot be changed unilaterally, which means that change depends on the agreement of (or consensus amongst?) those to whom conventions apply.

New conventions are developed, and others abandoned. In the former category may well be the right of the Prince of Wales to communicate and meet with ministers, to obtain information from them, to comment on their policies, and to argue for alternative policies (Brazier, 1995, 'The Constitutional Position of the Prince of Wales', *Public Law*, 401). The former parliamentary convention governing the rules under which the Table Office of the House of Commons refused to allow a written parliamentary question to a minister to be tabled if the minister had earlier refused to answer it has also disappeared, although ministerial conventions on this matter still operate (Second Report of the Public Service Select Committee, HC 313). Another recent innovation is the promulgation of 'concordats'. These are sometimes intended to govern the relationship between different organs of government. One of the several examples that occur in the context of devolution is the 'Concordat between HM Treasury and the Cabinet of the National Assembly of Wales' which clarifies the relationship between these bodies and expresses their mutual obligations. This could be seen as expressing new conventions. But there is also another type of 'concordat', an example of which is the 'Enforcement Concordat' dealing with the relationship between regulated commercial interests and enforcement bodies. This lacks the character of a convention in part because it merely sets out broad policy goals, for example that enforcement bodies should adopt a helpful and constructive approach, and that information should be published in plain language.

Conventions change their meaning incrementally as they are applied – that being one of their alleged advantages. On the other hand, there is often doubt about the status of certain practices. For example, since the late 1970s it has become apparent that a government need not resign merely because it suffers a major defeat. A formal Commons vote of no confidence is needed. This makes it very difficult to remove a government. There is uncertainty as to whether there is a convention embodying the 'mandate' doctrine – the idea that governments are bound to attempt to honour election promises. If this doctrine exists it would complete the 'democratic chain' between monarch and people. The status and functions of the Cabinet are also uncertain. Recent prime ministers have preferred to rely upon informal groups of advisors (see Chapter 13).

The need to evolve the constitution is not in itself a conclusive case for the existence of conventions because Parliamentary sovereignty ensures that any anachronistic laws can simply be repealed. However, there would have been political risks in incrementally curtailing the powers of the Crown by repeated legislative means which might have risked constitutional confrontation. Conventions can also offer advantages in a society in which constitutional reform often finds a low place in the public's (and thus the government's) view of political priorities.

### 2.4.4    Why are Conventions Obeyed?

There are many reasons why conventions are normally obeyed, not least because of the adverse political consequences which might result from their breach. This is unsurprising since conventions are traditionally regarded as a matter of political ethics. As we have seen, Dicey distinguished conventions from laws by the absence of judicial enforcement. However, this did not mean that Dicey was content with exclusively political redress for breach of convention, and his argument somewhat undermines his distinction between law and politics. He stated (1959, p. 439 *et seq.*) that conventions are not laws and so not enforced by the courts, but he argued that even the 'boldest political adventurer' would be restrained from breaching conventions because (at least in the case of some conventions) it would eventually lead to the offender coming into conflict with the courts and the law of the land (pp. 445–6). He gave as an example the consequences which might follow if Parliament did not meet at least once a year, or if a government did not resign after losing a vote of confidence. Dicey argued that the government would not have the statutory authority for raising (some) taxes, nor for spending money.

However, not all conventions can be similarly treated. For example, if the Speaker shows party political bias the consequences are more likely to be in the political arena. Moreover, the adversarial nature of politics means that even political sanctions are far from inevitable. The pressure of political opponents and party and the strength of prime ministerial support, as well as the reaction of the press, play a large part in determining the fate of a minister whose department's performance has been found wanting (Chapter 13). The absence of adverse political repercussions may fortify ministers who give parliamentary answers that are incomplete but, contrary to Dicey, even this failure is also unlikely to lead to a breach of the law. Indeed the absence of political consequences may in part explain why some conventions are not always obeyed.

It is, however, true that if some conventions were breached, Parliament might be compelled to intervene to prevent a recurrence. Most famously, this occurred after the Lords refused to pass the Finance Bill 1909, thereby disregarding the conventional principle that the Lords should ultimately defer to the wishes of the elected Commons. The Parliament Act 1911 removed the veto power of the Lords in respect of most Public Bills. If the sovereign (without ministerial advice) were to refuse to grant the royal assent to a bill passed by both Houses, the prerogative power to refuse would soon be removed by legislation.

It might also be suggested that conventions are obeyed because they are part of a shared and respected system of values. This is evident in the commonly accepted definitions of conventions which emphasise the consent upon which they depend for their existence (e.g. Sir Kenneth Wheare definition above, and see Munro, 1999, p. 61). Whilst the values which underpin conventional obligations are shared by those to whom they apply a breach is unlikely. The disregard of a widely shared political ethic might threaten the career of the offender, about which there might also be adverse publicity.

Conventions may be breached or qualified (depending on one's viewpoint) where there is a conflict between what is normally constitutionally expected and current political consensus or expediency. In 1975 the Prime Minister 'suspended' the principle of collective cabinet unanimity to allow ministers to express their views openly in a referendum campaign concerning membership of the EEC. Any referendum on the future of sterling as British currency might result in a similar temporary modification to collective ministerial responsibility. Political opponents argued after 1975 that this first so-called 'suspension' was a clear breach of a convention but, according to a counter-argument, conventions are sufficiently flexible to admit of exceptions where prevailing political consensus demands it.

### 2.4.5    Law and Convention

For Dicey, the distinction between legal and political rules depended on the absence of direct coercive legal power to enforce conventions. Jennings, by contrast, argued that law and convention share common characteristics, each resting ultimately on public acquiescence. But this does not explain the different attitude of the courts to conventions when compared with laws.

At one level it is possible to understand how laws and conventions differ. A law does not fall into desuetude, yet a convention can disappear if it is not followed for a significant period, or if it is broken without objection.

Munro (1999) points out that a breach of the law does not call into question its existence or validity. He adds that individual laws do not rest upon consent – an unpopular law or a widely disregarded law is nevertheless a valid law. But a convention is only valid if it is accepted as binding. Another difference is that laws emanate from definite sources – the courts and Parliament. In the case of conventions there is a lack of an authoritative source which might declare or establish the existence of conventions and provide for their interpretation, application and change. As Dicey indicated, there is no direct judicial remedy when a convention is breached but this is not so with conventions.

Nevertheless, Dicey's distinction between law and convention has been criticised as too rigid. Some laws are less binding than others. For example, procedural requirements stipulated by statute are sometimes 'directory only'. This means that such requirements need not always be obeyed (see Chapter 15). The immigration rules made under the Immigration Acts comprise a mixture of binding rules, general guidance and advice. Whether they are 'law' is debatable (see *Singh* v *Immigration Appeal Tribunal* (1986)). Nor can importance be a distinguishing factor. As we have seen, conventions deal with fundamental matters and laws might of course also do so. Thus conventions can be as important as laws; and some conventions may be more important than some laws. It must be conceded however that importance is irrelevant to the existence of a law but not to the existence of a convention. It is also sometimes said that conventions are different from laws because they lack certainty. Munro (1999) demonstrates that certainty is not the issue. He argues that some social rules, such as the rules of cricket, can be clearly stated but they are manifestly not laws. Moreover, many laws are uncertain and, whilst the courts certainly rely on precedent, they are free to depart from precedents in many cases.

Perhaps the crucial distinction between convention and law concerns the attitude of the courts. Many conventions function in a close relationship with laws since they direct how discretionary power will be exercised or prevent the exercise of anachronistic prerogative powers. Conventions provide principles and values which form the context of the strict law. The courts do not apply conventions directly. This means firstly, that there is no remedy in the courts for breach of a convention as such and that the views of a court as to whether a particular convention exists and what it means are not binding. The existence and meaning of a convention are matters of fact that must be proved by evidence and not matters of law for the court. On the other hand, the courts do not ignore conventions. A convention may form the political background against which a law has to be interpreted. For example, the convention of ministerial responsibility had enabled the courts to permit the powers of ministers to be exercised through civil servants in their departments, a principle that does not apply in other areas of government where statutory authority is required before powers can be delegated (*Carltona Ltd* v *Commissioner for Works* (1943)).

Two cases may help to illustrate the difference between law and convention in the courts. First, in *Reference Re Amendment of the Constitution of Canada* (1982) the Canadian Supreme Court, relying partly on British authority, recognised but refused to apply a convention. Under Canadian law, any amendment to the Canadian Constitution required an Act of the UK Parliament, following a request from the Federal Government of Canada. The Canadian government wished to amend the constitution so as to free itself from this legal link with Britain. The UK Parliament would automatically pass any legislation requested by Canada.

However, there were important Canadian conventions on the matter. These required that the governments of the Canadian provinces be consulted about, and give their consent to, any proposed changes in the constitution that affected federal/provincial relations. Some claimed that this had not been done. The Supreme Court was divided as to whether the convention in question existed. A majority held that it did, and went on to explain in some detail what the convention meant. Some of the judges doubted whether the court should have gone even this far, but as long as we remember that the court's view about the meaning of a convention is not in itself binding it seems acceptable. In any event a larger majority held that, whatever the convention meant, it could not affect the *legal* rule that empowered the Federal Government to resolve to seek an alteration to the constitution. Thus the convention could not be enforced by legal remedies. The judges also denied that a convention can ever crystallise into law, for example by becoming established over a period of years. This seems to be equally true of English law (see Munro, 1999, p. 72 *et seq.*).

The second case is *A-G* v *Jonathan Cape* (1975). The government sought to prevent publication of the diaries of Richard Crossman, a former Labour Cabinet minister. It relied upon the legal doctrine of breach of confidence. This involves balancing the confidential nature of any material against any public interest in favour of its disclosure. The government based its case upon the convention of collective Cabinet responsibility, arguing that this necessarily required that Cabinet business remain confidential to Cabinet ministers. The Lord Chief Justice, Lord Widgery, refused to apply the convention as such. He held that the convention was relevant only to the problem of deciding where the balance between confidentiality and the public interest lay. His Lordship held that the diaries could be published because they dealt only with matters of historical interest and did not concern the activities of Cabinet ministers still in office. Thus the convention was a crucial strand in the argument, but not the law itself.

However, the courts might develop the common law so as indirectly to incorporate the values currently expressed in conventions or convert important practices into rules of law. For example, the law of judicial review has been significantly affected by the convention of ministerial responsibility to Parliament (Chapter 14) and in *Carltona Ltd* v *Commissioner for Works* (above) the courts accepted the legitimacy of civil servants taking decisions that are in law the responsibility of the minister without reference to the minister personally. In *R* v *Secretary of State for the Home Department ex parte Ruddock* (1987) it was held that the practice of publishing the criteria governing the issue of warrants for telephone-tapping purposes created a legitimate expectation, enforceable in the courts, that these criteria would be observed before taps interception was permitted. A counter-argument to this kind of incorporation is that, if courts enforce conventions, their existence becomes 'fixed' as a matter of law, thus taking judges into the political arena and losing the flexibility which is supposed to be a reason for conventions.

### 2.4.6    Codification of Conventions

The argument surrounding codification of conventions is not unrelated to the arguments for a written constitution for the UK, and raises many of the same points. The case for codification often involves two distinct positions. The first asserts that conventions should both be codified and given legal force; a different argument asserts that conventions could be codified but without legal force. The latter argument asserts that conventions might be codified within an authoritative text with no legal status and so remain as non-legal political practices as at present. Even under this version, however, which has been adopted in Australia in relation to 34 constitutional practices, it is likely that the courts may cite those conventions which the process codified. (See C.J.G. Sampford, '"Recognize and Declare": an Australian Experience in Codifying Constitutional Conventions', 1987, *OJLS* 369). Such an approach would address the lack of precision in the scope of some conventions, and would enable us to say with certainty which usages are, and which are not, conventional. For example, the present lack of agreement about the conventional powers of the monarch to dissolve Parliament (Chapter 12) could damage the monarchy by accusations of political partiality. Establishing the certainty of conventions could safeguard the neutrality of those who apply them.

The more adventurous position involving codification *and* enactment arouses a number of concerns. The first is that such a model of codification would damage the flexibility of the constitution and inhibit its evolutionary role in maintaining the relationship between the constitution and contemporary political values. One of the purposes of conventions has been to annul anachronistic law. It would be undesirable if conventions were to become fossilised and so impede further constitutional change. This might even prevent the development of qualifications limiting the scope of some conventions (as in the case of the 'suspension' of collective Cabinet unanimity in 1975).

Moreover, as conventions are enforced as a matter of political dynamic, some argue that political flexibility might also be curbed if the courts were invited to pronounce on the breach of a conventional obligation. There are strong arguments that the demands of political morality ought to be a matter of collective decision reached through the medium of politics, and so fall outside the proper scope of the judicial function (non-justiciable). The codification of conventions, and indeed the blurring of the distinction between law and convention, might not in any case lead to judicial enforcement. To take the example of ministerial responsibility, we may conclude that apportioning blame is a political matter not a legal one. This means that the question of whether a minister's conduct in office is such that he or she should resign would seem to be a non-justiciable question, depending as it does on party support, the timing of the discovery, the support of the Prime Minister and Cabinet and the public repercussions. But the issue is not so clear if a minister were to deny an obligation to answer *any* questions in the House of Commons. What would prevent the court granting a declaration that such behaviour was unconstitutional? Would the arguments be equally as strong if a minister deliberately misled Parliament where resignation should be automatic? (See *Ministerial Code*, Section 1, para. iii; and the 2nd report of the Public Service Select Committee, 1995–6, HC 313, para. 26.)

There might also be practical difficulties in systematic codification. It would be impossible to identify all usages which are currently conventional, and immediately after a code was established, there would be nothing to prevent the evolution of new conventions.

The case for a systematic codification of conventions is not self-evidently of merit. One possible approach (but one which would not overcome all the difficulties mentioned above) might be to enact some of the most important and widely accepted conventions. This would place those selected outside the scope of the executive and locate more extensive power in Parliament. Constitutional development would then be a matter of statutory reform which itself would follow from more open debate and discussion.

In fact some of the main conventions have been enacted as law in the Scotland Act 1998, and the Government of Wales Act 1998 (below, Chapter 4). A limited and 'soft' version of codification currently operates where the conventions are expressed in instruments such as the *Ministerial Code*. This has the advantage of greater clarity, but it allows for future change since the *Code* can be amended at the discretion of the Prime Minister.

## 2.5 Constitutional Silence and Abeyance

The absence of a rule set out in a statute or case or embodied in a known convention might also be a source of the constitution in that it may indicate a deliberate choice to leave a question unanswered. Silence for example might indicate that the constitution prefers to leave an area free for the actors to do what they like subject perhaps to the ordinary private law. This is the Hobbesian notion of negative freedom lying 'in the silence of the law' (Chapter 1). The absence of legal or conventional rules governing the organisation of the central executive provides an example as does the absence of rules controlling government privatisation.

Silence might also encourage the opposite inference that government should have no freedom. For example, where a law sets out a list of rights to which it gives special treatment as is the case with the Human Rights Act 1998, Chapter 17). Do we assume that this is intended to be a comprehensive list or can other rights be recognised to which we can extend similar protection by analogy? More generally, where Parliament has not legislated in a particular area, does this mean that the common law should also refuse to go there, taking its lead from the democratic branch or is this an invitation for the common law to fill the gap (c.f. *Re Mckerr* (2004) where Parliament has legislated the common law should not fill any gap).

Constitutional silences are therefore ambiguous. Their most important function might be to discourage us from looking too closely into areas that are controversial or which raise unknowns and into which it might be wiser not to venture. In other words silence enables us to let sleeping dogs lie and invites disputing factions to take comfort in the belief that the constitution does not rule out their concerns. Examples include the question whether European law prevails over domestic law and whether Parliament can override certain basic principles of Scottish law (Chapter 7) and the extent of the Queen's personal powers (Chapter 12). This notion of silence is also embodied in the concept of a non-justiciable issue which the court refuses to determine (Chapter 12). Similarly there may be values in the constitution, personal privacy is an example, which cannot easily be embodied in clear rules so that they are best undefined as providing only a general sense of direction or an attitude (see Lord Hoffmann in *Wainwright* v *Home Office* [2003] 4 All ER 969, 979).

The risk of constitutional abeyance is that, without established guidelines, the pressure of disagreement might eventually erupt into open conflict, with the constitution powerless to resolve the dispute – the Hobbesian nightmare (Chapter 1). This was the case in the English civil war of the seventeenth century against a constitution that did not clearly define the powers of the monarch. It is arguably the case in Northern Ireland today where the devolution legislation, with its attempt to compromise between rival factions, has been suspended (Chapter 4). However it is arguable that a constitution and indeed law itself can work only within a broad consensus of beliefs and is irrelevant in situations of fundamental disagreement.

## Summary

- ▶ The UK constitution is embodied in individual statutes and in the common law which is claimed to derive from the values embedded in the community. Statutes and common law principles that are regarded as 'constitutional' are given special treatment but within a context of considerable uncertainty.

- ▶ The UK constitution is also embodied in customs and practices, the most important of which are called conventions. Conventions are pragmatically intertwined with law but are not directly enforceable in the courts. There is therefore no authoritative mechanism for interpreting, identifying or enforcing conventions.

- ▶ Conventions are of fundamental importance in the UK constitution. In their best light they enable the constitution to evolve pragmatically in accordance with changing political values. In their worst light they allow the government of the day and its favourites to manipulate the constitution in their own interests, for example by recruiting sycophantic academics to endorse a particular interpretation of a convention.

- ▶ There is disagreement about the definition of conventions. Accordingly, it is not always clear which forms of constitutional behaviour are conventions and which are mere practices. Conventions are binding rules of constitutional behaviour, whilst mere practices are not.

- ▶ Conventions are distinct from law firstly in that there are no authoritative formal tests for the validity of conventions and secondly because conventions are not directly enforced by the courts. However, there is no inherent difference in the content of laws and conventions and the courts use conventions, as they do moral principles, to help interpret, develop and apply the law.

- ▶ Some commentators have argued that conventions could be incorporated into the law, but even if this is achieved, how many such laws would be justiciable? Codification might offer certainty in respect of those conventions included in the code, but new conventions would be evolved after the code was introduced, and some flexibility in adapting existing conventions might be lost. There may be scope for extending 'soft' forms of codification, such as the *Ministerial Code*.

- ▶ Constitutional silences or 'abeyances' play a useful role mainly by avoiding confrontation in respect of issues that are inherently controversial.

# Exercises

**2.1** 'The British constitution presumes, more boldly than any other, the good faith of those who work it' (Gladstone). 'The constitution is "what happens"' (Griffith). Explain and compare these two statements.

**2.2** 'Parties have substituted for a constitution in Britain. They have filled all the vast empty spaces in the political system where a constitution should be and made the system in their own image' (Wright). Explain and criticise this statement.

**2.3** Constitutional conventions violate the fundamental republican principle of equal citizenship.' Discuss.

**2.4** To what extent is the UK constitution a common law constitution and how important is this in contemporary conditions?

**2.5** What is the relationship between law and convention? Does it serve a useful purpose to distinguish between law and conventions?

**2.6** What are the advantages and disadvantages of the UK's reliance on conventions. Should conventions be enacted into law?

**2.7** To what extent is silence a valuable constitutional device?

## Further reading

Allott, P. (1992) 'The theory of the British constitution', in Gross and Harrison (eds) *Jurisprudence: Cambridge Essays,* Cambridge, Cambridge University Press.

Bagehot, W. (1867) *The English Constitution,* 2nd edn, London, Keegan Paul, (1902) Chapter 1.

Barendt, E. (1998) *An Introduction to Constitutional Law,* Oxford, Clarendon Press, Chapter 2.

Economides, K. et al. (eds) (2000) *Fundamental Values*, Oxford, Hart Publishing, Chapter 12.

Foley, (1989) *The Silence of Constitutions,* London, Routledge.

Hennessy, P. (1995) *The Hidden Wiring: Unearthing the British Constitution,* London, Golancz, Prologue and Introduction.

Jaconelli, J. (1999) 'The Nature of Constitutional Convention', *Legal Studies,* **19**: 24.

Laws, J. (1989) 'The ghost in the machine: principles of public law', *Public Law,* 27.

Marshall, G. (1984) *Constitutional Conventions,* Oxford, Clarendon Press.

Munro, C. (1999) *Studies in Constitutional Law*, 2nd edn, London, Butterworth, Chapter 3.

Nolan, Lord and Sedley, Sir S. (eds) (1997) *The Making and Remaking of the British Constitution*, London, Blackstone, Chapter 2.

Porter, R. (1990) *England in the Eighteenth Century*, Harmondsworth, Penguin.

**Further reading cont'd**

Postema, G. (1986) *Bentham and the Common Law Tradition*, Oxford, Clarendon Press, Chapters 1, 2.

Sedley, Sir S. (1994) 'The Sound of Silence: Constitutional Law without a Constitution', *Law Quarterly Review,* **110**: 270.

Ward, I. (2000) *A State of Mind? The English Constitution and the Public Imagination*, Stroud, Sutton Publishing.

# Chapter 3

## An overview of the main institutions of the UK constitution

Small clusters of self-enclosed, self-serving groups on the peaks, and the public on the plain below. (Anthony Sampson, *Who Runs This Place?* 2004)

## Key words

- ▶ Legitimacy and different kinds of power
- ▶ Reason and tradition
- ▶ Dignified and efficient
- ▶ Parliamentary government
- ▶ Politics and law
- ▶ Democratic accountability and executive domination
- ▶ Political parties
- ▶ 'Trust': voluntary codes of conduct
- ▶ Civil Service impartiality
- ▶ Judicial independence

### 3.1 Introduction

The object of this chapter is to offer an overview of the structure of the UK constitution as a framework for more detailed discussion in the following chapters. A preliminary issue is what makes a constitution binding. This is sometimes called 'legitimacy'. A constitution is said to be 'legitimate' when taken as a whole it can be justified on the basis of widely accepted beliefs. For example, Locke thought the people had a right to rebel against an unjust constitution thus justifying the seventeenth-century English revolution against the Crown. However, some (e.g. Weber, 1864–1920) argue that 'legitimacy 'merely means that the constitution, of whatever kind including one based purely on force, is effective. UK law takes this pragmatic view in the context for example of recognising the legality of a rebellion (See *Madzimbamuto* v *Lardner-Burke* (1969): legality of a takeover of a British colony by a group of white settlers). According to this view our constitution is legitimate because those who wield effective power recognise it as such, although admittedly a general sense among the people that the constitution is morally good or at least that it is in their interests might help them stay in power.

Legitimacy therefore depends on a blend of three types of power none of which alone can suffice; firstly the power of brute force (*imperium*), secondly the power to pay and reward (*dominium*) and thirdly the power to persuade. 'Persuasion' for example might include appealing to some ideal such as religion in order to unite a community. Thus legitimacy depends partly upon what Ward (2000) has called 'the popular imagination'. This is not confined to formal legal texts and the pronouncement of officials but includes art, drama and literature such as novels, poetry and the press.

It is often said that the glue which holds our unwritten constitution together is the propensity of the British to subservience and deference to officialdom. Writing in the mid-nineteenth century, Walter Bagehot, (1902) regarded social class deference and superstition as the magic ingredients that animated the constitution. Bagehot took a jaundiced view of the political sophistication of ordinary people and thought that government could only work effectively if its authority was buttressed by traditional institutions which command people's imagination and make them deferential to the rulers.

Bagehot distinguished between what he called the 'dignified' and the efficient parts of the constitution. The dignified parts give the constitution its authority and encourage people to obey it. They involve the trappings of power and the mystique of ceremonial and ritual. According to Bagehot, the monarchy and Parliament constitute the main dignified elements of the constitution. The 'efficient' part of the constitution, which Bagehot located in the Cabinet and which depends on the political balance of forces at any given time, carries out the working exercise of power behind the scenes. From this perspective, all government boils down to an oligarchy of like-minded people in the form of a 'king' and his courtiers.

What is dignified and what efficient evolves over time. For example, the eighteenth-century Hanoverian kings lost public respect by becoming virtually party politicians. William IV in 1834 was the last monarch to dismiss a ministry which had the support of Parliament. Towards the end of her reign (1837–1901), Queen Victoria 're-dignified' the monarchy by distancing herself from political partisanship and introducing the kind of pomp and ceremony that characterises the UK monarchy today. It remains unclear however whether the monarch retains a vestige of political power (Chapter 12). The distinction between the dignified and efficient performs a useful function in a democracy by preventing working politicians from claiming to embody the state, a technique adopted by tyrants throughout history. For example, the monarch and Parliament have authority, the latter because it is elected while the government has power without authority in its own right.

On the other hand, the dignified element can reinforce tyranny by hiding reality. Indeed Bagehot thought that it would be dangerous to shed the light of reality upon the constitution. The 'noble lie' postulated by Plato in his *Republic* and designed to keep people happy with their designated roles, was that when humans were formed in the earth, the rulers had gold mixed with them, the military silver and the workers lead. Even Plato's pupils found this hard to swallow but, they thought that it is sometimes right to lie in the interests of the state. There is an element of the same thinking in the contemporary constitution. For example in *McIlkenny* v *Chief Constable of the West Midlands* [1980] 2 All ER 227 at 239–240, Lord Denning MR took the view that it was better for the 'Birmingham Six' to remain wrongly convicted than to face the 'appalling vista' of the police being found to be guilty of perjury, violence and threats. The Scott Report into the sale of arms to Iraq HC115 (1995–6) revealed that ministers and civil servants regarded it as being in the public interest to mislead Parliament, if not actually to lie, over government involvement in arms sales to overseas regimes.

## 3.2 ▶ Historical Outline

The purpose of this historical outline is to indicate some themes and issues which have influenced the contemporary constitution. All constitutions reflect competing myths or stories of how the constitution takes its particular form and how it is justified. Traditionalists claim that the UK constitution is the happy and pragmatic outcome of a gradual evolution towards freedom and democracy ordered by benevolent customs. Accordingly the monarchy, in the shape of the Norman Conquest of 1066, had usurped an earlier more democratic regime, 'the ancient constitution'. The King gradually gave way to Parliament as representing those worthy to have a stake in the community. Parliament steadily broadened its membership until eventually the people as a whole controlled it, with the courts benevolently protecting their rights. The collapse of the French Revolution at the end of the eighteenth century was regarded as an awful warning of the dangers of radical constitutional building. Abuses are unlikely, because, apart from the odd maverick, we can trust our rulers to be persons of high ability and integrity who can vouch for each other. They are also subject to political pressures to please at least enough of the public to keep them in office. Distrust for the written constitutional model survives today in the form, for example, of resistance to the European Union.

Another view is that the history of the constitution is driven by chance, circumstances and personalities in an endless power struggle. Both external and internal controls over government ebb and flow in response to particular incidents and problems and in accordance with changing political beliefs. There is no single driving force. 'Everything that happens is constitutional' (Griffith, 'The Political Constitution', 1979, *Modern Law Review* **42**(1), 19).

### 3.2.1    The Medieval Period

The main institutions of our constitution, the monarchy, parliament and the courts developed in the medieval period. The King was the most powerful warlord whose private army was based on the system of feudal land-holding. England had a centralised but flexible legal regime in the shape of the common law, a system of justice available to all deriving its authority from the King. There was also a tradition of local administration, in theory under the Crown but in practice allowed considerable independence.

Magna Carta (1215), extracted from King John by the leading barons, is usually taken to embody the principle that the King is subject to the law in the sense of the customs of the realm that protected the rights of the landowners and local communities. Magna Carta can also be depicted as a pragmatic deal struck between the King and powerful interest groups and many of its provisions were later abandoned. However it remains of great symbolic value as capturing the essence of the rule of law and accountable government (Chapter 5). It includes the principles of no taxation without representation, the right to a fair trial and no imprisonment or confiscation of property other than by law (which at the time meant common law custom).

Parliament was originally a meeting of influential persons summoned by the King, originally in the House of Lords, to give advice. The House of Lords, which dates from Saxon times, was composed of the great landowners. The House of Commons, which began to meet during the thirteenth century, consisted of representatives of the 'people' (in practice being chosen from influential local worthies). They were summoned by the King to legitimate demands for taxation in return for redressing the grievances of subjects. Parliament began to make laws originally on the basis that it was declaring the existing customs of the realm. Parliament also had the status of a High Court, able to give final rulings on the law and to 'empeach' public officials for misconduct. Empeachment, in which the House of Commons brings accusations before the House of Lords, remains possible but depends on a resolution of the House and is unlikely to be used today. However, subject to current reforms (below), the House of Lords still acts as a final court of appeal from most UK courts and each House has the power to punish those who offend against its internal rules (Chapter 9).

### 3.2.2    The Tudor Period

The Tudor period spanning the sixteenth century saw the emergence in main-land Europe of the modern concept of the state as a self-contained impersonal structure served by a bureaucracy and with absolute authority within its territory (Chapter 4). This replaced the more complex medieval regime in which Church, state and various interest groups such as landowners and trade groups co-existed uneasily. Throughout Europe the monarchy claimed to embody this absolute notion of the state although less so in England where the common law and Parliament provided counter-forces.

It was established by the sixteenth century that the two Houses of Parliament met separately, that Parliament could make new laws and that the King must ask the House of Commons for money in the form of direct taxation. The King was however entitled to raise indirect taxes such as duties on imports and could also confiscate and sell property and control franchises and monopolies such as the right to pursue certain trades.

The Tudor monarchs ruled with relatively little need to summon Parliament, partly by confiscating church property following the Reformation (1532–6) and partly from the proceeds of naval adventures, and levies on overseas trade. This period also saw the emergence of the modern type of executive comprising ministers, the most important of which were styled Secretaries of State; committees, notably the Privy Council comprising the monarch's favourites and exercising the formal powers of the Crown; and a bureaucratic structure of civil servants. The Privy Council remains today but, thanks to conventions, its functions are mainly formalities but nonetheless legally necessary.

During the sixteenth and seventeenth centuries, medieval ideas of limited monarchy within the common law clashed with the newer ideas of absolute monarchy and the nation state. Classical republican ideas of equal citizenship also surfaced (e.g. Sir John Harrington, 1561–1612) although these have not significantly influenced constitutional development in the UK. In the law courts the clash between Crown and Parliament was foreshadowed by controversy about the late medieval notion of the Crown's 'two persons', the one ('gubernaculum') concerned with protecting the realm and which claimed to be above the law; the other, ('jurisdictio'), an official whose day-to-day duties primarily concerned the enforcement of private rights and were subject to the law (see *Duchy of Lancaster Case* (1567). However it was widely accepted that only in Parliament could the King exercise the fullest lawmaking power.

### 3.2.3    The Seventeenth-century Revolution

The seventeenth century was a crucible of ideas. They include sovereignty, individual rights, representation of interests and, to a limited extent, democracy. The century was dominated by religious and financial conflicts between the Crown and Parliament. These led to the revolution of 1688 which was the foundation of the present constitution. The Stuart monarchs ran out of money and were under military pressure from Scotland and Ireland. They claimed the right to raise taxes without Parliament but respected the common law by subjecting their powers to scrutiny by the courts (see e.g. *Case of Proclamations*

(1611); *R v Hampden* (1637)). The judges were servants of the Crown but asserted their independence from the Crown in deciding cases (*Prohibitions del Roy* (1607). Nevertheless their position remained ambivalent since they could be dismissed by the King. For example Coke CJ's stand against royal interference in the *Case of Prohibitions* (above) was followed by his dismissal for taking a similar stand in 1616 in the *Commendum* case.

From 1629 Charles I attempted to rule without Parliament on the basis of taxes extorted from the rising middle classes. However, when he attempted in 1639 to impose the Anglican prayer book on the Scots, the resulting uprising forced him to summon Parliament in 1640 (the 'Long Parliament' which technically survived until 1660 albeit dormant for most of its life). A short-lived compromise was reached in 1641 when the Star Chamber and other special prerogative courts introduced by the Tudors to support an administrative state were abolished. These events left English legal culture with a deep suspicion of special jurisdictions over governmental matters and a preference for the ordinary courts.

Civil war broke out in 1642 resulting in victory for Parliament in 1646. There was a wide-ranging constitutional debate at Putney between the ruling conservative establishment of landowners led by Oliver Cromwell and the more radical army rank and file represented by the Levellers. The Levellers proposed a written constitution, 'The Agreement of the People', based on religious freedom, equality before the law and universal suffrage. However, Cromwell invoked custom and tradition in favour of more limited reforms. The Levellers were defeated by force in 1649.

In 1649 Charles I was executed on the authority of Parliament which was packed with army supporters. The House of Lords was abolished and a republic declared. In 1653 Parliament was expelled and a military dictatorship led by Oliver Cromwell as 'Lord Protector' introduced. However, after Cromwell's death in 1658 it seemed that chaos could best be avoided by restoring the traditional constitution. A self-appointed group of political leaders restored the Crown in 1660 in the form of Charles II, the heir of Charles I.

Charles II and his brother James II (1685–88) ruled on the basis that there had been no republic and the republican legislation was expunged from the statute book. A limited religious toleration was declared and a relatively liberal regime introduced. The uneasy stalemate was broken when James began to assert the interests of Catholics and to attempt to override Parliament. Catholicism was associated in the public mind with absolution, an association that still scars the constitution by preventing the monarch from being or marrying a Catholic.

The foundations of the modern constitution were laid by the 1688 revolution when James dissolved Parliament and fled the country. A self-appointed 'Convention Parliament' offered the Crown to the Protestant William of Orange and his wife Mary (James's daughter) who were backed up by the Dutch navy. In political terms the 1688 revolution was relatively conservative being a compromise designed to satisfy all influential interests. It was justified in two inconsistent ways. On a Hobbesian premise James II had abdicated leaving a power vacuum which, according to the common law doctrine of necessity, must be filled in order to avoid chaos. On the other premise, based on Locke, James had broken his trust (Chapter 1). This entitled the people to rebel. In the case of Scotland and Ireland, continuing support for the Stuart monarchs was crushed by force.

William and Mary accepted the Bill of Rights 1688 which dealt with various grievances against the Stuart kings. It prohibited the Crown from exercising key powers without the consent of Parliament, including the power to make laws, to tax, to keep a standing army in peacetime, and to override legislation. It also protected freedom of speech and elections in Parliament, secured frequent Parliaments, protected jury trial and banned excessive bail. William and Mary then summoned a Parliament which ratified the Acts of the Convention (Crown and Parliament Recognition Act 1689). The Act of Settlement 1700 provided for the succession to the Crown and gave superior court judges security of tenure, and therefore independence from the Crown. The Act of Settlement also linked Church and state by requiring the monarch to be a Protestant and not to marry a Catholic.

The 1688 settlement was not based on democracy nor the fundamental rights of the individual such as a century later would influence the French and American revolutions. If anything it confirmed the principle of aristocratic rule. The House of Lords was a powerful body and the House of Commons was largely made up of landowners and traders dependent on the patronage of the Lords. Thomas Paine, who fled the country in 1792 having been charged with sedition for denying that Britain had a constitution, said:

> What is [the Bill of Rights 1688] but a bargain which the parts of the government made with each other to decide powers. You shall have so much and I will have the rest; and with respect to the nation, it said, for your share, you shall have the right of petitioning. This being the case the Bill of Rights is more properly a bill of wrongs and of insult. (*The Rights of Man* (1791–2), (London, Penguin, 1987) p. 292)

### 3.2.4 The Eighteenth and Early Nineteenth Centuries: The Parliamentary System

The 1688 revolution had put the main legal and political structures in place. In law the King remained the executive branch of government. During the following two centuries political power moved away from the King to ministers in Parliament with policy made by the Cabinet. This was brought about almost entirely by conventions (Chapter 2).

At a time when most European states were absolute monarchies, the British constitution was widely regarded by overseas observers such as Montesquieu as a stable and liberal regime embodying the rule of law and a separation of powers between Parliament, the executive and the monarchy. From inside Britain however the picture was more blurred.

At first the monarch claimed to run the executive personally and to choose ministers although a convention existed from the outset that the Commons could dismiss a ministry of which it disapproved. The Crown ran what was in effect a political party known as the 'Court and Treasury Party' which it controlled by giving government jobs to its supporters and manipulating elections.

A significant difference from the modern Parliament was that the party system was looser than is the case today and the pros and cons of political parties were matters of lively controversy (e.g. lack of independence against rallying support for great causes). About half the MPs were independent of party allegiance. The main parties, the Whigs (broadly liberal, secular, progressive and republican) and the Tories (traditionalist, church, monarchical and conservative) alternated in forming governments but split and reformed several times and members frequently changed parties. One reason for the relative independence of MPs was that, unlike today, most MPs had private means and did not depend on their party for career advancement. Indeed an Act of 1710 (9 Anne c.5) imposed a property requirement on membership of the House of Commons (except for the eldest sons of peers and knights and the representatives of Oxford and Cambridge universities).

The electoral system was not democratic and bore little relationship to the distribution of the population. General elections did not necessarily relate to changes in government as is the case today but governments formed and reformed under royal and aristocratic influence. There was a property qualification to vote in the rural counties. In the boroughs (towns) the right to vote depended on local charters and customs. In many cases this was attached to particular property and could be bought. There were numerous 'rotten boroughs' which had only a handful of electors sometimes in the gift of particular families. At the other extreme the expanding cities had few representatives. Elections were largely controlled by aristocratic families with a power base both in the House of Lords and in local affairs. Thus royalty and ministers could influence the outcome of elections by giving jobs, pensions or contracts or by selecting candidates for seats. For example, a letter to the Prince Regent in 1813 asked:

> Have you any friends of the same sentiments desirous of securing seats for the next Parliament without trouble, opposition or even attendance? I will enter into

arrangements with them to their satisfaction, either for Ilchester, where I have reduced the voted to fifty two or for Grantham, where I own by inheritance and purchase the chief part of the Parish and have the Duke of Rutland at my command. My second question is, whether you can form an idea at what time the promise of the peerage will be realised to me? (A. Aspinall (ed.) *Letters of King George IV No 271*, Cambridge, 1938)

Some contemporary themes are emerging. Patronage today is exercised by the political parties who nominate candidates for election and recommend peerages. In the eighteenth century, civil servants were also appointed by patronage and many senior officials and judges were also members of Parliament. Then as now the permanent civil service was caught between two stools. On the one hand, efficiency required it to be distant from day-to-day politics. On the other hand, ministers required loyal servants. Various 'Place Acts' attempted a compromise by barring many categories of public official from membership of Parliament. Today, we tackle the problem by barring most public officials from sitting in Parliament and creating a category of 'special advisor' who is a civil servant with party political affiliations (below).

By the end of the eighteenth century the Crown's direct powers had been reduced but the modern conventions removing the Crown from political interference were not fully established until the late nineteenth century. The Crown must appoint the leader of the majority party as Prime Minister and must accept his choice of other ministers. Moreover the Crown must dissolve Parliament at the request of the Prime Minister who must so request if the government loses the confidence of the House of Commons. The Crown must act on the advice of ministers generally and must assent to all legislation presented by Parliament.

During the eighteenth century the notion of the 'mixed constitution' was promoted in which monarch, Lords and Commons acted as checks on each other in a balanced clockwork-like machine. For example Blackstone announced that the Royal Assent to legislation meant that the King could not propose evil but could prevent it and went on to eulogise the mutual checks between nobility, king and people which Parliament embodied (see this volume Chapter 6). Blackstone also emphasised the importance of the rule of law and the independence of the judges although in the eighteenth century this was ambivalent. In particular judges were politically appointed and were often members of Parliament and the Cabinet and, until the reign of George III (1760–1820), they had to be reappointed on the death of a monarch. Even today the highest appeal court is part of Parliament (below).

The courts were in theory open to all (who could afford the fees) and juries were on the whole reluctant to impose draconian penalties. The common law, albeit reluctantly, rejected slavery (*Somersett's Case* (1772)), and the courts protected property and freedom of expression (e.g. *Leach* v

*Money* (1765); *Entick* v *Carrington* (1765); *Wolfe Tone's Case* (1798)). The jury system was developed. Religious discrimination was reduced. The courts protected rights in the formal sense that whatever rights a person had were usually adjudicated impartially. However, the content of those rights was affected by draconian legislation passed in the interests of landowners, such as anti-poaching laws and a tax system that put the overwhelming burden upon consumption as opposed to property, thus penalising the poor (see E.P. Thompson, *Whigs and Hunters*, 1975). There were also ruthless measures against blasphemy and political offences including sedition, and against public disorder. These included the intermittent suspension of *Habeas Corpus* (an ancient procedure for ensuring the release of those unlawfully imprisoned).

Britain did not escape the social dislocations that were a prominent feature of the times but, for reasons that are not fully understood, managed to escape the revolutions that brought down many European regimes. A possible reason lay in the flexibility of our constitutional arrangements and the willingness of the aristocratic elite to give way gradually in the face of pressures for reform. Other reasons lay in the relative flexibility of the social class structure in Britain and with the deference of the English character.

Scotland, which had previously been a separate state under the same monarch, was united with England as a single state, Great Britain, with one Parliament (Acts of Union 1706). However, it is still debated whether Parliament has more limited powers in respect of Scotland than England (Chapter 7). The Act of Union with Ireland 1800 temporarily united Great Britain and Ireland as the UK. However, by 1921 most of Ireland had become an independent state. Northern Ireland, which from Tudor times had been occupied by Protestant settlers from England and Scotland, remains part of the UK. There is still no consensus as to the status of Northern Ireland.

### 3.2.5    The Nineteenth and Twentieth Centuries: Democracy and the Central State

During the nineteenth century the political and economic circumstances of Britain rapidly changed. Rural communities centring upon market towns and dominated by the great aristocratic landowners were overshadowed by large urban conurbations dependent upon industrial production and overseas trade. This led to a rapidly increasing urban population of wage earners, demands for democratic government and the provision of public services. Between the first Reform Act of 1832 and 1928 when women were given the franchise, Parliament gradually and reluctantly extended the right to vote. Many more electoral constituencies were created with an attempt to make these correspond to the distribution of the population. Secret ballots were introduced. These developments strengthened the party system producing the large, professional and tightly controlled parties that currently dominate the political process. The balance of power between Parliament and the executive increasingly moved in favour of the executive. MPs were increasingly becoming professional politicians dependent for their livelihood on party support. Elections became the mass campaigns with which we are familiar today. After the First World War the moderately radical Liberal party collapsed and the conservative Tories were confronted by the newly emergent Labour Party then representing working-class interests.

Utilitarianism and economics replaced law as the intellectual fashion (Chapter 1). For much of the nineteenth century free-market ideas were dominant but coupled with strong state activity to provide basic services and remedy injustices. Local authorities were created to provide the roads, utilities and public health services necessary to support business interests, but their powers were limited by the courts to prevent them providing more than basic welfare services (for example *A.G.* v *Fulham Corporation* (1921)).

The extension of democracy led to a debate about the place of the common law. Traditionalists regarded the common law as a hedge against tyranny while reformers such as Bentham despised the common law as an enemy of progress, democracy and efficient management. '[E]ighteenth century veneration for the law was giving way to pungent criticism of it' (Briggs, A., *The Age of Improvement*, 1783–1867 (London, Longman 1959) p. 92). During this period when Parliament began to be genuinely representative, the courts explicitly endorsed the principle of parliamentary supremacy. In relation to the common law it is arguable that the broad justice-based system that predominated during the eighteenth century was challenged by more formalistic rule-based conceptions of law that suited the development of capitalism and free markets in the nineteenth century. This was underpinned by the dominant religion which extolled the merits of hard work and duty.

During Queen Victoria's reign (1837–1901) the monarchy reshaped itself as a symbolic representative of the nation standing outside party politics. Power became increasingly concentrated in the House of Commons and the executive. Lord Salisbury, whose final administration ended in 1892, was the last Prime Minister to sit in the House of Lords. The Parliament Act 1911 resolved the matter in favour of the Commons by removing most of the powers of the House of Lords to veto legislation. However, the House of Lords retains significant influence. Its main function is now that of a revising and delaying mechanism.

Impelled by the demands of a larger electorate, the executive began to increase in size and range of discretionary powers as successive governments provided a wider range of welfare services such as education, public health, housing and social security payments. These could be delivered only through large bureaucratic organisations making numerous detailed decisions, guided by a plethora of rules and advised by technical specialists. An important landmark was the Northcote-Trevelyan Report of 1854 which led to the creation of a permanent, professional and non-party political civil service, appointed on merit – an ideal retained today.

During the twentieth century it became widely accepted that the state can regulate any aspect of our lives and that whether it should do so was a matter not for the constitution but for the everyday political contest. The traditional sources of law, Acts of Parliament and the courts, were supplemented by an array of tools which enabled the executive to act relatively quickly and informally but without detailed parliamentary scrutiny. These included delegated legislation made by government departments under powers given to them by statute and non-statutory rules issued by officials as 'guidance', strictly not binding in law but normally followed. Thousands of administrative tribunals staffed by government appointees were created to deal with the disputes generated by the expansion of state activity. Other bodies outside the traditional umbrella of parliamentary accountability were created to run services or to give advice. Executive control over Parliament increased. This was reinforced by the dependence of Parliament upon the specialised knowledge of the executive, and the dependence of members of Parliament upon the patronage of their party.

The constitution made only limited responses to these developments. It became increasingly apparent that the shape of the constitution can be determined by the government of the day. For example, the current Prime Minister, Tony Blair, has been reported as saying, 'people have to know that we will run from the centre and govern from the centre' (*Times Higher*, 22. April 2004). It was feared that the executive had outgrown the constraints both of the rule of law and of political accountability to Parliament. The *Committee on Ministers' Powers* (1932, Cmd 4060) and the *Committee on Administrative Tribunals and Inquiries* (1958, Cmnd 218) recommended marginal reforms which strengthened the powers of the courts and supplemented parliamentary scrutiny of the executive. These included a parliamentary committee to scrutinise such delegated legislation as statute required to be laid before Parliament (Statutory Instruments Act 1946), increased rights of appeal and the creation of a Council on Tribunals with powers to approve procedural rules for most administrative tribunals and statutory inquiries (Tribunals and Inquiries Acts 1958/1992). From the 1960s, various ombudsmen were set up to investigate complaints by citizens against government but without enforceable powers.

Recognising the inevitability of executive discretion and reluctant to appear to be challenging democracy, the courts usually deferred to political decisions, an attitude which was particularly strong after the Second World

War. In the inter-war period, both ends of the political spectrum were worried. Some believed that the executive had taken over, others that an individualistically minded judiciary would frustrate social reforms.

There were also concerns about democracy. In 1972 the UK became a member of what is now the European Union (European Communities Act 1972). Much European law has thereby become binding in UK law but is not made by an elected body and is subject only to limited democratic scrutiny (Chapter 8). Concerns were also raised that the electoral system puts minorities into power and enables the large political parties to control both the executive and Parliament (Chapter 10). These complaints amounted to fears that the constitution had degenerated into an oligarchy which did little more than allow the people to choose periodically between groups of cronies. Indeed in the eighteenth century, Rousseau (Chapter 1) asserted that the British were slaves except at election time. More recently Howard Davies, Director of the London School of Economics, remarked of democracy that:

> even where power has nominally rested with the populace at large, it has typically been wielded by a tightly defined group, usually rather a nasty one. (*Times Higher*, 23 April 2004)

During the late twentieth century and continuing today, there was a revival of the notion of the free market as the basis for delivering public welfare, and government began to disband its provision of public services such as utilities, transport, and housing in favour of private or semi-private bodies However, reluctant to give up power, government created a range of bureaucratic bodies to regulate the privatised bodies. At the same time the courts began to interfere more actively with government decisions in the interests of individual rights; a development supported by the enactment in 1998 of the Human Rights Act. Moreover some judges claimed the common law to be the basis of the constitution, even suggesting that the common law is capable of overriding Acts of Parliament in order to resist executive tyranny (see Laws, 1996, 'The Constitution, Morals and Rights', *Public Law*, 622; Woolf, 1985, *Protection of the Public: a new Challenge*).

## 3.3 The Structure of Modern Government

In the absence of a written constitution it is difficult to summarise the basic structure of the constitution. The following is an approximation:

- ▶ *Parliament*, the lawmaking branch, is usually regarded as 'sovereign' in the sense of having unlimited and ultimate power (Chapter 7).
- ▶ The UK constitution is a *constitutional monarchy*, meaning that there is a non-elected head of state who does not govern in person. The Crown is the symbolic head of state and also the formal head of the executive branch. The Crown governs through ministers chosen from members

of Parliament, can make law only in conjunction with Parliament and depends on Parliament for finance. However, although it cannot interfere with the legal rights of others except under powers given to it by Parliament or under certain powers known as the royal prerogative, the Crown as a person is otherwise free in law to do anything that an adult individual can do, although it is restricted by numerous conventions and traditions (Chapter 12).

▶ The UK constitution has an extreme *parliamentary character*. The leader of the majority party in the House of Commons is appointed by the Queen as Prime Minister to form a government from his or her supporters in Parliament. Thus whichever group controls Parliament is the most powerful actor in the constitution.

▶ *The executive* has a loose and fragmented structure. Parliament usually gives power to individual ministers, not to the Crown as such. Ministers are collectively and individually accountable to Parliament for government policy and the activities of their departments. Government departments are coordinated by the Prime Minister, the Cabinet and the Treasury (Chapter 13).

▶ *The courts* decide disputes, applying the law to particular cases, and in particular, review decisions made by the executive. They cannot interfere with the internal proceedings of Parliament since Parliament is at least co-equal with the courts (Chapter 9). They also create law in the form of the common law. The conventional and historically plausible view is that the common law must give way to Acts of Parliament but some commentators and judges challenge this (Chapter 7).

▶ No public authority can interfere with individual freedom or rights without power to do so under an Act of Parliament, royal prerogative or, occasionally, by a common law rule, for example police powers to prevent a breach of the peace (Chapter 18).

▶ The UK constitution is not fully democratic. The upper House of Parliament is unelected and the courts through the common law have lawmaking power although this is more limited than that of Parliament. It is assumed however that in the case of conflict the democratic element, namely the House of Commons, must have the last word.

### 3.3.1  The Authority of the Constitution: The Crown

In strict theory all legal power emanates from the Crown who as head of state is involved with all three branches of government. Indeed the history of our constitution can be described as an evolution from household servants to public officials. Strictly speaking, Acts of Parliament are made by the Queen following advice from Parliament and there is no other way she can make laws. Moreover, by convention the monarch cannot refuse the

Royal Assent to any bill properly presented by Parliament. Members of the judiciary are in law appointed by the Queen and act in the Queen's name since their powers historically derive from the royal functions of keeping order and doing justice. However, since the seventeenth century, the judicial function has been separate from the executive functions of the Crown (*Prohibitions del Roy* (1607) and it is settled that the Crown cannot establish new courts or interfere with judicial decision making.

The executive is still run in the name of the Crown but by convention the Queen must act through ministers supported by Parliament. Ministers can act through appointed civil servants who are also Crown servants but ministers remain legally and constitutionally responsible. Thus there is a tension between the dispersed way in which powers are allocated, which leads for example to rivalry between government departments and the legal theory that the Crown is a single entity. The Crown is treated as a single legal entity for the purpose of private law such as property ownership but statutory powers are usually exercised by ministers in their own right.

There are also certain powers vested in the Crown under the common law. These are known as the royal prerogative (Chapter 12). This is a residue of the powers of the medieval monarchs although some prerogatives can be justified as being necessary in any state, for example the power to declare war or to make treaties. Most royal prerogative powers are exercised by ministers, many of them by the Prime Minister. Because they do not require the support of laws made by Parliament they are relatively difficult to subject to democratic control as was recently illustrated by the controversy over the war with Iraq. As head of state, the monarch exercises ceremonial and symbolic functions such as signing important legal instruments, granting titles and honours and representing the UK abroad. More controversially, the Queen must exercise real political power in the form of her residual sovereignty if the normal system of parliamentary government collapses, for example if a Prime Minister tries to remain in office without the support of Parliament (Chapter 12).

The Crown also has certain legal immunities deriving from the mystique of monarchy. However the medieval maxim, 'the King can do no wrong' has been constantly reinterpreted to meet changing ideas and is no longer favoured in the context of the executive (Chapter 12 and see McIlwain, *Constitutionalism Ancient and Modern* (1947, London, Cornell University Press) Ch. IV). For example in *M* v *Home Office* (1993), it was held that the Crown, ministers, and the courts were separate entities and that ministers could not hide behind Crown immunity. Lord Templeman remarked that to hold otherwise would be tantamount to backtracking on the seventeenth-century revolution. However, the Queen cannot be held liable personally in a court nor probably even compelled to attend a court.

### 3.3.2 The Legislature: Parliament

In European democracies the legislature is invariably an elected assembly (Parliament) having either one (unitary) or two parts (bicameral), the latter being favoured by liberals to limit power and by republicans to disperse it. The UK Parliament is bicameral. The House of Lords is not elected but composed entirely of people appointed by various routes, ultimately by the Prime Minister (Chapter 10). Until 1999 membership of the Lords was dominated by the hereditary aristocracy, those whose title passes down their family after an initial appointment originally made by the monarch (below). By virtue of the House of Lords Act 1999, apart from a temporary rump, hereditary peers can no longer sit in the Lords, the members of which are now appointed by the Prime Minister as life peers or as office holders namely, senior judges and Church of England bishops. The House of Lords is subservient to the elected House of Commons (Chapter 11).

Parliament formally makes laws in the form of statutes. It also supervises and removes the executive. By convention the House of Commons chooses the leader of the executive, the Prime Minister, who is invariably the leader of the largest political party in the Commons. Thus although the law gives us a representative democracy (a candidate for election need not belong to any party), in practice we have a market democracy (Chapter 1) where competing parties take turns to form a government. In contemporary conditions it is rare that an independent candidate can attract sufficient public attention to win a seat in the Commons. Moreover, the electoral system itself favours large parties (Chapter 10). Parliamentary control over the executive is widely regarded as limited and ineffective. This is mainly due to party political factors which enable the executive to put pressure on members of Parliament (Chapters 9, 13).

Parliament also provides the executive with money by legislating to raise taxes and approving in broad terms the spending proposals of the government (Chapter 11). The historical relationship between the two Houses of Parliament and the Crown as regards finance is a central feature of the constitution. For example, since the Bill of Rights 1688 it has been established that the Crown cannot raise taxes except by Act of Parliament. Moreover the House of Commons plays the dominant part: 'the Crown demands money, the Commons grant it, and the Lords assent to the grant' (Erskine May, *Parliamentary Practice*, 21st edn, 1997, p. 723). However, parliamentary control over finances is probably ineffective in practice, since Parliament has not the time, the independence nor the expertise to scrutinise government accounts with any rigour. Control over government finance is primarily exercised by the Treasury (Chapter 13). According to Thomas Paine, this is like a criminal judging himself (*The Thomas Paine Reader*, Penguin, 1987, p. 225)

### 3.3.3    The Executive

Strictly speaking, the UK constitution has no concept of the executive as a discrete branch of government since Parliament can confer executive powers on anyone. The Crown forms the nearest we have to an executive. There are three kinds of member of the executive as part of the Crown. Firstly, there are about 100 ministers of various ranks, by convention appointed and dismissed by the Prime Minister, all of whom must be members of Parliament either on appointment or as soon as possible afterwards. (A Prime Minister might for example appoint a friend as a minister and then appoint that person to the House of Lords.) Secondly, there are appointed civil servants. Thirdly, there are appointed 'special advisors'.

The civil service comprises non-political servants of the Crown (other than the armed forces). It gives impartial advice to ministers and carries out the orders of ministers supposedly serving every government loyally whatever its political makeup. The civil service acts as a storehouse of knowledge and a stabilising influence in the constitution, counterbalancing the regularly changing body of elected politicians. It is therefore important that senior civil servants are independent of party politics, and are subject to a duty of confidentiality so that they can serve any kind of government. However, in the context of claims that a civil servant may owe a duty to the Crown above that owing to his or her government department, Sir Robert Armstrong, then head of the civil service, announced that for all practical purposes the Crown is the government of the day (Hennessy, *The Hidden Wiring*, p. 346). Moreover, the *Civil Service Code* (Cabinet Office, 1996) makes it clear that civil servants owe primary loyalty to ministers. There are about 1000 civil servants who have a direct imput into government policy and about 500,000 civil servants in all. The Prime Minister is the minister responsible for the organisation and discipline of the civil service.

#### 3.3.3.1 *Special Advisors*

Special advisors are party political advisors appointed personally by ministers and working closely with them. They were formally recognised by a government announcement in 1974 but have probably always existed. In March 2003 there were 81 special advisors of which 27 worked for the Prime Minister. They are temporary civil servants whose posts terminate with their minister. Unlike other civil servants they are not required to be politically impartial and some are empowered to give directions to civil servants (Civil Service Order in Council 1995). Their functions include advising ministers, briefing party members and officials, publicising government policies and drawing up or reviewing policies of both government and party (see *Ninth Report of Committee on Standards in Public Life* (Cm 5775, 2003); *Code of Conduct for Special Advisors* (2001), Cabinet Office). There is a concern that their activities, particularly in relation to communication with the media, may threaten the reputation of the civil service for impartiality. There is also a concern that permanent civil servants may be denied access to ministers and that their role will reduced to carrying out orders from special advisors. Some special advisors have attracted the label of 'spin doctors' (e.g. the controversy in 2003 relating to the publication of a case for attacking Iraq and the case of Jo Moore who advised that the day of the terrorist attack on the World Trade Center was 'a good day to bury bad news').

The constitutional problem is that the distinction between the political and the permanent parts of the executive has become blurred thereby upsetting an important balance. On the other hand, special advisors serve as a valuable link between the two elements. In its *Ninth Report* (2003) the Committee on Standards in Public life recommended that both the civil service and special advisors should be subject to a statutory regime which clarifies their respective constitutional roles and duties. In particular special advisors should be defined as a separate category distinct from civil servants and should not normally be given executive powers nor management or disciplinary powers over civil servants. Ministers should be personally accountable for the acts of their special advisors.

The Civil Service (No. 2) Bill currently before Parliament (Chapter 13) provides that no special advisor shall exercise executive powers and requires the Prime Minister to lay an annual report, including costs, before Parliament on the appointment, role and responsibilities of special advisors. It appears that special advisors will remain civil servants paid from public funds whereas it is arguable that as political advisors they should be financed by the political party.

There is little formal law regulating the internal organisation of the executive. Heavy reliance is placed on internal conventions and practices (Chapter 13). Coordination between government departments is supplied through the Prime Minister, in whom the making of government policy is increasingly centralised, and the Treasury which controls government finances and is the gatekeeper to parliament as far as claims for resources are concerned (ibid). The Cabinet, a committee of senior ministers chaired by the Prime Minister, is also a coordinating body which historically has been the final policy maker within the executive. In recent years, however, the Cabinet has become relatively insignificant, meeting only briefly to endorse decisions made elsewhere.

Executive powers are also conferred by statute on many miscellaneous specialised bodies, the powers of which depend on particular legislation and fluctuate with changing political fashion. Such bodies include the Housing Corporation (funds and regulates social housing providers), the Environment Agency, NHS Trusts, regulators of the public utility companies, the Financial Services Authority etc. Ministers may have substantial powers of control over such bodies including appointing their governing bodies, providing finance and giving directions. However, such bodies have no direct democratic accountability. Much intellectual energy has gone into labelling and categorising these bodies, for example 'QUANGOs' (quasi-autonomous non-governmental agencies), 'non-departmental public bodies', but there is no legal significance in these labels. Moreover, functions may be exercised on behalf of government by voluntary bodies such as housing charities. Such a body might be a public body for some purposes and not for others (see Chapters 4, 16, 17).

### 3.3.4 Appointing, Controlling and Removing Governments

As we saw in Chapter 1, the parliamentary system means that the people choose representatives to make laws on their behalf in Parliament while the executive is chosen and sustained by Parliament from its own members. We have also seen that the UK constitution has the anomaly that the upper House of Parliament is chosen by the executive. Parliament therefore has two conflicting roles, both supported by democratic credentials, one being to form the government, the other being to hold the government to account. This conflict creates serious tensions in the constitution which modern party loyalties reinforce (Chapters 11, 13).

In law the Queen appoints the government who are merely her servants. By convention she must invite the leader of the majority party in Parliament to form a government. He or she then becomes Prime Minister and appoints other ministers from members of Parliament, the most important ministers, particularly those directly concerned with finance, being members of the House of Commons. The Prime Minister can freely dismiss any minister.

According to the convention of ministerial responsibility, ministers are responsible to Parliament collectively for government policy and individually for the conduct of their departments. During the nineteenth century, when government was smaller and less complex, it was orthodox that a minister must formally take the blame when serious mistakes or misconduct occurred in his department. This is intended to create strong democratic responsibility and also encourages civil servants to give frank, independent and impartial advice. However, in contemporary circumstances where government departments are large and complex, with many functions hived off to semi-autonomous 'executive agencies', it is not possible for a minister to control everything that happens in his or her department. Ministers have therefore sought to weaken the principle of ministerial responsibility (Chapter 13).

Ministerial responsibility is an aspect of the democratic principle that the people should be able to get rid of governments that displease them and choose a new one. In order to prevent either Parliament or the executive from dominating the other, there is a balance in which Parliament can dismiss ministers collectively, and the Prime Minister can temporarily terminate Parliament. The Crown and the civil service provide the necessary element of continuity. As usual there is a mixture of law and convention:

▶ By law (Parliament Act 1911) Parliament terminates automatically at the end of five years from the date of the royal proclamation which summons it. Ministers remain in office until the new Parliament is elected by a general election which must be held within about three weeks of termination (Representation of the People Act 1985; Chapter 10). As soon as the election result is known then, by convention, if the government party cannot command a majority it must resign at once. (The brutal way in which this is managed, illustrated by media images of the defeated Prime Minister leaving his or her official residence on the day after polling day, provides a graphic illustration of democracy in action.)

▶ If a government is defeated in the House of Commons on a vote of confidence then by convention it must resign. If an alternative administration cannot command the support of a majority of the House then by convention the Queen must dissolve Parliament, leading to an election. However, given the force of party loyalty and the fact that MPs who vote against the government are voting for their own termination, such votes are rare. The most recent one was in 1974 when the Labour government had only a small majority which was exploited by the smaller parties.

▶ By convention the Prime Minister can at any time request the Queen to dissolve Parliament and she must normally do so. Again this leads to an election. This convention places considerable power in the hands of a Prime Minister since he has the fortunes of his party in his hands and thus reinforces the strong party political control exercised by the executive over Parliament (above).

▶ In exceptional circumstances where a Prime Minister acts grossly improperly the Queen might intervene and dismiss the government or dissolve Parliament. She appears to have unlimited legal power under the royal prerogative to do both without giving reasons. However the conventions, if any, that guide her power remain uncertain since there are no clear precedents (Chapter 12).

### 3.3.5 The Judiciary

The third branch of government is the judiciary. In a parliamentary system the distinction between the legislature and the executive is blurred but in any liberal system it is vital that the judiciary be independent of the other branches of government. However, independence is a slippery and relative concept. In this section I shall outline the main constitutional features of the judiciary. Further aspects particularly affecting judicial independence and reforms are discussed in Chapter 6. The Court system is regulated by statute (see Courts Act 2003, Courts and Legal Services Act 1990, Supreme Court Act 1981, Magistrates Courts Act 1980, Courts Act 1971). We are concerned primarily with England and Wales. Scotland and Northern Ireland have a separate court system although appeals from Northern Ireland and appeals in civil cases in Scotland are dealt with by the House of Lords (below).

The main courts are as follows:

▶ Superior Courts, whose judges enjoy greater independence, form the Supreme Court of Judicature – not to be confused with the new type of Supreme Court proposed by the government. This includes the High Court which deals with major civil cases and the Court of Appeal which in two divisions deals with civil and criminal appeals. These are staffed by High Court judges and Lords Justices of Appeal.

▶ Inferior courts include the Crown Court which deals with the more substantial criminal cases (and in certain respects has superior court status), county courts which deal with smaller civil cases, and magistrates courts which deal mainly with minor criminal cases. Professional judges in these courts are circuit judges who hear criminal cases in the Crown court and civil cases in the county court; district judges who hear some county court cases and criminal cases in the magistrates court. There are also lay magistrates sitting usually in panels of three supported by a professional Justices' Clerk who advises them and can also exercise certain judicial functions on their behalf. There are also part-time professional Assistant Recorders and Recorders who hear criminal cases in the Crown Court. These are normally practicing barristers, the post being a road to promotion to higher judicial office.

▶ There are also numerous special tribunals deciding matters allocated to them by statute, often involving disputes with government bodies, and there are military courts. Tribunals are supervised by an independent Council on Tribunals which is concerned to protect their independence from the executive (see Tribunals and Inquiries Act 1992). There is usually a right of appeal from a tribunal to the ordinary court system and the High Court can also review decisions of inferior courts and government departments (Chapter 14).

▶ The highest appellate court – in an anomalous position for historical reasons – is part of Parliament, namely the Appellate Committee of the House of Lords. This hears appeals from all the UK jurisdictions except

Scottish criminal cases. In practice, it is independent of Parliament as such. Twelve full-time Lords of Appeal in Ordinary (usually sitting in panels of five) are specifically appointed as judges and retired Law Lords also sit as required (Appellate Jurisdiction Act 1876). Non-legally qualified peers cannot sit. By convention the Law Lords do not participate in party political debate, although they occasionally speak on law reform matters and those affecting the judiciary. Indeed this kind of structured link between different branches of government is often regarded as desirable. However, current government proposals include replacing the Appellate Committee with a separate Supreme Court.

### 3.3.5.1 The Appointment and Dismissal of Judges

Judges of the Court of Appeal, the House of Lords, the Heads of the Divisions and the Vice Chancellor are appointed by the Queen on the advice of the Prime Minister (Appellate Jurisdiction Act 1876 s.2, Supreme Court Act 1981 s.10 and convention). Other judges are appointed by the Queen on the recommendation of the Lord Chancellor (Supreme Court Act 1981 s.10; Courts Act 1971 ss.16; 21 Courts Act 2003 s.22). The Lord Chancellor occupies an anomalous constitutional position being nominally head of the judiciary but also the government minister in charge of the court system and the presiding officer in the House of Lords. The government is currently proposing to reform the office of Lord Chancellor. Lay magistrates are appointed by the Lord Chancellor on behalf of the Queen (ibid. s.11). Magistrates clerks are appointed by the Lord Chancellor and, despite their judicial functions, are treated as ordinary civil servants without security of tenure (Courts Act 2003 s.2 (1), s.27). Specialist tribunals are appointed by ministers under particular statutes and, in the case of chairmen, sometimes from a panel nominated by the Lord Chancellor.

Judges of the main courts and some tribunals must be appointed from a pool of experienced practising lawyers. This contrasts with the position in other European countries where there is a separate judicial profession. The UK system has the advantage of drawing on talented people from outside government who are familiar with the workings of the court process. The disadvantage is that this might reinforce the perception of the legal system as a closed elite.

The process for appointing judges is not regulated by law. Traditionally the Lord Chancellor privately consults judges and other senior lawyers, and the senior judges who head each division of the courts apparently have a veto over appointments. This process creates the risk that the judiciary is regarded as a self-perpetuating body of cronies. There are also complaints relating to the limited gender and ethnic diversity of the judiciary (see Hale, 'Equality and the Judiciary', 2001, *Public Law* 489).

In recent years the appointments process has become more open. Appointments up to High Court level are advertised, the broad criteria are published (*Judicial Appointments*, HMSO, 1990) and the Lord Chancellor makes an annual report to Parliament. There is a non-statutory Commission for Judicial Appointments that reviews the operation of the system and hears complaints from disappointed candidates. However, appellate appointments are by invitation only and other appointments can be made by invitation (see Peach, *An Independent Scrutiny of the Appointment Processes of Judges and Queen's Council in England and Wales*, 1999). The present system is defended on the basis that only insiders have accurate knowledge of the pool of talent available. However, the government proposes an 'independent' Judicial Appointments Commission, comprising judicial and lay members, which would recommend appointments (Chapter 6).

Superior court judges, that is judges of the High Court and above, hold office during 'good behaviour'. This in itself is hardly conducive to independence since what matters is who decides whether they have misbehaved. They can be dismissed by the Crown following a resolution of both Houses of Parliament (another constitutional safeguard in the hands of the House of Lords), and probably then only for misbehaviour (Supreme Court Act 1981 s.11 (3); Appellate Jurisdiction Act 1876 s.6). An alternative interpretation of these provisions is that the Crown can dismiss a judge for misbehaviour without an address from Parliament, but on an address a judge can be dismissed irrespective of misbehaviour. In exceptional circumstances judges can be removed by the Lord Chancellor on medical grounds (Supreme Court Act 1981 s.11 (8)). Superior court judges must retire at 70 (Judicial Pensions and Retirement Act 1993). The salaries of superior court judges cannot be reduced except by statute although the executive could refuse to increase them. No judge has been subjected to these provisions since the nineteenth century when a judge was dismissed for embezzling court funds.

The bulk of the judiciary (about 97%) is inferior court judges. Inferior court judges do not have full security of tenure but are appointed by the Lord Chancellor under various statutes which make different provisions for dismissal. Part-time judges are appointed for fixed periods, and whether they are renewed is in the hands of the Lord Chancellor (see Courts Act 1971 s.21 (5)). Full-time circuit and district judges can be dismissed by the Lord Chancellor for incapacity or misbehaviour (Courts Act 1971 ss.17, 20). Lay magistrates can be removed by the Lord Chancellor for incapacity or misbehaviour, persistent failure to meet standards of competence prescribed by the Lord Chancellor and declining or neglecting their duties (Courts Act 2003 s.12). Magistrates clerks, in common with other civil servants, have no security of tenure but can, it seems, be dismissed broadly on the same basis as private employees. Tribunal members are usually appointed for fixed terms and can in some cases be dismissed only with the consent of the Lord Chancellor (Tribunals and Inquiries Act 1992 s.7).The Lord Chancellor also appoints Queen's Council who are senior practising lawyers and as such likely to benefit both in respect of their private practice and in terms of eligibility for judicial appointment from this government patronage. The Queen's Council system is currently under review.

### 3.3.6 The Police

The police have a claim to special constitutional status since they are authorised to use violence and are closely connected with the judicial process. It is therefore important that the police are seen to be independent of the executive. On the other hand, the police service is funded by taxation so that democratic accountability is desirable. An accommodation must be struck between these concerns.

The organisation of police forces has three aspects. These have led to complex and tension-ridden arrangements for police governance and accountability. First, there is the traditional status at common law of the 'constable' as an independent officer of the Crown with inherent powers of arrest, search and entry to premises, some common law and others statutory, and owing duties to the law itself to keep the peace (see Police Act 1996 s.10; *R* v *Metropolitan Police Commissioner ex parte Blackburn* [1968] 2 QB 118 at 136). Each police force is under the direction of its Chief Constable (in London the Metropolitan Police Commissioner) with regard to operational matters. All police officers and also prison officers are constables.

Second, there is a tradition that the organization of the police should be locally based and subject to democratic control so as to avoid the concentration of power associated with a 'police state'. Under the Police Act 1996, local police forces are organised on the basis of counties and amalgamations of county units. There are special arrangements in London comprising the Metropolitan Police and the City of London Police Force, limited to the square mile that technically comprises the City (Greater London Authority Act 1999). Each local force is answerable to a local police authority which comprises a mixture of local councillors, justices of the peace and persons appointed by the Home Secretary, with elected members a bare majority. The political balance of the elected members must reflect that of the council as a whole (Criminal Justice and Police Act 2001 s.105). The Chief Constable must have regard to the objects and targets set out in an annual plan made by the police authority (Police Act 1996 s.8). Police funding is a combination of central government grant and a levy (precept) on local taxation.

The police authority must maintain an 'efficient and effective police force' (Police Act 1996 s.6 (1)). Some argue that this gives the police authority political control since it allows them to specify how policing priorities should be ordered. The more widely held view is that it only requires the authority to provide material resources and to fix the budget for whatever policing policies are determined by the Chief Constable. However, s.7 enables a police authority to impose 'objectives' on its force consistent with any objectives imposed by the Home Secretary (below). The plan must also have regard to national objects and performance targets set out by the Home Secretary. The police authority appoints and removes the Chief Constable and certain other senior officers.

Third, the central government has large and increasing powers over police forces conferred by statute, usually upon the Home Secretary. These are subject to no specific constitutional principles but seem to be generated by pragmatic considerations and the desire of particular governments to exercise control. For example, the Home Secretary's approval is need for the appointment and removal of a Chief Constable and the Home Secretary can also require a police authority to suspend or remove a Chief Constable (Police Reform Act 2002 ss.32, 33). This was illustrated recently by the insistence of the Home Secretary against the will of the police authority that the Chief Constable of Humberside Police be suspended as a result of criticisms over failings of the force in relation to the Soham murder inquiry. The Home Secretary can also draw up a national policing plan (ibid. s.1), a code of practice for Chief Officers (s.2), and make regulations concerning resources including requiring the use of specified equipment (s.5).

Technical support may be too expensive to provide locally and modern crime is no respecter of local boundaries. There are therefore national bodies, including the National Police Data Bank, and the Mutual Aid Coordinating Centre, National Criminal Intelligence Service and the National Crime Squad (Police Act 1997). These bodies carry out police operations directly, operating formally by agreement with local forces. They are regulated by central boards, the membership of which strikes a balance between a minority of independent persons appointed by the Secretary of State, and nomination by chief officers and local police authorities from among their members. A Central Police Training and Development Authority has also been created (Criminal Justice and Police Act 2001), the objectives of which are decided by the Secretary of State who can also give it detailed guidance and directions. There is therefore a considerable momentum towards a national police force.

Originally the police themselves conducted most prosecutions. However, the Prosecution of Offenders Act 1985 created a separate Crown Prosecution Service which is under the control of the Director of Public Prosecutions (DPP). Crown prosecutors in local areas have powers to prosecute and conduct cases subject to discretion given by the DPP under the Act. The DPP is appointed by the Attorney-General who is answerable in Parliament for the Crown Prosecution Service. The Crown prosecutor has power to take over most criminal prosecutions (s.3) or to order any proceedings to be discontinued (s.23). Except where an offence can only be prosecuted by a person named in the relevant statute (for example the Attorney-General, or a specified public authority), any individual may bring a private prosecution, but the Crown Prosecution Service can take over such a prosecution (s.6 (2)).

The *Police Complaints Authority* has an independent role in investigating complaints against the police (see *R (Green)* v *Police Complaints Authority* (2004)).

### 3.3.7    The Privy Council

The Privy Council is the descendant of the medieval 'inner council' of trusted advisors to the King. Members are appointed by the Queen on the advice of the Prime Minister. Over the centuries the functions of the Privy Council were transferred either to Parliament or to ministers and the institution itself was left to wither. There are currently over 400 privy councillors including Cabinet ministers, senior judges and miscellaneous worthies who have attracted the approval of the Prime Minister. The Cabinet is sometimes said to be a committee of the Privy Council although there is no legal basis for this assumption. However Cabinet ministers are invariably appointed Privy Councillors and as such swear an oath of secrecy.

Apart from its judicial functions (below), the role of the Privy Council is largely formal. Its approval is needed for certain important exercises of the royal prerogative, known as prerogative orders in council, including for example the regulation of the civil service, and also for 'statutory orders in council' where Parliament gives power to the executive to make laws in this form. Approval is usually given by a small deputation of councillors attending the Queen. The Privy Council also confers state recognition and legal personality by granting charters to bodies such as universities and professional, scientific and cultural organisations. It can exercise some degree of supervision over such bodies.

Committees of the Privy Council have certain important functions. In particular the judicial committee is the final court of appeal from those few commonwealth countries who choose to retain its services, in which capacity it is familiar with broad constitutional reasoning. The judicial committee is made up from the Law Lords together with judges of the country under whose laws the appeal is heard. Importantly the judicial committee has jurisdiction over devolution issues including human rights matters under the Scotland Act 1998, the Northern Ireland Act 1998 and the Government of Wales Act 1998 (Chapter 4). It also has jurisdiction in respect of ecclesiastical courts, peerage claims, election petitions and appeals from the Channel Islands and the Isle of Man. Its former appeals jurisdiction in relation to the medical profession is now exercised by the Administrative Court (Chapter 16). Not being strictly a court, the judicial committee can give advisory opinions to the government (Judicial Committee Act 1833 s.4) although this is rare.

### 3.3.8 The Church of England

The relationship between church and state is ambivalent. On the one hand, neither Christianity nor any other religion is part of the law as such (*Bowman v Secular Society* (1917)). On the other hand, we do not have a formal separation between Church and state such as exists in, for example, France and the USA. The Church of England is the 'Established Church' and as such has certain links with the state. This is the result of the historical chance that Henry VIII was the founder of the Church of England. It is sometimes justified even by supporters of other religions on the basis that the Church provides religious services open to all without discrimination and that it helps the state to curb the extremes of religious fanaticism. The Scottish and Welsh churches do not have an equivalent status.

There are several particular connections between the Church of England and the state. First, the monarch is the nominal head of the Church, second, Church laws (Measures) have statutory force and must be approved by Parliament (see Church of England Assembly (Powers) Act 1919). There are also special ecclesiastical courts subject to control by the ordinary courts if they exceed their powers or act unfairly. Third, the Queen on the advice of the Prime Minister (which as usual is binding on her by convention) appoints bishops (see Ecclesiastical Jurisdiction Measure 1963). Fourth, the 26 most senior bishops are members of the House of Lords until retirement. Finally, everyone has certain rights in connection with baptisms, weddings and funerals. However, a Church body is not as such a public body (see *Aston Cantlow Parochial Church Council v Wallbank* 2003) but particular church functions available to the public such as weddings and funerals might be public functions and, as such, subject to control by the courts.

### 3.4 Standards in Government

The informal nature of much of the UK constitution, particularly at the higher levels, makes our arrangements heavily dependent on trusting those in power. A series of scandals from the 1980s exposed significant corruption, ambivalence and incompetence within central government and Parliament. Most prominent were the Westlands affair in 1987 where ministers and civil servants appeared to conspire against each other (see Treasury and Civil Service Committee, HC 92 (1985–6)) and the 'arms to Iraq' affair which involved allegations that ministers had tried to cover up breaches of UN sanctions against Iran (see Scott Report (1996, HC 115). There have also been allegations that MPs and ministers have received bribes from business interests; claims that favours are performed in return for donations to party funds, and conflicts between governmental media-management and civil service objectivity (see Butler Report, *Review of Intelligence on Weapons of Mass Destruction* (2004) HC 898).

A favoured mechanism for dealing with such allegations comprises non-legally binding codes of conduct policed by bodies appointed by the executive and working with varying degrees of informality with terms of reference drawn up by the executive, that is, the people who are to be investigated. Their reports are usually published. The Committee on Standards in Public Life was appointed by the Prime Minister in 1994 as a permanent committee. Its terms of reference included the UK Parliament, UK members of the European Parliament, central and local government and other publicly funded bodies such as the NHS. The Committee reports to the Prime Minister. It does not investigate complaints against individuals.

In its first report (Cm 2850, 1995) under the Chairmanship of Lord Nolan, the Committee promulgated seven 'Principles of Public Life' that subsequently became widely regarded as representing the core values of public service. They are 'selflessness, integrity, objectivity, accountability, openness, honesty, and leadership'. They are supported by what Nolan called 'common threads', these being mechanisms used to imbed the principles into governmental institutions. These are codes of conduct, independent scrutiny and guidance and education. These principles are enshrined in a series of codes (e.g. *Ministerial Code, Code for Special Advisors, Civil Service Code, Local Government Code, Code of Conduct for MPs, Code of Practice for Ministerial Appointments to Public Bodies*).

The Codes are not legally enforceable although Parliament has powers to enforce the MPs' Code. A Parliamentary Commissioner for Standards was created in 1996 to adjudicate upon questions arising out of MPs' interests and to report to the Standards and Privileges Committee of the House of Commons, thus creating enforceable although flawed adjudicative machinery (Chapter 9).

The 'Nolan' principles regarding public appointments are particularly important. Against the background of a tradition which permits ministers to choose whom they like to serve in important public positions, the Committee has promulgated principles of appointment on merit, according to open and published criteria that all public bodies should follow and with independent representation on appointment bodies. There is a Commission for Public Appointments created under the royal prerogative in 1995 which oversees the appointment process relating to a wide variety of public bodies and publishes a code of practice and annual reports. The long-standing

Civil Service Commissioners perform a similar role in relation to civil service appointments. There is also a House of Lords Appointments Commission which has an advisory role in relation to the Prime Minister's power to select members of the House of Lords (Chapter 10).

There are both advantages and disadvantages in voluntary codes of practice which might be compared with conventions in this respect (Chapter 2). Firstly, unlike conventions, codes of practice are written and may have an authoritative mechanism for settling disputes such as the Parliamentary Commissioner for Standards (above). However, unless there is an independent enforcement mechanism the vice of self-interest is likely to be associated with such codes so that they may not command public confidence. For example, the *Ministerial Code* is ultimately enforced only by the Prime Minister. Because the codes have no legal status, they cannot be enforced in the courts but, in the paternalistic British tradition, are invoked only at the discretion of officials and politicians – members of the selfsame groups whom the codes seek to control. The vagueness of many of the codes is also a mixed blessing. On the one hand, the codes are flexible and could produce negotiated outcomes which are practical and acceptable to the persons concerned. On the other hand, the flexibility of the codes enables them to be manipulated for party political purposes or self-interest.

In a recent consultation paper the Committee on Standards has warned that that the codes might be undermined by appearing to be overzealous or overbureaucratic and attracting public cynicism (see *Getting the Balance Right: Implementing Standards of Conduct in Public Life*, 2003). The Committee particularly emphasised the principle of 'proportionality' which concerns adjusting processes to the particular context taking account of the importance of the activity and the risks and costs involved. It also emphasised the importance of the culture of the particular organisation.

The Principles of Public Life have occasionally been incorporated into statute (e.g. Northern Ireland Act 1998 s.16(4); see Bridge in Economides et al. (eds), *Fundamental Values* 2000). There is a statutory electoral commission to ensure openness and accountability in the conduct of elections and campaign funding (Political Parties, Elections and Referendums Act 2000). There is also a commission to enforce standards in local government (Local Government Act 2000). More generally it has been suggested that the standards of public life could be absorbed into existing legal principles such as fairness, rationality, proportionality and respect for rights (see Oliver in Taggart (ed.) *The Province of Administrative Law* 1997).

## 3.5  Recent Reforms

Since the present Labour government took office in 1997 there have been a series of constitutional reforms. They remind us that in the UK constitutional change is produced merely by ordinary legislation in the hands of the government of the day. This is illustrated by the events of summer 2003 when proposals for abolishing the Lord Chancellor and creating a new Supreme Court were announced by the government incidentally to a routine 'reshuffle' of government posts (Chapter 6). If a constitution is to set the framework within which government operates then it is arguable that the mechanism for constitutional change should be to some extent outside the control of particular governments.

We shall discuss the individual reforms in their context but for convenience will list the highlights here:

▷ Substantial political and legal power has been devolved towards elected regional bodies in Scotland, Wales and Northern Ireland, each of which now has an elected government, albeit subordinate to the Westminster Parliament (Government of Wales Act 1998, Northern Ireland Act 1998 (currently suspended), Scotland Act 1998. It is an 'asymetrical' devolution in that each region has a different extent and structure of devolved government (Chapter 4). Limited powers have also been devolved to an elected mayor and Assembly in London (Greater London Authority Act 1999) and there are proposals to create elected assemblies in some English regions. However, an attempt to introduce a north eastern assembly was decisively rejected in a referendum in November 2004. It is noteworthy that all the new elected bodies have voting systems designed to reflect the distribution of votes more fairly than the simple 'first past the post' method that applies to Parliament itself (Chapter 10).

▷ Many of the human rights protected by the European Convention on Human Rights have been incorporated into UK law (Human Rights Act 1998) thereby allowing the courts to pronounce upon the compatibility of UK law with broader international ideas of human rights, although not to override Acts of Parliament (Chapter 17).

▷ Membership of the House of Lords is currently undergoing reform to remove the hereditary element although the details of this remain uncertain (House of Lords Act 1999; Chapter 10).

▷ The electoral process and the financial affairs of political parties have been subjected to limited regulation in order to ensure accountability and openness (Political Parties, Elections and Referendums Act 2000). Reform of the parliamentary voting system has not been pursued (see *Report of the Independent Commission on the Voting System* (The Jenkins Report), 1998, Cm 4090-1).

▷ The Freedom of Information Act 2000 gives the public access to some official documents but is widely regarded as weak, with the government retaining a veto (Chapter 19).

## Summary

▶ The historical development of the constitution has been evolutionary in the sense that the main institutions – Parliament and courts – have been hived off from the Crown and adjusted to changing circumstances. However, there has been continuous struggle for control of Crown and Parliament, culminating in the present system of party political domination.

▶ The Crown as the executive branch of government must be distinguished from the Queen personally as head of state. Statutory powers are normally given to individual ministers and the central government is therefore fragmented.

▶ Parliament comprises an unelected upper House with limited powers (House of Lords) and an elected lower House (House of Commons). Lawmaking is the legal responsibility of Parliament but in practice is dominated by the executive. The electorate chooses members of the House of Commons and the leader of the majority party forms the executive. The upper House is currently undergoing reform but there is disagreement as to what form this should take.

▶ Apart from ministers, the executive also comprises permanent civil servants who act as a source of impartial advice and carry out the instructions of ministers and special advisors who are personal, political appointees of ministers. There are tensions between these groups.

▶ According to the doctrine of ministerial responsibility, ministers are responsible to Parliament for the conduct of their departments and for agencies sponsored by their departments. The civil service is responsible to ministers but not directly to Parliament. Ministerial responsibility is becoming weaker and its scope and effect unclear.

▶ Parliament can give executive powers to anyone. In recent years executive powers have been distributed across a wide variety of public and private bodies This raises questions of accountability.

▶ Weaknesses in the traditional methods of accountability have led to attempts to formulate standards of ethical conduct for persons holding public office. These do not generally have legal status and are enforced within government itself.

▶ There are mechanisms to safeguard democracy against both legislature and executive. No government can last for more than five years without submitting to an election and that before then Parliament can remove a government (at risk in this case of its own dissolution). The executive can also dissolve Parliament but again must submit to a general election. These mechanisms are weakened by the executive domination of parliament produced, not by the law, but primarily by the strength of the political party system.

▶ The judiciary is usually regarded as subordinate to Parliament but has an ambivalent position by virtue of the common law. There is a tension between the judiciary and the executive arising out of the courts' powers of judicial review.

## Summary cont'd

▷ Senior judges have strong security of tenure. The appointment of judges is made by politicians. Recent reform proposals introduce the safeguard of an independent Judicial Appointments Committee to make recommendations but the position remains ambivalent (see Chapter 6).

▷ The police are regulated by an unstable combination of local and central government.

▷ The Church of England has particular constitutional links with the state but is not a state religion.

# Exercises

**3.1** To what extent is the historical development of the UK constitution an example of the triumph of democracy?

**3.2** What mechanisms enable the executive to dominate Parliament? Are there any counter mechanisms?

**3.3** Assess the arguments for and against abolishing the monarchy.

**3.4** What are the advantages and disadvantages of 'Codes of Conduct' compared with law and constitutional conventions as a method of ensuring governmental accountability?

**3.5** Bill, a High Court judge, is alleged to have been sexually harassing the junior staff of the High Court Registry. Parliament is not sitting and the Lord Chancellor advises the Queen to make an example of Bill by dismissing him forthwith. Advise Bill.

**3.6** Critically assess the present arrangements for appointing judges.

## Further reading

Committee on Standards in Public Life Reports, http://www.publicstandards.gov.uk.

Constitution Committee House of Lords *Changing the Constitution: the Process of Constitutional Change*, Fourth Report Session 2001–2, HL Paper 69, London, HMSO.

Finer, F., Bogdanor, V. and Rudden, B. (1995) *Comparing Constitutions*, Oxford, Clarendon Press, Chapter 2.

Forman, N. (2002) *Constitutional Change in Britain*, London, Routledge.

Hazell, R., Masterman, R., Sandford, M., Seyd, B. and Croft, J. (2002) 'The Constitution: Coming in From the Cold', *Parliamentary Affairs*, **55**.

Hennessy, P. (1995) *The Hidden Wiring: Unearthing the British Constitution,* London, Gollancz, Chapters 1, 8, Conclusion.

**Further reading cont'd**

King, A. (2000) *Does the United Kingdom Still Have a Constitution?*, London, Sweet & Maxwell.

Lyons, A. (2003) *Constitutional History of the United Kingdom,* London, Cavendish.

Nolan, Lord and Sedley, Sir S. (1997) *The Making and Remaking of the British Constitution*, London, Blackstone, Chapters 1, 3, 4, 5.

Oliver, D. (1995) 'Standards of conduct in public life: what standards?', *Public Law,* 497.

Oliver, D. (2003) *Constitutional Reform in the United Kingdom,* Oxford, Oxford University Press.

Ward, I. (2004) *The English Constitution: Myths and Realities,* Oxford, Hart Publishing.

Weill, R. (2004) 'We the British People', *Public Law* 380.

Wilson, Lord (2004) 'The Robustness of Conventions in a Time of Modernisation and Change', *Public Law* 407.

Woodhouse, D. (2003) 'Delivering Public Confidence: Codes of Conduct; A Step in the Right Direction', *Public Law* 511.

# Chapter 4

# The state and the regions of the UK

The England Team is the only team playing in the World Cup that is not a nation state: there is no political or cultural outlet for England's feeling of national identity. (*Observer*, 13 June 2004)

## Key words

- State, country and nation
- Statism and non-statism
- Citizens and subjects
- Federalism and devolution
- Asymmetric devolution

## 4.1 The Notion of the State

The term 'state' derives from 'status' and originally meant a recognised function in the overall scheme of things. In ancient Greece and Rome the 'city state' was regarded as an independent, self-governing community of like-minded people based on the republican values of citizen self-rule. The contemporary idea of the state has developed from this into what is inaccurately called the 'nation state'. There is no necessary connection between the idea of a nation and that of a state. A nation is a cultural, political and historical idea but not a legal concept. It signifies a relatively homogenous community marked out, for example, by a common language, common ethnicity, or shared cultural traditions. A state is defined by law and based on geographical boundaries. A nation may have a moral claim to be a state with its own laws and government, (see Lord Hoffmann in *A v Secretary of State* (2004)).

The 'nation state' has been the basic unit of political and legal organisation since the seventeenth century and the association of the two ideas has often been used by those in power as a means of inspiring loyalty. For example the constitution of Poland asserts that 'Supreme Power shall be vested in the Nation' (see also ECHR Art. 15 (Chapter 19)). On the other hand, many states have been created by military force, economic circumstances or political bargains. As the history of Ireland, the Balkan states and many African states sadly reveals, nationalistic sentiment and the artificiality of state boundaries sometimes generate violence and even genocide, both internationally and within a state. The term `country' has no legal significance and is often used loosely to refer either to a nation or to a state.

The notion of the state developed during the late sixteenth and early seventeenth centuries, primarily for military purposes in the context of constant territorial conflicts and influenced by the Hobbesian idea that a state needs a single ruler in order to guarantee security (Chapter 1). This was a reaction against the loose, medieval political structure of rival warlords, to some extent held together by the Church, and also against the re-emergence in the fifteenth century of democratic ideas of citizen self-rule. Throughout mainland Europe the state was represented by a monarch supported by a military and administrative structure and imposing law from above. Britain however retained the tradition that the ruler requires the consent of the 'community' although there has been considerable disagreement as to what is meant by 'community'.

During the eighteenth century, generated by Enlightenment ideas of scientific reason, secularism and equality, the state was regarded as an impersonal command structure designed to advance the general welfare. On the other hand, generated by nineteenth-century romanticism which, reacting against the violent aftermath of the French Revolution, feared the mechanical and impersonal aspects of Enlightenment rationality, the state was sometimes linked to nationalistic sentiments and used as a justification for invading other states or suppressing minorities. The culmination of this was the Second World War, one outcome of which was the creation of the European Union as an attempt at a legal system transcending states and nations (Chapter 8).

There has been no agreement as to the relationship between the state and the citizen. Hence different versions of democracy and of liberalism, republicanism and communitarianism (Chapter 1) have each influenced the constitution at different times. Liberalism is ambivalent towards the state: on the one hand, the individual is the basic concern of liberal law with the state envisaged as an organisation designed to protect individual liberty. On the other hand, a liberal state does not reject the notion of a nation cemented by shared values, thus threatening minorities within the state who may not accept those values. Moreover, under the influence of democracy, the state has become an all purpose organisation with no limitation other than the wishes of a majority as to the functions it might have.

The UK is a state in international law but it is not a nation. It has evolved through uncoordinated historical events. Its various units, mainly England, Northern Ireland, Scotland and Wales, have no international legal status but Northern Ireland, Scotland and Wales have some devolved government powers. England, although it was a nation state until it assimilated with Scotland in 1707, has no legal identity as such. English law applies in England and Wales. Scotland and Northern Ireland have their own legal systems which, not surprisingly, share much in common with English law although Scotland has also been influenced by the French civil law system. Acts of the UK Parliament apply to the whole of the UK unless specifically providing otherwise.

Unlike other European legal systems, English law has no concept of the 'state' as a legal entity. The Crown is our nearest equivalent but this means different things in different contexts (Chapter 12). England was an exception to the development of statist ideas in that the claims of the monarchy were successfully resisted by Parliament, culminating in the 1688 revolution which built on existing institutions. The revolution was presented as a revival of older ideas, sanctified by ancient institutions against both monarchy and republicanism. The historical trajectory of English constitutional politics was regarded as a continuous process of bargaining between the King and other interest groups represented by Parliament (Chapter 3).

In English law the concept of the state is used loosely to describe any governmental activity (e.g. state schools). Where legislation refers to the 'state' its meaning depends on the particular context, for example the community as a whole (*Chandler* v *DPP* (1964)), the 'sovereign power' (*General Medical Council* v *BBC* (1998)) or the executive branch of government (*D* v *NSPCC* (1978)). Sometimes the terms 'nation' and 'state' are used interchangeably, for example where the law refers to the 'National Health Service', 'the national interest' or 'national security' (see *Council of Civil Service Unions* (CCSU) v *Minister for the Civil Service* (1985)).

The non-statist nature of English law has at least the following important consequences:

▶ There is a distinction in statist constitutions between 'public law', which regulates the state itself and its relationship with citizens, and 'private law' which the state uses to regulate the relationship between its citizens. The UK constitution has not historically recognised such a distinction. It has been regarded as a strength of our constitution that a single system of law applies to officials and individuals alike. Thus, unless a particular law provides otherwise, officials have no special powers or status and are individually responsible for any legal wrongs they commit (Chapter 5). Thus the doctrine of *raison d'etat* as a general justification for government power is not recognised by English law (*Entick* v *Carrington* (1765)).

▶ The increasing powers given to governmental officials and the trend towards privatization (Chapter 3) have led to attempts to distinguish between public and private law and public and private bodies and functions, particularly in connection with judicial review of government action (Chapter 16), human rights (Chapter 17) and access to information (Chapter 19). For example, the government represents the whole community rather than any particular section of it and therefore carries special responsibility (see *R v IRC ex parte Unilever* [1996] STC 681 at 695; *R v Somerset CC ex parte Fewings* [1995] 1 All ER 513 at 524; *Reynolds v Times Newspapers* [1998] 3 All ER 961 at 1004). Conversely, in order to perform its duties, the government might have privileges not available to other bodies and so should be subject to particular legal controls. It cannot be assumed that a public body or public function will be defined in the same way in each context. For example, the Freedom of Information Act 2000 (Chapter 19) provides a list of public bodies which can be altered by ministers. The Government Resources and Accounts Act 2000 (Chapter 11) refers unhelpfully to a 'government department or a body exercising public functions' (s.7(3)). The Human Rights Act 1998 does not provide a definition (Chapter 17).

▶ One reason why we cannot clearly distinguish between the public and the private is that our non-statist tradition allows us to allocate governmental functions haphazardly between the central government proper (i.e. ministers) and other bodies specially created for the purpose and also to transfer functions to private bodies. We regard the distinction between functions that should be carried out by the state and those appropriate to the private sector as a political matter outside the law. There are some advantages in the UK approach. Particular decision-making bodies must be openly identified and cannot hide under the general state umbrella. There are also disadvantages in that there seems to be no constitutional principle to prevent public powers being farmed out to bodies that are not democratically accountable. Similarly there are no legal principles governing the question whether and on what terms the government can hand over assets to the private sector. Whether these are sold and at what price or given away and to whom depends on particular legislation or government practice.

▶ There may be a tension between the duty of a civil servant to the Crown, which is the nearest we have to a general concept of the state, and to particular ministers (Chapter 13).

▶ Our system of government is fragmented between different bodies and there is no single entity which can hold property or enter into legal transactions on behalf of the public. For legal purposes, the Attorney-General represents the government. Government powers and property are vested by particular legislation either in the Crown or in particular ministers or departments (Chapter 13).

▶ In a statist system the state is both a creation of the law and the producer of law. The judges are the authoritative interpreters of the law but not its creators. Judicial opinions are regarded as making more concrete the laws emanating from the state but do not traditionally have an independent lawmaking role. By contrast the historical basis of the common law gives the courts an independent basis of legitimacy. The authority of the common law lies in community values. In the common law system, the judges are regarded as individuals charged with doing justice. Judicial decisions are normally fully reasoned and dissents are commonplace.

## 4.2 Citizenship

In its general sense citizenship means full membership of a state. Citizenship can be distinguished from other relationships in that citizenship involves rights against and duties to the whole community as opposed to those concerning only people we know personally such as friends and family or rights arising by agreement. In the civic republican tradition (Chapter 1), citizenship is particularly associated with active participation in public life whereas 'liberal' citizenship primarily concerns the rights and entitlements of individuals against the state. The unpleasant side of citizenship is that it entails 'exclusion' in the sense of an unwelcoming attitude to those regarded as non-citizens, who in UK law are labelled 'aliens'. For example, Article 6 of the European Convention on Human Rights (the right to a fair trial) does not apparently apply to the expulsion of aliens (*R (G) v Immigration Appeal Tribunal* (2004)).

The notion of citizenship as it first emerged in Ancient Greece presupposed a small community roughly equal in wealth, and from similar social backgrounds. Indeed women, foreigners and slaves, comprising most of the population, were excluded. In today's larger and more diverse communities it is difficult to suppose that common values can be applied uniformly to all. Cultural practices and loyalties such as language and family customs militate against detailed notions of the rights and obligations of citizenship and engage the problems of liberal pluralism (Chapter 1).

A state can adopt any regime it wishes for its citizens. Although there is a status of 'British citizen', (below) those subject to the jurisdiction of English law are strictly speaking not citizens but 'subjects' of the Crown. A subject includes anyone within the territory of the UK since such a person can lay claim to the protection of the Crown. Despite the word commonly being associated with subservience, the notion of a 'subject' is sometimes said to give valuable protection in that it presupposes a relationship of mutual respect between ruler and ruled which is safeguarded by law. Thus in return for 'allegiance' (loyalty), the Crown is obliged under the common law to protect the rights of the subject and to keep the peace. In his speech on the scaffold (1649) Charles I announced that:

> I must tell you, that [the people's] liberty and freedom consists in having the government of those laws, by which their life and their goods may be considered most their own; 'tis not for having a share in government that is nothing pertaining to 'em. A subject and a sovereign are clean different things.

A problem with this view is that, unless the people can control the lawmaking process, how can they ensure that the laws do in fact protect their rights? On the other hand, an extreme view of citizenship such as that of Rousseau (Chapter 1) proclaims that a citizen must submit to the will of the majority, whatever that might be.

In English law citizenship is mainly concerned with the right to reside, rights concerned with political participation and sometimes access to public services and taxation. Other legal rights and duties depend on presence in the territory or sometimes, particularly in relation to health and welfare services, a more specific connection such as actual residence. In exceptional cases, notably the Channel Islands, non-citizens have restricted property rights.

UK citizenship law is complex due to the many changes that have been made in order to control immigration following the collapse of the British Empire and to assuage post-imperial guilt. It can only be sketched here. The British Nationality Act 1981 (BNA), as amended, is the main legislation. There is no legal concept of citizenship of any other unit within the UK. There is a notion of citizenship of the European Union. However, this merely endorses certain rights within member states which apply to citizens of other EU states.

The following have 'British' citizenship under the Act:

▶ Persons who were citizens or who by virtue of specified family connections (patrials) had the right of abode in the UK, under the regime that existed before 1983 (s.11).

▶ Those born or adopted in the UK (s.50). However, at least one parent must also be either a citizen or settled in the UK. If the parents are not married this must be the mother.

▶ Those descended from a British citizen (s.2). At the time of birth at least one parent must be a citizen other than by descent or be a citizen working abroad for the British government having been recruited in the UK or, in certain cases, working for the European Union having been recruited in a member state.

▶ Most persons connected with British colonies, other than certain military bases in Cyprus (formerly 'British Dependent Territories Citizens', now 'British Overseas Territories Citizens'), have a right to become full citizens (British Overseas Territories Act 2003). In the case of the Falkland Islands, over which the UK fought a war with Argentina in 1982, this is automatic (British Nationality (Falkland Islands) Act 1983).

▶ Some citizens of Hong Kong, which the UK surrendered to China in 1997, have certain rights to registration as British citizens (British Nationality (Hong Kong) Act 1997).

▶ Citizenship can be acquired by registration or naturalisation. Registration is a right available to persons born in the UK or who fulfil certain requirements of residence or parentage (BNA s.4). Naturalisation (s.6) is a matter for the discretion of the Secretary of State and is available to anyone, subject to requirements of residence, language, good character and 'knowledge of life in the UK' as determined in accordance with regulations made by the Home Secretary (Nationality, Immigration and Asylum Act 2002 s.4). Thus a communitararian and potentially illiberal element has been injected into the law.

▶ There are certain other categories which attract special privileges. These include Commonwealth citizens (BNA 1 s.37); British Protected Persons (BNA ss.38, 50 (1)), European citizens and citizens of the Republic of Ireland.

▶ All other persons are 'aliens'. Unless statute requires otherwise, while present in the UK, aliens (other than those from countries with whom we are formally at war) have the same rights and duties in English law as citizens.

▶ Citizenship can be renounced by registration with the Secretary of State (BNA s.12). However, registration becomes ineffective unless the person in question acquires citizenship of another state within six months. Apart from this, allegiance cannot be voluntarily surrendered (*R* v *Lynch* (1903)).

▶ The Home Secretary can by Order remove citizenship if he is satisfied that (1) that person 'has done anything seriously prejudicial to the interests of the UK or a British Overseas Territory' unless deprivation of citizenship would make the person stateless or (2) has acquired citizenship by fraud, false representation or concealment of a material fact. Reasons must be given for the Order and there is a right of appeal to an Immigration Adjudicator and thence, on a point of law and with permissions to the Immigration Appeal Tribunal and the Court of Appeal. If the Home Secretary certifies that the matter is one of security, foreign relations or 'otherwise in the public interest', the only appeal is to the Special Immigration Appeals Commission which involves restrictions relating to access to evidence (see Nationality, Immigration and Asylum Act 2002 s.4, replacing s.40 of the BNA 1981).

Citizenship is legally important mainly in the following respects:

▶ It confers a right of abode in the UK under immigration law (Immigration Act 1971 s.1). Certain commonwealth citizens who can trace historic connections with the UK also have a right of abode, which cannot be exercised by polygamous wives (Immigration Act 1988 s.2). European Union citizens also have certain rights of residence in the UK. Citizens of the Republic of Ireland are exempt from immigration control but can be expelled (Immigration Act 1971 s.1 (3)).

▶ British, Irish and Commonwealth citizens lawfully resident in the UK may vote in parliamentary and local elections (Representation of the People Act 2000).

▶ Non-citizens (other than Irish citizens) cannot be members of either House of Parliament (British Nationality Act 1981 Sched.7).

▶ Honours and titles cannot be conferred upon non-citizens.

▶ British citizens have a right to call upon the protection of the Crown when abroad, although this is not enforceable in the courts. The main consequence of the Crown's duty to protect British citizens abroad is that the Crown cannot require payment for such protection unless the person concerned voluntarily exposes him or herself to some special risk (see *China Navigation Co. Ltd* v *A-G* (1932); *Mutasa* v *A-G* (1980)).

▶ British citizens abroad are subject to special taxation laws.

▶ British citizens cannot generally be removed (deportation) or excluded from the UK. There are two exceptions. Firstly, anyone can be extradited to stand trial or serve a sentence in a commonwealth country or a state with which the UK has an extradition treaty (Extradition Act 2003); there are special arrangements with Ireland. Secondly, under emergency legislation relating to Northern Ireland, the Home Secretary can exclude or remove even a citizen from Great Britain (i.e. England, Wales and Scotland) who has not been 'ordinarily resident' for at least three years.

▶ Non-citizens can in certain circumstances be detained without charge unless they choose to leave the country (Anti-Terrorism, Crime and Security Act 2001, a provision recently held to be contrary to the ECHR (see Chapter 19)).

▶ All British citizens owe allegiance to the Crown wherever they are in the world (see *R* v *Casement* (1917)). Allegiance has two main practical consequences. Firstly, the Crown probably cannot plead the defence of 'Act of State' against a person who owes allegiance (Chapter 12). Second, the offence of treason is committed against the duty of allegiance. Aliens resident and perhaps even present in the UK also owe allegiance (*de Jager* v *A-G* (1907)). A person who holds a British passport apparently owes allegiance even if he has never visited the UK and even if the passport has been fraudulently obtained (see *Joyce* v *DPP* (1946)).

## 4.3 Federalism

The UK constitution is a 'unitary' constitution. A unitary state has an overriding supreme lawmaker which can devolve power to subordinate units but is free to take the power back. In a federal state such as the USA, the constitution divides power between a central federal government and separate state units in such a way that each unit is independent within its own sphere and neither can override the other. This requires above all a strong and independent Supreme Court to resolve differences between the two levels and imposes a legalistic framework upon the constitution. By contrast, devolved government (which includes local government) retains ultimate power at the centre but allocates defined functions to lower levels such as towns or regions, usually subject to powers of control, although there is sometimes constitutional protection for the local units. A federal system might also include devolved government, for example local government within each federal state. The extent to which powers are devolved varies considerably.

Historically, federalism developed in the interests of common defence by groups of states against foreign invaders. Federal and devolved governments both respond, but in different degrees, to the idea of group liberalism and particularly of national identity (Chapter 1), namely that within an overall framework the constitution should recognise the separate identities of different groups, in this case relying on the link between geographical areas and group identity. Federalism also gives effect to republican values of equality and division of power. Indeed James Madison, one of the founders of the US constitution, famously argued that large democratic units help to prevent domination by a faction. Mill argued (*Representative Government;* Chapter 15) that smaller devolved units encourage individuals to participate in public affairs. He suggested that the UK constitution did not require a federal framework since our culture was less obsessed with uniformity than that of continental countries (ibid. Chapter 13). This is a political debate relevant to the European Union (Chapter 8). However Mill also argued in favour of larger units since there may not be sufficient serious issues at local level to justify the time of competent public officials or attract the interest of talented people, and local elections may be more influenced by national than by local politics. Devolved government is therefore a pragmatic compromise between competing goods.

Within a federal constitution there is usually a single citizenship of the state as a whole. How powers are allocated between the different bodies varies according to the political concerns of the state in question. Usually the federal government is responsible for foreign affairs, defence and major economic matters, while private law issues are the responsibility of the states. Social matters such as housing, education and health may be divided between the levels. Sometimes, for example in the USA, particular matters are given to the federal level with the residue left with the states. In other cases the converse applies.

Federalism therefore gives effect to republican values of equality and division of power (Chapter 1). The relationship between a federal government and the states within it, is not, in law, one of superior and inferior, but of partnership. Each has its own sphere of activity and its own constitution, legislature and courts and it may be unlawful for one to trespass upon the other. The federal legislature is typically bicameral, one House representing the whole nation, the other representing the smaller units. A unitary state such as the UK may also have a bicameral Parliament but this is relatively unusual and its rationale debateable (Chapter 9).

Federalism is practicable where the component units have sufficient in common economically and culturally, for example a shared history or language, to enable them to cooperate, while at the same time each unit is sufficiently distinctive to constitute a community in its own right but not sufficiently powerful to aspire to a military role on the international stage. Thus a delicate balance must be struck. The USA and Australia are relatively successful federations whereas Canada, with its split between English-speaking and French-speaking regions, is less stable. Yugoslavia, with its many ethnic tensions, has been tragically unsuccessful. Indeed, as with any constitution, the actual disposition of power in a federation depends on political and economic factors so that the balance between centre and state may not be apparent from reading the constitution. Moreover, the term federal is not a legal definition but only an abstract model. There is no reason why any particular constitution should correspond neatly to the model. It is probably best to regard terms such as 'federal' or 'unitary' not as precise definitions, but as convenient points upon a political spectrum ranging from loose associations of countries for particular purposes to simple one-government states.

The UK is a union of what were the separate states of England, parts of Ireland and Scotland. Wales is a nation within the UK but has never been a state in its own right. Before the introduction of devolved government in 2000 (below) the internal affairs of Scotland and Wales were governed by the UK central executive with what has sometimes been regarded as overtones of colonialism. This took the form of 'administrative devolution' to ministers for Scotland, Wales and Northern Ireland. There was therefore no specific democratic power base or accountability mechanism linking the ministers to their regions (see Munro, *Studies in Constitutional Law*, (2nd edn 1999, p. 37 *et seq.*). Indeed the relevant minister might have an English constituency. Scotland and Northern Ireland have separate legal systems but the House of Lords and the Privy Council are final courts of appeal for all the UK jurisdictions.

Federalism has not been a serious element of UK politics (c.f. Olowofoyeku, 'De centralising the United Kingdom: the Federal Argument', (1999), 3 (1), *Edinburgh Law Review*, 57). Dicey, the influential Victorian constitutional lawyer strongly opposed federalism claiming that it tends to conservatism, creates divided loyalties and elevates legalism to a primary value, making the courts the pivot on which the constitution turns and perhaps threatening their independence (1915, p. 171). During the late nineteenth century there were some advocates of a federal UK as a way of avoiding home rule for Ireland.

The *Royal Commission on the Constitution* (1973, Cmnd 5460) argued against a federal constitution for the UK on the following grounds. First, lack of balance since the units are widely different in economic terms, with England being dominant. Second, a federal regime would be contrary to our constitutional traditions in that it would elevate the courts over political machinery. Third, the UK was thought to require central and flexible economic management since its resources are unevenly distributed geographically, much of its land area being thinly populated hills. Fourth, apart from Northern Ireland, regional issues were not high on the agenda of the main parties, which suggested that there was little public desire for federalism.

## 4.4 Devolution

The Royal Commission (above) asserted that government in the UK was over-centralised and recommended devolved government. Referendums were subsequently held in Scotland and Wales which foundered because they failed to obtain the required two-thirds majorities in favour of change. The Labour government that took office in 1997 was supportive of devolved government. Following further referendums which produced considerable public support for devolution in Scotland and significant but less support for devolution in Wales, legislation was introduced to give devolved powers to a Scottish Parliament, a Northern Ireland Assembly and, to a lesser extent, a Welsh Assembly. The devolved powers in Northern Ireland are currently suspended due to the absence of agreement between the different factions. In this chapter we shall outline the main provisions, dealing with particular aspects in their context in later chapters.

The devolution arrangements preserve the unlimited power of the UK Parliament to legislate for the devolved regions and to override laws made by devolved bodies. Thus there is no federal ingredient. However, as an issue of politics it would be difficult for Parliament to interfere with matters allocated to the devolved governments. There are also non-legally binding arrangements, 'concordats', between each UK government department and the devolved administrations. These put in place conventions for coordinating the activities of the governments, for example through a joint ministerial committee, and may buttress the kind of secretive informality that has long bedevilled UK government (see *Memorandum of Understanding and Supplementary Agreements*, 1999 Cm 4444, 2001, Cm 4806; see Rawlings, 'Concordats of the Constitution', 2000, 116 *Law Quarterly Review* 257, Trench 2004, *Public Law* 513).

The devolution arrangements are asymmetrical in the sense that they are different in each region and raise different constitutional issues. In the case of Scotland a major concern seems to have been to reduce the likelihood of national independence. In the case of Northern Ireland there is an aspiration towards an inclusive form of democracy reflecting the notion of group liberalism (Chapter 1). Devolution in Northern Ireland raises more fundamental issues than is the case elsewhere. This is partly because the arrangements are concerned with fundamental disputes about the legitimacy of the state itself and partly because they are influenced by the international concerns of relationships with the neighbouring Republic of Ireland. In the case of Wales, although the devolved powers fall significantly below those in the other regions, there is an aspiration towards substantive concerns of economic development and cultural identity reflecting communitarian values (Chapter 1).

The courts, ultimately the Judicial Committee of the Privy Council, are responsible for ensuring that the limits of the devolved powers are respected. The devolution legislation therefore marks a change of emphasise in our constitutional arrangements away from reliance upon informal and political methods and towards 'juridification'. This leads to the question of whether the devolution arrangements can be regarded as 'constitutional' and so subject to a special approach to interpretation (Chapter 1). We might envoke matters such as the importance of the devolved arrangements with respect to the fundamental concerns of the particular community. On this basis the Northern Ireland arrangements have a particularly strong claim to be regarded as constitutional. Indeed in *Robinson* v *Secretary of State for Northern Ireland* (2002) Lord Hoffmann asserted that the Northern Ireland Act 1998 is to be construed:

> against the background of the political situation in Northern Ireland and the principles laid down by the Belfast Agreement for a new start. These facts and background form part of the admissible background to the construction of the Act just as much as the Revolution, the Convention and the federalist papers are the background to construing the Constitution of the USA.

### 4.4.1  Scotland

Scotland was a separate nation state from 1010 until 1706 although after 1603 the Crowns of England and Scotland were united. Since the sixteenth-century Reformation there had been cultural assimilation between the two countries, but also quarrels between Catholics and Protestants. In 1689 Scotland offered its Crown to William and Mary on the same revolutionary terms as in England (Chapter 3). After quarrels between the two Parliaments the Treaty of Union 1706 abolished the separate Scottish and English Parliaments and created a Parliament of Great Britain. The treaty was confirmed by separate Acts of each Parliament (Act of Union with England 1706; Act of Union with Scotland 1706). The Acts of Union are still in force. They preserve the separate Scottish legal system and church and safeguard the private rights of Scottish subjects (below; Chapter 7). The Union was unpopular but was brought about by economic interest on the part of Scotland and fear of invasion on the part of England.

In relation to the continuing role of the UK government in respect of Scotland, there are special committees in Parliament to examine Scottish Affairs and a minister for Scotland accountable to the UK Parliament. Before 1998, Scotland was entitled to at least 71 seats in the UK Parliament, thus making it over-represented in terms of its population. Section 86 (1) of the Scotland Act 1998 abolishes this entitlement and places Scotland under the same regime as England in terms of the criteria for defining constituencies (Chapter 10). This is likely to reduce the number of Scottish MPs to about 59. The UK government also has substantial powers in relation to the devolved Scottish government.

The Scotland Act 1998 creates a devolved government for Scotland. It is modelled broadly on the UK's parliamentary system and the Act gives legal force to provisions similar to those which in England are in the form only of conventions. The Queen is the formal head of the Scottish government but acts through Scottish ministers. Whether in this statutory context the Queen has any personal discretion remains to be seen. Acts of the Scottish Parliament require the Royal Assent (Scotland Act 1998, s.28). There is a Scottish Parliament and a Scottish executive. However the Scottish executive has less power in relation to the Parliament than its UK counterpart. The UK Parliament retains its full power to make laws for Scotland (s.28 (7)). Indeed section 37 purports to empower the UK Parliament to override the Acts of Union (Chapter 7). Moreover, an Order in Council can alter the matters devolved to the Scottish Parliament (s.30).

The Scottish Parliament of 129 members is elected partly by proportional representation (see Chapter 10). Originally the Scottish constituencies were the same as those for the UK Parliament. However, by virtue of the Scottish Parliament (Constituencies) Act 2004, the link between the two has been severed in order to preserve the existing representation. The electoral system was designed to make the composition of the Parliament correspond more closely to public opinion than is the case with the UK Parliament and perhaps to reduce the likelihood that Scottish Nationalists might form a majority. The Scottish Parliament cannot alter these arrangements.

The Presiding Officer of the Parliament, elected by the House for the duration of the Parliament (s.19), has the constitutional function of submitting bills for royal assent, recommending the appointment of the First Minister and advising a dissolution (below). Subject to the devolution limits (below), royal prerogative powers and powers previously exercised by UK ministers are transferred to Scottish ministers (s.53). Most powers of ministers are of course conferred by the Scottish Parliament itself. The capacity of the Crown in relation to Scotland is separated from that in relation to the UK, in effect treating the two as separate entities so that they can enter into, for example, property transactions with each other (s.99). Similarly a corporate body exercises administrative functions for the Parliament (s.21).

The Scottish Parliament sits for a term of four years which must be followed by a general election, after which it must meet within seven days (s.2). It can be dissolved earlier by a two-thirds majority – an unlikely event – or where it fails to designate a First Minister within 28 days (s.3). This might arise where an administration finds itself deadlocked because of tensions within a coalition government (more likely than in the UK Parliament because of the proportionate electoral system). Thus, unlike the case with the UK Parliament, the executive cannot dissolve the Scottish Parliament.

The Scottish executive comprises the following:

▷ The First Minister is appointed and dismissed by the Queen on the nomination of the Parliament (s.45).
▷ Other ministers and junior ministers are appointed by the First Minister from members of the Parliament (MSP) subject to the approval of the Queen with the agreement of the Parliament (ss.47, 49, 87). They can be dismissed by the First Minister (ss.47 (3)b, 49 (4)b).
▷ Law officers, namely the Lord Advocate and the Solicitor General for Scotland. (There is an Advocate General for Scotland who is responsible for giving advice on Scottish matters to the UK government.) Appointment and removal of the law officers must be recommended to the Queen by the First Minister with the agreement of the Parliament (s.48).

The Parliament must nominate a First Minister within 28 days of any of the following events: a general election, the resignation of the First Minister, any other vacancy in the office and the First Minister's ceasing to be an MSP other than on a dissolution (s.46). The First Minister, all other ministers and the law officers must resign if the executive loses a vote of confidence (ss.45 (2), 47 (3), 48 (2) 49 (4)). When Parliament is dissolved a minister remains in office until dismissed but otherwise loses office on ceasing to be an MSP (ss.47, 49). If however the First Minister ceases to be an MSP he remains in office until a successor is chosen.

Ministers in the UK government cannot hold office in the Scottish executive (s.44 (3)). Scottish civil servants remain part of the UK home civil service but are appointed by Scottish ministers (s.51). Thus where the ruling political party in Scotland is different from that of the UK there may be a conflict of loyalty.

### 4.4.1.1 *Legislation*

The Scottish Parliament can legislate generally subject to the restrictions in the Act (s.28, s.29 Sched. 4). These are substantial and make it clear that this is devolution rather than federalism. Acts of the Scottish Parliament are technically subordinate legislation owing their validity only to the Scotland Act 1998 (see e.g. Human Rights Act 1998 s.21). They can therefore be set aside by the courts and can be overridden by any inconsistent UK legislation. The validity of the procedure leading to an enactment does not affect the Act's validity (s.28 (5)), but otherwise Acts of the Scottish Parliament that are outside its competence 'are not law' (s.28). However, the democratic character of the devolved lawmaking process provisions suggests that the court will be reluctant to interfere. Moreover, where a measure is ambiguous it must be interpreted narrowly in favour of its validity (s.101).

The following are the main restrictions on legislation:

▶ The Scottish Parliament cannot, except in minor respects (Sched. 4, para. 4), amend the Scotland Act itself.
▶ It cannot alter any law outside Scotland.
▶ It cannot override European law, nor, and significantly different from the UK Parliament, rights binding under the Human Rights Act 1998. UK ministers have the exclusive power to bring EC law into effect (ss.52, 54, 57 (2)).
▶ It has taxation powers limited to altering the basic rate of income tax by 3 pence in the Pound (s.73). However, most of its finance is derived from the UK government.
▶ Many important matters are 'reserved matters' on which only the UK Parliament can legislate (s.30, Sched. 5). They include important constitutional provisions including matters affecting the Crown (but not the exercise of the royal prerogative); the civil service; the registration and funding of political parties; the Union with England; the UK Parliament; the higher Scottish courts; international relations; defence and national security; treason; fiscal, economic and monetary policy;

currency; financial services and markets, money laundering; border controls; transport safety and regulation; media policy; employment regulation; certain health matters; and the regulation of key professions and social security.

▶ The Presiding Officer, who submits bills for Royal Assent (s.32), must decide whether a bill is within the powers of the Parliament (s.31). The Advocate General, the Lord Advocate or the Attorney-General can require a bill to be referred to the Privy Council (s.33). However, and somewhat controversially due to the 'colonial' flavour of such a power, the Secretary of State can prohibit a bill from being sent for Royal Assent where s/he: 'has reasonable ground to believe' that the bill would be incompatible with international obligations, or the interests of national security or defence, or would have an adverse effect on the law relating to reserved matters (s.35) (see also s.58 in relation to the Scottish executive).

▶ The UK government can make subordinate legislation remedying *ultra vires* Acts of the Scottish Parliament and the Scottish executive (s.107). Moreover, additional functions outside devolved matters can be given to Scottish ministers by Order in Council (s.63), for which they are accountable to the UK Parliament. The court can protect people who may have relied on invalid laws by removing the retrospective effect of the invalidity or suspending the invalidity to allow the defect to be corrected (s.102).

▶ The committee system within the Scottish Parliament is more pro-active than is the case with the UK Parliament (Chapter 11). Scottish committees can not only scrutinise the executive and revise legislation but can initiate legislation, and conduct inquiries which involve direct communication with the people.

After a slow start the Scottish Parliament has enacted a substantial amount of legislation, particularly concerning social matters and public services, that has markedly distinguished the regime from its English counterpart. These include free personal care for the elderly, rescue packages for fisheries and the victims of foot and mouth disease, land reform, mental health and freedom of information.

### 4.4.1.2 *The Courts*

Scotland has its own court system. However, civil appeals are decided by the House of Lords which has jurisdiction over the whole of the UK while criminal appeals are decided within the Scottish courts. Scottish criminal law is markedly different to that in England. However it is not obvious that there should be uniformity in the civil law (see *Mackintosh* v *Lord Advocate*

(1876); *R* v *Manchester Stipendiary Magistrate ex p. Granada Television Ltd* [2001] 1 AC 300 at 304.

Scottish judges appear to have stronger protection against political interference than their UK counterparts (Chapter 6). The most senior judges (the Lord President of the Court of Session and the Lord Justice Clerk) are appointed by the Queen on a recommendation from the Prime Minister on the nomination of the First Minister (s.95). Other judges are appointed on the recommendation of the First Minister. Senior judges can be dismissed only on a recommendation by the First Minister following a resolution of Parliament. The resolution can be made only on the basis of a written report from a tribunal, chaired by a member of the Privy Council who has held high judicial office, concluding that the judge is unfit for office on the grounds of inability, neglect of duty or misbehaviour. In the case of the Lord President and the Lord Justice Clerk, the Prime Minister must be consulted.

There is special provision for 'devolution issues'. These are (Sched. 6):

- whether the Parliament has exceeded its powers;
- whether a member of the executive has acted outside his devolved competence or violated the Human Rights Act or European Community law;
- any other question about whether a function is within devolved competence;
- any other question arising by virtue of the Act about reserved matters.

A devolution issue can initially be raised in any court by a party to the proceedings and the court can refer a devolution issue to a higher court (a court against which there is no appeal must do so). Proceedings can also be instituted in a Scottish court by the Advocate General or the Lord Advocate and in an English court by the Attorney-General (the chief law officer of the UK government). Where a devolution issue arises, the Advocate General and the Lord Advocate can also be parties to any proceedings in Scotland.

Devolution issues must be ultimately decided by the Privy Council either on appeal or by way of a reference from a lower court. In addition, the Lord Advocate, the Advocate General, the Attorney-General or the Advocate General for Northern Ireland can directly refer to the Privy Council any devolution issue arising in a case to which he is a party. Where a devolution issue arises before the House of Lords, it must be referred to the Privy Council unless the House in all the circumstances thinks that it is more appropriate to decide it itself. More generally it seems anomalous that human rights and EC matters are devolution issues since the same principles apply throughout the UK. Under current reform proposals a UK-wide Supreme Court will replace the House of Lords and the Privy Council in relation to devolution matters (Chapter 6).

### 4.4.2 Northern Ireland

The history of Ireland is complex and raises fundamental political issues about the sharing of political power in Northern Ireland and about its relationship with the UK. Disagreements centre upon divisions between the Catholic and Protestant communities and upon a history of imposed settlement from England and Scotland. Broadly speaking, the majority Protestant community prefers to remain an integral part of the UK while the Catholic community would prefer union with the neighbouring Republic of Ireland.

Ireland had been nominally subject to the English Crown from the tenth century. According to English law, laws made by the Irish Parliament had been subject to English statutes and to approval by the King in Council since 1494 ('Poyning's Law'). However, until Tudor times England effectively controlled only an area around Dublin called the Pale. Henry VIII and Elizabeth I attempted to extend English administration to the whole of Ireland, precipitating rebellion followed by confiscation of land and extensive settlement by English and Scots Protestants in what is now Northern Ireland. Cromwell's regime during the 1650s consolidated this policy with large-scale massacres. The conquest of Ireland was completed in 1690 when William III, in alliance with France and supported by the Pope, defeated the deposed Catholic King of England, James II, at the Battle of the Boyne.

After a series of violent rebellions against Protestant supremacy, the Acts of Union of 1800 joined Britain and Ireland into the UK thus creating the UK Parliament. The Irish Parliament was abolished in favour of Irish representation in the UK Parliament. The Acts of Union declared that the Union was to last 'for ever'. They also protected the United Church of England and Ireland but the repeal of this provision by the Irish Church Act 1879 has been upheld (*Ex parte Canon Selwyn* (1872)).

Unrest punctuated by periods of violence continued throughout the nineteenth and twentieth centuries. In the late nineteenth century the question of 'Irish home rule' was among the most important questions in UK politics. This had wider implications. It weakened the personal authority of the monarchy, who unwisely took sides in the dispute, and generated dispute about the most fundamental principles of the constitution including the balance of representation in the UK Parliament. No agreement was reached but the notion of parliamentary supremacy became a powerful symbol and federalism was strongly resisted. Dicey in particular was a strong supporter of the Union and thought that home rule would be possible only by abolishing Parliament.

The Government of Ireland Act 1920 partitioned Ireland between what is now the Republic of Ireland and the six counties of Northern Ireland. The Act introduced a devolved government in Northern Ireland. Section 75 provided that:

notwithstanding the establishment of the Parliament of Northern Ireland or anything contained in this Act, the supreme authority of the Parliament of the UK shall remain unaffected and undiminished over all persons, matters and things in (Northern Ireland) and every part thereof.

Originally there was proportional representation in the Parliament thus giving a voice to the Catholic minority, but this was abolished in 1929, allowing Protestant majority rule.

The Irish Free State (Constitution) Act 1922 gave the rest of Ireland internal self-government.

Outside Northern Ireland both measures were ignored and the Republic of Ireland created its own constitution based upon the sovereignty of the people. This constitution applied to the whole of Ireland although it was ineffective in the north. There were therefore conflicting legal orders, each being valid from its internal viewpoint. Eventually the UK recognised the independence of the republic (Ireland Act 1949) but provided that:

> in no event will Northern Ireland cease to be part of the UK without the consent of the Parliament of Northern Ireland. (s.1 (2))

From 1972, against a background of violent disturbances and terrorist activities, direct rule from Westminster was imposed on Northern Ireland and stringent emergency legislation introduced. A series of agreements attempted to engineer a compromise by creating machinery for inter-community negotiations (the *Anglo-Irish Agreement* 1985; the *'Downing Street Declaration'* (1994), Cm 2422). These led to the *Belfast* (or *'Good Friday'*) *Agreement* (1998 Cm 3883) between the two governments and the main political parties in Northern Ireland. This provides for the restoration of devolved government, the amendment of the Irish constitution so as to accept that Northern Ireland is currently controlled by the UK, and the creation of various consultative bodies representing the interests of the UK, Northern Ireland and the Republic of Ireland (North/South Ministerial Council, British-Irish Council, British-Irish Intergovernmental Conference).

The Good Friday Agreement was endorsed by 71% of voters in Northern Ireland and 94% in the Republic of Ireland in separate referendums. It makes devolution conditional upon the completion of the peace process and so the devolved institutions can be suspended. This is currently the case (Northern Ireland Act 2000). The main points of contention are the questions of renouncing violence and the decommissioning of weapons. Nevertheless we shall briefly outline the devolution arrangements.

The Northern Ireland Act 1998 attempts to ensure a balance between the competing communities. It is sometimes characterised as an example of deliberative democracy and liberal pluralism, (Chapter 1). It restricts the political freedom of the legislature and executive to a greater extent than is the case in the rest of the UK. The overriding power of Parliament to make law for Northern Ireland is not affected (s.5 (6)). Prerogative and executive power remains with the Queen who must act through Northern Ireland Ministers (s.23). Ministers are directly elected by the Assembly in accordance with the balance of the parties within it. Thus the system is very different from the UK's traditional system which concentrates power in the majority party leader. The Northern Ireland devolution is also significant in that it provides for the people to vote in a referendum to leave the UK, and it provides for another state, the Republic of Ireland, to participate in the affairs of Northern Ireland. The following are the main provisions of the Act:

▶ Northern Ireland remains part of the UK and that the status of Northern Ireland will be altered only with the consent of a majority of its electorate (s.1) If a referendum favours a united Ireland, the Secretary of State is required to 'make proposals' to implement this by agreement with the Irish government (s.1).

▶ There is a Northern Ireland Assembly elected by the single transferable vote (Chapter 10). The Assembly's powers are more limited than is the case with Scotland and the Secretary of State has stronger powers. The Assembly sits for a fixed four-year term but can be dissolved on a resolution supported by two-thirds of its members or if a Chief Minister or Deputy Chief Minister cannot be elected (s.32). If thirty members petition the Assembly in relation to any matter to be voted on, the vote shall require cross -community support (s.42).

▶ Acts of the Assembly require the Royal Assent and, as in Scotland, the validity of proceedings leading to an enactment shall not be questioned in the courts (s.5 (5)). Unlike the case in Scotland where this is a matter for the Presiding Officer of the Assembly, the Secretary of State submits bills for Royal Assent (s.14). He can refuse to submit a bill if he thinks it is outside the competence of the Assembly or contains provisions incompatible with international obligations, the interests of defence or national security, the protection of public safety or public order, or would have an adverse effect on the operation of the single market within the UK. The Secretary of State can also make an order remedying an *ultra vires* Act (s.80).

▶ As in Scotland provisions of the Assembly outside its competence are not law (s.6). Similar provisions apply in relation to control by the courts over devolution matters. The Assembly has general legislative power in relation to matters exclusively within Northern Ireland, subject to European Community law and to the rights protected by the Human Rights Act 1998. The Assembly can raise certain taxes but not the main taxes that apply generally throughout the UK. 'Excepted' and 'reserved' matters are listed in Schedules 2 and 3. The Assembly cannot legislate on excepted matters unless ancillary to other matters. It can legislate on reserved matters and on ancillary matters with the consent of the Secretary of State (ss.6, 8). Discrimination on the ground of religious belief or political opinion is outside the competence of the Assembly and certain statutes cannot be modified (s.7).

▷ The First Minister lacks the discretionary power of a UK Prime Minister to appoint or dismiss other ministers or dissolve the legislature. Instead there is a bipartisan arrangement ensuring that both unionists and nationalists play a part. The First Minister and Deputy First Ministers are elected jointly by the Assembly from its members. This requires not only a majority of the Assembly as a whole but also separate majorities of unionists and nationalists (s.16). The First and Deputy First Ministers hold office until a new election subject to both losing office if either resigns or ceases to be a member of the Assembly. Subject to a maximum of 10, which can be increased by the Secretary of State (s.17 (4)), and to the approval of the Assembly, the First and Deputy First Ministers jointly decide on the number of Northern Ireland ministers heading departments and forming a cabinet. Ministers are then nominated by the political parties from members of the Assembly in accordance with a formula designed to reflect the balance of parties in the Assembly (s.18).

▷ A minister can be dismissed by his or her party nominating officer and loses office on ceasing to be a member of the Assembly other than after a dissolution (s.18). Ministers collectively lose office when a new Assembly is elected, where a party is excluded on a vote of confidence, where a new determination as to the number of ministers is made or as prescribed by standing order (ibid.).

▷ Ministers and political parties can be excluded for up to 12 months (renewable) by the Assembly on the ground that they are not committed to peace or have otherwise broken their oath of office (s.30). The motion must have the support of at least 30 members (of a total of between 96 and 108) and must be moved by the First and Deputy First Ministers jointly or by the presiding officer of the Assembly if required to do so by the Secretary of State. The Secretary of State must take into account the propensity to violence and cooperation with the authorities of the excluded person. The resolution must have cross-party support.

▷ Ministers must take a pledge of office which includes a 'Ministerial Code of Conduct' (s.16 (10) Sched. 4). The code requires the 'strictest standards of propriety, accountability, openness, good community relations and equality and avoiding or declaring conflicts of interest'. Any direct or indirect pecuniary interests that members of the public might reasonably think could influence their judgement must be registered. The code is similar to the *Ministerial Code* for the UK ministers and requires compliance with the 'Nolan Principles of Public Life' (Chapter 3). In Northern Ireland, unlike the rest of the UK, it might therefore be enforceable in the courts.

▶ There are human rights and equal opportunities commissioners with powers to advise government and support legal proceedings.

### 4.4.3 Wales

Wales has strong cultural traditions but, unlike Scotland and Northern Ireland, has never had its own government or legal system. Wales was never a separate state but consisted of a number of principalities. The largest of these passed into English rule in 1084 (Statute of Wales) and the English local government system was imposed by the Statute of Rhuddlan (1284). England had subdued the whole of Wales by the sixteenth century (see Act of the Union of Wales 1536). A separate Welsh Assembly was abolished in 1689. English law applied throughout Wales and a single court system was introduced in 1830. Within Wales there are markedly different areas both economically and culturally, so that it is more difficult than in the case of Scotland to regard Wales as a country or a nation. Earlier proposals for Welsh devolution in the Wales Act 1978 were defeated by a referendum and the current proposals were only narrowly approved.

The emphasis of the Welsh arrangements is threefold: first, the strengthening of democratic accountability within Wales; second, stimulating economic development and encouraging sustainable development and equal opportunities (e.g. ss.115, 120, 121); third, representing Welsh interests at a national and international level (see *A Voice for Wales: The Government's Proposals for a Welsh Assembly*, 1997, Cm 3718). Relatively weak and flexible mechanisms have been devised for Wales which leave considerable discretion in the hands of UK ministers.

The Government of Wales Act 1998 creates a Welsh Assembly of 60 members elected by a method similar to that in Scotland (Chapter 10). However, the Welsh electoral system is less proportional than the Scottish system thus giving greater influence to the majority party. It sits for a fixed term of four years but, unlike the Scottish Parliament, cannot be dissolved earlier. Thus there is no provision for democratic control by means of a vote of confidence. Unlike the other devolved bodies, the Assembly has no lawmaking powers of its own. It can exercise only such legislative or executive powers as are transferred to it by Order in Council from UK ministers (s.22). Thus the powers and functions of the Welsh Assembly can be changed from time to time and its powers are subject to UK statutes. As subordinate legislation, laws made by the Assembly are invalid if they are contrary to the Human Rights Act 1998.

The Assembly exercises the functions that were previously exercised by the Welsh Office. These include agriculture, forestry, fisheries and food, environmental and cultural matters, economic and industrial development, education and training, health, housing, local government, social services, sport and tourism, town and country planning, transport, water and flood defences. The Assembly is required to prepare schemes dealing with sustainable development (s.121), and to promote equal opportunities (s.10(1)) and the Welsh Language (s.47). It must also sustain and promote local government and promote relevant voluntary organisations.

There is no separation of powers between the legislature and the executive, the executive being comprised of committees of the legislature on the local government model. As in Scotland civil servants are part of the UK home civil service (s.34 (2)). The powers exercisable under the Act are vested in the Assembly itself with flexible powers for delegation to committees and secretaries. The Assembly must elect committees, one for each of its functions as it determines, to which the executive will be responsible, and also an Audit Committee, and a Subordinate Legislation Scrutiny Committee. Because of the blurring of functions between executive and legislature, the Assembly committees are expected to be more pro-active than committees of Parliament and to be involved at every stage of the decision-making process rather than merely scrutinising after the event.

The Assembly must elect a First Secretary, analogous to a Prime Minister. The First Secretary appoints Assembly secretaries analogous to ministers. The First Secretary and the Assembly secretaries together comprise the Executive Committee. The Executive Committee can be made up from one party but there must be representation of minority parties on other committees.

There is an Auditor General for Wales who reports to the Assembly and a Welsh ombudsman. The National Audit Office can also scrutinise the Assembly's accounts and must work in cooperation with the Auditor General for Wales. The Secretary of State for Wales will continue to represent Welsh affairs at national level and in the Council of Ministers of the EU. The Secretary of State has a duty to consult the Assembly.

Much of the 1998 Act is preoccupied with rationalising the profusion of non-elected specialist public bodies (QUANGOs) that had developed in Wales. The Assembly has certain powers of control over Welsh local authorities and other bodies. These powers include in some cases the power of abolition or to transfer functions to the Assembly or a local authority. This is designed to meet widespread concerns about the lack of democratic accountability in Wales.

There is no separate court system although there is a division of the Administrative Court in Cardiff dealing with Welsh governmental issues. This could develop distinctive constitutional principles in the Welsh context. The UK Attorney-General also has responsibility for Wales. It seems that any court can invalidate decisions and legislation made by the Assembly. However, there are provisions similar to those in Scotland and Northern Ireland, for the Privy Council to deal with devolution matters by way of appeal or by a reference from the Assembly or the Attorney-General (Government of Wales Act 1998 s.109, sched. 7).

### 4.4.4 England

England, comprising 85% of the population of the UK, has no elected institutions of its own nor indeed a legal identity. England is governed by the central UK government. Therefore Scottish, Welsh and Northern Ireland members of the UK Parliament are entitled to vote in debates affecting exclusively English matters (the 'West Lothian' question, so-called after the constituency of Tam Dalziel, a relentless pursuer of the matter). For example the government won the recent vote in favour of increasing university tuition fees by virtue of its Scottish supporters even though students at Scottish universities do not pay fees. On the other hand, Scottish, Welsh and Northern Ireland voters are represented in the UK Parliament roughly in proportion to their population. This means that the UK Parliament, which retains unlimited power to legislate in relation to Scotland, Wales and Northern Ireland and provides most of their funding, is dominated by English MPs. Scotland, Northern Ireland and Wales receive from the central government substantially more money per head of the population than does England.

Central government powers relating to the English regions such as land use, transport and economic development are divided between the Departments of Transport, Local Government and the Regions (DTLR), the Department of Trade and Industry and the Cabinet Office. There are nine regional offices of central government charged with a coordinating role. There are also eight Regional Development Agencies (RDAs) wholly appointed by the Secretary of State and charged only with one purpose, that of advancing economic development including related matters of education and training (Regional Development Agencies Act 1998). RDAs are funded by the DTLR but accountable to the Secretary of State for Trade and Industry.

There is a limited form of regional devolution for the London region in the form of an elected mayor and Assembly (Greater London Authority Act 1999). The Assembly is elected on the basis of 'first past the post' (Chapter 10) together with an 'additional member' from a party list in accordance with the party's share of the vote, thereby reflecting public opinion to greater extent than is the case with local government and Parliament. The mayor and Assembly have certain executive powers in relation mainly to transport, land-use planning and local amenities.

The government proposes to offer a limited form of devolution to other English regions. The Secretary of State has power, after considering the 'level of interest' (undefined), to hold referendums in respect of the creation of elected regional assemblies in eight English regions (Regional Assemblies (Preparations) Act 2003). The Assemblies would be elected by a mixture of first-past-the-post and an additional member top-up on a similar basis to London (above). They would be funded by central government grant together with limited power to precept from local government taxation and some borrowing powers. They would not have lawmaking power. They would have strategic planning functions currently exercised by local government and unspecified administrative functions currently exercised by regional agencies of the central government. They would have 'targets set by central government (see *Your Region, Your Choice: Revitalising the English Regions*, 2002, Cm 5511). As with local government, it is doubtful whether regional assembles will have sufficient independence to be of constitutional significance. A proposal for a required assembly for North East England was rejected by 78% in a referendum in November 2004. It is unlikely that English devolution will be implemented.

## 4.5  Local Government

For many centuries there has been a strong tradition of local government in England. Although formally under the Crown, local officials, in particular Justices of the Peace, have exercised wide powers to keep order, provide local services and act as courts of law. Indeed it has been claimed that the dispersed and inefficient system of government that operated in the eighteenth and early nineteenth centuries was one of the factors that prevented the aristocratic dominance of English politics turning into the tyranny that led to the many revolutions that took place in Europe during that period. However, during the mid-nineteenth century, following the growth of democracy and under the influence of utilitarian ideas (Chapter 1), Parliament created the structure of elected local authorities charged with providing public services such as education, public health, leisure amenities, housing, land-use planning and transport that remains the basis of the modern system of local government. There is a mass of local government legislation of which the Local Government Act 1972 forms the basis.

Local authorities in England (the same applies in Scotland and Wales), are created by statute and therefore have only the powers and functions given to them by Parliament. As with Parliament itself, local councillors are elected by the first-past-the-post system which discounts all but the candidate with the largest number of votes thus ignoring the spread of votes. Local government is regulated in detail by the central government and by the Audit Commission. In many cases, notably land-use planning there is a right of appeal to central government against local decisions. By contrast, some constitutions specifically protect local government autonomy. For example, the Italian constitution protects regional and local autonomy according to the 'subsidiarity 'principle that decisions should be taken at the nearest possible level to those affected by them. (See also Carnwath 'The Reasonable Limits of Local Authority Power', 1996, *Public Law* 244.)

Local authority functions outside London are divided between county councils and district councils (metropolitan and non-metropolitan, see Local Government Act 1985). In some areas unitary authorities combine the functions of both levels (Local Government Act 1999). In rural areas there are parish councils (in Wales community councils), which have certain powers in relation to minor local amenities and have to be consulted upon planning matters. In London there are London Boroughs and the City of London Corporation.

Local authorities have a certain political claim to autonomy at least for the following reasons:

▶ They are directly elected and can therefore act as a separation of powers check on central government.

▶ They have certain tax raising powers over residents and businesses, the latter having no vote which can be capped by central government. However, about three-quarters of their finances are provided by central government and their other financial powers, in particular borrowing powers, are heavily circumscribed by central government (Local Government and Housing Act 1989).

▶ Services such as housing, education and environmental control should be administered flexibly in accordance with local circumstances. On the other hand, it is desirable for there to be similar basic services across the country, an issue that may trouble the courts (see e.g. *R v Gloucestershire County Council ex parte Barry* (1997) (Chapter 14)).

▶ Mill claimed (Chapter 1) that it is desirable in the interests of democracy and individual self-fulfillment for people to have closer contact with governmental bodies than is possible at central government level. In particular local democracy generates different political perspectives and healthy disagreement and debate.

▶ Local authorities are separate legal entities and can therefore claim the protection of the courts against improper intervention by central government (see e.g. *Secretary of State for Education and Science v Tameside MBC* (1977)). However this depends on how strongly the courts are prepared to read the values of local democracy into legislation a matter on which there is disagreement (see e.g. *R v Somerset County Council ex parte Fewings* (1995); *Roberts v Hopwood* (1925)).

Local government powers are so limited and circumscribed by the central government that it is unlikely that they contribute significantly to Mill's ideals. Indeed Mill recognised that, because of the low quality of the available personnel, significant public functions could not effectively be discharged at local level. Although there has been a marginal increase in local independence to spend small sums of money (Local Government Act 2000), local government is of little constitutional significance, being primarily a delivery mechanism for central policies. Local elections usually attract a very low turn out (about 25%) and the votes may reflect attitudes to central government rather than local issues.

## 4.6   The Channel Islands and the Isle of Man

The Channel Islands and the Isle of Man have special constitutional status, being neither part of the UK nor colonies or overseas territories. Their status derives from the royal prerogative, The Channel Islands are subject to the Crown as successor to the Duke of Normandy and have their own legislatures (the 'States'), their own courts, and are self-governing as to their internal affairs. Parliamentary supremacy was extended to the Channel Islands by a Prerogative Order in Council of 1806. However, there is a presumption of interpretation that an Act will not apply to the Channel Islands in the absence of express words or necessary implication. The common law does not apply and, subject to prerogative and statutory legislation, their law is local customary law. However, because the Channel Islands and the Isle of Man are directly subject to the Crown, the important protection provided by the judicial review powers of the High Court applies to both (see *Ex parte Brown* (1864); *Ex parte Anderson* (1861)).The Channel Islands are not members of the European Union but there are special treaty arrangements. Channel Island citizens are British citizens (British Nationality Act 1981 ss.1, 11, 50 (1)).

The position of the Isle of Man is broadly similar, although the Crown's rights seem to derive from an ancient agreement with Norway, confirmed by statute (Isle of Man Purchase Act 1765 (repealed)). Legislation made by its legislature, the Tynewald, must be assented to by the Queen in Council. (See generally *Royal Commission on the Constitution* 1973 Part XI and Minutes of Evidence VI, pp. 7, 13, 227–34; *X v UK* (1981), ECHR.)

## 4.7 British Overseas Territories

In the majority of former UK overseas territories all ties with UK law have been severed by Acts of Parliament (e.g. Canada Act 1982; Australia Act 1986). The UK retains a handful of dependent territories (formerly called colonies). The main dependent territories are Anguilla, Bermuda, British Virgin Islands, Cayman Islands, Falkland Islands, Gibraltar, Montserrat, the Pitcairn Islands, St Helena, the Turks and Caicos Islands. In principle, dependent territories are subject to the full force of parliamentary sovereignty and can be governed under the royal prerogative. However, certain rules determine the extent to which English law applies. If the colony was acquired by settlement, then the settlers carry the common law with them. If the colony is acquired by conquest or agreement (cession) so that it has its own population then, once a representative legislature has been established, English law does not apply unless the Crown reserves the right to legislate (*Campbell* v *Hall* (1774)). Moreover, under the Colonial Laws Validity Act 1865 all representative legislatures have full lawmaking power, including the power to alter their own constitution, powers and procedure subject to the UK Parliament (see *Liyanage* v *R* (1967)). However, there are no requirements as to the composition of the 'representatives' in question.

## 4.8 Note: The State and International Relations

It is often argued that the state is no longer appropriate as the basic constitutional unit. Pressures from within that favour devolution to areas of regional identity and pressures from outside, have in this view weakened the legitimacy of the state. It is also pointed out that we live in a 'global' economy supported by electronic communication and dominated by organisations that can operate in many countries to a large extent outside the control of their host countries. These developments can be rationalised by the assumption that states have passively 'consented' to them. However, they contain no democratic mechanisms. Indeed it has been suggested that democracy and the rule of law can flourish only at the margins within a society where there is a large measure of stability and consensus (see Harden, R., *Liberalism, Constitutionalism and Democracy*, Oxford, OUP, 1999). Moreover, globalisation is a one-way street which involves the 'developed' liberal world imposing its ideas on the allegedly undeveloped world but rarely, if ever, the other way round. National security also has a global dimension (see *Secretary of State* v *Rehman* (2002)).

Methods of imposing constitutional order on such an unruly world include asserting the rule of law by means of international legal codes enforced through international courts and through mechanisms for deliberative or participatory democracy by interest groups including voluntary bodies (Non Governmental Organisations or NGOs). However in order to be legally binding these mechanisms must be incorporated within the law of individual states. In the case of the UK, an international treaty cannot be enforced unless it is first enacted by Parliament (*The Parlement Belge* (1879). This leads to controversy concerning whether the resulting legislation should be interpreted literally according to domestic principles or in the light of more flexible international approaches (see *Brind* v *Secretary of State* (1991)). Furthermore, international principles are often couched in vague language so as to secure the acceptance of communities with different political and cultural perspectives. For example, the European Union Treaty has acknowledged the importance of the 'diversity' of the member states through the concept of 'subsidiarity' (Chapter 8). Under the Council of Europe, the European Court of Human Rights has developed the doctrine of 'margin of appreciation' to cater for different understandings of human rights in different states (Chapter 17).

## Summary

- ▶ The UK constitution has no unified concept of the state. This leads to a fragmented system of government but may protect individual freedom.

- ▶ Citizenship entitles a person to reside in the UK and has certain other miscellaneous consequences. There is no legal concept of the citizen corresponding to the republican notion of equal and responsible membership of the community.

- ▶ The UK constitution does not distribute power geographically as a method of limiting the power of the state or enhancing democracy. It favours a strong central authority. The UK is therefore not a federal state.

- ▶ Legislative and executive power has been devolved to elected bodies in Scotland and Northern Ireland but without significant tax raising powers. The UK Parliament has reserved the power to legislate in respect of many matters and has a general power to override the devolved assemblies. Their legislation is subordinate legislation, which is invalid if it exceeds the limits prescribed by the devolution statutes. In particular, unlike a UK statute, legislation violating the Human Rights Act 1998 is invalid.

- ▶ A more limited devolution applies to Wales. Executive and subordinate legislative power, delegated specifically by the UK Parliament, has been devolved to an elected Welsh Assembly. The Welsh language, sustainable development and equal opportunities are specifically protected.

- ▶ Elections to the devolved bodies are by proportional representation.

- ▶ The Scottish executive is structured according to the UK parliamentary system. However the balance of power is more in favour of the Parliament than is the case in the UK system. The Welsh system is structured more on

**Summary cont'd**

the model of local government. The Northern Ireland system is primarily concerned to achieve a balance between different political factions and is more restrictive than is the case with Scotland.

▶ The Privy Council is the final appeal court on 'devolution issues' including human rights cases although the UK government also has the power to intervene.

▶ There is no devolved government in England. Local government is subject to comprehensive central control. Regional Development Agencies have been created but these are appointed bodies charged only with particular economic goals and thus lacking essential attributes of democratic government. There is a proposal to introduce elected regional assembles with limited powers.

▶ There has been considerable discussion about the allegedly reduced importance of the state in constitutional law and politics. However, the state in as much as it reflects a genuine political and entity remains a key element in international affairs and is the form and context into which international rules are translated and applied.

# Exercises

**4.1** What are the advantages and disadvantages of the 'state' as a legal entity?

**4.2** Assess the importance of citizenship in the UK constitution. Do we have a liberal concept of citizenship? Does citizenship protect members of minorities?

**4.3** What is a federation? Outline the advantages and disadvantages of a federal structure.

**4.4** Compare the arguments for devolution within the UK with those in favour of a federal UK.

**4.5** What are the main differences between the devolved powers of Scotland, Wales and Northern Ireland and what are the reasons for those differences? Which region has the greatest degree of autonomy?

**4.6** Compare the balance of power between the legislature and the executive in Scotland with that in the UK government.

**4.7** What are the constitutional problems of devolution to the English regions?

# Further reading

Bogdanor, V. (1999) 'Devolution: decentralisation or disintegration?', *Political Quarterly,* **70**: 185.

Bogdanor, V. (ed) (2003) *The British Constitution in the Twentieth Century*, London, The British Academy, Chapter 15.

Bogdanor, V. (2004) 'Our New Constitution', *Law Quarterly Review,* **120**: 242.

Brazier, R. (1999) 'The Constitution of the United Kingdom', *Cambridge Law Journal,* **58**: 96.

Dyson, K. (1980) *The State Tradition in Western Europe*, Oxford, Martin Robertson, Chapters 1, 4.

Hadfield, B. (1999) 'The Nature of Devolution in Scotland and Northern Ireland: key issues of responsibility and control', *Edinburgh Law Review,* 3.

Hazell, R. (1999) 'Re-inventing the Constitution: can the state survive?', *Public Law* 84.

Hazell, R. (2001), 'The English Question: can Westminster be a proxy for an English Parliament?' *Public Law,* 268.

Himsworth, C. (1996) 'In a State no Longer: the End of Constitutionalism', *Public Law* 639.

Jowell, J. and Oliver, D. (2000) *The Changing Constitution*, 4th edn, Oxford, Oxford University Press, Chapter 5.

McAlester, D. (2001) 'Wales: Labour's devolution dilemma', *Parliamentary Affairs,* **54**: 156.

Merinos, P. (2001) 'Democracy, Governance and Governmentality: civic public space and constitutional renewal in Northern Ireland', *Oxford Journal of Legal Studies,* **21**: 287.

O'Neill, M. (2001) 'Judicial Politics and the Judicial Committee: the devolution jurisprudence of the Privy Council', *Modern Law Review,* **64**: 603.

O'Neill, M. (2004) *Devolution and British Politics,* Harlow, Pearson, Introduction, Chapters 6, 7, 9, 12, 13, 14, 15.

Rawlings, R. (1998) 'The New Model Wales', *Journal of Law and Society,* **25**: 461.

Rawlings, R. (2001) 'Taking Wales Seriously', in Campbell, Ewings and Tomkins (eds), *Sceptical Essays on Human Rights*, Oxford, Oxford University Press.

Walker, D. (2000) 'Beyond the Unitary Conception of the United Kingdom Constitution', *Public Law,* 384.

Walker, D. (2002) 'The Idea of Constitutional Pluralism', *Modern Law Review,* **65**: 317.

# Chapter 5

# The rule of law

Every law is contrary to liberty. (Jeremy Bentham)
The rule of Law, the enemy alike of dictatorship and anarchy, the friend by whose good offices authority and liberty can alone be reconciled.
(Lord Hailsham)

## Key words

▶ Government by law and government under law
▶ Law and freedom
▶ Law and discretion
▶ Law and reason
▶ Law and democracy
▶ Law and liberalism
▶ Law and equality
▶ The virtue of general rules
▶ Form and substance

## 5.1 Introduction: The Function of the Rule of Law

The rule of law, sometimes equated with the idea of 'constitutionalism', has been widely proclaimed as a pillar of constitutional thought. Its most basic meaning is that all power in a community should be subject to general rules: according to Aristotle, and many times repeated, 'a government of laws not men'. However, since laws are made by 'men' and can have any content it is difficult to understand what this means. By laws Aristotle was referring to the established customs and traditions of his city rather than the kinds of rules issued by modern governments. The rule of law is asserted for example in the Treaty on European Union and the Canadian *Charter of Rights and Freedoms*. It is much invoked by United Kingdom courts (below). Moreover, the concepts of the rule of law, individual freedom and democracy are often linked, for example in the European Convention on Human Rights (see *Klass* v *Federal Republic of Germany* (1979); *Young, James and Webster* v *UK* (1982)), and in the proposed European Union Constitution which extols 'democracy, equality, freedom and the rule of law'. The rule of law is not a 'law' in itself but is a moral and political aspiration that influences our attitude to the law. Thus it is not necessarily a contradiction to say that an Act of Parliament , although itself a law, might violate the rule of law.

There is widespread disagreement as to what the rule of law means and of its value. At one extreme it has been claimed that the rule of law is a good idea irrespective of the content of any particular law since it acts as a restraint on a despot and prevents officials from picking on individuals. At the other extreme the rule of law is often regarded as rhetoric merely signifying a law of which the speaker approves. In the middle, associated with liberalism (Chapter 1), are claims that the rule of law entails certain good things other than the bare principle that government should be subject to rules. As with other concepts which we meet in constitutional law, we must be careful to ensure that participants in the discussion are using the term rule of law in the same sense. Indeed there is no reason to take for granted that a user of words intends to give them a precise meaning.

The rule of law comes at a price. It has been associated with the notion of pedantic adherence to formalism, logic, linguistic niceties and tedious protracted courtroom procedures enriching lawyers at the expense of desirable social or economic outcomes, and overlooking qualities such as sympathy and mercy. On the other hand, a liberal, while recognising these defects, might regard them as a price worth paying for protection against arbitrary power. Hobbes (Chapter 1) would regard even bad laws as better than violence or endless argument, given that humans have been unable to invent a better solution.

Discussion of the rule of law has been dominated by two themes. Firstly there is the association, republican in origin, of law with 'reason' and 'equality'. Courts justify their decisions, and so the legitimacy of violence, by public reasoning, based upon logically and consistently applying rules derived from an authoritative source and,where these are uncertain, from values which are proclaimed as widely accepted in the community. For example, when Aristotle famously pronounced that that it is better for the law to rule than for any of the citizens to rule (*Politics* III.16, 1087a) he was probably referring to understandings about justice among an elite group of 'citizens' with common values and traditions designed to bring about their own collective good.

Secondly the 'enlightenment' or liberal version of the rule of law regards the notion as concerned with devices that control government in the interests of individual liberty. This version, originating with Locke and Montesquieu in the seventeenth century (Chapter 1), envisages government as concerned primarily with policing and employs the stereotype of aggressive officials who must be resisted. For example Montesquieu (1689–1755) famously asserted:

> Constant experience shows us that every man invested with power is apt to abuse it, and to carry his authority as far as it will go ... To prevent his abuse it is necessary from the very nature of things that power should be a check to power. A government may be so constituted, as no man shall be compelled to do things to which the law does not oblige him, nor forced to abstain from things which the law permits. (*The Spirit of the Laws*, 1761)

Neither theme sits easily with contemporary ideas about government. In particular they do not cater for the demands of a democracy that government should provide a wide range of public services which the law should facilitate as well as control. For example Bentham, the leading utilitarian (Chapter 1), was unhappy with what he called 'Judge and Co'. He thought that laws should be no more than guidelines, and in the end should give way to his master principle of the greatest happiness of the greatest number. He thought it particularly strange that courts should be bound by precedent since to him this merely reproduces errors. Nor does the 'reason' model easily cater for the diversity of ways of life, beliefs and values that is found in a modern community where people with many different ethnic, religious and social interests live together. In particular the liberal idea of the rule of law has been attacked from communitarian and democratic standpoints on the ground that, by focusing on individual rights, it sets up conflicts and discourages us from cooperating with each other.

Even within a liberal framework the rule of law contains contradictions. On the one hand it can be presented as a device to control power by making powerful bodies keep to rules. On the other hand it can reinforce existing power by requiring people to obey bad laws. Part of the rhetoric of the rule of law, derived from Hobbes (Chapter 1), insists that there is an obligation to obey even bad laws for the sake of public order. However, the rule of law is not necessarily an absolute and might give way to other more important values.

Attempts have been made to link the idea of the rule of law to democracy. For example it is claimed that by ensuring that officials keep within the powers given to them by the people, the rule of law is both the servant and policeman of democracy. However, although in European culture there is a historical connection between these groups of ideas, if anything the notion of the rule of law seems to be at odds with democracy in that it usually depends on decisions being made by an elite of unelected judges (see Chapter 17). Furthermore the production of laws does not require a democratic lawmaker. The law can be the policeman and servant of any regime. Certainly a democratically inclined law can protect values such as freedom of the press and fair voting rights without which democracy would be flawed. However the rule of law as such would be equally satisfied by a law which restricted these freedoms. We must therefore be careful to distinguish the rule of law as such from what we might consider to be 'good' law.

The three main versions of the rule of law in the context of the UK are as follows. They will be discussed in more detail later. A broad distinction can be made between the rule of law as government *by* law (versions 1 and 2), and the rule of law as government *under law* (version 3).

1. *The core rule of law* (often called the 'thin' rule of law): government by law in the form of general rules as opposed to the discretion of the ruler. This implies the idea of reason since reason is required to make and follow rules. It also implies 'equality' in the sense that everyone who falls within a given rule must be treated the same in accordance with it. For example Montesquieu favourably contrasted monarchy with despotism on the basis that although both are the rule of one person, monarchy is rule according to law, and therefore reason, whereas a despotism is rule according to the irrational whim of the ruler.
2. *The amplified rule of law* ('thick' rule of law). The core rule of law generates unease since even a vicious law such as one requiring the extermination of all members of an unpopular group seems to satisfy its requirements. It is therefore claimed that certain ideas relating to justice, such as independent courts, are inherent in the notion of law as guiding conduct and that these at least moderate bad laws. It is not claimed that these are absolute values which cannot be overridden by other factors; nor do they guarantee that any given law is a good law.
3. *The 'extended' rule of law.* This is the most ambitious version. It claims that law encapsulates the overarching values of the community – in our case assumed to be liberal values – in the care of impartial judges (see Allan, 2001). It claims also to link law with republican ideas of equal citizenship. In as much as this version of the rule of law relies upon vague and contestable concepts such as equality and freedom, it conflicts with the core rule of law (above).

## 5.2　Historical Background

The idea of the rule of law was asserted by Aristotle in the third century BC (above). In England the rule of law is claimed to go back to the Anglo-Saxon notion of a compact between ruler and ruled under which obedience to the King was conditional upon the King respecting customary law. The English version stresses government under law and also the common law as law made by independent courts. Magna Carta (1215) is said to have reinforced the principle that the state can act only through law. By endorsing Magna Carta, the King was forced to commit what were previously unwritten customs to formal writings. Although Magna Carta did not itself hold for long, its symbolic effect was immense:

> no freeman shall be taken or imprisoned or be disseissed of his freehold, or liberties or free customs or be outlawed or exiled or in any wise destroyed ... but by ... the law of the land. (See Thompson, *Magna Carta: Its role in the Making of the English Constitution*, 1972).

The rule of law was famously invoked by the thirteenth-century jurist Bracton as 'a bridle on power':

the King should be under no man but under God and the Law because the Law makes him King.

This was a conscious break from the Roman law tradition which regarded law as the will of the ruler. Although Bracton accepted that in the sphere of government the King had some autocratic powers (the royal prerogative), he regarded the King as confined by law in respect of decisions concerning the rights of subjects.

The rule of law was asserted against the King in the seventeenth century. This time emphasis was placed on the connection between the courts and reason. According to Coke CJ the rule of law protected both ruler and subject, the ruler against criticism, the subject against tyranny: 'The golden and straight metwand of the law and not the uncertain and eroded cord of discretion.' (*Institutes* Part 4, 37,41 (c.1669), see also *Prohibitions del Roy* (1607) 12 Co. Rep. 63). Later in the seventeenth century, John Locke (Chapter 1), an ally of Parliament against the King, equated law, reason and freedom which, as we saw in Chapter 1, has its dangers.

> Law in its true notion is not so much the limitation as the direction of a free and intelligent agent to his proper interest and prescribes no further than is for the general good of those under that law ... for all the power the Government hath being only for the good of the Society, as it ought not to be Arbitrary and at Pleasure, so it ought to be exercised by established and promulgated Laws: that both the People may know their duty, and be safe and secure within the limits of the law, and the Rulers too kept within their due bounds not to be tempted by the Power they have in their hands, to imploy it to such purposes, and by such measures, as they would not have known and own not willingly. (*Second Treatise on Government*, (1690), VI: 57, IX, 137)

During the eighteenth and early nineteenth centuries the constitution was particularly influenced by the rhetoric of the rule of law. The constitution was regarded as a delicately balanced machine held in place by law; as George III put it, 'the most beautiful balance ever framed' (Briggs, *The Age of Improvement*, 1959, p. 88). The rule of law protected individual rights imagined as being grounded in ancient common law tradition.

> The poorest man may in his cottage bid defiance to all the forces of the Crown. It may be frail, its roof may shake, the wind may blow through it, the storm may enter, the rain may enter, but the king of England cannot enter. (Lord Brougham, *Historical Sketches of Statesmen in the Time of George III*, 1845)

It was widely asserted that the relative stability and economic prosperity enjoyed by Britain during that period was connected with a commitment to the rule of law. By contrast France with its

> demagoguary, revolt, beheadings and ... unruly mobs stood in English 'common sense' as a dreadful warning of all that can go wrong, a sort of conceptual opposite to England's altogether more sensible ways. (Pugh, in Halliday and Karpick

(eds), *Lawyers and the Rise of Western Political Liberalism: from the Eighteenth to the Twentieth Centuries*, 1997, p. 168)

However, the eulogies of the rule of law were consistent with harsh and repressive Acts of Parliament such as the suspension of Habeas Corpus in 1794 and 1798, the notorious anti-poaching 'Black Acts' (see Thompson, *Whigs and Hunters*, 1975), and the Corresponding Societies Act 1799 which outlawed radical political and cultural organisations.

With the expansion of democracy that took place from the mid-nineteenth century, influential lawyers such as Dicey (below) attempted to reformulate and defend the traditional idea of the rule of law against what they perceived as threats from both democratic ideas and the authoritarian influences of continental Europe (Chapter 4). In 1928 the Lord Chief Justice Lord Hewart published *The New Despotism* in which he asserted that the rule of law was under threat from the executive. This led to the establishment of the *Committee on Ministers Powers* (the Donoughmore Committee) whose terms of reference were 'to report what safeguards were desirable or necessary to secure the constitutional principles of the sovereignty of Parliament and the supremacy of the law'. Described as having 'the dead hand of Dicey lying frozen on its neck', the Committee's report (1932, Cmnd 4060) gave the constitution a clean bill of health albeit with a powerful dissent from Laski. The Committee recommended some strengthening of the powers of Parliament in relation to delegated legislation and asserted the importance of control by the courts over the executive.

Subsequently the rule of law became associated with a belief that conservative and liberal-minded judges were determined to frustrate the more collectivist polices of left-wing governments (see Griffith, *The Politics of the Judiciary*, 4th edn, 1991). More recently with the introduction of the Human Rights Act 1998 there has been a revival of interest in the rule of law as a means of bringing together the ideas of law, liberalism and democracy (see Poole, 2003).

## 5.3  The Core Rule of Law: Government by Law

The basic or core meaning of the rule of law is government *by* law in the sense that government operates through definite general rules announced in advance and made by a recognised lawmaker. In particular the government should itself be bound by the laws that it makes until it changes them in the authorised way. This associates law with the goods of freedom and equality (Chapter 1). As Hayek asserted:

> stripped of all technicalities this means that government in all its actions is bound by rules fixed and announced beforehand – rules which make it possible to foresee with fair certainty how the authority will use its coercive powers in given circumstances, and to plan one's life accordingly.

There is an obvious flaw with this version of the rule of law in that discretion cannot be eliminated. Firstly, the lawmaker has discretion as to what laws to make. Even if there are constitutional rules limiting the lawmaker's discretion, whoever has the power to change the constitution has a complete discretion as to its content. Secondly, many laws are to a greater or lesser extent vague in meaning. A judge therefore has a discretion when applying them which, as Pope immortalised, can be used to suit the interests of those in power (*Horace Imitated: Satire I of Book II*):

> Envy must own, I live among the great,
> No pimp of pleasure, and no spy of state.
> With eyes that pry not, tongue that ne'er repeats,
> Fond to spread friendships, but to cover heats;
> To help who want, to forward who excel;
> This, all who know me, know; who love me, tell;
> And who unknown defame me, let them be
> Scribblers or peers, alike are *mob* to me.
> This is my plea, on this I rest my cause –
> What saith my counsel, learned in the laws?
> F. Your plea is good; but still I say beware!
> Laws are explained by men – so have a care.
> It stands on record, that in Richard's times
> A man was hanged for very honest rhymes.
> Consult the statute: *quart.* I think it is,
> *Edwardi sext. or prim. et quint. Eliz.*
> See *libels, satires* – here you have it – read.
> P. *Libels and satires!* Lawless things indeed!
> But grave *Epistles* bringing vice to light,
> Such as a king might read, a bishop write;
> Such as *Sir Robert* would approve? – F. Indeed?
> The case is altered – you may then proceed;
> In such a cause the plaintiff would be hissed;
> My lords the judges laugh, and you're dismissed.

To self-styled 'critical' legal scholars the vagueness of law is a fundamental objection to the idea of the rule of law which they regard as a mask for naked power. The standard liberal reply is that vagueness is a matter of degree and in some circumstances is to be welcomed (see Kutz,'Just Disagreement: Indeterminacy and Rationality in the Rule of Law', 1994, **103** *Yale Law Journal* 997). Most laws in practice have a widely accepted meaning. And even where laws are vague, there are widely accepted standards of 'practical reasoning': consequences, moral values, analogy with precedents, appeals to widely shared feelings etc. Even though many values may be ultimately incommensurable (Chapter 1) so that there is no objective 'right' answer, it is at least possible to justify a particular solution which would be widely accepted. Moreover a liberal is suspicious of too much certainty as dangerously repressive. Disagreement is to be welcomed as protecting freedom provided that there is a means of peacefully settling disputes in a particular case. The liberal perspective on the rule of law therefore concentrates on fair procedures rather than outcomes.

Thirdly, discretion may be desirable in many contexts particularly that of welfare liberalism (Chapter 1). It is widely recognised that the provision of public services must involve the exercise of discretion in individual cases where the circumstances are too various, unpredictable or complex to be encapsulated in rules. For example, it would be difficult to lay down detailed rules in advance governing access to public services such as health or education. Resources are limited and hard choices have to be made between competing goals. The courts take the view that such choices are for the political rather than the legal process (Chapter 15, see e.g. *R v Cambridge Health Authority ex parte B* (1995): experimental medical treatment).

Discretion is also desirable to lighten the burden of the strict law. The rule of law may therefore conflict with other valuable impulses such as sympathy and compassion. The police do not have to prosecute everyone. The Revenue may release a taxpayer from a tax burden. There must also be wide emergency powers to some extent outside both law and democracy to deal with unforeseen and exceptional threats. Hobbes regarded security as the highest duty of the state and even the European Convention on Human Rights can be derogated from to meet an emergency (Human Rights Act 1998 s.14).

None of this excludes the rule of law altogether. The law can prescribe broad guidelines within which decisions must be made and, in particular, lay down procedures policed by the courts which must be followed to ensure that government keeps within the rules it makes (Chapter 14). Emergency powers can be hedged with legal safeguards, for example a requirement that they lapse after a set period and are supervised by the courts (even if we do not resort to the device of the Roman republic that declared officials to be outlaws who could be killed on sight if they attempted to use emergency powers beyond the needs of the emergency).

A fundamental criticism of the core rule of law relates to the formalistic attitude of mind that it promotes, namely the assumption that moral and political values can be reduced to definite rules which are given the appearance of objectivity. Utilitarians such as Bentham regard the rule of law as getting in the way of achieving good public purposes, pointing to what they regard as lawyers' delays and formalism which puts processes over outcomes and favours the wealthy and articulate who can most easily gain the ear of the courts. Bentham thought that the rule of law encourages the rich and powerful to harass people who cannot fight back. If the core rule of law were comprehensively applied then not only would lawyers, a specialised and unelected elite, be in a position to impose their own preferences upon the rest of us but the values of society would be frozen.

To its supporters, the formalism of the rule of law is a valuable achievement of the human mind as an upholder of equality and dignity: a defence not only against tyrants but also against well-meaning busybodies. Formalism also ensures that courts and public officials have to justify their decisions. For example, in *Taylor v Thames Valley Chief Constable* (2004) the Court of Appeal stressed the fundamental principle that a policeman must give clear reasons for arresting someone; Sedley LJ [58] basing this on the value of human dignity (see also *Christie v Leachinsky* (1947).

### 5.3.1     The Rule of Law and Freedom

It is sometimes asserted, notably by Hayek (below) that the core rule of law is inherently supportive of freedom. Montesquieu and Locke thought that freedom means doing what the law allows. Since laws can have any content and are enforced by violence, this seems paradoxical. As Hobbes put it, 'freedom lies in the silence of the laws' and in *The Pilgrim's Progress* Bunyan asks:

> (h)e to whom thou was sent for ease, being by name legality, is the son of the Bondwoman … how canst thou expect by them to be made free?

However, if there is a rule there must be a zone of freedom, even if a small one, outside its limits. This is why E.P. Thompson (*Whigs and Hunters*, 1975) claims that the rule of law is an 'unqualified human good'. A wholly evil regime would have no reason to stick to rules. In this sense the core rule of law links with the republican notion that freedom means that others have no power to control me. For example, a slave whose master in fact allows him to do as he likes, without being required by law to do so, is nevertheless not free since the master retains the power of control. Thus the reliance of the UK constitution on conventions and other voluntary mechanisms supported only by the goodwill of persons in power (Chapter 2) belongs to the world of the kind slavemaster rather than the rule of law.

A more substantial link between the rule of law and freedom relies on 'positive freedom', meaning self-mastery and the opportunity, using reason, to exploit the good things in life available to us (Chapter 1). As Hobbes recognised, without law this would be impossible since there would be no security or stability to enable us to plan our lives. We would not therefore be able to exercise our natural freedom. This is also what Montesquieu had in mind (above). However, as Berlin points out (Chapter 1), the danger of positive freedom is that a tyrant or zealot might attempt to impose its own view of the good life upon us claiming that it is doing only what we would rationally desire and therefore that it is enabling us to exercise 'time' freedom.

Hayek however claims that *in itself* the rule of law guarantees freedom. He claims that a government which accepts the rule of law would not enact repressive laws since these would harm its own supporters and also that we are free to plan our lives around laws and so avoid them. However, short of freedom to commit suicide, this does not seem to work, for example, in the case of a law that imposes military conscription for all adults. The explanation seems to be that Hayek takes the notion of *generality* very seriously. Firstly, he claims that the general rules must be logically consistent with each other. However, this would surely mean that the law would protect only those freedoms approved of by the lawmaker. For example, I cannot exercise my freedom to go about my business in a public place if your freedom to hold a public procession obstructs my way (Chapter 18). A general law might equally well authorise anyone who holds a procession to be jailed or might remove objectors to the procession off the streets.

Secondly the laws must apply equally to all and not favour any particular social and economic objective. In Hayek's world the law could not for example allocate welfare benefits or support to industry unless everyone got the same. These requirements rule out large areas of state activity involving discretionary powers. Hayek recognised that his proposals are likely to lead to economic inequality and perhaps hardship but assumes that these are outweighed by the advantages of individual freedom. In common with many economic liberals, Hayek also believed that the certainty created by the rule of law would encourage wealth creation and that the poor would be better off than under alternative regimes. There is no historical evidence either way in relation to these matters (see Gray, *Hayek on Liberty*, 2nd edn, 1986; Gray, *Liberalisms*, 1988).

Objectors to the core rule of law regard it as favouring an impoverished idea of freedom. They claim that freedom is of little value unless people have the resources to fulfil themselves by exercising choices. They further claim that the core rule of law obstructs this in that it favours the status quo, formal but not substantive equality and the interests of the wealthy (see e.g. Horowitz, 'The Rule of Law: an Unqualified Human Good? '(1977) 86 *Yale Law Review*, 561). This view seems to rest on trusting the motives and ability of officials to deliver good things without the inconvenient restraints of the law.

## 5.4 The 'Amplified' Rule of Law: Law as Guiding Conduct

Some writers argue that, if it is to fulfill its function of guiding conduct, the notion of law as rules necessarily implies certain moral principles which are inherent in the idea of government by rules. The American legal theorist Fuller, (*The Morality of Law*, 1969) provides the most well-known Fuller's list of principles includes the following:

▶ generality
▶ promulgation so that laws can be known in advance (e.g. *R (Anufrijeva)* v *Secretary of State* (2003): decision to refuse asylum seeker status took effect from the date when the claimant was informed of it)
▶ non-retroactivity (e.g. *R* v *Secretary of State for the Home Department ex parte Pierson* (1998): retrospective alteration of prison sentence)
▶ clarity (e.g. *Merkur Island Shipping Corp.* v *Laughton* (1983): excessively complex legislative drafting)
▶ consistent application (e.g. *R* v *Horseferry Rd Magistrates Court ex parte Bennett* (1994): fair trial not given to person brought before the court by kidnapping even if court process itself is fair)
▶ the practical possibility of compliance (e.g. *R* v *Secretary of State for Social Services ex parte Joint Council for the Welfare of Immigrants* (1996): regulations which deprived asylum seekers of welfare benefits unless they claimed asylum status at the port of entry would frustrate their right of appeal. However, Parliament subsequently validated the regulations (Asylum and Immigration Act 1996 s.11)
▶ constancy through time (frequent changes in the law might offend this)
▶ officials must comply with the rules (*M* v *Home Office* (1993)
▶ Raz (1977) includes open access to independent courts and a right to legal advice (e.g. *R* v *Lord Chancellor ex parte Witham* (1997): increases in legal fees denied access to courts for low-income people; see also Lord Millett in *Cullen* v *Chief Constable RUC* [2004] 2 All ER 237 253; Lord Woolf in *M.* v *Secretary of State* [2004] 2 All ER 863, 873).

This gives protection to the individual – by interpreting legal rules in the light of these principles but without evaluating whether the *content* of a particular law is good or bad. Indeed it is consistent with hideously repressive regimes although Thompson (above) argues that fidelity to the rule of law at least makes such regimes better than they otherwise would be. Nor does the rule of law claim that its requirements are absolute. A retrospective law might for example occasionally be desirable to deal with a particularly serious social problem, and the normal requirements of the rule of law may be compromised if security is at stake, provided that the protection is overridden as little as possible and safeguards are in place. For example in *Brown* v *Stott* [2001] 2 All ER 97, 128 Lord Hope said:

> The rule of law requires that every person be protected from invasion by the authorities of his rights and liberties. But the preservation of law and order on which the rule of law also depends, requires that those protections should not be framed in such a way as to make it impracticable to bring those who are accused of crime to justice. The benefits of the rule of law must be extended to the public at large and to the victims of crime also.

The case concerned the right to a fair trial under Article 6 of the European Convention on Human Rights, the House of Lords holding that the normal right to remain silent was overridden by a requirement to disclose the name of the driver of a car in connection with a drunk driving charge. This was because of the social importance of road safety coupled with the fact that other safeguards ensured a fair trial.

## 5.5   The Extended (Liberal) Rule of Law: Government Under Law

This version of the rule of law overlaps with but goes beyond the amplified rule of law (above). It claims somewhat extravagantly that law provides the overarching values of the community against which acts of government must be quantified. In the case of the UK this is said to mean liberal democracy (see e.g. Allan, 2001). The ordinary meaning of democracy as government with the consent of the people (Chapter 1) has no special connection with liberalism. However, it is argued that democracy is supported by liberal values such as freedom of expression and association which must be secured by law lest the majority, driven for example by a charismatic leader or by panic reaction to an emergency, hands over its power to a dictator, as happened in Germany in 1933.

A further dimension is to link the rule of law in the sense outlined above with the common law. Badged as 'the principle of legality' this claims to restrain 'bad laws' by interpreting legislation and evaluating executive action in the light of common law values, assumed to be liberal, so as to require Parliament to use very clear language if it wishes to override them and so be accountable. In *R* v *Secretary of State for the Home Department ex parte Simms* (1999), the House of Lords prevented the government from restricting a prisoner's access to a journalist through whom he intended to publicise his claim that he was wrongfully convicted. Lord Steyn remarked that:

> in these circumstances even in the absence of ambiguity there comes into play a presumption of general application operating as a constitutional principle ... This is called the 'principle of legality'. (See also Lord Hoffmann's speech, *R (Anufrijeva)* v *Secretary of State* (2003); Lord Steyn, *R* v *Secretary of State for the Home Department ex parte Pierson* [1998] AC 539, 575.)

The values concerned would include, for example, freedom of expression, property rights, non-discrimination, open government and fair democratic processes as well as the rights included in the 'amplified' rule of law (above). In *R (Middleton)* v *West Somerset Coroner* (2004) the victims of a misuse of state power in relation to the treatment of prisoners were held to be entitled to an effective public inquiry to apportion blame (see Lord Bingham [5]).

The suggested link between liberal values, the rule of law and the common law seems to be twofold. Firstly the common law is not merely imposed from the top by a lawmaker but is generated by disputes freely brought before the courts by individuals and requires the exercise of power to be rationally justified. Secondly there is the idea that the law must be applied according to the understanding of those subject to it as equal citizens. In this respect the common law's independence from government means that it can plausibly claim to represent the values of the community. For example, according to Allan (2001, p. 62):

> (t)he principle that laws will be faithfully applied, according to the tenor in which they would reasonably be understood by those affected, is the most basic tenet of the rule of law: it constitutes that minimal sense of reciprocity between citizen and state that inheres in any form of decent government, where law is a genuine barrier to arbitrary power.

This brings in a republican dimension but, as we saw in Chapter 1, republican and liberal perspectives may conflict – republicanism having an authoritarian slant. Sir John Laws, a leading contemporary judge, has linked the common law specifically to liberal claims by drawing on philosophical principles which appear to combine liberal and republican perspectives. ('The Constitution: Morals and Rights', 1996, *Public Law* 622, 623; c.f. Irvine, 1996, *Public Law* 636). He asserted that, because the courts derive their powers from the common law and have no electoral mandate to pursue any particular policy, they must fall back on what he considered to be the only possible moral position, namely individual freedom.

> (The) true starting point in the quest for the good constitution consists in ... the autonomy of every person in his sovereignty.

Thus he argued in favour of independent judges as the guardians of values such as freedom, equality, certainty and fairness against elected governments (see also Laws, 'Law and Democracy', 1995, *Public Law* 72; Laws in Forsythe (ed.) *Judicial Review and the Constitution*, 2000).

However, such philosophical assumptions are controversial and concepts such as freedom and equality are inherently vague. As we saw in Chapter 1 liberalism comes in several competing forms so that attempts to impose a liberal orthodoxy seem dogmatic. Moreover, the common law derives its legitimacy not from abstract philosophy but from community values, whatever they happen to be. It is therefore not necessarily liberal. Although confined by the accumulation of precedent, the common law arguably tracks the opinions of the dominant group in the legal community at any given time (in particular the judges). While legal education and tradition secure a certain conformity there is no reason to assume that the precedents are sufficiently clear or the values of the community sufficiently uniform and stable to form a credible basis for coherent liberal principles. The extended rule of law may therefore be no more than the temporary preferences of a fashionable group of lawyers. Indeed liberal values are not peculiar to courts but pervade all political debate. Other bodies may have political aims but must still balance these against notions of justice to the individual. There seems to be no reason to assume that the courts are any better able to do this than an elected assembly since the primary job of the courts is to apply rules not to decide what the rules should be.

## 5.6 Dicey's Version of the Rule of Law

There is a particular English version of the rule of law famously promoted by A.V. Dicey (1915) which still influences the way lawyers conceive the constitution. Dicey's version of the rule of law favours the rights of the individual against government aggression, which he claims are embedded in the common law. Dicey formulated a threefold version of the rule of law as follows:

1. *The absolute supremacy or predominance of 'regular' law as opposed to arbitrary power and the absence of discretionary authority on the part of government.*

   No man is punishable or can be lawfully made to suffer in body or goods except for a distinct breach of law established in the ordinary legal manner before the ordinary courts.

This means firstly that no official can interfere with individual rights without the backing of a specific law. For example in *R* v *Somerset CC ex parte Fewings* [1995] 1 All ER 513, Laws J said (at 524) that the principles that govern the application of the rule of law to public bodies and private persons are 'wholly different' in the sense that:

   the freedoms of the private citizen are not conditional upon some distinct and affirmative justification for which he must burrow in the law books ... But for public bodies the rule is opposite and so of another character altogether. It is that any action to be taken must be justified by positive law.

Laws J described this as one of the 'sinews' of the rule of law. However, it only applies to acts that interfere with traditional legal rights such as private property. It is therefore ill equipped to deal with the many ways in which modern governments operate. For example in *R* v *Secretary of State for Health ex parte C* (2000), it was held that a government department was entitled to place a man's name on a child-abuse blacklist without giving him a prior right to be heard. Although entry on the register harmed the individual by destroying his job prospects, his legal rights were not infringed since in English law there is no right of privacy as such.

Dicey believed that officials should not have wide discretionary powers. For example, in *Rantzen* v *Mirror Group Newspapers* (1994) the Court of Appeal condemned the wide discretion given to juries to fix the amount of damages in libel cases as violating the rule of law. We have already suggested that it is impossible and undesirable to avoid discretion. Indeed, Dicey did not rule out all discretionary power but only 'wide arbitrary or discretionary power of constraint'. He insisted on limits to and controls over the exercise of discretion. These include guidelines based on the purposes for which the power is given and standards of reasonableness and fairness. In other words, the rule of law is a broad guide to the values which should underpin the law.

2. *Equality before the law*
Equality has several different meanings. Dicey was not concerned with most of them. Indeed as an opponent of votes for women, he was concerned to preserve some forms of inequality. Dicey's version of equality before the law was concerned with limiting the power of officials in favour of individual legal rights. According to Dicey, everyone whether high official or ordinary citizen is subject to the same law administered by ordinary courts.

He did not mean that no official has special powers. This would have been obviously untrue. Dicey had two specific ideas in mind. Firstly, he meant only that officials as such enjoy no special protection, so that if an official abuses his power, he is personally liable to anyone whose property rights or personal freedom he violates just as if he were a private citizen. For example, in *M v Home Office* (1993) it was held that a minister cannot refuse to comply with a court order on the basis that he is a servant of the Crown. However, there are exceptions. In particular, judges are immune from personal liability in respect of their actions in court (Chapter 6), the Crown has immunities based on the doctrine of 'Act of State' (Chapter 12) and the Queen is completely immune from legal liability. Thus Dicey's principle is merely a presumption which can be overcome by showing some justification for an inequality.

Secondly, Dicey meant that disputes between government and citizen are settled in the ordinary courts according to the ordinary law rather than in a special governmental court applying special rules. In this respect Dicey compared English law favourably with French Law where there is a special system of law and courts dealing with the powers of government (*droit administratif* enforced by the *Conseil D'Etat*). Dicey thought that special administrative courts would give the government special privileges and shield the individual wrongdoer behind the cloak of the state. However, Dicey later came to believe that, in view of the increasing power of the executive, he may have been too optimistic about the ordinary courts' ability to protect the individual and began to cast around for other solutions (see (1915) *Law Quarterly Review*, **31**).

Nevertheless this aspect of Dicey's teaching has had great influence upon the UK constitution. Until as recently as the 1970s there was resistance to the idea of special courts and judges to deal with disputes involving governmental powers. Since 1977 however, there has been a special procedure for challenging government decisions albeit within the ordinary court system (Chapter 16). However, in partial vindication of Dicey, attempts to distinguish between public law and private law have floundered (ibid.). There are also numerous 'special' systems of law, such as social security law and immigration law, which deal with disputes between the individual and the state. These are administered by specialist tribunals outside the ordinary courts which often include lay people. Such tribunals are speedier, cheaper, more informal, and even sometimes more expert than the 'regular courts'. However, they are usually subject to the supervision of the ordinary courts and the rule of law requires that attempts to exclude the ordinary courts be strongly resisted (e.g. *Anisminic* v *Foreign Compensation Commission* (1967); Chapter 7).

Sometimes the principle of equality backfires. For example in *Malone* v *Metropolitan Police Commissioner* (1979) it was held that, at common law, the police are free to tap telephones since there was no legal prohibition against a private person doing so (a gap in the law that was subsequently closed by statute, Chapter 19). More recently it was held in *Harrow LBC* v *Qazi* (2003) that a local authority can rely on its property rights as a landlord in order to evict a tenant. It is arguable that a principle of equality is not adequate to remedy abuses of the wide-ranging powers of modern government, for example the refusal of a welfare payment or of a council home, which have no parallel in the world of private citizens.

3. *The constitution is the 'result' of the ordinary law*
Dicey's third meaning of the rule of law derives from the common law tradition. He believed that the UK constitution, not being imposed from above in the form of a written constitution, was the result of decisions by the courts in particular cases, and was therefore embedded in the very fabric of the law and backed by practical remedies. According to Dicey this strengthens the constitution. Moreover, because the common law developed primarily through the medium of private disputes, it also biases the constitution against governmental interests by treating private law, with its concentration on individual rights, as the basic perspective. Perhaps Dicey's version of the rule of law shows only that he trusted judges as a hedge against the popular democracy which he feared.

The seminal case of *Entick* v *Carrington* (1765) illustrates the three aspects of Dicey's rule of law. The Secretary of State ordered two King's Messengers to search for Entick, accused of sedition, and to bring him with his books and papers before the Secretary of State. Entick sued the Messengers. The court held that the plea of 'state necessity' was unknown to the common law because there was no statute or common law precedent from which it could be derived, that the practice of issuing general warrants giving officials wide discretion was unlawful and that the Messengers had no specific statutory authority regarding the particular papers that they seized.

On the other hand, in *R v IRC ex parte Rossminister Ltd* (1980) Parliament gave a general power to tax officials to enter and search private premises which the courts upheld, rejecting *Entick v Carrington* as irrelevant antiquarianism. This illustrates the tension between the common law and parliamentary supremacy (Chapter 7). The matter depends essentially on how far the judges are willing to interpret statutes as being subject to common law principles. As we have seen however, since *Rossminster* the common law has been more strongly applied (above).

## 5.7 The International Rule of Law

Since the Second World War there have been several attempts to draw up internationally binding codes of basic human rights and to promote liberal values under the banner of the rule of law. These have turned the rule of law into a virtually meaningless umbrella for whatever goods the parties to the conventions wish to support. For example the *Declaration of Delhi* (1959), an unofficial pronouncement of the International Commission of Jurists, proclaimed that the rule of law is intended to establish 'social, economic, educational and cultural conditions under which [individuals' ] legitimate aspirations and dignity may be realised'.

Other international instruments include the United Nations *Universal Declaration of Human Rights* (1948) and various regional charters. There is an International Criminal Court to deal with war crimes, crimes against humanity and genocide but the USA has not accepted its jurisdiction. Of most direct concern to UK law is the European Convention on Human Rights (ECHR) which drew heavily on the UN declaration (above). The ECHR came into effect in 1952 under the auspices of the Council of Europe as a response to the fascist and communist atrocities that had disfigured much of the twentieth century. Individuals have a right to petition the European Court of Human Rights in respect of violations by states. Under the Human Rights Act 1998, most provisions of the Convention have belatedly been made binding in UK law although they do not override Acts of Parliament (Chapter 17). The rule of law is central to the workings of the ECHR. For example, exceptions to the rights protected by the convention must be 'prescribed by law'. In this context 'a norm' cannot be regarded as a law unless it is formulated with sufficient precision to enable a citizen to regulate his conduct.

The idea of the rule of law comes under particular stress when there is a clash between different legal regimes, in particular between international and domestic law. International law as such is not automatically part of UK law, which has adopted a 'dualist' approach. This means that an international treaty, if it is to alter domestic law, must first be incorporated by statute into UK law. However, customary international law is recognised by the common law but can be excluded by statute (*Chung Chi Cheung* v *R* [1939] AC 160 at 168; at 177). Thus a treaty which embodies customary law may be part of UK law whether or not it is enacted.

*R* v *Bow Street Magistrate ex parte Pinochet Ugarte (No. 3)* (1999) shows the difficulties of applying international values in the context of the domestic rule of law. Pinochet was the former head of state of Chile making a private visit to the UK. The Spanish government requested that he be extradited to Spain to stand trial in respect of murders and torture which he was alleged to have organised in Chile during his term of office. The Torture Convention 1984, as translated into English law by the Criminal Justice Act 1988, requires a state to either prosecute or extradite an alleged offender. Pinochet relied on the international doctrine of state immunity, according to which a head of state cannot be tried in a domestic court. Complete immunity applies to serving heads of state. Immunity also applies to former heads of state but only in relation to official acts committed while they were in office.

The House of Lords, unusually comprising seven judges, eventually held that Pinochet was not entitled to immunity. However, their Lordships took different routes to their conclusions. Lords Browne-Wilkinson, Hutton, Saville and Phillips held that the matter depended on the 1988 Act but, because it was intended to implement a treaty, the Act must be construed in the light of that treaty. They held that state-sponsored torture violated fundamental principles of international law which Chile had accepted by signing the convention. Torture was therefore not to be regarded as part of the official functions of a head of state which the immunity protected. They held, however, that Pinochet could only be extradited for offences which were alleged to have taken place after 29 September 1988 which was the date on which the Criminal Justice Act 1988 came into force. This was therefore a bland compromise between international and domestic principles perhaps reflecting the 'amplified' rule of law (above)

Lord Millett, supported partly by Lord Hope and Lord Hutton, took a more radical approach, perhaps reflecting the 'extended' rule of law (above). He argued that, irrespective of the Act, torture was an international offence under a developing customary international law and was therefore unlawful at common law. For him there was no immunity even in respect of crimes committed before the 1988 Act. Similarly Lord Hutton said that 'certain crimes are so grave and so inhuman that the international community is under a duty to bring to justice a person who commits such crimes' (at 163).

Lord Goff, dissenting, took the 'core' rule of law perspective grounded in the traditions of English law. He read the texts more strictly than the others, holding that the State Immunity Act 1978 s.20 gives immunity to a former head of state in respect of official acts wherever committed. He was not prepared to rule out torture as an official act. In this connection he emphasised legal certainty, pointing out the difficulty of drawing lines between different kinds of wrongdoing and the problems that might be faced by former heads of government who ventured into countries the interests of which they had damaged while in office.

## Summary

▶ Constitutionalism means limited government and includes the ideas of the rule of law and the separation of powers as means of restricting and controlling government. The rule of law is an umbrella for assorted ideas about the virtues of law mainly from a liberal perspective. They centre upon law as reason and law as a means of controlling aggressive government. They do not fit easily with ideas of democracy, nor with government as a provider of welfare services nor with communitarian ideas.

▶ The rule of law in its core sense emphasises the importance of general rules as binding on government and citizen alike. The core sense of the rule of law is morally ambivalent since it can also be regarded as an efficient tool of tyranny.

▶ In an amplified sense, the rule of law requires the law to reflect certain basic values derived from the nature of rules as guides to conduct. However, these are also consistent with repressive laws.

▶ In an extended sense, the rule of law is claimed to be the guardian of the basic liberal values of the community entrusted to the courts because of their role as guardians of impartial reason. It is claimed to be translated into rights such as non-discrimination, freedom of expression, and access to government information. However there is no reason to believe that these values or reason itself are the prerogative of courts and they have to be accommodated against social goals of elected governments. Why courts should do this is a theme to be pursued in later chapters.

▶ The rule of law as expounded by Dicey has significantly influenced the UK constitution. Dicey advocated that government discretion should be limited by definite rules of law, that the same law could in general apply to government and citizen alike, and that Britain does not need a written constitution because, in his view, the common law made by independent courts with

## Summary cont'd

practical remedies provides a firmer foundation for individual rights. This has greatly influenced the thinking of the legal profession, but may be unsuited to the control of modern government. It is also difficult to reconcile the rule of law in this sense with the principle that Parliament has unlimited power which can be harnessed by a strong executive.

▶ Other modern ideas of the rule of law include the increasing importance of international treaties which attempt to establish codes of fundamental rights and freedoms that governments should respect.

# Exercises

**5.1** Do you agree with Thompson that the rule of law is an 'unqualified human good'?

**5.2** To what extent is Dicey's version of the rule of law of value today?

**5.3** 'The Rule of Law functions as a clear check on the flourishing of a rigorous democracy. Attempts to characterise the rule of law as the butler of democracy are false and misleading' (Hutchinson and Monahan). Critically discuss.

**5.4** To what extent, if at all, is the rule of law conducive to freedom?

**5.5** Does the rule of law have a substantive content in terms of individual rights?

**5.6** 'The principle that laws will be faithfully applied, according to the tenor in which they would reasonably be understood by those affected is the most basic tenet of the rule of law'(Allan). Discuss critically.

**5.7** Do the following violate the rule of law?

(i) The Queen being exempt from legal liability.
(ii) A statute banning press criticism of the Prime Minister.
(iii) A statute which states that an allegation relating to the conduct of the security services cannot be made in the ordinary courts.
(iv) A statute which gives a discretion to the Education Secretary to decide what courses shall be taught in universities.

**5.8** 'The rule of law clearly forms an essential element of liberal democracy and plays its part in providing a theoretical basis for an independent judiciary but it forms only one side of a balanced constitution' (Carol Harlow). Explain and critically discuss.

# Further reading

Allan, T. (1999) 'The rule of law as the rule of reason: consent and constitutionalism', *Law Quarterly Review*, **115**: 221.

Allan, T. (2001) *Constitutional Justice: a Liberal Theory of the Rule of Law*, Oxford, Oxford University Press, Chapters 1, 2, 3, 4.

Barber, N. (2001) 'The academic mythologies', *Oxford Journal of Legal Studies*, **22**: 369.

Craig, P. (1997) 'Formal and substantive concepts of the rule of law: an analytical framework', *Public Law*, 467.

Endicott, T. (1999) 'The impossibility of the Rule of Law', *Oxford Journal of Legal Studies*, **19**: 1.

Griffiths, J.A.G. (2000)'The Brave New World of Sir John Laws', *Modern Law Review* **63***:*159.

Hayek, F. (1960) *The Constitution of Liberty*, Chicago, Henry Regnery Co., 133–61, 205–19.

Horowitz, M.J. (1977) 'The Rule of Law: An Unqualified Human Good?', *Yale Law Journal*, **86**: 15.

Hutchinson, A. and Monahan, P. (1987) (eds) *The Rule of Law Ideal or Ideology*, Toronto, University of Toronto Press.

O'Donovan, K. (1989) 'Engendering Justice: Women's Perspectives and the Rule of Law', *University of Toronto Law Journal*, **39**: 127.

Poole, T. (2002) 'Dogmatic Liberalism? T.R.S.Allan and the Common Law Constitution', *Modern Law Review*, **65**: 463.

Poole, T. (2003) 'Back to the Future: Unearthing the Theory of Common Law Constitutionalism', *Oxford Journal of Legal Studies*, **66**: 435.

Raz, J. (1977) 'The Rule of Law and its Virtue', *Law Quarterly Review*, **93**: 93.

Summers, R.S. (1993) 'A Formal Theory of the Rule of Law', *Ratio Juris*, **6**: 127.

Tivey, L. (1999) 'Constitutionalism and the political arena', *Political Quarterly*, **70**: 175.

Waldron, J. (1989) 'The Rule of Law in contemporary legal theory', *Ratio Juris*, **2**: 79.

# Chapter 6

## The separation of powers

> Political liberty is nothing else but the diffusion of power. (Lord Hailsham)

## Key words

- ▶ Different meanings of separation of powers
- ▶ Checks and balances
- ▶ Responses to different political pressures
- ▶ Separation of powers and judicial independence
- ▶ Separation of powers and mixed government
- ▶ Democracy and separation of powers
- ▶ Parliament and the courts
- ▶ Partnership

### 6.1 Montesquieu's Doctrine of the Separation of Powers

Article 16 of the (French) *Declaration of the Rights of Man* (1789) states that 'a society where rights are not secured or the separation of powers established has no constitution'. It is widely believed that in all societies there is a natural tendency for power to gravitate towards a single personal leader under whatever title (king, president, prime minister etc.). The doctrine of the separation of powers attempts to combat this by providing mechanisms to make it difficult for any single power group to dominate and to ensure that government action requires the cooperation of different groups, each of which helps to keep the others within bounds. The doctrine is particularly associated with republican thinking but also supports the liberal values of the rule of law (Chapters 1, 5).

It is perhaps less important how the functions, of government are divided than that they should be divided. However, the division that has found most favour is that proposed by Montesquieu (1689–1755) who divided government into three branches or institutions corresponding to basic functions of government, namely the legislature, the executive and the judiciary. The legislature makes the laws, the judiciary settles disputes, and imposes sanctions for breaking the law, the executive enforces and puts the law into effect.

Montesquieu was a leading proponent of both the republican tradition and the individualistic form of liberalism (Chapter 1), being concerned to protect individual freedom. However, Montesquieu was no democrat and placed faith in aristocratic government subject to limits. His idea of limits on power was what he called 'dissonant harmony'. He believed that disagreement was a healthy feature of politics and that the need for different interests to cooperate would prevent any power being used excessively. As he famously stated 'power must be checked by power'.

Montesquieu thought that if any two of the three functions fall into the same hands the outcome is likely to be tyranny. According to the doctrine of the separation of powers, each branch has different functions but each uses its power to police the limits of the others. Conversely, within the limits of its powers, each branch should be independent of the others. For example, judicial review exists both to police the limits of executive power and to protect the executive within those limits (Chapter 14). As Nolan LJ put it in *M v Home Office* [1992] QB 270, 314,

> The proper constitutional relationship between the executive and the court is that the courts will respect all acts of the executive within its lawful province, and that the executive will respect all decisions of the court as to what its lawful province is.

The balance between the three powers depends on the particular fears and worries of the political system in question. For example, Rousseau and Mill (Chapter 1) emphasised the distinction between lawmaking in the sense of general rules which should be approved by the people, (in the case of Mill, through elected representatives), and individual decisions in the hands of 'experts' who must be limited and controlled by the people.

Montesquieu feared the legislature most. He vested the executive in the monarchy believing that this gave the constitution stability and continuity. The executive and legislature would, according to Montesquieu, check each other. For instance the executive could not make laws or obtain finance without the support of the legislature but in Montesquieu's view the legislature could not remove the executive. Montesquieu thought it appropriate that the executive should summon the legislature as and when needed but did not explain how an abuse of this power might be dealt with. However, in the UK constitution the meeting of the legislature is protected by statute and convention and the legislature can remove the executive (Chapter 9).

In the contemporary UK we regard the executive as the most dangerous branch in that it commands the resources of the state, including the use of force, and is in a position to dominate the legislature. Indeed, by the end of the nineteenth century Mill, influenced by de Toqueville's writing on the emerging American democracy, feared:

> the only despotism of which in the modern world there is real danger-the absolute rule of the head of the executive over a congregation of isolated individuals all equal and all slaves. (*Autobiography*, 1873)

More recently the desirability of an independent judiciary has been emphasised as a check on both an increasingly powerful executive and, apparently, the people (Chapter 17).

## 6.2 The Mixed Constitution

Montesquieu also insisted on a separation between class interests as another kind of check and balance. This reflects the idea of the 'mixed constitution' based on Aristotle's three forms of government, namely monarchy, aristocracy and democracy (Chapter 1). Aristotle believed any single form of government was unstable leading to a permanent cycle of disasters. In particular democracy – in the sense of the rule of the majority – leads to anarchy which is overcome only by the intervention of a dictator who will eventually be overthrown by force in favour of either aristocracy or democracy, each of which in turn will collapse. He therefore favoured a blend of democracy and aristocracy: democracy to provide consent, aristocracy to provide stability and wise leadership. Aristocracy meant literally 'rule by the best', by which Aristotle meant an educated group wealthy enough to be independent.

The early Roman republic adopted similar ideas ('power in the people, authority in the Senate' – Cicero), but was later replaced by dictatorship ('what pleases the prince has the force of law'). To Montesquieu, all three elements of the mixed constitution should be represented in the legislature since this was the supreme body. As with the separation of powers, each element would check the others. The monarch could veto legislation but not initiate it: 'prevent wrong but not do wrong'. The aristocratic and the elected elements would have to agree to make changes in the law.

Montesquieu, an aristocrat himself, believed that an aristocracy based on inheritance produced an independent, educated and leisured class who would protect freedom and curb the democratic element ('liberty is the stepchild of privilege') while the other elements of the constitution could prevent the aristocracy from using their powers selfishly. Montesquieu claimed to base his theory on the British constitution. He particularly admired the British constitution in that the executive power was centred upon the Crown and our legislature had two parts, one (the House of Lords) being aristocratic. However, in Montesquieu's time the conventions that removed power from the Crown in favour of ministers who were also members of the legislature had not yet crystallised. Moreover, Montesquieu may not have appreciated that the English constitution gave Parliament unlimited power over the Crown.

Blackstone (1723–80) an influential compiler of English law also praised the mixed constitution although he possibly underestimated the dominant influence held by the aristocracy of his day.

Herein indeed consists the true excellence of the English government that all the parts of it form a mutual check upon each other. In the legislature the people are a check on the nobility and the nobility a check upon the people ... while the king is a check upon both which preserves the executive power from encroachments. And this very executive power is again checked and kept within due bounds by the two Houses ... For the two Houses naturally drawing in two directions of opposite interest, and the prerogative in another still different from them both, they mutually keep each other from exceeding their proper limits ... like three distinct powers in mechanics, they jointly compel the machine of government in a direction different from what either acting by itself would have done ... a direction which constitutes the true line of the liberty and happiness of the country. (*Commentaries on the Laws of England*, 1787, edn, OUP, pp. 154–5)

The mixed constitution remains a significant element of the formal legal structure in the form of the monarchy and the House of Lords. However, politically the monarchy and the House of Lords are relatively impotent. It is worth remembering that originally aristocracy simply meant government by the 'best'. The hereditary principle which was the historical basis of the House of Lords was rationalised on the ground that inherited land-holding gave a powerful interest in the government of the country through which the lower classes enjoyed 'virtual representation'. Today an automatic link between inheritance and political influence is no longer acceptable, at least openly, as giving political power. Indeed since the Life Peerages Act 1958 anyone can be appointed to the House of Lords for life by the Queen on the advice of the Prime Minister, a power which is apparently immune from review by the courts. This reform was intended to enlist some of the 'best' into Parliament. However, life peerages can be awarded without any reason at all.

There are currently proposals to remove the aristocratic element from the House of Lords (Chapter 10). However, fear of democracy remains alive and many people are attracted by the idea of a non-elected part of the legislature (particularly if it includes themselves). This raises the difficulty of who we can trust to identify the 'best' so as to avoid Aristotle's corruption of aristocracy into an oligarchy of cronies. Unfortunately it has not proved possible to agree.

## 6.3 Other Kinds of Separation

It is worth noting that there are other kinds of separation of powers which serve the same function of preventing the concentration of power. Examples are as follows:

▶ Between elected politicians and appointed civil servants providing expert skills (Chapter 13). Mill's approach is broadly the form of representative democracy (Chapter 1) practised in the UK. Mill thought that most governmental functions should be entrusted to experts with democracy through elected representatives providing the elements of consent and control (*On Representative Government*). This serves a similar purpose to the mixed constitution of placing a buffer between raw democracy and government. The people's only legal power is to choose at intervals an individual as a representative for each locality in the House of Commons out of which the executive is formed by conventions over which the people have no control.

▶ Between the 'dignified' and the 'efficient' parts of the constitution (Chapter 3), for example the Queen and ministers.

▶ Between central and local government. However, in the UK local government is entirely subordinate to central government (Chapter 4).

## 6.4 Judicial Independence

Judicial independence is an aspect of the rule of law in its own right. It overlaps with but goes beyond the separation of powers. Separation of powers concerns the independence of the judicial system from other branches of government. Judicial independence requires the independence of individual judges from any pressures that threaten not only actual impartiality but also the appearance of impartiality. Article 6 of the European Convention on Human Rights includes both elements by requiring 'a fair and public hearing … by an independent and impartial tribunal established by law.' For example, in *Millar* v *Dickson* (2002) the Privy Council found a violation of Article 6 where the prosecuting authority, the Scottish Lord Advocate, was also responsible for renewing the appointment of a temporary judge even though there was no complaint about the actual impartiality of the judge in question. As Lord Hope stated ([2002] 3 All ER 1041, [41]):

> Central to the rule of law in a modern democratic society is the principle that the judiciary must be, and must be seen to be independent of the executive.

Beyond the separation of powers judicial independence also requires that judges should be protected against attacks on their conduct in court. They are immune from personal actions for damages in respect of acts within their powers or done in good faith (*McC* v *Mullan* (1984), Courts Act 2003 ss.31–35). Superior court judges may enjoy complete immunity (*Anderson* v *Gorrie* (1895)). Anything said in court by judges, advocates and witnesses is absolutely privileged against an action in libel and slander but advocates are not protected against liability for negligence (see *Trapp* v *Mackie* (1979), *Arthur JS Hall* v *Simons* (2000)). Judicial independence also requires that judges should not have any personal conflict of interest in relation to the parties before them (Chapter 15).

Judicial independence is an uncertain concept. It requires judges to be protected against external pressures but does not mean that they should not be accountable for their actions. Accountability has different meanings. It means firstly that a decision maker must explain and justify its actions and secondly that a decision maker might be penalised if its actions fall short of required standards. Judges are to some extent accountable in the first sense, which does not conflict with independence. They normally sit in public and, except in the case of juries (below), and magistrates courts, written reasons are given for decisions. Thus judicial decisions are open to scrutiny by the media. A three-tier appeal system and review by the High Court of decisions of inferior courts also contribute to accountability as does the Criminal Cases Review Commission which deals with miscarriages of justice. Judges occasionally give evidence on general matters to parliamentary committees.

## 6.5 The Separation of Powers in the UK

The separation of powers has been endorsed by contemporary UK judges (e.g. Lord Templeman in *M v Home Office* [1993] 3 All ER 537, 540; Lord Mustill in *R v Secretary of State for the Home Department ex parte Fire Brigades Union* [1995] 2 All ER 244, 267–8; L and Hoffmann in *R (Pro-Life Alliance) v BBC* [2003] 2 All ER 977, 997) while others have recognised it as applying at least between the legislature and the judiciary (Lords Nicholls and Hope in *Wilson v First County Trust* [2003] 4 All ER 97, 116, 130; Lord Diplock in *Duport Steels v Sirs* [1980] 1 WLR 142, 157; Sir John Donaldson in *R v HM Treasury ex parte Smedley* [1985] 1 All ER 589, 593).

However, there is little agreement as to whether the separation of powers is a helpful idea or what it means in the UK. Indeed some, for example Jennings (*The Law and the Constitution*, 1959), argue that there is no important difference between the three functions; the executive and judicial being essentially a more detailed kind of lawmaking. Others (e.g. Marshall, 1971) argue that the separation of powers is an umbrella for a miscellaneous collection of principles, each of which can be justified on its own terms, for example judicial independence (above). On the other hand Barendt (1995) and Munro (1999) regard the doctrine as an important organising and critical principle. However, this debate may be confused because different protagonists are using the concept of the separation of powers in different senses and for different purposes.

It seems clear that the ideas of the separation of powers (and the mixed constitution, above) have influenced the UK constitution but that this has been in an unsystematic, incomplete and pragmatic way in which the balance of forces is unstable. Most obviously there are indeed three branches of government, with broadly separate functions: the legislature (Parliament), the executive (the Crown) and the judiciary. All three historically originated with the Crown (Chapter 3) but are now treated as separate institutions. *M v Home Office* (1993) concerned whether the court could treat the Home Secretary, a minister of the Crown, as in contempt of court for disobeying a court order. The court rejected the argument that, because the courts and ministers were both historically part of the Crown, the Crown would in effect be in contempt of itself. Simon Brown J ( [1992] 4 All ER 97 at 107), citing Montesquieu, pointed out that at least since the seventeenth century the courts had been recognised as an institution separate from the Crown itself and that there were three branches of government with which the Queen had a symbolic relationship. Moreover, a minister exercising powers conferred on him by law was not to be treated as part of the Crown since to do so, as Lord Templeman remarked ([1993] 3 All ER 537, 540), would undo the consequences of the Civil War.

The thrust of the contemporary debate appears to set up the judiciary in alliance with the legislature against the executive. Therefore we put stress on an independent judiciary without necessarily adopting Montesquieu's full blown doctrine. Indeed Montesquieu recognised that there might be an overlap between the legislature and the executive although emphasising that there should be some separation:

> But if there were no monarch, and the executive power should be committed to a certain number of persons selected from the legislative body, there would be an end then of liberty. (The Spirit of the Laws, 1761).

In *R v Secretary of State ex parte Fire Brigades Union* [1995] 2 All ER 244, Lord Mustill said at 267:

> it is a feature of the peculiarly British conception of the separation of powers that Parliament, the executive and the courts each have their distinct and largely exclusive domain. Parliament has a legally unchallengable right to make whatever laws it thinks right. The executive carries on the administration of the country in accordance with the powers conferred on it by law. The courts interpret the laws and see that they are obeyed. This requires the courts to step into the territory which belongs to the executive, not only to verify that the powers asserted accord with the substantive law created by Parliament, but also that the manner in which they are exercised conforms with the standards of fairness which Parliament must have intended. Concurrently with this judicial function Parliament has its own special means of ensuring that the executive in the exercise of delegated functions, performs in a way that Parliament finds appropriate. Ideally it is these latter methods which should be used to check executive errors and excesses; for it is the task of Parliament and the executive in tandem, not of the courts, to govern the country. In recent years however, the employment in practice of these specifically Parliamentary remedies has on occasion been perceived as falling short and sometimes well short of, of what was needed to bring the performance of the executive in line with the law and with the minimum standards of fairness implicit in every Parliamentary delegation of a decision making function. To avoid a vacuum in which the citizen would be left without protection against a misuse of executive

powers the courts have had no option but to occupy the dead ground in a manner and in areas of public life, which could not have been foreseen 30 years ago.

This relates to the notion of the 'harmonious' constitution which treats the separation of powers as a safety mechanism, requiring intervention by one or other of the institutions in order to restore the balance of the constitution where harmony is breaking down. For example, according to Lord Mustill, when power is concentrated in an overactive executive with a frail parliamentary opposition it may be important for the courts to be more active than usual in exercising their powers (see Verde, *The Harmonious Constitution* (2000) PhD Thesis, University of Newcastle upon Tyne).

Related to the above, two glaring violations of the separation of powers can be highlighted in the UK constitution. Firstly, our common law system means that the judges are also lawmakers and their function is not confined to interpreting laws made by others. There are certain checks and balances, although these depend on the judges restraining themselves. One such is the judges' duty to follow precedent so as to limit the possibility of making up new law according to a judge's personal preferences. Another is the fact that the judges must make their law only in the context of the particular case before them. Another is the supposed principle that a court must ultimately defer to Parliament (Chapter 7). In *W.H. Smith Do It All Ltd* v *Peterborough* [1991] 4 All ER 193 at 196, Mustill LJ remarked that:

> according to the doctrine of the separation of powers as understood in the UK, the legislative acts of the Queen in Parliament are impregnable.

The second violation of the separation of powers gives our constitution one of its most important characteristics. By convention, ministers who lead the executive must also be members of Parliament (Chapter 3). This contrasts with presidential systems such as that of the USA under which the leader of the executive is separately elected and cannot be a member of the legislature. Some countries have adopted compromises between these extremes. In the UK therefore, depending on the political and personal forces of the day, without checks and balances, either the executive is subordinate to Parliament or (more likely) the executive dominates Parliament.

Bagehot (*The English Constitution*) claimed that the 'almost complete fusion' between the executive (by which he meant Cabinet ministers) and the legislature was the 'efficient secret' of the constitution. However, although Bagehot's writings have been highly influential, his analysis is widely regarded as oversimplified ('a television man before his time'). For example, there are various devices which attempt to ensure that neither the executive nor Parliament can completely dominate the other. Moreover, the functions and processes of the two branches are not fused. Ministers must publicly announce and defend their polices in Parliament whereas executive decisions are taken in secret by self-selected groups.

A problem with attempts to apply the separation of powers to the UK constitution is that the doctrine has different aspects which might conflict. The examples given throughout the book should be examined with this in mind. The separation of powers includes the following distinct but overlapping aspects:

▶ *functional separation* meaning that it is possible to define legislative, judicial and executive functions as conceptually separate
▶ *institutional separation* meaning that each of the three institutions should exercise its functions independently and should be protected against interference from the others
▶ *separation of personnel* meaning that no one should be a member of more than one branch so as to avoid conflicts of interest and the accumulation of power
▶ *checks and balances* meaning that each branch should have powers to police the others. This raises a potential conflict with institutional separation.

In the following sections I shall identify important examples of these different forms of separation of powers.

### 6.5.1　Functional Separation

This assumes that the three functions of government can be conceptually distinguished in the sense that activities of lawmaking, judging and carrying out executive tasks are different in significant respects irrespective of who carries them out. This is a controversial theoretical issue but constitutional thinkers have, since the time of Aristotle, agreed that there is at least a distinction between the making of general rules, which requires the participation of a wide a range of people, and the implementation of those rules in individual cases, which requires professional expertise and impartiality. This idea unites, for example, Locke, Rousseau and Mill despite their different ideas as to the purpose of government (Chapter 1).

I shall assume that, in most cases at least, we can distinguish between the three functions. A lawmaker issues general rules, a judge acts as referee by applying rules to a dispute while the executive enforces the law and makes government policy. Indeed, the executive function is open-ended, comprising anything that is neither judicial nor legislative. It includes proposing new laws, providing information and advice, making agreements and managing property and institutions, in these respects overlapping with private functions.

Whether a matter is executive or judicial may depend not on any natural quality it has but on the mechanism chosen to deal with it. For example,

....posing a penalty in connection with a court ruling is part of the judicial function (see Lord Steyn in *R (Anderson)* v *Secretary of State* (2002)) but arguably an 'administrative penalty' imposed mechanically, such as a parking ticket, is not. Nor arguably is a decision based on government policy such as refusing planning permission for a new building. A grant of planning permission creates a new right but a judicial function, strictly speaking, is meant only to determine existing rights under the law. However if the same decision was made by applying a rule, for example a right to planning permission for any house within a defined zone, it could be regarded as a judicial function. Moreover, unlike a minister or a traffic warden, a court exercising a judicial function cannot initiate action but must respond to disputes which others bring before it. Thus the judiciary is often claimed to be the 'least dangerous branch', having no weapons at its disposal and having no particular axe to grind.

Montesquieu's threefold functional distinction modified that made by Locke who distinguished between legislative, executive and what he called 'federative' functions but treated the judicial function as a particular aspect of the executive. Federative functions are concerned with the conduct of foreign affairs. Even though foreign affairs are nowadays considered to be part of the executive function, the notion of federative function remains useful. It is associated with the special powers formally vested in the sovereign and labelled the royal prerogative (Chapter 12). Foreign affairs have special characteristics which make them unsuitable for legal controls, involving as they do matters outside the reach of any single legal system and often requiring swift political action or negotiation not reducible to rules.

### 6.5.2    Institutional Separation

This means that the three functions are entrusted to separate institutions which should not interfere with each other. In the past the UK constitution has been lax in this respect but recently there has been a tendency to strengthen this aspect of the separation of powers in relation to the judiciary.

#### 6.5.2.1 *Parliament and the Executive*
There is overlap between Parliament and the executive in that while Parliament has no executive functions (except in relation to its own internal affairs), the executive is involved in lawmaking. The role of Parliament is mainly reactive, that of scrutinising and criticising measures put to them by the executive. Since the UK constitution does not adopt the liberal principle of minimal government recommended by the likes of Hayek (Chapter 1), Parliament has neither the time nor the expertise even to scrutinise all the laws that may be desirable. Thus many laws are enacted with no significant parliamentary input, MPs merely voting blindly for their party.

Sometimes statutes authorise ministers to alter other statutes by means of delegated legislation: the 'Henry VIII Clause' (see Barber, N., Young, A., 2003, *Public Law* 112). Indeed there are many laws, known as 'delegated' or 'subordinate' legislation, made directly by government departments under powers delegated to them by statute; a practice that is widely accepted as inevitable. Indeed delegated legislation far outnumbers statutes. Unlike statutes, delegated legislation can be set aside by the courts under their judicial review powers (Chapter 14).

The separation of powers is acknowledged in the case of international treaties by the principle that, as merely an act of the executive, a treaty cannot alter legal rights until it has been enacted by Parliament (*Maclaine Watson* v *DTI* (1988); *The Parlement Belge* (1879) see Chapter 4 note). However, the courts interpret the law, at least where it is unclear, in the light of a presumption that treaty obligations should be honoured (*Garland* v *BREL* [1983] 2 AC 251, 277; *A-G* v *BBC* [1981] AC 303, 354).

### 6.5.2.2 *Parliament and the Courts*

Parliament and the courts avoid interfering with each other. Under Art. 9 of the Bill of Rights 1688, an important part of the revolutionary settlement (Chapter 3), the courts cannot interfere in parliamentary proceedings or challenge statements made in Parliament (Chapter 9). They can however use Parliamentary proceedings as background information (below). In relation to its own composition and internal affairs the House of Commons has exclusive power to decide disputes and punish offenders.

There is no parliamentary scrutiny of the judiciary, such as committee hearings, and Parliament has no role in judicial appointments. Cases in progress should not be discussed in Parliament except in relation to matters of national importance or the conduct of ministers (see Erskine May, *Treatise on the Law, Privilege, Proceedings and Usage of Parliament*, 22nd edn, 1997, pp. 383–4, 542–3). Ministers do not answer questions on legal matters. No reflection must be cast on a judge's personal character, competence or motives except on a substantive motion for his dismissal, although backbenchers, but not ministers, may criticise individual judgements.

### 6.5.2.3 *The Executive and the Courts*

The courts have power to review executive decisions but are concerned to ensure that they do not enter into the sphere that properly belongs to the executive by deciding questions of economic and social policy or the allocation of resources or pursuing government policy goals in deciding cases. How this balance is struck is a controversial question and various devices are used by the courts to help them in the task (Chapters 15, 17). As Lord Hoffmann pointed out in *R (Pro Life Alliance)* v *BBC* [2003] 2 All ER 977 (which concerned whether the courts or Parliament through the BBC should determine questions of taste and decency), this is a matter of law in support of the separation of powers not of 'deference' to the executive as it is sometimes described.

The executive sometimes makes judicial decisions when it decides for example whether a given person is entitled to a welfare payment or to a school place. Indeed ministers are often required to decide appeals against government decisions, even those in which their own department has an interest. However, the practice of ministers determining planning appeals does not violate the right to a fair trial under the European Convention on Human Rights, at least where the decision is one based on policy, provided that there is the safeguard of judicial review (*R (Alconbury)* v *Secretary of State* (2001); Chapter 14). Moreover, what the separation of powers importantly requires is that each body should have the *last word* in relation to its particular function. Thus Parliament can approve, veto, or alter laws proposed to it and the judiciary can review executive action and has the last word as to what a law means.

The Lord Chancellor's department as part of the executive controls the administrative and financial aspects of the courts. Under the Courts Act 2003, s.1 the Lord Chancellor has a general duty to ensure an 'efficient and effective' court system (but not, at least expressly, a fair and independent one). The courts must bid for public money just like any other department so that, for example, legal aid (an essential element of access to justice) competes for resources with other government departments (Access to Justice Act 1999). Reliance on public money attracts regulation based on efficiency and 'value for money', which could distort the judicial process in favour, for example, of taking short cuts. In a 'judicial-centred' model of the separation of powers such as that in the USA, the judges themselves are given a budget within which they control the administration of the courts.

Magistrates clerks have certain judicial functions in connection with criminal proceedings and also advise magistrates on the law participating in their private deliberations. Under the Courts Act 2003 they are treated as civil servants under the control of the Lord Chancellor and without security of tenure. They can be transferred between magistrates courts. The Act makes some concession to their independence by providing that when exercising judicial functions they are not subject to directions from the Lord Chancellor (s.29).

It has been held that the activities of magistrates clerks do not violate judicial independence provided that the clerk advises only on matters of law and procedure not the actual decision, and that any matters that the parties might wish to comment upon are raised in open court (*Clark (Procurator Fiscal Kircaldy)* v *Kelly* (2003)). It is difficult to see how these protections are safeguarded given that the deliberations are in private. In *Kelly* the Privy

Council relied on the right of appeal, the 'well understood conventions' and the clerk's professional code as safeguards.

It is important for judicial independence that judges have no duty to advise the executive. However, judges sometimes accept appointment to hold inquiries into matters of public concern which may involve politically sensitive issues involving the executive such as the *Scott Report into Arms Sales to Iraq* (HC 115, 1996) and the Hutton Inquiry (2004) into the suicide of a government advisor in the context of the decision to invade Iraq. This practice violates the separation of powers by requiring the judge to respond to terms of reference dictated by the executive, so raising suspicions of bias. Indeed in some countries such as the USA and Australia the practice is regarded as unconstitutional (see Drewry, 'Judicial Inquiries and Public Reassurance' [1996] *Public Law* 368; Woodhouse, 'Constitutional and Political Implications of a UK Supreme Court', [2004] *Legal Studies* 140).

Traditionally judges have not participated in public debate (see McMurdo, M. 'Should Judges Speak Out?' Judicial Conference of Australia 2001, (http://www.jca.asn.au)). However, in 1987 the Lord Chancellor relaxed the notorious 'Kilmuir' rules, made in 1959 by the then Lord Chancellor, which restricted such participation and the matter is now left to the discretion of the individual judge. This has sharpened the conflict within the office of Lord Chancellor, who must represent both government policy and the judges (see http://www.dea.gov.uk/judges).

Reflecting the inherent conflict between justice and security, there is a conflict of functions between the Home Secretary and the judiciary in that the Home Secretary has played a part in fixing the length of time to be served by prisoners given life sentences by a court. In a series of cases, see *R (Anderson)* v *Secretary of State* (2002), both the European Court and the UK courts have held that such a conflict of functions is contrary to Art. 6 of the ECHR, denying the citizen a right to a fair trial by an independent court. It was stressed in *Benjamin* v *UK* (2002), 13 BHRC 287, [36], that the involvement of the executive in sentencing:

impinges on the fundamental principle of the separation of powers and detracts from a necessary guarantee against the possibility of abuse.

The Home Secretary retains some discretionary power in relation to the release of prisoners serving fixed sentences of 15 years or more (Criminal Justice Act 1991 ss. 35, 50). This as been upheld as non-discriminatory (Chapter 17) but the Court of Appeal has left the general question open (see *R (Clift)* v *Secretary of State* (2004)).

Another vital safeguard is that juries should not be vetted by the executive (*R* v *Crown Court at Sheffield ex parte Brownlow* (1980)) and cannot be required to give reasons for their verdicts or punished for giving or failing to give a verdict (*Bushell's Case* (1670)). It is an offence for anyone to publish information as to what was said in a jury room (Contempt of Court Act 1981 s.8 (1)).

### Separation of Personnel

This means that, in view of the risk of bias or conflict of interest, the same persons must not be members of more than one of the three branches or exercise more than one function. This principle has traditionally been applied pragmatically and not consistently. We have already seen that the UK constitution does not comply with this, most importantly by its requirement that ministers must also be members of Parliament, a principle that in theory strengthens executive accountability to Parliament but in practice, due to the subservience of MPs, enables the executive to dominate Parliament. There are however examples of the separation of personnel. No more than 95 ministers can be members of the Commons (House of Commons (Disqualification) Act 1975 s. 2 (1)), thus preventing the government from packing the Commons with sycophants. Moreover, certain kinds of official (civil servants, police, regulators, members of the armed forces, etc.) cannot be members of the Commons (ibid. s.1; see Chapter 10).

The judiciary has a stronger but still incomplete separation of personnel. The holders of most judicial offices cannot be members of the House of Commons (House of Commons Disqualification Act 1975 s.1). However, as we have seen, the highest appellate body is the Appellate Committee of the House of Lords, and its judges are full members of the House. This has been justified on the grounds that it injects legal perspective into the proceedings of the House and enables judges to benefit from an understanding of the legislative process. However it is difficult to see the point of this membership. Lord Bingham remarked that a member of a legislative chamber is valued for his or her ability to speak out whereas a good judge is valued for caution and reticence (*Constitution Unit Spring Lecture*, UCL, 2002). Indeed there are conventions restraining the law lords from participating in party political controversies and speaking on matters that might affect future cases (*Hansard* HL col. 419, 22 June 2000). Indeed they rarely speak at all in the House, none doing so in 2000 and only one in 2001.

The Lord Chancellor, often described as a walking contradiction of the separation of powers, is an office created by Edward the Confessor (1042–1066). As the King's secretary and the holder of ecclesiastical office ('the conscience of the king'), during the medieval period the Lord Chancellor became primarily concerned with legal processes in respect of which he was both judge and an administrator. The Lord Chancellor is part of all three branches of government although his involvement has fluctuated over the years. He is the nominal head of the judiciary but in practice rarely sits as judge. He is the Cabinet minister responsible for the courts, the legal profession and legal aid and, as such, head of a large spending department as well as making most judicial appointments, disciplining judges and being responsible for the organisation of the courts. Since the 1960s the executive work of the Lord Chancellor's Office has vastly increased. The Lord Chancellor also presides over the House of Lords but, unlike the Speaker of the Commons, has no disciplinary powers since the House is supposed to regulate itself collectively (Chapter 11).The Lord Chancellor is in formal status superior to the Prime Minister and has a higher salary and pension than other ministers (Lord Chancellor's Pension Act 1832).

Like other ministers, the Lord Chancellor is appointed and dismissed by the Prime Minister and has no security of tenure. Unlike the case with other judicial offices, there are no specific qualifications for appointment. For example, the current Lord Chancellor is a barrister who was formerly a flatmate of the Prime Minister.

There is a therefore a potential conflict of interest in certain of the Lord Chancellor's functions Indeed it could be argued that, where the Lord Chancellor sits as a judge at least in relation to a matter involving the government, the right to a fair trial under the Human Rights Act 1998 is compromised (see *McGonnell* v *UK* (2000): Bailiff of Guernsey). On the other hand, the conflicts between the interests of justice and those of other government policies, most clearly law and order and security, are inherent in any government. Indeed it is arguable that the overlapping roles of the Lord Chancellor support rather than infringe the separation of powers by acting as a buffer or lubricant between the three branches. As a member of the House of Lords, and therefore unelected, he has a certain independence from party politics. As a spending minister he can ensure that the judiciary is properly resourced, and as a judge can bring expertise and protect judicial appointments and discipline against executive interference. On the other hand, as a member of the Cabinet, the Lord Chancellor is bound by collective responsibility (Chapter 13) and has no security of tenure to stand up to the Prime Minister.

The Attorney-General also has conflicting roles, being a member of the government and its chief legal advisor and also playing a part in the judicial process (Chapter 13). The Attorney has powers to bring legal proceedings against public authorities on behalf of the public interest and to consent to many kinds of prosecution including political offences under official secrets and public order legislation. The Attorney can also intervene by means of a *nolle prosequi* to prevent criminal proceedings. The Attorney's powers to take legal action are apparently not subject to judicial review (see *Gouriet* v *UPOW* (1978)) so that the possibility of politically biased action goes unchecked.

The Scott Report (HC 115 1996) revealed an official culture in which the advice of the Attorney-General was treated as if it had legal force, a practice condemned by the court in *R* v *Brown* (1993). Moreover, the Attorney is regarded as having a private lawyer–client relationship with the government so that his advice can be made public only with the consent of the government. The combination of these principles allowed for example the current government to claim that it was lawfully entitled to invade Iraq on the basis of partly undisclosed advice from the Attorney-General.

### 6.5.4 Checks and Balances

This involves each branch having some control over the others but also requires each branch to be protected against undue interference by the others, thus entailing the need for pragmatic compromise. The checks and balances concept may therefore conflict with other aspects of the separation of powers. In the UK checks and balances might take the form of law or convention and, in keeping with the 'insider' tradition, many checks and balances such as the various commissions and committees dealing with standards of government are informal and not legally enforceable (Chapter 3). There are examples of checks and balances throughout the book. Some highlights will briefly be mentioned here.

▶ The Queen in an emergency could invoke her royal prerogative powers to dismiss the Prime Minister, dissolve Parliament or refuse to dissolve Parliament.

▶ The Prime Minister can advise the Queen to dissolve Parliament but it must meet again within a year.

▶ The executive must resign if it loses the support of Parliament, leading to a dissolution if an alternative government cannot command the support of Parliament.

▶ The executive makes judicial appointments on the basis that a democratic element is desirable in order to prevent the existence of a self-perpetuating clique. This is widely accepted as appropriate (see *Campbell and Fell* v *UK* (1984)). A stronger political imput such as the hearings by Congress used in the USA would create a risk that judicial appointments and behaviour would be politically partisan. On the other hand, since judges make decisions with political consequences and have considerable scope to be influenced by political preferences, it is arguable that their political views should be brought into the open. At present there is no statutory mechanism for independent scrutiny of judicial appointments such as exists in many countries, although reform in this respect is proposed (below).

▶ The executive and Parliament play a part in appointing and dismissing judges by means of mechanisms which themselves contain checks and balances (Chapter 3). For example, superior court judges can be dismissed only by a resolution of both Houses of Parliament. Proposals for reforms to the method of appointing judges also embody an elaborate system of checks and balances between ministers and the proposed judicial appointments commission (below).

▶ Area courts or 'boards' scrutinise, review and make recommendations to the Lord Chancellor in relation to his function of managing the court system (Courts Act 2003). These are appointed by the Lord Chancellor, drawn from prescribed categories (at least one judge, two lay magistrates, two persons with local knowledge of the court system and two representatives of local residents). They have no security of tenure. The Lord Chancellor must also make an annual report to Parliament.

▶ The courts provide a check over the executive by means of judicial review, where they try to draw a line between the legality of government action, which they are entitled to police, and the merits of government action, which is a matter for Parliament (Chapter 14). However, the limits of judicial review are vaguely defined. As Lord Mustill pointed out in *R* v *Secretary of State for the Home Department ex parte Fire Brigades Union* (1995) (above), there is a tendency for judicial intervention to expand to fill the 'dead ground' where other safeguards fall short.

▶ The Humans Rights Act 1998 attempts to strikes a balance between the three branches by requiring the courts to scrutinise acts of all three branches that violate the main provisions of the European Convention on Human Rights, subject to Parliament's power to override Convention rights by using very clear language (Chapter 17).

▶ More generally the courts check Parliament since they have power to interpret statutes and can do so in the light of the moral values associated with the rule of law (Chapter 5). Thus interpreting statutes is more than merely seeking to obey what Parliament intended (even if the idea in itself makes sense) but is an independent function (Chapter 5). On the other hand, the intentions of the democratic branch must be respected so that a compromise must be struck based on the limits of interpretation. In *Duport Steels Ltd* v *Sirs* [1980] 1 All ER 529 at 551, Lord Scarman said:

> the constitution's separation of powers, or more accurately functions, must be observed if judicial independence is not to be put at risk ... confidence in the judicial system will be replaced by fear of it becoming uncertain and arbitrary in its application. Society will then be ready for Parliament to cut the power of the judges.

He meant that that the judges must observe the law by sticking to the language of legislation even at the expense of their own views of justice or policy. However language is often unclear. The courts therefore assume that Parliament must have intended its language to be understood in the context of widely shared assumptions about the principles and values of the constitution (Chapter 5). These in turn may not be clear or may be derived from the values held by a narrow group of powerful people such as lawyers. An important corrective in this context is the rule of law idea that an enactment should be read as those subject to it are likely to understand it.

Once a statute has been enacted therefore, Parliament loses control of its meaning in favour of the courts. In this connection the case of *Pepper* v *Hart* (1993) raises problems. The House of Lords held that, where the language of an Act is ambiguous, the court can look in *Hansard* (the official record of the proceedings of the House), and perhaps in other official documents, at statements made by the promoters of the Act in Parliament (usually ministers), in order to see what they intended. This threatens the separation of powers by putting the executive in a privileged position over both Parliament and the courts. A statute is the collective enterprise of Parliament over which the executive should not have special control. Moreover, the use made of proceedings in Parliament raises issues relating to the protection of Parliament against outside interference (Chapter 9).

Apart from *Pepper* v *Hart*, background material such as official reports used in preparing the statute (legislative history) could always be looked at but only for the purpose of discovering the context in which a statute was passed and ascertaining its broad purpose. Indeed in *Wilson* v *First County Trust* [2003] 4 All ER 97 [60], Lord Nichols suggested that *Pepper and Hart* does no more than extend this principle to statements made in Parliament itself. *Wilson* itself concerns the particular approach to statutes required where the Human Rights Act 1998 is involved (Chapter 17).

Later cases have taken a cautious approach to *Pepper* v *Hart*, emphasising that it is for the courts to decide what a statute means and that the statements of ministers, however explicit, cannot control the meaning. Moreover, such statements have not generally proved helpful and should be resorted to only where the legislation is obscure, ambiguous or would lead to absurd results, and then only if the statements to be used are clear (*R* v *Secretary of State for Environment, Transport and the Regions ex parte Spath Homes* (2000); *Wilson* v *First County Trust* (above), [58], [59], [139], [140]). It has been also suggested that *Pepper* v *Hart* applies only where the executive attempts to enforce a statute in a way which contradicts what it previously said in Parliament (*R* v *Secretary of State ex parte Spath Homes* [2001] 1 All ER 195, 226-227, *Wilson* v *First County Trust* (above), [113], [140]). Thus the doctrine becomes a weapon in defence of Parliament against the executive and, as such, a constitutional check and balance.

## 6.6 Proposed Reforms

In 2003 the government introduced a Constitutional Reform Bill containing proposals intended to rationalise aspects of the judicial branch in relation both to institutional separation and personnel arrangement (see *Constitutional Reform: a Supreme Court for the United Kingdom* CP 11/03 (July 2003), *Constitutional Reform: a New Way of Appointing Judges* CP 10/03 (July 2003), *Constitutional Reform: reforming the Office of the Lord Chancellor* CP 13/03 (2003)). The bill introduces a more formal separation of powers. However, rather than the traditional conflict model of the separation of powers, the reforms are couched in terms of 'partnership' between the courts and the executive.

> The Lord Chief Justice and I are determined that the successful partnership between my department and the judiciary should be sustained and entrenched for future generations. (Lord Falconer, Lord Chancellor and Secretary of State for Constitutional Affairs; see *New Law Journal* 26 March 2004, p. 442)

The first proposal is to create a separate Supreme Court to replace the Appellate Committee of the House of Lords, thereby separating the courts from Parliament. Serving judges would be disqualified from participating in the business of the House of Lords. The second proposal was to abolish the office of Lord Chancellor in favour of a Secretary of State for Constitutional Affairs. However the Office of Lord Chancellor is now apparently not to be abolished, but its duties are to be modified. The third proposal is to introduce an independent element into the judicial appointments process. Administration and supervision of the judiciary will be split between the Department of Constitutional Affairs and the Lord Chief Justice. Financial control will remain with the government. At the time of writing the future of the bill is uncertain.

The bill had unusually been referred to a Select Committee of the House of Lords (see HL Paper 125 (2004)). There was considerable disagreement in the Committee on fundamental issues, particularly in relation to the Supreme Court and abolition of the Lord Chancellor. The bill also embodies the main elements of a 'concordat' between the Judges' Council and the government concerning the division of functions between executive and judiciary (Department for Constitutional Affairs, 2004). At present its progress remains unclear.

The reform proposals can be criticised from three directions. First, some might regard them merely as cosmetic tinkering, ignoring wider questions of principle such as the independence and accountability of the judges, whether positive measures should be taken to widen the pool from which judges are selected, whether the Supreme Court should be confined to important constitutional issues and whether it should be able to overrule Acts of Parliament. It is widely recognised that the courts are increasingly required to adjudicate on the lawfulness of government action and should therefore be seen to be independent, an idea that sits uneasily with that of partnership. Second, traditionalists might regard the reforms as expensive, disruptive, and unnecessary in the light of the (to them) successful accommodation achieved by the existing arrangements. Third, those with a utilitarian bent might consider the proposals a wasted opportunity for fine tuning of detailed matters such as the reorganisation of the mechanisms for appeals.

### 6.6.1 The Supreme Court

It is not proposed that the Supreme Court's powers will differ from those of the existing House of Lords. It will comprise 12 judges as now sitting in panels (the outcome of a case might depend on how a panel is selected). The minister can increase the number of judges. The court will have some administrative independence being able to make its own procedural rules and will have substantial financial autonomy similar to that of a non-ministerial government department (Chapter 13).

The main reasons for the proposal are to ensure a separation of powers between legislature and judiciary and to enhance public understanding of and confidence in the judicial system. Article 6 of the European Convention on Human Rights, as it has been applied by the European Court (Chapter 17), requires courts not only to be independent but to appear to be so. Moreover, the Human Rights Act, the strengthening of the courts' powers of judicial review of the executive, devolution and the impact of European Union membership mean that the courts have greater political significance than has traditionally been the case. It is arguable that, since the court will no longer be a part of Parliament, the proposal will shift the constitutional balance in favour of the courts and might even make it easier to justify the courts overriding Acts of Parliament.

Much of the argument in favour of the status quo consists of the familiar reliance on custom and trust. Opponents of the proposal point out that there is no requirement of a formal separation of powers in the UK constitution and emphasise Parliament's historical role as a court. Moreover, there seems to be no evidence one way or another about lack of public confidence in the present arrangements, and it is not doubted that the House of Lords is independent in practice. It is sometimes argued that the Law Lords inject a valuable perspective into Parliamentary debates and contribute to the romantic idea of Parliament as a meeting of all the interests of the realm. However, by convention the Law Lords do not participate in party political debates and, in common with other judges, avoid expressing opinions relating to matters likely to come before them in litigation.

It has also been pointed out that the House of Lords has special protection against the executive in relation particularly to finance and that arrangements should be made to protect the new court against such political pressures (see House of Lords, 2003). The link with the House of Lords may be partly retained in that Supreme Court judges may be appointed to it on retirement.

Special considerations apply in respect of the devolved regimes of Scotland, Northern Ireland and Wales. Ordinary appeals from those regimes currently go to the House of Lords as do all English appeals. However, appeals on devolution matters (Chapter 4) go to the Privy Council, the membership of which is almost the same as that of the House of Lords. The Privy Council will remain to hear overseas appeals but its jurisdiction in devolution matters will be transferred to the Supreme Court, thereby perhaps encouraging a systematic constitutional and human rights jurisprudence. On the other hand, there might be loss of the local perspective. However, an amendment is proposed to safeguard the separate identity of the jurisdictions in the case law of the Supreme Court and appointments to the court must take into account the need for representation of the jurisdictions.

### 6.6.2 The Lord Chancellor

The main reason for abolishing the Lord Chancellor has been an increasing perception of the conflict within his three roles as head of the judiciary, head of the government department responsible for the court system and member of the House of Lords (above). Under the original bill the Secretary of State as an ordinary minister will exercise the executive functions of Lord Chancellor, sometimes in consultation with the Lord Chief Justice, to ensure an 'efficient and effective court service' but will not hold judicial office nor necessarily be a lawyer. As an ordinary spending minister he will be accountable to the House of Commons. He will also have a role in judicial appointments (below). The Lord Chief Justice will be the 'President' of the judiciary with responsibility for making procedural rules (subject to consultation with the minister), for education and training and for assigning judges to particular cases. Disciplining judges will be the joint responsibility of the Secretary of State and the Lord Chief Justice. The House of Lords will decide for itself who is to preside over its sittings.

At the heart of government is a conflict between the values of justice and those of law and order. The main worries about the proposal are therefore as follows. Firstly, there will be no person with a specific constitutional duty to speak on behalf of the judiciary. Secondly, that an ordinary minister may have insufficient political weight to protect the judiciary against interference by other ministers. Thirdly, there is a tension between the Lord Chancellor's role as champion of the law, safeguarded by the relative independence of the House of Lords (Chapter 9), and the desire for a minister in charge of an important spending department to be democratically accountable to the Commons. Other objections to the abolition of the Lord Chancellor are based on the notion that our constitution should evolve according to custom and tradition and not be engineered. It is argued that the antiquity of the office is evidence that it is good. On the other hand, the Lord Chancellor is a political appointment without security of tenure, no different from any other Cabinet minister and there is no legal guarantee of his independence. Moreover, since it is widely accepted that the Lord Chancellor can no longer sit as a judge, the office is in any case radically changed.

The bill includes a vague duty on ministers and officials to 'uphold the continued independence of the judiciary', and 'not to seek to influence particular judicial decisions through any special access to the judiciary'. The Secretary of State for Constitutional Affairs must have regard to the need to defend that independence, to the need for the judiciary to have 'the support necessary to enable them to exercise their functions' and to the need for 'the public interest in regard to matters relating to the judiciary or otherwise to the administration of justice to be properly represented in decisions affecting those matters' (Clause 1). None of this excludes the possibility that judicial independence can be outweighed by other factors. The Select Committee of the House of Lords thought that a duty to uphold the 'rule of law' should be included. The main argument against this appears to be the absence of agreement as to what is meant by the rule of law (Chapter 5).

In July 2004 the House of Lords voted against the proposal to abolish the Lord Chancellor. It appears that the government will accept this but at the time of writing it remains unclear what functions and powers the office will retain.

### 6.6.3 Judicial Appointments

The bill introduces a Judicial Appointments Commission with power to advertise vacancies, scrutinise candidates and recommend appointments but with ministers having a limited veto. In the case of appointment to the Supreme Court, there will be a special five-person commission including members from Northern Ireland and Scotland and with at least one lay person.

There is broad support for this aspect of the reforms. It is generally accepted that, in a democracy, elected politicians should have a say in the appointment of senior judges. Most judicial appointments will be made by the Queen on the recommendation of the minister (or Lord Chancellor). In the case of the Supreme Court, the recommendation is by the Prime Minister who must, however, recommend the name put to him by the minister.

The Commission will be formally independent both of the executive and judiciary, comprising judges and a majority of lay people. It will be independent from politicians being appointed by the Lord Chief Justice, the Commissioner for Public Appointments and the Chairman of the Commission, who will not be a lawyer. Appointments must be based 'on merit' and with a threshold of 'good character'. The minister in consultation with the Lord Chief Justice is to publish general 'Guidance' for judicial appointments but the bill does not propose any additional criteria relating for example to diversity such as are used in other official appointments. There will be a Judicial Appointments Ombudsman to investigate complaints and report to the minister as to whether the procedures are properly followed.

The Commission will submit a report to the minister containing a single name which he can either accept, reject on the ground that the person is unsuitable for office, or require the panel to reconsider on both unsuitability and merit grounds. He must give written reasons. The Commission cannot put up a rejected name again but the minister can exercise each of these options once only.

## Summary

▶ The doctrine of the separation of powers means that government power should be divided up into legislative, executive and judicial functions, each with its own distinctive personnel and processes, and that each branch of government should be checked so that no one body can dominate the others.

▶ In Montesquieu's version the separation of powers is complemented by the idea of the mixed constitution in which different class interests checked and balanced each other particularly in the legislature. There is a vestige of the mixed constitution in the institutions of monarchy and the House of Lords. However, the idea of the mixed constitution shorn of its historical association with a hereditary aristocracy might still be valuable as providing a check over crude majoritarian democracy linking with the idea of deliberative democracy.

▶ The separation of powers comprises separation of function, of institutions and of personnel and includes the notion of checks and balances. The particular blend in any given case depends on the preoccuptions of the particular country. There is little agreement among writers as to whether the separation of powers is a valuable idea or in what sense it applies in the UK. Separation

## Summary cont'd

of powers ideas have influenced our constitutional arrangements but in a pragmatic and unsystematic way.

▶ In the UK there is no strict separation of personnel particularly between the legislature and the executive worries about executive domination are the main driving force. There are also concerns about the relationship between the courts and Parliament in particular in the context of the use that the courts should make of things said in Parliament.

▶ The question of judicial independence can be regarded as an aspect of the separation of powers but could be considered an issue in its own right irrespective of other aspects of the doctrine. There is a tension between judicial independence and ensuring that judges are accountable.

▶ Current reform proposals are an attempt to strengthen the separation of powers by creating a Supreme Court to replace the Appellate Committee of the House of Lords, injecting an independent element into judicial appointments and abolishing the office of Lord Chancellor. It could be that aspects of these reforms strengthen institutional separation but weaken checks and balances.

# Exercises

6.1 Does the idea of the mixed constitution have contemporary value?

6.2 Distinguish and illustrate the possible different meanings of the separation of powers.

6.3 It is sometimes said that the UK constitution embodies a 'fusion' between the legislature and the executive. Do you agree? Is it desirable that the composition of the executive and legislature be separate?

6.4 Are there adequate safeguards for both judicial independence and judicial accountability in the UK constitution?

6.5 Explain the significance of *Pepper* v *Hart* in connection with the separation of powers.

6.6 The replacement of the Appellate Committee of the House of Lords will 'put the relationship between the executive, the legislature and the judiciary on a modern footing, which takes account of peoples' expectations about the independence and transparency of the judicial system' (*Constitutional Reform: A Supreme Court of the United Kingdom,* Dept of Constitutional Affairs, 2003). Discuss.

**6.7** Assess the arguments for and against the abolition of the office of Lord Chancellor.

**6.8** 'It is a serious flaw in the Consultation Paper that, insofar as it adopts any constitutional principle, it appears to choose the doctrine of the separation of powers not the independence of the judiciary' (Lord Hobhouse, *The Law Lords' Response to the Government's Consultation Paper on Constitutional Reform*, HL 2003). Explain and critically comment in the light of the Constitutional Reform Bill 2004.

**6.9** 'A spirit of partnership between the judiciary, the legislature and the executive is essential' (Lord Woolf, Lord Chief Justice, Squire Centenary Lecture, Cambridge 2004). Discuss in relation to the Constitutional Reform Bill 2004.

## Further reading

Barber, N. (2001) 'Prelude to the Separation of Powers', *Cambridge Law Journal*, **61**: 59.

Barendt, E. (1995) 'Separation of powers and constitutional government', *Public Law*, 599.

Barendt, E. (1998) *An Introduction to Constitutional Law*, Oxford, Clarendon Press, Chapter 7.

Cooke, Lord (2003) 'The Law Lords: An Endangered Heritage', *Law Quarterly Review*, **119**: 49.

Department of Constitutional Affairs (2004) *The Lord Chancellor's Judiciary Related Functions* (http://www.dca.gov.uk/consult/lcoffice/judiciary.htm).

Ewing, K.D. (2001) 'The Unbalanced Constitution' in Campbell, T., Ewing, K.D. and Tompkins, A. (eds) *Sceptical Essays on Human Rights*, Oxford, Oxford University Press.

House of Lords (2003) *The Law Lords' Response to the Government's Consultation Paper* (http://www.parliament.uk/documents/upload/JudicialSCR071103.pdf).

Legal Studies (2004) Special Issue, *Constitutional innovation: the creation of a Supreme Court for the United Kingdom; domestic, comparative and international Reflections*. 2, 3, 5,7,8, 9,10.

Le Sueur, A. (2003) 'New Labour's (surprisingly quick) steps in Constitutional Reform', *Public Law*, 368.

Marshall, G. (1971) *Constitutional Theory*, Oxford, Clarendon Press, Chapters V, VI, VII, IX.

Munro, C.R. (1999) *Studies in Constitutional Law*, 2nd edn, London, Butterworths, Chapter 9.

**Further reading cont'd**

Steyn, Lord (1997) 'The weakest and least dangerous department of government', *Public Law,* 84.

Steyn, Lord (2001) 'Pepper and Hart: a Re examination', *Oxford Journal of Legal Studies,* **21**: 59.

Steyn, Lord (2002) 'The Case for a Supreme Court', *Law Quarterly Review,* **118**: 382.

Steyn, Lord (2003) 'Creating a Supreme Court', *Counsel,* Oct. 2003, 14.

Woodhouse, D. (1998) 'The Office of Lord Chancellor', *Public Law,* 617.

# Chapter 7
## Parliamentary supremacy

Whoso has sixpence is sovereign (to the length of sixpence) over all men ... A Parliament speaking through reporters to Buncombe and the twenty-seven millions, mostly fools. (Thomas Carlyle, 1795–1881)

## Key words

▶ Political and legal supremacy
▶ Self-embracing sovereignty?
▶ The common law as foundational?
▶ Interpreting or overriding?

### 7.1 Introduction

The doctrine of parliamentary supremacy or sovereignty maintains that Parliament, in the sense of Queen, House of Lords and House of Commons acting together, has unlimited legal power to enact any law. It is important at the outset to emphasise that parliamentary supremacy is a legal principle meaning that a law made by Parliament must conclusively be accepted as binding, in the sense of enforceable, by the courts. However, we should not take the extreme legalistic position and claim that this has nothing to with political supremacy since the fact that Parliament has enacted the law means that the community has indicated that it is important enough to justify the use of violence and therefore that it has priority over other rules. Moreover, acceptance of parliamentary supremacy gives out the signal that, in common with Hobbes (Chaper 1), we are prepared in principle to concede the state unlimited control over our lives. On the other hand, the doctrine of parliamentary supremacy has nothing to say about any political, moral or economic constraints there might be on the laws that Parliament makes. Even here however we might be concerned if the law is out of step with political reality.

In the absence of a written constitution the foundations of the doctrine of parliamentary supremacy, resting as they do on no more than widespread acceptance, look frail.

The doctrine has recently been challenged from several directions. Firstly, it is argued that that in practice Parliament is subservient to the executive. However, there seems to be little force in this since members of Parliament have chosen to defer to the executive and there is no legal or compelling political reason why they should continue to do so. Secondly, it has been argued that international legal requirements, notably those of the European Union, restrict parliamentary supremacy. Thirdly, it has been argued that pressures from within, for example Scottish devolution, mean that the legal doctrine is out of line with political reality and should be amended. Fourthly, it is argued that, because legislation made by Parliament has to be applied by the courts if it is to be enforced, the supreme authority is the common law which 'conferred' sovereignty on Parliament and can therefore take it away again. However, there is no logical reason why the common law should not have surrendered to Parliament. As Hobbes recognised, all authority ultimately depends on nothing but community acquiescence which could be to anything. A moderate version of the common law argument is that there is 'dual' sovereignty between Parliament and the courts according to which the one is supreme in making the law, the other in saying what it means.

Even if it is true that political power tends to end up in the hands of a single leader, there is no logical reason why there should be a single *legal* sovereign with unlimited powers. For example, in the USA power is carefully divided so that no single entity has unlimited legal power. Even the last word, the power to change the constitution, is divided in complex ways between different groups who must agree to make the change. However, as Hobbes also realised, it may be necessary as a last resort to give absolute power to a single body to deal with an emergency, including the power to decide whether an emergency exists. Even here however safeguards can be put in place (Chapter 19).

## 7.2 Historical Outline

In the absence of a written constitution and any logical or political imperative, the question of what is the fundamental principle of the constitution can only be settled historically. At least since Tudor times, parliamentary supremacy has been the orthodox doctrine. Indeed as early as the fourteenth century it became clear that the king could not exact taxes without the permission of Parliament, and from this power base Parliament could control the making of laws. A statute of Edward III (14 Edw. III, stat.ii.c.1) declared that the nation:

> should be no more charged or grieved to make any common aid or sustain charge except by the common assent of the prelates, earls, barons, and other magnates and commons of the realm and that in Parliament ... Nor does the king by himself or by his ministers impose tollages, subsidies or any other burdens whatsoever on his subjects, nor change the laws nor make new ones without the concession or assent of his whole realm expressed in Parliament.

By the sixteenth century it had become clear that Parliament could change the common law. Even the Tudor monarchs, who developed a strong central executive, recognised that the full power of the Crown could be exercised only in combination with Parliament. In 1543, Henry VIII declared

We be informed by our judges that we at no time stand so highly in our estate Royal as in the time of Parliament wherein we as head and you as members are conjoined and bound together into one body politic.

The most convincing example of this was the Reformation Parliament (1529–36) which destroyed the medieval social order by making the Church part of the English state.

We have already discussed the seventeenth-century struggle between the King and Parliament (Chapter 3). Even during that period the issue was the extent of the King's powers to act alone. It was not seriously doubted that Parliament, in the sense of King, Lords and Commons combined as representing the whole realm, had unlimited power. Parliamentary supremacy is sometimes said to derive from the 1688 revolution. (see *Pickin v BRB* (1974)). However, the revolution established only that Parliament was superior to the king and did not deal explicitly with the relationship between Parliament and the common law. A realistic assessment might be that the courts accepted the doctrine of parliamentary supremacy in return for security of tenure which they were given by the Act of Settlement 1701.

Seventeenth-century dicta, notably Coke CJ in *Dr Bonham's Case* (1610), and *Day v Savidge* (1615), and even post-revolutionary dicta (*City of London v Wood* (1710); *Forbes v Cochrane* (1824)), could be read as asserting that an unreasonable Act of Parliament is void. By the middle of the eighteenth century this had been 'revised' in favour of the modern compromise that the courts interpret statutes so as to avoid an unreasonable or unjust meaning (see Blackstone, 1776, Comm. 91, 160). Blackstone also emphasised the importance of the legislature being 'less corrupt' than the executive thus anticipating the modern position that Parliament might be too corrupt to use its sovereignty against the executive.

By the nineteenth century, parliamentary supremacy met the political needs of the day. It conformed to the extension of democracy and the increasing need for drastic governmental powers of intervention in a changeable industrial society. Case law emerged in support of parliamentary supremacy during the middle of the nineteenth century (e.g. *Lee v Bude and Torrington Railway Co.* (1871); *Edinburgh and Dalkeith Railway Co. v Wauchope* (1842)) which has been consistently confirmed since (see *Manuel v A-G* (1983); *Pickin v British Railways Board* (1974)).

## 7.3 The Meaning of Parliamentary Supremacy

According to Dicey (1915, pp. 37–8):

The principle of parliamentary sovereignty means neither more nor less than this, namely that Parliament has, under the English constitution, the right to make or unmake any law whatever; and further that no person or body is recognised by the law of England as having a right to override or set aside the legislation of Parliament.

This has three aspects which do *not* stand or fall together. Firstly, Parliament has unlimited lawmaking power in the sense that it can make any kind of law. Secondly, the legal validity of laws made by Parliament cannot be questioned by any other body. Thirdly, one Parliament cannot bind a future Parliament.

Dicey tried to split sovereignty into separate legal and political elements, arguing that Parliament was legally sovereign in the sense that the courts must obey it, but not politically sovereign. Dicey described legal sovereignty as 'the power of law making unrestricted by any legal limit' and contrasted this with political sovereignty, as in the sense of the body 'the will of which is ultimately obeyed by the citizens of the state' (1915, p. 70). He recognised both 'internal' and 'external' political limits on the lawmaker. Internal limits are limits inherent in the attitudes of the people who make up Parliament. The political and moral pressures imposed by constitutional conventions, patronage and party discipline are internal limits. The external limits consist in what those subject to the law are prepared to accept. Parliament cannot in practice pass any law it wishes, and its laws might be condemned as morally or politically bad or even as unconstitutional in a broad sense. Dicey thought that political sovereignty lay in the electorate.

Parliamentary supremacy is concerned only with an Act of Parliament (a statute). An Act of Parliament, as the preamble to every Act reminds us, is an Act of the monarch with the consent of the House of Lords and the House of Commons: the Queen in Parliament. In certain circumstances, however, the consent of the House of Lords can be omitted under the Parliament Acts of 1911 and 1949 (Chapter 11). Even if we believe that the House of Commons is the political sovereign, a resolution of the House of Commons has in itself no legal force, except in relation to the internal proceedings of the House (*Bowles* v *Bank of England* (1913); *Stockdale* v *Hansard* (1840)).

Dicey's legal sovereign is therefore divided, comprising three bodies, namely Queen, Lords and Commons. Only in combination can they exercise the power of Parliament. It is not the absolute sovereign of Hobbes for whom the sovereign must be a single unit (Chapter 1). Thus Blackstone, who defended parliamentary supremacy in the eighteenth century, linked the doctrine with that of the mixed constitution (Chapter 6). Indeed at the time Dicey first wrote (1885), the House of Lords had substantial power to block legislation. Dicey's doctrine does not therefore depend on the doubtful assumption that there must be a single ultimate source of power. Indeed Dicey denied that there was a logical need for an ultimate sovereign (1915, p. 143), merely pointing out that the evidence suggested that we have in fact adopted the doctrine of parliamentary supremacy.

We will now examine the three facets of parliamentary supremacy.

### 7.3.1 Freedom to Make Any Kind of Law

Parliament can make any laws it likes irrespective of fairness, justice and practicality; hence Sir Ivor Jennings's famous example that Parliament can make it an offence for Frenchmen to smoke in the streets of Paris (*The Law and the Constitution*, 5th edn, London, University of London Press, 1959, p. 170). The UK courts are bound to obey a statute applying anywhere and whether or not the relevant overseas courts would recognise it is immaterial (e.g. *Manuel* v *A-G* (1983)). It has been said that Parliament cannot make a man a woman, or a woman a man, but this is misleading. The so-called laws of nature are not rules at all. They are simply facts which occur in a predictable pattern. A statute which enacted that all men must be regarded as women and vice versa would no doubt be impractical, but would be legally valid.

Dicey relied on examples of valid statutory provisions that are arguably grossly unjust. However, these examples do not prove that the courts would apply a statute that they consider even more unjust. All Dicey was saying is that the evidence to date was consistent with parliamentary supremacy. Modern cases continue to support Dicey. They include retrospective legislation (*Burmah Oil Co. Ltd* v *Lord Advocate* (1965); War Damage Act 1965); statutes conflicting with international law, (see *Mortensen* v *Peters* (1906), *Cheney* v *Conn* (1968)), or with fundamental civil liberties, (see *R* v *Jordan* (1967)). *Pickin* v *British Railways Board* (1974) goes further since the House of Lords expressly affirmed that the courts must obey any law made by Parliament and could not even examine whether the legislation had been made in good faith in accordance with the proper parliamentary procedures.

### 7.3.2 Parliament Cannot be Overridden

Turning to the second limb of Dicey's formulation – that no other body can override Parliament – firstly, international courts such as the European Court of Human Rights or the European Court of Justice do not have the power to declare an Act of Parliament invalid. Secondly, in the event of a conflict between a statute and some other kind of law, the statute must always prevail. However, this leaves open the possibility that a statute itself might authorise some other lawmaking authority to override statutes. This was probably achieved by the European Communities Act 1972 (below) but still leaves it open to Parliament to repeal the Act in question, thereby cutting away the authority of the other body.

### 7.3.3 Parliament Cannot Bind its Successors

As regards Dicey's third limb, a statute cannot be restricted even by another statute. This is a vital principle, emphasised particularly by republicans at least since the seventeenth century, that no generation should be able to tie the hands of the future. For example, Edmund Burke argued that the 1688 revolution had permanently enshrined a constitution which included the House of Lords. Thomas Paine answered this as follows:

> Every age and generation must be as free to act for itself, in all cases as the ages and generations which preceded it. The vanity and presumption of governing beyond the grave is the most ridiculous and insolent of all tyrannies. (Foot and Kramnick (eds) *The Thomas Paine Reader*, 1987, p. 204)

However, Parliament could bind its successors by abolishing itself, having first created a body with more limited powers or by handing over power to a dictator.

The approach traditionally taken by the English courts makes it relatively easy to override earlier statutes. This is the 'implied repeal' doctrine according to which a later statute that on an ordinary reading is inconsistent with an earlier statute impliedly repeals the earlier statute to the extent of the inconsistency. The court is not required to attempt to reconcile the two, and it is irrelevant that the earlier Act states that it cannot be repealed: *Vauxhall Estates Ltd* v *Liverpool Corporation* (1932); *Ellen Street Estates Ltd* v *Minister of Health* (1934). The *content* of the two statutes must be directly inconsistent. Therefore in *Thoburn* v *Sunderland City Council* (2002), a 1985 statute which allowed goods to be sold in pounds and ounces did not impliedly repeal section 2 (4) of the European Communities Act 1972 which empowered ministers to make regulations altering Acts of Parliament for the purpose of implementing EC law. Regulations were later made requiring only metric units (the 'Metric Martyrs' case).

The implied repeal doctrine, although consistent with parliamentary sovereignty, is not essential to it. It is merely a particular approach to interpretation and there is nothing to prevent a statute from requiring the courts to interpret legislation as overriding another statute only if express or very clear language is used, thus putting a partial brake on change. An example might be a 'notwithstanding' clause, stating that a particular statute shall be repealed only by an Act which expressly states that it is to apply 'notwithstanding' the bill of rights. Similarly section 3 of the Human Rights Act 1998 requires all other statutes to be interpreted in accordance with the rights protected by the Act 'if it is possible to do so' (Chapter 17). The implied repeal doctrine therefore does not apply. In *Thoburn* v *Sunderland City Council* (2002) Laws LJ suggested that the same applies to 'constitutional statutes' (below).

## 7.4 The Ingredients of an Act of Parliament

The courts obey, not Parliament as an institution but a law which counts as a valid 'Act of Parliament'. Two questions arise from this. First, what rules create an Act of Parliament? Second, to what extent can the courts investigate whether these rules have been obeyed? There are complex procedural rules for producing statutes but not all of them affect the validity of a statute. Three kinds or levels of rule can be distinguished:

1. There is the basic definition of a statute as a document that received the assent of the three institutions that comprise the Queen in Parliament. The basic procedural requirements for passing an Act are usually the consents of the three elements, i.e. Queen, Lords and Commons. The Royal Assent signed by the Queen is usually notified to each House separately as a formality but can be pronounced by commissioners before both Houses assembled in the House of Lords (Royal Assent Act 1967).The preamble to a statute invariably recites that the required assents have been given.

   A court is not bound by a document that does not appear on its face to have received the necessary assents but conversely must accept the validity of a document that does so appear (*Prince's Case* (1606); *Hall* v *Hall* (1944)). This is called the 'enrolled Act rule' and precludes the courts from investigating whether the proper procedures have been complied with (*Edinburgh and Dalkeith Railway* v *Wauchope* (1842); *Manuel* v *A-G* (1983)). The official version of a statute was traditionally enrolled upon the Parliament Roll. Today there is no Parliament Roll as such, but two official copies of the Act are in the House of Lords' Library and the Public Record Office.

2. A second layer of rules regulates the relationship between the three institutions. Some are conventions with which the courts are not concerned, for example the rule that the monarch cannot refuse the Royal Assent. Others are statutory. For example the Parliament Acts of 1911 and 1949 restrict the power of the House of Lords to refuse its consent to a bill passed by the Commons. In principle the court should be able to decide whether these rules have been obeyed. However, the Parliament Act 1911 foresaw this possibility, and excluded it by providing that a certificate given by the Speaker under the Act, to the effect that the requirements of the Act have been complied with, is 'conclusive for all purposes and shall not be questioned in any court of law' (Parliament Act 1911 s.3). Similarly, the Regency Act 1937 provides that the Royal Assent can be given by a regent if the monarch is under 18, or ill, or in certain other events. In this case the court may be able to investigate whether the Act has been properly applied on the basis that the enrolled Act rule (above) only applies to the normal Act of Parliament.

3. Thirdly, there is a complex network of rules concerning the composition and procedure of each House. These include the various stages of passage of a bill, voting procedures, and the law governing qualifications for membership of either House. They comprise a mixture of statute, convention and the 'law and custom of Parliament' enforced by the House itself. It is settled that ordinary courts have no jurisdiction to enquire into any matters related to the internal affairs of the House. Quite apart from the enrolled Act rule (above), these are matters of parliamentary privilege and are exclusively within the jurisdiction of the House itself. This is true even if it is alleged that the House has violated a statute, or that a bill has been introduced fraudulently (see *Pickin* v *British Railways Board* (1974)).

## 7.5 Challenging Parliamentary Supremacy

There are various arguments that Parliament can, in particular contexts, be legally limited. Each stands on its own feet so that the acceptance of any one of them, except possibly the common law claim (below) does not affect any other aspect of the doctrine.

### 7.5.1 Grants of Independence

If Parliament were to pass an act giving independence to a piece of territory currently under UK jurisdiction, such as Wales, could a later Act revoke that independence? For example the Canada Act 1982 s.2 provides that 'no Act of the United Kingdom Parliament passed after the Constitution Act 1982 comes into force shall extend to Canada as part of its law'. Although as matter of political reality, the answer is no unless the territory in question either consents or is conquered by force, the legal answer is yes as far as the UK courts are concerned (*British Coal Corporation* v *R* (1935), *Manuel* v *A-G* (1983)). There is however a dictum by Lord Denning in *Blackburn* v *A-G* (1971), that legal theory must give way to practical politics. All his Lordship seems to be saying is that it would be, in a practical sense, impossible for Parliament to reverse a grant of independence. On the other hand, a legal principle that is so out of line with common sense might well be worth reconsidering.

### 7.5.2 Acts of Union: Was Parliament Born Unfree?

The modern UK Parliament is the result of two treaties. First, the Treaty of Union with Scotland, 1706, created the Parliament of Great Britain out of the former Scottish and English Parliaments. The treaty required, among other things, that no laws which concern private rights in Scotland shall be altered 'except for the evident utility of the subjects within Scotland'. There were also powers securing the separate Scottish courts and Presbyterian Church 'for all time coming'. The new Parliament was created by separate Acts of the then Scottish and English Parliaments, giving effect to the treaty (see Act of Union with Scotland 1706). Some Scottish lawyers therefore argue that Parliament was 'born unfree', meaning that the modern Parliament cannot go beyond the terms of the Acts that created it. They suggest that the protected provisions of the Act of Union cannot be altered by Act of Parliament. In effect, the Union created a new Parliament which, in relation to the protected Scottish provisions, does not necessarily have the quality of supremacy inherent in the former English Parliament (see Munro, 1999, pp. 137–42; Upton, 1989, *Law Quarterly Review*, **105**: 79). Another view is that parliamentary supremacy is an evolving doctrine which developed after the Acts of Union.

In the case of Northern Ireland there was a Treaty of Union in 1798, which preserved certain basic rights in Ireland, including the continuance of the Protestant religion and the permanence of the Union itself. The Treaty was confirmed by the Act of Union with Ireland 1800, which created the UK Parliament. The Act covered the whole of Ireland but what is now the Republic of Ireland later left the Union. It might be argued that the Northern Ireland Act 1998 s.1, which provides for the Union to be dissolved if a referendum so votes, would be invalid as contrary to the Act of Union. The 1998 Act makes no express reference to the Act of Union with Ireland, s.2 merely providing that the Act overrides 'previous enactments'. Political circumstances in Northern Ireland make this ambiguity understandable.

The crucial provisions of the Scottish Union have not been altered, but s.37 of the Scotland Act 1998 expressly states that the provisions of the Act are to take priority over the Act of Union. This leaves open the question whether an Act can do this at all. The issue has surfaced in a few cases in all of which an Act of Parliament was obeyed. In *Ex parte Canon Selwyn* (1872) (Ireland), the court denied that it possessed the power to override a statute.

In two Scottish cases, *MacCormick* v *Lord Advocate* (1953) and *Gibson* v *Lord Advocate* (1975), the Scottish courts were able to avoid the issue by holding that no conflict with the Acts of Union arose. However, in both cases the argument in favour of the Acts of Union was regarded as tenable, particularly by Lord Cooper in *MacCormick*. However his Lordship, with the apparent agreement of Lords Keith and Gibson, suggested that the issue might be 'non-justiciable', that is, outside the jurisdiction of the courts and resolvable only by political means. On this view a statute that flouts the Acts of Union may be unconstitutional but not unlawful. In both cases the courts left open the question whether they could interfere if an Act purported to make drastic inroads into the Act of Union, for example by abolishing the whole of Scottish private law (see also *Sillers* v *Smith* (1982)). Thus the courts carefully steered around a constitutional abeyance (Chapter 2).

### 7.5.3    The Redefinition Theory

This is an attempt to circumvent the rule that Parliament cannot bind its successors. The argument has various labels, sometimes being called the 'new view', sometimes the 'entrenchment' argument, sometimes the 'manner and form' theory and sometimes the distinction between continuing and self-embracing sovereignty. It has attracted considerable academic discussion and can draw support from certain overseas cases (see below). Apart from a brief discussion by Slade LJ in *Manuel v A-G* (above) it has not yet surfaced in the English courts.

The redefinition argument is essentially that, if Parliament can do anything, it can prescribe and change what counts as a valid Act of Parliament and in so doing make it difficult to change an Act that it 'entrenches'. It can be supported as follows:

1.  There must be rules of law that tell us what counts as an Act of Parliament and these must be logically prior to Parliament which can speak only through these rules. These rules therefore define Parliament: without them Parliament is merely a rabble of individuals. I outlined earlier what they are, namely that an Act of Parliament requires the consent of the Queen, the Lords, and the Commons.
2.  The courts are obliged to apply only a law that has a valid pedigree in this sense. A document which purports to be an Act of Parliament but which has not been passed according to these basic rules has no legal force.
3.  The crucial question therefore is whether an Act of Parliament itself can modify the rules which prescribe what counts as an Act of Parliament. If Parliament can do anything then we must concede that it can indeed do so. Suppose for example a statute enacts a bill of rights and goes on to say that 'no law shall be passed that is inconsistent with the bill of rights nor shall this statute be repealed expressly or impliedly without a referendum of the people'. What Parliament has done in this example is to add to the existing requirement of Queen, Lords and Commons a further requirement of a referendum. An entrenched statute can therefore still be repealed but not without the special procedure.
4.  Those who reject the above argument argue that if Parliament ignores the special procedure, the courts will simply obey the most recent Act of Parliament and thus treat the special procedure as impliedly repealed. However, this misses the point since a document that has not been produced under the special procedure is not a valid statute and so must be ignored, just as an ordinary law would be ignored if it did not have the Royal Assent. Parliament would remain supreme but would,

for the purpose of the statute that it is intended to protect, now mean for Queen, Lords, Commons and referendum.

5. Some would go further and argue that the special 'entrenching' provision could consist of a procedure within the traditional Parliament, for example a two-thirds majority of the Commons being required to repeal a particular statute. However, this weaker form of entrenchment seems to fall foul of the rule that the courts cannot inquire in the internal procedures within each House.

On the other hand a statute could expressly empower the courts to investigate the internal procedures.

Judicial support for the redefinition theory exists but is slender. It has been accepted in two commonwealth cases (*A-G for New South Wales* v *Trethowen* (1932) and *Bribery Commissioner* v *Ranasinghe* (1965)) (Privy Council) and in a South African case (*Harris* v *Minister of the Interior* (1952)). *Trethowen* went so far as to suggest that the court could grant an injunction to prevent a bill being submitted for the Royal Assent if it did not comply with the entrenched procedure. This seems unlikely to apply in England since the courts have consistently refused to interfere with the conduct of parliamentary proceedings. The issue would arise in the UK if a court were asked to obey a document that fails to comply with an entrenched provision.

These cases are ambiguous authority. *Trethowen*, *Ranasinghe* and *Harris* have been explained on the basis that the legislatures in these countries were not truly supreme in the same way as the UK Parliament. Thus in *Trethowen* and *Harris* a UK Act had established the powers of the legislatures in question, and in *Ranasinghe* the relevant entrenching power was contained in a written constitution. On the other hand, in *Trethowen*, the relevant UK Act (the Colonial Laws Validity Act 1865) provided that the New South Wales Parliament had complete lawmaking power as far as internal matters were concerned. However, when *Trethowen* reached the Privy Council it was emphasised that the case turned on the fact that a subordinate legislature was involved (see [1932] AC at 526). In *Harris* the Statute of Westminster 1931 had given the South African Parliament unlimited lawmaking power. Moreover, the court stressed that its reasoning did not assume that the Parliament was in any sense subordinate. Indeed in both *Trethowen* and *Ranasinghe* there were dicta that the same arguments might apply to the UK Parliament. It was said in *Ranasinghe* (at p. 198) that the entrenched clause argument does not limit parliamentary supremacy, but merely changes the way in which that supremacy must be exercised.

The issue also arose in *Manuel* v *A-G* (1983). A peculiarity of the Canadian Constitution was that certain changes to it could only be made by the UK Parliament. Canada wished to enact a new constitution free from this remnant of empire. A group of Canadian Indians brought an action in the English courts arguing that the Canada Act 1982 (a UK Act giving effect to Canada's wishes) was invalid because it was passed without the request or consent of Canada's Indian nations whose consent was arguably required under s.4 of the Statute of Westminster 1931, a UK statute. Megarry J at first instance applied the traditional principle that no court can refuse to obey an Act of Parliament and struck out the action. However, the Court of Appeal avoided grappling with the problem of parliamentary supremacy by pointing out that s.4 did not say that that actual consent was required, but only that the Act must 'declare' that the relevant consent had been given. The Canada Act contained the required declaration and whether or not it was true was therefore legally irrelevant. The Court of Appeal was prepared at least to recognise the possibility that if an Act stated that a consent must actually be given, then an attempt to pass an Act without that consent could be invalid even from the UK perspective.

It has also been suggested that the UK Parliament has redefined itself several times. Thus, the Parliament Acts 1911 and 1949 provide that in certain circumstances a bill can receive the Royal Assent without the consent of the House of Lords. Under the Regency Act 1937 the powers of the monarch can be exercised by certain other people when the monarch is indisposed or absent. However, none of this legislation places any limitations upon the powers of Parliament. Moreover, even if these provisions can be regarded as redefining Parliament, there is no need for a court to follow the logic of this to its conclusion so as to permit any kind of redefinition. On the other hand, the argument at least opens the way to the redefinition possibility.

The most formidable challenge to the 'redefinition' argument comes from Professor H.W.R. Wade (1955). Wade argues that the meaning of 'Parliament' is 'fixed' by a rule which is 'above and beyond the reach of Parliament'. Parliament cannot simply make itself supreme, so there must be some independent explanation of why it is so. Wade argues that the explanation lies in the events of 1688 which created the fundamental rule of our constitution, a rule that is unique in character, a 'grundnorm': essentially a political principle standing outside and above the ordinary legal system and giving it its validity. Wade goes on to argue that, because this rule gave Parliament its power, it cannot be altered by Parliament, so that Parliament remains as monarch, Lords and Commons, and any attempt to redefine Parliament, for example, by adding a referendum, would be ineffective. Thus, paradoxically, Wade supports the traditional notion that Parliament can do anything by admitting that there is one thing Parliament cannot do, that is to alter its own definition.

Wade regards laws passed under the Parliament Acts 1911 and 1949 (which has been used only 5 times), as not being truly Acts of Parliament, but special forms of delegated legislation. Indeed, according to this argument the 1949 Act, which limited the delaying period even further, might be invalid on the basis that a delegated body cannot enlarge its own powers, at least without clear authority to do so (*R v Burah* (1878)). For the same reason the House of Lords could not be abolished under the Parliament Act machinery. Indeed, if Wade's 'higher law' argument is accepted, it may not be possible lawfully to abolish the House of Lords at all.

Wade accepts that the doctrine of parliamentary supremacy could in political reality be abolished, but would regard this as a revolution, that is, the introduction of an entirely new basic principle. How will we know whether such a revolution has taken place? Wade would place the matter in the 'keeping of the courts', so that if the courts were to accept the redefinition theory this would authoritatively signify the 'revolution'. From this Wade concludes (1980, p. 37) that one way to ensure that a bill of rights prevailed over a later statute would be to make the judges swear a new form of judicial oath, one of loyalty to the bill of rights rather than to justice according to law. Those such as Sir John Laws who support the rule of law ideal that the courts are the guardians of constitutional values have rallied behind Wade's argument (below, and Chapters 5, 6).

There are difficulties with Professor Wade's argument. For example why should there be a single grundnorm at all? In particular why should the meaning of parliamentary supremacy be frozen in time as of 1688? Could the doctrine rather be seen as one of continuous evolution? Moreover, the notion of revolution is usually confined to a change that is either violent or entirely outside the existing framework of law. A change brought about in accordance with the existing rules, which is the basis of the redefinition argument, is surely worth distinguishing from a revolution. Indeed, it seems a misuse of language not to do so. Moreover, even if we accept the idea of Wade's 'higher rule' this does not exclude the redefinition theory. Why should the higher rule, supposedly made by those in charge of the 1688 revolution, not authorise its creature – Parliament – to alter the rule itself? Wade believes that the courts can alter parliamentary supremacy just as Parliament can authorise ministers to make regulations altering future statutes, but denies that Parliament can do so. Neither logic nor practical politics, nor indeed historical evidence, points inevitably to this. At this rarefied level, politics and law are inextricably intermingled. If the courts accept a 'redefinition of Parliament' Wade would call it a revolution. Others might regard the court as having resolved a basic ambiguity within the existing constitution, sometimes described as 'continuing or self-embracing sovereignty'. In either case the ultimate criterion is public opinion.

### 7.5.4  The European Union

The European Union and its powers were created by a series of treaties between the member states. Member states are obliged under the treaties to give effect to those community laws that are intended by the Communities to be binding within domestic law. However, the law of the European Union (strictly speaking, the law of the European Community which is the institutional backbone of the Union) is applied to the legal systems of each member state in accordance with the laws of that state. It is sometimes argued that the UK has therefore surrendered part of parliamentary supremacy (see *Blackburn* v *A-G* (1971)). If this is right then a democratic body has committed the sin of trying to bind the freedom of future generations. We shall discuss the effect of EC law in more detail in Chapter 8 but will outline the matter of sovereignty here.

In English law a treaty as such cannot change the law but must first be incorporated into an Act of Parliament. The European Communities Act 1972 incorporated EC law into the UK constitution. Another Act of Parliament could repeal the 1972 Act, the question being how strong would be the language required to do so. The European Communities Act 1972 s.2 (4) states that 'any enactment, passed or to be passed ... shall be construed and have effect subject to the foregoing provisions of this section'. The provisions referred to require among other things that the English courts must give effect to certain laws made by European bodies (s.2 (1)). Section 3 of the Act also requires UK courts to follow the decisions of the European Court of Justice which is the court of the EC. Not surprisingly this court favours the supremacy of the EC (see *Costa* v *ENEL* (1964)). However, the significance of EC law depends entirely on UK constitutional law and in particular on the common law's attitude to parliamentary supremacy (see *Thoburn* v *Sunderland City Council* (2002) [57]–[59]). On the one hand, there is no reason why parliamentary supremacy should not be abandoned in favour of EC law. On the other hand, the evidence is at present inconclusive.

The effect of the above provisions seems to be that a UK statute, even one passed after the relevant EC law, must give way to EC law. This is often described as 'disapplying' an Act. There is a strong presumption of interpretation that the clearest language is needed to displace the primacy of EC law. The doctrine of implied repeal is therefore displaced but, as we said earlier, this is not essential to parliamentary supremacy. Normally therefore if a UK statute is inconsistent with a directly applicable EC law, the EC law must be applied. *R* v *Secretary of State for Transport ex parte Factortame* (1990), concerned a clash between the European Treaty and the Merchant Shipping Act 1988. Lord Bridge said at 140: 'By virtue of s.2 (4) of the Act of 1972, Part II of the 1988 Act is to be construed and take effect subject to directly enforceable community rights ... This has precisely the same effect as if a section were incorporated in ... the 1988 Act ... which enacted that the provisions were to be without prejudice to the directly enforceable community rights of nationals of any member state of the (EC).' (See also *Equal Opportunities Commission* v *Secretary of State* (1994). Lord Bridge's dictum indicates that the matter is still one of interpretation. A statute that unambiguously states that it is to override European law will arguably prevail (see *Garland* v *British Rail Engineering Ltd* (BREL) (1983), c.f. Wade (1996) 112 *Law Quarterly Review* 568 regarding *Factortame* as a constitutional revolution). Thus, there is a general obligation to interpret UK legislation to conform to EC laws thereby avoiding possible conflicts. *Thoburn* v *Sunderland City Council* (2002) accepted that the doctrine of implied repeal has to that extent been excluded.

### 7.5.5  The Common Law

As we saw in Chapter 5 the courts do not interpret statutes mechanically but will apply them in the context of the 'rule of law' which embodies respect for fundamental values and individual rights. There are many presumptions of statutory interpretation, the overall effect of which is that Parliament must use very clear language if it wishes to override values of fairness and justice developed by the courts. The difficulty is to draw the line between interpretation of and outright disobedience to a statute. *Anisminic Ltd* v *Foreign Compensation Commission* (1969) is sometimes regarded as a judicial attempt to subvert Parliament under the cloak of interpretation. The applicant challenged a ruling by the Commission that it was not eligible for compensation under a statutory scheme. The governing Act included an ouster clause designed to protect the Commission against challenge in the courts. This stated that a 'determination' of the Commission 'under the Act' shall not be questioned in any court of law. Nevertheless the House of Lords, applying a presumption that the jurisdiction of the courts should not be excluded, allowed the challenge on the ground that a ruling which was flawed by an error of law was a nullity and so did not count as a 'determination under the Act' within the meaning of the ouster clause. This reasoning has been criticised as collapsing the distinction between interpreting a statute and overriding one.

The contrary argument is that Parliament legislates in the knowledge of basic common law values, which, in accordance with the rule of law, it can be taken to accept unless it clearly states otherwise (see *R* v *Secretary of State ex parte Pierson* (1998) per Lord Steyn, *R* v *Secretary of State ex parte Simms* (1999) per Lord Hoffmann. Far from being radical, the *Anisminic* reasoning was fully documented in the old cases. Therefore Parliament could have anticipated the line that the court might take and have used tighter language if it wanted to exclude challenge, thereby making explicit that it was overriding widely shared values. This compromise has been rationalised by claiming that there is 'dual sovereignty' between Parliament and the courts. For example in *X Ltd v Morgan Grampian Publishers Ltd* [1990] 2 All ER 1 at 13, Lord Bridge referred to the 'twin foundations' of the rule of law namely 'the sovereignty of the Queen in Parliament in making the law and the sovereignty of the Queen's courts in interpreting and applying the law'. In *Hamilton v Al Fayed* [1999] 3 All ER 317 at 320, Lord Woolf MR referred to 'the wider constitutional principle of mutuality of respect between two constitutional sovereignties'.

Indeed some writers such as Allan (below) suggest that the courts might actually strike down or at least disapply an Act of Parliament that violates basic constitutional values such as access to the courts. This issue links with Wade's view (above) that parliamentary sovereignty is 'in the keeping of the courts'. As we have seen, a few cases such as *Dr Bonham's Case* (1610) suggest this possibility but at least since Tudor times there has been no serious challenge to parliamentary supremacy. Nevertheless in the absence of a written constitution it is not possible to exclude judicial rejection of the doctrine. Indeed, the courts themselves inevitably have to decide the limits of their own powers when a case comes before them (Chapter 6). Thus it has been said:

> whoever hath an absolute authority to interpret any written or spoken laws, it is he who is truly the lawgiver and not the person who just spoke or wrote them. (Bishop Hoadley's sermon preached before the King, 1717)

While the courts have pushed interpretation a long way they have not yet overridden an Act of Parliament. Contemporary judges in the main support ultimate parliamentary supremacy but are sometimes ambivalent. For example in *R v Lord Chancellor's Department ex parte Witham* [1997] 2 All ER 779 at 783, Laws J asserted that:

> In the unwritten legal order of the British State, at a time when the common law continues to accord a legislative supremacy to Parliament, the notion of a constitutional right can in my judgement inhere only in this proposition that the right in question cannot be abrogated by the state save by specific provision in an Act of Parliament ... General words will not suffice. And any such rights will be creatures of the common law, since their existence would not be the consequence of the democratic process but would be logically prior to it.

*Thoburn v Sunderland City Council* (2002) [62]–[64] Laws LJ stated that a 'constitutional statute' would be similarly protected, in the sense of a statute 'which conditions the legal relationships between citizen and state in some general overarching manner, or enlarges or diminishes the scope of what are now regarded as fundamental rights'. There are also extra-judicial suggestions that parliamentary supremacy may be conditional on compliance with fundamental values (see Woolf, 1995; Sedley, in Nolan and Sedley, 1997, p. 26).

Allan (2001) argues that it is inconsistent with the political assumptions of a liberal society on which the rule of law is based that the legislature, or indeed any part of the government, should be all powerful all being subject to the same overarching principles. Allan claims that, in the common law tradition, the courts have the duty to protect the fundamental values of the society. Relying on the fact that the court is concerned not with the statute generally but with its application to the individual case, Allan suggests that the court can legitimately hold that a statute which appears to be grossly unjust in the particular context does not apply to the particular case. This approach could be reconciled with parliamentary supremacy on the basis that Parliament cannot foresee every implication of the laws it makes and can be assumed to respect the rule of law. In *Cooper* v *Wandsworth Board of Works* (1863), Byles J put the matter more strongly when he said that 'the justice of the common law will supply the omission of the legislature'.

Those supporting the courts might argue in favour of the high standard of public reasoned argument practiced in the courts and the relative objectivity and independence of judges. A much canvassed argument is that the representative democracy which gives Parliament its legitimacy is an imperfect democracy and does not necessarily reflect the views of a majority of voters (see *R* v *Secretary of State ex parte Fire Brigades Union*, (1995); Chapter 6). In particular Parliament has become dominated by the executive. Thus the usual defence of Parliament, that it can make laws which are informed by a wider range of opinions than are available to a court and which carry the consent of those subject to them, can be presented as hollow. On the other hand, it seems somewhat bizarre to remedy a failure of democracy by suggesting an even more undemocratic mechanism.

Those supporting Parliament (e.g. Waldron) might point to the indignity of political decisions being made on their behalf by people we have not chosen and also the fact that judges are not accountable. They might also deny that the legal attitude to liberal issues should have a privileged status whereas Parliament comprises a larger cross-section of the community that can make a better informed decision. The liberal values that the rule of law embraces are widely accepted but they are not peculiar to law. They are applied by all public decision makers but in different ways in different contexts. Moreover, such ideas as freedom and equality are the source of much disagreement which judges are not qualified to resolve.

Dicey thought that the rule of law and parliamentary supremacy supported each other (1915, Chapter 3). He argued that Parliament is not a single body but three entities defined by law, each of which checked the other. He thus relied on the mixed constitution. Secondly, he pointed out that Parliament could act only through the medium of law. It has no executive powers and depends on independent courts to apply and interpret its laws. The courts need not give a statute the meaning that Parliament itself would have placed upon it and can bring rule of law values and legal ideas of 'reason' to bear. This relies on the separation of powers (Chapter 6). Thirdly, the rule of law 'necessitates' parliamentary supremacy in that the executive cannot interfere with the individual without obtaining legal powers from Parliament, again a separation of powers argument. A democrat might also argue that the parliamentary rules provided by law ensure that a wide range of opinions can be taken into account as part of the lawmaking process and that Parliament cannot be interfered with by nondemocratic forces. In this sense the rule of law supports parliamentary supremacy. On the other hand, Parliament, if it is indeed supreme, could change the law by abolishing all democratic and separation of powers safeguards, including those provided by the courts.

Dicey's view depended on the pivotal role which he thought that the House of Lords played in checking the excesses of democracy and upon his assumption that the common law was the guardian of basic values. Today the House of Lords is subordinate to the Commons and, as we have seen, there is no longer widespread agreement, if there ever was, as to what the values of the constitution should be. In his later years Dicey realised that the power of political parties, an increasingly diverse electorate, external threats and the need for governments to provide expensive public services put the traditional place of Parliament as the centre of the constitution into question.

## 7.6 Conclusion

The doctrine of parliamentary supremacy rests on frail foundations. There seems to be no logical answer to the question whether the common law or any other source of authority can override Parliament. Both kinds of law ultimately depend on nothing more than public acceptance. Thus the answer lies in empirical evidence and in political argument. For example, there is still controversy in the USA as to whether the Supreme Court in *Marbury* v *Madison* (1803) was right to hold that a written constitution entitles the courts to rule upon compliance with it.

Parliamentary supremacy was a historical response to political circumstances and it does not follow that the same response is appropriate today. The period during which Dicey promoted the doctrine (before the First World War) was one of relative political stability and economic prosperity for the UK. The people, or at least the majority, were benefiting from the spoils of empire, and belief that Parliament backed by consensus values could deliver stability and prosperity was still plausible. Popular revolution as experienced elsewhere had been staved off by cautious reforms. Latterly, different forces, both domestic and international, have arisen which have made parliamentary sovereignty appear parochial, politically unreal and intellectually threadbare. These forces include the global economy, devolution, membership of the European Union and other international obligations, and the increasing powers of the executive over Parliament. There is no longer a political consensus that Parliament should be legally unlimited and no compelling legal reason why it should be.

## 7.7 Note: Delegated Legislation

The doctrine of parliamentary supremacy concerns Acts of Parliament. In practice, however, most English legislation consists of delegated or subordinate legislation. Unlike Acts of Parliament delegated legislation, in common with other executive actions can be challenged in the courts (Chapter 14). Delegated legislation comprises laws made outside Parliament, usually by ministers but also by the Privy Council, and by statutory bodies such as local authorities. Laws made by the devolved governments are also subordinate legislation. Such lawmaking is possible only under powers which are conferred by an Act of Parliament (the 'parent' Act). It is commonplace for a statute to lay down a general principle and then to confer power upon a minister to make detailed rules fleshing out the principle. Delegated lawmaking powers are sometimes very wide, and often permit the minister to implement or alter Acts of Parliament past or future (the 'Henry VIII' clause, e.g. European Communities Act 1972 s.2 (4), (above), Deregulation and Contracting Out Act 1994, Pollution Prevention and Control Act 1999) (see Barber, N. and Young, A. [2003] *Public Law* 112).

Delegated legislation has often been criticised on constitutional grounds and is an infringement of the separation of powers. Delegated legislation can be made without the public and democratic processes represented, albeit imperfectly, by Parliament. However, it is difficult to imagine a complex and highly regulated society that could function effectively if all laws had to be made by Parliament itself (see *Committee on Ministers Powers* (1932), Cmd 4060). Most delegated legislation is subject to a limited amount of parliamentary scrutiny (see Chapter 11).

Delegated legislation comes under many names, including, for example, regulations, orders, directions, rules, bylaws. Little hinges on the terminology used. However, a compendium term, 'statutory instrument', applies to most delegated legislation made by ministers and to Statutory Orders in Council (Statutory Instruments Act 1946). Statutory instruments must be formally published, and, in accordance with the rule of law, it is a defence in criminal proceedings to show that an instrument has not been published and that it is not reasonable to expect the accused to be aware of it (ibid., s.4). However, it seems that failure to publish does not affect validity for other purposes (see *R* v *Sheer Metalcraft* (1954)).

# Summary

▶ The doctrine of parliamentary supremacy provides the fundamental legal premise of the UK constitution. The doctrine means that an Act of Parliament must be obeyed by the courts, that later Acts prevail over earlier ones, and that rules made by external bodies, for example under international law, cannot override Acts of Parliament. It does not follow that Parliament is supreme politically although the line between legal and political supremacy is blurred.

▶ Parliamentary supremacy rests on frail foundations. Without a written constitution it is impossible to be sure as to its legal basis other than as an evolving practice which is usually said to depend on the 1688 revolution. It is possible to maintain that the common law is really supreme.

▶ Parliament is itself a creature of the law. The customary and statutory rules which have evolved since medieval times determine that, except in special cases, Parliament for this purpose means the Queen with the assent of the House of Lords and House of Commons. The courts can determine whether any document is an Act of Parliament in this sense, but cannot inquire into whether the correct procedure within each House has been followed.

▶ The doctrine has two separate aspects: first, that the courts must obey Acts of Parliament in preference to any other kind of legal authority, and second, that no body, including Parliament itself, can place legal limits upon the freedom of action of a future Parliament. The first of these principles is generally accepted, but the second is open to dispute.

▶ The implied repeal doctrine is sometimes promoted as an aspect of parliamentary supremacy but is merely a presumption of interpretation.

▶ The doctrine of parliamentary supremacy is subject to considerable attack:

- grants of independence to dependent territories; these can probably be revoked lawfully in the eyes of UK courts
- the possibility that parts of the Acts of Union with Scotland and Ireland are unchangeable: this is probably outside the courts' jurisdiction
- the 'redefinition' argument proposes that by altering the basic requirements for lawmaking Parliament can effectively limit itself, just as it could if it abolished itself in favour of a more limited body
- the idea that Parliament limited the freedom of future Parliaments in relation to certain laws made by the European Communities. The implied repeal principle has been modified but Parliament probably retains the ultimate power to override an EC rule.
- the role of the common law as constituting 'dual sovereignty' through the court's exclusive power to interpret Acts of Parliament leading to argument that parliamentary supremacy is conditional upon acceptance by the courts. This links with the extended version of the rule of law which was discussed in Chapter 5. The question of the ultimate source

## Summary cont'd

of power cannot be answered within the legal system alone but depends on public acceptance.

▶ Dicey attempted to reconcile parliamentary supremacy with the rule of law by pointing out that Parliament is defined by law and can act only through the instrument of law so that independent judges interpret its legislation. This relies on the separation of powers.

▶ Acts of Parliament must be distinguished from delegated legislation. The latter can be set aside by the courts on the ordinary grounds of judicial review.

# Exercises

7.1 Trace the development of the doctrine of parliamentary supremacy. Has it a secure legal basis?

7.2 To what extent, if at all, has the doctrine of parliamentary supremacy been affected by the 'redefinition theory'?

7.3 'Every age and generation must be as free to act for itself, in all cases as the ages and generations which preceded it. The vanity and presumption of governing beyond the grave is the most ridiculous and insolent of all tyrannies' (Thomas Paine). Discuss.

7.4 Marshal the arguments for and against the proposition that the UK Parliament cannot repeal the Act of Union with Scotland.

7.5 To what extent is it useful to distinguish between legal and political sovereignty? Do you agree with Dicey's attempt to do so?

7.6 Consider the validity and effect of the following provisions contained in (fictitious) Acts of Parliament:

(i) 'There shall be a bill of rights in the UK and no Act to be enacted at any time in the future shall have effect, in as far as it is inconsistent with the bill of rights, unless it has been assented to by a two-thirds majority of both Houses of Parliament and no Act shall repeal this Act unless it has the same two-thirds majority.'

(ii) 'No bill shall be introduced into either House of Parliament which purports to affect the established Church of England unless it recites on its face that it has the prior approval of the Synod of the Church of England.'

(iii) 'There shall be no parliamentary elections for 50 years.'

(iv) 'This Act shall apply notwithstanding any contrary rule of European Community law'.

**7.7** 'The sovereignty of Parliament and the supremacy of the law of the land – the two principles which pervade the whole of the English constitution may appear to stand in opposition to each other, or to be at best countervailing forces. But this appearance is delusive' (Dicey). Discuss.

**7.8** In *X Ltd* v *Morgan Grampian Publishers Ltd* [1990] 2 All ER 1 at 13, Lord Bridge referred to the 'twin foundations' of the rule of law namely 'the sovereignty of the Queen in Parliament in making the law and the sovereignty of the Queen's courts in interpreting and applying the law'. In *Hamilton* v *Al Fayed* [1999] 3 All ER 317 at 320, Lord Woolf MR referred to 'the wider constitutional principle of mutuality of respect between two constitutional sovereignties'. Critically discuss.

**7.9** 'Whoever hath an absolute authority to interpret any written or spoken laws, it is he who is truly the lawgiver and not the person who just spoke or wrote them' (Bishop Hoadley's sermon, preached before the King, 1717).

## Further reading

Allan, T. (1997) 'Parliamentary sovereignty: law, politics and revolution', *Law Quarterly Review,* **113**: 443.

Allan, T. (2001) *Constitutional Justice,* Oxford, Oxford University Press, Chapter 7.

Allan, T. (2002) 'Constitutional Foundations', *Cambridge Law Journal,* 87.

Bradley, A. (2000) in Jowell, J. and Oliver, D. (eds) *The Changing Constitution,* 4th edn, Oxford, Oxford University Press.

Craig, P. (2003) 'Constitutional Foundations, the Rule of Law and Supremacy', *Public Law* 92.

Elliott, M. (1997) 'Reconciling Constitutional Rights and Constitutional Orthodoxy', *Cambridge Law Journal,* **56**: 474.

Goldsworthy, J. (1999) *The Sovereignty of Parliament: History and Philosophy,* Oxford, Oxford University Press, Chapters 1, 2, 9, 10.

Goldsworthy, J. (2001) in Campbell, T., Ewing, K.D. and Tompkins, A. (eds), *Sceptical Essays on Human Rights,* Oxford, Oxford University Press.

Laws, Sir J. (1993) 'Is the High Court the guardian of fundamental constitutional rights?', *Public Law* 59.

Laws, Sir J. (1995) 'Law and Democracy', *Public Law* 72.

MacCormick, N. (1978) 'Does the United Kingdom have a constitution? Reflections on MacCormack v Lord Advocate', *Northern Ireland Law Quarterly,* **29**: 1.

MacCormick, N. (1993) 'Beyond the sovereign state' *Modern Law Review,* **56**: 1.

Marshall, G. (1971) *Constitutional Theory,* Oxford, Clarendon Press, Chapter 3.

Munro, C.R. (1999) *Studies in Constitutional Law,* 2nd edn, London, Butterworth, Chapters 5, 6.

**Further reading cont'd**

Nolan, Lord and Sedley, Sir S. (1997) *The Making and Remaking of the British Constitution,* London, Blackstone Press, Chapter 6.

Wade, H.W.R. [1955] 'The basis of legal sovereignty', *Cambridge Law Journal,* 172.

Winterton, G. (1976), 'The British Grundnorm: Parliamentary Supremacy Re-examined', *Law Quarterly Review,* **92**: 591.

# Chapter 8

# The European Union

> Europe has never existed. It is not the addition of national sovereignties in a conclave that creates an entity. One must genuinely create Europe.
> (Jean Monnet, 1888–1979)

## Key words

- ▶ Federation or confederation?
- ▶ Democratic accountability
- ▶ Variable geometry
- ▶ Politicised court?
- ▶ Supremacy?
- ▶ Market liberalism
- ▶ Balance of power between members

In this chapter we shall discuss the main legal principles relating to the European Union as they affect the UK constitution. We shall therefore not discuss the internal workings of the EU except from this perspective. Readers should also refer to Chapter 7 which discusses the impact of the EU on parliamentary supremacy.

## 8.1  The Nature of the European Union

What was originally called the European Communities or the Common Market was created after World War II as an aspiration to prevent further wars in Europe and to regenerate the European economies. The prototype was the European Coal and Steel Community created by the Treaty of Paris 1951. The other communities were created in 1957 by two Treaties of Rome. They are the European Community (EC) (formerly called the European Economic Community) and the European Atomic Energy Community. In 1992, under the Maastricht Treaty, the European Union was created as an umbrella political organisation. However, the legal powers are exercised by the communities, the Union as such having no legal identity. The various legal institutions are shared by the communities and some of them, but not the European Court, are used by the Union although the legal basis for this is unclear.

The founder members were France, Germany, Italy, Luxembourg, Belgium and the Netherlands. The UK became a member in 1972 and, by virtue of the European Communities Act 1972, laws made by EC bodies are binding in English law. There are now 25 members including former communist countries, thereby altering the original balance and introducing a wide range of economic, political, cultural and religious perspectives which challenge the old-fashioned republicanism and liberalism blend of the founder members. Members who joined at later dates are Austria, Denmark, Finland, Greece, Ireland, Portugal, Spain and Sweden. The following joined in 2004 under the Nice Treaty (2000): Cyprus, Czech Republic, Estonia, Hungary, Latvia, Lithuania, Malta, Poland, Slovakia and Slovenia. Bulgaria and Romania will join in 2007 and Turkey wishes to join.

The EC is by far the most important of the communities and responsible for most of the legal and political activity. The objectives of the communities were originally exclusively economic, primarily to encourage free trade between member states, but the organisation was heavily influenced by a desire to protect agricultural interests espoused principally by France. This has left the EU with a heavy financial burden in that about 65% of its budget is still devoted to agricultural subsidies. The interests of the European Union have steadily widened, partly by a process of interpreting the existing objectives liberally and partly by the member states formally agreeing to extend the areas of competence of the EC. In particular, the Single European Act of 1986 made environmental protection a separate area of competence. The Union has also developed a substantial security and foreign policy perspective. The political dynamics of the EU are generated firstly by tensions between European Union institutions and national governments that wish to retain their sovereignty and secondly by tensions between large and small nations. There are few areas of UK law that are immune from EC influence which was famously described by Lord Denning as an 'incoming tide' (*Bulmer* v *Bollinger* (1974)).

The Single European Act of 1986 marked a significant increase in the powers of the EC by increasing the matters that could be decided by majority vote, thereby reducing the power of individual states to protect their independence by vetoing measures to which they objected. By the Treaty on European Union (Maastricht Treaty) of 1992 the political but not the legal dimensions of the communities have been subsumed within the broader notion of the 'European Union', a process which was consolidated by the Amsterdam Treaty in 1997. Since *Maastricht* there has been substantial political concern that the process of European integration should be restrained, not least because the European Union is widely regarded as undemocratic. Indeed, the Amsterdam Treaty (1997) introduced safeguards and flexibility arrangements in favour of national governments which can opt out of certain provisions. Involvement in the European enterprise is therefore multi-layered, sometimes described as 'variable geometry'.

The *Maastricht* Treaty also instigated progress towards monetary union, including the creation of an independent European Central Bank. There is now a single European currency, the 'Euro', which is regulated by the European Central Bank (Art. 4). The UK does not participate in this. Those states within the 'eurozone' are subject to central economic regulation by the European Central Bank which has no formal democratic accountability. The possible effect of the single currency upon the powers of the UK Parliament is one reason why the decision whether or not to join the Euro is widely regarded as raising important constitutional issues. The current government has promised that the decision will be taken only after a referendum. There is also freedom of movement between the mainland European Union states under the Schenken Agreement. The UK is not a party to this.

The treaties, which were amended and consolidated with effect from February 1 2003 by the *Nice* Treaty (above) arguably form a crude constitution. The main treaty from a legal perspective is the EC Treaty, the successor to the original Treaty of Rome. The European Union is based on the Treaty of European Union (TEU) (Maastricht, 1993). The treaties are 'framework treaties' that allow the institutions to develop laws and policies, and indeed other institutions for the purpose of closer integration between the member states. The aims of the EC set out in Art. 2 of the EC Treaty are as follows:

> to promote throughout the Community a harmonious, balanced and sustainable development of economic activities, a high level of employment and of social protection, equality between men and women, sustainable and non-inflationary growth, a high degree of competitiveness and convergence of economic performance, a high level of protection and improvement of the quality of the environment, the raising of the standard of living and quality of life, and economic and social cohesion and solidarity among Member States.

All EC acts must fall within the powers conferred by the EC Treaty and cannot go beyond 'what is necessary for achieving the objects of this Treaty' (Art. 5). However, by virtue of Art. 308 the Council acting unanimously can create additional powers:

> if action by the Community should prove necessary to attain, in the course of the operations of the common market, one of the objectives of the Community and this treaty has not provided the necessary powers.

In some cases, notably aspects of agriculture, the EC has 'exclusive competence' in which case member states cannot legislate independently in the areas in question, at least once the EC has decided to intervene. This as a device similar to a federal constitution (Chapter 4). In other cases the principle of 'subsidiarity' applies (Art. 5). This requires the Community to intervene 'only if and in so far as the objects of the proposed action cannot be achieved by the Member States and can therefore, by reason of the scale or effects of the proposed action, be better achieved by the community.' The absence of logic and the vagueness of this formulation is obvious.

In 1991 the European Court of Justice, which is charged not only with securing compliance with the law but also with advancing the aims of the communities, described the Treaty as a 'constitutional charter' based on the rule of law. It emphasised that individuals as well as states are the subjects of community law although in fact, individuals other than those employed by the EC have only limited rights to instigate proceedings in the court (see *Opinion on the Draft Agreement on a European Economic Area* [1991] ECR 1-6084; see also Mancini, 'The Making of a Constitution for Europe' in Keohan and Hoffman (eds) *The New European Community: Decision Making and Institutional Change*, 1991).

There is currently a proposed European Constitution agreed in 2004 which will rationalise the complex treaty provisions, and revise the internal voting arrangements and distribution of powers in order to cater for the enlarged membership. It recites the familiar litany of rhetorical and conflicting claims in favour of liberal democracy and the rule of law, fundamental rights, subsidiarity, national identity of member states, and the supremacy of EC law. Some of this defies understanding, for example:

> Convinced that thus united in its diversity Europe offers them the chance of pursuing, with due regard for the rights of each individual and in awareness of their responsibilities towards future generations and the Earth the great venture which makes it a special area of human hope. (Preamble)

It also asserts the principle of supremacy of EC law:

> The constitution and law adopted by the Union's institutions in exercising competences conferred on it, shall have primacy over the laws of the member states. (Art. 1-5a)

However this cannot in itself affect the legal position which depends on the constitution of each member state. To a certain extent, all member states have already accepted the supremacy of EC law.

The constitution creates a fixed-term President of the Council (below) and a minister responsible for foreign affairs, makes the European Union a legal entity capable of entering into international treaties in its own right and introduces a Charter of Rights. As regards the controversial matter of foreign policy, the constitution requires members to conform to an agreed European Union policy, thereby affecting a basic aspect of sovereignty. It must be approved by all member states including the UK and is unlikely to take effect, if at all, in the forseeable future.

## 8.2 Community Institutions

The Community has lawmaking, executive and judicial powers which are blended in a unique way that does not correspond to traditional notions of the separation of powers or liberal democracy. The primary concern is to provide a balance between the interests of the Community as such and those of the member states. Only democracies can be admitted to membership There are no clear lines of accountability. Power is divided between institutions, some of which share the same functions. Such democratic accountability as there is takes the forms of (i) a limited degree of accountability to an elected 'European Parliament', and (ii) arrangements made under the constitutions of the individual states. The balance between the different bodies, particularly in relation to the Parliament, varies according to the treaty provision under which a particular issue arises.

The main institutions are as follows (Art. 7):

▶ The Council of Ministers including the European Council
▶ The European Commission
▶ The European Parliament
▶ The European Court of Justice (ECJ)
▶ The Court of Auditors (not discussed here)

Other important community institutions include the Committee of Permanent Representatives (COREPER), which comprises senior officials who prepare the Council's business and are very influential, and the European Central Bank (Art. 8). There are also advisory and consultative bodies, notably the Economic and Social Committee and the Committee of the Regions.

### 8.2.1 The Council of Ministers

This is the primary lawmaking body. The Council's main function is to approve or amend laws proposed by the European Commission, although in some cases it can ask the Commission to make a proposal (Art. 208). It also decides the budget and adopts international treaties and is responsible for ensuring that the objectives of the treaty are attained. The Council is made up of a minister representing each member state who must be authorised to commit the government. The membership fluctuates according to the business in hand. A president holds office for six months, each member state holding the office in turn.

The Council is biased towards national interests rather than towards an overall 'community view'. The community view is represented by the Commission (below), creating a distinct kind of separation of powers and a recipe for political tension. The way in which Council decisions are made is therefore all-important. Certain decisions, albeit a shrinking category, must be unanimous, thus permitting any state to impose a veto. An increasing number of decisions are made by a 'qualified majority', whereby votes are weighted according to the population of each state. Sometimes a simple majority suffices. According to a convention agreed in 1966 and known as the Luxembourg Convention, where very important interests of a member state are in issue the Council should vote unanimously. It is however arguable that, given the increasing use of qualified majority provisions in the treaties, this convention is losing its political legitimacy.

The European Council, which is a twice yearly meeting of heads of state and the president of the Commission, previously existed outside the treaties but was 'legalised' by the Single European Act (now Art. 4). Its function is to 'provide the Union with the necessary impetus for its development and shall define the general political guidelines thereof'. The Council as such has no lawmaking power but nevertheless seems to tip the balance of power away from the supra-national elements of Commission and Parliament towards the inter-governmental element.

### 8.2.2     The European Commission

The Commission represents the interests of the communities as such. It is required to be independent 'beyond doubt' of the member governments (Art. 213). Its members are chosen by agreement between the member governments and currently comprise one member from each state. Each commissioner is appointed for a renewable term of five years, in order to correspond with the life of a parliament. Prior to the nomination of the other commissioners, the president of the Commission is nominated for a two-year term by the member states after consulting the European Parliament. The president has a right to object to individual nominees (Art. 217) and the appointment of the commissioners as a whole must be approved by the Parliament (Art. 214(2)). The president assigns departmental responsibilities (Directorates-General) to the other commissioners who are required to conform to the political direction of the president (Art. 219). Members of the Commission cannot be dismissed by their governments or the president during their terms of office (Art. 214) so that, unlike a head of government, the president has little political leverage. Commissioners can be compulsorily retired by the European Court on the ground of inability to perform their duties (Art. 216), and the whole Commission can be dismissed by the Parliament (Art. 201). The main functions of the Commission are as follows:

- ▶ To propose laws or political initiatives for adoption by the Council. The Council or the Parliament can request the Commission to submit proposals (Arts 192, 208).
- ▶ To make laws itself either directly under powers conferred by the treaty or under powers delegated to it by the Council.
- ▶ To enforce community law against member states, and the other community institutions. The Community has no police or law enforce-

ment agencies. The Commission enforces the law by issuing a 'reasoned opinion', negotiating with the body concerned and, if necessary, initiating proceedings in the Court (Art. 226). The judgements of the Court are enforced through the laws of member states.

▶ To administer the union budget.

▶ To negotiate with international bodies and other countries (Arts 228, 229–31).

Neither Council nor Commission is directly accountable democratically. Laws can be initiated only by the non-elected Commission but must be validated by the Council which is essentially a reactive body. Moreover, because membership of the Council fluctuates it is vulnerable to being dominated by the permanent officials of the Commission. The effective operation of the system therefore depends on a threefold informal network of understandings between Commission, Council and Parliament, which has a consultative role (below).

### 8.2.3 The European Parliament

The European Parliament does not make law but was created as an 'advisory and supervisory' body (Art. 189). It injects a limited but increasing democratic element. Its seats (to a maximum of 700) are allocated in proportion to the population of each member state. Elections are held every five years. Since 1979 MEPs have been directly elected by residents of the member states, the detailed electoral arrangements being left to each country.

Elections to the EU Parliament in Britain are on the basis of a closed party list (European Parliamentary Elections Act 2002). There are 87 seats divided into electoral regions (9 for England, 1 each for Scotland, Wales and Northern Ireland with 71, 8, 5 and 3, members respectively). Each party lists its candidates in order of preference and votes can be cast either for a party or for an individual standing separately. The seats are allocated in the order set out on the list by the parties in proportion to the share of the vote achieved by each party.

The Parliament is required to meet at least once a year and in practice meets roughly once each month, alternating, expensively, between Strasbourg and Luxembourg. Its members vote in political groupings and not in national units (see Art. 191). Under the Treaty, MEPs are required to be independent of national policies and not to act under instructions from any outside source. Freedom of speech and proceedings within the Parliament are protected but, unlike the UK Parliament, the European Parliament does not seem to enjoy privilege against interference from the courts. The European Court of Justice can review the legality of its activities (*Grand Duchy of Luxembourg* v *Parliament* (1983)).

Its main functions are as follows:

▶ It has the right to be consulted by the Council on many legislative proposals. In some cases it has a right of veto. In limited cases it can request the Commission to propose legislation (Art. 190).

▶ It approves the Union budget and can amend the part of the Union budget that is not devoted to compulsory functions. This means that the Parliament has little control over most of the budget and no realistic control over the overall level of Community spending, or its distribution between the member states. It can veto the whole Union budget (Art. 272).

▶ It approves the appointment of the Commission and the admission of new member states. It must be consulted on the choice of the Commission's president and on the appointment of certain other senior officials.

▶ By a two-thirds majority that is also an absolute majority of all members it can dismiss the entire Commission but not individual members of it (Art. 201).

▶ It can question members of the Commission orally or in writing. Commissioners often appear before its committees although it has no legal power to compel this.

▶ It can hold committees of inquiry into misconduct or maladministration by other EC bodies (Art. 193). It appoints an ombudsman to investigate complaints by citizens, residents or companies based in member states against EC institutions, other than the Court (Art. 195).

▶ Any citizen, resident or company based in a member state can petition it on a matter which comes within the Community's field of competence and affects him, her or it directly (Art. 194).

Apart from the Parliament's limited powers the fragmented nature of community decision making makes parliamentary accountability weak, a problem compounded by the fact that the implementation of community laws and policies is carried out by national governments. The lawmaking processes increasingly require a web of consultation between Parliament, Council and Commission (below). This blurs the lines of accountability. Moreover, party organisation is relatively weak. These factors may encourage an ethos of consensus and self-interest rather than robust accountability. The accountability of MEPs is itself weak since elections are in large constituencies and there is no relationship between an individual member and the voter. Given its limited powers it is not surprising that the turnout for elections to the Parliament is low (around 25%). (See Meny and Knapp, *Government and Politics in Western Europe*, 1998.)

In some legislative contexts the role of the Parliament has been significantly strengthened (Arts 251, 252). There are two procedures. Firstly, applying mainly to monetary union matters, the 'cooperation' procedure permits a parliamentary input at an early stage and requires a unanimous vote of the Council if Parliament either rejects its policy or proposes amendments with which the Commission disagrees. Secondly, relating to most economic, social and environmental matters but not to agricultural matters, the 'co-decision' procedure gives the Parliament a veto which it must exercise by an absolute majority. In the event of a deadlock between the Parliament and the Council, there is provision for a joint conciliation committee made up of equal numbers of each, with the Commission as mediator. If agreement still cannot be reached, the parliamentary veto stands.

### 8.2.4 The European Court of Justice

The European Court of Justice (ECJ) comprises judges appointed by agreement between the governments of the member states. Unlike national judges, they have little security of tenure, being appointed for a renewable term of six years and dismissible by the unanimous opinion of the other judges and advocates-general (Statutes of the Court, Art. 6). As well as the judges there are eight advocates-general who provide the Court with an independent opinion upon the issues in each case (Art. 222). The opinion of the advocates-general is not binding on the Court, but is highly influential.

One judge is appointed from each member state and sittings are as a 'Grand Chamber' of 11. They elect a president for a renewable period of three years. Appointments must be made from those eligible for the highest judicial office in each member state and also from 'jurisconsults of recognised competence' (EC Treaty, Art. 223). This permits such persons as academic lawyers or social scientists to be appointed. There is also a Court of First Instance (sitting in panels of three or five). This hears cases of kinds designated by the Council (unanimity is required). There are no specific qualifications for appointment to the Court of First Instance other than being a person 'whose independence is beyond doubt and who possesses the ability required for judicial office'. The Court of Justice hears appeals on a point of law from the Court of First Instance.

The Court's task is to ensure that 'in the interpretation and application of the EC treaty the law is observed' (Art. 220). The 'law' consists of the treaties themselves, the legislation adopted in their implementation, general principles developed by the Court, the *acquis communitaire*, which is the accumulated and developing inheritance of community values and general principles of law common to the member states including the European Convention on Human Rights (Treaty on European Union, Art. 2). There is also 'soft law' which is not binding but must be taken into account. Soft law includes 'declarations and resolutions adopted in the community framework; international agreements and agreements between member states connected with community activities' (see Europe Documents No. 1790 of 3 July, 1992, p. 3). It has been suggested that parts of the EU system are 'entrenched' in the sense that not even the Treaty itself could be altered in defiance of them. However in *Grau Gromis* (1995) the ECJ accepted that 'the Member States remain free to alter even the most fundamental parts of the Treaty'.

The main jurisdiction of the ECJ is as follows:

(i) Enforcement action against member states who are accused of violating or refusing to implement European law (Art. 226). These proceedings are usually brought by the Commission, but can be brought by other member states subject to having raised the matter before the Commission (Art. 227). The Commission first gives the member state a chance to state its case. The Court can award a lump sum or penalty payment against a member state which fails to comply with a judgement of the Court that the state concerned has failed to fulfil a treaty obligation (Art. 228). This is an important strengthening of the enforcement powers of the Court.

(ii) Judicial review of the acts or the failure to act of community institutions (Arts 230, 231, 232). This can be brought by other institutions and by member states. An individual or private body can bring an action only in special circumstances where the community act in question is directed to the individual in person or is of 'direct and individual concern to him or her' (see for example *Salamander v European Parliament* (2000)). In contrast to its reluctance to permit individuals to sue the EC under this provision, the Court has been liberal in supporting individual rights against national governments (below).

(iii) Preliminary rulings on matters referred to it by national courts relating to the interpretation of the Treaty and the validity and interpretation of acts of community institutions and of the European Central Bank (Art. 234). This is the lynchpin of the ECJ's role as a constitutional court and is how actions brought by private persons would normally be dealt with. Any national court, where it considers that a decision on the question is necessary to enable it to give judgement, may request the ECJ to give a ruling on a question of community law (Art. 177). The role of the European Court is confined to that of ruling upon the question of law referred to it. It then sends the matter back to the national court for a decision on the facts in the light of the Court's ruling. A court against whose decision there is no judicial remedy in national law (that is, the highest appeal court or any other court against which there is no right of appeal or review) must make such a request (ibid.). All UK courts are obliged to obey any community law that is made binding on them by community law (see European Communities Act 1972 s.2 (4)) and are required to follow decisions of the ECJ (ibid., s.3 (1)). The power to give preliminary rulings does not apply to the Court of First Instance.

It may be difficult to decide whether a reference can or should be made. The parties have no say in the matter (*Bulmer* v *Bollinger* (1974)). A court need not make a reference if it thinks the point is irrelevant or 'reasonably clear and free from doubt' (the *acte-claire* doctrine) nor if 'substantially' the same point has already been decided by the ECJ (see *CILFIT SI Ministro de la Sanita* (1983)). In *R* v *International Stock Exchange ex parte Else (1982) Ltd* [1993] 1 All ER 420 at 422, Bingham LJ said that 'if community law is critical to the decision the court should refer it if it has any real doubt'. Furthermore, the court can take into account the convenience of the parties, the expense of the action, and the workload of the European Court (ibid.) (*Van Duyn* v *Home Office* [1974] 3 All ER 178 at 1986; *Macarthys Ltd* v *Smith* (1979); *Customs and Excise* v *Samex* [1983] 1 All ER 1042 at 1055–6).

It may be difficult to decide whether the law is sufficiently clear to entitle the UK court to decide for itself. Much depends upon how English legal culture responds to the different reasoning methods of the ECJ, that is whether the UK court approaches the problem by way of our traditional 'literal' approach to questions of interpretation, or takes a broader approach, focusing on the 'spirit' as opposed to the letter of the law in the continental manner (see *Henn and Darby* v *DPP* (1981)). The same applies to the question of whether a decision in the matter is 'necessary' for the resolution of the case. We may not know this until we know what the relevant community law means.

The Court has no jurisdiction over what are currently called 'second-pillar' matters (foreign and security policy) since these are political matters for the European Union not the communities as such. Its jurisdiction over 'third-pillar' matters (cooperation in criminal matters) depends on the consent of the state concerned but it has no jurisdiction in respect of the operations of the police and other law enforcement agencies (Art. 35.5). However, in other areas, for example freedom of trade, the Court can interfere with police activities so as to require the police to give priority to EC aims (see *R* v *Chief Constable of Sussex ex parte International Trader's Ferry* [1999] 1 All ER 109 at 155).

It is often said that the glue that holds together the communities and the member states in a constitutional framework is the rule of law represented by the ECJ. The Treaty itself is not explicit as to the relationship between the ECJ and the law of the member states, but the ECJ has developed several principles which have enabled it to give primacy to EC law over national law. According to some commentators the ECJ has, in defiance of the normal values of judicial impartiality and democracy, taken upon itself the political agenda of promoting European integration by becoming not only the judge but the police force of the European enterprise. It has attempted to enlist national courts in this enterprise, by requiring them to defer to EC law and by conferring on individuals European law rights that are enforceable in national courts. On the other hand it has injected some democratic principles into EC law albeit in a sporadic fashion (see Mancini and Keeling (1994) *Modern Law Review*, **57**: 175).

## 8.3 Community Law and National Law

Sections 2 and 3 of the European Communities Act 1972 require UK courts to apply EC law in accordance with the decisions and general principles of the ECJ. We saw in Chapter 7 that the doctrine of parliamentary supremacy has been modified by the 1972 Act to the extent that a UK statute cannot impliedly override or repeal an EC law of a kind that is enforceable in a domestic court. Thus where the language of a UK statute conflicts with such an EC law, the EC law prevails. However, an express provision in a UK statute might override an EC law so that ultimately parliamentary supremacy prevails. The main concern of this chapter is which EC laws are directly enforceable.

The relationship between the UK constitution and the European Union involves a clash of constitutional tradition between the pragmatic, common law, politically driven constitution of the UK and the civil law approach which is driven by abstract concepts familiar to the continental jurists. There are different ways of approaching the relationship between EC law and national law. One is to regard EC law as a distinct system with its own principles and methods of reasoning, in which the courts must participate by applying European methods as if they were federal courts. Another would be to regard EC law as 'processed' into English law under the authority of the European Communities Act 1972, to be approached in much the same way as other legislation in the light of the reasoning methods of English law The choice between these two approaches influences the extent to which the courts are willing to subordinate UK law to EC ideas.

There seems to be no consistent practice among the English judges and examples of both approaches can be found. In *Mayne* v *Ministry of Agriculture* (2001), it was held that UK regulations implementing an EC Directive do not apply to future amendments of the Directive unless they are clearly worded as doing so and in *R* v *Poole BC ex parte Beebee* (1991): a minimalist approach to implementation of environmental directive was taken. However in *Berkeley* v *Secretary of State* (2000) Lord Hoffmann emphasised the importance of giving effect to EC law's environmental purposes.

There is also a 'spillover effect' whereby rights initially established for European purposes are later extended to domestic contexts on the basis that it would be unjust for domestic law to be more restrictive than EC law (e.g. M v *Home Office* (1993): interim relief against the Crown). More generally it has been said that involvement with Europe has accelerated the tendency to approach the interpretation of legislation from a broad purposive perspective as opposed to the narrow linguistic perspective traditionally favoured by the English courts (Lord Steyn in R *(Quintavalle)* v *Secretary of State* [21]: regulation of cloning).

Some EC measures take effect 'without further enactment' (European Communities Act 1972 s.2 (1)) and are automatically part of UK law. These will be discussed below. In other cases there has to be a conversion to UK law, usually in the form of a statutory instrument (ibid., s.2 (2)). Certain measures, including taxation, the creation of new criminal offences, and retrospective laws, can only be implemented by an Act of Parliament (ibid., Schedule 2). The remedy against a state that fails to implement a measure of this type is an action by the Commission in the ECJ following protracted and secretive interchanges (above).

The main kinds of EC legal instrument are as follows (Art. 249):

(i) *The Treaty.* Treaty provisions are sometimes directly enforceable in the UK courts (below).

(ii) *Regulations.* These are general rules, which apply to all member states and persons. All regulations are 'directly applicable' and as such are automatically binding on UK courts except where a particular regulation is of a character that is inherently unsuitable for judicial enforcement.

(iii) *Directives.* A Directive as such is not automatically binding but is sometimes so (below). It is a requirement to achieve a given objective but leaves it to the individual states to specify how that objective is to be achieved by altering their own laws. A Directive may be addressed to all states or to particular states. A time limit is usually specified for implementing the Directive.

(iv) *Decisions.* These are addressed to specific persons or organisations including member states and are 'binding in their entirety on those to whom they are addressed'.

(v) *Opinions and Recommendations.* These do not have binding force. However the ECJ has power under Art. 228(6) to give an opinion at an early stage of a matter, for example in relation to a proposed treaty.

(vi) *International Agreements.* The EC has power to enter into international agreements which might be binding if they are intended to confer rights on individuals.

**8.3.1** Direct Applicability and Direct Effect

'Direct effect' must be distinguished from 'direct applicability' which applies only to EC regulations. The difference between the two concepts is that regulations are always binding, whereas 'direct effect' depends upon the quality of the particular EC instrument. It has been suggested that the ECJ developed the direct effect doctrine in order to make use of domestic law enforcement agencies as a means of compensating for the weak enforcement provision offered at EC level through the Commission (see Craig, 1992; Weatherill, 1995, p. 101 *et seq.*).

Where the direct effect doctrine applies, the national court must give a remedy which, as far as possible, puts the plaintiff in the same position as if the directive had been properly implemented. This might for example require national restrictions to be set aside, or national taxes to be ignored or national rules that are stricter than a Directive covering the same ground to be set aside (see e.g. *Defrenne* (1976) – retirement restrictions; *Pubblico Ministerio* v *Ratti* (1979) – excessive labelling requirements).

Direct effect applies to the Treaty and to Directives. A Treaty provision that has direct effect is enforceable against anyone upon whom its provisions impose an obligation. Directives however can be enforced only 'vertically', that is, against a public authority or 'emanation of the state', but not 'horizontally' against a private person (see *Marshall* v *Southampton Area Health Authority (No. 1)*(1986); *Faccini Dori* v *Recreb* (1995)). The reason seems to be that the state, which, as we saw above has the primary duty to implement a Directive, cannot rely on its failure to do so; an argument that it would be unfair to apply to a private body. It also follows that the state cannot rely on an unimplemented directive against an individual (see *Wychavon D.C.* v *Secretary of State* (1994)).

What is meant by an emanation of the state? It will be recalled that the UK has no legal concept of the state but relies on separate bodies linked in a variety of ways to the central government. For the purpose of direct effect, any public body seems to be regarded as an emanation of the state (*Marshall* v *Southampton Area Health Authority* (No.1) (1986)). A public body must (i) exercise functions in the public interest subject to the control of the state, and (ii) have special legal powers not available to individuals or ordinary companies (see *Foster* v *British Gas* (1990)). All the activities of such a body, even those governed by private law, for example employment contracts, seem to be subject to direct effect. The privatised utilities of gas, electricity and water are probably emanations of the state but it is unlikely that the privatised railway companies would be, since although they are subject to state regulation and receive state subsidy they have no statutory obligation to perform public duties nor significant special powers (see *Doughty* v *Rolls Royce* (1992)).

To have direct effect, an instrument must be 'justiciable', meaning that it is of a kind which is capable of being interpreted and enforced by a court without trespassing outside its proper judicial role. In essence, the legal obligation created by the instrument must be certain enough for a court to handle. The tests usually applied are as follows (see *Van Duyn* v *Home Office* (1974)):

(i) The instrument must be 'clear, precise and unconditional'. It must not give the member state substantial discretion as to how to give effect to it. For example in *Francovich* (1993) a Directive concerning the treatment of employees in an insolvency was not unconditional because it left it to member states to decide which bodies should guarantee the payments required by the Directive (see also *Gibson* v *East Riding DC* (2000): Directive about paid leave did not make clear what counted as working time). However, the fact that a Directive leaves it to the state to choose between alternative methods of enforcement does not prevent it from having direct effect if the substance of the right is clear from the Directive alone (*Marshall (No. 2)* (1993)). The European Court interprets the precision test liberally, bearing in mind that apparent uncertainty could be cured by a reference to the court (see Craig, 1992).

(ii) The instrument must be intended to confer 'rights'. A problem arises here in respect of purely 'public' interests, such as some environmental concerns, for example wildlife conservation. It is arguable that a body with a public-law right sufficient to give standing in national law to challenge the government's action, for example a pressure group, could rely on the direct effect doctrine. In other words the 'rights' requirement is no more than an aspect of the general principle that the directive must concern matters appropriate for a court.

(iii) The time limit prescribed by a Directive for its implementation must have expired.

### 8.3.2 Indirect Effect

Even where a European law lacks direct effect, the courts must still take account of it. Article 10 requires member states to 'take all appropriate measures' to fulfil European obligations, and Article 249 requires that the objectives of Directives be given effect. The traditional attitude of the courts has been that domestic legislation should be interpreted to fit European law only where the relevant European rule had direct applicability or direct effect, or where the domestic rule was specifically passed to give effect to European law and then only where the domestic law was unclear (see *Litster* (1990), *Finnegan* (1990), *Duke* (1990), *Webb* v *EMO* [1992] 4 All ER 929 at 940).

Doubt has been cast on this by the decision of the ECJ in *Marleasing* (1992). The court held that all domestic law, whether passed before or after the relevant community law, must be interpreted 'so far as possible' in the light of the wording and purposes of the Directive in order to achieve the result pursued by the latter'. However *Marleasing* involved a law (in the Spanish civil code) which could be interpreted in different ways. It is uncertain therefore whether clear, unambiguous domestic law must give way to a European rule. In *Webb* v *EMO (Air Cargo) (UK) Ltd* (1992), Lord Keith said that *Marleasing* applies to laws passed at any time provided that their language is not distorted. In *Ghaidan* v *Mendoza* (2004) [45], which concerned an analogous provision in the Human Rights Act 1998 (Chapter 17), Lord Steyn accepted that *Marleasing* created a strong obligation.

### 8.3.3   State Liability

Even where a Directive does not have direct effect, an individual may be able to sue the government for damages for failing to implement it. This was established by the ECJ in *Francovich* v *Italy* (above) where the Directive was too vague to have direct effect. Nevertheless the court held that damages could be awarded against the Italian government in an Italian court. The court's reasoning was based upon the principle of giving full effect to EC rights. This is a powerful and far-reaching notion. In order to obtain damages, (i) the Directive must confer rights for the benefit of individuals; (ii) the content of those rights must be determined from the provisions of the Directive (a certain degree of certainty is therefore needed); (iii) there must be a causal link between breach of the Directive and the damage suffered (see also *R* v *Secretary of State for Transport ex parte Factortame (No. 4)* (1996), *(No. 5)* (2000)).

In domestic law, damages cannot normally be obtained against the government for misusing its statutory powers and duties (see *Barrett* v *Enfield Borough Council* (1999)). The *Francovich* principle, which was subsequently accepted by the House of Lords (*Kirklees MBC* v *Wickes Building Supplies* (1992)), is therefore of great significance. *Francovich* leaves the procedures for recovering damages to national courts, but any conditions must not make recovery impossible or excessively difficult. There may also be a developing principle that legal remedies must be equally effective in each member state (below).The *Francovich* principle also avoids the 'vertical' enforcement rule (above). Failure to implement a Directive against a private person would entitle the plaintiff to sue the government.

### 8.3.4   Effective Remedies

There is also an obligation to give effective remedies to protect rights in EC law. The courts originally took the view that this obligation merely required that the remedies available in European cases should be no worse than in equivalent domestic cases. However, it now appears that the courts must sometimes provide better remedies in relation to European rights than would be available domestically. In *Factortame* (No. 2) (1991), the House of Lords accepted a judgement of the European Court of Justice that required the court to issue an interim (temporary) injunction against the Crown in order to suspend the operation of a statute, which, contrary to a European Directive, prohibited the applicants from fishing in UK waters. At that time, interim relief against the Crown was thought not to be possible in UK law. The government argued that the protection given was the same as that which domestic law would give in similar circumstances, that is, none. The ECJ however held that there is an overriding requirement that the remedy must be effective to protect the European right and the court should consider whether in the circumstances an injunction should issue (see also *Johnston* v *Chief Constable of Royal Ulster Constabulary* (RUC) (1986)).

It remains to be seen how much freedom a member state has in adjusting its remedies to its own circumstances. For example, in *Factortame* the court still had a discretion whether to issue the injunction based upon the justice and convenience of the circumstances. The English courts are very cautious about issuing interim injunctions and will do so only as a last resort (see *R* v *HM Treasury ex parte British Telecommunications plc* (1996)). The governing principle is that the remedy must be adequate and effective, but member states can choose among different possible ways of achieving the object of a Directive.

## 8.4 Democracy and the European Union

Although a democratic government is a requirement of membership perhaps the most fundamental constitutional problem of the EU is the 'democratic deficit'. As we have seen powers are fragmented between the Council and the Commission with the latter as the driving force. Neither of these institutions are directly accountable democratically. The European Parliament has a significant role but has limited powers.

Some of the founders of the European Communities such as Jean Monnet (1888–1979) were paternalistic idealists who had little interest in democratic processes, assuming perhaps that the 'European spirit' could gradually be infused into public opinion by example and propaganda. When the European Communities Act 1972 was passed by the UK Parliament, the driving forces were the desperate economic plight of the UK, coupled with the romantic adulation of European culture by the then Prime Minister, Edward Heath. No serious attention was paid to the democratic credentials of the Community structure.

The European Union relies mainly on the democratic processes of the member states. In the UK proposed EC legislation is scrutinised by Parliament although it may not have any power of veto or amendment. Council and Commission documents are made available to both Houses, ministerial statements are made after Council meetings, questions can be asked, and, in addition to the ordinary departmental committees, there are select committees in each House to monitor EU activity. The House of Lords Select Committee is particularly well regarded and, in addition to scrutinising new legislation, makes wide-ranging general reports on the European Union.

As regards the executive, accountability is weakened in that there is no government department specifically dealing with the EU which depends on the normal machinery of government (Chapter 13). However the main departments have European Sections. The Foreign Office acts as a coordinating body and a junior minister is responsible for 'Europe'. Thus there is a complex network of negotiating machinery involving the competing interests of the UK and the European Union, the UK and other member states and interdepartmental rivalries with Parliament on the sidelines. In keeping with the ethos of UK government, the operation of European Union matters relies on informal contacts between unelected officials.

There may be a convention that no UK minister should consent to an EC legislative proposal before a debate has taken place, unless there are special reasons which must be explained to the House as soon as possible. However, this is not consistently followed. In practice, the volume of EC legislation is greater than the time available and much European business is conducted without MPs having the opportunity to consider it in advance (see HC Deb., 30 October 1980, col. 843–4). Ministers in their capacity as members of the Council are probably not bound by resolutions of the House of Commons.

There is one specific democratic constraint. By virtue of the European Parliamentary Elections Act 1978, s.6, no treaty which provides for an increase in the powers of the European Parliament can be ratified by the UK without the approval of an Act of Parliament. It is perhaps ironic that this provides protection only against the elected element of the EC.

The European Union is dedicated to particular social and economic goals centring upon the protection of free trade. It is thus wedded to market liberalism which is not necessarily consistent with democracy or with other forms of liberalism (Chapter 1). Although the goals of the European Union have become progressively wider, they are not compatible with the premise that democracy is about governing with the consent of the people and cannot be tied to any particular substantive goals. Nevertheless Article 10 provides that:

member states shall take all appropriate measures, whether general or particular, to ensure fulfilment of the obligations arising out of this treaty or resulting from actions taken by the institutions of the Community. They shall facilitate the achievement of the Community's tasks. They shall abstain from any measure that could jeopardise the attainment of the objectives of the Treaty.

This seems to impose an obligation to place EU goals above democracy (see *Internationale Handelsgesellschaft* Case [1970] ECR 1125 at1135). It has been described as imposing a moral obligation on member states and even as 'the sort of spiritual and essentially vacuous clause that is more commonly found in constitutional orders such as that of Nazi Germany' (Ward, 1996, p. 65).

Democracy depends on wide access to information about governmental activity. Until recently, European Union institutions were notoriously secretive. However Art. 255 of the Treaty and Regulation No. 1049/2001 have created a limited public right of access to European Parliament, Council and Commission documents including documents both drawn up by them and received by them. This applies to any citizen of the Union (i.e. a citizen of a member state) and to any person residing in or having a registered office in a member state. There is however a long list of exceptions relating to most important community activities (Art. 4). They include security, defence and military matters, international relations, financial monetary or economic policy, privacy and the integrity of the individual. Commercial interests, legal matters, inspections, investigations and audits are also excepted, subject to a public interest test. Internal documents are excepted if disclosure would seriously undermine the decision-making process, again subject to a public interest test. This is a familiar reason for claiming secrecy and raises the suspicion of self-protection (see Chapter 19). No specific enforcement measures are provided.

However, the Court has taken a vigorous attitude to the right to information. In *World Wildife Fund for Nature* v *Commission* (1997), which concerned information about Commission policy on environmental protection, the Court of First Instance held that, although at the time there was only a voluntary undertaking to disclose information, having adopted it, the Commission is bound to respect it. The court also held that exceptions should be interpreted restrictively so as not to inhibit the aim of transparency and that the Commission must give reasons for refusing to disclose information. The Court has also refused to accept blanket immunity for particular kinds of information and required the Commission to balance the public right to know against a clear public interest in secrecy in the particular case (see *JT's Corporation* v *Commission* (2000); *Van der Val* v *Netherlands* (2000)).

## 8.5 Federalism and the European Union

The European Union is difficult to fit into a coherent constitutional structure. In addition to the conflicts already mentioned, there is a conflict between the ideal of European integration and that of national identity. For example, Article 6 of the EC Treaty requires national identity to be respected. This tension suggests the possibility of a federal model since, as we saw in Chapter 7, federalism is intended to reconcile this kind of tension by marking out spheres of independence for each unit. While some idealists, notably Jean Monnet, pursued the agenda of a federal Europe, the thrust of the original initiative was towards the pragmatic integration of economic policy as the basis of evolution towards what the treaties call 'ever closer union' but with no agreed final destination.

The EU has certain features of federalism in that the powers and purposes of the communities are defined in the Treaty with the member states having residual autonomy in other areas. Some EC law overrides incompatible domestic law and, under the doctrine of 'pre-emption', member states may not legislate in areas reserved to the Community at least in cases where the Community has actually exercised its powers (see *Commission* v *UK* (1981)).

On the other hand, the Union has no elected government nor an enforcement arm of its own. It cannot raise taxes and depends on the courts and the executives of the member states to enforce its will. There is a concept of citizenship of the European Union which applies to citizens of the member states (Art. 17) but this gives only limited rights, namely free movement within the Union, within the requirements of the Treaty, and the right to stand or vote in local government elections and in elections to the European Parliament on the same terms as nationals.

A delicate balance has to be struck between harmonising the law throughout the Community and catering for particular national needs, so that individual states can sometimes depart from normal community requirements (for example individual states can sometimes opt out of EC laws on the basis of special circumstances). There are also transitional provisions ('multi-speed' or 'variable geometry' arrangements) in which a core of members participate leaving others to opt in later if at all (for example monetary union, social welfare provisions and immigration arrangements). It is therefore doubtful whether there exists in Europe that delicate balance between diversity and unity on which a federal system depends. The policy of widening membership of the EU is likely to increase this problem.

In these respects the European Union is more like a confederation or an inter-governmental body rather than a genuine supra-national body. Indeed the German Supreme Court has held that ultimate power remains with the member states (see *Brunner* v *European Union Treaty* (1994)). On the other hand, its laws are directly enforceable against individuals. The European Union is therefore best regarded as a unique legal order not reducible into other forms.

The tension between the interests of the member states and those of the Union is expressed ambiguously through the concept of 'subsidiarity' which was introduced by the Maastricht Treaty (TEU Art. 2, EC Treaty Art. 5). Subsidiarity is a vague term with no agreed meaning which can be used to serve different political interests. Historically, subsidiarity is an authoritarian doctrine used by the Catholic Church to legitimise a hierarchical power structure. Subsidiarity can also be regarded as a pluralist liberal principle that decisions should be made at a level as close as possible to those whom they affect.

The version of subsidiarity in the EC Treaty (Art. 5) concerns the distribution of powers between the Community and national governments:

> In areas that do not fall within its exclusive competence, the Community shall take action, in accordance with the principle of subsidiarity, only if and so far as the objectives of the proposed action cannot be sufficiently achieved by the Member States and can therefore, by reason of the scale or effects of the proposed action, be better achieved by the Community ... Any action by the community shall not go beyond what is necessary to achieve the objects of this treaty.

This formulation is vague (e.g. the notions of 'sufficient' and 'better' and the non-sequitur between them). It is unlikely to be directly enforceable in law but, may operate at a political level thereby indirectly influencing the law. However there is another definition of subsidiarity in Art. 2 of the Maastricht Treaty which is not only internally contradictory but seems to clash with that in Art. 5 as 'a new stage in the process of creating an ever closer union in which decisions are taken as near as possible to the citizen' (however, Art. 2 seems to give priority to the Art. 5 version). Moreover, doctrines such as those of the supremacy of EC law and pre-emption are difficult to reconcile with subsidiarity.

## Summary

▶ The European Union and within it the European Community (EC) exists to integrate key economic and increasingly social policies of member states with the aim of providing an internal 'common market', of creating a powerful European political unit, and of reducing the risk of war within Europe. The constitution of the EU is an evolving one aimed at increasing integration between its member states. The EU has three main policy areas or 'pillars', these being economic development, common foreign and security policy and cooperation in justice and home affairs. Only the first pillar, together with immigration matters, is regulated by law, most laws being made by the EC. EC law raises conflicts between democratic values and the existing goals of the community, between the independence of the member states and the integrationist goals of the EU and between the different legal cultures of the common law and civil law traditions.

▶ EC law has been incorporated into UK law by the European Communities Act 1972, which makes certain EC laws automatically binding in the UK, requires other laws to be enacted in UK law either by statute or by regulations made under the 1972 Act, and obliges UK courts to decide cases consistently with principles laid down by the European Court of Justice. In some cases questions of law must be referred to the ECJ. The ECJ has developed the role of constitutional court and is sometimes regarded as being a driving force for integrationist policies which enlist national courts in the project of giving primacy to European law.

▶ The other main policy and lawmaking bodies are the Council of Ministers, which is the main lawmaking body; the European Council of Heads of State, responsible for policy direction; the appointed European Commission, which proposes laws, makes some laws, supervises the implementation of policy, carries out research and takes enforcement action; and the elected European Parliament, which is mainly a consultative and supervisory body but has certain powers of veto. Taken together these bodies are meant to balance the interests of national governments and those of the Union as such, but not to follow strict separation of power ideas. There is only limited democratic input into the EC lawmaking process.

▶ Law and policy-making power are divided between the Council and the Commission with the Commission as the driving force but the Council having the ultimate control. Voting sometimes has to be unanimous but there is increasing use of qualified majorities where voting is weighed in favour of the more populous states. The Parliament does not initiate laws but has certain powers of veto and can sometimes suggest amendments.

▶ Not all EC law is directly binding on member states. 'Regulations' are binding. Other laws including the Treaty itself are binding if they satisfy the criteria of 'direct effectiveness' created by the European Court. Directives must also satisfy the criteria of 'direct effectiveness' and can have direct effect only against public bodies (vertical direct effect) but not against private bodies (horizontal direct effect). However, the concept of 'indirect effect', which requires domestic law to be interpreted so as to conform to EC law, may alleviate this. The government may also be liable in damages if its failure properly to implement an EC law damages an individual in relation to right created by the EC law in question.

Membership of the Union may not have fundamentally altered the doctrine of parliamentary supremacy, but the UK courts have accepted that a statute which conflicts with a binding EC rule must be 'disapplied'. There is a general political principle – perhaps an emerging convention – in favour of the supremacy of Union law.

# Exercises

**8.1** Explain the constitutional structure of the European Union. To what extent is it federal?

**8.2** It is a requirement of membership of the EU that the member state must have a democratic form of government, but it has often been remarked that the EU would not satisfy the conditions for membership of itself. Do you agree?

**8.3** What powers does the UK Parliament possess in relation to European Union policy?

**8.4** To what extent are (a) the Council of Ministers and (b) the European Commission accountable for their decisions?

**8.5** Explain the relationship between UK courts and the European Court of Justice. To what extent is the ECJ a constitutional court?

(a) What is the purpose of the direct effect doctrine and what are its main limitations?

(b) An EC Directive requires member states to ensure that compensation is paid to part-time workers who are made redundant. The compensation must be paid by the employer. The UK has not implemented the Directive. Jeff, a part-time employee of Dodgy Burgers plc, is made redundant. His employer refuses to pay him compensation. Advise Jeff as to his rights, if any.

**8.6** Explain the constitutional implications of the *Marleasing* case.

**8.7** Parliament wishes to put right injustices suffered by women. It passes an Act which permits women to be paid more than men for the same work. Assume that a directly effective European Union law requires women to be paid the same as men for the same work and discuss the following:

(i) Gail is paid the same as John for the same work and seeks a remedy (a) in an English court (b) in the European court.

(ii) Would your answer differ if the Act said that 'this Act is applicable notwithstanding any decision of the European Court of Justice, or any powers of European Union Law or any powers of the European Communities Act 1972'?

**8.8** Gervase has suffered lead poisoning. It has been established that this has been caused by a reaction in a water softener manufactured by Hydros, a Greek company. The retailer from whom it was purchased has gone into liquidation, and it was not insured. The reaction was one not generally known of at the time the water softener was supplied to Gervase, but some six months earlier an article had appeared in a Japanese scientific magazine which described reactions of this kind in laboratory tests of the filter material used in the water softener.

When Gervase sues Hydros under the Purchasers Protection Act 1990 (fictitious), Hydros admits that the water softener was defective, but relies on s.4 (1)(c) of the Act, which provides a defence to such an action where 'the state of scientific and technical knowledge at the time (time of supply) was not such that a producer of products of the same description as the product in question might be expected to have discovered the defect if it had existed in his products while they were under his control'. Section 5 of the Act also limits damages under the Act to £5,000. Gervase claims that he has suffered injuries worth £10,000 due to his being unable to pursue his job as a self-employed taxi driver for six weeks.

The Act was passed to implement the EC Purchasers Protection Directive (fictitious). Gervase wishes to rely on Article 7(e) of the Directive which provides a defence only where 'the state of scientific and technical knowledge at the time when he put the product into circulation was not such as to enable the existence of the defect to be discovered'. Advise Gervase as to the rules by which any conflict between the Act and Directive will be resolved and the procedures involved.

## Further reading

Bogdanor, V. (2000) in Jowell, J. and Oliver, D. *The Changing Constitution*, 4th edn, Oxford, Oxford University Press.

Craig, P. (1992) 'Once Upon a Time in the West: Direct Effect and the Federalization of EEC Law', *Oxford Journal of Legal Studies,* **12**: 453.

Craig, P. (1997) 'Directives: Direct Effect, Indirect Effect and the Construction of National Legislation' *European Law Review*, 519.

Harden, I. and McGlynn, C. (1996) 'Democracy and the European Union', *Political Quarterly*, 32.

Hartley, T. (1996) 'The European Court, Judicial Objectivity and the Constitution of the European Union', *Law Quarterly Review*, **112**: 411.

Michael, J. (1996) 'Freedom of Information Comes to the European Union,' *Public Law*, 31.

Munro, C.R. (1999) *Studies in Constitutional Law,* London, Butterworth, Chapter 6.

Shaw, J. and More, G. (eds) (1995) *New Legal Dynamics of European Union,* Oxford, Clarendon Press.

Walter, N. (1995) 'European Constitutionalism and European Integration', *Public Law,* 266.

## Further reading cont'd

Ward, I. (1996) *A Critical Introduction to European Law,* London, Butterworth, Chapters 1, 2.

Weatherill, S. (1995) *Law and Integration in the European Union,* Chapters 1, 2, 4, 6.

Weiler, J. (1993) 'Journey to an Unknown Destination: A Retrospective and Prospective of the European Court of Justice in the Arena of Political Integration', *Journal of Common Market Studies,* **31**: 417.

# Part II

# Government Institutions

# Chapter 9

# Parliament: constitutional position

The virtue, spirit and essence of a House of Commons consists in its being the express image of the feelings of the nation. It was not instituted to be a control *on* the people. It was designed as a control *for* the people.
(Edmund Burke)
They [Parliament] are a lot of hard-faced men who look as if they had done very well out of the war. (Stanley Baldwin, Prime Minister 1923–29, 1935–37)

## Key words

- Executive domination
- Sustaining and controlling government
- Mixed constitution: the need for a second chamber
- Tension between separation of powers and rule of law
- Conflicts of interest

## 9.1 Introduction

The word 'Parliament', which meant a parley or conference, entered into official language about the middle of the thirteenth century. It described a formal meeting summoned by the King between himself and the elite members of society for the purposes of advising him and legitimising his tax demands on the people (Chapter 3). A dominant feature of the contemporary UK constitution is its extreme parliamentary system. Derived from conventions under which its leader (the Prime Minister) is chosen, the executive depends on the support of Parliament and all ministers must be members of Parliament. The Crown can make law only in conjunction with Parliament and by convention cannot veto any law duly presented by Parliament. Broadly, the history of Parliament is that of power struggles between the Crown and Parliament and between the two Houses of Parliament. The House of Commons had triumphed over the Crown in the sense of the monarch, and over the House of Lords, but the Crown, in the sense of the executive, appears to have re-emerged for the time being as the winner.

The traditional function of Parliament as endorsed by conservatives such as Burke and also liberals such as Mill (Chapter 1) has been to represent the people against the Crown. In contemporary circumstances its role has become closer to that of a back-up to the executive government, a recruiting ground for ministers and a process for legitimating executive action. Most laws are proposed by the executive so that the activities of Parliament are reactive and conflicting: to sustain the executive by authorising the raising and spending of funds, to hold the executive to account and to scrutinise, approve or amend legislation. This reflects Mill's ideal of representative democracy as government by experts subject to control by the people. Parliament also acts, in a mechanical fashion as a way of translating the popular vote into the appointment of an executive, since, again by convention, whoever commands a majority in the House of Commons is entitled to form a government. As we shall see, by virtue of the distortions of the electoral system, a popular majority does not necessarily translate into a parliamentary majority.

Although the legal supremacy of Parliament probably remains in place, its political power and prestige has declined in recent years. This is the result of an accumulation of factors, some new, others long standing, which together raise doubts as to whether Parliament is still the most important institution of the constitution. These factors include:

▶ the increasing influence of international lawmaking which in practice restricts national legislatures. Examples are the European Union, NATO, the World Trade Organisation and World Bank, and the European Convention on Human Rights
▶ at the other end of the scale the devolution of powers, albeit to differing extents, to the nations within the UK
▶ the increase in the power of the executive
▶ powerful political parties funded by business interests
▶ a more assertive and activist judiciary.

The UK version of the Parliamentary system gives exceptionally strong powers to the executive, particularly to the Prime Minister (Chapter 13), and although in law omnipotent, Parliament is, politically, correspondingly weak. The main reason for the dominance of the executive is the strong party system that has developed in UK politics since the early twentieth century. Thus our constitution could be regarded as a party/market democracy (Chapter 1). Legal arrangements support this in that the first-past-the-post voting system, which applies to Parliamentary elections, supports strong large parties by making it difficult for small parties to win seats (Chapter 10). As a matter of practical politics the party leaders are in a position to pressurise their supporters in the House of Commons, partly because, like the eighteenth-century aristocracy (Chapter 3), they can influence the choice of election candidates and partly because there are many opportunities of patronage through appointments as ministers or to influential committees. Control of parliamentary business and the timetable in the House of Commons are largely in the hands of the government party although the independent Speaker, who chairs the sittings of the Commons, exercises a certain moderating influence being responsible for ensuring fair debate and protecting the interests of minorities (Chapter 11). Parliament can exercise its will only by voting and each party has a highly organised 'whip' system dedicated to enforcing party discipline and persuading members to vote in the required way. In some circumstances, usually where matters of personal conscience are in issue, there may be a 'free' vote. Arguably, however, a member of the Commons should not be pressurised in any respect (below).

Executive domination is also aided by the Parliament Acts 1911 and 1949 (below) which prevent the unelected House of Lords from vetoing legislation introduced in the Commons. Most members of the House of Lords sit for life and are therefore less susceptible than members of the Commons to party pressures and their procedures are less dominated by the party machines. On the other hand, by convention appointments to the Lords are for the Prime Minister although there is an advisory appointments commission to combat the corruption that has historically played a part in such appointments (Chapter 3). Indeed, perhaps the most crucial check over the executive available in our parliamentary system – ignoring the claim that the courts supply a check – is that Parliament must terminate after five years (below) so that the government must submit to a general election and resign if it loses its majority. This statutory provision (Parliament Act 1911 s.7) cannot be altered without the consent of the House of Lords so that, to some extent, it is entrenched against the executive.

However, executive domination of Parliament must not be overstated. Parliament, although dominated by members of the executive, remains a separate institution with large powers of its own and protection against executive interference which it could use were it so minded. Its current subservience is voluntary. Government proposals must be publicly explained in Parliament and ministers must justify their decisions in public if required to do so by Parliament. The Opposition is a formal institution protected by the law of parliamentary procedure – a government and Prime Minister in waiting. It has a duty to oppose government policy, short of actually frustrating the governmental process, and forms a 'shadow cabinet' ready to take office immediately.

While there is no law to this effect, it is often claimed that a member of Parliament has a duty to exercise an independent judgement on behalf of all his or her constituents and not merely those who voted for him or her (Chapter 1). However, in practice, many MPs mechanically support the party that sponsors them. Under the general law it is unlawful for a member of a public body to be bound by a prior commitment to party policy (*Bromley LBC* v *GLC* (1983); Chapter 14). In the case of an MP, however, Parliamentary privilege prevents the courts from intervening (below).

There is funding designated by the House of Commons ('Short Money', named after the MP who proposed it) for the parliamentary work of opposition parties. This is determined by a formula based on the number of seats and votes the party received in the previous election (in 2003/04 the amount was £11,765.20 plus travel expenses. There is also funding for the Opposition leader's office (£548,101.65) The funding of the House of Commons, and of individual MPs' salaries and support, is also determined by the House as a separate charge on public funds (Chapter 11) and so is relatively independent of the executive. In practice, however, recent opposition parties have been extremely weak as a result of internal conflicts and failure to recover from damaging election defeats.

## 9.2 The Meeting of Parliament

Parliament is summoned and dissolved by the Crown under the royal prerogative, the alleged abuse of this power being a major contribution to the seventeenth-century revolution. The modern law is overlaid by statute and convention, its foundations being established by the 1688 revolution. The main principles are as follows. They give considerable power to the Prime Minister but also contain important checks over the executive.

▶ 'Parliament ought to be held frequently' (Bill of Rights 1688, Art. 13) and must meet at least once every three years (Meeting of Parliament Act 1694). By convention Parliament meets annually backed by administrative necessity, for example to authorise tax and public spending (Chapter 11).

▶ Parliament must automatically end at the expiry of five years from the date of its writ of summons (below) (Septennial Act 1715; Parliament Act 1911). This triggers a general election (Chapter 10). The five-year period is intended to strike a balance between the desire for MPs to be independent of the temptation to pander to populist pressures and the need to ensure that they do not go native and forget their dependency on the voters.

▶ Within the five years Parliament may be dissolved by the monarch (law) on the advice of the Prime Minister (convention). Dissolution triggers a general election which must be held, according to a complex formula, within about three weeks of the dissolution proclamation (Representation of the People Act 1985, Sched. 1). (The same proclamation dissolves Parliament and summons a new one.) This is one of the main sources of prime ministerial power. However, it is possible that in certain extreme cases the monarch can exercise personal choice whether or not to dissolve Parliament (Chapter 12). A Parliament usually lasts for about four years, dissolution being timed for the political advantage of the Prime Minister. It is sometimes suggested that Parliament should sit for a fixed term, thus removing a Prime Minister's power to call an election to suit his or her own party. This could, however, paralyse a weak government (see *Royal Commission on the Constitution*, Cmnd 5460, 1969–73).

▶ A Prime Minister whose government is defeated on a vote of confidence in the House of Commons must resign. Unless an alternative leader can be supported by the existing House of Commons, which is most unlikely, the outgoing Prime Minister must also ask for a dissolution of Parliament, which the monarch must normally grant (Chapter 12). This principle also gives the Prime Minister power over Parliament in that Parliament cannot dismiss the Prime Minister without dismissing itself.

A 'Parliament' is divided into 'sessions'. These are working periods of a year usually running from November (about 170 sitting days). Sessions are 'prorogued' by the monarch under the royal prerogative. Each session is opened by the monarch, with an Address from the Throne which is written by the government and outlines its legislative proposals. A general debate on government policy takes place immediately afterwards. Within a session, each House can be adjourned at any time by resolution of the House. The Speaker can suspend individual sittings of the Commons. Adjournments apply to daily sittings and to the breaks for holidays and over the summer. The rump of the session following the summer break is used to finish outstanding business. Most public bills that are not completed by the end of a session lapse, this being another lever available to the executive. In practice Parliament is either prorogued or adjourned (below) a few days before being formally dissolved.

There is machinery for recalling each House by proclamation while it stands prorogued (Parliament (Elections and Meetings) Act 1943 s.34) and also under emergency legislation (Civil Contingencies Act 2004). An adjourned Parliament can be summoned by proclamation (Meeting of Parliament Act 1870) and also by the Speaker and the Lord Chancellor (who presides over the House of Lords) at the request of the Prime Minister or perhaps at the request of the leader of the Opposition. However, it does not seem to be possible for ordinary MPs to recall Parliament in order to debate any crisis that may arise while Parliament is not sitting. Government has many powers under the royal prerogative, notably to deploy the armed forces and even to declare war, which it can exercise without reference to Parliament.

## 9.3 The Functions of Parliament

### 9.3.1 The House of Commons

The main functions of the Commons are as follows:

▶ *Choosing the government* indirectly by virtue of the convention that the person who commands a majority of the Commons is entitled to form a government. The Commons has no veto over individual appointments nor can it dismiss individual members of the government (another prime ministerial power).

▶ *Sustaining the government* by supplying it with funds and authorising taxation. The size and complexity of modern government means that parliamentary control over government cannot be exercised directly. Parliamentary approval of the executive's budget and accounts is largely a formality. Detailed scrutiny and control over government spending takes place mainly within the government itself through the medium of the Treasury (Chapter 13). However, a substantial parliamentary safeguard is provided by the National Audit Office, headed by the Comptroller and Auditor General (Chapter 11). This is an aspect of a modern tendency to create specialised supervisory bodies while preserving constitutional propriety by making them formally responsible to Parliament.

▶ *Legislating.* Any member can propose a bill but, in practice, the parliamentary timetable is dominated by government business and legislation is usually presented to Parliament ready drafted by the executive. This is why Bagehot thought that the absence of a strict separation of powers made the UK constitution an effective machine for ensuring government by experts. There are certain opportunities for private members' bills but these rarely become law (Chapter 11).

▶ *Supervising the executive.* By convention ministers are accountable to Parliament and must appear in Parliament to participate in debates, answer questions and appear before Committees (Chapter 13). The House of Commons can require a government to resign by a vote of no confidence. These sanctions are rarely used since the resignation of government is likely to result in a general election, putting the jobs of MPs at risk.

▶ *The redress of grievances* raised by individual MPs on behalf of their constituents. There are certain opportunities to raise grievances in debates (Chapter 11) but they are usually pursued by correspondence with ministers or by the Parliamentary Ombudsman. By convention every constituent has a right of access to his or her MP, which can be exercised by visiting Parliament if necessary.

▶ *Debating matters of public concern.* Again, there are limited procedural opportunities for such debates.

### The House of Lords

The House of Lords comprises some 695 persons. It is unusual among second chambers in the following respects:

▶ Its members are not elected. Most of them are appointed by the Crown, including 12 serving law lords, on the advice of the Prime Minister. There are also 26 senior Church of England bishops. Thus in many cases membership is compulsory, although attendance is not.
▶ Members other than the bishops sit for life.
▶ Members receive no payment other than expenses.
▶ Members have no constituencies and are accountable to no one. About 25% of the members are independent of political parties.
▶ By long-standing practice the proceedings of the House are regulated by the House itself, without formal rules or disciplinary sanctions, members being treated as bound by 'personal honour'.

A common justification for a second chamber is to represent the different units of a federal system with the first chamber representing the popular vote, as for example in the US. The conventional justification for the existence of a second chamber in the UK is that it acts as a revising chamber to scrutinise the detail of legislation proposed by the Commons and to allow time for second thoughts, so acting as a constitutional safeguard against the possible excesses of majoritarianism and party politics.

However, being undemocratic, the position of the House is controversial. It could be depicted as a constitutional abomination, as a valuable ingredient of a mixed constitution or as an anomalous relic which from a pragmatic perspective might nevertheless have some useful functions. The Parliament Act 1911 removed the power of the House of Lords to veto most legislation and its preamble stated that this was a precursor to replacing it by a second chamber 'constituted on a popular basis' and for 'limiting and defining' its powers. However, there has been no agreement as to how that should be done and at present the House Lords is in limbo (Chapter 10). In 2000 the Wakeham Commission (*A House for the Future: Royal Commission on the House of Lords,* (Cm 4534) endorsed the conservative view that the House of Lords should remain subordinate to the Commons (thus ensuring the clear democratic accountability of the government), that it should provide constitutional checks and balances and that it should provide a parliamentary voice for the 'nations and regions of the United Kingdom'. At present no agreed proposals for further reform of the House of Lords have emerged – a pattern that has been repeated since 1911.

According to Wakeham, the functions of the second chamber include, and should continue to include, the following:

▶ To provide advice on public policy, bringing a range of perspectives to bear which should be broadly representative of British society and in particular provide a voice for the nations and regions of the UK and for ethnic minorities and interest groups.

▶ To act as a revising chamber scrutinising the details of proposed legislation within the overall polices laid down by the Commons. By convention, supported by the Parliament Acts 1911 and 1949 (Chapter 11), the House of Lords does not discuss matters of government finance, this being a prerogative of the Commons (R. Brazier, 'The Financial powers of the House of Lords', 1998, *Anglo American Law Review* 17(2): 131).

▶ To provide a forum for general debate on matters of public concern without party political pressures.

▶ To introduce relatively uncontroversial legislation or private bills as a method of relieving the workload of the Commons. Any bill other than a financial measure can be introduced in the Lords.

▶ To provide ministers, supplementing those in the House of Commons. By convention, the Prime Minister and other senior ministers heading large spending departments must be members of the Commons. The Lord Chancellor is a member of the House of Lords and, as we have seen, current proposals to abolish the office of Lord Chancellor are faced with a dilemma between the relative independence of the office in the House of Lords and the desirability of such an important government department being accountable to the Commons (Chapter 6).

▶ To provide committees to discuss general topics, such as the European Communities Committee and the Science and Technology Committee. Such reports are highly respected.

▶ To permit persons who have made a contribution to public life, other than party politicians, to participate in government. Life peerages provide the mechanism for this. The contemporary House of Lords is dominated by former officials, politicians and leading members of the elite professions and business interests. These are largely white, male, elderly and affluent.

▶ To act as a constitutional check by preventing a government from prolonging its own life, in respect of which the Lords has a veto (above). The consent of the Lords is also needed for the dismissal of senior judges (Chapter 3).

▶ To act more generally as a constitutional watchdog. It has no specific powers for this purpose but has a Constitutional Committee which examines the constitutional implications of bills brought before the House. The Lord Chancellor is also the minister responsible for constitutional affairs (Chapter 6).

▶ To act as the highest judicial appellate body, although this is currently in question (Chapter 6).

These functions can be pursued in the House of Lords partly because its procedure and culture differ significantly from the Commons. In particular, party discipline is less rigorous and the House of Lords is less partisan than the Commons. Members of the House of Lords (other than bishops of the Church of England sitting as such) are life members removable only by statute and are therefore less susceptible to political pressures than MPs. The House as a whole controls its own procedure, making it relatively free from procedural constraints, and is subject to less time pressure than the Commons. Its members have considerable accumulation of experience and knowledge. The House of Lords cannot therefore easily be manipulated by the government, is attractive to external lobbyists and can ventilate moral and social issues in an objective way. Occasionally members of the House of Lords will respond to their individual consciences, or to public opinion, and defeat government proposals.

## 9.4 Parliamentary Privilege and Standards

It is important that a legislature can control its own affairs and be protected against disruption and interference both by outsiders and from within its ranks. Interference by the Crown with parliamentary business was an ingredient of the seventeenth-century revolution and at the beginning of every Parliament the Speaker symbolically asserts the 'ancient and undoubted privileges' of the House of Commons against the Crown. The House of Lords also has its privileges, which it polices collectively, but does not have the power to punish.

Some parliamentary privileges are mainly of historical or symbolic interest. These include the collective right of access of the Commons to the monarch. Members of the Commons also enjoy immunity from civil, as opposed to criminal, arrest during a period from 40 days before to 40 days after every session. In the case of peers, the immunity is permanent and seems to be based on their status as peers rather than membership of the House (*Stourton v Stourton* (1963)). Now that debtors are no longer imprisoned, civil arrest is virtually obsolete, being concerned mainly with disobedience to court orders. There is no privilege preventing a civil action against an MP in his or her private capacity (*Re Parliamentary Privileges Act 1770* (1958)). Members and officers of both Houses have automatic exemption from jury service (Juries Act 1974) and the House can exempt members from giving evidence in court.

The two most important privileges are (i) the collective privilege of each House to control its own composition and procedure, and (ii) freedom of speech. We shall discuss these below. We shall also discuss the conflicts that have arisen between Parliament and the courts over parliamentary privilege. At present there is an uneasy stalemate. Parliament has never accepted that the courts have the power to decide what are the proper limits of its privileges. The ordinary courts accept that Parliament has the exclusive power to regulate its own internal affairs, but claim the right to determine the limits of other privileges (that is, those affecting the rights of people outside the House) but not to interfere with how established privileges are exercised.

### 9.4.1 Contempt of Parliament

Breach of a specific parliamentary privilege should be distinguished from 'contempt' of Parliament. A parliamentary privilege is a special right or immunity available either to the House collectively (for example to control its own composition and procedure) or to individual members (for example freedom of speech). Contempt is a general term embracing any conduct, whether by MPs or outsiders,

> which obstructs or impedes either House of Parliament in the performance of its functions or which obstructs or impedes any member or officer of the House in the execution of his duty or which has a tendency directly or indirectly to produce such results. (Erskine May, *Parliamentary Practice*, 22nd edn, 1997, p. 108)

This is very wide. It includes, for example, abuses by MPs of parliamentary procedure, disruption in the House, improper or dishonest behaviours by MPs, and harassment of, or allegations against, MPs in newspapers. Contempt not only protects the 'efficiency' of the House but also its 'authority and dignity'.

A controversial aspect of contempt of Parliament concerns public access to parliamentary information, which arguably should be unrestricted except where the disclosure would harm the public interest. However, parliamentary committees often sit in private, and 'leaks' of reports of select committees have been prohibited since 1837, although action is only likely to be taken if the leak causes substantial interference with the function of a Committee. The House of Commons has waived any more general right to restrain publication of its proceedings and has authorised the broadcasting of its proceedings, subject to a power to give directions. It has also undertaken generally to use its contempt powers sparingly (HC 34, 1967–8, para. 15).

Perhaps the most striking feature of contempt of Parliament is that Parliament accuses, tries and punishes offenders itself. The ordinary courts have no jurisdiction over the internal affairs of Parliament (below) and there are no independent safeguards for the individual. This is on the one hand, an assertion of a version of the separation of powers (Chapter 6) but, on the other hand, it seems to violate rule of law values and the ECHR (see *Demicola v Malta* (1992)) concerning the right to be judged by an independent court. The immunity of Parliament from interference by the courts is reinforced by the Human Rights Act 1998 which provides that Parliament, except the House of Lords in its judicial capacity, is not a public body for the purpose of the Act (s.6 (3); Chapter 17). This prevents an action being brought against Parliament under the Human Rights Act.

The procedure for dealing with a contempt of Parliament, or a breach of privilege, is as follows (see HC 417, 1976–7):

1. Any member can give written notice of a complaint to the Speaker.
2. The Speaker decides whether to give priority over other business.
3. If the Speaker decides not to do so, the member may then use the ordinary procedure of the House to get the matter discussed. This would be difficult in practice.
4. If the Speaker decides to take up the matter, the complaining member can propose that the matter be referred to the Committee of Standards and Privileges or that some other action be taken, for example an immediate debate. A select committee can in certain cases refer a contempt against itself direct to the Committee (HC Deb. vol. 94, col. 763–4, 18 March 1986).
5. The Committee (17 senior members) investigates the complaint. Witnesses are examined but there is no right to legal representation. The procedure is entirely up to the Committee. The accused has no legal right to a hearing nor to summon or cross-examine witnesses.
6. The Committee reports back to the House, which decides what action to take. This could range from a reprimand, through suspension or expulsion from the House, to imprisonment for the rest of the session, renewable indefinitely. The House of Lords can imprison for a fixed term and can also impose a fine. The Nicholls Report on Parliamentary Privilege (HL 43-1, HC 214-1, 1998–9) recommended that punishment of non-members should be a matter for the ordinary courts and limited to a fine (see Leopold, 1999, *Public Law* 604).
7. The Speaker also has summary powers to deal with disruptive behaviour in the House, or breaches of the rules of debate. He or she can exclude MPs and others from the Chamber until the end of the session (HC Standing Orders 24–6), and make rulings on matters of procedure. The Lord Chancellor presides over the House of Lords, but has no procedural or disciplinary powers.

The conduct of MPs and the justice and effectiveness of the internal disciplinary process came into the public spotlight during the 1990s when several MPs were accused of accepting payments to give favours to outside interests. The Nicholls Committee recommended that the procedure be reformed in favour of stronger procedural rights reflecting contemporary standards of fairness relating to the right to a fair trial. In its Eighth Report (2002), Cm 5663), the Committee on Standards recommended that no one party should have a majority on the Standards and Privileges Committee, that ministers' aides should not serve as members, that there should be an investigatory panel with an independent Chair, and that full reasons should be published for every decision.

### 9.4.2 'Exclusive Cognisance'

Although the qualifications for being a member of Parliament are fixed by statute, each House has the exclusive right to decide who shall actually sit, to regulate all internal proceedings, and to expel members. In accordance with the separation of powers (Chapter 6), no legal process is possible in respect of any matter before the House and no one can be prevented from placing a matter before Parliament (see *Bilston Corporation* v *Wolverhampton Corporation* (1942)). Conversely, the courts cannot order a minister to present a matter to Parliament even where a change in the law is required by European law (*R* v *Secretary of State for Employment* (1992)). The courts cannot decide whether the procedures in Parliament for enacting legislation have been properly followed (*Pickin* v *BRB* (1974); Chapter 7).The courts can however examine proceedings in the House for the limited purpose of obtaining factual information for example as to the purpose of a statute or in the circumstances contemplated by the controversial case of *Pepper* v *Hart* (1993), see Chapter 6. However, it is for the court to interpret a statute on the basis of general legal principles presumed to identify the intention of Parliament as a whole and the meaning placed on a bill by individual speeches in Parliament is not conclusive (*Wilson* v *First County Trust* (2003)). Moreover approval by the House of delegated legislation or a government decision, except as part of a statute, cannot make valid something unlawful (*Hoffman La Roche* v *Trade and Industry Secretary* (1974)). Resolutions of the House of Commons cannot alter the general law (*Stockdale* v *Hansard* (1839); *Bowles* v *Bank of England* (1913)).

In *Bradlaugh* v *Gossett* (1884)), Charles Bradlaugh, a well-known free-thinker, had been duly elected to the Commons. The House refused to let him take his seat because it deemed that as an atheist he had no statutory right to take the oath. In fact, the courts had previously ruled in his favour (*Clarke* v *Bradlaugh* (1881)). Nevertheless, the court held that it had no power to intervene since this was a matter exclusively to do with the internal procedure of the House. On the other hand, the courts have claimed that the Commons has no control over those outside the House itself, and that

Parliament cannot interfere with court processes (*Ashby* v *White* (1703)). Thus there seems to be a stalemate since Parliament has never accepted that the courts can intervene in any of its processes (below).

What counts as an internal proceeding in Parliament? On one view anything which happens within the precincts of the Houses of Parliament (the Palace of Westminster) is protected. In *R* v *Grahame-Campbell ex parte Herbert* (1935), the Divisional Court held that the House of Commons bar was exempt from the liquor licensing laws and so could sell drinks without restriction. However another explanation of this case is that the Palace of Westminster, a royal palace, enjoys Crown immunity from statute law (Chapter 12). Another view is that immunity applies only to the official business of the House. This will be discussed in the next section in connection with freedom of speech. On this view, ordinary criminal offences unconnected with parliamentary business taking place in the precincts should fall within the ordinary law, although the Sergeant at Arms may control the entry of law enforcement officials into the Palace of Westminster.

### 9.4.3 Freedom of Speech

This is the central privilege of an MP, who must be at liberty to speak and write without fear of interference from outside bodies. On the other hand, as with any liberty, the price to be paid is that some MPs might abuse this freedom to make untrue allegations against persons who cannot answer back or to violate privacy as in the '*Child Z*' case (HC 1995–6, vol. 252, paras 9, 10) where a child was named in defiance of an order of the Court of Appeal.

Article 9 of the Bill of Rights 1688 (part of the revolution settlement for the purpose of protecting MPs against the Crown) states that:

> The Freedom of Speech or Debates or Proceedings in Parliament ought not to be impeached or questioned in any court or palace out of Parliament.

Article 9 has been interpreted widely as not only excluding civil and criminal proceedings but also preventing parliamentary materials from being used as evidence in court proceedings (*Church of Scientology* v *Johnson-Smith* (1972): MP sued for defamation; evidence of his statements in Parliament could not be used). However, the Defamation Act 1996 s.13 amended the Bill of Rights in order to accommodate Neil Hamilton, a Conservative MP, who wished to sue a newspaper for defamation, relying upon parliamentary material for the purpose. Section 13 permits an MP to use things said in Parliament in evidence, provided that the MP waives his or her own immunity. This illustrates the frailty of constitutional principle against party political government. Indeed the Nicholls Committee pointed out that s.13 was a distortion of the constitution in that

Art. 9 exists in the public interest to protect Parliament and is not a provision which individual MPs should be able to waive in their own interests. The Committee therefore proposed that Art. 9 should be waived only by each House.

In *Hamilton v Al Fayed* (1999) the Court of Appeal adopted a narrower interpretation of Art. 9. It held that Art. 9 does not exclude the use of parliamentary material in court but only prohibits the court from penalising or criticising anything said or done in parliamentary proceedings. For example, evidence of something a minister said in Parliament cannot be used to determine whether he is exercising his statutory powers improperly (*R v Secretary of State for Trade ex parte Anderson Strathclyde* [1983] 2 All ER 233 at 238–9), although it can be used as evidence of what his policy is. In addition, statements made by the proposers of a bill in Parliament may be used by courts to ascertain the factual or policy background to a statute and for the limited purposes contemplated in *Pepper v Hart* (Chapter 6). In *Pepper v Hart* the House of Lords took the view that the purpose of Art. 9 was only to prevent MPs from being penalised for what they said in the House (see also *Prebble v Television New Zealand* (1995) and Leopold, 1981, *Public Law* 316).

*'Freedom of Speech or Debates or Proceedings'*: This includes questions asked by an MP in the House whether written or oral, committee proceedings, and written documents published by Order of the House (Parliamentary Papers Act 1840, s.2). Extracts from such documents enjoy only 'qualified' privilege, meaning that they must be made in good faith. Broadcasts of parliamentary proceedings also have qualified privilege (Defamation Act 1952, s.9) as do other unofficial reports and broadcasts such as press reports or parliamentary sketches, provided that they are not merely selective extracts but reasonably comprehensive (*Wason v Walter* (1868); *Cook v Alexander*, (1974)).

*'In Parliament'*: The meaning of 'in Parliament' has not been settled. In 1688, it was no doubt thought that the phrase was self-explanatory. However, the work of a modern MP is not confined to work within the Chamber or even in committees. Much of an MP's time is spent in writing letters, and attending meetings in the UK and abroad with pressure groups, local authorities, business organisations, foreign officials, etc. MPs also meet or write to ministers and constituents. Anything said in the Chamber as part of the business of the House, and in committees or reports related to the business of the House, is certainly protected. Parliamentary committees often visit places around the country, and interference with their proceedings wherever they take place is a contempt of Parliament (for example disturbance at Essex University, 1969 HC 308, 1968–9). At the other extreme, party political speeches by MPs in their own constituencies are not

protected, nor are writings in the press, or TV interviews, nor election matters. It is arguable that speech, even within the House itself, that is unrelated to parliamentary business enjoys no privilege (see *Re Parliamentary Privileges Act 1770* (1958)). In 1976, in the *Zircon* affair, the Committee of Privileges ruled that the showing to MPs within the precincts of a film about a secret security project was not protected by privilege and could therefore be the subject of an injunction (see HC 365, 1986–7). In *Rivlin* v *Bilankin* (1953) a libellous letter about a private matter was posted in a letter box within the precincts. It was held in a short unreasoned judgement that the letter was not protected by privilege.

The main area of doubt concerns things said or written by MPs outside the House as part of their duties on behalf of their constituents, for example a letter complaining to the Secretary of State about a National Health hospital. In the case of *Strauss* (1956), the House of Commons by a tiny majority (218–213) rejected a recommendation by the Committee of Privileges that such letters should be protected by parliamentary privilege. *Strauss* concerned a complaint about the activities of the London Electricity Board. This was not a central government department so the minister to whom Strauss wrote was not directly responsible to Parliament for its day-to-day activities. It is not clear what the reasons for the Commons resolutions were, and the vote may have been on party lines. The *Strauss* view certainly seems narrow and artificial and in later reports the Committee of Privileges has recommended that Strauss be overturned. This has not been implemented. On the basis of *Strauss*, a letter from an MP is privileged only if it is to do with a matter currently being debated in the House or is the subject of an official parliamentary question. In 1967 a Select Committee on Parliamentary Privilege (1967–8, HC 34) recommended that privilege be widened to include all official communications by an MP, but the Nicholls Committee, above, favoured the narrow view. In contemporary circumstances it is likely that any extension of privilege will be made by statute. For example, a decision by an MP to refer a matter to the Parliamentary Ombudsman has absolute privilege (Parliamentary Commissioner Act 1967 s.10 (5)).

'*Impeached or questioned*': Parliament takes the view that it is contempt even to commence legal proceedings by serving a writ upon an MP in respect of a matter which Parliament considers to be privileged. This is a direct challenge to the courts, since if this view is right then the courts have no power to decide the limits of parliamentary privilege. We shall discuss this below.

'*Out of Parliament*': Article 9 prevents interference with the freedom for speech of MPs by any outside body. Legal actions, bribes and threats are the most obvious illustrations (below), but other kinds of pressure also constitute contempt. This could include, for example, publishing MPs' home telephone numbers (*Daily Graphic* case (HC 27 1956)), accusing MPs of drunkenness (*Duffy's Case* (HC 129 1964–5)), or making press allegations of conflict of interest by MPs). However Art. 9 has not been used against media criticism of political speeches by MPs. Nor does Art. 9 prevent courts or other bodies from looking into matters which are also before Parliament, provided that the parliamentary processes or things said in them are not criticised (see *Hamilton* v *Al Fayed* (1999)). The Human Rights Act 1998 might also restrain an expansive interpretation of Art. 9. Although an action could not be brought against Parliament itself, the court is required to interpret all legislation including Art. 9, 'if it is possible to do so', in a way that conforms to the rights set out in the Act, one of which is freedom of expression (s.3).

Independently of the Bill of Rights, an MP performing his official duties inside or outside the House is protected by qualified privilege which is an aspect of the general law of defamation (Chapter 18; for example *Beach* v *Freeson* (1972): complaint to Lord Chancellor about solicitors). This may include media interviews (*Church of Scientology* v *Johnson-Smith* (1972)) but does not apply to party political activities such as election campaigns. Qualified privilege does not ensure that MPs are entirely immune but covers only statements made in good faith. It applies only to defamation, whereas full or 'absolute' parliamentary privilege covers every kind of legal action. Also, qualified privilege is a defence to an action so that the MP must subject himself to the burden of legal proceedings. Even if he eventually wins, the expense and uncertainty of litigation may discourage an MP from speaking freely. It is apparently a contempt of Parliament even to begin legal proceedings against an MP in respect of a matter protected by full parliamentary privilege.

None of this affects limitations placed upon members' freedom of speech by Parliament itself, for example by rules of procedure, or possibly by party discipline within the House. Indeed, these restrictions are themselves immune from control by the courts because of the 'exclusive cognisance' privilege (above). The Speaker, who presides over the House of Commons, has a duty to control procedure impartially. Internal rules exist to prevent MPs misusing their privilege of freedom of speech, for example by attacking people who cannot answer back, or by commenting upon pending legal proceedings. For example, 'the invidious use of a person's name in a question should be resorted to only if to do so is strictly necessary to render the question intelligible and the protection of Parliamentary privilege should be used only as a last resort', and 'in a way that does not damage the good name of the House' (see HC Deb. vol. 94 col. 26, 17 March 1986; P. Leopold, 1986, *Public Law* 368).

### 9.4.4  Standards of Conduct in the Commons

Following the recommendations of the First Report of the Committee on Standards in Public Life (1995 Cm 2850) there is a *Code of Conduct for MPs* (HC Session 1996–7, 24 July 1996). In keeping with parliamentary privilege, this is policed by the House itself (below). The protection of parliamentary privilege entails the risk that an MP might abuse his or her privilege for personal gain. It is not clear whether the general law of corruption applies to an MP (see Leopold in Oliver and Drewry, 1998 and R. Greenaway [1998] *Public Law* 357). The traditional role of an MP is to be an independent representative of his or her constituents and to speak in Parliament in furtherance of the general public interest, thus reflecting Rousseau's ideal of the general will. Several factors may threaten the independence of an MP.

First and foremost there are party loyalties. Secondly many MPs are sponsored by outside bodies, including trade unions and business interests, who may contribute towards their election expenses, research and administration costs and to local constituency expenses. Some MPs accept employment as paid or unpaid 'consultants' to businesses and interest groups such as the Police Federation, or hold company directorships. MPs are also frequently offered 'hospitality', or gifts, or invited on expenses-paid 'fact-finding' trips. There are also 'all party' subject groups of MPs which involve relationships with outside bodies (see HC 408, 1984–5). Except in the case of a private bill, a member is free to vote on a matter in which he has a personal interest.

The position is particularly difficult where an MP acts as a paid advisor to an interest group such as a trade union or a drugs company, and is dismissed for not advocating the employer's interests in Parliament. This happened in the *Brown Case* in 1947 – an MP sponsored by a trade union. The Committee of Privileges voted that a contract could not require an MP to support or represent his sponsor's interests in Parliament, nor could the sponsor punish the MP for not doing so. However, it was not contempt to dismiss a consultant if, for whatever reason, the employer or sponsor was unhappy with his services. This somewhat evasive compromise does not seem to take the matter much further. It would be a contempt to threaten to dismiss an MP unless he took a certain line in Parliament, but not, apparently, to dismiss him after the event. Arguably, pressures from local constituency parties would also be contemptuous.

It is often said that sponsorships and consultancies enable MPs to keep in touch with informed opinion outside Westminster and to develop specialised knowledge. They also enable MPs without private means to supplement their parliamentary salaries. The process of enacting legislation is also helped by consultation with interested parties. There is much 'lobbying' of civil servants, and it is desirable that this should be counterbalanced by MPs having their own access to outside interests. On the other hand, there is a danger that an MP might cease to be independent and become a hired hand, paid to advocate his patron's cause. MPs might also spend time on activities such as sitting in company boardrooms which may generate little understanding of social problems and where the time would be better spent helping their constituents.

Since the seventeenth century, resolutions of the House have declared that certain kinds of external influence are in contempt of Parliament. The latest distinction seems to be between promoting a specific matter for gain, which is forbidden, and acting as a consultant generally, which is acceptable. There have been many resolutions attempting to capture this elusive matter. The latest resolution (1995), which amends a resolution of 1947 (HC 816 1994–5) and is incorporated in the *Code of Conduct for MPs* (above), states that:

> It is inconsistent with the dignity of the house, with the duty of a Member to his constituents, and with the maintenance of the privilege of freedom of speech for any member of this House to enter into any contractual agreement with an outside body, controlling or limiting the Member's complete independence and freedom of action in Parliament or stipulating that he shall act in any way as the representative of such outside body in regard to any matter to be transacted in Parliament; the duty of a Member being to his constituents and to the country as a whole, rather than to any particular section thereof: and that in particular no Members of the House shall, in consideration of any remuneration, fee, payment or reward or benefit in kind, direct or indirect, which the Member or any member of his or her family has received is receiving or expects to receive –
>
> (i) advocate or initiate any cause or matter on behalf of any outside body or individual, or
> (ii) urge any other Member of either House of Parliament, including Ministers, to do so by means of any speech, Question, motion, introduction of a bill, or amendment to a motion or a Bill.

The *Guidance to the Resolution* published by the House of Commons (1997) makes it clear that MPs can be sponsored by outside bodies and can freely take up constituency problems relating to bodies with which they are connected. In 1974 it was resolved that MPs should disclose any relevant financial interests in debates, committees and communication with ministers and civil servants and there have been resolutions requiring declarations concerning membership of delegations on overseas visits (see *Code of Conduct*). A further resolution (1995) restricts the extent to which any member with a paid interest may participate in, or accompany, a delegation to Ministers or public officials. A member should not initiate, or participate in, or attend any such delegation where the problem to be addressed affects only the body with which the member has a relevant interest, except when that problem relates primarily to a constituency matter (*Guidance* HC 1997).

There are also criminal offences involving members of public bodies. Corruption is a common law offence and there are also statutory offences under the Public Bodies (Corrupt Practices) Act 1889 and the Prevention of Corruption Act 1916, s.4 (2). These offences seem wide enough to include cases where MPs are offered bribes (but see *Royal Commission on Standards of Conduct in Public Life*, 1976, Cmnd 6524). However, an MP might sometimes be protected by Article 9 of the Bill of Rights (above). Nevertheless in *R v Greenaway* (1998) a Conservative MP had accepted a bribe to use his influence to help a person acquire UK citizenship. The court held that parliamentary privilege did not apply because the offence occurred when the bribe was received and therefore the court did not need to investigate what went on in Parliament itself.

MPs are required to enter information about their financial interests in a Register of Members' Interests, a practice which Enoch Powell condemned as unconstitutional, claiming that an unlawful qualification has been added for serving as an MP. The register itself has been held (oddly) not to be protected by parliamentary privilege (*Rost v Edwards* (1990)). The categories of interest required by the register have been strengthened in response to the Nolan Committee and include provision of services such as consultancy, company directorships, employment or offices, professions and trades, names of clients, financial sponsorships, overseas visits as an MP, payments received from abroad, land or property, shareholdings and 'any interest or benefit received which might reasonably be thought by others to influence the member's actions in Parliament'. As a result of a recommendation by the Committee on Standards, the value of an interest must now be disclosed and in the case of paid employment or sponsorship, the amount of time involved. According to the register only one in five MPs is without an external source of income, endorsing what Sedley (2001), *London Review of Books*, 15 Nov, 11) calls a culture of moonlighting which would be unacceptable in any ordinary job one can think of, and affirming the legitimacy of accepting retainers from outside interests.

Following the First Report of the Committee on Standards in Public Life (1995, Cm 2850) the House of Commons appointed a Parliamentary Commissioner for Standards empowered to investigate complaints of misuse of the Commons register and to report to the Standards and Privileges Committee of the House of Commons (HC Standing Orders (Public Business) (1995) No. 150). The Commissioner can also investigate complaints by MPs and the public concerning the *Code of Conduct* and give advice to MPs. Its decisions, being subject to parliamentary privilege are not subject to judicial review (*R v Parliamentary Commissioner for Standards* (1998)). The Commissioner cannot investigate the interests of ministers acting as such. There is no independent mechanism for this purpose although Parliament can order an independent inquiry into 'a matter of urgent importance', (Tribunals of Inquiry (Evidence) Act 1921). In practice governments prefer voluntary inquiries of their own. Parliament can appoint and dismiss the Commissioner. In 2001 Elizabeth Filkin did not have her contract renewed. She had attracted a reputation as an assiduous investigator. In its Eighth Report (2002, Cm 5663) the Committee on Standards recommended that the independence of the Commissioner be strengthened. The Commissioner should be appointed for a non-renewable term of 5–7 years, should have the power to call for witnesses and documents and should not be an employee of the house.

### 9.4.5 Standards in the House of Lords

There is a 'custom' that the House of Lords should not be subject to formal rules regulating standards but should rely on the 'personal honour' of members (see Fifth Report of Select Committee on Procedures of the House (HL 1994–5) No. 98). However no reason has been offered as to why members of the Lords are more honourable than members of the Commons. The reason perhaps lies in the UK constitution's underlying distrust of democracy. The House of Lords appears to have no disciplinary sanctions and, with the possible exception of treason, a member could not be deprived of a peerage or suspended or expelled for misconduct without statutory authority. The Letters Patent issued by the Crown that create a peerage confer a legal right to sit in the House of Lords. It is customary for membership of the House of Lords not be regarded as a full-time commitment and many members have outside business and professional interests including full-time jobs. The current proposals for reform of the House of Lords have not decided whether members should be paid.

Since 1995 there has been a limited voluntary register of members' financial interests. The Seventh Report of the Committee on Standards (2000, Cm 4903) recommended that there should be a House of Lords *Code of Conduct* and a compulsory register of members interests although both should be laxer than the equivalent House of Commons arrangements. The recommendation was founded on the belief that public confidence should be the overriding concern and that public opinion would not look favourably upon a voluntary register. However, there would be no obligation to disclose the amount of payment and, while disclosure of consultancies and lobbying interests should be compulsory, disclosure of other interests should be voluntary, the test being interests which 'members consider may affect the public perception of the way in which a member discharges his or her parliamentary duties'. This was implemented in 2002 (see HL Deb. 24 July 2001, col. 1849).

## 9.4.6 The Courts and Parliamentary Privilege

As we have seen, the courts are not prepared to intervene in the internal affairs of the House. On the other hand, where parliamentary activity involves the rights of persons outside the House, the courts have claimed the power to intervene at least to the extent of deciding whether the privilege asserted by Parliament exists. In a famous eighteenth-century controversy that asserted basic rule of law values, the courts held that parliamentary officers have no power to deprive citizens of voting rights: 'where there is a right there is a remedy' (*Ashby* v *White* (1703), see also *Paty's Case* (1704)). In *Stockdale* v *Hansard* (1839) it was held that parliamentary privilege did not protect reports published by order of the House from being the subject of libel actions. The subject matter of these disputes is only of historical interest. Parliament no longer controls elections and *Stockdale* v *Hansard* was soon reversed by statute (Parliamentary Papers Act 1840). Nevertheless, the general principle about the power of the courts remains valid.

Parliament has never accepted that *Stockdale* v *Hansard* was correctly decided, and has never withdrawn the claim to be the exclusive judge of its own privileges. In *The Sheriff of Middlesex Case* (1840), which was a sequel to *Stockdale* v *Hansard*, Parliament imprisoned the two holders of the office of Sheriff for enforcing the court's judgment in *Stockdale* v *Hansard*. Not surprisingly, the Sheriffs applied to the court for release, but the court, including Lord Denman, who had decided *Stockdale* v *Hansard* itself, held that it was powerless to intervene. Parliament had the undoubted right to commit to prison for contempt and it did not have to give reasons. Unless some improper reason was disclosed on the face of the committal warrant, the court must assume that Parliament was acting lawfully, even though the judges knew otherwise. Therefore, by relying on the *Sheriff of Middlesex Case*, Parliament can arbitrarily imprison anyone it likes. Whether this principle will be taken advantage of in modern times rests with Parliament's, or the courts', political sense. The courts are unwilling to take action that might be considered as trespassing on Parliament's preserves. Parliament too has shown restraint in asserting claims to privilege (for example the *Strauss* case mentioned above). This standoff between courts and Parliament could be regarded as an example of the dual sovereignty which it is claimed that the separation of powers requires. Indeed, in characteristic fashion it has been claimed that there is a voluntary, mutual respect between the two institutions (*Hamilton* v *Al Fayed* [1999] 3 All ER 317, 333–4).

The Nicholls Report suggested the enactment of a code of parliamentary privilege to include modest reforms largely intended to clarify the relationship between Parliament and the courts. In addition to the recommendations that I have already mentioned they include the following:

▶ 'place out of Parliament' for the purposes of Art. 9 should be defined to include courts and tribunals empowered to take evidence on oath but not tribunals of inquiry if both Houses so resolve;

▶ there should be an offence of abuse of public office which should include MPs;

▶ MPs should be subject to the criminal law relating to corruption;

▶ members of the Lords should be compellable before Commons committees;

▶ Parliament's 'exclusive cognisance' should be confined to 'activities directly and closely related to the business of the House';

▶ Contempt by non-members should be dealt with by the ordinary courts;

▶ Freedom from arrest should be abolished.

## Summary

▶ The House of Lords originated as the King's council of leading landowners of the realm. It subsequently evolved into a lawmaking body in partnership with the Commons. After the 1688 settlement the House of Lords was regarded as holding the constitutional balance of power, but by the twentieth century it had become subordinate to the elected House of Commons. The Lords were given a new lease of life by the introduction of Life Peers in the 1960s, but the constitutional role of the House remains controversial. By convention and law the Lords must ultimately defer to the Commons. We mentioned the House of Lord's functions as a limited but relatively independent constitutional check and balance.

▶ We sketched the historical development of the House of Commons, starting with its medieval origins in the practice of the King seeking advice from trusted local representatives, and concluding after the First World War when the Commons became a fully representative chamber. We emphasised the development of the relationship between the House and the Crown, pointing out that the executive and the party system now dominate the Commons.

▶ There is a network of laws and conventions to ensure that Parliament meets annually and that it can remove the government. However, the government can dissolve Parliament subject to the possibility of the overriding powers of the Crown, which are discussed in Chapter 11, and MPs cannot hold the government to account during the long periods when Parliament is not sitting.

▶ We outlined the functions of Parliament, these being not to initiate legislation but to scrutinise legislation, provide the executive with finance, hold the executive accountable, debate matters of public concern and redress grievances. We pointed out that the executive is usually too powerful and complex for Parliament to be effective. However, at least Parliament is a public forum in which the executive can be forced to justify its actions.

## Summary cont'd

▶ The functions of the House of Lords include:

(i)   Revising and delaying legislation introduced in the Commons (other than financial legislation);

(ii)  Dealing with relatively uncontroversial legislation, and with business overflowing from the Commons;

(iii) Providing a forum for debate of matters of general concern;

(iv)  Providing a political base for government ministers who do not possess seats in the Commons;

(v)   Providing a method of rewarding those deemed meritorious by the government;

(vi)  Acting as a constitutional safeguard should a government attempt to extend its own life or dismiss the judiciary;

(vii) Acting as a final appellate court.

Because of the control over the Commons exercised by the executive, a second chamber is desirable but there is no agreement as to how the hereditary element in the Lords should be replaced. At present the House of Lords is accountable to no one.

The rules of procedure and of party discipline in the House of Lords are more relaxed than is the case with the Commons.

▶ We examined Parliament's power to protect itself against interference from without and within through the law of parliamentary privilege and its powers to punish for contempt. Parliament can enforce its own privileges free from interference by the ordinary courts.

▶ We discussed the parliamentary privileges, based on the separation of powers of exclusive control over its own procedures and freedom of speech drawing attention to its possible limits in terms of what counts as parliamentary proceedings and to the separate matter of qualified privilege in the law of defamation.

▶ We discussed the safeguards against conflicts of interest by MPs including the Register of Interests and the Parliamentary Commissioner for Standards. We referred to the difficulty of distinguishing between lobbying on behalf of an interest and using specialist knowledge to present a case in the public interest.

▶ We discussed the relationship between the courts and parliamentary privilege, drawing attention to the unresolved conflict as to who decides whether a claimed privilege exists. This conflict may depend on the extent of Parliament's power to commit for contempt.

# Exercises

**9.1** What is the constitutional justification for the House of Lords?

**9.2** 'The executive has undue control over the summoning and dismissal of Parliament.' Discuss.

**9.3** 'It is not unduly idealistic to regard the integrity of Members' judgement, however constrained it may be by the party system, and the devotion of their time to the job to which they have been elected, as fundamental values worth not only protecting but insisted on' (Sedley). Discuss in relation to the outside interests of MPs and peers.

**9.4** In what circumstances is an MP immune from legal action in respect of things he or she says or writes?

**9.5** To what extent does the power of Parliament in relation to contempt of Parliament comply with the rule of law?

**9.6** Rat, a member of Parliament, is employed on a salary by the Institute of Top Executives, a right-wing pressure group, to represent the Institute in Parliament. During a debate, Rat makes a speech calling for higher taxation of executives' salaries, and accusing various members of the Institute of tax evasion. He later circulates copies of this speech to members of his local constituency party. Dog, the chairman of the Institute, who is one of those accused of tax evasion, seeks your advice as to whether the Institute can dismiss Rat as its parliamentary representative, and as to whether he should bring a libel action against Rat. Advise Dog.

**9.7** George is a member of Parliament. A constituent sends George a letter accusing the management of a local nuclear power station of negligence in relation to safety standards. George, who is employed as a consultant by a company involved in the promotion of renewable sources of energy, passes on the letter to the minister responsible. The manager of the power station hears about the letter and issues writs for libel against (i) the constituent, and (ii) George.

The manager also alleges that George has taken bribes from a company specialising in wind power generators to ask questions in the House.

Discuss.

**9.8** Bulldog, MP, asks Fox, the Minister of Health, in the House of Commons, a question in which he strongly criticises the manner in which the National Health Board deals with the problem of 'lengthy waiting lists for hospital treatment and allocation of hospital beds'. In a later letter to Fox, Bulldog makes further and more serious allegations concerning the conduct of the an individual hospital manager. The solicitor to the NHB advises the Board that

Bulldog's letter is defamatory. Acting on this advice, the NHB issues a writ for libel against Bulldog while Parliament is in session. Contending that this is a matter of parliamentary privilege over which the court has no jurisdiction, Bulldog refuses to enter an appearance or to defend the action. Meanwhile, the House of Commons resolves that any judge, counsel or party who takes part in such proceeding will be guilty of contempt.

Discuss the position of Bulldog and any possible action that may be taken against (i) the members of the National Health Board, and (ii) any solicitor or counsel who proceeds with the libel action against Bulldog.

# Further reading

Archer, P. (2000) 'The House of Lords, Past, Present and Future', *Political Quarterly*, **70**: 396.

Blackburn, R. (1989) 'The Summoning and Meeting of New Parliaments in the United Kingdom', *Legal Studies*, **9**: 165.

Brazier, R. (1989) 'The Constitutional Role of the Opposition', *Northern Ireland Law Quarterly*, **40**: 131.

Dickson, B. and Carmichael, P. (eds) (1999) *The House of Lords: Its Parliamentary and Judicial Roles*, Oxford, Hart Publishing.

Lock, G. (1985) 'Parliamentary Privilege and the Courts', *Public Law*, 64.

Munro, C.R. (2000) *Studies in Constitutional Law*, 2nd edn, London, Butterworth, Chapter 7.

Norton, P. (1993) *Does Parliament Matter?*, Harvester, Wheatsheaf.

Oliver, D. and Drewry, G. (eds) (1998) *The Law and Parliament*, London, Butterworth.

Riddall, P. (2000) 'The Second Chamber: In Search of a Complementary Role', *Political Quarterly*, **70**: 404.

Wakeham, Lord (2000) *A House for the Future: Royal Commission on the House of Lords*, Cm 4534, London, HMSO.

Weir, S. and Beetham, D. (1999) *Political Power and Democratic Control in Britain*, London, Routledge.

# Chapter 10

# The composition of Parliament and parliamentary elections

Britain has been said to be a party democracy rather than a Parliamentary Democracy. (Budge, Crewe, McKay, Newton, *The New British Politics*, 450)

## Key words

▶ Legitimacy
▶ Different kinds of democracy
▶ Majorities and representation
▶ Conflicting functions of elections
▶ Fair elections and freedom of expression

## 10.1 Introduction

The composition of Parliament raises fundamental questions. Firstly, about the legitimacy of the constitution: to what extent in relation to the functions outlined in Chapter 9 does the legislature have public consent and confidence? Secondly, about the nature of democracy: which of the different kinds of democracy outlined in Chapter 1 best captures our arrangements? Can a non-elected element in the legislature be justified on grounds of efficiency? Do the voting rules cater for the different functions expected of Parliament? Thirdly, there are questions concerning the relationship between democracy and other liberal values. What restrictions should there be on the right to vote or to stand for election or to participate in an election campaign? Liberal freedoms such as freedom of expression and republican rights such as participation (Chapter 1) may conflict with the aspiration of equality.

## 10.2 The House of Lords

Almost anyone can be a member of the House of Lords. Aliens (Act of Settlement 1700 s.3), persons under 21 (SO 2), undischarged bankrupts (Insolvency Act 1986 s.427 (1)) and persons convicted of treason until their sentence is served (Forfeiture Act 1870 s.2) cannot sit in the House of Lords. Members can apparently be removed only by statute.

There is no legal limit on the size of the House of Lords. Before the House of Lords Act 1999 there were about 1,349 members, making the House of Lords the largest legislative chamber in the world. The 1999 Act reduced this to 695 by ejecting 654 of the 746 hereditary peers. The numbers will remain similar if the current proposals for reform (below) take effect. This still makes the House of Lords one of the largest second chambers in the world, eclipsed, according to Kellner (*Evening Standard* 8 Nov 2001), only by Kazakhstan and Burkina Faso. Germany's Bundesrat has 69 members and the US Senate 100. In Europe, Italy, with 326, comes nearest to the UK. Small upper chambers could be justified on the basis that, having more limited powers than the lower House, they can be more cohesive and more focused.

The dominant feature of the House of Lords is that none of its members is elected, all being chosen by the executive in one form or another. Protocol 3 of the European Convention on Human Rights (ECHR) requires states to hold free elections to the legislature. In *Matthieu-Mohun* v *Belgium* (1988), the ECHR held that this requires at least one chamber to be elected. However, one of the judges went further and stated that the elected element must comprise a majority of the legislature and the non-elected element must not have greater powers than the elected element. The present House of Lords seems to violate the majority requirement, there being currently 659 members of the House of Commons.

The membership of the House of Lords comprises the following:

▶ **The lords spiritual**

The lords spiritual comprise the archbishops of Canterbury and York, the bishops of London, Durham and Winchester, and 21 other diocesan bishops of the Church of England, these being the senior in order of appointment. Bishops are appointed by the Queen on the advice of the Prime Minister, the practice being that he chooses one from a list of nominations provided by the church authorities. The bishops vacate their seats in the Lords on ceasing to hold office. They are not peers and can vote in parliamentary elections. Dignitaries from other faiths can be appointed to the House of Lords as ordinary peers.

▶ **Hereditary peers**

Until the House of Lords Act 1999, the hereditary peers formed a majority, thereby both biasing the House of Lords in favour of conservative interests and being difficult to justify on the basis of democratic principles. Hereditary peers are persons on whom, or on whose ancestors, the monarch has conferred various ranks, namely dukes, duchesses, marquises, earls, viscounts and barons, specifying that the peerages can be inherited by the peer's descendants. No reason need be given for the conferring of a peerage and it is unlikely that the conferring of honours or titles is subject to judicial review. Allegations are made from time to time that peerages are used to bribe supporters or to get rid of dead wood in the House of Commons or even sold.

'Peers of the United Kingdom' derive their titles from grants made after the Acts of Union with Scotland and Ireland. 'Peers of England' were created before the union with Scotland in 1706 and 'peers of Great Britain' were created between 1707 and the union with Ireland in 1801. Scottish peerages are those created before 1707 (Peerage Act 1963 s.4). Irish peers derived from the pre Union era cannot sit in the Lords but can be elected to the Commons (*Earl of Antrim's Petition* (1967)). A peeress in her own right can sit in the House of Lords but only since the Peerage Act 1963.

At common law a peer cannot surrender his or her peerage (*Re Parliamentary Election for Bristol SE* (1964)). However, under the Peerage Act 1963 a hereditary peerage can be disclaimed for life. The peerage must be disclaimed within 12 months of succeeding to it (one month if the new peer is a member of Parliament) or within 12 months of coming of age. The succession to the peerage is not affected. A peer who disclaims his or her title cannot again become a hereditary peer but could be appointed a life peer (below).

The government is proposing to reform the composition of the House of Lords (below). As an initial measure the House of Lords Act 1999 provides that no one shall be a member of the House of Lords by virtue of a hereditary peerage. This is subject to an exception, negotiated to prevent the peers from rejecting the Act. Under the exception the House elects 90 peers together with the Earl Marshall and the Lord Chamberlain who are royal officials. The elected peers comprise 75 peers elected on the basis of party balance (currently 42 Conservatives, 28 cross-benchers without party membership, 3 Liberal Democrats and 2 Labour), together with 15 elected as deputy speakers and committee chairs. The elected peers sit for life. Other peers can now stand for and vote in elections to the House of Commons.

### ▶ Life peers

Life peers are appointed by the Crown, on the advice of the Prime Minister, with the rank of baron. Originally life peers could not sit in the House of Lords, but under the Life Peerages Act 1958, enacted in order to regenerate the House of Lords, they can now do so. Life peerages are intended to enable hand-picked people to play a part in public life and also to be a way of countering the apparent conservative bias represented by the hereditary peers. In practice, a radical element has not emerged. Life peerages are often bestowed on retired public officials who have served loyally, or on retired members of the House of Commons, particularly those who have held high government office. They are used more as a reward for past services, or as a device for ridding the Commons of unwanted members than as means of infusing the House with new blood. Occasionally a life peerage is created for a person who has performed public services or whom the Prime Minister wishes to appoint as a minister. This may cause political problems arising out of a lack of perceived legitimacy. There are currently about 470 life peers in the House of Lords.

In an extreme case, where for example a Prime Minister attempts to flood the Lords with his or her cronies, the monarch could perhaps reject the Prime Minister's advice in relation to appointments. Where a Prime Minister seeks to act undemocratically, it is arguable that the monarch has a duty to act as the ultimate constitutional check. On two important occasions the monarch reluctantly agreed to appoint sufficient peers to secure a government majority. These were the Reform Act 1832, which extended the parliamentary franchise, and the Parliament Act 1911, which reduced the powers of the House of Lords. In both cases the House of Lords was threatening to obstruct the Commons. In the case of the 1911 Act, George V agreed to appoint the peers only if the government's policy was submitted to a general election.

Pending reform of the House of Lords, the Prime Minister's conventional power to appoint life peers is subject to a non-statutory House of Lords Appointments Commission. Appointed by the House (see *Hansard* HL 4 May 2000, col. 181W), it vets all proposals for appointment as a life peer and also administers a new process for non-party political appointments (the so-called 'people's peers'). However, its decisions are no more than advisory. The commission comprises a cross-bench peer as Chair, together with three peers nominated by the main parties and three 'independent' persons. Its terms of reference embody the Nolan principles of impartiality, integrity and objectivity. Any British or Irish citizen over 21 can apply for appointment. The criteria for appointment are a record of 'significant achievement', 'independence of political parties' and 'an ability to contribute to the work of the House' (see http//www.houseoflordsappointmentscommission.gov.uk).

The last of these criteria invites preference to be given in the manner of a private club to those with whom the existing members feel personally comfortable. Most of the life peers appointed under the new regime have been persons prominent in public life and likely to be personally known to members of the appointing committee. As a result of the 1999 Act and the appointment of life peers, it seems that the political balance of the House of Lords is now held by Liberal Democrats and cross-benchers.

▶ **Lords of Appeal in Ordinary**
These currently comprise 12 judges specifically appointed for the purpose from which are drawn the highest appellate tribunal as the Appellate

Committee of the House of Lords. The same judges also sit as members of the Judicial Committee of the Privy Council which is strictly part of the executive. They are life peers and can sit and vote in the House after they give up their judicial office from which they must retire at 70 (Judicial Pensions and Retirement Act 1993). By convention, the law lords do not participate in party political debate while holding judicial office but may speak on questions of law reform. Other peers who hold or who have held high judicial office, notably the Lord Chancellor in defiance of the separation of powers, can also be members of the Appellate Committee. Proposed reforms were discussed in Chapter 6.

### 10.2.1 Attendance in the House of Lords

Many members of the House of Lords have little interest in politics and do not regularly sit. This may introduce unpredictability into the handling of business. Members can claim daily expenses for attendance and it is possible that a flood of members may descend on the House on a particular occasion in search of personal advantage. The influence of erratic attendees can be decisive, as was the case in 1987 when the House was flooded with Conservative peers to support the abolition of local property taxes in favour of a 'poll tax' on individual residents (subsequently abolished). Standing Order 20 enables a peer to apply for leave of absence. The Order requires a peer to state an affirmative intention to attend. Peers granted leave of absence are not expected to attend for the remainder of that Parliament, although one month's notice can be given of termination of leave of absence. There are however no sanctions against peers who disregard the attendance rule.

### 10.2.2 House of Lords Reform

Attempts to reform the Lords have foundered, partly because of disagreement as to what the role of the House should be as well as to its composition, and partly because the matter has not had high political priority. Mill (Chapter1) argued (*On Representative Government*, Chapter 13) that a second chamber should primarily act as a partial check on the majority and should ideally embody

> the greatest number of elements exempt from the class interests and prejudices of the majority, but having in themselves nothing offensive to democratic feeling.

This suggests an elected chamber chosen by a method of election different from that for the Commons but one drawing on popular support. However, Mill also thought that in every constitution there should be a centre of resistance to the predominant power – 'and in a democratic constitution, therefore, a nucleus of resistance to the democracy'. He recommended including experts in a second chamber, recruited primarily from persons distinguished in the public professions, such as the judiciary, armed forces and civil service. However, although he thought that the question of a second chamber was relatively unimportant, it could be justified (in both liberal and republican terms) on the basis of the corrupting effect of absolute power and as a mechanism for producing compromise. Mill's preferred solution was proportional representation in the House of Commons (below) which would make it more difficult for any majority faction to be dominant.

In a unitary system such as that of the UK, a wholly elected house might either duplicate or rival the House of Commons, thereby weakening the accountability of the government. On the other hand, an entirely appointed Chamber would lack public credibility and reinforce the patronage that currently undermines the constitution. Furthermore, there is no consensus as to who should make appointments to the House and on what basis. The hereditary element is said to have the advantage of independence but at the price of legitimacy. An attractively democratic possibility would be random selection from the whole adult community, as is currently the case with jury service. However, this raises many practical and economic problems and is probably unrealistic (see Phillipson, 2004, *Public Law* 352).

The Parliament Act 1911 began the process of reform by removing the power of the House of Lords to veto public bills introduced in the Commons, other than a bill to prolong the life of a Parliament (Chapter 11). The Bryce Conference of 1917–18 (Cd 9038) attempted to tackle the problem of the composition of the House of Lords but was unable to agree. In 1958 the introduction of life peers reinvigorated the House to a certain extent, particularly in relation to the work of its committees. In 1968 an all-party conference proposed removing voting rights from most of the hereditary element and introducing the concept of 'working peers', mainly life peers, who would form a permanent nucleus of the House. The bill to introduce these reforms was abandoned because of backbench opposition from both sides of the House.

The present Labour government is reforming the House of Lords in two stages. Stage 1 comprised the House of Lords Act 1999 (above). Stage 2 remains unrealised. The report of the Royal Commission on the House of Lords (the Wakeham Report (2000)) was broadly accepted by the government (*Hansard* HL 7 March 2000, col. 919), but attracted widespread criticism for its conservatism and lack of rigour. The Commission looked at the House of Lords in isolation from wider questions of constitutional reform and did not therefore question the role and powers of the House of Commons nor those of the executive. Wakeham endorsed the existing roles of the House of Lords as subordinate to the Commons, providing limited checks on the executive, a revising mechanism for legislation and a 'constitutional long-stop' to force the government to have second thoughts. Wakeham's governing principles (Wakeham, 2000, 31) seem to be:

> the capacity to offer council from a range of sources ... broadly representative of society in the UK at the beginning of the 21st century ... It should give the UK's constituent nations and regions, for the first time a formally constituted voice in the Westminster parliament.

The electorate is not to be trusted to produce these outcomes but must be paternalistically protected against itself.

Wakeham rejected the extremes of an all-elected second chamber and one comprised of 'experts'. Wakeham thought that a wholly elected second chamber might produce the 'wrong sort of people', reinforce party political control, result in 'voter fatigue' and either gridlock or rubber-stamp the Commons thus weakening governmental accountability. Wakeham rejected random selection apparently because of the risk of appointing persons who would not 'fit in'. Wakeham rejected the notion of a 'council of the wise', recognising that government is about accommodating disagreement and is necessarily political.

Perhaps updating the classical 'mixed constitution', Wakeham therefore proposed a House comprising a balance of representatives from the main interests in the community with about one third elected. Elections would be on a fifteen year cycle, with one third being elected every five years to ensure that the outcome did not duplicate elections to the Commons. An independent statutory commission would appoint all other members, taking account of regional, ethnic, gender and religious concerns.

The subsequent progress of the reforms is one of confusion. A government White Paper (2001, *The House of Lords: Completing the Reforms*, Cm 5291) broadly adopted Wakeham's proposals but weakened them in favour of a larger element of government control over the House of Lords. This was not well received and was followed by proposals from the Public Administration Committee (Fifth Report 2001–2, HC 494–1), the House of Commons and the political parties for different permutations of elected and appointed members. In 2002 a Joint Committee of both Houses set out seven options ranging from complete election to complete appointment, all of which were rejected by the Commons (HL 17, HC 171 2002–3). In July 2003, the government announced that it would, in the medium term, confine itself to making the House of Lords effective in its present form. In September 2003, the government announced that it would introduce a bill to remove the remaining hereditary peers and set up a statutory appointment commission. This would select members according to the distribution of votes at the previous general election with 20% being non-party appointments. At the time of writing these reforms have not been put into place.

### 10.3 Membership of the House of Commons

Anyone can be a member of the House of Commons other than the following:

- aliens other than citizens of Ireland;
- people under 21 (Family Law Reform Act 1969 Schedule 2 para. 2);
- mental patients (Mental Health Act 1983 – there are provisions for removing MPs under this Act);
- members of the House of Lords;
- clergy ordained by bishops in the Churches of England and Ireland, ministers of the Church of Scotland and Roman Catholic priests (see *Re MacManaway* (1951));
- Debtors made bankrupt, until five years after discharge unless the discharge certifies that the bankruptcy was not caused by the debtor's misconduct; persons convicted of election offences (below);
- persons convicted of treason, until expiry of the sentence or pardon (Forfeiture Act 1870);
- persons convicted of an offence and sentenced to prison for more than one year while actually in prison or unlawfully at large (Representation of the People Act 1981) – this was designed to prevent convicted terrorists in Northern Ireland from standing;
- persons holding certain public offices (House of Commons (Disqualification) Act 1975.

The last of these disqualifications is an example of the separation of powers. One element of the seventeenth-century conflict between Crown and Parliament was the Commons' fear that the Crown might bribe members by giving them jobs. The Act of Settlement 1700 therefore provided that nobody who held Crown office or a place of profit under the Crown could sit in the Commons. This would of course have prevented ministers from sitting, and the constitution would have had a strict separation of powers. This part of the Act was repealed by the Succession to the Crown Act 1707. However, there are limits upon the number of ministers who can be members of the Commons, thus giving the Commons a degree of independence. These are as follows:

(i) Under the House of Commons (Disqualification) Act 1975 not more than 95 ministers may sit and vote;

(ii) The Ministerial and Other Salaries Act 1975 (as amended) fixed the salaries of the various grades of minister, and limits the number of paid ministers of the government to 83 plus about 30 other specialised political office-holders such as whips; and also four Law

Officers. However, a government can increase its loyalists in the House by appointing unpaid parliamentary secretaries.

(iii) The House of Commons (Disqualification) Act 1975 debars certain other holders of public office from sitting in the Commons. The main examples are as follows:

- Full-time judges of various kinds.
- Regulators of privatised utilities.
- Civil servants.
- Members of the regular armed services and police (other than specialised forces such as railway police).
- Members of foreign legislatures. However, by virtue of the Disqualifications Act 2000, a member of the Irish legislature (the Oireachtas) can be a member of the Commons.
- Members of certain public boards and undertakings.
- Holders of the offices of Steward or Bailiff of the Chiltern Hundreds or of the Manor of Northstead. These are meaningless titles in the gift of the Chancellor of the Exchequer. There are no specific rules entitling MP's to resign or retire but a successful application for one of these offices has the same effect.

In the event of a dispute about a disqualification, the Judicial Committee of the Privy Council may make a declaration on the application of any person (s.7). The House may also refer a matter to the Privy Council for an opinion (Judicial Committee Act 1833, s.4). The House has the statutory power to disregard a disqualification if it has been subsequently removed (for example by the MPs resigning from a disqualifying post (s.6 (2)).

## 10.4 The Electoral System

### 10.4.1 The Purpose of Elections

We can assess the electoral system only in relation to its aims. Is it (a) to secure democratic local representation; or (b) to produce effective government; or (c) to produce 'accountable' governments? No electoral system has yet been thought up that successfully combines all of these aims. Underlying these conflicting aims is the difference between 'representative democracy' and 'market democracy' outlined in Chapter 1. Moreover, the process of electing representatives is the only democratic mechanism regularly provided by the UK constitution (referendums on particular issues are occasionally offered by particular governments) so that participatory democracy is excluded. Indeed, there is no provision for entrenching electoral rights so that the arrangements governing elections are made by ordinary statutes under the control of the government of the day. Protocol 1 Art.

3 of the European Convention on Human Rights provides a general and vague standard, limited to representative democracy:

> Free elections at reasonable intervals by secret ballot, under conditions which will ensure the free expression of the people in the choice of the legislature.

Until well into the nineteenth century the prevalent belief was that only landowners had a sufficient stake in the realm to vote, the majority of the population enjoying 'virtual representation' through the property owners. During the nineteenth century the extension of voting rights to non-property owners was slowly and reluctantly conceded, resisted by liberal arguments that the freedom of talented people to develop themselves would be curtailed by the inflated demands of the masses. Democracy was also resisted by the likes of Dicey who thought that it was unpredictable and Matthew Arnold (1822–88). Arnold believed in a grand overarching concept of the public good and recommended an 'authority of culture' by which he seemed to mean a monarchy or the Platonic ideal of a wise ruling class (Arnold, *Culture and Anarchy*, ed. Dover Wilson 1960). This approach is still canvassed in the context of reform of the House of Lords (above).

There is a divergence between the law of the electoral process and practical politics. The legal basis of democracy in the UK is that the electorate in each constituency chooses an individual to represent the constituency in the House of Commons. However, as we have seen, by convention the House of Commons chooses the leader of the executive who is the party leader commanding a majority in the Commons. The party system therefore encourages the electorate to vote essentially for a party with the question of effective democratic representation being subsidiary. Elections are therefore fought and funded between the parties on a national battlefield. Dicey, however, believed that a 'parliamentary executive must by the law of its nature follow, or tend to follow, the lead of Parliament' (1915, p. 484).

The European Convention on Human Rights (above) does not require any particular kind of electoral system, thus endorsing the principle that elections may have different aims. An electoral system must not discriminate against particular groups of citizens although a particular political party cannot apparently challenge the electoral system on the basis that it is at a disadvantage (see *Lindsey* v *UK* (1979); *Matthieu-Mohun* v *Belgium* (1987); *Liberal Party* v *UK* (1982)). The courts are likely to adopt a low level of review in relation to electoral machinery because of sensitivity to the separation of powers.

Election law is found primarily in the Representation of the People Act 1983 and the Parliamentary Constituencies Act 1986. Important changes were made by the Representation of the People Act 2000 and the Political Parties, Elections and Referendums Act 2000.

## 10.4.2 The Electoral Commission

The Electoral Commission was a response to the concerns of the Fifth Report of the Committee on Standards in Public Life (Cm 4057, 1998) relating to the financing of political parties. It was created by the Political Parties, Elections and Referendums Act 2000 with a wide-ranging remit to supervise the conduct of elections and the financial affairs of political parties, thereby bringing what had previously been regarded as private concerns into the open. The Commission registers political parties and keeps records of their accounts and of donations to them. It reports and advises upon the conduct of elections and referendums and provides for public access to information relating to the financial affairs of political parties. It is empowered to facilitate public education relating to current electoral systems in the UK and the European Union. Finally, the Electoral Commission is empowered to arrange schemes for alternative methods of voting such as, for example, electronic and postal ballots, making voting facilities available in shops or extending voting times.

The Electoral Commission is independent of the executive. It is appointed by the Queen on an Address from the House of Commons which must have the support of the Speaker after consultation with the party leaders (s.3). Its members must not be members, officers or employees of political parties nor holders of elective office. Nor must they have had such connections nor been registered party donors (below) within the last ten years (s.3 (4)). The Electoral Commission is supplemented by an advisory Speaker's Committee which comprises relevant ministers and backbench MPs (s.2) and an advisory Parliamentary Parties Panel comprising persons appointed by the parties who must include at least two MPs (s.4).

## 10.4.3 General Elections and By-elections

Electoral law is governed primarily by the Representation of the People Acts 1983 and 1985. The timetable and other procedural matters are set out in 'Parliamentary Election Rules' in Sched. 1 of the 1983 Act. A general election must be held within about three weeks from the proclamation which summons a new Parliament (Chapter 9). Writs are sent from the Crown to designated returning officers in each constituency. The returning officers are responsible for the election, but registration officers, who are normally local authority chief executives, make the detailed arrangements. There are detailed rules for designating returning officers, but where a constituency is a whole county or a whole district, the returning officer is the sheriff of the county or the chairman of the district council. In England this is one of the few remaining duties of the sheriff, who prior to Tudor times was the representative of the Crown in local areas.

A by-election takes place when there is an individual vacancy in the House. The House itself decides whether to fill the vacancy, and by convention the motion is proposed by the party to which the former member belonged. Unfortunately there is no time limit for this. When the House is not sitting the Speaker can issue the writ (Recess Elections Act 1975).

### 10.4.4 Candidates

It is important that any law restricting the ability of people to stand for Parliament or form a political party does not violate the general principle of free election. For example, an individual with an axe to grind or a single interest party should be as free to stand as one of the major national parties, despite the undoubted inconvenience to the latter. The law is therefore concerned with fairness between candidates and with preventing fraud, disruption or confusion.

Subject to the disqualifications above, anyone can stand for Parliament who can provide a deposit of £500 (to be forfeit if one-twentieth of the total vote is not won) and is supported by ten signatures (Representation of the People Act 1983 Sched. 1). However, no one can be nominated unless their nomination paper states either that they stand in the name of a qualifying registered party under Part II of the Political Parties, Elections and Referendums Act 2000 or that they do not purport to represent any party (s.22). The latter applies to candidates standing as independents, or the Speaker seeking re-election or if the nomination paper provides no description. For the purposes of the Act a political party is any organisation or person that puts up candidates for electoral office (s.40). A one-person party is therefore possible.

Each political party must be registered with the Electoral Commission. In order to qualify for registration, the party must provide its name, its headquarters address and the names of its leader, treasurer and nominating officer, although these can be the same person. It can also provide the name of its campaign officer and if it does so the campaign officer will have some of the responsibilities of the treasurer (s.25). It must also have a scheme approved by the Commission for regulating its financial affairs. The Commission can refuse to register a party on the following grounds: duplication of or confusion with existing names, names having more than six words, names being obscene or offensive or where publication would be an offence, names in a script other than roman, or containing words prohibited by the Secretary of State (s.28). This seems to create a significant possibility of executive censorship. Similar rules apply to party emblems (s.29).

A registered political party is subject to accounting and audit requirements (Political Parties, Elections and Referendums Act 2000 Part III). Its accounts must be lodged with the Electoral Commission and must be available for public inspection (s.46). For the first time the law has acknowledged that political parties are more than private clubs and that they should be subject to external financial controls. On the other hand, this creates a risk of state interference with political freedom. Hence, despite a substantial body of opinion in favour, there is no public funding of political parties' election campaigns. However, grants of up to two million pounds are available from the Electoral Commission to parties represented in Parliament by at least two members to develop policies (Political Parties, Elections and Referendums Act 2000 s.12).

### 10.4.5  Qualifications to Vote

In general the law relating to eligibility to vote has become progressively more liberal, partly in response to a steady decline in turnout at general elections. For example, at the election of 2001 the turnout was less than 60%, the government being elected by only 25% of the electorate, thus raising serious questions of legitimacy.

To be eligible to vote, a person must be: (i) 18 years of age on the date of the poll; (ii) either a British citizen or a 'qualifying' Commonwealth citizen; (iii) not subject to any legal incapacity (below); (iv) registered on the electoral register for the constituency (Representation of the People Act 2000 s.1). A qualifying Commonwealth citizen is one who either does not require leave under immigration law to enter the UK or who has leave.

To qualify for registration a person must be:

▶ 18 years of age or due to be 18 within 12 months beginning on the first of December following the date of the application for registration.
▶ Resident in a dwelling in the constituency on the date of the application for registration.

'Residence' means the person is normally living at the address in question as his or her home. This is a question of fact and seems to focus on whether the dwelling is the applicant's home for the time being as opposed to his being a guest or a lodger for some particular purpose (see *Hipperson* v *Newbury Electoral Officer* (1985) – temporary residents). According to section 3 (2) of the Representation of the People Act 2000:

> regard shall be had in particular to the purpose and other circumstances, as well as to the fact of his presence at or absence from the address on that date ... for example, where at any particular time a person is staying at any place other than on a permanent basis he may in all the circumstances be taken to be at that time (a) resident there if he has no home elsewhere, or (b) not resident there if he does have a home elsewhere.

Temporary absence at work or attendance on a course at an educational institution does not interrupt residence if either the applicant intends to return to actual residence within six months and will not be prevented from doing so by performance of that duty or the dwelling would otherwise be his permanent residence and he would be in actual residence (s.3 (3)). Temporary periods of unemployment can be ignored (s.3 (4)). A student might therefore choose between two possible residencies, (*Fox* v *Stirk* (1970)).

There are special registration provisions for the benefit of certain people who have to be absent from their normal residence for long periods. These include overseas electors who have been resident in the UK during the last 20 years (Representation of the People Act 1985), persons in mental hospitals, unconvicted prisoners, merchant seamen, members of the armed forces (service voters) and certain other public employees. Moreover, under the Political Parties, Elections and Referendums Act 2000 s.6, persons in mental hospitals, unconvicted prisoners and the homeless, as an alternative to establishing residence on normal principles, can make a 'declaration of local connection' in relation to any constituency. Detained offenders are not resident where they are detained (ss.4, 5).

### 10.4.5.1 *Incapacities*

Even if they are on the electoral register, the following have no right to vote:

▶ Members of the House of Lords other than bishops sitting ex officio.
▶ Convicted prisoners and persons detained in mental hospitals as offenders (except for contempt of court or refusing to pay a fine), including persons unlawfully at large (Representation of the People Act 2000 s.2). However, in *Hirst* v *UK (No. 2)* (2004) the European Court of Human Rights held that the blanket exclusion for prisoners violates the right to free elections (above) depriving some 700,000 people of the right to vote. The government claimed (as if on republican grounds, see Chapter 1) that the exclusion was a punishment and designed to uphold respect for civic responsibility and the rule of law. The court held that an automatic absolute bar was not acceptable, there being no legitimate policy reason for excluding all convicted prisoners irrespective of such matters as the nature of the offence or length of sentence. The prisoner in question was serving a life sentence and had already served its punitive element; his continuing detention was because he was regarded as dangerous. This in itself should not necessarily disqualify him. The government had argued that decisions as to the franchise were political and should be decided by Parliament. However, the court pointed out that there should be a considered debate in the legislature rather than unquestioning reliance on tradition. The government has not yet responded to this ruling.

- ▶ Persons convicted of election offences (corrupt practices – five years; illegal practices – five years in the particular constituency).
- ▶ Persons lacking the mental capacity to vote.
- ▶ Illegal immigrants and asylum seekers waiting for a decision (Political Parties, Elections and Referendums Act 2000 s.2).

### 10.4.6 The Voting System

There are problems with the workings of voting systems as reflections of democratic values. Firstly, a system that always produces a genuine majority government may be impossible to achieve. For example, in an election where there are three candidates, different majorities might prefer A to B, B to C and C to A.

Secondly, the electoral system for Parliament: 'first past the post', or 'relative majority', is a 'plurality' system giving the seat to the candidate with the largest number of votes which need not be an overall majority. Plurality systems are defective in terms of democratic representation in that they ignore the votes for all but the winning candidate so that minorities have no representation. Smaller parties face particular difficulties. For example, in 2001 Labour won 62.6% of the seats with 40.7 of the vote, the Conservatives won 25.2% seats on 31.7%, the Liberal Democrats won 8.0% seats on 18.3% and other parties won 4.2% on 9.3%. In 1951 Labour won more votes than the Conservatives, but lost the election. In 1974 the opposite happened. In 1983 and 1987 the Liberal party gained 25% of the votes but 3.5% of the seats.

Another reason why a majority in Parliament may not reflect the majority of the voters is that the constituencies do not contain the same number of voters (below), so that it takes fewer voters to elect a candidate in some seats than in others. About three-quarters of the seats are 'safe seats' for either Labour or the Conservatives where the MP is effectively chosen by party activists. The system broadly favours the Labour party since Labour votes are more evenly distributed across the country, including the larger cities which have several constituencies with relatively small populations. Conservative seats tend to have more voters and are concentrated in rural or suburban areas.

The Blake Commission on Electoral Reform (Hansard Society, 1976) castigated the voting system as producing flagrant 'minority rule' and at the same time suppressing other minorities. (In Parliament itself the members always vote by simple majority in a straight, yes/no way between two propositions. The combination of these two forms of voting means that any particular law may command the support of only about 20 per cent of the public.)

On the other hand, the first-past-the-post system is simple and transparent, offering voters a clear choice. It encourages accountable governments which are supported by substantial numbers of voters. A party stands or falls as such at an election and it must answer on its own record. It cannot blame any minority parties, and, unlike systems with proportional representation (below), governments cannot change without the consent of the electorate (below).

### 10.4.7 Other Voting Systems: the Devolved Governments

The choice between voting systems is between the incommensurables of strong government, fairness, reflecting the majority will and protecting minorities. Complex systems of proportional representation (PR) are widely used in an attempt to achieve fairness and protect minorities. They rely on mathematical formulae to make the outcome correspond more closely to the distribution of the vote. All have advantages and disadvantages and no voting system has yet been devised that reconciles the competing demands on it. For example, PR systems favour negotiations between political parties and produce unstable governments held together by shifting alliances between small and large parties, thus weakening accountability. On the other hand, first-past-the-post favours party confrontation, producing instability of a different kind when successive strong governments constantly undo the policies of their predecessors. Arguably, however, a degree of instability is desirable in a liberal society where there is no agreement as to the right answer to social and political problems (Chapter 1).

There are several variations of PR. The main forms are as follows:

▶ *The Party List:* Under the 'closed list system' the voter chooses only the party, individual seats being allocated by the party in accordance with the party's share of the vote. The party list system has been said to destroy the principle of local representation and to put excessive power into the hands of party leaders. In Germany, a party must secure at least 5% of the overall vote or win three constituencies to gain 'list' seats. Thus extremist minorities are prevented from holding the balance of power. This method is widely used throughout Europe and for elections to the European Parliament. A version of it, the *additional member* system, is used for elections to the Scottish Parliament, the Welsh Assembly and the London Assembly (see Scotland Act 1998 ss.1–8; Government of Wales Act 1998 ss.1–8; Greater London Authority Act 1999 s.4). A proportion of candidates (73/129 in Scotland, 40/60 in Wales) are first elected on the first-past-the-post principle. This is topped up by a second vote for other candidates on a party list basis representing eight regions in Scotland and five regions in Wales. Each region is allocated an 'electoral region figure'. In the case of individual candidates, this is simply the total number of votes cast for that person. In the case of a party, the electoral region figure is the number of votes won by that party, divided by one plus the number of seats won by the party in the constituency elections. The candidate or party with the highest electoral region figure wins the first seat. The second and subsequent seats are awarded on the same basis, in each case after a recalculation to take account of seats already won. Thus the fewer the seats won by a party in the constituency elections, the better the chances of winning a seat in the top-up election. There is a single London constituency. The second vote can be either for an individual candidate or for a registered political party.

▶ *The Single Transferable Vote:* This is probably the method that most reflects voting preferences but loses the single-member constituency. It is used for elections in Northern Ireland where, as we have seen, the desire to neutralise conflicting political forces dominates the constitutional arrangements (Chapter 4, see Northern Ireland Act 1998 ss.8, 28, 34). Each constituency can elect a given number of members. Votes are cast for candidates in order of preference. There is an 'electoral quota' for each constituency, calculated according to a formula based on the number of voters divided by the number of seats. The quota is the winning post. A candidate who obtains the quota based on first preferences is elected. Any surplus votes over the quota are transferred to other candidates according to the second preference expressed on the winning candidate's voting slips. This may produce more winners who reach the quota. The process is repeated until all the seats are filled. If no candidate reaches the quota the candidate with the lowest number of votes is eliminated and his votes distributed among the other candidates. This system enables voters to choose between different candidates within the same party since all seats within a constituency could be fought by each party. It also prevents wasted votes and protects minorities.

There are also voting systems which do not achieve PR but which attempt to produce a candidate with majority support where there are three or more candidates. The main example is the *alternative vote* system. The candidates are voted for in order of preference and there are several rounds. After each round the candidate with the lowest vote is eliminated and his votes distributed among the others until a winner with a clear overall majority emerges. If there is still a deadlock a winner might then be chosen by lot. This system seems unfair in that it takes account of the second preferences only of those who supported losing candidates. It is the system used for elections for the Mayor of London (Greater London Authority Act 1999 s.4).

The alternative vote system was recommended for Britain as long ago as 1910 by the Royal Commission on Electoral Systems. In 1998 the *Independent*

*Commission on the Voting System* (Cm 4090) chaired by Lord Jenkins, a Liberal Democrat victim of the simple majority system, recommended the introduction of a voting system which combined the alternative vote in single-member constituencies, topped up from a party list. It appears, however, that the first-past-the-post system will remain for elections to the UK Parliament for the foreseeable future. It is unlikely to be in the interests of an incumbent government to change the electoral system.

### 10.4.8 Voting Procedures

Voting is traditionally in person at a designated polling station. However, 'absent voters' are permitted to vote by post or proxy (Representation of the People Act 2000, Sched. 4). Any person otherwise qualified to vote is entitled to a postal vote. A person on the register but no longer resident in the constituency can have an absent vote. A proxy vote applies in special cases. These include service and overseas voters, disabled people, people with work or education commitments and people who have to make a long journey. The government is currently encouraging the use of postal and electronic voting.

The ballot is secret in the sense that the vote itself is cast in privacy. However, there is no protection for postal votes and by comparing the registration number on the voting slip with the register of electors, it is possible for officials to discover how a voter cast his vote. Indeed, this is necessary to prevent multiple voting. The Act contains provisions intended to prevent ballot papers being examined, except for the purpose of detecting election offences (see Representation of the People Act 2000 Schedule 1).

### 10.4.9 The Constituencies

The outcome of a general election is usually determined by a relatively small number of 'marginal constituencies' in which no one party has a substantial majority. Voting patterns in the UK are significantly influenced by geographical considerations, so that the boundaries of the constituencies are crucial, as is the number of constituencies in each region. Moreover, the population is not evenly dispersed. Therefore some constituencies will contain more voters than others, so that each vote does not carry equal weight.

There is semi-independent machinery for fixing electoral boundaries (Parliamentary Constituencies Act 1986). This requires four boundary commissioners for England, Wales Scotland and Northern Ireland to make proposals for altering constituency boundaries. This function is to be taken over by the Electoral Commission working through boundary committees (Political Parties, Elections and Referendums Act 2000 s.14). A wide range of criteria are used and the Commissioners have considerable discretion.

There must be a review of the number and boundaries of constituencies at intervals of between 10 and 15 years. A review may take several years to complete and once made could well be out of date. A report is submitted to the Home Secretary who is required 'as soon as may be' to lay the report before both the Houses of Parliament, together with a draft Order in Council giving effect to it (s.2 (5)). Each House must approve the Order which is then submitted to the Queen in Council. It then becomes law.

The criteria are as follows (Schedule 2):

1. The total number of seats in the UK but excluding Northern Ireland must not be substantially greater or less than 613.
2. Wales must have at least 35 constituencies and Northern Ireland a minimum of 16 and a maximum of 18, but normally 17. The effect is that Wales is represented more generously than England and Northern Ireland in terms of population.
3. There must be a separate 'City of London' constituency.
4. Each country has an 'electoral quota'. This is a rough average of voters per constituency. It is calculated by dividing the total electorate by the number of constituencies on the date when the Commission begins its review. It cannot be updated during the course of a review. For England the quota is roughly 65,000. The electoral quota is one factor to be taken into account but, because of the many factors that have to be balanced, few constituencies correspond exactly to the quota although in recent years the extent of variation has become less.
5. Other factors to be taken into account are as follows:
   (i) Conformity to local government boundaries.
   (ii) Local ties.
   (iii) The inconvenience involved in altering boundaries except to comply with local government boundaries.
   (iv) Special geographical considerations including the size, shape and accessibility of a constituency.

These factors may point in different directions and it is a matter for the Commission how to rank them. The Commission is not required 'to aim at giving full effect in all circumstances to the rules' (Schedule 2, para. 7). However, the rules relating to the number of constituencies seem to have the highest priority. Inconvenience and local ties can be balanced against any of the rules, but 'special geographical considerations' are related only to the 'local government boundary' and the 'electoral quota' factors.

The report and the Order in Council can be challenged in the courts but the chances of success are small. The time factor is important. As we have seen, no court can interfere with parliamentary procedure, so that the Home Secretary could not be prevented from laying an order before the House (see

*Harper* v *Home Secretary* (1955)). A court could perhaps require a Home Secretary to lay an order, in order to prevent him delaying a report which does not favour the government party.

A court could review the completed Order in Council since approval by Parliament as such cannot save something which is unlawful. However, by virtue of s.4 (7) the validity of any Order in Council which purports to be made under the Act and which recites that approval was given by each House 'shall not be questioned in any legal proceedings'. The effect of 'ouster' clauses of this kind is controversial and is affected by the Human Rights Act 1998 (see Chapter 17). This form of words would, because of the word 'purports', probably prevent the court from setting aside the Order in Council.

A report must therefore be challenged before it is submitted to the Home Secretary. Even here the chances of success are slim because of the Commission's wide discretion. The court will defer to the subjective judgement which the Commission is required to make. Indeed, even if the Commission does act improperly, for example by ranking the various factors capriciously, the court would not normally make an order that prevents the report from going to Parliament. At most it would make a declaration (a non-binding opinion, see *R* v *Boundary Commission for England ex parte Foot* (1983)).

### 10.4.10 The Conduct of Election Campaigns

This chapter is concerned with parliamentary elections but the same principles apply to the various other elections that are now held in the UK. The election conflict at constituency level has always been closely regulated by law designed to ensure fairness between the candidates campaigning in their local arenas. The law was open to the charge that it does not allow for national party politics with its massive financial backing from private donors, nor for modern methods of campaigning, including the intensive use of the national and international media. The Political Parties, Elections and Referendums Act 2000 attempts to bring the law up to date by addressing this reality (see *The Funding of Political Parties in the United Kingdom*, Cm 4443, 1999). Reflecting the Nolan principles of public life, the Act attempts to bring greater openness and accountability to the financing of political parties and national campaigns.

#### 10.4.10.1 *Campaign Expenses*

There are controls over the money spent on campaigning during the election period. The law is designed to ensure that no candidate has an unfair advantage or can buy votes (see *R* v *Jones* (1999)). In the USA, restrictions upon election expenses have been held to violate freedom of speech (*Buckley* v *Valeo* (1976)). The counter-argument is that equality of resources in elections is a better safeguard of free speech in the long run. The main principles are as follows:

▶ For most purposes the election period begins with the date of the proclamation announcing the dissolution of Parliament and ends with the date of the poll (e.g. Political Parties, Elections and Referendums Act 2000 Sched. 10).

▶ Every candidate must have an election agent who is accountable for the conduct of the candidate's campaign. A candidate can appoint himself as agent. There are controls over receipts and expenses out of the candidate's own pocket (Representation of the People Act 1983 ss.73, 74).

▶ There is a maximum limit upon the amount that can be spent on behalf of any candidate in respect of 'the conduct or management of a election' (Representation of the People Act 1983 s.76; Political Parties, Elections and Referendums Act 2000 s.132). This depends primarily on the size of the constituency and amounts to about £10,000 at a general election and £100,000 at a by-election (where there is less national support, (see below). There is no fixed definition of an election expense. Some expenditure, for example to canvassers, on posters (except to advertising agents), on hiring vehicles to take people to vote, and on broadcasting from abroad, is banned completely (ss.101–12). Candidates are entitled to use schools and public buildings for meetings (ss.95, 96). Each candidate can also send one election address to each voter post-free. Reasonable personal expenses can be incurred (s.18).

▶ The Political Parties, Elections and Referendums Act 2000 extended controls over expenditure by registered political parties at national level. This applies during the 'campaign period' which is 365 days, ending with polling day. Thus the artificiality of distinguishing between promoting the party and promoting the individual candidate that surfaced in earlier cases may no longer arise (see *Grieve* v *Douglas-Home* (1965); *R* v *Tronah Mines Ltd* (1952); *DPP* v *Luft* (1977). Firstly, all campaign expenditure must be authorised by the party treasurer, his or her deputy, or other responsible officer delegated by the treasurer (s.75). Campaign expenduiture includes party political broadcasts, advertising, other than leaflets giving personal information about candidates, market research, rallies, press conferences and transport (Sched. 8). Secondly, there are overall limits on expenditure based on the number of constituencies contested up to a limit of £810,000 in England, £120,000 in Scotland and £60,000 in Wales (s.79). The Treasurer must deliver a return of expenditure to the Electoral Commission (s.83) which must be made available for public inspection (s.84).

▶ There are also provisions regulating payment by third parties on behalf of candidates during the campaign period. No expenditure over £500 can be incurred 'with a view to' promoting a candidate without the authority of the candidate or his agent thus counting as part of the candidate's expenses (Representation of the People Act 1983 s.75; Political Parties Elections and Referendums Act 2000 s.131, c.f. *Bowman* v *UK* (1998)). There are exceptions for newspapers and broadcasting.

▶ The Political Parties, Elections and Referendums Act 2000 introduced the concept of 'controlled expenditure' applying at a national level. Controlled expenditure is the production or publication of material which is made available to the public and which can reasonably be regarded as intended to promote any candidate (including prejudicing another candidate) even if the material serves some other purpose as well (s.85). For example, a leaflet put out by a pressure group in favour of banning hunting might be controlled expenditure if one of the candidates was associated with the issue of hunting.

Controls apply to expenditure made within the campaign period (above) (Political Parties, Elections and Referendums Act 2000 Sched. 10 Para. 3). It is an offence to incur controlled expenditure above certain limits unless it is made by a 'recognised third party'(s.94). The limits are £10,000 for England and £5000 for the other regions. A recognised third party can incur expenditure up to £793,500 for England, £108,000 for Scotland, £60,000 for Wales, £27,000 for Northern Ireland (Sched. 10). There are certain exceptions to these limits which include newspaper editorial matter, broadcasts, personal expenses and the value of services provided free by individuals (s.87).

A recognised third party must be an individual resident in the UK or on the electoral register, or a registered political party, company, trade union, building society, friendly society, partnership, or unincorporated association, for example a pressure group (s.88).

▶ Controls also apply to donations to political parties. These controls are not intended to outlaw donations as such but to bring them into the open and ensure accountability. Suspicions concerning secret donations particularly from overseas sources have tainted both main parties. 'Donation' is widely defined to include gifts, sponsorship, subscriptions, fees, expenses, non-commercial loans and the provision of non-commercial services (s.50). A registered party cannot accept a donation if it is not made by a 'permissible donor' or if it is anonymous (s.54 (2)). However, trusts established before 27 July 1999 are exempt (s.55 (5)).

A permissible donor must be registered to vote in the UK or be a business, trade union or registered political party based in the UK. In the case of a company, the shareholders must have approved the donation and the amount must be disclosed in the directors' report (s.140, Sched. 19). There are some exceptions to the duty of disclosure. These include voluntary services provided by an individual, donations of not more than £200, various payments made under statute, payments to MPs by the European Parliament, and the hire of stands at party conferences for a payment deemed reasonable by the Commission.

The party must report relevant donations to the Electoral Commission: in the case of donations amounting to more than £5000, on a quarterly basis and weekly during an election campaign if the party is fielding a candidate (ss.63, 65, 68, 96). The Electoral Commission keeps a public register of donations and other controlled expenditure although this must not include the address of a donor who is an individual (s.69). Impermissible donations must be returned or if the donor cannot be identified, given to the Commission (s.56). The court can order a donation to be forfeited (s.58). Similar controls apply to donations to recognised third parties (Sched.11).

#### 10.4.10.2 *Broadcasting and the Press*

It is widely believed that modern elections are won or lost on television. There are therefore rules which attempt to ensure that the parties are treated fairly. These work reasonably well in the traditional two-party context. Indeed, they are in some respects very stringent.

▶ Political advertising is unlawful except for party political broadcasts made by agreement between the British Broadcasting Corporation (BBC), OFCOM and the main parties (see Communications Act 2003 s.333). This prevents the worst excesses of wealthy parties. Only registered political parties can make party political broadcasts (Political Parties, Elections and Referendums Act 2000 s.37). Political broadcasting programmes are excluded from counting as election expenses (s.75 (1)).

▶ There is a general duty on OFCOM to preserve good taste and balance and impartiality in all political broadcasting (Communications Act 2003 s.6). The BBC is not governed by statute but operates under a royal charter and an agreement with the Home Office. However, OFCOM can regulate the BBC in accordance with Charter and Agreement (Communications Act 2003 s.198). The Agreement and the Code of Practice prescribed by OFCOM forbid the expression of editorial opinion about matters of public policy excluding broadcasting matters. The independent broadcasters are protected by the European Convention on Human Rights in respect of the right of freedom of expression (Chapter 17). However, as a public body the BBC is probably not entitled to such protection. In principle the broadcasters' duties are enforceable by the courts. On the other hand, the idea of political impartiality is both vague and complex and the courts are reluctant to interfere in party political matters. For example, must there be balance within the context of every specific subject? How much coverage should minority parties enjoy? It is unlikely that a court would intervene with the broadcasting authority's decision except in a case of bad faith or complete irrationality (see *Wilson* v *IBA* (1979); *R* v *Broadcasting Complaints Commission ex parte Owen* (1985); *R (Pro Life Alliance)* v *BBC* (2003)).

▷ There are strict controls over broadcasts about particular constituencies. An item in which any candidate 'takes part' (which means 'actively participate' (*Marshall* v *BBC* (1979)) cannot be broadcast without all the candidates' consent (s.93 (1)).

▷ It is an illegal practice for a person to 'use or aid, abet, counsel or procure' the use of broadcasting stations outside the UK for electoral purposes except where the matter is to be retransmitted by one of the domestic broadcasting companies (s.93). However, this may not prevent overseas stations from directly broadcasting to voters via satellite television.

## 10.4.11 Election Disputes

There is an Election Court comprising two High Court judges. Either a voter or a candidate may within three months of the election lodge a petition to the court. The court can disqualify a candidate, order a recount or scrutiny of the votes, declare the result of the election, void the election and order a fresh election (Representation of the People Act 1983 s.159). The court's decision takes the form of a report to the Speaker which the House is bound to accept (s.144 (7)).

Election offences are either 'corrupt' or 'illegal' practices. These involve the offender being disqualified as a candidate or prevented from sitting in Parliament. The extent of the disqualification depends upon whether it is a corrupt practice (ten years everywhere) or an illegal practice (five years in a particular constituency). 'Innocent' illegal practices can be overlooked (s.167). A corrupt practice involves dishonesty, improper pressure on voters, or excessive expenditure. Illegal practices concern breaches of various statutory requirements relating to agents, premises, advertising, broadcasting and other matters. Where an election offence is involved, separate criminal proceedings may be taken in an ordinary court in relation to the offence. Conviction disqualifies a person from membership of the House, and the Speaker must declare the seat vacant.

## Summary

▶ The House of Lords is unelected and with nearly 700 members is one of the largest legislatures in the world – this is thought to be inappropriate to its functions. The composition of the House of Lords is to be further reformed. The government has proposed that the House mainly remains unelected but with an elected element of one fifth. A further one fifth should be chosen by an independent commission but most of the House should be nominated by the political parties and appointed by the Prime Minister. As yet no further reforms have been made.

▶ The voting system for parliamentary elections is currently the simple plurality, first-past-the-post system. Voting systems must cater for the incommensurables of effective government, accountable government and democratic representation. We asked whether the electoral system is adapted to its modern task of choosing governments, whether it is truly representative of public opinion and whether it is fair to all candidates. We briefly compared different kinds of voting system including the alternative vote and PR. Variations of PR are used in elections to the regional legislatures and to the European Parliament. This is likely to create political tensions within the UK.

▶ We discussed the machinery for regulating constituency boundaries. This is given a certain amount of protection against political interference but proposals for changes must be approved by the House of Commons. It is difficult to challenge decisions made by this process in the courts.

▶ The law governing the conduct of elections, which had previously ignored national politics in favour of the individual election at local level, has recently been reformed to regulate campaign expenditure at national level including spending by third parties on election campaigns and donations to and sponsorship of political parties. The independent Electoral Commission has wide responsibilities in relation to the finances of political parties and the conduct of elections. This is intended to bring greater openness and accountability to political parties.

▶ We discussed controls over election broadcasting. These are designed to ensure fairness between the parties in accordance with their popular support and are more stringent than are restrictions over the press.

## Exercises

**10.1** 'The capacity to offer council from a range of sources ... broadly representative of society in the UK at the beginning of the 21st century ... It should give the UK's constituent nations and regions, for the first time a formally constituted voice in the Westminster parliament' (Wakeham Report).

To what extent does the House of Lords as it is at present meet these requirements?

**10.2** Why is reform of the House of Lords so difficult?

**10.3** 'The UK electoral system is undemocratic.' Discuss.

**10.4** Explain the basis on which parliamentary constituencies are designated. Do the present arrangements contain adequate safeguards against political manipulation?

**10.5** 'There is now an overwhelming case for legislation regulating expenditure on a national (election) campaign' (Rawlings). 'Restrictions on the conduct of elections violate basic rights of free expression.' Do you consider that the Political Parties, Elections and Referendums Act 2000 has adequately addressed these competing concerns?

**10.6** A general election is expected to take place within the next eighteen months. The Campaign for Free University Education proposes to distribute leaflets and to hold meetings during the election campaign in various university towns. Jerry, a wealthy businessman resident in the USA, wishes to make an anonymous donation of one million pounds to any political party that will campaign to withdraw the UK from the European Union. Discuss the legality of these proposals.

**10.7** 'Reforms of the electoral system through the introduction of a single transferable vote ... would revitalise the operation of political processes and make a major contribution to the development of a more accountable, effective system and a more influential citizenry' (Oliver). Discuss.

# Further reading

Bogdanor, V. (1999), 'Reforming the Lords: a Sceptical View', *Political Quarterly*, **70**: 375.

Budge, I., Crewe, I., McKay, D. and Newton, K. (2004) *The New British Politics*, 3rd edn, London, Pearson, Chapters 16, 17.

Committee on Standards in Public Life (1998) *The Funding of Political Parties in the United Kingdom* Cm 4057-I.

Constitutional Commission, *Options for a New Second Chamber*, (London, Constitutional Commission 1999).

Jones, B., Kavanagh, D., Moran, M. and Norton, P. (2004) *Politics UK*, 5th edn, London, Pearson, Chapter 8.

Lardy, H. (2000), 'Democracy by Default: The Representation of the People Act 2000', *Modern Law Review*, **64**: 63.

McClean, I. (2000) 'Mr Asquith's Unfinished Business', *Political Quarterly*, **70**: 382.

Phillipson, G. (2004) 'The "greatest quango of them all"', *Public Law*, 352.

**Further reading cont'd**

*Report of the Independent Commission on the Voting System*, (Jenkins Report) (1998) Cm 4090-1, London, HMSO.

Reports of the Electoral Commission; www.electoralcommission.gov.uk.

Russell, M. (2000) *Reforming the House of Lords: Lessons from Overseas*, Oxford, Oxford University Press.

Russell, M. and Cornes, R. (2000) 'The Royal Commission on the House of Lords: A House for the Future?', *Modern Law Review*, **64**: 82.

Shell, D. (2000) 'The Future of the Second Chamber', *Political Quarterly*, **70**: 390.

Wakeham, (2000) *A House for the Future*, Royal Commission on the House of Lords Cm 4534.

Webb, P. (2001) 'Parties and Party Systems: Modernisation, Regulation and Diversity', *Parliamentary Affairs*, **54**: 308.

# Chapter 11

# Parliamentary procedure

*The minister, whoever he at any time may be, touches it as with an opium wand and it sleeps obedience. (Thomas Paine, The Rights of Man, Pt. 2)*

## Key words

▶ An adversarial process
▶ Publicity
▶ Executive domination
▶ Self-regulation
▶ Uncertain role of Upper House

## 11.1 Introduction

Parliamentary procedure has four main purposes: first to enable different interests to combine in a single outcome such as a statute, second to make the executive accountable, third to redress the grievances of constituents and fourth to prevent outside interference. Parliamentary procedure is based upon standing orders, customs and conventions and rulings by the Speaker who presides over the House of Commons. The authoritative manual of parliamentary procedure is Erskine May, *Parliamentary Practice* (22nd edn, 1997). The finance administration and staffing of the House of Commons are supervised by the House of Commons Commission which comprises a group of MPs chaired by the Speaker (House of Commons (Administration) Act 1978). It does not have a government majority and is therefore independent of the executive.

Parliamentary procedure is adversarial, presupposing a government and opposition constantly in conflict. The rectangular layout of the Chamber, and indeed of the Palace of Westminster itself, reflects this. Other European legislative chambers are characteristically semi-circular in layout representing a more conciliatory ethos with the parties, usually elected by proportional representation, merging into each other. The adversarial nature of the procedure is mitigated by what are known as 'usual channels'. These involve informal cooperation between the parties so as to ensure that the procedures operate smoothly and fairly. For example, absences from votes may be arranged in 'pairs' so as to maintain party balance. Whips have the responsibility of enforcing party discipline and liaising between the government and backbench MPs. The government Chief Whip, although not a cabinet member, frequently attends cabinet meetings.

The government is usually able to dominate the business of the House of Commons. In some countries, influenced by the doctrine of separation of powers, there are provisions which prevent the procedure from being controlled by the executive. In the UK, the parliamentary timetable is determined by the government under Standing Order 13 which, usually, gives priority to government business. The government also exercises influence over MPs through party discipline and patronage and through influencing the membership of committees (below). While the number of paid ministers is limited by statute (Chapter 10), the government can appoint an unlimited number of unpaid parliamentary aides who are required under the convention of collective responsibility to support the executive. This device can be also be used to remove an independently minded individual from a departmental select committee, membership being limited to backbenchers. The Chief Whip advises the Prime Minister upon the careers of ministers and MPs.

A report from a Hansard Society Commission, *The Challenge for Parliament; Making Government Work* (Newton, 2001), suggested that there are 'serious gaps in the working of accountability to Parliament'. The Commission recommended in particular that departmental select committees should have greater freedom from government interference and that backbench MPs should have their own career structure to make them independent of government patronage. An attempt by the government in 2001 to remove two independently minded select committee members was defeated by the House as a whole, illustrating that ultimately the House does have the power needed to preserve some independence from the executive.

The House of Lords regulates its own procedure which is less adversarial and party dominated than the Commons. There is also less reliance on formal procedural rules. The Lord Chancellor presides over the House of Lords as well as speaking for the government. The Lord Chancellor does not have the disciplinary powers available to the Speaker, his only power being to put a question to the vote (SO 18). The House of Lords has no power to suspend or expel a member. The House of Lords is subservient to the Commons but the limits of this are not clear. Under the Parliament Acts 1911 and 1949 the Lords can delay most bills introduced in the Commons for a certain time (below) and this gives them a certain measure of legitimacy. By convention, the Lords are not entitled to oppose the will of the Commons in relation to financial measures, nor, according to the 'Salisbury Convention', where a Commons' proposal gives effect to a commitment in the government's election manifesto or possibly to other important government policies.

The Wakeham Report (Chapter 10) did not propose major changes in the constitutional role of the second chamber. It emphasised that the House of

Commons should remain the superior body and that the holding of government to account in the context of the second chamber meant no more than requiring government to explain and justify its actions. Wakeham rejected extending the powers of veto of the second chamber to constitutional matters. Instead it recommended that the committees of the second chamber be strengthened by the addition of a Constitutional Committee perhaps with a human rights sub-committee.

## 11.2 The Speaker

The office of Speaker, the 'first commoner', symbolises the historical development of the House of Commons particularly in the seventeenth century. The Speaker presides over meetings of the Commons and is the intermediary between the House and the Crown. The Speaker represents the rights of the House against the Crown, controls the procedure, keeps order and is responsible for protecting the rights of all groups within the House, particularly those of minorities. He or she has considerable discretion. The Speaker makes procedural rulings, decides who shall speak, and has summary powers to suspend members or to terminate a sitting. In terms of the conduct of particular proceedings, the Speaker need not normally give reasons for decisions (see SO 31, 42, 45). The Sergeant at Arms is the enforcement agency responsible to the Speaker.

The Speaker is elected, from its membership, by the House at the beginning of each Parliament. The 'father of the house', the longest serving member, runs the election. Traditionally a newly elected Speaker has to be dragged to the chair, reminding us that this was once a dangerous post. The Speaker is required to be impartial between the political parties. He/she cannot therefore represent his/her constituency in debates nor fight elections under a party banner. There is also a deputy Speaker and deputies to him. One of these presides when the House is sitting as a Committee.

## 11.3 Legislative Procedure

Parliament debates each bill in a process that distinguishes between general principles and detail. Parliamentary debates consist of a motion, and question proposed by the Chair in the same form as the motion. Following debate the question is put and voted upon, the result being expressed as a resolution or order. At any stage there may be amendments proposed but in all cases issues are presented to the House one at a time for a yes or no vote by a simple majority. This reflects the confrontational nature of Parliament and also ensures that the voting is on a majoritarian basis. The main distinctions are between public bills and private bills. There are also special arrangements for financial measures.

### 11.3.1 Public Bills

A public bill is a bill intended to alter the general law. The formal procedures in the House are only the tip of the iceberg. Any member can propose a bill ('a private member's bill') but almost all public bills are promoted by the government and introduced by ministers. Private members' bills are unlikely to suceed without government support. Twelve Fridays are provided in each session to private members' bills (SO 13 (4)). Priority is determined by a ballot, held annually, for which only backbenchers are eligible. Only the first six in the ballot have a realistic chance of success because, of the twelve Fridays, six are devoted to bills in their later stages. Sometimes the winners adopt bills proposed by others, for example outside pressure groups or even the executive. A private member can also get a bill debated under the '10 minute rule' (SO 19). This involves a motion twice a week that leave be given to present a bill. A short debate takes place. There is little prospect of the matter going any further, the essential aim being to publicise an issue. Nevertheless, some important social reforms have been made by private members' bills, including abortion legislation, the abolition of the death penalty, and divorce reform. However, all had government support in the form of time allocation and drafting assistance.

Before their formal introduction, public bills go through various processes within the administration involving the formulation of policy and principles and consultation with outside bodies. When these have been completed the bill is sent to Parliamentary Counsel for drafting. Some bills, particularly those dealing with commercial matters, are drafted with the aid of outside lawyers. The relationship between the draftsmen and the government is similar to that of lawyer and client. The draftsmen work under considerable pressure of time and there is continuous consultation with government departments. Some bills relating to reform of the general law are prepared by the Law Commission.

Important bills may be foreshadowed by Green Papers, which are consultation documents, or by White Papers, which state the government's concluded opinions. Both are published. Recently, important bills have been published as draft bills for 'prelegislative' discussion by Parliament and with public consultation before the formal process is started (see Kennon, 2004, *Public Law* 477). The final version of a bill is approved by the Legislation Committee of the Cabinet and then introduced into Parliament. Except for financial measures, which must be introduced by a minister in the Commons, a bill can be introduced into either the House of Lords or the House of Commons. The same stages apply in each House. Relatively uncontroversial bills are likely to be introduced in the House of Lords.

The stages of a public bill are as follows:

- *First reading:* this is a formality which ensures that the bill is printed and published.
- *Second reading:* at which the main principles of the bill are discussed. In theory, once a bill has passed this stage its principles cannot later be challenged. However, 'wrecking' amendments are sometimes introduced (for example by addition of the word 'not') with a view to neutralising a bill. Manipulating fine dividing lines is part of the parliamentary art. Occasionally second reading is dealt with by a special committee.
- *Committee stage:* the bill is examined by a standing committee, with a view to suggesting detailed amendments. Unlike a select committee which exists for the whole of a Parliament (below), a standing committee is set up only for the purpose of a particular bill. Its membership of around 50 is based upon the strength of each party in the House, so that it is difficult for amendments to be made against the wishes of the government. Opponents of a bill sometimes deliberately cause delays by discussing matters at length in committee. However, the chairman has power to decide which amendments should be discussed and a 'business sub-committee' allocates time for discussion. The parliamentary draftsman may be present and civil servants or experts might be called to give evidence. Sometimes a bill is referred to a committee of the whole House. This might happen, for example, when the bill is uncontroversial or at the opposite extreme where it is of profound political significance.
- *Report stage:* the result of the committee's deliberations is returned to the House which can then vote upon the amendments and consider further amendments. The Speaker can select the amendments to be debated. The report stage can be dispensed with where the bill has been discussed by a committee of the whole House.
- *Third reading:* this is the final vote on the bill. Only verbal amendments are usually possible at this stage but the bill as a whole can be opposed.
- The bill is then sent to the other House. If amendments are there suggested it is returned for further discussion, 'Lords, Amendments Considered'. If there is disagreement between the two Houses the Parliament Acts procedure can be triggered (below).
- Otherwise the bill is sent for Royal Assent. This is usually notified by commissioners to each House separately (Royal Assent Act 1967). Some bills are assented to at the prorogation ceremony that ends each session. By convention, the monarch must always assent, except possibly in the unlikely event of the Prime Minister's advising to the contrary. In this

case, however, the government would be at odds with the Commons and so required to resign.

Once a bill has received the Royal Assent it becomes law. However, it is often provided that an Act or parts of it shall take effect only when a minister so orders. A minister's decision whether or not to bring an Act into effect is subject to judicial review (see *R v Secretary of State for the Home Department ex parte Fire Brigades Union* (1995)). It is also common for an Act to confer power on ministers to make detailed regulations without which the Act itself cannot operate. These might include a 'Henry VIII clause' under which a minister is empowered to alter other statutes.

### 11.3.2 Private Bills

A private bill is one directed to particular persons or places, for example a bill to build a new section of railway line. It is a somewhat antiquated notion and today most powers directed to specific persons or places are exercised by the executive under various powers conferred by general legislation (below). Private bill procedure allows Parliament to amend proposals and is therefore suitable for very important private schemes. Although private bill procedure involves outside elements, it is still wholly within parliamentary privilege. Therefore the courts cannot intervene on the ground that the procedure has not been properly followed or even that there has been fraud (*Pickin v BRB* (1974)).

The private bill procedure involves the following:

(i) Advertisement of the proposals in the locality.
(ii) A petition and a copy of the bill to be lodged in Parliament by 27 November each year. This is the equivalent of first reading.
(iii) Notification to persons affected. The bill's promoters must do this and persons affected are entitled to petition against the bill.
(iv) Second reading. This is to discuss whether the bill is contrary to national policy.
(v) The committee stage before a special committee of the Commons or the Lords. At this stage those who petitioned against the bill can appear represented, if they wish, by counsel. The procedure is similar to that of a court and evidence can be called and witnesses cross-examined. Public bill procedure is therefore slow and expensive.
(vi) Report stage and third reading and Royal Assent are similar to those for public bills.

A public bill with a private element is called a 'hybrid bill'. For example, the Aircraft and Shipbuilding Bill 1976 nationalised these industries and was, as such, a public bill but it exempted certain named firms from its proposals. A hybrid bill is subject to the public bill procedure until the committee stage when it is examined by a select committee in the same manner as a private bill.

Private bill procedure has been much criticised, not only because it is slow but because it fails to provide opportunities for the public to be directly involved in debating schemes which may have serious environmental impact, for example new railway lines. There is however a range of alternative procedures with less and sometimes no parliamentary input. These enable public bodies such as local authorities or utility companies to obtain powers to override private rights. The main examples are as follows:

▶ The Transport and Works Act 1992 applies primarily to large rail and waterway projects. The Act allows a Secretary of State to authorise projects after consulting local authorities and affected parties and including an environmental assessment. A public inquiry must be held into objections. The Secretary of State can also refer proposals of national importance to Parliament for debate.

▶ Provisional Orders made by Ministers, again following a public local inquiry, are confirmed by a provisional order confirmation bill, the committee stage of which involves a select committee at which interested parties can be heard. Thus there is an element of detailed parliamentary scrutiny.

▶ 'Special parliamentary procedure' involves a ministerial order which is subject to a public inquiry and also to a hearing before a special parliamentary committee. It can be debated on the floor of the House. This procedure is less cumbersome than private bills or provisional order confirmation bills but gives the authority of Parliament to sensitive proposals (for example the sale of certain National Trust land).

▶ Many projects such as new highways can be authorised, without Parliament, by ministerial order made under general legislation, usually following a local public inquiry (for example Acquisition of Land Act 1981). It has been held that, because these procedures are political rather than judicial, they do not violate the right to a fair trial under the European Convention on Human Rights, provided that the safeguard of judicial review is available (see *Alconbury Developments* v *Secretary of State* (2001).

### 11.3.3 Government Control Over Procedure: Cutting Short Debate

If a public bill has not become law by the end of a session it lapses. This allows the government to pressurise its supporters into acquiescence. However, the practice has recently been changed to allow some bills to be carried over into the next session. This must be authorised by a resolution of the House. Moreover, discussion of a bill can be timetabled by the cross-party Programming Committee under a 'programme motion' (see *Modernisation Select Committee Report*, 1997–8, HC 543). There are other procedural devices available to both Houses, but most importantly in the Commons, to cut short the time spent on debate. These usually depend upon a vote of the House and in the Commons are therefore under the control of the government. Recently, as part of the 'modernisation' of Commons' procedures, the use of these devices has been replaced by government's timetabling of the discussion on a bill, thereby further increasing executive control. The older procedural devices are as follows:

▷ *Closure:* A motion that the question be now put (SO 35). The Speaker can also cut short debate when (s)he thinks there has been adequate discussion (SO 67). Except in the case of private members' bills closure motions are rare.

▷ *Guillotine:* A minister may propose a timetable for a bill. The guillotine procedure may prevent parts of a bill being discussed at all. Conversely, where a government is weak, a defeated guillotine motion can destroy a bill.

▷ *'Kangaroo'* (SO 41): The Speaker at report stage or the chairman of a committee selects clauses or amendments for discussion.

▷ There are also procedural devices available in specific contexts (see Griffith and Ryle, 1989, *Parliament*, p. 219).

### 11.3.4    House of Lords Legislative Procedure: The Parliament Acts

Procedure in the Lords is under the control of the House collectively and is more consensual. Bills other than those involving government taxation or expenditure can be introduced in the House of Lords. A bill introduced in the House of Commons and passing all its stages goes to the House of Lords. The procedure is broadly similar except that the committee stage usually takes place before a committee of the whole House.

Under the Parliament Acts 1911 and 1949 the House of Lords can delay most legislation only for one session, that is for roughly one year. After the second session, the bill can receive the Royal Assent without the consent of the Lords. If the Commons amends a bill after it has come back from the Lords in the first of the two sessions, then it may not count as the same bill, unless the amendments were suggested by the Lords. One year must elapse between the second reading of the bill in the Commons in the first session and its third (the final) reading in the second session. In the case of a 'money bill' the Lords can delay only for one month, provided that the bill is sent to them at least one month before the end of a session. A 'money bill' is a public bill which deals *exclusively* with either central government taxation or central government spending, borrowing or accounts. The certificate of the Speaker that a bill is a money bill is conclusive for all purposes (1911 Act s.3). This definition is fairly narrow since few bills deal exclusively with these matters. The Speaker must certify that the Parliament Act's procedure has been followed and his certificate cannot be challenged. The Parliament Act procedure has been little used (see Welsh Church Act 1914; Government of Ireland Act 1914; Parliament Act 1949; War Crimes Act 1991; European Parliamentary Elections Act 1999; Sexual Offences (Amendment) Act 2000; Hunting Act 2004). Usually, while the Lords sometimes delay bills, they have in the end given way to the Commons.

The Parliament Acts do not apply to certain kinds of legislation. These are as follows:

▶ local and private bills;
▶ bills confirming Provisional Orders (above);
▶ bills introduced in the House of Lords;
▶ a bill to prolong the life of Parliament. Because of this exemption the House of Lords retains the key constitutional role of preventing a government from avoiding an election by prolonging its own life.
▶ The Parliament Act procedure may possibly not apply to a bill to abolish or to reduce the powers of the House of Lords (see Chapter 7). The Wakeham Commission (see Chapter 10) proposed that it be made clear by a simple amendment to the Parliament Acts that the Parliament Acts should not apply to a bill that affects the composition or powers of the House of Lords. Wakeham rejected any other extension of the Lords' power of veto on the ground that this might risk upsetting the supremacy of the Commons. Wakeham emphasised that, in the context of the House of Lords, the vague concept of accountability means primarily that the Lords should provide a mechanism to make the government think again, rather than to overrule the government.

## 11.4 Financial Procedure

It is a fundamental principle embodied in both law and convention that the House of Commons controls public finance and that proposals for public spending can be initiated only by the Crown: 'The Crown demands money, the Commons grant and the Lords assent to the grant' (Erskine May, Parliamentary Practice, 22nd edn 1997, 732–6). On the other hand, modern government finance is so large and complex that such control may be unrealistic. The Commons scrutinises taxation and expenditure proposals very superficially. In practice the most substantial control over government finance is exercised internally by the Treasury (Chapter 13).

The dependence of the executive on money voted by the people is an essential feature of a democratic constitution. The Crown comes to the Commons to ask for money. Hence financial measures can be proposed only by the Crown, and the Commons can reduce the estimates but not increase them (see SO 46). The survival of a government depends upon the Commons voting it funds, and the refusal of the Commons to do so is the equivalent of a vote of no confidence so that the government must resign. By convention, the House of Lords cannot amend measures relating to central government finance and, as we have seen, can delay money bills only for one month.

Financial procedure is based on an ancient distinction between 'ways and means' – raising money – and 'supply' – allocating money to the purposes of the executive. This may be somewhat artificial since the two are closely related. By virtue of the Bill of Rights 1688 the Crown cannot raise taxation without the consent of Parliament. The basis of the principle that the Crown cannot spend money without the consent of Parliament is partly long-standing custom endorsed by the common law (*Auckland Harbour Board* v *R* (1924)), and partly statute in that payments into the Consolidated Fund, the government's bank account, require statutory authority (Exchequer and Audit Departments Act 1866 s.11).

Taxation and expenditure – the 'estimates' – must first be authorised by resolutions of the House of Commons (SO 48). Amendments cannot be made outside the terms of the resolution, thus strengthening the government's hand. The enactment of the legislation itself is a formality, any serious discussion having taken place earlier when the government presented its public spending proposals according to a timetable of its choosing.

There are three main financial measures. Firstly, the Finance Act raises taxation. The Royal Assent to a taxation measure is expressed in the words: '*La Reyne remercie ses bons sujets, accepte leur benevolence et ainsi le veult*' (The Queen thanks her good subjects, accepts their kindness and thus assents), as opposed to the normal '*La Reyne le veult*'. Secondly, an Appropriation Act, usually in May, allocates amounts out of the consolidated fund to the Crown according to the estimates ('votes') presented for each government department for the current financial year, that is, until the following April. It also confirms spending which has been authorised provisionally by other legislation for the current and previous years. Thirdly, Consolidated Fund Acts authorise interim spending until the following Appropriation Act and may also authorise additional spending from time to time. In the case of these financial measures, the committee stage takes the form of a committee of the whole House.

### 11.4.1    Taxation Procedure

The key taxation event is the annual 'budget' resolution proposed by the Chancellor. This speech includes the Chancellor's views on the economy and overall strategy and proposals for tax changes. It therefore sets the general economic framework of government policy. The budget resolution is followed by the annual Finance Bill. This includes taxes (notably, income tax) that must be authorised afresh each year. These annual taxes are enforced and administered under permanent legislation (Income and Corporation Taxes Act 1988). Some taxes, mainly indirect taxes such as customs duties, are authorised by permanent legislation although their rates can be changed at any time. Constitutional principle is preserved in the case of EC law by the requirement in the European Communities Act 1972 that EC laws affecting taxation, for example V.A.T, must be implemented by a statute.

The effect of the budget resolution is that the budget's main tax proposals become law with immediate effect, but lapse unless embodied in a Finance Act that becomes law by a specified time. This is 5 August if the speech is in March or April, otherwise within four months (Provisional Collection of Taxes Act 1968). This procedure illustrates the basic constitutional principle that resolutions of the Commons cannot by themselves change the law but need statutory backing (*Bowles* v *Bank of England* (1913)).

Central government money does not come exclusively from taxation. Governments borrow large sums of money in the form of bonds and on the international money market. Money is also raised from landholding, investments both in the UK and overseas, and from trading activities. These sources of finance are not subject to detailed parliamentary scrutiny although statutory authority is required in general terms for borrowing (National Loans Fund Act 1968).

### 11.4.2    Supply Procedure

Most public expenditure must be authorised annually by the Appropriation Act which approves the government's estimates. These are made under the supervision of the Treasury which in practice provides the main method of controlling government finances (Chapter 13). They include 'votes' setting out the government's proposed allocation of funds between departments. Thus the Commons approves both the global sum and the executive's broad priorities. However, the Appropriation Act is in very short and general terms, merely listing the broad functions of each government body to be financed, allocating a global amount, designating a grant from the consolidated fund and setting a limit to 'appropriations in aid', that is, money that can be raised from fees and charges etc. Moreover, the Act deals only in cash so that contemporary methods of 'resource accounting' imposed by the Treasury may not fall properly within parliamentary controls (see Daintith and Page, 1999, p. 166). The Act appears to authorise payment to the Crown rather than to the individual department, thus reinforcing the Treasury's power to control other departments by presiding over the allocation of funds. However, in *R v Lords Commissioners of the Treasury* (1872) it was said *obiter* that the Treasury is obliged to pay the sums in question.

The Public Accounts Committee admitted in 1987 that parliamentary control over the estimates is largely a formality (HC 98, 1986–7, para. 2). The annual Appropriation Act and Consolidated Fund Acts are usually passed without debate. Debates on the estimates have been replaced by twenty 'opposition days' which allow the opposition parties to raise anything they wish, and by special 'adjournment debates' following the passage of the Acts. The latter allow issues to be discussed without a vote.

There is an arcane debate as to whether the Appropriation Act alone is sufficient to make lawful particular items of expenditure which fall within its general provisions. This is worth briefly considering as it raises wider concerns as to the role of internal understandings and influences as against legal constraints in the constitution (see Daintith and Page, 1999, pp. 35, 174, 203–6). One view is that, in addition to the Appropriation Act, specific powers must be conferred either by statute or under the royal prerogative. In other words, the Appropriation Act is addressed only to the executive and authorises the Crown to use the government's bank account for purposes which are lawful. On the other hand, if an act of the Crown does not involve interfering with the legal rights of others why should the Crown require specific powers since as a person it can do anything that the law does not forbid including, presumably, spending its money? On this argument the Appropriation Act which puts the money into the Crown's hands should be a sufficient legal basis for spending thus supporting Treasury power.

It seems clear that where a statute does in fact confer specific spending powers, as is usually the case, this must be obeyed and cuts down any general power derived from the Appropriation Act (see for example *R v Secretary of State for Foreign Affairs ex parte World Development Movement* (1995); *R v Secretary of State for the Home Department ex parte Fire Brigades Union* (1995)). However, a later Appropriation Act could validate past unlawful. expenditure. A Concordat in 1932 between the Treasury and the Public Accounts Committee (see Treasury, *Government Accounting*, 1989, Annex 2.1.) assumed that an Appropriation Act could override limits in other statutes but stated that it was 'proper' that permanent spending powers and duties should be defined by particular statutes. Other government statements are inconsistent (see Daintith and Page, 1999, p. 205). It may be that the courts would be reluctant to read general provisions in an

Appropriation Act as overriding specific provisions in other Acts (see *Fisher v R* (1901)).

Some items of expenditure are permanently authorised by particular statutes. These are called consolidated fund services. They include judicial salaries, royal expenses, European Community payments and interest on the national debt. The Government Trading Act 1990 gives permanent authority to the financing of certain commercial services such as the Post Office by means of a Trading Fund. In practice most government spending is the subject of long-term commitments (for example pensions), thus leaving little flexibility.

## 11.5 Supervision of the Executive

This depends upon the doctrine of ministerial responsibility (Chapter 13) and relies in the last resort upon the convention that the House of Commons can require the government to resign. In modern times the role of Parliament has been weakened by the party system and the difficulty of obtaining information from the government. It should also be remembered that not all government activity requires formal parliamentary authority. This includes royal prerogative powers, including the making of treaties and other matters concerning foreign affairs (Chapter 12), commercial and property transactions carried out under private law powers, national security and the use of the armed forces where additional expenditure is not involved. Parliamentary scrutiny is also limited by the practice of conferring decision-making power to semi-independent bodies outside the central government.

The main procedures for scrutiny of the executive are as follows:

▶ *Questions* (SO 50). These can be written or oral. About 45 minutes each day are allowed for oral questions to ministers. The Prime Minister has one session of 30 minutes. Any MP can put down a question. In other cases there is a rota of three ministers per day but members must ballot for the privilege of asking an oral question. Except in the case of Prime Minister's Questions, advance notice must be given but a member may ask one unscheduled supplementary question. Civil servants who brief ministers are skilled in anticipating possible supplementaries which need only bear a tenuous relationship to the main question. For example: Q. 'What are the Prime Minister's engagements for the day?' S. 'Why is he not visiting X where another hospital has been closed?' Conversely, sycophantic questions by government supporters are frequently asked. Oral questions are probably of value only as a means of ensuring that ministers present themselves in public. They are of limited value as a means of obtaining information.

By convention, ministers must provide the information requested but can refuse to answer on various grounds including expense and the 'public interest' and cannot be pressed upon a refusal to answer. Some matters are excluded. These include matters relating to the monarchy, to litigation in process and to personal criticism of a judge. Moreover, answers can be perfunctory and incomplete although ministers must not 'knowingly' mislead Parliament and must correct any inadvertent error at the earliest opportunity (see *Ministerial Code*, Chapter 13). Apart from the Prime Minister, ministers have about two weeks' advance notice. Questions can be put in writing without limit and the answers are recorded in *Hansard*, the official parliamentary journal. A 'Private Notice' question can be asked by any member without prior warning, which requires a minister to answer. This must however be of an 'urgent character' and relate either to matters of public importance or to the arrangement of business (SO 17 (3)).

▶ *Debates*. There are various opportunities for debating general matters: all involve limited time. However ministers must respond if required and thus debates require government to present itself in public.

(i) *Adjournment debates:* These can be on any matter for which a minister is responsible. The most common is a half-hour daily adjournment debate which can be initiated by a backbencher. There is a weekly ballot (SO 9). There can also be adjournment debates following passage of a Consolidated Fund or Appropriation bill (above), emergency adjournment debates (which are rarely permitted), and 'recess' debates in which miscellaneous topics can be debated for up to three hours. Amendments cannot be moved to adjournment motions, so adjournment motions can be used by the government to restrict the Opposition. Adjournment debates do not result in a formal vote, and a minister's response cannot be questioned.

(ii) *Opposition days* after the proceedings on the annual Appropriation Act (above).

(iii) *Emergency debates:* To open the debate the support of 40 members or a vote of the House is required (SO 20). The Speaker must hold that the matter is urgent and relates to the responsibilities of ministers. Only three minutes are allowed for the application.

(iv) The debate following the Queen's Speech at the opening of a session.

(v) *Censure motions:* By convention, a government is expected to resign if defeated on a censure motion (also called a no-confidence motion). The government must provide time to debate the motion.

Until the 1970s the convention also seemed to include other government defeats on important matters, but the latter seem no longer to require resignation (HC 870 Deb. 71–2, 1974). The possibility that a government can be defeated on a major part of its programme but also remain in office strengthens a weak government by providing a safety valve for dissidents within its party. Since 1964 a government has resigned only once following a censure motion (1979). On that occasion the government was a minority government, again a rare event. A no-confidence motion has no particular form. Either government or Opposition can declare any vote to be one of confidence. In today's conditions the procedure seems to be essentially a publicity stunt. However, such a vote does require the government to publicly defend itself.

(vi) The budget debate.

(vii) Ministerial statements which can be followed by questions and discussion. The Speaker can require a minister to attend and make a statement.

(viii) *'Westminster Hall'*: Introduced as part of the modernisation programme, this is a parallel chamber which sits in a large committee room on three weekdays. It is intended to be a supplement to the main chamber as a forum for debates initiated by backbenchers on less contentious business for which time might not be easily found in the main chamber. In particular it can be used for adjournment debates (above). Decisions must be unanimous and otherwise are referred to the main House. Ministers must be available to respond every other week whereas in the main chamber they must respond if required to any debate.

### 11.5.1 Supervising Expenditure

Money raised by central government goes into the 'consolidated fund'. The control of spending from the consolidated fund is the responsibility of the Commons but, given the size and complexity of modern government this is clearly an impossible task for an elected assembly. In practice, direct parliamentary control over expenditure is very limited. Substantial controls are, in characteristically English fashion, imposed within the government machine itself by the Treasury and are an example of the importance of internal rules based on a mixture of statute, royal prerogative and the inherent power of any employer to administer its workforce (see Chapter 13).

In medieval times, the Court of Exchequer supervised government spending, but the modern courts have relinquished this responsibility in favour of Parliament. The courts are therefore reluctant to interfere with central government spending decisions which are subject to parliamentary scrutiny (see *Nottinghamshire CC v Secretary of State* (1986)). However, in *R v Secretary of State for Foreign and Commonwealth Affairs ex parte World Development Movement* (1995) a Foreign Office decision to give a large grant to the Malaysian government for the Pergau Dam project was set aside by the Court of Appeal on the basis that the project had had no economic justification and that there was an ulterior political motive. In that case the governing legislation specifically required that the decision be based on economic grounds, which, crucially, the court equated with 'sound' economic grounds.

The expenditure of central departments and other public bodies related to the centre is scrutinised on behalf of Parliament by the Comptroller and Auditor General. The Comptroller is appointed by the Crown on a motion from the House of Commons proposed by the Prime Minister with the agreement of the Chair of the Public Accounts Committee (Exchequer and Audit Depts Acts 1866–1957; National Audit Act 1983 s.1). The Comptroller is an officer of the Commons and has security of tenure similar to that of a High Court Judge (See Exchequer and Audit Dept Act 1866). The Comptroller and Auditor General is not directly concerned with the merits of government policy but only with the efficient and economical use of money (National Audit Act 1983, ss.6, 7). However it is difficult to separate these two concerns.

The Comptroller is supported by the National Audit Office (NAO) which is responsible for scrutinising the accounts of central government departments and also those of some outside bodies dependent on government money, such as universities. The NAO carries out two kinds of audit. 'Certification Audit' is based on financial accounting practice. 'Value for Money Audit' is based on the wider concerns of the 'economy, efficiency and effectiveness' of government expenditure (National Audit Act 1983 s.6). This is not meant to include the substantive merits of government policy, although the line between them may be difficult to draw. The NAO is also concerned with matters of 'regularity, legality, propriety and probity'.

The Comptroller reports to the Public Accounts Committee of the House of Commons. This committee carries out an annual scrutiny of government accounts and its report is debated by the Commons. It thus provides a key mechanism for the control of government finance and for government accountability in general.

## 11.5.2 Scrutiny of Delegated Legislation

The practice of delegating lawmaking powers to the executive is necessary, given the complexity of modern government and the pressure upon parliamentary time. Most delegated legislation is detailed and highly technical. It would be impracticable to subject all delegated legislation to detailed democratic scrutiny so that the law is necessarily a compromise. Thus delegated legislation is subject to a limited degree of parliamentary control by being laid before one or both Houses for approval. Unlike a bill, Parliament cannot usually amend delegated legislation.

Originally the laying process was haphazard, but as a result of public concern about 'bureaucratic tyranny' (see *Report of Committee on Ministers' Powers*, 1932, Cmnd 4060) limited reforms were made by the Statutory Instruments Act 1946. Most delegated legislation takes the form of a statutory instrument which subjects it to the Act. A statutory instrument made after the 1946 Act came into force is defined as such if it is made by Order in Council or if the parent Act expressly provides. Thus there is no legal obligation on governments to comply with the controls in the 1946 Act. Moreover, a statutory instrument has to be laid before the House only if its parent Act so requires. The 1946 Act also requires that statutory instruments must be published 'as soon as may be' unless there is a special excuse for not doing so (s.3). Failure to publish may not make the instrument invalid but provides a statutory defence to prosecution, provided that the accused was unaware of the instrument and that no reasonable steps had been taken to publicise it (s.3 (2); see *R v Sheer Metalcraft Ltd* (1954)).

The laying procedures typically require only that the statutory instrument be 'laid on the table' of the House in draft or in final form for 40 days subject to annulment by a vote of the House – the 'negative' procedure. The fate of the instrument therefore depends upon the chance of a member's seeing the document and securing a debate. Some instruments are required to be laid for information only, Parliament having no power to annul them. A small number of important statutory instruments are made subject to an 'affirmative' procedure under which there must be a positive vote in order to bring them into effect.

The Parliament Acts do not apply to delegated legislation so that the House of Lords has the power to veto a statutory instrument. It has done so only once in the last 30 years when it vetoed a measure that would deny free mailing for candidates in the election for the mayor of Greater London (*Hansard*, HL 20 Feb. 2000, col. 136). The Wakeham Committee (see Chapter 10) and the government have proposed that this power be removed in favour of a delaying power only.

The Joint Committee on Statutory Instruments is responsible for scrutinising statutory instruments laid before Parliament. The scrutiny committee is not concerned with the political merits of the instrument but is required to draw the attention of Parliament to specified constitutional matters. These are as follows:

(i)   Does the instrument impose taxation or other forms of charge?

(ii)   Does it exclude control by the courts?
(iii)  Is it retrospective without the express authority of the parent Act?
(iv)   Has there been unjustifiable delay in laying or publishing it?
(v)    Is there doubt as to its legal validity or does it appear to make some unusual or unexpected use of the powers under which it was made?
(vi)   For any special reason does its form or purport call for elucidation?
(vii)  Does its drafting appear to be defective?
(viii) Any other ground other than those relating to policy or merits.

### 11.5.3   Select Committees

A select committee is appointed, for the whole of a Parliament, from back-benchers. There are three main kinds: firstly, there are committees charged with investigating the expenditure, administration and policy of the main departments and reporting to the House (SO 130). There is no Prime Minister's Committee as such but the Prime Minister voluntarily appears before the Liaison Committee which is composed of the Chairs of the other committees. The Security and Intelligence Committee is made up of MPs but is appointed by and reports to the Prime Minister (Chapter 19).

Secondly, there are committees dealing with important general concerns. These include broadcasting, environmental audit, food standards, European scrutiny, public accounts, public administration, regulatory reform, statutory instruments. Thirdly there are committees dealing with matters internal to the House such as standards and privileges, modernisation, and procedure. There is also the Speaker's Committee which deals with electoral matters (Political Parties, Elections and Referendums Act 2000). Finally, there are joint committees of the Lords and Commons. These include human rights, statutory instruments, financial services and markets and House of Lords reform.

The work of the departmental select committees is coordinated by the Liaison Committee which selects the members in proportion to party representation in the House. In practice, however, it appears that the membership is selected according to instructions from party whips. The chairmanship is a matter for negotiation between government and opposition. Select committees may also recruit outside advisers such as academics. They interview witnesses but have little real ability to probe deeply. Time, party discipline, the doctrine of ministerial responsibility and the rules of parliamentary procedure combine to frustrate their activities. In principle, a select committee has power to call for 'persons and papers' at any time, even when Parliament is not sitting, and failure to attend or refusal to answer questions could be a contempt of the House. However, enforcement would require a resolution of the House and the committee can do little on its own (see HC 353, 1991–2, paras 20–21).

Particular problems are as follows:

▶ Members of the House of Lords, being protected by their own privilege, cannot be required to attend.
▶ Ministers can probably not be required to attend nor to answer questions without an Order of the House.
▶ Committees have no power to demand papers from government departments. An Address to the Queen (in respect of a secretary of state) or a formal Order from the House is required.
▶ Select committees have no independent research resources.
▶ Ministers have relied on traditional notions of ministerial responsibility as a means of shielding the inner workings of government from parliamentary scrutiny, slightly tempered by a general undertaking by ministers to cooperate with committees, for example by explaining why evidence cannot be given. Civil servants are protected by ministerial responsibility and probably cannot be required to attend without the consent of ministers. Even where they do attend, their evidence has been limited to describing their 'actions' taken on behalf of ministers as opposed to their 'conduct' generally. Thus civil servants cannot give evidence about cabinet matters, nor the consultation process within government, nor the advice they gave to government, nor policy alternatives. Indeed, ministers have sometimes forbidden civil servants from appearing, in particular on the grounds of national security, 'good government' and 'excessive cost'. However, this remains controversial (see Chapter 13).

Select committees have drawn public attention to important issues and have exposed weaknesses in governmental policies and procedures. Their capacity to do this may have a deterrent effect on government departments. On the other hand, their reports do not necessarily lead to action or even to debate in Parliament and they are not tools for extracting information. To this extent the view of the Procedure Committee that select committees have been a modest success in requiring government to explain itself is perhaps a little sanguine (HC 19, 1989–90, paras 356–7). On the other hand the backbench composition of select committees and their practice of seeking consensus have given them a certain independent status.

Except for committees of the whole House and some minor committees, all House of Lords committees are select committees which can therefore accumulate expertise. Select committees in the House of Lords deal with subjects rather than departments, reflecting the role of the upper House as a forum for the detailed discussion of important issues free of immediate party pressures. The Science and Technology Committee, the European Committee and the Environmental Committee are particularly well regarded.

## 11.6 Redress of Grievances

Overlapping with Parliament's duty to supervise the executive is the duty of members of Parliament and the right of Parliament collectively to seek the redress of the grievances of subjects of the Crown. Procedurally this depends upon opportunities being made available to backbench members to raise individual grievances. One problem is the possibility of conflicts with party interests, another is the lack of resources, including time. No parliamentary time is reserved for the redress of grievances as such. An MP is able to give publicity to a grievance by placing it on the parliamentary record. Apart from that, the process is haphazard.

The main procedures available are questions, adjournment debates, and, perhaps most effectively, informal communications with ministers, although, as we have seen, the latter are not always protected by parliamentary privilege (Chapter 9). All these suffer from the inability of an individual MP to force disclosure of information. Early Day Motions can also be used. This procedure allows an MP to put down a matter for debate without a fixed date. Early Day Motions are hardly ever debated. Their function is to draw public attention to a particular issue. They may be supported by a large number of members across parties, amounting in effect to a petition.

There are other miscellaneous opportunities by way of business questions and points of order, both of which allow members briefly to draw attention to matters which concern them. These must, strictly speaking, relate to the internal procedures of the House, but the Speaker customarily gives considerable latitude. Finally, there are public petitions which members can present on behalf of their constituents. These are published in *Hansard*.

These examples suggest that a sophisticated knowledge of the procedures of the House can be used tactically to some effect. On the other hand, it is easy for an MP to avoid following up a complaint from a constituent, by passing it to another agency. However, members habitually deal with grievances outside the formal parliamentary framework, acting in effect as generalist welfare offices. A letter from an MP is likely to be dealt with at a higher level in the civil service hierarchy than would otherwise be the case. On the other hand, MPs lack the expertise and resources to be in a position to follow up complaints in detail.

### 11.6.1 The Parliamentary Commissioner for Administration

The Parliamentary Commissioner for Administration (PCA) investigates on behalf of Parliament complaints by citizens against the central government and certain other bodies controlled by the central government (Parliamentary Commissioner Act 1967; Parliamentary and Health Services Commissioners Act 1987; Parliamentary Commissioner Act 1994). Popularly known as the 'ombudsman', the PCA enjoys similar salary and security of tenure to a superior court judge. The PCA has a discretion whether or not to investigate any particular case although this is subject to judicial review (see *R* v *Parliamentary Commissioner ex parte Dyer* (1994)). Investigations are private (s.7 (2)). This may be advantageous by encouraging greater frankness by those being investigated. The PCA can see documents and interview civil servants and other witnesses and the normal plea of government confidentiality cannot be used (s.8 (3)). However, Cabinet documents can be excluded (s.8 (4)) and the PCA must not name individual civil servants. There are also Local Government Commissioners who reports to the local authority concerned; the governing legal principles being in several respects similar (Local Government Act 1974).

There are considerable limitations on the powers of the PCA as follows:

▶ Important areas of central government activity are excluded from its jurisdiction. These include foreign affairs, state security (including passports), legal proceedings, criminal investigations, government contracts, commercial activities other than compulsory purchase of land (but statutory powers exercised by contractors under privatisation arrangements are within the ombudsman's jurisdiction), civil service employment matters and the granting by the Crown of honours, awards and privileges.

▶ The PCA can investigate allegations of 'injustice in consequence of maladministration' (s.5 (1)). Maladministration is not defined but means broadly some defect in the process of decision making: 'bias, neglect, inattention, delay, incompetence, inaptitude, perversity, turpitude, arbitrariness and so-on' (the 'Crossman Catalogue' 734 HC Deb. col. 51, 1966). The PCA cannot directly question government policy nor the merits of the exercise of a discretion (s.12), see *R* v *Local Commissioner ex parte Bradford City Council* (1979).

▶ Complaints must be in writing within 12 months of the decision complained of.

▶ Complaints must be made to a MP. This is intended to preserve the constitutional principle that the executive is responsible to Parliament. It is up to the MP whether to request the PCA to intervene. There has been considerable criticism of this rule. MPs, it has been suggested, prefer to take the credit for redressing grievances themselves and may therefore be reluctant to refer to the ombudsman. Conversely, MPs may be unclear about the PCA's power and refer inappropriate cases, or even pass the buck by referring cases indiscriminately.

▶ The PCA cannot normally investigate cases where the citizen has a legal remedy but he has a discretion to do so. It should however exercise this broadly, taking account of matters such as the claimant's means (see *R v Local Commissioner for Administration ex parte Liverpool City Council* (2001)).

▶ The PCA has no power to enforce its findings. Unlike the local ombudsman it does not have the sanction of publicity. Its only power is to report to the MP who enlisted its aid. If it has found injustice caused by maladministration and considers that it has not been remedied, it may also lay a report before Parliament. Reflecting the convention of ministerial responsibility, it is for the minister concerned to decide whether to give effect to the recommendations, for example by compensating the victim of the injustice, or improving departmental procedures. Government departments have usually accepted the PCA's recommendations but much depends on the attitude of the House of Commons. The Public Administration Committee monitors the PCA.

# Summary

▶ Procedure in the House of Commons is regulated by standing orders and by the Speaker who has a duty to safeguard all interests. We outlined the lawmaking procedure as it applies to public bills and private bills. We then looked at the procedural framework within which the Commons attempts to make legislation, hold the government to account, control public finance, and redress citizens' grievances. The timetable is largely under the control of the government as are procedural devices for cutting short debate. However, there are opportunities for backbenchers and the opposition to intervene.

▶ There are mechanisms for approving government spending and taxation proposals and for scrutinising government expenditure, notably the office of Comptroller and Auditor General and the Public Accounts Committee. In general, however, the House of Commons is not equipped for the detailed control of government expenditure. In recent years the emphasis has switched to internal controls over expenditure through the Treasury (Chapter 13).

▶ Other devices for parliamentary control of the executive include specialist select committees and the Parliamentary Commissioner for Administration. These devices have implications for ministerial responsibility. This is because (i) they involve investigating the activities of civil servants; and (ii) they raise questions about the relationship between ministers and the House of Commons. Select committees provide a valuable means of publicising issues but have weak powers and are subject to influence by the executive. The extent to which select committees can scrutinise the activities of executive agencies is unclear.

▶ Delegated legislation is often required to be laid before the House although, unless the affirmative procedure is used, it may not get serious scrutiny. The Joint Committee on Statutory Instruments monitors delegated legislation on constitutional grounds.

## Summary cont'd

▶ The House of Lords regulates its own procedure. The Lord Chancellor presides but does not have the disciplinary powers available to the Speaker. Subject to these considerations, procedure in the Commons is dominated by the government through its power to propose business and its control of a majority of votes. Government proposals take up most of the available time. Members of Parliament have no privileged access to government information so that their debate is not especially well informed.

▶ The conventional assessment of Parliament is that it has become subservient to the executive, primarily because its members have capitulated to party loyalty, reinforced by the electoral system and by the dual role of ministers as members of both executive and Parliament. Parliament, according to this view, is at its worst as a method of controlling government finance, poor at supervising the executive and lawmaking but better at redressing individual grievances, although this owes a lot to the work of members outside the formal parliamentary procedures. On the other hand, Parliament provides a forum where the executive must defend itself in public and expose the strengths and weaknesses of its leaders. The possibility of defeat in an election may encourage members to distance themselves from an unpopular government and act as a limited constitutional check.

# Exercises

**11.1** Explain and illustrate the difference between a public bill, a private bill and a hybrid bill. What parliamentary procedures apply in each case?

**11.2** 'The main democratic service provided by Parliament is that it forces the government to defend itself in public.' Discuss.

**11.3** 'The key to democracy is the power to control public finance.' Is the UK constitution democratic in this sense?

**11.4** Explain the extent to which the government of the day can control the parliamentary process.

**11.5** Examine the strengths and weaknesses of select committees and parliamentary questions as a means of controlling the executive.

**11.6** Compare the procedures of the House of Commons and House of Lords. To what extent do these reflect the different constitutional functions of the two Houses?

**11.7** Explain the constitutional differences between the Parliamentary Commissioner for Administration and the Parliamentary Commissioner for Standards (Chapter 9).

**11.8** The government proposes to introduce the following measures at the beginning of the parliamentary session 2005–6. The House of Lords has declared its firm opposition to all of them. Advise the government.

▶ A bill to extend the life of the present Parliament to 2008. This bill has the support of 70% of the public in an opinion poll.

▶ A bill to increase the taxation on country houses. In order to comply with an EC Directive, the bill must become law by the end of 2006.

▶ A bill to replace hereditary peers by persons elected by the readers of the *Sun* newspaper.

▶ A statutory instrument imposing restrictions upon rural fishing rights.

## Further reading

Brazier, R. (1988) 'The Financial Powers of the House of Lords', *Anglo American Law Review*, 131.

Clothier, C. (1986) 'The Value of an Ombudsman', *Public Law* 204.

Cowley, P. and Stuart, M. (2001) 'Parliament: a Few Headaches and a Dose of Modernisation', *Parliamentary Affairs*, **54**(3): 442.

Daintith, T. and Page, A. (1999) *The Executive in the Constitution*, Oxford, OUP, Chapter 4.

Giddings, P. (ed) (1995) *Parliamentary Accountability*, Basingstoke, Macmillan – now Palgrave Macmillan.

Harden, I. (1993) 'Money and the Constitution: Financial Control Reporting and Audit', *Legal Studies*, **13**: 16.

Harden, I. et al. (1994) *Audit, Accounting Officers and Accountability: The Pergau Dam Affair, Public Law* 526.

Hennessy, P. (1995) *The Hidden Wiring*, London, Gollancz, Chapter 6.

Jones, B., Kavanagh, D., Moran, M. and Norton, P. (2004) *Politics UK*, 5th edn, Harlow, Pearson, Chapter 17.

Jowell, J. and Oliver, D. (2003) *The Changing Constitution*, 5th edn, Oxford, Oxford University Press, Chapter 8.

Newton, Lord (2001) *The Challenge for Parliament: Making Government Work*, London, Hansard Society.

Riddell, P. (2000) *Parliament under Blair*, London, Politico.

Rogers, R. and Walters, R. (2004) *How Parliament Works*, 5th edn, Harlow, Pearson, Chapters 3, 6, 7, 8, 9, 10, 11, 13.

Waldron, J. (1999) *Law and Disagreement*, Oxford, Oxford University Press, Chapters 2, 3, 5.

Weir, S. and Beetham, D. (1999) *Political Power and Democratic Control in Britain*, London, Routledge.

# Chapter 12

## The Crown

> The fool had stuck himself up one day, with great gravity, in the King's Throne; with a stick, by way of sceptre in one hand, and a ball in the other: being asked what he was doing? He answered 'reigning'. Much of the same sort of reign I take it, would be that of our Author's Democracy.' (Jeremy Bentham, *A Fragment of Government*, 1776, Chapter 2, para. 34)

## Key words

- Crown and monarch
- Crown and government
- Personal and political powers
- Special and ordinary powers
- Justiciability
- Democratic accountability
- Legal immunities

### 12.1 Introduction: The Nature of the Crown

We saw in Chapter 4 that UK law has no concept of the state as an entity and sometimes uses the notion of the crown as a substitute. However, the crown is an obscure concept, particularly as to whether the Crown and the Queen are the same. The Queen/Crown is (i) part of the legislature albeit with at most a veto; (ii) the formal executive of the UK as a whole and of the devolved governments of Wales, Scotland and Northern Ireland; (iii) head of the Church of England; (iv) head of the armed forces; (v) source of the authority of the judiciary (vi) prosecutor. The Queen also has primitive ceremonial and symbolic functions representing Bagehot's 'dignified' constitution as a focus of authority.

The Queen has a range of important powers collectively known as the royal prerogative. These are common law powers and derive historically from the monarch's personal command of the government. Some of the more draconian powers were abolished in the seventeenth century and all prerogative powers are subject to parliamentary supremacy. Moreover, most of the Queen's legal powers are limited by convention. Most importantly, she must always assent to a bill properly put before her, must appoint as Prime Minister the person who commands support of a majority in the House of Commons, and in dissolving Parliament and exercising any other power she must normally act on the advice of the Prime Minister or other appropriate minister. It is in any case contemporary practice for statute to confer powers directly on individual ministers, thus creating our characteristic fragmented form of government (Chapter 13). Sometimes, however, statutory powers are conferred on the Crown as such (e.g. Bank of England Act 1998 s.1 (2): appointment of governor of Bank). As the ultimate source of power, the Queen might exercise her residual personal powers in time of crisis (below). Property is usually vested in the Crown as such, since not all government departments have their own legal identity (Chapter 13).

The historical process of removing power from the monarch (Chapter 3) has left us with ambiguities and confusions concerning the legal nature of the Crown and its relationship with the executive. It is not clear whether the 'Crown' means the Queen personally, or a corporate body with one member, namely the Queen, or a kind of company synonomous with the executive or merely a 'brand name' with no legal identity as such (see *M v Home Office* (1993), including dicta in the lower courts, and McLean, (2004), *Oxford Journal of Legal Studies* 129).

The Crown means different things in different contexts: for example, when speaking of the head of state we refer to the Queen, but when speaking of the executive we refer to the Crown. The prosecution of offenders is carried out in the name of the Queen representing the state, but independently of the executive. It may be that there is no legal significance in the terminology: for example, the Scotland Act 1998 refers to the executive power as vested in 'Her Majesty' (s.52). However, the Crown in its official capacity must be separated from the Queen since, under the Crown Proceedings Act 1947 (below), the Crown can be sued but not the Queen in her personal capacity.

The Crown is often said to be a corporation *sole*. A corporation sole is an office that is a legal entity which exists permanently, separate from the individual who holds the office at any given time and thus not being affected by the death of the office holder. An alternative view, which accommodates the reality of modern government, is that the Crown is a corporation *aggregate* akin to a company. In *Town Investments Ltd v Department of the Environment* (1977) the question arose whether an office lease taken by a minister, using the standard formula 'for and on behalf of her majesty' was vested in the minister or the Crown, since in the latter case it would be immune from taxation. The House of Lords held that the lease was vested in the Crown. Lord Diplock thought that the Crown was a fiction describing the executive. Lord Simon of Glaisdale said that the expression 'the Crown' symbolises the powers of government that were formerly wielded by the wearer of the crown, and reflects the historical development of the executive as that of offices hived off from the royal household. He stated that the legal concept best fitted to the contemporary situation was to consider the Crown as a corporation aggregate headed by the Queen and made up of 'the departments of state including ministers at their heads'. His Lordship added two riders: 'First the legal concept still does not correspond to the political reality. The Queen does not command those legally her servants. On the contrary she acts on the formally tendered collective advice of the Cabinet.' Secondly, 'when the Queen is referred to by the symbolic title of "Her Majesty" it is the whole corporation aggregate which is generally indicated. This distinction between "the Queen" and "Her Majesty" reflects the ancient distinction between "the King's two bodies", the "natural" and the "politic"' (see *Duchy of Lancaster Case* (1567) 1 Plow 325 at 327). Sir Robert Armstrong, a former Cabinet Secretary, said that 'for all practical purposes, the Crown is represented by the government of the day' (Hennessy, *The Hidden Wiring*, 1995, p. 346).

Moreover, there is not one Crown but many (*R v Secretary of State for Foreign and Commonwealth Affairs ex parte Alberta Indian Association* (1982)). Australia, New Zealand and Canada each recognise the Crown as their Head of State. The office happens for historical reasons to be held by the Queen of the UK, but in each case she has a separate title and responsibilities. The Queen is also Head of the Commonwealth, a title of symbolic importance which carries no legal powers, but probably still has political significance. Indeed, a conflict could arise between the Queen's role as Head of the Commonwealth and her duty to accept the advice of the British government. For example, in the mid-1980s the Commonwealth, contrary to the wishes of the UK government, wanted to ban sporting and trade links with South Africa because of apartheid.

Ministers and officials are servants of the Crown but are not the Crown itself. They should therefore have no special immunity in litigation and can be sued for their personal wrongs just like anyone else. In *M v Home Office* (1993), the Home Secretary attempted to rely on crown immunity in order to deport an immigrant in defiance of a court order. The House of Lords held that he was liable in his official capacity for contempt of court. In that case, however, Parliament had conferred the power in question directly upon the Secretary of State, whereas in *Town Investments* (above) the lease had been made 'for and on behalf of her majesty'.

In *R v Preston* [1993] 4 All ER 638 at 663 Lord Mustill remarked:

The Crown as the source of authority means that the UK has never found it necessary to create the notion of the 'state' as a single legal entity

This could be said to support liberal ideas of freedom in that power is divided between separate bodies of which the Crown is merely one, rather than concentrated in a Hobbesian leviathan (Chapter 1). If we were to abolish the monarchy then a different explanation would have to be found as to the basis of legal power. This could lead to a written constitution. Thus, even though the role of the monarch herself is relatively insignificant, the monarchy remains the keystone of the constitution.

## 12.2 Succession to the Monarchy

Under the 1688 settlement Parliament conferred on itself the power to appoint the sovereign. The Act of Settlement 1700 provides that the Crown is to be held by the direct descendants of Princess Sophia (the grand-daughter of the deposed James II). The holder of the Crown must be a Protestant and must not marry a Catholic. The rules of descent are based upon the medieval law governing succession to land. Preference is given to males over females and to the elder over the younger. The land law rules required sisters to hold land equally (co-parcenaries). However, in the case of the Crown, the first-born prevails (although the matter has not been litigated). Since the point of these rules is that they are arbitrary, in the sense that personal merit or public choice is irrelevant, we need not pursue them further. The succession has been altered only once when Edward VIII abdicated in 1936 (His Majesty's Declaration of Abdication Act 1936). It is not settled whether the monarch has the power to abdicate without an Act of Parliament. Since monarchy is a status conferred by law and without a voluntary act, the answer is probably not. The Crown's titles are also determined by statute (Royal Titles Act 1953).

When the monarch dies, the successor immediately and automatically becomes monarch. A special Accession Council, composed mainly of members of the House of Lords, proclaims this. The proclamation is later confirmed by the Privy Council. Whether these bodies have a power of veto is unclear. Certainly the subsequent coronation ceremony has no legal significance, being purely symbolic and theatrical. If the monarch is a minor, ill, or absent abroad, the royal functions are exercised by a regent or councillors of state (see Regency Acts 1937–53). In such cases certain bills cannot be assented to – most importantly a bill for altering the succession to the Crown.

## 12.3 Financing the Monarchy

Even in her private capacity the Queen is exempt from taxes unless statute specifically provides otherwise. The Queen has, however, entered into a voluntary agreement to pay tax on current income and personal capital. The expenses of the monarchy and of those members of the royal family who perform what they regard as public duties are funded from the Civil List in return for the monarch surrendering to Parliament the hereditary income from Crown property. The Civil List is an amount granted by Parliament at the beginning of each reign. It consists of an annual payment that can be increased by statutory instrument made by the Treasury, subject to veto by the House of Commons (Civil List Acts 1952–75). However, under the Civil List Act 1975, the Treasury can make additional payments a practice that would make the monarchy equivalent to an ordinary government department. This is not currently implemented. However, many of the royal expenses are funded directly by government departments, such as the upkeep of Crown buildings, security, travel and entertaining political dignitaries.

## 12.4　The Powers and Functions of the Monarchy

Since 1688 the functions and personal powers of the monarchy have gradually been reduced. The 1688 revolution left the monarch in charge of running the executive but dependent upon Parliament for money and lawmaking power. The monarch retained substantial personal influence until the late nineteenth century, mainly through the power to appoint ministers and to influence elections in the local constituencies. Until after the reign of George V (1910–34) monarchs occasionally intervened in connection with ministerial appointments and policy issues. The abdication of Edward VIII (1936) probably spelt the end of any political role for the monarch.

The modern functions of the monarchy can be outlined as follows:

1. *To symbolise the nation*, participating for this purpose in ceremonies and public entertainments. It is often said that the popularity and public acceptance of the monarchy is directly related to the fact that the monarch has little political power and is primarily an entertainer. It is not clear why a modern democracy requires a personalised 'leader'. There is a strong element of superstition inherent in the notion of monarchy, hence the importance of the link between the monarch and the Established Church.
2. *To 'advise, encourage and to warn'*. The monarch, supported by a private secretary, has access to all government documents and regularly meets the Prime Minister. The monarch is entitled to express views in private to the government but there is no convention as to the weight to be given to them.
3. *Certain formal acts*. The monarch must normally accept the advice of ministers. These include:
    - (i)　Assent to statutes.
    - (ii)　Orders in Council.
    - (iii)　Appointments of ministers, ambassadors, bishops and judges.
    - (iv)　Royal proclamations, for example dissolving and summoning Parliament or declaring a state of emergency.
    - (v)　Ratifying solemn treaties.
    - (vi)　Granting charters to universities, professional bodies, etc. These bestow the seal of state approval and also incorporate the body in question so that it can be treated as a separate person in law.
    - (vii)　Awarding peerages, honours and medals.

In certain cases it is believed that the monarch can and indeed must exercise personal power. There is little precedent. There are internal Cabinet Office guidance documents on the matter but the fact that unpublished sources have any weight at all is a sad reflection on the culture of those who exercise power. The governing principle seems to be that the head of state is the ultimate guardian of the constitution and must intervene where the normal machinery of government has broken down. Important occasions calling for the intervention of the monarchy are as follows:

▶ *The appointment of a Prime Minister.* The Queen must appoint the person who can form a government with the support of the House of Commons. This usually means the leader of the majority party as determined by a general election. Nowadays each party elects its leader. In the unlikely event of a majority not being found, the existing Prime Minister must probably be permitted to attempt to form a government. Failing that, the Queen should summon the leader of the next largest party. If that fails, there is disagreement as to what should happen, and in particular as to whether the monarch has any personal discretion. The Queen should attempt to find someone else capable of commanding a majority, but it is not clear whom, if anyone, she should consult. For example, should she consult the outgoing Prime Minister? Alternatively the Queen should dissolve Parliament, causing another election. The guiding principle seems to be that she must try to determine the electorate's preference.

▶ *The dismissal of a government and the dissolution of Parliament.* If a government is defeated on a vote of confidence in the House of Commons but refuses to resign or to advise a dissolution, the Queen could probably dismiss the government. This has not happened in Britain since 1783, but happened in Australia in 1975. In such a case the Opposition, if it could form a majority, could be placed in office or the Queen could dissolve Parliament, thus putting the case to the people through an election. It has been suggested that the Queen could dismiss a government that violates a basic constitutional principle, for example by proposing legislation to abolish elections. In order to dissolve Parliament the Queen would require a meeting of the Privy Council. It would therefore be convenient as a temporary measure for her to appoint the Leader of the Opposition as Prime Minister, who would then formally advise her in favour of a dissolution (see *Adegbenro v Akintola* [1963] AC 614 at 631).

▶ *Refusing a dissolution.* This possibility arises because of the convention that the Prime Minister may advise the monarch to dissolve Parliament. The Queen might refuse a dissolution if the Prime Minister is acting clearly unconstitutionally, for example if a Prime Minister whose party lost a general election immediately requested a second dissolution or where a Prime Minister falls personally foul of his party. Unfortunately there are no clear-cut precedents. It is likely that the Queen could refuse a dissolution only where there is a viable alternative government and a general election would be harmful to the national interest, although it seems difficult for anyone, let alone the Queen, to make such a judgement. A dissolution has not been refused in Britain this century but one was refused by the Governor-General of Canada in 1926. The Governor-General's decision was later rejected by the electorate.

▶ *The Queen might refuse a prime ministerial request* to appoint peers to the House of Lords where the reason for the request is to flood the Lords with government supporters. The precedents (1832 and 1910–11) suggest that the monarch would have to agree to such a request but only after a general election. This matter is therefore closely connected with the power to dissolve Parliament.

▶ *The Royal Assent.* The monarch has not refused assent to legislation since 1709. It appears to be a strong convention that Royal Assent must always be given. However the Queen might refuse Royal Assent where the refusal is on the advice of the Prime Minister, for example in the unlikely event of a private member's bill being approved by Parliament against the wishes of the government. Here two conventions clash. It is submitted that the better view is that she must still give assent because the will of Parliament has a higher constitutional status than that of the executive.

## 12.5 Crown Immunities

The Crown has special privileges in litigation. At common law no legal action would lie against the Crown in respect of its property rights and contracts, or in respect of injuries caused by the Crown (torts). Nor was the Crown bound by Acts of Parliament. This obvious gap in the rule of law was avoided by the Crown's practice of voluntarily submitting to the jurisdiction of the courts. In the case of actions involving property and contract this was through a procedure called a 'petition of right'. In the case of a tort, the individual Crown servant who committed the tort could be made liable and, where it was not clear who was responsible, the Crown would nominate a defendant, for example where a visitor to military premises was accidentally injured. In either case the Crown would pay the damages. Dicey did not regard crown immunity as seriously threatening the rule of law, pointing out that the individual Crown servant could always be held liable and that in practice the Crown would usually be willing to stand behind its employees. This seems a little flimsy.

There is also the obscure maxim 'the king can do no wrong'. This principle goes beyond the still existing procedural rule that the monarch cannot be made personally liable. It means that wrongdoing or bad faith cannot be attributed to the Crown. For example, the Crown at common law could not be liable for wrongs committed by its employees because unlawful acts of its employees were necessarily committed without its authority. However, the maxim has never prevented the courts from deciding whether a particular action falls within the lawful powers of the Crown. Invalid acts are not the same as wrongful acts (see *Dunlop* v *Woollahra MC* (1982)).

The Crown Proceedings Act 1947 was an attempt to rationalise this area of law and in particular to subject the Crown to legal liability, as if it were a private person, for breaches of contract, for the wrongs of its servants and for injuries caused by defective Crown property, etc. Section 1 permits action for breach of contact against the Crown; Section 2 permits action in tort, but only where a private person would be liable in the same circumstances. However, the Act still leaves the Crown with several special privileges. The most important are as follows:

▶ *No court order can be enforced against the Crown*, so that the plaintiff's right to damages depends upon the Crown voluntarily paying up. Similarly no injunction lies against the Crown nor against a crown servant acting on behalf of the Crown (Crown Proceedings Act 1947 s. 21). However, this applies only in civil law cases involving private rights. In judicial review cases where the legality of government powers are in issue and also in cases involving the enforcement of EC law (Chapter 8), ministers cannot claim Crown immunity (*M* v *Home Office* (1993)).

▶ *In an action for breach of contract the Crown can plead 'executive necessity'*. This means that it can refuse to comply with a contract where it has an overriding power to take some action in the public interest (see the *Amphitrite Case* (1921); *Commissioners of Crown Lands* v *Page* (1960)). It is unlikely that a court would challenge a minister's view of executive necessity, provided that a plausible justification is given. However, it is not correct to state that the Crown cannot be bound by any contract that hinders its freedom of action, since all contracts do this. There must either be some definite prerogative power that overrides the contract, or the contract must conflict with a statutory duty. For example, governments cannot cancel contracts without compensation merely because of policy changes.

▶ *In the case of action in tort* the 1947 Act contains several restrictions. The main ones are as follows:
   (i) The Crown is not liable for the acts of its 'officers' unless the individual officer was appointed directly or indirectly by the Crown

and paid wholly from central government funds (s.2 (6)). (The term 'officer' includes all Crown servants and ministers.)

(ii) The Crown is not in any circumstances liable for wrongs committed by 'judicial' officers (s.2 (5)): that is, judges or members of tribunals. A person exercising judicial functions also enjoys considerable personal immunity (below; Chapter 17).

(iii) Until 1987 a member of the armed forces injured on duty by another member of the armed forced or while on military property could not sue the Crown if the injury was pensionable under military regulations (s.10). This caused injustice because it was irrelevant whether or not the victim actually qualified for a pension. The Crown Proceedings (Armed Forces) Act 1987 abolished this rule but the Secretary of State can restore it in times of war or national emergency, see *Matthews* v *Ministry of Defence* (2003).

▶ *The Crown is not bound by an Act of Parliament unless it expressly or by necessary implication binds the Crown*. Necessary implication is a strict notion. It is not sufficient to show that the Crown is likely to cause unfairness and inconvenience or even that the exemption is against the public interest (*Lord Advocate* v *Dumbarton District Council* (DC) (1990)). It has to be established that the statute would be unworkable unless the Crown were bound (see *Cooper* v *Hawkins* (1904) – speed limit did not bind Crown). It is debatable whether the Crown can take the benefit of statutes, even though it is not bound by them. For example, the Crown can evict a tenant free of statutory restrictions, but could the Crown as a tenant resist eviction by a private landlord by relying on the same statutory rights that it can ignore as a landlord?

▶ *Act of State*. The Crown is not liable for injuries caused in connection with bona fide acts of government policy, provided that the action is authorised or subsequently ratified by the Crown (for example *Nissan* v *AG* (1970) – British troops billeted in Cyprus hotel: not an act of policy); *Buron* v *Denman* (1848) – British naval officer setting fire to barracks in West Africa in order to liberate slaves: Crown subsequently confirmed the action).

The defence of Act of State cannot apply within the UK except against 'enemy aliens', that is, citizens of countries with which we are formally at war (*Johnstone* v *Pedlar* (1921) – US citizen maltreated: Crown liable). This is because the Crown owes a duty to protect everyone who is even temporarily on British soil. Indeed, for the same reason the defence may not be available against a British subject anywhere in the world. In *Nissan's* case (above) the House of Lords expressed divided views on the point (see also *Walker* v *Baird* 1892)); *Johnstone* v *Pedlar* (above)). On the other hand, it seems unfair to favour people with no substantial link with the UK merely because they happen to hold British passports. The Human Rights Act 1998 applies to acts done by the UK government in overseas territory under its control (*R* (*Al Skeini*) v *Secretary of State* (2004): treatment of prisoners in Iraq).

In a broader sense certain high-level policy acts directed at other countries are also called Acts of State, for example, making treaties, declaring war, recognising new governments or granting diplomatic immunity (see Diplomatic Privileges Act 1964). These are exercises of sovereign powers with which the courts will not interfere. British subjects along with others may be incidentally affected by this kind of Act of State. For example, in *Cook* v *Sprigg* (1899) the Crown annexed Pondoland and refused to honour railway concessions granted to British subjects by the former government (see also *West Rand Central Gold Mining Co* v *R* (1905)). Indeed, this kind of Act of State may affect rights in domestic law. For example, a formal declaration by the Crown as to the existence of a state of war (*R* v *Bottril ex parte Kuechenmeister* (1947)), the recognition of a foreign government (*Carl Zeiss Stiftung* v *Rayner and Keeler Ltd (No.2)* (1967)) and the conferring of diplomatic immunity (*Engelke* v *Musmann* (1928); *Mighell* v *Sultan of Johore* (1894)) are not challengeable in the courts even though they might invalidate existing obligations or prevent legal actions.

## 12.6 The Royal Prerogative

The royal prerogative is a collection of special powers, rights and immunities vested in the Crown that is not conferred by Parliament. Identifying each of these powers and their scope is problematic since there is no authoritative source. This uncertainty is a concern because, as a matter of constitutional principle, those exercising power should be able to identify authority justifying its exercise.

Because the sovereign acts on the advice of ministers, many prerogative powers have become powers exercisable by ministers. These powers include some that are amongst the most significant powers possessed by government, for example a decision to deploy troops and the power to make a treaty are prerogative powers. The constitutional problem concerns a lack of democratic control over officials claiming to act under the prerogative. Decisions taken under the prerogative are essentially decrees with no formal accountability other than the limited possibility of judicial review. In some cases however, notably that of immigration control, prerogative powers have been overlaid by statutory arrangements. Where this applies the prerogative is to that extent overridden.

Although ministers are conventionally responsible to Parliament, at least one Prime Minister has expressed the view that 'It is for individual Ministers to decide on a particular occasion whether and how to report to Parliament on the exercise of prerogative powers' (HC Deb. 1 Mar. 1993, col. 19W). The absence of statutory controls has become controversial. There was, for example, no legal requirement for the government to gain parliamentary approval to send British troops to Iraq in 2003, although there is probably now a convention requiring this. Whether the convention extends, for example, to the deployment of troops in a peace keeping role as opposed to armed conflict is unclear. The absence of any statutory requirement for parliamentary approval thus raises profound questions in a modern democracy (see Fourth Report of the Public Administration Select Committee, 2003-04, HC 422 *Taming the Prerogative: Strengthening Ministerial Accountability to Parliament*). Similarly there are few democratic safeguards in relation to the treaty-making power: a ministerial signature, without Parliamentary approval, is all that is legally required to make a treaty. The UK constitution is perhaps unique in allowing government such extensive and imprecise powers that are not granted by the legislature.

The royal prerogative originated in the special rights and powers available to the monarch under the common law. Medieval legal theory did not regard the Crown as either the source of law or above the law, but did confer special rights on the monarch. Some of these were based upon the position of the monarch as chief landowner within the feudal system. Others derived from the responsibility of the monarch to keep the peace and defend the realm. This duality may have corresponded to the distinction drawn in seventeenth-century cases between the 'ordinary' and the 'absolute' prerogatives, the latter being discretionary powers vested in the king and arguably beyond the reach of the courts (see *Bates Case* (1606)). Today a similar distinction is represented as one between the personal and the political prerogatives, although this distinction probably has no legal consequences since prerogative powers as such are no longer immune from judicial review (below).

### 12.6.1    Historical Sketch

While individual monarchs have attempted to exploit prerogative power, on the whole the prerogative has been subject to the rule of law. From the sixteenth century, theories of absolute monarchy became dominant in Europe, but were less influential in England (Chapter 3). During the Tudor period (1485–1603) much law was made by royal proclamation and it is a matter of scholarly controversy as to when statute was regarded as necessary. A statute had at that time the status of an authoritative court judgement concerned with declaring rather than changing the law. Social regulation fell within the prerogative: for example, a proclamation of 1546 closed London brothels, and one of 1530 prohibited the publication of unauthorised religious books. Another proclamation of 1530 required 'vagabonds and beggars' to be stripped and beaten. It could however be argued that these exercises of power were not examples of true lawmaking but either fell within established common law rights of the Crown or concerned the enforcement of existing law.

In 1611 it was made clear that the King can legislate only within areas of prerogative allowed to him by the general law (*Case of Proclamations* (1611)). The debate therefore shifted to exploring the limits of the prerogative. The Stuarts attempted to extend the prerogative and to impose taxes and override the ordinary law. However, even they submitted themselves to the courts and, in a series of famous cases punctuating the political conflicts of the time, the scope of the prerogative was inconclusively argued (for example *Bates Case* (1606); *R* v *Hampden* (1637); *Godden* v *Hales* (1686)). Given that the judges were dismissable by the Crown, these cases were not always consistent. The ultimate solution was military (Chapter 3).

The conflict between King and Parliament was resolved by the 1688 settlement. The Bill of Rights outlawed certain aspects of the prerogative including the power to suspend laws without parliamentary consent. The power to dispense with laws (that is, to free individuals from penalties) was abolished only 'as it hath been assumed and exercised of late', thus preserving the prerogative of mercy which is exercised in modern times by the Home Secretary. The Bill of Rights also banned taxation under the royal prerogative. Modern judges have taken this further by refusing to imply a power to tax directly or indirectly unless very clear statutory language is used for the purpose (see *AG* v *Wilts United Dairies* (1921); *Congreve* v *Home Office* (1976); *Macarthy and Stone Ltd* v *Richmond Borough Council* (1991)).

The 1688 settlement provides the framework of the modern law. This can be summarised as follows:

▶ In principle the royal prerogative remains but must give way to statute.
▶ No new prerogatives can be created (*BBC* v *Johns* (1965)) but new applications of existing prerogatives are possible.
▶ The prerogative can be controlled by the courts, although the extent of such control depends upon the type of prerogative power in question and the context (see below).

Prerogative powers can be exercised either directly by ministers or by prerogative orders in council. The latter require a formal meeting of the Privy Council (a quorum of four) in the presence of the monarch.

### 12.6.2 Prerogative or Prerogatives?

Influenced by Locke and Blackstone, Lord Denning in *Laker Airways Ltd* v *Department of Trade* (1977) considered that the Crown had a general discretionary power to act for the public good in certain spheres of governmental activity for which the law had otherwise made no provision. This suggests that the state may benefit from a single, overarching power to interfere in private rights where it perceives an important public benefit may result, especially in times of emergency. This interpretation is, however, inconsistent with *Entick* v *Carrington* (1765). Here the court emphatically rejected a claim of 'executive necessity' that officers of the state had a general power to enter and search private property in the absence of express statutory or common law powers (see also *R* v *IRC ex parte Rossminster* (1980)). Lord Denning's views were not supported by the other members of the Court of Appeal. They are also fundamentally inconsistent with ideas of limited government. The better view is that, although the Crown has certain discretionary powers in relation to emergencies, such as the requisitioning of property (below), the prerogative comprises a finite number of distinct powers rather than one general power to act for the public good. However, considerable challenge to notions of limited government in relation to ministerial action arises because as a person in law the Crown may do anything that is not prohibited by statute or the common law.

### 12.6.3     Modern Prerogative Powers

The prerogative powers are of central importance in our modern constitution. There is no authoritative list of prerogative powers. However, in October 2003, the Public Administration Committee (PAC) of the House of Commons published a list supplied by the government of what it believed to be the main prerogatives (Fourth Report, Session 2003–04). It also took the view that some prerogative powers, for example the power to press men into the navy, may have lapsed through disuse. Similarly the ancient writ of *ne exeat regno*, which prevents persons, from leaving the country, is sometimes regarded as obsolete. However, there is no doctrine of obsolescence in English law (see *Felton* v *Callis* (1969); *Parsons* v *Burk* (1971)).

The PAC's list includes the following. Firstly, in relation to domestic affairs:

- Appointment and dismissal of ministers;
- The summoning, prorogation and dissolution of Parliament;
- Royal Assent to bills;
- The appointment and regulation of the civil service;
- The commissioning of officers in the armed forces;
- Directing the disposition of the armed forces in the UK;
- The appointment of Queen's Counsel (senior barristers). The Crown appoints judges by statute (Chapter 3);

- The prerogative of mercy (which is used to remedy errors in sentence calculation);
- The granting of honours;
- the granting of royal charters to bodies such as universities, learned societies, charities or professional associations which gives the body the status of a legal person and signifies state approval of its activities;
- Crown immunities (above).

Secondly, in relation to foreign affairs where considerable flexibility is needed so that these prerogatives are not generally subject to legal control (below):

- The making of treaties;
- The declaration of war;
- The deployment of the armed forces on operations overseas;
- The recognition of foreign states;
- The accreditation and reception of diplomats.

The PAC's list did not mention certain other established prerogatives. These include the government of overseas territories, the granting and revoking of passports, and the Attorney-General's prerogative power to institute legal proceedings in the public interest and to stop criminal proceedings by issuing a *nolle prosequi*.

There is also the possibility that the Crown has a residual power to keep the peace within the realm, for example by issuing the police with weapons (*R v Secretary of State ex parte Northumbria Police Authority* (1988) and similarly to enter upon, take and destroy private property in an emergency although compensation may be payable if the property is taken in peacetime for public use (see *Burmah Oil Co. v Lord Advocate* (1965); War Damage Act 1965). In relation to emergencies, however, the prerogative has largely been superseded by statute (Chapter 19). The security services also operate within a broad statutory framework, but many of their powers were formerly prerogative powers. Similarly immigration control, the administration of charities and the care of children and mental patients are now governed by statute.

Finally there are miscellaneous prerogatives based on feudal landholding. The most important of these are the Crown's ownership of the seashore and tidal waters and the Crown's rights to ownership of certain living creatures, notably swans.

### 12.6.4 Two Kinds of Prerogative Power?

There is ambiguity as to what a prerogative power is. Blackstone (1723–1780), whose view seems to be technically correct, regarded the prerogative as confined to the special powers of the Crown. The Crown also has ordinary common law powers such as ownership of property but these exist because the Crown has the status of an ordinary adult person. Unlike the special prerogative powers (*imperium* power), the Crown cannot do anything under the ordinary powers that a private individual could not do. These powers cannot therefore violate the rights of others. This links with Dicey's idea of the rule of law (Chapter 5) according to which all are subject to the same general law. Nevertheless the economic power available to the Crown (sometimes called *dominium* power) is substantial; for example, a defence contract or health service contract made with the Crown could affect the livelihoods of millions. Indeed, Dicey himself described the prerogative as including *all* the non-statutory powers of the Crown, including the 'private law' powers of ownership, employment contracting, etc., possessed by the Crown as a person in common with everyone else (1915, p. 429).

Blackstone's distinction seems unreal in as much as all Crown powers are important politically, and in the way they are exercised are indistinguishable from powers which Blackstone would regard as genuine examples of the prerogative. The Crown may be a property owner in common with others but its economic and political power surely put it in a special position and call for additional controls, particularly if, following Locke (Chapter 1), we believe that government holds all its powers subject to public duties. There is much to be said for Dicey's view and for treating all non-statutory powers of the Crown alike.

The modern cases seem to support Dicey. In *Council of Civil Service Unions* v *Minister for Civil Service* (1985) (also known as the GCHQ case), the House of Lords treated the control of the civil service as part of the royal prerogative, holding that they could review the validity of an Order in Council's varying the terms of employment of certain civil servants. Lord Diplock expressed the view that the distinction between special and ordinary powers of the Crown is artificial and would regard all common law powers of the Crown as part of the prerogative. In *R* v *Criminal Injuries Compensation Board ex parte Lain* (1967) a government scheme to pay compensation to the victims of crime was treated as a matter of prerogative, thus enabling the court to review errors of law made by the board which was set up to run the scheme. The scheme was financed out of money provided by Parliament but was not then statutory. Since anyone can give away money, this scheme would not count as royal prerogative under the Blackstone definition.

### 12.6.5    Parliamentary Scrutiny

As common law powers, prerogative powers do not need to be authorised by Parliament. In this sense there is a gap in democratic accountability.

However, some parliamentary control is possible, firstly because all government functions depend on money which must be authorised by Parliament (Chapter 11) and secondly through the doctrine of ministerial responsibility (Chapter 13). These methods of control are inherently weak since Parliament has insufficient resources adequately to scrutinise government spending and there is in any case normally an automatic majority for the executive. Moreover, by convention the Prime Minister cannot be questioned about advice given to the sovereign concerning certain prerogative powers, such as the grant of honours, the appointment and dismissal of privy councillors and the dissolution of Parliament. The reason for this is that the exercise of these powers involves the personal discretion of the monarch, even though the monarch must usually act on the advice of the Prime Minister. Whether their exclusion is justifiable upon any basis other than the mystique that has traditionally attached to the prerogative is debatable. They involve wide discretionary powers, but that in itself could be an argument *for* rather than against political accountability.

Most other prerogative powers, such as the deployment of the armed forces, do not need formal parliamentary approval unless specific extra money is required. (However, additional government spending is usually met out of a general contingency fund or a vote retrospectively made by Parliament, Chapter 11). Thus opportunity for democratic accountability for the exercise of this power is limited. The Public Administration Select Committee is presently consulting on whether to recommend reform which, as part of a possible scheme to place all prerogative powers on a statutory basis, would normally require express consent of the House of Commons before the armed forces were sent into combat.

Other prerogative powers relate to foreign relationships, national security matters and the prerogative of mercy on which ministers sometimes refuse to be questioned. However, Parliament, if it wished, could insist on investigating. In some cases the exercise of a prerogative power must be confimed by statute. These include treaties which alter the existing law and certain EU treaties (Chapter 8).

### 12.6.6 Judicial Control

Traditionally the courts exercised only limited control over the prerogative. If a prerogative power was disputed a court could determine whether it existed, and (if it existed) what it empowered the executive to do, but the monarch (that is, a minister) was the only judge of how to exercise the power. For example in the *Saltpetre* case (1607) the King was held to have the power in an emergency to enter private land, and to be the sole judge of both whether an emergency existed and what measures to take (see also *R v Hampden* (1637); *A-G v de Keysers Royal Hotel* (1920)). The court's approach was contradictory. A power limited to emergencies (as in *Saltpetre*) was not really limited at all if its holder can conclusively decide what counted as an emergency.

The courts have developed sophisticated rules for judicial review of the exercise of statutory powers, based on notions of fairness, reasonableness and relevance (Chapter 14). These do not (in theory at any rate) entitle the courts to make the government's decisions for them but are designed to ensure that government keeps within the limits of its powers and complies with basic moral standards. Is there any reason why the same should not apply to the prerogative?

As a result of the speeches in the House of Lords in *Council of Civil Service Unions v Minister for the Civil Service* (1985) *(CCSU)*, the courts have asserted a jurisdiction over executive power, including a prerogative power, unless restricted by Parliament. In other words, decisions made under the authority of prerogative powers are, in principle, reviewable on the same basis as decisions made under a statutory power. But this does not mean that this jurisdiction will always be exercised. The power must be of a 'justiciable' nature, which means that it must be suitable for the courts' scrutiny. This is no longer resolved by looking at the source of the power (statute or prerogative) but upon its subject matter and its suitability on the facts of the particular case.

In *CCSU* ([1985] AC 374, at p. 418), Lord Roskill gave the following as indicative and non-exhaustive examples of powers that would not be reviewable:

> Prerogative powers such as those relating to the making of treaties, the defence of the realm, the prerogative of mercy, the grant of honours, the dissolution of Parliament and the appointment of ministers as well as others are not, I think susceptible to judicial review because their nature and subject matter are such as not to be amenable to the judicial process. The courts are not the place wherein to determine whether a treaty should be concluded or the armed forces disposed in a particular manner or Parliament dissolved on one date rather than another.

However, in later cases this number of non-justiciable, or 'forbidden areas' has been curtailed. If the subject matter of the decision concerns the rights or legitimate expectations of individuals, the matter is more likely to be justiciable, and this is so even if the context relates to diplomacy and foreign affairs. For example, the power to issue a passport is reviewable, because it is merely an administrative decision affecting the right of individuals and their freedom of travel (*R v Secretary of State for Foreign and Commonwealth Affairs ex parte Everett* (1989)). Other powers held to be reviewable are the powers to grant a pardon (*R v Secretary of State for the Home Department ex parte Bentley* (1993), *A-G of Trinidad and Tobago v Lennox Phillips* (1995)); to make *ex gratia* payments to the victims of crime (*R v Criminal Injuries Compensation Board ex parte P* (1995)) and to farmers affected by the foot and mouth epidemic (*National Farmers Union* v *Secretary of State for the Environment, Food and Rural Affairs* (2003)); the issue of warrants for telephone tapping (*R* v *Secretary of State for the Home Department ex parte Ruddock* (1987), see now the Regulation of Investigatory Powers Act 2000 which replaces the prerogative in this respect); and the policy of discharging homosexuals from the armed services (*R* v *Ministry of Defence ex parte Smith* (1996)), as well as the decision to alter the terms of employment of civil servants (*CCSU* – above). The court may also examine the *vires* of legislation made under the prerogative for the government of British colonies (*R (Bancoult)* v *Secretary of State for the Foreign and Commonwealth Office* (2001)).

The courts have even gone so far as to hold that an outright refusal to make diplomatic representations on behalf of a subject whose human rights were being violated whilst detained overseas might be reviewable, and furthermore, that judicial review would lie in an extreme case of this kind if the individual's legitimate expectations were breached or the Foreign Office behaved unreasonably. (See *R (Abbasi)* v *Secretary of State for Foreign Affairs* (2002) concerning an application on behalf of a British citizen detained indefinitely by the US at Guantanamo Bay without access to either a lawyer or a court.)

The courts accept, however, that the subject matter of some decisions and the factual context in which the decision is reached mean that some cases necessarily fall within the 'forbidden areas'. The main reasons for this concern the unsuitability of the judicial process to matters which have wide political consequences. This is particularly the case if adjudication would be damaging to the public interest in the field of international relations, defence or national security or in relation to decisions affecting contraversial matters central to the democratic process, where objective rules are not appropriate. Many prerogative powers are exercised at the highest political levels; many of them concern foreign affairs and emergencies and most of these involve wide subjective discretion This means that the conduct of high-level diplomacy between governments will not normally be reviewable: for example, at a time of significant international tension and when diplomacy was still proceeding, the court would not declare the meaning of UN Resolution 1441 and whether it authorised states to take military action in the event of non-compliance by Iraq with its terms. The court was concerned that to have done so would have compromised Britain's negotiating position (*CND* v *Prime Minister of the United Kingdom* (2002)).

The disposition of the armed forces and the Attorney-General's powers to commence legal actions have also been held to be unreviewable (see *Chandler* v *DPP* (1964); *Gouriet* v *UPOW* (1978)). Similarly, the court will not consider whether a treaty-making power has been unlawfully exercised, nor review the content of a treaty (*R* v *Secretary of State for Foreign and Commonwealth Affairs ex parte Rees-Mogg* (1994); *Blackburn* v *A-G* (1971)). The

*Abbasi* case (above) reminds us, however, that even in the context of international diplomacy, and perhaps also similar cases of high-level policy, there may be limits beyond which judicial review may be available; and this principle is capable of extension. Nevertheless, it is likely that some of the powers mentioned by Lord Roskill, such as the power to appoint and dismiss ministers, or the dissolution of Parliament, could never be justiciable in the absence of a fundamental remodelling of the separation of powers (see Harris, 2003, *Cambridge Law Journal* **62**: 631).

**12.6.7** Prerogative and Statute

Since Parliament is sovereign, statute can abolish a prerogative power by express words or by necessary implication (*British Coal Corporation* v *The King* (1935); *De Morgan* v *Director General of Social Welfare* (1998)). Subsequent repeal of that statute may permit the prerogative to revive although it will depend on the construction of the statute making the repeal (see *A-G* v *de Keysers Royal Hotel* (1920) at 539; *Burmah Oil* v *Lord Advocate* (1965) at 143).

Problems arise where Parliament has enacted statutory provisions dealing with the same subject matter as the prerogative without expressly abolishing the prerogative powers. Sometimes the statute will expressly preserve an overlapping prerogative so that the two can operate in tandem but this is not always the case. Where an area of governmental activity is subject to both a statutory and a prerogative power, the statutory power may supersede the prerogative power (see *A-G* v *de Keysers Royal Hotel Ltd* (1920); *Laker Airways Ltd* v *Department of Trade* (1977)). Whether or not it does so is a matter of interpretation of the statute in question. First, it depends on whether the statute is intended to bind the Crown (see above), and secondly, whether the statute is intended to replace the prerogative. If the entire area of governmental activity that could be regulated under the prerogative is covered by a statute, it is the statute that prevails. In the *De Keyser* case the question concerned whether the property owners were entitled to compensation after their hotel was occupied by the armed forces in wartime. The Crown took possession ostensibly under a statute which conferred an enforceable legal right to compensation. It was nevertheless argued on behalf of the Crown that it had a prerogative power to take possession of land during an emergency and that no compensation was payable as of right under this prerogative power. The House of Lords upheld the property owners' claim, holding that the occupation of the hotel had taken place under statutory powers. The prerogative had been superseded by a comprehensive statute regulating this field of governmental activity, and it would be meaningless for the legislature to have imposed limitations on the exercise of governmental power if these could merely be bypassed under the prerogative.

Where the statute co-exists with a prerogative power, it seems that the government cannot choose whichever power is most favourable to it: the principle that it cannot use a prerogative power to evade safeguards conferred by statute applies. In the *Laker Airways* case the Department of Trade was held to be bound by a statute regulating the licensing of civil airlines which required an element of competition. It could not therefore rely on its prerogative power arising under a treaty to remove the licence of an entrepreneur, thereby preventing him from setting up a cut-price airline between London and New York. Provisions regulating the circumstances in which revocation could occur existed in the statute, but these had been circumvented unlawfully by the purported use of the prerogative.

More recently the courts have taken a different and controversial approach where prerogative and statute co-exist. In *R v Secretary of State ex parte Northumbria Police Authority* (1988), the prerogative was not put into abeyance where an apparently comprehensive system of statutory powers existed. Here it was held *obiter* that the Home Secretary could use a prerogative power to supply the police with weapons, even though statute placed local authorities in charge of providing police resources. The court said that the prerogative power was suspended only when its exercise was inconsistent with a statutory power. *De Keyser's* case was treated as an example of inconsistency. Purchas LJ suggested that the *De Keyser* principle is qualified where executive action is designed to benefit or protect the individual. In such cases the exercise of prerogative power will be upheld unless statute unequivocally prevents this.

This decision was somewhat surprising since the relevant statute contained no saving for the prerogative. Vincenzi (1996) is critical of it, arguing that the decision is an unprecedented example of the courts' permitting the Crown to disregard statutory provisions in its perception of the public interest. He identifies a tension with the Bill of Rights that prohibits the Crown from suspending or dispensing with statute.

*R v Secretary of State for the Home Department ex parte Fire Brigades Union* (1995) may support Vincenzi's view. The Secretary of State had power to make a commencement order bringing legislation into force that was intended to establish a particular regime for compensation for victims of crime. It was held that he could not refuse to bring the statute into effect in order to establish a different scheme under the prerogative. However, as their Lordships remarked, the case is not strictly speaking an example of a conflict between statute and prerogative. The statute was not yet in force and the gist of their Lordships' reasoning was that, by committing himself to the prerogative scheme, the minister had disabled himself from bringing the statute into force. Thus *Fire Brigades* case is authority that the *De Keyser* principle – that statute ousts the prerogative – does not apply where a

statute has been enacted but not yet brought into force. Here the prerogative power continues to exist, but subject to the important limitation that it
must not be exercised in a manner which, in substance, conflicts with the
intention of Parliament.

### 12.6.8    Prerogative and Human Rights

The Human Rights Act 1998, s.21 enacts that an Order in Council made
under the royal prerogative is 'primary legislation' for the purposes of the
1998 Act. This means that the court cannot set aside any exercise of the
prerogative made by an Order in Council that conflicts with a right
protected under the European Convention on Human Rights (Chapter 17).
If the government chose to amend it, the Order would be subject to the 'fast
track' procedure, although ministers have the power to amend Orders in
Council as they think fit anyway.

A further consequence of s.21 is that a public authority is only bound to
act in accordance with convention rights unless conflicting primary legislation requires it to act otherwise (s.6). Since an Order in Council is deemed
by s.21 to be 'primary legislation', a public authority that acts in accordance
with its terms would appear to act lawfully even if in breach of a convention right (see further Billings and Ponting, 'Prerogative Powers and the
Human Rights Act: elevating the status of Orders in Council', 2001, *Public
Law* 21).

### 12.6.9    Reform

In its Fourth Report in Session 2003–04, the Public Administration
Committee favoured enhanced democratic control of the royal prerogative
powers exercisable by ministers. Accordingly, it recommended that that
there should be a public consultation exercise on ministerial prerogative
powers which should contain proposals for legislation to provide greater
parliamentary control over all the executive powers enjoyed by ministers.
Its recommendation continued, 'This exercise should also include specific
proposals for ensuring full parliamentary scrutiny of the following Ministerial prerogative actions: decisions on armed conflict; the conclusion and
ratification of treaties; the issue and revocation of passports.'

Lord Lester of Herne Hill recently introduced the Executive Powers and
Civil Service Bill 2003 in the House of Lords. One of its major purposes was
to place 'executive powers' exercisable by ministers under the authority of
Parliament. It defined these as rights and powers under the royal prerogative, but the definition excluded a number broadly related to powers that
belong to Her Majesty in her personal capacity or to any member of the
royal family. The purpose of the bill was that no executive power should be

exercised without parliamentary authority. As a 'general rule' this authority would have been conferred by the bill itself, subject to two exceptions where actual authority would normally be required. These included the ratification of treaties and instances in which it is proposed to commit the UK to direct participation in any war, international armed conflict or international peace-keeping activity.

At present the texts of treaties requiring ratification are laid before Parliament, but the reform would have required Parliament to be provided with additional explanatory and justificatory material explaining what the purposes of a particular treaty are, why it is considered to be beneficial and a cost/benefit analysis. Certain treaties (for example those requiring a change in the domestic law or where the private rights of individuals or corporations are affected) would only be ratified if approved by a resolution of each House.

The bill provided that in the case of either the treaty-making or deployment power, action could be taken without parliamentary approval in cases of emergency, provided that the Prime Minister notified each House of Parliament and provided reasons for the decision to treat the case as an emergency. These parts of Lord Lester's bill have not survived parliamentary scrutiny. It remains to be seen whether the government will introduce a bill to implement similar recommendations of the Public Administration Committee.

## Summary

- In this chapter we first discussed the meaning of the term Crown. The Queen as head of state must be distinguished from the Crown as the executive. It is not clear whether the Crown is a corporation sole or a corporation aggregate.

- Succession to the throne depends entirely on statute, thus reinforcing the subordinate nature of the monarchy.

- The monarch has certain personal political powers which should be exercised in times of constitutional crisis. These include the appointment of a Prime Minister, the dissolution of Parliament and the appointment of peers.

- At common law the Crown was immune from legal action. Some of this immunity has been reduced by the Crown Proceedings Act 1947, but the Crown is still immune from enforcement and has certain special defences including 'Act of State' and 'executive necessity' in contract. There is however no general doctrine of state necessity as justifying interference with private rights. Certain acts of the Crown give rise to immunity from legal liability.

## Summary cont'd

▶ The Crown's executive powers derive from three sources:

(i) Statutes

(ii) The royal prerogative – that is, the residue of special common law powers peculiar to the monarch. While many prerogative powers have been surrendered or are obsolete, some, notably in foreign affairs, remain important. The prerogative cannot be used to make law or raise taxation. No new prerogative powers can be created. Prerogative powers can be reviewed by the courts unless they concern a 'non-justiciable' subject matter such as foreign relationships. While prerogative powers require public funding and are therefore subject to some parliamentary scrutiny, in practice, political control over prerogative power is limited.

(iii) Powers possessed by virtue of the fact that the Crown is a legal person with basically the same rights and duties as an adult human being. The Crown can therefore make contracts, own property, distribute money, etc. There is a dispute as to whether this kind of power is part of the royal prerogative. The exercise of these powers can be reviewed by the courts and is subject to general methods of parliamentary accountability.

The prerogative must give way to statute although the scope and extent of this is unclear.

# Exercises

12.1 Compare the royal prerogative with parliamentary privilege (Chapter 9), with reference to (i) its purposes; (ii) its history and sources; and (iii) the extent to which it can be controlled by the courts.

12.2 To what extent are royal prerogative powers subject to legal and political controls? How, if at all does judicial control of the prerogative relate to the separation of powers?

12.3 To what extent does the Crown enjoy special privileges or immunities in litigation?

12.4 Advise the Queen in the following cases.

(i) There has just been a general election in the UK. The existing government has obtained the largest number of seats in the Commons but without an overall majority. The Opposition is negotiating with a minority party to form a government. The Prime Minister refuses to resign.

(ii) What would be the position if the Opposition had obtained the largest number of seats in the Commons, and the government was negotiating with the minority party?

(iii) The government is defeated in a vote on the Annual Finance Act. The Prime Minister refuses to resign.

(iv) The Prime Minister has just been sacked as party leader. However, due to an agreement with the Opposition and a minority party, he could still command a small majority in the Commons.

**12.5** Critically discuss proposed reforms of the prerogative powers.

**12.6** The Government of Carribia, an independent Commonwealth country, is overthrown by a rebel force, 'The People's Front'. Cane, the displaced Prime Minister of Carribia, requests the aid of the British government. British troops are sent to Carribia and are authorised under an agreement between the British government and Cane to 'use all necessary measures to restore the lawful government of Carribia'. During the British troops' campaign on the island they requisition buildings owned by Ford, an American citizen, for use as a military depot, and destroy the home of Austin, a British citizen, in the belief that it is being used as a base by the rebels. Ford and Austin sue the British government for compensation. Discuss.

Would your answer differ if Carribia was a UK dependent territory?

**12.7** Ruritania is an independent member of the Commonwealth. The UK Queen is the Queen of Ruritania. Last week a military coup in Ruritania succeeded in capturing the palace occupied by the Governor-General who represented the Queen. The military commander requests the Queen to abdicate in favour of himself as King. The situation in Ruritania is currently uncertain, and forces loyal to the Queen are attempting to secure control. The British government advises the Queen not to abdicate. The Commonwealth Secretary-General advises her to abdicate. What would you advise?

# Further reading

Blackburn, R. (1999) 'Monarchy and the Royal Prerogative', in Blackburn, R. and Plant, R. (eds) *Constitutional Reform*, London, Longman.

Bogdanor, V. (1995) *The Monarchy and the Constitution*, Oxford, Oxford University Press.

Brazier, R. (1999) *Constitutional Practice*, 3rd edn, Oxford, Oxford University Press, Chapter 9.

Harris, J. (1992) 'The Third Source of Authority for Government Action', *Law Quarterly Review*, **109**: 626.

Hennessy, P. (1995) *The Hidden Wiring*, London, Gollancz, Chapter 2.

Jones, B., Kavanagh, D., Moran, M. and Norton, P. (2004) *Politics UK*, 5th edn, Harlow, Pearson, 16.

**Further reading cont'd**

Jowell, J. and Oliver, D. (eds) (2000) *The Changing Constitution*, 4th edn, Oxford, Oxford University Press, Chapter 8.

Loveland, I. (2003) *Constitutional Law, Adminstrative Law and Human Rights: a Critical Introduction*, 3rd edn, London, Butterworths, Chapter 4.

Munro, C.R. (1999) Studies in Constitutional Law, 2nd edn, London, Butterworths, Chapter 8.

Nairn, T. (1988) *The Enchanted Glass: Britain and its Monarchy*, London, Hutchinson.

Sunkin, M. and Payne, S. (eds) (1999) *The Nature of the Crown: a Legal and Political Analysis*, Oxford, Clarendon Press.

Vincenzi, C. (1998) *Crown Powers, Subjects, Citizens*, London, Pinter.

# Chapter 13

# Ministers and departments

> Institutions tend to protect their own and to resist criticism from wherever it may come. (Lord Hope in *R* v *Shaylor* [2002] 2 All ER 477, 509)

## Key words

- ▶ Fragmented government
- ▶ The pre-eminence and vulnerability of the Prime Minister
- ▶ Accountability and responsibility
- ▶ Chain of accountability: policy and operations
- ▶ Independence of civil service
- ▶ Internal controls and democracy

## 13.1 Introduction

The subject matter of this chapter, particularly in respect of the powers of the Treasury, illustrates the influence of internal practices and understandings in the hands of the unelected officials who safeguard the continuity of government and the corresponding weakness of democratic controls.

## 13.2 The Powers of the Prime Minister

The powers of the Prime Minister, which derive mainly from convention (other powers may be added by statute), have evolved gradually since the middle of the eighteenth century, corresponding to the decline in the powers of the monarch. The office, which dates from the early eighteenth century, was originally that of Cabinet chairman deputising for the monarch, and acting as an intermediary between the monarch and the government. The Prime Minister is appointed by the Queen and by convention must be a member of and enjoy the support of the House of Commons. In practice the Prime Minister is always the leader of the party with the largest number of seats in the Commons. This was originally designed to limit the power of governments, but modern party discipline has had the opposite effect.

The powers of the Prime Minister are scattered in convention, statute, custom and practice, royal prerogatives and 'nods and winks'. The Prime Minister exercises important prerogative powers. These include the appointment and dismissal of ministers and other important public offices, the dissolution of Parliament, overall responsibility for security, control of the civil service and the mobilisation of the armed forces. The Prime

Minister also has specific statutory powers in sensitive political areas (e.g. Police Act 1997 s.9; Intelligence Services Act 1994 s.2; National Minimum Wages Act 1998; National Audit Act 1983 s.1).

The main conventions that secure the pre-eminent power of a Prime Minister are as follows:

▶ The Prime Minister appoints and dismisses all government ministers and determines their status and pecking order. S/he also has powers of appointment in relation to senior judges and many other important public posts (a mixture of statute and convention).

▶ The Prime Minister controls the Cabinet agenda, formulates its decisions and allocates government business. In this way cabinet discussion can be bypassed and matters entrusted to selected prime ministerial supporters, smaller groups of ministers, or civil servants or indeed anyone chosen by the Prime Minister since there is no constraint on a Prime Minister taking advice from anyone.

▶ Except for the unlikely events of intervention by the monarch, empeachment by Parliament and removal by his or her party under its rules for electing a leader, there is no formal machinery to get rid of a Prime Minister. A vote in the House of Commons of no confidence can only bring down the government as a whole.

▶ The Prime Minister may advise the Queen to dissolve Parliament. Thus the Prime Minister can choose the date of a general election, holding his or her colleagues' careers to ransom.

▶ The Prime Minister is also Minister for the Civil Service.

▶ The Prime Minister is head of the internal security services.

▶ The Prime Minister is the channel of communication between Queen and government.

▶ The Prime Minister is the main spokesperson for the nation and as such has unique access to the media. The Prime Minister's press office holds a key position. There is a danger that, in terms of public perception and therefore legitimacy, the Prime Minister is perceived as a head of state, thereby eclipsing the monarchy. Ministers' energies are centred upon their own departmental interests. Few have the time or knowledge to concentrate upon issues outside their departmental concerns.

Apart from the unlikely event of empeachment, the main limits upon the power of a Prime Minister lie in the checks and balances that prevent the Prime Minister using powers arbitrarily. These include:

▶ The Queen's power to intervene in extreme cases (Chapter 12).

▶ The risk of dismissing Cabinet ministers who may enjoy political support in their own right. In practice, a Prime Minister's freedom to appoint ministers may be limited by party considerations. The Cabinet is full of rivals for power. A Prime Minister could not impose his or her will over a united Cabinet that enjoys substantial support in the Commons. If a Prime Minister requested the Queen to dissolve Parliament in such circumstances, she might be entitled to refuse the request.

▶ The absence of a separate prime ministerial department (apart from a Private Office). However, Prime Ministers may have a substantial staff of independent special advisors brought in from outside the regular civil service.

▶ A Prime Minister could be deposed as party leader and therefore lose the support of the Commons. Everything therefore depends upon the political balance between the particular holder of the office and the party. The influence of senior backbench MPs may be significant. The resignation of Margaret Thatcher in 1989 provides an example.

## 13.3 The Cabinet

The Cabinet is the policy-making body of senior ministers which formally coordinates the work of government departments (see Haldane Committee, 1917, Cmnd 9230). It is doubtful whether it is underpinned by convention or is merely a creature of practice. The Cabinet has no legal powers as such. However, statute law recognises the status of the Cabinet by protecting cabinet secrecy (Health Service Commissioners Act 1983 s.12; Parliamentary Commissioner Act 1967 s.8 (4)) and sometimes powers can be exercised only by a minister of cabinet rank (Data Protection Act 1998 s.28 (10). The Cabinet no longer appears to be an effective political force, having deteriorated in recent years from being the primary policy-making body to a role which seems largely that of confirming decisions made elsewhere, in particular by informal groups coordinated by the Prime Minister and other individuals.

According to the *Ministerial Code* (below), the business of the Cabinet and ministerial committees consists in the main of: (i) questions which significantly engage the collective responsibility of the Government because they raise major issues of policy or because they are of critical importance to the public; and (ii) questions on which there is an unresolved argument between departments.

The Cabinet originated in the seventeenth century as a group of trusted privy councillors called together to give confidential advice to the monarch. The term was originally one of abuse and referred to the King's 'closet' or anteroom. An attempt was made in the Act of Settlement 1700 to prevent 'inner caucuses' from usurping the functions of the Privy Council, but the provisions were never implemented and were later repealed. George I (1714–27) leaned particularly heavily on party leaders, and from his reign on the monarch ceased to attend cabinet meetings substituting the Prime Minister. During the reign of George III (1760–1820) the convention emerged that the monarch should generally consult the Cabinet. The eighteenth-century Cabinets served the vital purposes of ensuring that the executive could command the support of the Commons and as a means of presenting the monarch with a united front. From a mid-nineteenth-century perspective Bagehot regarded the Cabinet as the pivot of the constitution and its driving force.

Cabinets usually comprise between 20 and 30 ministers including the heads of the main government departments and certain other senior office-holders. Other ministers and civil servants often attend cabinet meetings for particular purposes, notably the Chief Whip who forms a link between the government and its backbench supporters. Under the Ministers of the Crown Act 1975, the Lord Chancellor and three other cabinet members must be drawn from the House of Lords.

Cabinet business is frequently delegated to committees and sub-committees or informal groups of ministers and other persons such as civil servants and political advisors. This is an inevitable consequence of the complexity of modern government and is an important method by which the Prime Minister can control the decision-making process. There are two kinds of formal cabinet committee: (i) ad hoc committees set up on a temporary basis to deal with particular problems and (ii) named permanent committees, for example defence and overseas policy, economic strategy and legislation. The names and membership of these committees are published (*http://www.cabinet.office.gov.uk*). The Butler Report into the failure of intelligence leading to the war against Iraq (2004, *http://www.butlerreview.org.uk*), criticised the contemporary practice of policy making by informal groups including unelected persons selected by the Prime Minister without written records and without the Cabinet being fully informed.

Collective cabinet responsibility (below) ensures that every member of the government is bound by decisions approved by the Cabinet whether or not the full Cabinet has discussed them. Thus it is sometimes said that the Cabinet has become merely a rubber stamp or 'dignified' part of the constitution, the key decisions being made elsewhere. The secrecy surrounding the workings of the Cabinet is also an aspect of collective responsibility and makes objective analysis difficult. Other practical limits upon cabinet power are that its meetings are relatively short (about two hours per week), its members have departmental loyalties, and its agenda and procedure are controlled by the Prime Minister.

The Cabinet Office services and coordinates the work of the Cabinet and records its decision for implementation by departments. The Deputy Prime Minister is currently the minister responsible for the Cabinet Office. It comprises about 100 civil servants headed by the Cabinet Secretary who also coordinates other Whitehall committees and designates most of their chairmen and, as head of the civil service, reports to the Prime Minister. Arguably these three roles create fundamental conflicts of duty.

The *Ministerial Code* (1997, revised 2001; *http://www.cabinet-office.gov.uk/ central/2001/mcode*) issued by the Cabinet Office provides a general framework for the conduct of ministers which we shall draw upon in context. As we saw in Chapter 2 the legal status of the Code is unclear illustrating the informal nature of the constitution. It might have the status of convention but is arguably merely practice except in as much as it includes formal resolutions of Parliament, established conventions or Orders made under the prerogative.

## 13.4 Ministers

A minister is defined by the Ministers of the Crown Act 1975 as an office-holder under Her Majesty. It is for the Queen on the advice of the Prime Minister to designate the number and titles of ministers. Some ministers have separate legal personality as corporations sole. By convention, a minister must be a member of Parliament and most ministers, particularly those in major spending departments and the Treasury, must be members of the House of Commons. As we saw in Chapter 6, there are statutory limits on the number of paid ministers who can sit in the Commons so as to prevent a Prime Minister flooding the House with his or her supporters. There are about 100 ministers, ranked as follows.

▶ *Cabinet ministers:* Most cabinet ministers head departments but some offices are traditionally without departments and can be assigned to special or coordinating work by the Prime Minister. These include the Chancellor of the Duchy of Lancaster and the Lord President of the (Privy) Council. The Leader of the House of Commons is responsible for managing government business in the House. The most important departments are headed by Secretaries of State. These are the successors of the powerful officials created by Henry VIII to control the central government.

▶ *Ministers of state and parliamentary under-secretaries of state* (where the head of the department is a Secretary of State).

▶ *Parliamentary secretaries:* These are mainly recruited from the House of Commons and assist more senior ministers with political and administrative work.

▶ *Parliamentary private secretaries:* These are members of Parliament who act as unpaid assistants to individual ministers. They are not ministers for the purpose of counting the number of ministers who may sit in the House of Commons (Chapter 10).

▶ *Whips:* These control party discipline and provide a channel of communication between government and backbenches. They are formally officers of the roual household. The Chief Whip is not a member of the Cabinet but attends cabinet meetings and consults with the Prime Minister on matters such as the appointment of ministers.

## 13.5 Government Departments

By convention a minister must head each department in order to preserve ministerial responsibility. There are no constitutional requirements relating to the organisation of government departments. They can freely be created, abolished or amalgamated by the government. The only statutory limitations concern restrictions upon the number of ministers who can sit in the House of Commons (Chapter 10) and miscellaneous provisions relating to particular offices, notably the Lord Chancellor. The organization of departments is sometimes regarded as one of 'royal prerogative' but could also be the right of the Crown, as of any private organisation, to organise itself as it wishes, thus illustrating a possible weakness in our non-statist constitution. In the nineteenth century, committees of the Privy Council or special bodies were set up to deal with new governmental responsibilities but, as the work of government increased, separate permanent departments headed by ministers were created. These have been expanded, abolished, split up or combined as circumstances dictated without apparent constitutional constraints.

Some government departments and ministers, notably the Treasury and the Lord Chancellor, trace their origins back to medieval times. The Home Office and Foreign Office are nineteenth-century creations of the royal prerogative. The other departments are either statutory or, as is more common, set up by using the prerogative to create a Secretary of State (see below). Some departments such as the Inland Revenue and the Customs and Excise have substantial administrative and financial independence, with powers conferred directly upon them. They are known as non-ministerial departments. However, a minister remains constitutionally responsible for them.

Because English law has no umbrella concept of the state (Chapter 4), provision must be made for transferring rights and liabilities between different departments. These problems are dealt with by standardised legislation (e.g. Ministers of the Crown Act 1975; Civil Service (Management Functions) Act 1992; Deregulation and Contracting Out Act 1994). Special statutory arrangements exist between the Crown in Scotland, which has its own government and the Crown in relation to the UK as a whole (Scotland Act 1998 s.99; below). There is however the curiosity that since the office of 'Secretary of State' is in law a single office, the various

Secretaries of State can interchange functions and assets without the need for legislation. Other ministers can delegate the exercise of their powers to any civil servant within their department but not to other ministers (*Carltona* v *Commissioner for Works* (1943); *Lavender* v *Minister of Housing* (1970)). However, under the Civil Service (Management Functions) Act 2002, a minister can transfer the management of civil servants to any other Crown servant. This is intended to allow ministers to create semi-independent executive agencies.

For purposes of litigation a list of appropriate departments is maintained by the Treasury. In cases of doubt the Attorney-General represents the Crown (Crown Proceedings Act 1947, s.17).

### 13.5.1 The Treasury

The Prime Minister is the First Lord of the Board of the Treasury, a body that never meets. By convention, the Chancellor of the Exchequer is the responsible minister. The Treasury is an overlord and coordinating department in the sense that it is responsible for the economy as a whole, allocates finance to government departments, supervises their spending and is responsible for the tax gathering bodies, the Inland Revenue and the Customs and Excise Commissioners.

The Treasury has special constitutional significance and its activities provide a good illustration of the mix of legal and informal controls that typify the UK constitution and make the exercise of power obscure. There is a general 'understanding', the basis of which lies in internal practices based on 'ancient authority' that the Treasury both authorises and polices departmental expenditure (see Daintith and Page, 1999, pp. 109–26). Harden et al. (1996) describe this as a 'self-regulatory system relying on trust and elite consensus'. The support of the Public Accounts and Public Administration Committees of the House of Commons also legitimises Treasury power. Article 10 of the *Ministerial Code* requires government departments to consult the Treasury in relation to spending proposals. Thus the Treasury can strongly influence if not control the spending priorities of other departments.

The Treasury plays the traditional role of gatekeeper to Parliament in which it authorises and presents government spending and taxation proposals. Parliament depends on an initiative from the Treasury since, by custom of the House of Commons, the Crown's recommendation is required for all taxation and public expenditure. Although the annual Appropriation Act lists the sums requested on behalf of each department it is arguable that Parliament votes money to the Crown rather than to any particular department (Chapter 11). This gives the Treasury a powerful lever since it can approve allocations to individual departments. The Treasury fixes the overall levels of expenditure for each department and sets standards against which the effectiveness of spending is measured. It approves spending proposals by departments either in general or in relation to especially sensitive items.

Treasury pre-eminence is backed by some particular legal powers. Firstly, the Treasury has statutory power to approve payments from the Consolidated Fund and the National Loans Fund (the government's main bank accounts) and to place limits on other sources of income such as fees and charges (Government Resources and Accounts Act 2000, ss.2, 3). Secondly, the Treasury approves the form and method of the accounts of government departments (ibid., ss.5, 7). Under these powers the Treasury is in a position to decide what counts as public assets and expenditure and thereby to determine the extent to which public bodies can raise private money. Thirdly, the Treasury can authorise additional payments to departments (ibid., s.6) and many items of expenditure require Treasury consent under particular statutes.

The Treasury appoints an accounting officer for each department who is responsible for the management of the department (Exchequer and Audit Department Act 1866 s.22). This is usually the Permanent Secretary of the Department and in the case of an executive agency, its chief executive. The Comptroller and Auditor General examines departmental accounts and reports unauthorised expenditure to the Treasury which can either authorise it or report the matter to Parliament (Exchequer and Audit Departments Act 1921 s.1).

Under the Anti-terrorism, Crime and Security Act 2001 ss.4 and 5, the Treasury can freeze the assets of any person resident in the UK or of any UK citizen or company if it reasonably believes (a) that action to the detriment of the UK economy (or part of it) has been or is likely to be taken; or (b) action constituting a threat to the life or property of one or more UK nationals has been or is likely to be taken, in both cases either by an overseas government or by an overseas resident. The freezing order can prevent benefits being paid to the government or resident in question or to any person the Treasury reasonably believes has assisted or is likely to assist them. These powers are therefore not limited to terrorists but could, for example, be used to protect trade interests against overseas competition.

The Bank of England has some statutory independence. A statutory body, it administers the government's bank account and also those of the other main banks (Bank of England Act 1998). Subject to the statutory objectives of maintaining price stability, supporting the economic policies of the government and complying with inflation targets set by the Treasury, it is responsible for monetary policy (primarily fixing interest rates) and for issuing currency. Its directors are appointed by the Crown and can be dismissed on prescribed grounds with the consent of the Chancellor of the Exchequer and, 'in extreme economic circumstances', it is subject to directions from the Treasury. The bank is subject to parliamentary scrutiny by the Treasury Committee and is required to publish the minutes of its monetary policy committee, an annual report and an annual inflation report. However, it is unlikely that, in the absence of a plain violation of statute, fundamental matters of general economic policy would be subject to judicial review (c.f. *R v HM Treasury ex parte Smedley* (1985): payments contrary to statute).

## 13.6 The Law Officers

The Attorney-General is the chief law officer, and is assisted by the Solicitor-General. As party politicians, the law officers raise questions about the separation of powers. They are entitled to consult other ministers but by convention act independently. The Attorney-General has the following functions:

(i) representing the government in legal proceedings including intervening in any legal proceedings to put the government's view;

(ii) giving legal advice to the government which the government claims to be entitled not to make public on the questionable analogy of a lawyer and client relationship;

(iii) under various statutes to consent to the prosecution of certain offences and under the prerogative to interfere to prevent a prosecution (*nole prosequi*);

(iv) to bring legal proceedings on behalf of the general 'public interest', either on his own initiative or on the application of any member of the public (a relator action). This might include an action against a public authority. The Attorney-General's decision whether or not to intervene cannot be challenged in the courts (*Gouriet v Union of Post Office Workers* (1978));

(v) To refer questions of law to the Court of Appeal where an accused person has been acquitted of a criminal offence or to request a more severe sentence for a convicted person. The extent to which the A-G is influenced by the wishes of the government is obscure. For example, in relation to government attempts to suppress the media (Chapters 18, 19) his two roles as government lawyer and representative of the public interest are inseparable. We have only the predictable assertions of successive attorneys that they can be trusted. In 1924 the government fell because the Attorney acted on instructions from the government in relation to a prosecution of an anti government journalist (see Edwards, 1984).

## 13.7 Ministerial Responsibility

We have frequently referred to the doctrine of ministerial responsibility. This is a central principle of the constitution, defining both the relationships between ministers and Parliament and that between ministers and civil servants. It is entirely a matter of convention. Comparable principles operate in the devolved institutions on a statutory basis. In the National Assembly for Wales, Assembly secretaries are individually responsible to the Assembly, as is the Executive Committee as a whole (Government of Wales Act 1998 s.56). Scottish ministers are responsible to the Scottish Parliament (Chapter 4).

Ministerial responsibility has two aspects which are not entirely consistent, these being collective and individual responsibility. 'Responsibility' is sometimes used interchangeably with 'accountability'. Both terms have a range of meanings. They include obligations to provide an explanation, information, acknowledgement, review, and redress. Sometimes resignation may also be expected. The particular combination appropriate to any given case depends on the circumstances (see Barberis, 1998).

Supplementing ministerial responsibility, there are mechanisms, such as the Freedom of Information Act 2000 (when fully in force), the Citizens' Charter initiatives and the *Code of Practice on Access to Government Information* (1997), which also inform the notion of openness and accountability. The public accountability of government is a necessary and basic characteristic of any democratic system and ill-informed debate will not be effective. More generally, the openness and accountability of government is required by the Fourth and Fifth principles of public life set out by the Committee on Standards in Public Life (Chapter 3).

Ministerial responsibility does not mean that Parliament (except in its capacity as lawmaker) can give orders to ministers or lay down policies. Parliament does not itself govern and to this extent there is a separation of powers. Ministerial responsibility means only that ministers must discharge their duties in a manner which has the continued support of the Commons, and they must give an account of their actions and decisions. If the Commons so votes on a motion of confidence, the government must resign. Opposition MPs, as well as those of the minister's own party influence ministers in their decisions and exert pressure for changes in government policy. Ministerial responsibility also provides information to arm opponents in the adversarial conduct of British political debate. Indeed, it is a characteristic of the parliamentary system of government that there is a continuing struggle on the part of MPs to gain more information than ministers are willing to provide.

The doctrine of ministerial responsibility developed during the eighteenth and nineteenth centuries, corresponding to the rise of the House of

Commons and the decline in the power of the Crown. Its original purpose was as a weapon against the monarch by achieving coherence amongst politicians holding divergent views. On its face the convention can be acclaimed as a device to ensure accountable government. An alternative view is that the convention favours 'strong' government because it allows ministers to govern with little effective parliamentary supervision or interference since Parliament has neither the will nor the resources to hold ministers effectively to account (see Flinders, 'The Enduring Centrality of Individual Ministerial Responsibility within the British Constitution', 2000, *Journal of Legislative Studies*, **6**: 73). It can also be argued that the doctrine of collective ministerial responsibility could contribute to a general public disenchantment with politics if ministers are seen to vote in support of policies they are believed not to support (see B. Winetrobe, 'Collective Responsibility in Devolved Scotland', 2003, *Public Law* 24).

Ministerial responsibility may also be out of line with the practices of modern government, in particular the techniques of privatisation and devolved public management. In this context the convention actually shields government from public accountability because the impugned decision may have been taken in an agency that has been hived off from central government. Although in principle the minister remains fully responsible, the vague meaning of responsibility enables ministers more easily to evade blame the further away they are from the location of decision making. The party system and the tradition of secrecy within the civil service have also played a part in breaking the chain of accountability through Parliament to the electorate.

### 13.7.1  Collective Responsibility

Collective responsibility applies to the Cabinet and probably to all government ministers. It was developed originally so that government and Parliament could put up a solid front against the King. It suggests collegial government which is at odds with the legal basis of government with powers given to individual ministers. It has four aspects:

(i)   It requires all ministers to be loyal to the policies of the government, whether or not they are personally concerned with them (solidarity). Collective responsibility therefore applies even though many important decisions are made by sub-committees or informal groups selected by the Prime Ministers (which can include unelected persons, indeed anyone) and are not fully discussed by the Cabinet as a whole.

(ii)  It requires the government as a whole to resign if defeated on a vote of confidence in the House of Commons or if the Prime Minister resigns.

(iii) It requires that cabinet and government business be confidential.

(iv) It operates to protect ministers against personal responsibility since collective responsibility can be used to justify individuals avoiding blame. For example the Butler Report into intelligence failures relating to Iraq (2004, *http://www.butlerreview.org.uk*), absolved all ministers and civil servants from blame for misleading the public on the basis that the various falsehoods were 'collective' (Butler himself was a former head of the civil service). Collective responsibility and individual responsibility (below) are therefore in conflict.

The drastic sanction of a vote of confidence is the only method by which Parliament can enforce collective responsibility, but governments have rarely been defeated in this way in modern times. In 1924 Ramsay MacDonald's Labour government resigned, and in 1979 so did James Callaghan's Labour government. Both were minority governments.

Modern ideas of party solidarity make collective responsibility virtually meaningless as a method of control over governments, but very important as a method of asserting prime ministerial power and ensuring secrecy within the government since cabinet discussions are confidential (see *Ministerial Code*, Cabinet Office 2001, para. 17). A minister is not entitled to disclose what went on in cabinet nor to disclose any disagreement he may have with his colleagues. Resignation is also required before a minister can speak out on a particular issue. Nevertheless, as a convention, collective responsibility may be adapted to new circumstances. The Prime Minister can apparently modify it over a particular issue (for example, membership of the EEC (1975)).

The relationship between a Prime Minister and cabinet has an important impact on how well collective responsibility works in practice. There are tensions between a collegial style and a prime ministerial style of government. The collegial model of government, which emphasises the participation of all cabinet ministers in decision making, disguises the dominance of the Prime Minister in the formulation of policy (above) which tends to blur the difference between a parliamentary and a presidential system (Chapter 1).

There are no formal checks and balances. The extent to which the Prime Minister can exercise an authoritarian style depends on the composition and mood of the Cabinet, the attitude and cohesion of the party, and that of the Commons, the temper of the electorate and not least the personal style of the Prime Minister. If undue reliance is placed on a select group of senior ministers (the 'inner cabinet'), or unelected 'cronies', if too many 'private deals' are struck with individual ministers, or if too many controversial policies are effectively formulated in cabinet sub-committees, ministers may feel less inclined to loyalty. Some consensus amongst ministers may be necessary if only to avoid political embarrassment or ministerial resignations. Serious embarrassment can result where senior ministers resign having concluded that the workings of the Cabinet have strayed unacceptably far from the collegial model. Michael Heseltine resigned during the Westland affair in 1986. Similarly, Geoffrey Howe's resignation over EC policy in 1990 resulted from his concern about the Prime Minister's apparent distaste for collective decision making. This resignation played a pivotal role in ending Mrs Thatcher's tenure of No. 10 Downing Street.

It is uncertain how far collective responsibility applies to those junior ministers who have no legal status as ministers of the Crown, and who do not even nominally participate in the decision in question. It would appear, however, that the same 'conform or go' rule can be applied by a Prime Minister. Thus the government is assured of the 'payroll vote' from about 100 MPs who hold government office and from the whips. It seems that a junior minister cannot accept individual responsibility for departmental errors, because this is a responsibility that lies with the Secretary of State. Junior ministers account to Parliament on behalf of the minister. However, a constitutional duty binds even junior ministers to resign in the event of serious misjudgement (for example Edwina Currie and the salmonella affair).

It could be argued that collective responsibility is no different from the solidarity expected within any organisation. Ministers can discuss policy differences in private, confident that all will support the decision which is eventually reached. The presentation of a single view also adds authority to the government's position because it disguises the coalition nature of many governments. This argument begs the question whether government can be compared with, say, a large private sector company. Governments exist on behalf of and for the benefit of the people. Constitutional doctrines should therefore be assessed only in the light of their advantage to the public. Collective responsibility can be defended on the ground that it strengthens both the authority and the accountability of the government which stands or falls together. On the other hand, given that an important value of democratic government is to manage disagreement without suppressing it, it may be desirable for government not to speak with a single voice but to recognise the provisional nature of any decision reached. Collective responsibility can also protect an individual minister when things go wrong.

### 13.7.2 Individual Responsibility

Individual ministerial responsibility is concerned with the relationship of a minister to Parliament and also that between a minister and a civil servant. Ministerial responsibility protects civil servants from direct public responsibility, since they owe their loyalty to the government, and especially the minister in charge of their department (see *Civil Service Code*, revised 1999; *Notes of Guidance on the Duties and Responsibilities of Civil Servants in Relation to Ministers*, 1985 – the Armstrong Memorandum).

Most specifically, ministerial responsibility requires that ministers provide information to Parliament by means of answers to parliamentary questions, formal ministerial statements and letters to MPs, and that civil servants appear before Parliament only with the permission of ministers and on terms set by ministers. Beyond that its meaning and scope are unclear. As we shall see, there have been many recent reforms to the convention, but these reforms do not extend to giving outside bodies such as the Parliamentary Commissioner for Standards a responsibility in respect of ministerial conduct.

Sir Edward Bridges, the Permanent Secretary to the Treasury, expressed the classical interpretation of the doctrine in 1954 after the *Crichel Down* affair (quoted in the Second Report of the Public Service Committee, 1995–6, HC 313 para. 8). He stated that a minister is responsible to Parliament for the exercise of all executive powers and every action taken in pursuance of those powers. This emphasises that a minister must always answer questions and give a full account of the actions of his department. This is so whether or not the minister is personally at fault for what has gone wrong, and has been subject to only limited exceptions related *inter alia* to commercial confidence, national security and some macro-economic issues. The classical doctrine does not, however, satisfactorily resolve the question of when, as a constitutional requirement, a minister's 'responsibility' also entails a duty to take the blame for departmental errors, if necessary by resignation. One interpretation of the convention is that resignation is required for every serious departmental error regardless of the personal blame of the minister. As we shall see, modern practice does not support this ministerial vicarious liability. The burdens of government have become so extensive and so complex that ministers have been unwilling to resign, even for serious errors by their officials. Direct personal involvement or systematic failure is almost certainly now required but the reality is probably that the matter depends on whether the minister can command party political support.

Ministers have attempted to limit their responsibility by making various distinctions. Firstly, it has been claimed that responsibility applies only to 'policy' mistakes as opposed to 'operational' errors, which are deemed to be failures properly to implement policy. This has particularly been evident following the radical restructuring of government, with the majority of civil servants working in semi-detached Executive or Next Steps Agencies under the day-to-day direction of chief executives with only limited departmental control (below). This restructuring has tended to confuse lines of account-ability. Similar problems can be identified where a quango stands between the minister in charge of policy formulation and the delivery of a service, such as was the case with the Qualifications Agency and the examination boards in assessing AS/A2 qualifications during the so called 'exams crisis'. It seems, however, that ministers do not always escape blame where serious errors occur in such cases (see McCaig, 'School Exams: Leavers in Panic', *Parliamentary Affairs* 2003, **56**(3): 471).

The policy/operational dichotomy is a vague one. Indeed, the two are often inextricably interconnected. The effect has been to make it more diffi-cult for Parliament to find out who is to blame when problems arise. For example, is prison overcrowding policy or operation? Further, even if a matter can be classified *ab initio* as 'operational' as soon as adverse political consequences arise the same matter may mutate into one of policy, causing confusion as to whether (and if so when) responsibility shifts from a chief executive to a minister. An example of this concerned the deaths of immi-grant workers in Morecombe Bay in 2004 which was connected with inef-fective administration of immigration controls. The example of the Child Support Agency illustrates some ministerial reluctance to accept blame where inadequate agency performance is partly attributable to such matters as inadequate funding (a matter for ministers under *Taking Forward Conti-nuity and Change* Cm 2748). Conversely, ministers can exploit confusion by intervening where they perceive electoral gains as in the events leading up to the dismissal of Derek Lewis the head of the prison service following alle-gations of interference by the Home Secretary in the detailed adminstra-tion of the service (see the Learmont Report, Cm 3020, Oct. 1995; the House of Lords Public Service Committee Session, 1997–8, 55 para. 341). Ministers may also interfere in 'operational' matters whilst declining to answer ques-tions about them, claiming that such matters fall within the responsibility of the chief executive. Moreover, since it is the minister who decides what is policy and what is operation, ministers can effectively determine the extent of their constitutional responsibilities. The House of Lords Select Committee (above) concluded that it was not possible effectively to separate policy from operations and that such a division was not desirable (ibid. para. 348).

Secondly, ministers have distinguished between 'accountability' and 'responsibility'. This seems to divorce the circumstances in which a minister must give to the House an explanation of the actions of their department (accountability) from cases in which a minister must accept the blame for departmental mistakes and resign (responsibility). In *Taking Forward Conti-nuity and Change* (Cm 2748, pp. 27–8) the government stated that Parliament can always call a minister to account for all that goes on his department, but it added that a minister cannot be responsible in the sense of having personal knowledge and control of every action taken, and cannot be personally blameworthy when delegated tasks are carried out incompetently or errors of judgement are made at an operational level.

The accountability/responsibility distinction was rejected in 1986 by the Public Service Committee of the Commons (HC 313, 1995–6, paras. 21, 32) but accepted by the Scott Inquiry (*Report of the Inquiry into the Export of Defence Equipment and Dual-Use Goods to Iraq and Related Prosecutions*, HC 1995–6), 115 Section K vol. IV; see also Scott, 1996, *Public Law* 410). It demands that ministers must be prepared to offer a complete explanation of any error to Parliament. The duty embraces an obligation to offer reasons by way of justification in the face of criticism. This is so even if there is no obligation to resign.

Experience reveals, however, that ministers have not always been willing to give a full account of their actions. Notoriously, the conclusion of the Scott Inquiry was that there were numerous examples of ministers failing to give full information about the policies, decisions and actions of government regarding arms sales to Iraq (K8.1 para. 27) and that this had undermined the democratic process (D4.56–D4.58). Answers to parliamentary questions in the affair had been 'designedly uninformative' because of a fear of adverse political consequences if the truth were revealed (D3.107).

Following revelations of this kind in the Scott Report about the manner in which both ministers and civil servants had interpreted their constitutional functions, it became clear that there should be a renewed commitment to the doctrine of individual responsibility combined with a need to clarify the obligations entailed by it and, in particular, to ascertain the matters about which ministers must answer questions. This led to resolutions of the House of Commons and House of Lords on ministerial accountability (HC Debs, vol. 292 cols 1046–7, 19 March 1997; HL Debs, cols 1055–62, 20 March 1997. The resolutions are in similar but not identical terms). The resolutions led to the adoption by the Labour government of the *Ministerial Code* (above). This incorporates the resolution of each House (para. 1, sub-paras (ii)–(v)).

Section 1 of the Code reminds ministers that they can only continue to hold office for as long as they have the support of the Prime Minister. The Code then states that the Prime Minister (and not the respective Houses of Parliament) 'is the ultimate judge of the standards of behaviour expected of a Minister and the appropriate consequences of a breach of those standards'. This suggests that the Code envisages that the Prime Minister is both a setter of standards and responsible for their enforcement. For that reason the statement reads rather oddly in the context of the resolutions. The Code then expresses the following principles of ministerial conduct (which are mostly in the terms of the resolutions).

1. Ministers of the Crown are expected to behave according to the highest standards of constitutional and personal conduct. In particular they must observe the following principles of ministerial conduct:

   (i) Ministers must uphold the principle of collective responsibility;

   (ii) Ministers have a duty to Parliament to account, and be held to account, for the policies, decisions and actions of their Departments and Next Steps Agencies;

   (iii) It is of paramount importance that Ministers give accurate and truthful information to Parliament, correcting any inadvertent error at the earliest opportunity. Ministers who *knowingly* mislead the Parliament will be expected to offer their resignation to the Prime Minister; (emphasis added)

   (iv) Ministers should be as open as possible with Parliament and the public, refusing to provide information only when disclosure would not be in the public interest, which should be decided in accordance with relevant statute, and the Government's *Code of Practice on Access to Government Information*;

   (v) Similarly Ministers should require civil servants who give evidence before Parliamentary Committees on their behalf and under their directions to be as helpful as possible in providing accurate, truthful and full information in accordance with the duties and responsibilities of civil servants as set out in the Civil Service Code.

The respective resolutions of each House are of fundamental importance because ministerial responsibility is no longer an unwritten convention which can be varied at will by the government of the day; ministerial responsibility is now a rule of Parliament. The terms of the resolutions are not, however, without difficulty. As Woodhouse observes (1997), satisfying the terms of the resolutions may not be unduly burdensome. Ministerial judgement will still govern what it means to be 'as open as possible' and when disclosure 'would not be in the public interest'. This means that the problems of interpretative ambiguity still remain, and that the doctrine of ministerial responsibility remains somewhat elusive. It can also be asked whether a minister who deliberately misleads Parliament has sufficient integrity to offer resignation to the Prime Minister? And what is the effect of the statement that the Prime Minister is the ultimate judge of the appropriate standards of behaviour? Does this merely restate the political reality that loss of office inevitably follows the loss of prime ministerial support for a beleaguered minister or does it hint at a diminished role for Parliament? Could a future Prime Minister amend the Code in a manner inconsistent with the resolutions?

The *Code of Practice on Access to Government Information* was also revised in 1997 to create a clear statement of the presumption in favour of disclosure of information and included revisions to limit the scope of the exemptions under which information could be withheld. The need for this had been effectively heralded by the Scott Report (above) which stated that the accountability/responsibility divide was only constitutionally acceptable provided that there was a 'consequent enhancement of the need for ministers to provide ... full and accurate information to Parliament' which is vital to effective accountability (K8.16). The *Code of Practice* which, subject to the Freedom of Information Act 2000, continues to apply, includes exemptions in Part II which permit information to be withheld (e.g. defence, security and international relations, immigration and nationality, information of economic sensitivity, and internal discussion and advice such as cabinet papers). Under a further reform, the Table Office now only prevents the tabling of parliamentary questions if the minister has refused to answer the same question in the same session.

Officials are bound by the *Civil Service Code* (below) which includes guidance on giving evidence to select committees. *Guidance to Officials on Drafting Answers to Parliamentary Questions* (HC Debs vol. 285, 1996–7, col. 53W) emphasises that if information is to be withheld, and a parliamentary question cannot be fully answered, the answer must itself make this clear and explain the reasons in equivalent terms to those in the *Code of Practice*. This is important because it emphasises that information can only be withheld on limited grounds. However, there is compelling evidence that some departments have been slow to meet required standards; many are refusing access to information without citing the relevant exemption in the Code (see Ninth Report of the Public Administration Committee (PAC) HC 1086 Session 2001–02 and most recently Third Report of PAC, Session 2003–04).

MPs have expressed frustration that ministers are not always prepared to provide full and timely answers to parliamentary questions. Responses were sometimes delayed, incomplete or even irrelevant (see e.g., HC Deb 21 March 2002 vol. 382, cols 137 *et seq.* WH; and HC Deb 8 January 2004 vol. cols 151 *et seq.* WH; Second Report of the PAC, Session 2000–01 (HC 61), para. 29; Ninth Report of the PAC, Appendix 3 above). As far as excessive delay was concerned, Parliament has agreed that MPs should be restricted to asking a maximum of five 'named day' or priority questions a day, which should remove some of the pressure on civil servants in preparing responses to parliamentary questions.

But this does not conclude the issue because ministers and civil servants were also alleged to be making an undue and excessive use of the 'disproportionate cost' exemption in the *Code of Practice* that allows for a refusal to provide information on the ground that collecting the information sought would be too expensive. There are also concerns surrounding the commercial confidentiality exemption under the *Code of Practice*. Per annum, £50 billion is spent on public/private partnerships about which there is limited accountability because the commercial confidentiality exemption restricts the ability of MPs in their use of parliamentary questions to probe how this public money is spent.

Notwithstanding the reforms following the Scott Report, there has been an instance of a civil servant falsifying answers to parliamentary questions (see HC Deb, 5 Mar 2002, col. 275W). The Parliamentary Ombudsman has also found that the government had, in one instance, failed to meet its obligations relating to open government under the Code of Practice. The government did not accept the Ombudsman's recommendations. The Ombudsman formally recorded disappointment that a ruling made under the Code of Practice had not been respected in a special report in November 2001 (see 'Declarations made under the Ministerial Code of Conduct', HC 353 session 2001–02). This refusal may support claims that the codification of standards of ministerial conduct since Scott has not been fully effective.

In England there is no coercive machinery to compel a minister to offer a prompt, relevant and full answer. The Speaker has recommended that members who receive inadequate departmental responses should press the minister concerned, or raise it with the chair of the PAC (HC Deb, 28 November 2001, vol. 375, col. 971) but these proposals seem to be inadequate. It is by no means clear that ministers will respond to being 'pressed' as repeated questioning does not always succeed. MPs who consider that information has been withheld in breach of the Code of Practice may refer the matter to the Parliamentary Ombudsman for investigation. Access to the Ombudsman is indirect so a complainant would have to seek the assistance of a fellow MP who could refer the matter. There is evidence that recourse is increasingly being made to the Ombudsman where MPs conclude that ministers are withholding information in breach of the Code. (See Third Report of the PAC, Session 2003–04).

Accountability may be more effective in the devolved Parliaments. In Scotland a complaint by an aggrieved MSP that a minister has breached the Scottish Ministerial Code by improperly refusing to disclose information may be made to the First Minister. If this avenue was not fruitful the complaint could be referred by the MSP to the Presiding Officer as a dispute between MSPs. If the Presiding Officer were either unwilling or unable to resolve the matter he may decide to refer it to the Scottish Parliament's Standards Committee, which could by motion recommend that a member's rights and privileges be withdrawn if the complaint were upheld. However, ministerial openness seems less controversial than in Westminster. Only one complaint about this was made against a Scottish minister during 2002 and this was not upheld.

In Wales the Committee on Standards of Conduct receives and investigates complaints referred to it by the Presiding Officer relating to the conduct of any member of the National Assembly for Wales. If the complaint is substantiated, in its report to the Assembly, the Committee may 'recommend' action in appropriate cases.

More generally, the relationship between ministers and civil servants can cause an 'accountability gap'. This is because accountability can break down where a minister blames a civil servant for some failure and subsequently directs that individual not to appear before a select committee (this is permitted under the Cabinet Office document *Departmental Evidence and Response to Select Committees* (1997)). Notoriously, the Secretary of State for Trade and Industry refused to allow the civil servants involved in aspects of the Westland affair to appear before the Commons Defence Select Committee (see HC 519, 1985–6, Cmnd 9916, 1986). This problem has in part been addressed in the parliamentary resolutions. Although civil servants still give evidence to select committees under the direction of ministers, the minister must insist that civil servants be as helpful as possible in providing accurate, truthful and full information. (HC resolution para. (iv) above). As we have seen, however, Parliament still lacks power to compel ministers to answer questions and cannot require civil servants to give evidence to select committees.

The principles of open government are placed on a statutory footing by the Freedom of Information Act 2000 from January 2005 although there are wide exemptions in relation to information at ministerial level (Chapter 19).

### 13.7.2.1 *Resignation*

The issue of ministerial resignation engages both collective and individual responsibility. This is because where resignation takes place it saves fellow ministers from having to offer support for the beleaguered minister under the principle of collective ministerial responsibility. The question of ministerial resignation may be regarded as having received undue emphasis; more weight is now attached to other facets of responsibility such as a duty to provide information to Parliament as well as a duty to provide an explanation and redress where errors are made. Nevertheless the issue of resignation remains important.

It is sometimes believed that a minister should resign if serious errors are identified in his or her department. Characteristically of conventions, such a convention, if it ever existed seems to have been destroyed by disuse. The *Crichel Down* affair (Cmd 9220, 1954), which involved serious official misconduct in relation to government appropriation of land, was once thought to have required resignation, but is not now considered to support such a wide proposition. Sir Thomas Dugdale's resignation in that case probably owed more to political misjudgement and a lack of parliamentary support.

Of twenty-seven cabinet resignations since 1982, thirteen were the result of misconduct or corruption in office, seven misconduct in private life, five political disagreement, one voluntary and only one, Lord Carrington (following an intelligence failure in relation to the Falkland Islands), apparently as a response to the convention of formally accepting responsibility for departmental errors (Budge et al. (eds), 2004, p. 146). David Blunkett, the Home Secretary, remained in office following a number of serious breaches of security at Buckingham Palace since he was not personally to blame but resigned in 2004 as a result of personal accusations.

It has been said that

> the true convention … is hang on for as long as you can. How long a minister hangs on depends on his stock of political capital. (Dowding, *The Civil Service*, 1995, p. 169)

It is therefore necessary to separate a *constitutional* duty to resign from *political* pressures to resign (Scott, 1996, *Public Law* 410). It seems that resignation is only *constitutionally* required in two categories of case:

(i) where a minister has *knowingly* misled Parliament (except in the very limited cases where this is justified: The Public Service Committee, 2nd Report, 1995–6, HC 313 para. 32; see also Scott, 1996, *Public Law* 410 at 421; *Ministerial Code*)

(ii) the minister is personally to blame for a serious departmental error (Sir Richard Butler in evidence to Scott, Feb. 9 1994, Transcript pp. 23–4).

One recent resignation suggests the possibility that loss of office may also result where a minister has not volunteered a full disclosure of information to a ministerial colleague who has then unwittingly misled Parliament (see the Inquiry by Sir Anthony Hammond QC into the 'Hinduja Passport Affair', HC 287, Session 2000–01 para. 5.128). Ms Beverley Hughes resigned in April 2004 after wrongly denying that she had been warned that UK officials in eastern Europe had become increasingly disturbed by the scale of bogus visa applications. Her denial appears to have been an unwitting error, which means that she was not obliged to resign under the Code. However, there were signs of a withdrawal of prime ministerial support as the issue was seized on by the Opposition (*Telegraph* 2 April 2004).

An honest but unreasonable belief in the accuracy of information given to Parliament can be a lifeline to beleaguered ministers. Scott found that Mr Waldegrave unreasonably clung to the view that government policy governing the sale of arms to Iraq had been reinterpreted but that it had not changed (D3.123–124). Waldegrave did not resign. Similar questions arose after Lord Falconer's refusal in 2001 to resign in respect of the funding and sale of the Millennium Dome.

The second case where resignation is required embraces both serious personal misconduct and serious error in the minister's department in which the minister is implicated. Examples of the former include the case of Peter Mandelson who, in 1998, did not disclose that he had received a substantial private loan from a fellow minister whose business affairs were subject to investigation by Peter Mandelson's department (see also the Blunkett resignation (2004) concerning the giving of favours for personal reasons). Private misconduct unrelated to a minister's duties might also lead to resignation but perhaps only where the minister becomes politically vulnerable (for example David Mellor in 1992 following adverse publicity about his private life). Woodhouse argues that personal indiscretions fall within the ambit of conventional requirements because they affect the public credibility of the minister concerned ('Ministerial Responsibility in the 1990s: When do Ministers Resign?', 1993, *Parliamentary Affairs* 46: 277).

Raw politics rather than constitutional obligation may be the best explanation of ministerial resignations. Even in cases of personal misjudgement or serious policy failure, resignation will be influenced by pragmatic concerns of the gravity of the issue, party support for the beleaguered minister, including that of senior backbenchers (e.g. Blunkett (above)), the timing of the discovery of the error, the support of the Prime Minister and Cabinet and the public repercussions of the fault. The extent to which a minister's behaviour sidetracks the media from other news favoured by party managers may also be important. Norman Lamont kept his post as Chancellor of the Exchequer after sterling was withdrawn from the exchange rate mechanism in 1992 notwithstanding that this amounted to a serious reversal of a central strand of government policy. James Callaghan, his predecessor during the 1967 devaluation crisis, was less fortunate. Perhaps it is significant that Parliament was not sitting during the 1992 crisis.

## 13.8  Civil Servants

### 13.8.1  The Constitutional Position

The civil service is a professional, permanent and independent part of the executive, giving the constitution continuity and stability. Its purpose is:

> to assist the duly constituted government in formulating policies of the government, carrying out decisions of the government and in administering services for which the Government is responsible. (*Civil Service Code*, 1999, para. 1)

On the one hand, the civil service must offer impartial advice and expertise to governments of all political colours (ibid. paras 5, 9). On the other hand, it is required to carry government instructions with complete loyalty (ibid. para. 2). The argument that UK civil servants should have wider duties to the Crown as distinct from duties to the government of the day has not succeeded (see House of Commons Public Services Committee Ministerial Accountability and Responsibility, 1995–6, HC 313, para. 169).

There is therefore a tension from two directions. One is the complaint from ministers (perhaps weak ones) that they are dominated or subverted by their civil servants. The other, largely from civil servants, is that there are risks of political interference with the impartiality and influence of the civil service, particularly through ministerial involvement in appointments and also through the influence of special advisors and other persons recruited informally by ministers (Chapter 3). In some countries, notably the USA, most senior civil servants are political appointees and change with each incoming President. This has the advantage of a unified government geared to the political outcomes voted by the electorate but lacks checks and balances.

The main principles governing the conduct of the civil service are set out in the *Civil Service Code* (1999 *www.cabinet-office.gov.UK/central/1999/cscode.htm*). Reflecting a long tradition, this is in very general terms and does not comprise a set of rules to be applied directly. It sets out 'the constitutional framework within which civil servants work and the values which they expected to uphold' (Cabinet Office, *The Civil Service: Taking Forward Continuity and Change,* 1995, para. 2.8). The Civil Service Code has the legal status of primary legislation being imposed by prerogative Order in Council (*Civil Service (Amendment) Order in Council 1997*). It can also be incorporated in the terms of service of individual civil servants. Following the recommendations of the Committee on Standards in Public Life (Ninth Report, Cm 5775, 2003), civil service bills have been introduced to give statutory force and so democratic legitimacy to some of the existing principles relating to the civil service. The Civil Service (No. 2) Bill does not incorporate the Code as such but empowers the minister for the civil service to issue codes for civil servants and special advisors (Clause 8). Under the bill the process becomes more open than under the prerogative. Proposals to issue a code or make amendments must be published, representations from any person must be considered and the proposals can be annulled by Parliament.

### 13.8.2      Legal Status of a Civil Servant: Appointment, Dismissal and Discipline

There is no authoritative legal definition of a civil servant. The Civil Service Bill Clause 1, reflecting the Tomlin Commission on the Civil Service (Cmnd 3909, 1931), refers to:

> 'the civil service of the State' as including every person who serves the Crown in a civil capacity, other than the holder of judicial or political office, and whose remuneration is paid wholly and directly out of moneys provided by Parliament.

Presumably 'civil' here is to be contrasted with military. The armed forces are of course also Crown servants paid from parliamentary funds but are subject to a distinctive legal regime. The police may 'serve' the Crown but are not civil servants because they are paid partly out of local funds. Under the bill, the minister for the civil service can make regulations including other categories as civil servants.

As with other basic constitutional principles the position of a civil servant is governed by tradition and by a pragmatic mixture of prerogative, common law and statute. Rules controlling the civil service are sometimes made by prerogative Orders in Council which have the status of primary law but may also take the form of instructions issued by ministers. Management of the civil service is vested in the Prime Minister as minister for the civil service (*Transfer of Functions (Treasury and Civil Service) Order 1995*, SI 1995 no. 269; *Civil Service Order in Council 1995*). The Cabinet Office coordinates and supervises the civil service with each department being managed by its accounting officer. The accounting officer's activities can be directly examined by Parliament by means of the Public Accounts Committee and the Comptroller and Auditor General (Chapter 12).

The independent Civil Service Commission has the general functions of monitoring the appointments process and to decide appeals brought by civil servants under the Civil Service Code (below). The Commission is appointed by the Queen on the advice of the Prime Minster but reports directly to the Queen, thereby being unusually independent of the executive. It publishes and maintains the *Recruitment Code* for the Civil Service, and audits and reports on the operation of the Civil Service Code. It also makes an annual report to Parliament. Under the Civil Service (No. 2) Bill, the Commission will be placed on a statutory basis.

Following a practice dating from the nineteenth century (Chapter 3) and designed to replace a tradition of patronage and nepotism, permanent civil servants are appointed on merit by open competition (above). In the case of senior appointments, ministers can be consulted but by convention do not make the decision. Senior appointments must be approved by the Civil Service Commission (*Civil Service Order in Council, 1995*, Art. 5 (1)). However, there are exceptions to the principle of appointment on merit (see *Civil Service Order in Council, 1995, Recruitment Code*). They include special advisors (below) and appointments made directly by the Crown, such as the Governor of the Bank of England. Other exceptions such as short-term appointments or appointments in special circumstances are policed by the Civil Service Commission (see *Civil Service Order in Council 1995*, Art. 6).

Members of public bodies outside the civil service are also appointed on merit by a process requiring independence and open competition (see First, Fourth and Sixth reports of Committee on Standards in Public Life). There are concerns relating to ministerial patronage and interference in relation to such appointments and the sycophantic tendencies of the objects of such patronage. Some 11,000 appointments made by ministers to non-departmental public bodies (NDPDs), public corporations and regulatory bodies are monitored by a Public Appointments Commission under the royal prerogative (Order in Council July 16 2002) which has drawn up a code of practice (2004); there is also a commissioner for NHS appointments. The principles include independent assessors and 'proportionality' which enables simplified procedures to be used in the case of less important appointments (see Fourth Report of Public Administration Select Committee Session 2002–03, *Government by Appointment: Opening up the Patronage State*, HC 135); *Getting the Balance Right*, Committee on Standards, 2004).

The relationship between the Crown and a civil servant is usually said to be governed by the royal prerogative. According to this view a civil servant has no contract of employment and cannot enforce the terms of his employment other than those laid down by statute (*Civil Service Code* para. 14). At common law the Crown can dismiss a civil servant 'at pleasure', that is, without notice and without giving reasons (*Dunn v R* (1896)). This is consistent with the view that there is no contract. On the other hand, it has been held that there can be a contract between the Crown and a civil servant but that, as a matter of public policy, the contract can be overridden by the Crown's power to dismiss the civil servant at pleasure (*Riordan v War Office* (1959), but see *Reilly v R* (1934)). On this second analysis the terms of the employment such as pay and conditions are enforceable against the Crown.

Modern cases have stressed that there is no inherent reason why the relationship cannot be contractual (see *Kodeeswaren v A-G for Ceylon* (1970); *R v Civil Service Appeal Board ex parte Bruce* (1988); *R v Lord Chancellor's Department ex parte Nangle* (1992)). The Employment Act 1988, s.30, deems there to be a contract between the Crown and a civil servant for the purpose of making a civil servant liable for industrial action. Whether or not there is a contract, it seems clear that the Crown can still dismiss at pleasure and that a contractual term which says otherwise is not enforceable. This can be regarded as a matter of public policy.

Civil servants, like other citizens may be protected by judicial review. However in *Nangle* (above) it was held that judicial review did not apply to internal disciplinary decisions unless a formal adjudicative process is involved (c.f. *Bruce* (above) and *R v Civil Service Appeals Board ex parte Cunningham* (1991)). Moreover, internal remedies must be used before resorting to the courts. Most civil servants are also protected by statutory unfair dismissal rules administered by industrial tribunals (Employment Rights Act 1996 s.191). 'Unfair dismissal' is not the same as unlawful dismissal and the only enforceable order that an industrial tribunal can make is one of compensation. Special machinery applies to security issues. A minister can, by issuing a certificate, remove any category of Crown employee from the employment protection legislation on grounds of national security (Employment Rights Act 1996, s.193). A civil servant who is suspected of being a security risk is given a special hearing, but without the normal rights of cross-examination and legal representation, before a panel of 'three advisors'. These usually comprise two retired senior officials and a High Court judge.

Questions arise when a civil servant considers that his or her integrity is compromised, for example by being required to act for politically partisan purposes or possibly to break the law. Obeying the orders of a superior is not a defence in English law. The orthodox doctrine is that civil servants owe an absolute duty of loyalty to ministers (above) and the *Civil Service Code* imposes an absolute obligation of confidentiality. This is of course necessary to ensure that governments of different political complexion can work confidently with civil servants. There are however internal mechanisms to enable civil servants to express issues of conscience. These include a right of appeal to the independent Civil Service Commission and special provisions relating to the Official Secrets Act (Chapter 19). Judicial review may also be available (see *R* v *Shaylor* (2002)).

The political activity of civil servants is restricted according to the level of the individual in the policy-making hierarchy. The majority are unrestricted except while on duty or in uniform or on official premises. An 'intermediate' group can take part in political activities with the consent of their head of department. This includes clerks, typists and officials performing specialist non-political jobs. A 'restricted' group of senior officials directly involved in policy making cannot take part in national politics at all but can indulge in local politics with the consent of their head of department. However, whole departments can be exempted. Civil servants are also prohibited from taking gifts or doing other things that could create a conflict between their private interests and their official duties. A retired civil servant requires government approval before accepting employment with private sector organisations that are likely to have dealings with the government. (See *Civil Service Pay and Conditions Code*, Fifth Report of Treasury and Civil Service Committee, HC 1989–90, HMSO.)

### 13.8.3 Special Advisors

Special advisors are party political advisors appointed personally by ministers and working closely with them. They were formally recognised by a government announcement in 1974 but have probably always existed. In March 2003 there were 81 special advisors of which 27 worked for the Prime Minister. They are temporary civil servants whose posts terminate with their minister. Unlike other civil servants they are not required to be politically impartial and some are empowered to give directions to civil servants (Civil Service Order in Council 1995). Their functions include advising ministers, briefing party members and officials, publicising government policies and drawing up or reviewing policies for both government and party (see *Code of Conduct for Special Advisors*, 2001, Cabinet Office). They therefore serve as a link between the political and the permanent parts of the government. In recent years special advisors have become a more dominant element in government. There is a concern that their activities, particularly in relation to communication with the media, may threaten the reputation of the civil service for impartiality. There is also a concern that permanent civil servants may be denied access to ministers and that their role will reduced to carrying out orders from special advisors.

The constitutional problem is therefore that the distinction between the political and the permanent parts of the executive has become blurred, thereby upsetting an important balance. On the other hand, special advisors serve as a valuable link between the two elements. In its Ninth Report (2003) the Committee on Standards in Public life recommended that both the civil service and special advisors should be subject to a statutory regime which clarifies their respective constitutional roles and duties. In particular, special advisors should be defined as a separate category distinct from civil servants and should not normally be given executive powers nor management or disciplinary powers over civil servants. Ministers should be personally accountable for the acts of their special advisors.

### 13.8.4 Civil Servants and Ministerial Responsibility

Under the *Carltona* doctrine (*Carltona* v *Commissioner for Works* (1943)), a minister can lawfully exercise any of his statutory powers through a civil servant in his department and need not personally exercise any power, unless statute specifically so requires (e.g. Immigration Act 1971 s.13 (5), Regulation of Investigatory Powers Act 2000 s.59). The decision remains that of the minister, the civil servant and the minister being indivisible in law (see also *Bushell* v *Environment Secretary* (1981), *R (Alconbury)* v *Secretary of State* (2001)). It is not clear how far this principle depends on the power of control over civil servants available to ministers, the convention of ministerial responsibility itself or simply the unreality of ministers being capable of acting personally in every case. Nor is it clear how far the courts can control the internal arrangements made by a minister. In *Olahinde* v *Secretary of State* (1990) the House of Lords held that a deportation decision could be made by an immigration officer on behalf of the Secretary of State. However, Lord Templeman remarked (at 397) that the person exercising the power must be 'of suitable seniority in the Home Office for whom the minister accepts responsibility' (c.f. *Re Golden Chemical Products Ltd* (1976) denying judicial control).

The classical doctrine of ministerial responsibility has been that there is no direct link between civil servants and Parliament. Sir Edward Bridges (above) stated that as civil servants have no powers of their own, and so cannot take decisions or do anything except and in so far as they are subject to the direction and control of ministers, a civil servant has no direct responsibility to Parliament and cannot be called to account by Parliament (although ministers were never expected to defend official action of which they either disapproved or had no prior knowledge – HC Debs 5th series vol. 530 col. 1285, 20 July 1964).

Civil servants are therefore accountable to ministers, and ministers accountable to Parliament. In particular, advice given to ministers by civil servants cannot be disclosed without the permission of ministers and, according to the government, civil servants appear before parliamentary committees only with the consent of their ministers (below). Ministers therefore shield civil servants from Parliament. In return, civil servants are loyal to ministers and owe no other allegiance, thus emphasising the minister's own accountability to Parliament (see Seventh Report of Treasury and Civil Service Committee, 1985–6, HC 92, and Cmnd 9841, 1986 – government's reply).

The Scott Inquiry (above) revealed how in practice civil servants have sometimes acted independently of ministers, or in the expectation of subsequent ministerial ratification of their actions (Scott, 1996, HC 115 para. D3.40). This exposed the constitutional fiction that civil servants only give advice to ministers. Civil servants concealed important questions from ministers and may even have defied ministerial instructions (Scott, paras D2.398, see Lewis and Longley, 1996). Indeed, in 1994 the permanent secretary in the Overseas Development Department disclosed to the Public Accounts Committee that ministers had overridden his advice (*Times*, 18 January 1994). Moreover, as we saw above, ministers have attempted to pass responsibility to civil servants, firstly by distinguishing between policy and operational matters and secondly by distinguishing between 'accountability' as a duty to explain and 'responsibility' as liability to take the blame (Fifth Report from Treasury and Civil Service Select Committee, *The Role of the Civil Service* HC 27, 1993–4, para. 120).

It has long been accepted that, as accounting officer, the permanent head of a department must appear before the relevant parliamentary committee. It has never been settled whether select committees can require civil servants to attend to answer questions. In 1986 the Defence Select Committee claimed the absolute right to secure attendance from civil servants (HC 519, 1985–6). However, a compromise has been arrived at whereby ministers are enjoined to permit civil servants to appear but subject to restrictions (see para. 37, *Departmental Evidence and Response to Select Committees*, Cabinet Office, January 1997, replacing the so called 'Osmotherly Rules'). This document exhorts civil servants to be as forthcoming as possible in providing information under the *Code of Practice on Access to*

*Government Information*. Information can, however, be withheld in the public interest, which should be determined in accordance with the law and the exemptions set out in the Code. Moreover, civil servants cannot disclose or discuss the advice they gave to ministers, only the action they took on behalf of ministers.

The reorganisation of government has further placed the classical model under strain. This is most notably the case in the relationship between ministers and chief executives of Executive Agencies. Ministerial responsibility was intended to apply equally to the work of EAs which remain subject to the scrutiny of the PCA and the relevant select committee. However, the principle underlying the respective functions of the agencies and the departments is that autonomy for service delivery should reside with the agency, whilst policy matters should be reserved for the department acting under ministerial control. Framework agreements made between the agency and the sponsoring department (sometimes with the Treasury as a party) constitute the relationship between the two. The framework agreement contains the corporate strategy and financial arrangements under which the agency will work.

A chief executive is appointed (as a temporary civil servant) to be responsible for the day-to-day management of the agency, which is staffed by civil servants. The chief executive is responsible to the minister but, as accounting officer, also appears before select committees to answer MPs' questions about the functioning of the agency over which he or she has day-to-day management. Controversially, this suggests that a convention *may* have been emerging under which agency chief executives are directly responsible to Parliament in their own right (but see below).

The traditional assertion that civil servants advise ministers and act on their behalf has therefore been radically altered. MPs have also been encouraged to approach chief executives directly on behalf of their constituents, and chief executives answer written parliamentary questions. The answers are published in *Hansard* to avoid the bypassing of Parliament which might have occurred if chief executives responded directly to individual MPs (see, for example, Fifth Report of the Treasury and Civil Service Committee, (above) col. 53 para. 170).

In 1997 the House of Lords Select Committee on Public Service (above) identified a need for a re-examination of the relationship between ministers and civil servants, but expressed the view that there should be no distinction between the constitutional responsibilities of chief executives and other civil servants. This would mean that when they answer written parliamentary questions or appear before select committees they do so on behalf of their ministers. The Committee stated emphatically that ministers remain accountable for what goes on in agencies just as in their departments.

However, there remain concerns that when chief executives appear before select committees they are subject to the direction of their minister under the *Departmental Evidence and Response to Select Committees* (Cabinet Office, January 1997) which would limit their competence as witnesses and Parliament's ability to investigate.

Finally, the *Carltona* principle (above) may not apply to civil servants in executive agencies who are not directly under the control of a minister (see Freedland, 'Government by Contract and Public Law', 1994, *Public Law* 86). In *Williams v Home Office (No. 2)* (1981) the court drew a distinction between acts done by civil servants in the exercise of statutory functions conferred on ministers, and routine management matters, saying that the latter are not to be regarded as the act of ministers. This is questionable in terms of the traditional doctrine of ministerial responsibility, but perhaps represents a more realistic view of the nature of modern government.

## Summary

▶ As a body the Cabinet has been reduced in power in recent years, with decisions being effectively made by smaller groups within and outside the Cabinet and by departments of the executive.

▶ There are few constitutional laws or conventions concerning the detailed distribution of functions between departments. Political and administrative considerations rather than constitutional principle determine the number, size, shape and interrelationship of government departments. The creation of bodies outside the framework of the Crown is of greater constitutional and legal significance.

▶ The convention of ministerial responsibility is central to the UK constitution. We discussed its two limbs with their several branches. Collective responsibility means that all members of the government must loyally support government policy and decisions and must not disclose internal disagreements. Individual responsibility means that each minister is answerable to Parliament for all the activities of the department under his control. It also means that civil servants are not personally accountable. From these principles follow: (i) the traditional notion of the civil service as anonymous and politically neutral having a duty to serve with unquestioning loyalty governments of any political complexion; (ii) the secrecy that pervades the British system of government.

▶ Many people believe that the traditional doctrine of ministerial responsibility is out of line with the practices of modern government and effectively shields the government from accountability. In particular: (i) Cabinet decisions are rarely made collectively; (ii) many government bodies are not directly controlled by ministers, the creation of executive agencies reinforcing this; (iii) civil servants are increasingly expected to make political decisions and to be responsible for the financial management of their allotted activities; (iv) public functions are

## Summary cont'd

increasingly being given to special bodies or private bodies. Thus the traditional chain of accountability between Parliament, ministers and civil servants is weakened.

▶ In law, civil servants are servants of the Crown. They can be dismissed 'at pleasure', that is, without notice and without reason being given. However, the modern cases suggest that there can be a contractual relationship between the Crown and a civil servant and that a civil servant can be protected by the law of judicial review.

▶ In the light of the convention relating to ministerial responsibility, civil servants are regarded as servants of the government of the day with an absolute duty of loyalty to ministers. Their advice to ministers is secret and they appear before Parliament only with the consent of ministers. They are supposed to be non-political and neutral, responsible for giving ministers objective advice and for carrying out ministerial orders.

▶ The internal arrangements for the carrying-out of government business involve entrusting individual civil servants with considerable decision-making responsibility and in recent years with financial accountability within the government machine. Many civil servants work in executive agencies, hived off from the central departmental structure and outside the direct control of ministers. This has led to tensions between traditional ideas of ministerial responsibility and the actual channels of accountability and has raised problems in connection with the supposed distinction between policy and operational matters. Ministerial responsibility is also weakened by the practice of entrusting public functions to specialised NDPDs operating to varying extents independently of the central government.

# Exercises

13.1 Consider whether the relevant laws and conventions support Bagehot's view that the Cabinet is the central institution of the UK Constitution.

13.2 Does the *Ministerial Code* clarify the doctrine of ministerial responsibility?

13.3 'Ministerial responsibility is, in practice, an obstacle to the availability of information and to the holding of government to account' (Oliver). Discuss.

13.4 To what extent can Parliament and the public scrutinise the activities of a civil servant?

13.5 When should a minister resign?

13.6 Critically evaluate the constitutional significance of special advisors.

13.7 The government creates an executive agency to regulate motorway service areas. The Secretary of State for Consumption delegates to the agency his statutory powers to ensure the 'adequate provision of motorway services'. Under a contract made with the Secretary of State, the agency promises to achieve certain 'targets', including a clean environment. The agency employs Grasper plc to run the Naff Service Area. Due to cuts in its funding from the Secretary of State, the agency does not check Grasper's performance but increases its chief executive's annual 'performance bonus' by 100%. A newspaper subsequently discovers that many of the catering staff at the Naff Service area are illegal immigrants and that several of them have contracted food poisoning. In response to a parliamentary question, the Secretary of State asserts that the matter is no concern of his and he knows nothing about it. He also refuses to permit the agency chief executive to appear before the Select Committee for Consumption. Discuss.

## Further reading

Barberis, P. (1998) 'The New Public Management and a New Accountability', *Public Administration*, **76**: 451.

Bogdanor, V. (ed.) (2003) *The British Constitution in the Twentieth Century*, London, British Academy, Chapter 8.

Brazier, R. (1999) *Constitutional Practise*, 3rd edn, Oxford, Oxford University Press, Chapters 5, 6, 7.

Budge, I., Crewe, I., McKay, D. and Newton, K. (2004) *The New British Politics*, 3rd edn, Harlow, Pearson, Chapters 5, 6.

Daintith, T. and Page, A. (1999) *The Executive in the Constitution*, Oxford, Oxford University Press, Chapters 1–6.

Dowding, K. and Wun-Taek, K. (1998) 'Ministerial Resignations', *Public Administration*, **76**: 411.

Edwards, J. (1984) *The Attorney General, Politics and the Public Interest*, London, Sweet & Maxwell.

Harden, I. (1993) 'Money and the Constitution, Financial Control, Reporting and Audit', *Legal Studies*, **13**: 16.

Harden, I., White, F. and Hollingsworth, K. (1996) 'Value for Money and Adminstrative Law', *Public Law* 661.

Hennessy, P. (1995) *The Hidden Wiring*, London, Gollancz, Chapters 3, 4, 5, 8.

Jowell, J. and Oliver, D. (2003) *The Changing Constitution*, 5th edn, Oxford, Oxford University Press, Chapters 5, 6.

Lewis, N. (1998) 'A Civil Service Act for the United Kingdom', *Public Law* 463.

Lewis, N. and Longley, D. (1996) 'Ministerial Responsibility. The Next Steps', *Public Law* 490.

Woodhouse, D. (1997) *In Pursuit of Good Administration, Ministers, Civil Servants and Judges*, Oxford, Clarendon Press.

# Part III

# The Citizen and the State

## Chapter 14

# Judicial review: Grounds of review, I: Illegality and *ultra vires*

> In modern Britain, where no agreement exists on the ends of Society and the means of achieving those ends, it would be disastrous if courts did not eschew the temptation to pass judgement on an issue of policy. Judicial self-preservation may alone dictate restraint. (Lord Parker, Lord Chief Justice, 1959)

## Key words

▶ Legality and merits
▶ Law, fact and policy
▶ Respect for democracy
▶ Context-sensitive review
▶ Political objectivity of courts
▶ Discretion and duty
▶ Substantive and procedural standards

### 14.1 Introduction: The Constitutional Basis of Judicial Review

Judicial review, sometimes called the supervisory jurisdiction, is the High Court's power to police the legality of decisions made by public bodies. As usual an accommodation must be struck between competing concerns. On the one hand, the rule of law has been said to require that the legality of government action be:

> subject to review by independent and impartial tribunals ... The principles of judicial review give effect to the rule of law. They ensure that administrative decisions will be taken rationally in accordance with a fair procedure and within the powers conferred by Parliament. (per Lord Hoffmann in *R ((Alconbury)* v *Secretary of State* [2001] 2 All ER 929, 981)

On the other hand, judicial review operates within the context of parliamentary accountability of the executive and the various mechanisms, such as the ombudsman and the National Audit Office that give effect to it. Both the separation of powers and the European Convention on Human Rights require the courts to check misuse of power by the executive but also to avoid trespassing into the political territory of the government. Judicial review is regarded as a last resort method of challenge and there are procedural barriers intended to prevent its being too easily taken up (Chapter 16).

The courts claim not to be concerned with the 'merits' of government action, that is whether it is good or bad, but only whether governmental decisions fall within their authorising legislation and meet legal standards of fairness and 'reasonableness'. However, we shall see that these legal standards are open-ended, shading into questions of merit and that there is considerable room for debate as to the proper limits of the courts' powers.

Since 1977 judicial review cases has been heard by the Administrative Court, which is part of the Queen's Bench division of the High Court. This follows a special flexible procedure designed to cater for the public interest that actions against the government should be dealt with quickly and without trespassing into the legitimate area of government freedom. (Chapter 16). However, following the 'Woolf' reforms of civil procedure (2000) which were designed to increase the efficiency of ordinary litigation, the difference between the Administrative Court and other proceedings, while still significant, is less than was previously the case.

Judicial review applies to all public bodies other than the High Court itself and Parliament. In *Council of Civil Service Unions (CCSU)* v *Minister for the Civil Service* (1985), it was suggested that some matters are 'non-justiciable' meaning not appropriate for judicial review. This might be because of their political sensitivity or because the courts lack the expertise to deal with them or because the legal process may be unsuitable owing to the wide range of matters involved. Examples, mostly involving the royal prerogative, include the dissolution of Parliament, the appointment of ministers, the granting of honours, the making of treaties and other matters concerning relationships with overseas governments (see Chapter 12).

Moreover, the judicial review principles are flexible in that the intensity of review, the range of grounds available or the selection of remedies varies with the context. In controversial areas or in matters particularly appropriate to democratic decision making, or where the matter involves expertise outside that of the courts, while not excluding review entirely, the courts may allow a wide discretion to the government decision maker. For example, the courts apply strict standards to judicial bodies, such as tribunals that determine legal rights, but are less willing to interfere with a decision that involves the discretionary allocation of scarce resources, for example whether or not to treat an NHS patient (see *R* v *Cambridge Health Authority ex parte B* (1995)). The courts also respect the sphere of accountability of the executive to Parliament although some judges are more deferential to this than others (see the disagreement in *R* v *Secretary of State for the Home Department ex parte Fire Brigades Union* (1995)). As early as 1911 one judge at least was expressing doubts about ministerial responsibility (see *Dyson* v *A-G* (1911)).

The courts usually defer to a minister's opinion as to what national security requires but will at least ensure that the matter is genuinely one of national security (*CCSU* v *Minister for the Civil Service* (1985)). Other cases where the courts are cautious include electoral matters (*R* v *Boundary Commission for England ex parte Foot* (1983); child care (*R* v *Harrow LBC ex parte D* (1990)); academic matters (*Page* v *Hull University Visitor* (1993) compare *Clark* v *University of Lincolnshire and Humberside* (2000)); and voluntary regulatory bodies (*R* v *Panel on Takeovers and Mergers ex parte Datafin plc* (1987)), although there is usually no protection for unfair procedures and certainly not for bad faith.

The legal basis of judicial review is disputed and reflects the wider debate as to the nature of our constitution (Chapers 5, 7). There is a large but somewhat repetitive literature on this issue (the main viewpoints are collected in Forsythe, 2000). One perspective bases judicial review upon the common law and packaged as 'the rule of law', according to which powerful bodies must act in accordance with basic values of fairness and rationality (*Dr Bonham's Case* (1610); *Bagg's Case* (1615); *Cooper* v *Wandsworth Board of Works* (1863)). This draws inspiration primarily from liberal and republican ideas (Chapter 1). The other perspective – the *ultra vires* doctrine – relies on the doctrine of parliamentary supremacy and assumes that, because most government powers are created by Act of Parliament, the courts' role should be confined to ensuring that powers are exercised within the limits set out by Parliament. Thus the *ultra vires* doctrine requires the court to respect democratic principles. Rather tediously, both approaches seem to fit the facts and the historical evidence is inconclusive. Both approaches conform to possible meanings of the separation of powers. The *ultra vires* approach is more heavily biased towards the functional separation aspect of that doctrine; the common law towards checks and balances (Chapter 6).

The *ultra vires* approach accepts that the judges are developing their own principles but claims that Parliament intends that principles of judicial review be implied into the exercise of statutory powers because Parliament can be assumed to respect the rule of law as developed by the courts. In other words the *ultra vires* doctrine concerns an assumed intention of Parliament as opposed to a *specific* intention as to meaning of given legislation. Forsythe (1996) therefore suggests that the *ultra vires* doctrine is a useful 'fig leaf' which gives constitutional respectability to what is happening and at least reminds us that Parliament has the last word. Indeed, there are many presumptions of statutory interpretation which require courts to assume that Parliament intended to act fairly while allowing the court considerable room to decide what this means (Chapter 7). Judicial review may be regarded as an extension of this.

There are substantial judicial dicta in support of the *ultra vires* doctrine as the basis of judicial review (*Boddington* v *British Transport Police* [1998] 2 WLR 639, 650, 655, 662; *Credit Suisse* v *Allerdale BC* [1996] 4 All ER 129, 167; *Page* v *Hull University Visitor* [1993] 1 All ER 97 at 107. On the other hand, in *CCSU* v *Minister for the Civil Service* (1985), Lord Diplock famously classified the grounds of judicial review independently of the *ultra vires* doctrine, under the three broad heads of 'illegality, irrationality and procedural impropriety'.

Forsythe's fig leaf could be taken to hide something we would prefer not to see, namely that the *ultra vires* doctrine is an empty vessel for whatever happens to be the prevailing judicial fashion. The notion of a 'general intention' to go along with a package of judge-made law seems to be no more than a fiction, giving us no guidance as to the law to be applied in any given case. The common law version claims to be more honest. It asserts that the courts develop the law, subject to Parliament's being able to override the courts by using clear enough language (Chapter 7). It does not ignore the intention of Parliament. Firstly, a decision which is *ultra vires* in the sense that it violates a particular statutory requirement or limitation or is based on irrelevant considerations is invalid under both theories. Secondly, the common law approach would claim that broader grounds of review such as unreasonableness or unfairness (below) are free-standing, but that, by using clear language, Parliament can exclude any ground of review just as Parliament can change any common law rule such as a rule of contract law. There is therefore no inconsistency with parliamentary supremacy. Indeed neither the *ultra vires* approach nor the common law approach necessarily commits us to any particular attitude on the question of parliamentary supremacy. The difference between them is that, according to the common law view, Parliament *tolerates* judicial review whereas on the *ultra vires* view Parliament somehow *authorises* judicial review.

The common law approach also frees up judicial review so that its principles might apply to bodies whose powers do not derive from statute. For example, it is settled that royal prerogative powers and other non-statutory powers exercised by public bodies are subject to judicial review (*CCSU* v *Minister for the Civil Service* (1985), *R* v *Panel on Takeovers and Mergers ex parte Datafin plc* (1987)). The common law might also be the basis for extending judicial review principles, similar to those applied to government, to powerful private bodies (such as sports regulatory bodies, powerful commercial companies etc.) which exercise control over aspects of public life (e.g. *McInnes* v *Onslow-Fane* (1978)). Proponents of the *ultra vires* doctrine accommodate this possibility by suggesting that there need not be a single basis for judicial review. Thus the practice of judicial review depends on political choice rather than an abstract conceptual theory. On the other hand, the chosen theory cannot be ignored since it influences how decisions are made.

## 14.2 Appeal and Review

Judicial review must not be confused with an appeal. An appeal is a procedure which exists only under a particular statute or, in the case of a voluntary body, by agreement. An appeal allows the appellate body to decide the whole matter again, unless the particular statute or agreement limits the grounds of appeal (e.g. Tribunals and Inquiries Act 1992 s. 11: questions of law only). An appeal therefore may involve a thorough reconsideration of the whole decision whereas judicial review is concerned only with ensuring that legal standards are complied with. Depending on the particular statute, an appellate body might be a court, tribunal, minister or indeed anyone. A claim for judicial review as such is possible only in the High Court.

An appellate body can usually substitute its decision for the first instance decision, although in some cases its powers are limited to sending the matter back to be decided again by the lower body.

In judicial review proceedings, unless there is no doubt as to the right decision, the court cannot make the decision itself but must send the matter back to the decision maker with instructions as to its legal duties.

Unlike a right of appeal which can be raised only in the body specified, the invalidity of government action can be raised not only in the Administrative Court but, by way of 'collateral challenge', in any proceedings where the rights of a citizen are affected by the validity of government action (e.g. *Boddington* v *British Transport Police* (1998): defence to prosecution for smoking contrary to railway bylaws alleged to be *ultra vires*). This is because an unlawful government decision is of no effect in law (void/nullity) and can be ignored thus vindicating the rule of law (*Entick* v *Carrington* (Chapter 5)). In the case of an appeal the offending decision is fully valid until the appeal body changes it.

The concept of nullity does not always lead to a just solution. For example in *Credit Suisse* v *Allerdale BC* (1996) a local authority successfully relied on the argument that a guarantee which it had given was *ultra vires* so as to prevent the guarantee being enforced against it (see now Local Government (Contracts) Act 1997). In *DPP* v *Head* (1959) a man charged with having sexual relations with a patient 'detained' under the mental health Acts was able to argue that because the patient's detention order had not been made according to the required formalities, she was not 'detained' under the relevant Acts.

## 14.3 Classification of the Grounds of Review

Unfortunately there is no general agreement on how to classify the grounds of review and the text books take different approaches. The grounds themselves are broad, vague and overlapping, a conspicuous example of this being *Wheeler* v *Leicester City Council* (Chapter 15). In the following sections I shall organise the grounds of judicial review on the basis of Lord Diplock's classification in *Council of Civil Service Unions* v *Minister for the Civil Service* (1985) that is, under the three heads of 'illegality, irrationality and procedural impropriety'. However, the Diplock categories tell us little in themselves and do not avoid overlaps. Indeed the House of Lords has emphasised that the heads of challenge are not watertight compartments but run together (*Boddington* v *British Transport Police* (1998). It might however be helpful at this point to provide a checklist.

1. **Illegality**
   - 'Narrow' *ultra vires* or lack of jurisdiction in the sense of straying beyond the limits defined by the statute.
   - Errors of law, and (in certain cases) errors of fact.
   - 'Wide' *ultra vires* in the sense of acting for an ulterior purpose, taking irrelevant factors into account or failing to take relevant factors into account.
   - Fettering discretion.

2. **Irrationality**
   - '*Wednesbury*' unreasonableness. This could stand alone or be the outcome of taking an irrelevant factor into account.
   - Proportionality at least under the Human Rights Act 1998.

3. **Procedural Impropriety**
   - Violating important statutory procedures.
   - Bias.
   - Lack of a fair hearing.
   - Failure to give reasons for a decision.

In this chapter we shall discuss illegality. The other, broader grounds are discussed in Chapter 15.

## 14.4 'Narrow' *ultra vires*

A decision is *ultra vires* if it is outside the language of the statute. In the case of courts and judicial tribunals the terminology of 'lack' or 'excess' of jurisdiction means the same as *ultra vires*. A distinction is sometimes made between lacking jurisdiction at the outset, so that the decision maker has no power to deal with the matter at all, and straying outside jurisdiction by some subsequent defect. In most cases, however, this distinction does not matter (see *Anisminic Ltd* v *Foreign Compensation Commission* (1969)).

A famous example of *ultra vires* which raises its main issues is *A-G* v *Fulham Corporation* (1921). A local authority had power to provide a 'wash-house' for local people. It interpreted this as authorising the provision of a laundry service for working people who could leave washing to be done by staff and delivered to their homes. This was held to be unlawful in that 'wash-house', according to the court, means a place where a person can do their own washing. This raises questions as to the assumptions that the courts bring to the task of interpreting statutes. For example, the court might have been influenced by a prejudice against local bodies spending taxpayers' money on welfare services. If the court had read the statute against an assumption of democratic freedom principle, the outcome might have been different. More recently in *Bromley LBC* v *GLC* (1983) the House of Lords held that an obligation to provide an 'efficient and economic' public transport service meant that the council could not subsidise the London Underground for social purposes. Among other lines of reasoning it was held that 'economic' meant that there was an obligation to break even financially (see also *Prescott* v *Birmingham Corporation* (1955): free transport for pensioners held *ultra vires* under a power to charge such fares as the council thought fit). To be sure the courts' interpretation in all these cases was a possible reading of the statute but was it the only possible interpretation?

As we saw in Chapter 7, where the scope of a statute is unclear, the courts rely on presumptions of interpretation which point them in a particular direction. These presumptions, derived from broad ideas of the rule of law (Chapter 5), are applied unless overridden by clear statutory language. They can reflect the courts' perception of community values although this does not necessarily reflect public opinion. Examples include *R* v *Secretary of State for the Home Department ex parte Simms* [1999] 3 All ER 400 at 412: freedom of expression; *Congreve* v *Home Office* (1976); *Macarthy and Stone* v *Richmond LBC* (1991): no taxation without statutory authority; *R* v *Secretary of State ex parte Pierson* (1998): retrospective use of powers; *Raymond* v *Honey* (1983): prisoner's rights; *R* v *Lord Chancellor ex parte Witham* (1997): access to justice; *Hall* v *Shoreham UDC* (1964): private property rights; *R* v *Secretary of State for Social Services ex parte Joint Council for the Welfare of Immigrants* (1996): destitution).

These presumptions appeal to individualistic liberals but some of them have been criticised by 'welfare liberals' as attempts to counter policies based on the collective public interest (Chapter 1). They have been reinforced by the Human Rights Act 1998 which imposes a strong obligation to interpret all legislation so as to conform with rights embodied in the European Convention on Human Rights (Chapter 17).

There is some leeway in the *ultra vires* doctrine in favour of the government. The courts will permit an activity that, although not expressly authorised by the statute, is 'reasonably incidental' to something that is expressly authorised (e.g. *A-G* v *Crayford UDC* (1962): voluntary household insurance scheme reasonably incidental to power to manage council housing because it helped tenants to pay the rent). However, the courts take a strict approach which impacts particularly on local democracy. For example, in *Macarthy and Stone* v *Richmond LBC* (1991) a charge for giving advice in connection with planning applications was held not to be incidental to the authority's planning powers. Giving advice was not expressly authorised and was itself an incidental function. The House of Lords took the view that something cannot be incidental to the incidental. In *Hazell* v *Hammersmith and Fulham BC* (1992), it was held that interest swap arrangements – made by several local councils to spread the risk of future changes in interest rates – were not incidental to the council's borrowing powers because they concerned debt management rather than borrowing as such (cf. *R* v *Richmond LBC ex parte Watson* (2001)). The Local Government Act 2000 has to some extent reacted to these cases by broadening local government powers but subject to central control thus illustrating the continuous interplay between law and politics.

## 14.5 Errors of Law

The question whether the court can review decisions on the ground of legal or factual errors has caused problems. There is a clash of principle. On the one hand, if the court can intervene merely because it considers that a decision is wrong, it would be trespassing into the merits of the case and violating the separation of powers. From this perspective the question is not so much whether there was a mistake but who should have the last word on the matter (see *R* v *Nat Bell Liquors* (1922): false evidence not reviewable). On the other hand, the rule of law surely calls for a remedy if a decision maker makes a clear mistake. The courts have therefore adopted a compromise. Almost all errors of law and some errors of fact can be challenged. However, they have reached this position only after much technical wrangling.

A rationale that was popular in the nineteenth century is the doctrine of the 'jurisdictional' or 'collateral' or 'preliminary' question. According to this doctrine, if a mistake relates to a state of affairs which the court thinks that Parliament intended should exist objectively before the official assumes power to make the decision, then the court will interfere if it thinks that the required state of affairs does not exist. For example in *White and Collins* v

*Minister of Health* (1939), the Secretary of State had power to acquire land 'other than a garden or parkland'. It was held that the court could interfere if it thought that the minister had wrongly decided whether the claimant's land was parkland, (see also *R* v *Hackney Rent Tribunal ex parte Keats* (1950): tribunal had power to reduce rent for dwelling-house property let as business). The doctrine can be justified on the rule-of-law ground that a minister should not be allowed to expand his own powers (see Farwell J in *R* v *Shoreditch Assessment Committee* [1910] 2 KB 859 at 880). However, there seems to be no logical way of deciding which of many issues that a decision maker has to decide are 'preliminary' in this sense. Nevertheless the doctrine still exists (below).

A second device that flourished during the 1960s but has largely been superseded is the doctrine of 'error of law on the face of the record' or patent error (*R* v *Northumberland Compensation Appeal Tribunal ex parte Shaw* (1952)). This allows the court to quash a decision if a mistake of law can be discovered from the written record of the decision without using other evidence. This could not be squeezed into the *ultra vires* doctrine and decisions tainted by patent error are only 'voidable', that is, valid unless and until formally quashed by the court. This provides a practical compromise by allowing obvious mistakes to be rectified without reopening the whole matter. Many bodies were required to give written reasons for their decisions as part of the record (now Tribunals and Inquiries Act 1992 s.10), and the courts were liberal in what material they regarded as part of the record. However, mistakes of fact could not be challenged at all.

As a result of the speeches of the House of Lords in *Anisminic Ltd* v *Foreign Compensation Commission* [1969] 2 AC 147 (above), notably that of Lord Reid, the older doctrines have been made largely redundant in relation to errors of law. *Anisminic* appears to have made all errors of law reviewable, at least in principle. The FCC adjudicated on claims to compensation for war damage in connection with an Arab–Israeli war. Under the regulations, which were densely drafted, the owner of the damaged property and its 'successor in title' must be British subjects. The FCC had interpreted the term 'successor in title' as including a purchaser. This led it to refuse compensation to the claimant who had sold its property to an Egyptian company. The House of Lords held that as a matter of law a purchaser was not a successor in title. Therefore an irrelevant matter had been taken into account that Parliament did not intend, namely the Egyptian company. According to a majority of their Lordships, this made the decision not just wrong but outside the FCC's jurisdiction.

*Anisminic* has been widely taken as deciding that any mistake of law makes a decision *ultra vires* in that all such mistakes could be presented as taking an irrelevant factor into account. It therefore invites the courts to investigate the decisions of public bodies in considerable depth. However, there are dicta denying that all errors of law should be jurisdictional and it is not clear that their Lordships in *Anisminic* intended to go so far (see *South East Asia Fire Brick Sdn BHD* v *Non-Metallic Mineral Products Manufacturing Employees Union* (1981); *Pearlman* v *Keepers of Harrow School* (1979)). However, the wide reading of *Anisminic* has been endorsed, at least as a general principle by the House of Lords, in *Re Racal* (1981), *O'Reilly* v *Mackman* (1982), and *Page* v *Hull University Visitor* (1993).

The courts have to some extent drawn back. They have used the argument that some questions raise specialised issues or involve a mixture of matters of law, fact and opinion with which the courts should not interfere unless the approach taken by the decision maker is completely unreasonable (I shall discuss later what is meant by unreasonable). For example, in *Re Racal Communications* (1981) Lord Diplock suggested that *Anisminic* did not apply to decisions of courts where questions of law and questions of fact were inextricably mixed up. In *Page* v *Hull University Visitor* (1993) it was held that the specialised rules of universities could be conclusively interpreted by the University Visitor. More generally, *Anisminic* has not been applied to mistakes of fact which arguably should not be reviewable because the primary decision maker is usually in a better position than the court to discover the facts.

It is not always easy to distinguish between questions of law, questions of fact and questions of opinion. The latter are only reviewable if the decision maker acts unreasonably (Chapter 15). A question of law basically involves the meaning and usually the application of a rule. A question of fact involves the existence of some state of affairs or event in the world outside the law and depends on evidence. A question of opinion is where on the same evidence more than one view can reasonably be taken (*Lord Luke* v *Minister of Housing and Local Government* [1968] 1 QB 172): whether a building harmonised with its surroundings). However, the courts may treat some apparently legal questions of interpretation as matters of fact or opinion where they concern broad everyday notions or involve value judgements or matters of degree (see e.g. *Pulhoffer* v *Hillingdon BC* (1986): 'homeless'; *R* v *Monopolies and Mergers Commission ex parte South Yorkshire Transport* (1993): 'substantial' part of the UK; *Edwards* v *Bairstow* (1956): 'trade'; *Brutus* v *Cozens* (1973): 'insulting'; *R* v *Radio Authority ex parte Bull* (1997): 'political nature'; *Shah* v *Barnet LBC* [1983] 2 AC 309, 341: 'ordinarily' resident).

## 14.6 Errors of Fact

We have seen that errors of fact are not normally reviewable but there are exceptions.

▶ The doctrine of the preliminary question (above) applies to errors of fact where it is sometimes called the 'precedent fact' doctrine. This allows the court to decide the question of fact for itself. For example, in *Khawaja* v *Secretary of State for the Home Department* (1983) the Home Secretary could deport an 'illegal immigrant'. The House of Lords held that the court could decide whether the appellant was in fact an illegal immigrant and was not limited to deciding whether the minister's decision was unreasonable. The problem is to decide what kind of case falls within the doctrine. This depends upon the statutory context. In *Khawaja* the court was influenced by the fact that the decision involved personal freedom, so that a high level of judicial control was required. By contrast, in *Bugdaycay* v *Secretary of State* (1987) the question was whether the applicant was a genuine asylum seeker. Here the decision was heavily laden with subjective political judgement and the court was not prepared to treat the matter as one of precedent fact.

▶ A finding of fact which is completely unreasonable and without any evidential basis is reviewable (*Ashbridge Investments* v *Minister of Housing and Local Government* [1965] 1 WLR 1320, 1326). In *R* v *Criminal Injuries Compensation Board ex parte A* [1999] 2 AC 330, 344 Lord Slynn said that 'misunderstanding or ignorance of an established and relevant fact' is reviewable, but emphasised that this is no more than an application of ordinary review principles. (See also *Secretary of State for Education and Science* v *Tameside MBC* [1977] AC 1014 at 1017.) By contrast judicial review does not include a reinvestigation of *disputed* facts unless the decision is perverse (*Adan* v *Newham BC* (2002)). In other words, the courts will not attempt to investigate factual disagreements or to weigh evidence but will intervene in clear cases

▶ The matter has been complicated by Art. 6 of the European Convention on Human Rights which applies to UK law under the Human Rights Act 1998. Article 6 confers a right to a fair trial where 'civil rights and obligations' are in issue. The question arises whether the limited right to challenge findings of fact available in UK law is sufficient to satisfy Art. 6, which requires a right to challenge an administrative decision before a body with 'full jurisdiction' (*R (Alconbury)* v *Secretary of State* (2001)). The English courts have taken the view that judicial review may suffice in certain circumstances.

The first question is what is meant by a 'civil right and obligation'. Although some judges have preferred to confine the term to disputes about private law rights such as property rights, the European Court has taken a broader view which includes claims to 'public rights' against public bodies. The meaning of this is not clear. The underlying principle seems to be that the decision in question must either interfere with the existing property rights or personal rights of the individual, or have serious and direct adverse physical or economic consequences for the individual. For example in *Feldbrugge* v *the Netherlands* (1986), a claim to health insurance from the state on proof of certain facts was held to concern a civil right (see also *Salesi* v *Italy* (1998)). In *Tre Tractorer Aktebolag* v *Sweden* (1989) it was held that the revocation of a liquor licence engaged a civil right. In *Runa Begum* v *Tower Hamlets London BC* (2003), the House of Lords assumed but specifically did not decide that a discretionary decision by a local authority to provide accommodation for a homeless person engaged civil rights. By contrast, if a government decision involves a refusal to award a benefit that was not enjoyed before or to which the citizen has no special claim, or if a decision is purely advisory in its effect, a civil right may not be engaged.

Assuming that a civil right is engaged, the limited scope of judicial review in relation to findings of fact has sometimes been held to satisfy Art. 6. The UK courts have reduced the notion of 'full jurisdiction' to the virtually meaningless 'full jurisdiction to deal with the case as the nature of the decision requires' (see *Runa Begum* v *Tower Hamlets London BC* [2003] 1 All ER 731, 736 per Lord Bingham). They have made a distinction between, on the one hand, a decision where a citizen has a definite entitlement on proof of certain facts (e.g. to a pension based on prescribed contributions) and, on the other hand, a decision where the facts are part of a larger policy or politically orientated process where the decision maker has to balance facts against competing considerations and has a discretion as to the outcome, for example a local authority decision whether to grant planning permission for a new house in the countryside. The existence of safeguards for the individual within the administrative process is also relevant (see *Bryan* v *UK* (1995))

In the first 'factual' kind of case, judicial review is not normally a sufficient safeguard and, unless the initial decision is made by a body independent of government such as a court, a statutory right of appeal is required which can examine all questions of fact. In the second, 'policy', kind of case it has been held that the interests of democracy, and utilitarian considerations of efficient decision-making, and of respect for the machinery chosen by Parliament require a more flexible and less formal approach. In this case judicial review may suffice as a safety net (see *Runa Begum* v *Tower Hamlets London BC* (2003); *R (Alconbury)* v *Secretary of State* (2001)). It can be decided which category a case falls within only by looking closely at the particular decision-making process and its goals. It is clear however that the wider the view that is taken on the question of the meaning of 'civil right' (above) the more plausible it is that the case will fall within the 'policy' category.

## 14.7 'Wide' *Ultra Vires:* Improper Purposes and Irrelevant Considerations

These aspects of illegality arise in the context of discretionary powers and are sometimes labelled abuse of discretion. Even though the decision maker keeps within the express language of the statute, its motive may be improper or it may be influenced by irrelevant factors or it may overlook relevant factors. This applies even where the statute appears to give the decision maker an unrestricted, subjective discretion using such expressions as 'if the minister thinks fit' since even the widest discretionary power is in principle reviewable and it is for the court to decide what factors are relevant and what are the purposes of the Act (*Padfield* v *Minister of Agriculture* (1968): a minister acting under a particular statutory power must not be influenced by wider political considerations that do not advance the policy of the Act).

There is some flexibility. Firstly, the court will not set aside a decision if the irrelevant consideration would not have made any difference to the outcome. In this sense the line between legality and merits is blurred (see *R v ILEA ex parte Westminster City Council* (1986); *R v Secretary of State for Social Services ex parte Wellcome Foundation* (1987)). In the context of improper purposes this is sometimes expressed as the 'dominant purpose' test. For example, in *Westminster Corporation* v *London and North Western Railway* (1905), the local authority had power to construct public lavatories. It incorporated a subway into the design of its lavatories. This was held to be lawful on the basis that the subway was merely incidental to the lavatories. Although it could be used by people to cross the street it was also an appropriate method of reaching the lavatories. By contrast, in *Webb* v *Minister of Housing* (1965), the local authority had power to construct coast protection works. It incorporated a promenade into the scheme, compulsorily acquiring a number of houses for the purpose. This was held to be unlawful on the ground that more land was acquired than was needed for an adequate coast protection barrier. The whole scheme was invalid and the good part could not be separated from the bad. Similarly in *R v Lewisham LBC ex parte Shell UK Ltd* (1988), the council decided to boycott Shell's products on the ground that Shell had interests in South Africa which, at the time, was subject to apartheid. It was held that the policy have been lawfully justified on the ground of promoting good race relations in the borough. However, as the council had tried to persuade other local authorities to adopt a similar policy it had gone too far, its purpose being to put pressure on Shell. In *Porter* v *Magill* (2002), a local authority had embarked upon a policy of selling off its housing. It concentrated sales in marginal electoral wards with a view to attracting votes. The House of Lords held that the policy could not be justified on the basis of legitimate housing purposes. A democratic body can hope for an electoral advantage as the incidental outcome of its policies (and probably choose between alternative legitimate policies for electoral reasons), but it cannot distort policies in order to seek electoral advantage.

Secondly, unless the statute plainly requires the factors in question to be taken into account, the decision maker may have discretion to decide what is relevant in the particular circumstances particularly where the statute confers power in broad terms. The court will interfere only where the authority exerises its discretion unreasonably (below). For example, in *R v Somerset County Council ex parte Fewings* (1995), the local authority had statutory power to manage land 'for the benefit, improvement or development of their area'. It made an order banning deer hunting on its land, the majority of councillors voting for this on the ground of cruelty. The Court of Appeal held that the ban was unlawful on the ground that the council had not considered the governing statutory provisions at all. However, the court also took the view that had the council properly addressed the statute, it could but did not have to take into account the moral question of cruelty (see also *R (Khatum) v Newham London BC* (2004)).

In order to decide what factors are relevant, the starting point as always is the language of the particular statute. For example in *R v City of Westminster Housing Benefit Review Board* (2001), legislation required the housing benefit authority to reduce a claim when it considered that the rent was unreasonably high, 'having regard in particular to the cost of suitable accommodation elsewhere'. The board interpreted this as preventing it from taking into account the claimant's personal circumstances, including his wife's pregnancy and his reduced income as an asylum seeker. The House of Lords held that personal circumstances were relevant pointing out that the phrase 'in particular' invited other factors to be considered. Lord Bingham said that '(i)n the absence of very clear language I would be very reluctant to conclude that the board were precluded from considering matters which could affect the mind of a reasonable and fair minded person'.

It would also be relevant to take into account government advisory circulars related to the subject matter of the decision and the submissions of people affected by the decision. However, this does not mean that the decision maker must give any particular weight to a given matter or opinion. Subject to an overriding requirement to act 'reasonably' (below) and to special considerations where the Human Rights Act 1998 applies (Chapter 17), the decision maker can choose which to prefer, provided that a relevant consideration is not completely ignored. For example in *Tesco Stores* v *Secretary of State for the Environment* (1995) the House of Lords held that a planning authority could give 'nil' weight to an offer from Tesco to contribute to the building of a new road in the area in return for planning permission.

It is for the claimant to establish that irrelevant considerations have been taken into account and the failure of a minister to justify a decision is not in itself evidence of this. In deciding what factors are relevant, the court can look at background evidence, for example official reports which influenced the legislation in question, and also things said in Parliament (*Brind v Secretary of State* (1991)). However, statements made in Parliament cannot be used as evidence that a minister has acted improperly in relation to a decision made outside Parliament since this would violate the protection given to parliamentary proceedings by Art. 9 of the Bill of Rights 1688 (Chapter 9) (see *R* v *Secretary of State for Trade ex parte Anderson Strathclyde Ltd* [1983] 2 All ER 233, 238–9). An unequivocal statement as to the scope of a provision might however be binding (*R* v *Secretary of State for the Environment, Transport and the Regions ex parte Spath Homes* (2001)).

The relevant consideration doctrine can therefore be used to protect important interests. In *R (Bulger)* v *Secretary of State* (2001), the court, drawing on international obligations, held that in fixing the length of time a convicted child offender must serve, the Secretary of State must take into account the welfare of the child and keep its progress and rehabilitation under review. In *R* v *Secretary of State for the Home Department ex parte Venables* (1997) it was held that public opinion, in the shape of an opinion poll in the *Sun* newspaper, was not relevant where the Secretary of State was charged with the judicial duty of reviewing the sentence in a notorious child murderer case, since his judicial function must be exercised by his independent judgement. The courts have also held that local authorities should concern themselves with local issues as opposed to general issues of national or international politics (see *R* v *ILEA ex parte Westminster City Council* (1986); *R* v *Lewisham LBC ex parte Shell UK Ltd* (above)).

The courts are therefore policing the boundaries of the democratic process. In earlier cases, the courts appeared to be restricting the powers of local authorities in order to compel them to conserve the taxpayers' money by adopting 'business principles' in fixing wages, fares and prices at the expense of local democratic freedom (*Roberts* v *Hopwood* (1925); *Prescott* v *Birmingham Corporation* (1955); *Bromley LBC* v *GLC* (1983)). However, it has also been stressed that the scope of what is relevant should be responsive to changing community values (see *Pickwell* v *Camden BC* (1983)).

In *R* v *Secretary of State for Foreign and Commonwealth Affairs ex parte World Development Movement* (1995) the court perhaps went too far into the merits of government action. The government had statutory power to give financial aid to other countries for 'economic' purposes. It decided to give a grant to Malaysia for the Pergau Dam project. The Court of Appeal held that Parliament must have intended the word 'economic' to include only 'sound' economic decisions so that the court was entitled to infer that the decision had been made primarily for an ulterior purpose (perhaps of facilitating an arms sale arrangement). This seems to come very near to interfering with the merits of the decision since the court could deepen its investigation into any statutory function by saying that Parliament must have intended that function to be carried out 'soundly'. On the other hand, parliamentary scrutiny of public spending did not expose the misdeeds in this case so that the court's role may be justifiable as the only available constitutional check.

## 14.8 Fettering Discretion

Officials fetter their discretion by binding themselves, for example by a rigid rule, to make a particular decision without being prepared to consider departing from the rule in an individual case. This is unlawful and could be considered as an example of a failure to take all relevant factors into account (*R v Port of London Authority ex parte Kynoch* (1919)). Officials are of course bound by rules contained in legislation but where legislation gives them a discretion as to how to decide a particular case they must consider the case on its merits. An official can be influenced by general rules or policies drawn up within the government as a guide to decision making. Indeed it would be unlawful to ignore such guidance, provided of course that its content was relevant. Indeed government would be impracticable without them. Moreover, the principle of fairness requires that people be treated equally, thereby requiring general guidelines.

Nevertheless, unless a rule is laid down by or under statute, officials must always keep an open mind by considering whether in any given case an exception should be made. This is a vital protection for the individual against official intransigence. As Lord Reid put it in *British Oxygen Co. v Ministry of Technology* [1971] AC 610, 625:

> a Ministry or large authority may have had already to deal with a multitude of similar applications and then they will almost certainly have evolved a policy so precise that it could well be called a rule. There can be no objection to that, provided that the authority is always willing to listen to anyone with something new to say.

For example in *R v Secretary of State for the Home Department ex parte Hindley* (2000), a 'whole life tariff' set by the Home Secretary for a convicted murderer was lawful, provided that it was open to periodic review. On the other hand, the courts are not normally concerned with the weight to be given to any particular factor so that, short of tying their hands completely, officials can give preference to policies or rules, departing from them only in exceptional cases. Examples of unlawful fetters include the following:

▶ Rigid application of government policies or party political policies without making an independent judgement (*R* v *Waltham Forest LBC ex parte Baxter* (1988); *R* v *Local Commissioner for Administration ex parte Liverpool City Council* (2001)).

▶ Electoral mandates (*Bromley LBC* v *GLC* (1983)). Agreements and contracts that contradict a statutory obligation (*Ayr Harbour Trustees* v *Oswald* (1883); *Stringer* v *Minister of Housing* (1971); compare *R* v *Hammersmith and Fulham LBC ex parte Beddowes* (1987)).

▶ Advice given by officials (*Western Fish Products* v *Penwith District Council* (1981)); thus the doctrine of estoppel, under which in certain circumstances a person is bound by a promise or statement on which another relies, does not apply to governmental decisions made under statute.

▶ Acting under the dictation of another body (*Lavender* v *Minister of Housing* (1970)) but consulting another body and even relying on the decision of another body unless an objection is raised is lawful (see *R* v *GLC ex parte Blackburn* (1976)).

### 14.8.1 Legitimate Expectations and Fettering Discretion

By ensuring that the decision maker takes all relevant factors into account, the fettering discretion doctrine sometimes protects the citizen. However, it also protects the general public interest by allowing a public body to override promises or assurances that it has given to a citizen. This may be unjust to the citizen so that law creates a dilemma. The concept of 'legitimate expectation' confronts this dilemma. First recognised by Lord Denning in *Schmidt* v *Secretary of State for Home Affairs* (1969), a legitimate expectation arises where the citizen has been led to believe by a statement or other conduct of the government that he is singled out for some benefit or advantage of which it would be unfair to deprive him. The expectation might be generated by a promise or assurance either announced generally (*A-G for Hong Kong* v *Ng Yuen Shiu* (1983): letter stating interview would be given before deportation); *R* v *Secretary of State for the Home Department ex parte Khan* (1985): Home Office circular stated that adoptions of children from abroad would be allowed in certain circumstances), or given specifically to an individual (*Preston* v *IRC* (1985): letter concerning tax affairs).

A legitimate expectation must single out the claimant or a group of which the claimant is a member. It usually depends on a particular statement or promise and cannot be inferred merely from the general context, (*Re Westminster City Council* (1986)) nor from unofficial statements such as election address or media interviews. However, a legitimate expectation might be generated by a practice whereby people in the same position as the applicant have been given a benefit in the past (*CCSU v Minister for the Civil Service* (1985). There is apparently no legitimate expectation that the government will honour an international treaty obligation (*R v DPP ex parte Kebeline* (1999)). Although Art. 9 of the Bill of Rights 1688 prevents the courts from holding a minister liable for anything said in Parliament, a statement made in Parliament might be used as evidence in judicial review proceedings and might even create a legitimate expectation (see *Wilson v First County Trust* [2003] 4 All ER 97 [140].

In *R v North Devon Health Authority ex parte Coughlan* (2000), Lord Woolf took the view that an enforceable legitimate expectation should be confined to one or a few people. This relates to the issue of equality. Where the undertaking in question is given to particular individuals, there is a strong argument that these deserve special consideration. However, an expectation is often generated by a general policy announced in a circular, or a general practice. It is arguable that, where the claimant relies on an announcement or practice directed to the public at large, the claimant must show that s/he has acted on the expectation so as to incur expense or other detriment (see *R v Jockey Club ex parte RAM Racecourses* [1993] 2 All ER 225 at 236–240); *R v Secretary of State for Education ex parte Begbie* (2000); contrast *R v Minister of Agriculture ex parte Hamble Fisheries* (1995).

The statement that gives rise to the expectation must be clear and unambiguous and it must be reasonable for the claimant to rely upon it (see *Preston v IRC* (above)). Furthermore, where an assurance is given to an individual, the individual must have disclosed all relevant information (*R v IRC ex parte MFK Underwriting* (1990). Moreover, where the individual is relying on a general government policy, the statutory context might exclude a legitimate expectation (e.g. *Findlay v Secretary of State for the Home Department* (1985), parole policy, *Begbie* (above): admission to school).

What is the legal effect of a legitimate expectation? The expectation confers a heightened claim to the benefit in question but not an absolute right (*O'Reilly v Mackman* (1982)). Sometimes, as in *Shiu*, and *CCSU* (above), the expectation itself may be to have a fair procedure, such as being consulted or given a hearing before a decision is made. In other cases it may be substantive, that is to an actual benefit or permission. However, even a substantive expectation cannot bind the decision maker absolutely to honour it since this would result in an unlawful fettering of discretion and frustrate the democratic will of Parliament. The courts have therefore come to an unstable compromise between these competing concerns.

Firstly, unless it relates to a matter outside the statutory power in question, a legitimate expectation of some benefit is a relevant consideration which must be taken into account in making a decision (*R (Theophilus)* v *Lewisham BC* (2002): student grant to study abroad). Secondly, a legitimate expectation will entitle the claimant to a fair hearing and reasons to be given before the benefit is refused or withdrawn (*R* v *Secretary of State for Health ex parte United States Tobacco International Inc.* (1992)). Thirdly and more controversially, it may be that the government must honour the expectation unless this would frustrate the purpose of a statute or cause serious public harm. This would be an exception to the general principle mentioned earlier that the courts cannot interfere with the weight which the decision maker gives to the various factors to be taken into account.

In *Khan* (above) where the government stated by letter that certain policies concerning overseas adoptions would be followed, Lord Parker CJ suggested that

> vis-a-vis the recipient of such a letter, a new policy can only be implemented after such recipient has been given a full and serious consideration whether there is some overriding public interest which justifies a departure from the procedures stated in the letter. (at 48)

This is ambiguous. On the one hand, even where the expectation is substantive, the claimant might be entitled only to a hearing. Apart from this, the court would intervene only if the government could offer no rational reason for its change of policy. On the other hand, it might require the government not merely to provide a reason for changing its policy but to advance a strong justification for doing so.

The cases are conflicting. The possibility of a substantive legitimate expectation was accepted in *R* v *Secretary of State for the Home Department ex parte Ruddock* (1987) where it was held that the minister had in fact complied with the expectation. It was however rejected in *R* v *Secretary of State for Health ex parte United States Tobacco International Inc.* (above). In that case the government had encouraged the company to manufacture snuff in the UK. After the company had incurred expense on its investment the government withdrew its permission on medical advice. It was held that any legitimate expectation could not override the government's statutory power. However, the company was entitled to a hearing on the health issue and an opportunity to persuade the government to change its mind.

On the other hand, in *R* v *Minister of Agriculture ex parte Hamble Fisheries* (1995), Sedley J gave stronger effect to a substantive legitimate expectation. This concerned a claim to retain the benefit of a fishing licence in the face of a change in a policy designed to conserve fishing stocks. Sedley J suggested that a legitimate expectation creates a binding obligation that could only be overridden if the objectives of the statute could not otherwise be achieved, a matter to be assessed by the court. However, in *R* v *Secretary of State for the Home Department ex parte Hargreaves* (1997), the Court of Appeal condemned the 'heretical' doctrine of Sedley J, holding that a legitimate expectation did not prevent a change of policy being no more than a factor which the decision maker should take into account.

Nevertheless in *R v North Devon Health Authority ex parte Coughlan* (2000), the Court of Appeal held that a severely disabled resident of a local authority nursing home could hold the local authority to a previous assurance that it would be her home for life. The authority proposed to close the home in order to transfer nursing care to the local authority. The Court of Appeal held that the assurance created an enforceable legitimate expectation which only an overriding public interest could displace. The scope of this is not clear. In particular the right to respect for home and family life (European Convention on Human Rights Art. 8) was in issue, thereby raising the threshold of review. Moreover, although the decision to close the home had financial consequences for the authority, it was not the application of a government policy. In *R v Secretary of State for Education ex parte Begbie* (above) the Court of Appeal attempted a compromise based upon identifying circumstances where it would be 'an abuse of power' to overide an expectation. In particular the court should not interfere where the matter raised issues in the 'macro political field' which affected large numbers of people.

The legitimate expectation debate therefore sets the individual claim to respect against the majoritarian public good. The law cannot combine these goods and so reaches an untidy accommodation usually by offering the individual a hearing which might persuade the authority to change its mind. Another compromise solution would be to pay compensation to the victim. Unfortunately there is no right to compensation in UK law for unlawful administrative action as such.

## 14.9 Duty and Discretion

The converse problem to that of fettering discretion sometimes arises. This is where an authority claims to have a discretion when the statute itself appears to impose an absolute duty. It arises most frequently when a local authority fails to provide a benefit, for example a welfare payment, medical treatment or housing, on the ground that it does not have sufficient resources and must prioritise between different kinds of need. If the court were to order the authority to perform the duty, the rule of law would be asserted and political pressure put on the government to come up with the necessary resources. There may also be inequity where different standards are applied in different local areas. On the other hand, the court cannot command the impossible. Moreover, the imposition of a duty inhibits democratic choice. Different priorities between areas reflect the workings of democracy. Thus in *Southwark LBC* v *Tanner* [2001] 1 AC 1, 9, 10, Lord Hoffmann warned against judicial intervention in

a field which is so very much a matter for the allocation of resources in accordance with democratically determined priorities.

The courts are required to interpret the statute in order to determine whether the duty is intended to be absolute (mandatory) or permissive. Words such as 'shall' or 'may' are indicative but not conclusive and the whole statutory context must be examined. For example in *R (G)* v *Barnet LBC* (2004), the House of Lords held that the duty imposed on local authorities by the Children Act 1989 to safeguard and promote the welfare of children in need, provide only broad aims which the authority should bear in mind. This is sometimes labelled a 'target duty' reflecting the fact that all needs cannot realistically be met in full. The Act therefore gave the authority a discretion to choose between competing demands and to take cost into account. The court will interfere only if the discretion is exercised unreasonably (Chapter 15). The majority also held that the duty was not enforceable as such by individuals. (See also *R* v *Gloucestershire County Council ex parte Barry* (1997); *R* v *East Sussex CC ex parte Tandy* (1998); *R* v *Sefton MBC ex parte Help the Aged* (1997); *R* v *Newham London Borough Council ex parte Begum* (2000) Palmer (2000) *Oxford Journal of Legal Studies* **20**: 63).

# Summary

▷ Judicial review is constitutionally ambivalent. On the one hand, it supports the rule of law, parliamentary supremacy and democracy by enabling the courts to police the limits of government power. On the other hand, the courts are open to the complaint based on the separation of powers that they are interfering with the decisions of democratically elected bodies. The basis of this complaint is that the courts interpret the legislation in question in the light of their own values and presumptions of interpretation which are not necessarily democratic.

▷ Judicial review is not concerned with the merits of a government decision but whether the decision maker has kept within legal limits and followed broad principles of fairness and rationality. The grounds of judicial review are loosely classified under the heads of illegality, irrationality and procedural impropriety. This chapter concerns illegality which includes *ultra vires* in a narrow sense, errors of law, taking irrelevant considerations into account or failing to take relevant considerations into account and fettering discretion.

▷ The constitutional basis of judicial review is contested. According to one view it depends on the *ultra vires* doctrine. The alternative view is that judicial review is a freestanding part of the common law but subject to parliamentary supremacy. Proponents of the *ultra vires* doctrine cater for the fact that much of the law is actually judge-made by claiming that Parliament intends legislation to be interpreted according to principles of the rule of law.

▶ Review for mistakes of fact is limited since this might involve a reviewing court going outside its proper sphere. Clear errors of fact may be reviewable and an error of fact might also fall within one of the other grounds, e.g. irrationality (Chapter 15). The interpretation of broad subjective terms in a statute may be classified as mixed questions of law and fact to limit review. Limitations on review for mistakes of fact may raise the question of the right to a fair trial under the European Convention on Human Rights.

▶ Fettering discretion concerns the application of a self-created rigid rule, policy or undertaking etc. in a case where, under a statute, the decision maker must exercise a discretion. A decision maker can adopt guidelines but cannot treat them as absolutely binding. The doctrine of 'legitimate expectation' attempts to deal with the injustice that may arise where a public official departs from an undertaking which the citizen believes to be binding. There is also an issue as to whether a statute confers a discretionary power or an absolute duty. Where a decision involves the use of scarce resources the courts may use the concept of a 'target duty' to allow the exercise of discretion.

# Exercises

**14.1** 'The simple proposition that a public authority may not act outside its powers (*ultra vires*) might fitly be called the central principle of administrative law', Wade and Forsythe, *Administrative Law*. Discuss.

**14.2** Critically discuss the relationship between judicial review and (a) parliamentary supremacy; (b) the separation of powers.

**14.3** Explain the significance of legitimate expectations in relation to the rule against fettering discretion.

**14.4** To what extent does the *ultra vires* doctrine permit the courts to assess government action on the basis of their own political views.

**14.5** Under the Sports Act 2002 (fictitious), the Minister of Sport has power, 'where he considers it necessary in the interest of public safety and good order, to require the admission of paid spectators to any sporting event to be subject to showing membership cards at the entrance'. The Minister also has power to revoke any such membership cards. The Minister, interpreting 'sport' as including any activity which is competitive, has made an order requiring entrance to chess competitions to be subject to the showing of membership cards. There has been some evidence of disorder at the events. The Minister has been advised that chess events are an important source of the opposition party's finances. In another case, a civil servant has revoked the membership cards of all the members of a football club because the club has failed to provide an all-seating stadium. The club is in the third division and the present stadium is very rarely more than half full. Discuss.

14.6 Under the Lifestyle of the Community Act 2004 (imaginary), local authorities 'shall ensure that landlords within their areas provide essential services to premises occupied as residences by their tenants'. Tenants who are dissatisfied with action taken by their local authority may apply for an internal review carried out by one of the authority's senior staff. A, who has a tenancy of a bed-sitting room in a house owned by B complains to the local authority that the television set in his room provided by B does not work properly. The authority rules that A is not a tenant but only a lodger and that repairing a TV is not 'essential'. It also maintains that it does not have the sufficient financial resources to enforce claims of this kind since all its available money is allocated for the renovation of run-down houses. A applies for an internal review. This upholds the original decision. Advise A as to any legal rights he might have against the local authority.

## Further reading

Allan, T. (2003) 'Constitutional Dialogue and the Justification for Judicial Review', *Oxford Journal of Legal Studies*, **23**: 129.

Barber, N. (2001) 'The Academic Mythologians', *Oxford Journal of Legal Studies*, **21**: 369.

Craig, P. (1992) 'Legitimate Expectations: a Conceptual Analysis', *Law Quarterly Review*, 79.

Craig, P. (2004) 'The Common Law, Shared Power and Judicial Review', *Oxford Journal of Legal Studies*, **24**: 237.

Craig, P. and Bamforth, N. (2001) 'Constitutional principle, Constitutional Analysis and Judicial Review', *Public Law*, 763.

Endicott, T. (1994) 'Questions of Law', *Law Quarterly Review*, **114**: 292.

Forsythe, C. (1996) 'Of Fig Leaves and Fairy Tales: the Ultra Vires Doctrine, the Sovereignty of Parliament and Judicial Review', *Cambridge Law Journal*, **55**: 122.

Forsythe, C. (ed.) (2000) *Judicial review and the Constitution*, Oxford, Hart Publishing (includes some articles cited here).

Forsythe, C. and Elliot, M. (2003) 'The Legitimacy of Judicial Review', *Public Law*, 286.

Halpin, A. (2001) 'The Theoretical Controversy Concerning Judicial Review', *Modern Law Review*, **64**: 500.

Hare, I. (1998) 'Separation of Powers and Error of Law', In Forsythe, C. and Hare, I. (eds) *The Golden Metwand and the Crooked Cord*, Oxford, Clarendon Press.

Jowell, J. (1999) 'Of Vires and Vacuums: the Constitutional Context of Judicial Review', *Public Law*, 448.

**Further reading cont'd**

Laws, Sir J. (1995) 'Law and Democracy', *Public Law*, 72.

Oliver, D. (1998) 'A Negative Aspect to Legitimate Expectations', *Public Law*, 558.

Sales, P. and Steyn, A. (2004) 'Legitimate Expectations in English Public Law: An Analysis', *Public Law*, 564.

Woodhouse, D. (1995) 'Politicians and the Judiciary: a Changing Relationship', *Parliamentary Affairs*, 401.

Woolf, Lord (1998) 'Judicial Review: The Tensions Between the Executive and the Judiciary', *Law Quarterly Review*, **114**: 579.

# Chapter 15

# Judicial review: Grounds of review, II: Beyond *ultra vires*

## Key words

▶ Procedures and outcomes
▶ Varying intensity of review
▶ The appearance and the reality of justice
▶ Minimum levels of protection

This chapter continues the discussion in Chapter 14 but concentrates on grounds of review that are less directly linked to the notion of ultra vires and which therefore raise issues of the proper limits of the courts' role.

## 15.1 Irrationality/Unreasonableness

Irrationality or 'unreasonableness' is an overriding ground of review which applies to all government decisions. It can be used to challenge the exercise of discretion or findings of law and fact. Although the question of what is reasonable must, as always, be decided in the context of the particular statutory power, this ground of review operates as an external control in that it draws on values not directly derived from the statute itself. Indeed, the notion of 'unreasonableness' is so vague that it seems to invite the court to impose its own opinion of the merits for that of the decision maker.

In order to avoid appearing to violate the separation of powers, the courts have struggled to give the notion of unreasonableness a limited meaning. The main result has been to create a multi-level approach in which the intensity of judicial scrutiny varies with the context, the main factors being the seriousness of the decision in relation to the rights of the individual and, pulling in the other direction, the extent to which the decision maker's powers involve controversial social, economic, political or moral judgements.

The starting point and base line is usually called '*Wednesbury* unreasonableness' after Lord Greene's speech in *Associated Provincial Picture Houses Ltd* v *Wednesbury Corporation* (1948). Lord Greene MR emphasised that the court will interfere only where a decision is so unreasonable that no reasonable authority could have made it, not merely because it thinks it is a bad decision. Another way of putting it is that the decision must be 'beyond the range of responses open to a reasonable decision maker' (*R* v *Ministry of Defence ex parte Smith* [1996] 1 All ER 257 at 263; see also *R* v *Chief Constable of Sussex ex parte International Traders Ferry Ltd* [1999] 1 All ER 129 at 157). In *CCSU* v *Council of Civil Service Unions* [1984] 3 All ER 935 at 951, Lord Diplock said that the courts will interfere only where a decision has no rational basis or 'is so outrageous in its denial of accepted moral standards that no sensible person who has applied his mind to the question to be decided could have arrived at it'.

Lord Diplock's test is often used to justify not interfering with a decision. For example in *Brind* v *Secretary of State for the Home Department* (1991), the government banned live media interviews with supporters of the IRA. The House of Lords held that, although the ban was probably misguided, it had some rational basis as a means of denying publicity to terrorists and was therefore valid (see also *R* v *Radio Authority ex parte Bull* [1997] 2 All ER 561, 577). On the other hand, although successful challenges for unreasonableness are rare, they seem to fall short of irrationality. For example in *Hall* v *Shoreham Urban District Council* (1964), a local authority planning condition required the plaintiff to dedicate a road to the public. This was held to be 'unreasonable' because it amounted to the confiscation of property without compensation. However, the condition was hardly perverse or irrational given that the plaintiff stood to make considerable profit out of the permission.

A more flexible approach to unreasonableness is to ask whether a reasonable decision maker in the light of the material properly before him could reasonably justify his decision. This enables the court to apply different levels of scrutiny in different contexts, what Laws LJ in *R (Mahmood)* v *Secretary of State* called a sliding scale: 'the graver the impact of the decision upon the individual the more substantial the justification that will be required'. This approach therefore requires the court to consider the weight given to the relevant factors It is sometimes called 'heightened scrutiny' or 'heightened *Wednesbury*'. Its main effect seems to require the decision maker to show that it has placed particularly close attention – 'anxious scrutiny' – to the interests of the individual in question (see *Bugdaycay* v *Secretary of State* [1987] 1 All ER 940, 952; *R* v *Ministry of Defence ex parte Smith* (above); *R* v *Lord Saville* (1999)).

Heightened *Wednesbury* in itself gives little guidance as to when the court will intervene. For example in *R* v *Ministry of Defence ex parte Smith* (above), the Court of Appeal refused to interfere with a decision to ban practising homosexuals from serving in the army. The court recognised that the decision affected fundamental rights of the individual and therefore called for 'anxious scrutiny' but also thought that the court was not in a position to assess the specialist needs of military service and should therefore defer to the views of the military establishment. The decision of the UK courts was later held to violate the European Convention on Human Rights (below). Perhaps Lord Diplock's reference (above) to widely shared moral values provides the best guide and links with the rule of law ideas discussed in Chapter 5.

At the other end of the scale, where a decision depends on social, economic or political factors or matters 'remote from ordinary judicial experience', the court should, as a matter of practical reality, be cautious in interfering. In cases of this kind, where human rights interests are not at issue, the courts may revert to Lord Diplock's basic rationality test, interfering only where a decision is entirely capricious – an approach sometimes called 'super-Wednesbury' (e.g. *Nottinghamshire CC v Secretary of State for the Environment* (1986); *Hammersmith and Fulham LBC v Secretary of State for the Environment*(1990): central grants to local government. National security cases are also subject to a low level of review (see Chapter 19).

Unreasonableness may overlap with other grounds of review. In *Wheeler v Leicester City Council* (1985), a local authority refused to allow a rugby club to use its playing field. This was because the club had not prevented certain of its members from touring in South Africa during the apartheid era. The House of Lords held that the council had acted unlawfully. This could be regarded as an unreasonable infringement of individual freedom, or as a decision based upon an improper political purpose, or as an unfair decision in that the matter had been prejudged. Today *Wheeler* would probably be explained on human rights grounds, a perspective which was raised in the Court of Appeal but which the House of Lords avoided.

### 15.1.1 Proportionality

In cases subject to the Human Rights Act 1998 (Chapter 17), a more stringent standard of review applies in the form of the doctrine of 'proportionality', familiar in many European countries and under different labels eg. 'hard look', 'strict scrutiny' in North American law. It also applies in EC law. Broadly speaking a decision is proportionate only if it meets an important public goal (a 'pressing social need') and in doing so violates the right in question as little as possible. As Lord Diplock rather ponderously put it in *R v Goldsmith* [1983] 1 WLR 151 at 155, proportionality 'prohibits the use of a steam hammer to crack a nut if a nutcracker would do.'

The requirements of proportionality provided by the Privy Council in *De Freitas v Ministry of Agriculture* (1999) have been widely adopted. Whether:

(i)     The legislative objective is sufficiently important to justify limiting a fundamental right. It is a difficult question as to whether the court or an elected body should decide this but under the Human Rights

Act, unless the language of the statute makes it impossible to interpret it other than as violating the right, the court has the last word (Chapter 17).

(ii) The measures designed to meet the legislative object are rationally connected with it.

(iii) The means used to impair the right or freedom are no more than is necessary to accomplish the objective. An important matter would be for example whether there are alternative safeguards for the right in question.

Proportionality therefore requires the court to assess the weight of competing factors (see Lord Steyn in *R v Secretary of State for the Home Department ex parte Daly* [2001] 3 All ER 433 [27]. Before the new climate of opinion generated by the Human Rights Act 1998, English judges had objected to proportionality on the ground that it takes the court too far into the political merits (see *Hone v Maze Prison Visitors* [1988] 1 All ER 321 at 327–9; *Brind v Secretary of State for the Home Department* (1991); *Tesco Stores v Secretary of State for the Environment* (1995); *R v Chief Constable North Wales Police ex parte AB* (1998)). Therefore English law has sometimes fallen foul of the ECHR because it has failed to reach the standard of necessity required by the proportionality doctrine. For example *Smith* (above) was condemned by the European Court of Human Rights in *Smith and Grady v UK* (2000). It was held that the *Wednesbury* threshold of unreasonableness was too high to satisfy the European Convention because it excluded any consideration of whether the interference with the applicant's rights answered a pressing social need or was proportionate to the national security and public order aims pursued.

A recent illustration of proportionality is *R (Roberts) v Parole Board* (2004). A prisoner serving a mandatory life sentence applied for parole. The Parole Board refused to give his lawyer certain information provided by an informer concerning drug dealing but instead appointed a 'Special Council' who had no contact with the prisoner to represent the prisoner's interest in relation to this evidence. The reason for so doing was that the informer feared for his safety if his identity became known. It was held that the decision to appoint the Special Council was proportionate. The informer's fears were based on objective grounds, there was a strong public interest in protecting the source of evidence, the prisoner's interests were safeguarded by the court and there was no other way of protecting the source.

It has been suggested that proportionality should apply beyond Human Rights Act cases and should be considered as an aspect of the unreasonableness principle applicable to cases where important rights are in issue and also perhaps in cases involving legitimate expectations (above).

In *Smith* (above) proportionality and *Wednesbury* produced different outcomes. In many cases, the two are likely to produce the same outcome. For example in *R* v *Barnsley Borough Council ex parte Hook* (1976), a market trader was dismissed by the market manager for the relatively minor wrong of urinating in the street. This was held to be an unreasonably severe penalty.

*R* v *Secretary of State ex parte Daly* (2001) provided a useful discussion of the matter. It was government policy that a prisoner's confidential correspondence with his lawyer could be examined in the prisoner's absence in order to ascertain that it was genuine. The House of Lords held that, although the policy satisfied the bare rationality test, it was contrary to Art. 8 of the European Convention on Human Rights (respect for correspondence). A reasonable minister could not have concluded that the policy was necessary for the legitimate goal of keeping order in prisons. The House emphasised that the court must 'anxiously scrutinise' the decision to ensure that the minister gave proper weight to the right at stake. Lord Bingham based his reasoning firstly on the common law, heightened *Wednesbury* approach that there was no reasonable justification for the policy. However, he also said that, under the Human Rights Act, 'domestic courts must go beyond the ordinary standard and themselves form a judgement whether a convention right has been breached, conducting such an inquiry as is necessary to form that judgement' ([2001] 3 All ER at 455).

Lord Cooke [32] went beyond the human rights context. He described the *Wednesbury* case as 'an unfortunately retrogressive decision in English administrative law, in so far as it suggested that only a very extreme degree (of unreasonableness) can bring an administrative decision within the scope of judicial invalidation'. He emphasised that the level of interference should vary with the subject matter. 'It may well be, however, that the law can never be satisfied in any administrative field merely by a finding the decision under review is not capricious or absurd.'

In *R (Alconbury)* v *Secretary of State* [2001] 2 All ER 929 at 976 Lord Slynn stated that proportionality was different from *Wednesbury* but emphasised that 'the difference in practice is not as great as is sometimes supposed'. He thought that proportionality and *Wednesbury* should not be kept in separate compartments and that 'even without reference to the 1998 Act the time has come to recognise that this principle is part of English Administrative law, not only in when judges are dealing with community acts but also when they are dealing with acts subject to domestic law.' (See also *Council of Civil Service Unions* v *Minister for the Civil Service* [1984] 3 All ER 935 at 950 per Lord Diplock; *R (Association of British Civilian Internees; Far East Region* v *Secretary of State* [2003] QB 1397 [35]: suggesting *Wednesbury* be replaced by proportionality.)

However, even in a proportionality case involving human rights, the court will sometimes give a wide 'margin of discretion' to the government. This applies to matters regarded as unsuitable for judges to evaluate either because the courts lack the relevant knowledge or because they raise controversial political issues or because they raise wide issues which the legal process cannot handle. Such matters include security, social and economic policy, the allocation of public money and issues of public taste (see Chapter 14). Even here the court will require the decision maker to provide some objective justification, although this might be minimal.

> When anxiously scrutinising an executive decision that interferes with human rights the court will ask the question, applying an objective test, whether the decision maker could reasonably have concluded that the interference was necessary to achieve one or more of the legitimate aims recognised by the Convention (per Lord Phillips MR in *R (Mahmood)* v *Secretary of State* (2001) [32].

Proportionality and the margin of discretion will be discussed further in Chapter 17.

## 15.2 Procedural Impropriety

### 15.2.1 Statutory Procedural Requirements

This topic illustrates the elastic nature of contemporary judicial review. Failure to comply with a procedural requirement laid down by statute (such as time limits, consultation or giving required information or notice) could make a decision *ultra vires* and so void. However, the courts are reluctant to set aside a decision on purely technical grounds. Traditionally the courts have tried to rationalise this by distinguishing between 'mandatory' (important) and 'directory' (unimportant) procedural requirements by reference to the language of the governing statute. Recently they have modified this approach in favour of a flexible response to the particular context. Using their discretionary power to withhold a remedy, the courts will set a decision aside for procedural irregularity only if the harm or injustice caused to the applicant by the procedural flaw outweighs the inconvenience to the government or to innocent third parties in setting the decision aside (see e.g. *Coney* v *Choyce* (1975); *London and Clydesdale Estates Ltd* v *Aberdeen District Council* (1979); *R* v *Immigration Appeal Tribunal ex parte Jeyeanthan* (1999)).

However the courts may not allow administrative efficiency to override a statutory right of the public to be consulted. In *Berkeley* v *Secretary of State for the Environment* (2000), the House of Lords held that a local authority was required to make environmental information relating to a planning application for a football stadium available to the public even though the council successfully argued that it already had adequate environmental evidence to enable it to make a proper decision. Lord Hoffman in particular, reflecting the broad concept of democracy, suggested that public consultation was an end in itself and not merely an instrument of effective decision making.

Another important statutory procedural requirement is the rule against delegation. An official (or indeed anyone) who is entrusted with power to make a decision should not in principle transfer that power to someone else (*delegatus non potest delegare*). Applying this principle strictly would cause administrative breakdown and many exceptions have been made. Its only strict application is to courts and other judicial tribunals who adjudicate upon disputes relating to legal rights (*Barnard* v *National Dock Labour Board* (1953)).

Exceptions to the rule against delegation are as follows:

▶ The *Carltona* doctrine that a minister can act through a civil servant in his department (Chapter 13). This can be rationalised as not a true exception in that constitutionally the minister and civil servant are one (see *R (Alconbury)* v *Secretary of State* (2001)).

▶ Many local authority functions can be delegated by statute to committees, sub-committees, officers and other authorities but not to individual councillors or to outside bodies unless authorised by statute (see Local Government Act 1972 s.101; *R* v *Port Talbot BC ex parte Jones* (1988)).

▶ Many governmental functions can be transferred to private bodies (Deregulation and Contracting Out Act 1994 ss. 61, 69).

▶ Functions involving little discretion can be delegated, and the courts seem ready to imply statutory authority to delegate in cases where it would be inconvenient for the decision maker to do everything himself (*Provident Mutual Life* v *Derby City Council* (1981); *Nelms* v *Roe* (1969)).

▶ Fact finding, making recommendations and giving advice can be delegated, but the decision maker must not merely 'rubber stamp' the advice he is given. He must have enough information before him, e.g. a summary of evidence, to make a genuine decision (*Jeffs* v *New Zealand Dairy Board* (1966)).

### 15.2.2 The Right to a Fair Hearing

This ground of review is of ancient common law origin and is central to the idea of the rule of law. Until the early twentieth century, the courts applied a broad principle, traceable to the seventeenth century and usually labelled 'natural justice', namely that anyone whose rights were affected by an official decision was entitled to advance notice of a decision and a fair hearing before an unbiased judge (e.g. *Bagg's Case* (1615), *Dr Bonham's Case* (1610), *Cooper* v *Wandsworth Board of Works* (1863)). The advance of the democratically supported administrative state produced a more cautious judicial approach. *Local Government Board* v *Arlidge* (1915) marks a turning point where Dicey felt that even the rule of law was at risk. In *Arlidge* the House of Lords held that, in the case of administrative decisions (in that case a house closure order), provided that it complies with minimum standards of fairness, the government can decide for itself what procedures to follow, the citizen's protection lying not in the courts but in ministerial responsibility to Parliament (see also *Board of Education* v *Rice* [1911] AC 179, 182, but contrast *Dyson* v *A-G* (1911).

The courts then refused to apply natural justice to decisions other than those which they labelled 'judicial'. For this purpose 'judicial' means the impartial application of rules to settle a dispute about the parties' existing rights, narrowly defined; essentially what a court does. Thus the courts took a crude separation of powers approach which excluded natural justice from political, discretionary and policy orientated decisions which the court labelled 'administrative'. This excluded much of the welfare state from natural justice since the conferring of benefits such as education and housing does not strictly affect existing rights. It also excluded government powers such as planning, compulsory purchase and other forms of licensing which, although they affect rights, are usually discretionary. The main area left for natural justice was where a formal tribunal or inquiry determined a specific dispute but even this caused problems in the case of public inquiries held as part of a larger discretionary process leading to a political decision, for example to build a new road (see e.g. *Franklin* v *Minister of Town and Country Planning* (1948)).

However, in *Ridge* v *Baldwin* (1964), a case which marks the beginning of the contemporary renaissance of judicial review, the House of Lords returned the law to its older rationale. The Chief Constable of Brighton had been dismissed by the local police authority without a hearing. The authority had statutory power to deprive him of his position for incapacity or misconduct but not otherwise. The House of Lords held that he was entitled to a hearing for two reasons: (i) he had been deprived of a public office; (ii) the power to dismiss was limited by statute so that the authority did not have a complete discretion. Lord Reid emphasised that, irrespective of whether it is judicial in the above sense, a government decision that causes serious harm to an individual ought in principle to attract the right to be heard.

Since *Ridge* v *Baldwin*, a right to a hearing is no longer limited to judicial functions. The courts have extended it into most areas of government, including for example prison management (*R* v *Hull Prison Visitors ex parte St Germain* (1979); *Leech* v *Parkhurst Prison Deputy Governor* (1988)). Although the expression natural justice is still sometimes used it has become interchangeable with 'fairness' (see *Re HK* (1967)). However, the concept of 'judicial' is still relevant since a judicial decision will certainly attract a right to a hearing and this may be of a higher procedural standard than in the case of an administrative decision (below).

The courts have introduced limits to the right to be heard. These are based on pragmatic factors and include the following:

▶ 'Fairness' concerns the protection of persons who are adversely affected by government action, and not the idea of democratic participation in government. Thus the right to be heard may not include access to policy information (see *Bushell* v *Secretary of State for the Environment* (1981); *Hammersmith and Fulham LBC* v *Secretary of State for the Environment* (1990)). Similarly, advisory or preliminary governmental decisions do not attract a right to be heard unless the decision has direct adverse consequences for the individual's rights (*Norwest Holst* v *Trade Secretary* [1978] Ch 201: decision to start an investigation, no right to be heard; compare *Furnell* v *Whangarie High Schools Board* [1973] AC 660: suspension of teacher pending investigation, hearing required).

▶ A judicial decision to remove existing legal rights usually attracts a hearing, but the refusal of a discretionary benefit in the public interest, where the claimant has no specific entitlement, may not (see *Schmidt* v *Secretary of State for Home Affairs* (1969): extension of immigration permit; *McInnes* v *Onslow-Fane* (1978): refusing a referee's licence; *Findlay* v *Secretary of State for the Home Department* (1985): parole, change in policy). However, a decision to refuse a benefit which can only be made on limited grounds or which involves accusations of misconduct or bad character, or which affects a right protected under the Human Rights Act 1998 will attract a hearing (see *R* v *Gaming Board ex parte Benaim and Khaida* (1970); *R* v *Secretary of State for the Home Department ex parte Fayed* (1997)).

▶ Other factors might override the right to a hearing. In particular, national security (*CCSU* v *Minister for the Civil Service* (1985)). The need to act in an emergency will also exclude at least a prior hearing (*R* v *Secretary of State for Transport ex parte Pegasus Holdings Ltd* (1989): air safety). A hearing might be excluded where a decision affects so many people that a hearing would be impracticable, or where large numbers compete for scarce resources, for example applications for university places, or in respect of general decisions such as school closures which do not concern the interests of the persons affected. On the other hand, where a policy decision, for example to close an old people's home, directly relates to the interests of the persons concerned, there may be a collective right to be consulted, although not necessarily a hearing in individual cases (see *R* v *Devon County Council ex parte Baker* (1995).

▶ A hearing may be excluded when the court thinks that the outcome of the decision was not affected, so that no injustice has been done. There have been judicial warnings against this which seem to violate the basic principle that the courts are concerned with legality, not merits. Indeed, one reason for a right to be heard is that we cannot be certain that justice is done unless we have heard all points of view (see *Ridge* v *Baldwin* (1964); *John* v *Rees* (1969); *R* v *Environment Secretary ex parte Brent LBC* [1983] 3 All ER 321 at 357; *Cheall* v *Apex* (1983)). However in *Cinnamond* v *British Airports Authority* (1980), a group of Heathrow airport taxi drivers who had been repeatedly warned about allegations of misconduct had their licences withdrawn without a hearing.

The same flexible concept of 'fairness' also determines the ingredients of a hearing. There are no fixed requirements. Subject to any statutory requirements, a decision maker can fix its own procedure provided that it is 'fair' in the circumstances of the particular case (see *Lloyd* v *McMahon* [1987] 1 All ER 1118 at 1161). The requirements of a fair hearing are therefore flexible and to this extent *Arlidge* (above) remains important. Perhaps the law has become too flexible, with the disadvantage that 'fairness' does not necessarily imply a definite right to a hearing. For example in *Calvin* v *Carr* (1980), the plaintiff, a racehorse trainer, was suspended from the course because of accusations of tampering. The Privy Council held that a combination of factors meant that he was not entitled to be heard. These included the need to act quickly to preserve the integrity of the sport, the fact that he could appeal when he would be given a full hearing, and the fact that he had agreed to the regulations under which the decision was made.

The following factors are particularly important:

▶ The more serious the consequences for the individual, the higher the standard of hearing that is required. To this extent the notion of a judicial decision (above) remains important. At one end of the scale, preliminary or advisory investigations at best entitle a person to be told only an outline of any accusations against him and to answer them (*Maxwell* v *Trade Department* (1974); *R* v *Commission for Racial Equality ex parte Cotterell and Rothon* (1980)). At the other end of the scale, a person accused of misconduct or whose rights are in issue is normally entitled to see all the evidence and to cross-examine witnesses (*R* v *Army Board ex parte Anderson* (1992)). Administrative convenience cannot justify refusing to permit a person to call witnesses although the tribunal does have a residual discretion in the matter (*R* v *Hull Prison Visitors ex parte St Germain (No. 2)* (1979)).

▶ Fairness is a *minimum* standard to be balanced against the government's right to decide its own procedure. An oral hearing is not necessarily required (*Lloyd* v *McMahon* (1987) and formal rules of evidence are not required, fairness demanding only that the evidence be relevant and that the parties have a chance to comment on it (*Mahon* v *Air New Zealand* (1984)). There is no automatic right to legal representation but the decision maker must not adopt an absolute rule on the matter and must allow representation where a person cannot effectively present his own case (*Hone* v *Maze Prison Visitors* (1988), cf. *Enderby Town Football Club* v *FA* (1971)). If an inquiry is held, as is the case with planning and other land use decisions, the decision maker cannot subsequently take new factual material into account without giving the parties an opportunity to comment (see *Elmbridge BC* v *Secretary of State for the Environment* (2002).

▶ Problems of unfairness might arise where an individual is confronted with those who claim special knowledge but are reluctant to have this challenged. An expert decision maker can rely on his own accumulated experience without having to disclose this to the parties. Expert assessors are sometimes used to help judges and other decision makers; these need not disclose their advice in advance. Where the judge disagrees with it, on an important matter he should give the parties a chance to comment (*Ahmed* v *Governing Body of Oxford University* (2003)).

▶ As we have seen, a legitimate expectation (Chapter 14) might confer a right to be heard. However, the courts will give effect to a legitimate expectation only where it would be fair in all the circumstances (*R* v *Liverpool City Council* (1974)). It is questionable whether the notion of legitimate expectation adds anything to the general concept of fairness.

### 15.2.3   The Bias Rule

The idea of an impartial and independent judge is a fundamental aspect of the rule of law. However, complete impartiality is impossible to realise since not only is bias inherent in human nature but many kinds of decision-making process inevitably involve conflicts of interest. In particular, politicians required by democracy to make decisions are likely be influenced by party political considerations. The law therefore has to compromise, and has done so by distinguishing between different kinds of decision and different kinds of bias.

The decision maker need not actually be biased – this would fall under the head of irrelevant considerations (Chapter 14). The bias rule is concerned with the risk or appearance of bias, hence the well-known dictum of Lord Hewart in *R* v *Sussex Justices ex parte McCarthy* [1924] 1 KB 256 at 259 that 'justice must not only be done but must manifestly and undoubtedly be seen to be done'. The rationale is not only that of fairness to the parties but also of public confidence in the integrity of the decision- making process. The main principles are as follows.

A direct personal financial interest, however small, will *automatically* disqualify the decision maker, the law conclusively presuming bias (*Dimes v Grand Junction Canal Co.* (1852): Lord Chancellor held shares in company appearing before him; *R v Hendon RDC ex parte Chorley* (1933): local councillor had financial interest in development for which planning permission was sought. See also *R v Camborne Justices ex parte Pearce* [1955] 1 QB 41 at 47). An exception is where no other decision maker is qualified to act, in which case Parliament must be taken to have impliedly authorised the bias (*Wilkinson v Barking Corporation* (1948); see also Supreme Court Act 1981 s.11: judges as taxpayers). Also an insignificant (*de minimis*) interest might be ignored (*Locobail (UK) Ltd v Bayfield Properties Co.* (2000).

In *R v Bow Street Magistrates Court ex parte Pinochet (No. 2)* (1999), the House of Lords extended automatic disqualification to a case where a judge is a member of an organisation that is party to the case even though there is no financial element. Lord Hoffman, a law lord, was an unpaid director of a charitable subsidiary of Amnesty International, a human rights pressure group, which was a party to an appeal concerning whether to extradite a former President of Chile to Spain to face charges of torture and genocide (see Chapter 5). *Pinochet* has been criticised on the ground that there is an important distinction between 'interest' where the judge stands to gain personally so that he is a judge in his own case and should automatically be disqualified, and 'favour' where the judge might prefer a particular outcome and where a more flexible approach may be appropriate (Olowofoyeku, 2000). Other common law jurisdictions have confined automatic disqualification to strictly financial interests (ibid.) and, bearing in mind that *Pinochet* was a case of especial political significance it is unlikely that its rationale will be extended (see *Locobail (UK) Ltd v Bayfield Properties Co.* (2000)).

In other cases a more flexible approach is taken. The courts have tried to find a form of words which, on the one hand, reflects the interest of public confidence in the impartiality of the decision maker, and on the other, blocks challenges for flimsy or ill-informed suspicions (see *Lawal v Northern Spirit* [2004] 1 All ER 187, [14]). The current formula asks whether in the view of a 'fair minded and informed observer' taken as knowing all the circumstances, there is a 'real possibility' or 'real danger' of bias (*Porter v Magill* (2002)).

This formula emerged from *R v Gough* (1993) which replaced two earlier tests (that often produced the same outcome). These were firstly a strict 'reasonable suspicion' test according to which any suspicious factor as it appeared to a reasonable hypothetical observer might disqualify the judge even though if all the circumstances were known the observer might be reassured; secondly, the more liberal 'real likelihood' test allowed the reviewing court to decide for itself whether in all the circumstances bias was likely. The *Gough* test compromised between the two. It did not include the device of the hypothetical outsider but nor did it require an overall balance, only a 'real danger' of bias. However, *Gough* seemed to be out of line with the European Convention on Human Rights and the practice in other English speaking countries (see Olowofoyeku, 2000). In particular under *Gough* the court might be too trusting of other decision makers, sharing the 'insider' view of public life.

The *Gough* test was therefore modified by *Medicaments and Related Classes of Goods (Re) (No. 2)* by introducing the standpoint of the imagined attitude of a hypothetical outsider. It is questionable whether this makes any difference since the outsider's opinion is made up by the court. Each case depends on its particular circumstances. For example in *Gough* (above) the accused's brother was a neighbour of a jury member who did not, however, recognise him. The jury was not disqualified. It was perhaps crucial that the accused had accepted the jury-person's explanation since, unlike the other grounds of review, bias can be waived by the claimant. In *Porter* v *Magill* (above), a local government auditor investigating allegations of bribery had made a provisional press announcement endorsing the allegations. His later formal report confirmed his findings. The House of Lords held that he was not disqualified since the reasonable observer could assume that an experienced professional was capable of being impartial. By contrast in *Medicaments* (above) a *lay* member of the Restrictive Practices Court was applying for a job with a firm one of whose members often appeared as an expert witness before the court. The Court of Appeal held that she was disqualified even though she had taken steps to minimise the conflict of interest.

In *Locobail (UK)* v *Bayfield Properties* (2000) the Court of Appeal attempted to give general guidance. It stressed that general objections based on religious, racial, ethnic or national characteristics, gender, age class, political views, membership of organisations, income, and sexual orientation would not normally disqualify and that there must be a more specific connection with the case. It disqualified a judge who had written polemical articles in legal journals attacking the practices of insurance companies in circumstances similar to those in a case before him.

In the culture of personal networking that applies in the UK, allegations of bias are characteristically met by claims that professional practices ensure integrity. For example in *Taylor* v *Lawrence* (2002), it was held that a judge was not disqualified where a solicitor appearing before him had recently transacted family business on his behalf. Lord Woolf remarked [61-64] that an informed observer can be expected to be aware of 'the legal traditions and culture of this jurisdiction' with the implication that this would be reassuring. However, *Lawal v Northern Spirit* (2004) suggests a less complacent approach. The claimant was appealing to the Employment Appeal tribunal in respect of an allegation of racial discrimination by his employer. The senior counsel for the employer had previously sat as a part- time judge with one of the lay members of the tribunal. The House of Lords held that the reasonable outsider might well suspect that the relationship could bias the lay member. Lord Steyn [22] warned against complacent assumptions of professional integrity pointing out that:

> the indispensable requirement of public confidence in the administration of justice required higher standards today than was the case even a decade or two ago. The informed observer of today could perhaps be expected to be aware of the legal traditions and culture of this jurisdiction ... But he might not be wholly uncritical of that culture.

Readers might apply the contemporary test to the following older cases in all of which the decision makers were disqualified; *R v Liverpool Justices ex parte Topping* (1983): justices had printout of the accused's previous convictions; *Metropolitan Properties v Lannon* (1968): rent tribunal chairman advised his father in a dispute with the same landlord; *Hannam v Bradford City Council* (1970): member of a local authority committee adjudicating on a teacher's dismissal was also a governor of the school in question – disqualified even though had absented himself from relevant governor's meeting; *R v Barnsley Borough Council ex parte Hook* (above): market trader dismissed by market manager who had also discovered the offence.

In the case of administrative decisions taken by politicians, conflicts of interest arising out of political policies or out of competing responsibilities may be built into the system by statute. In this kind of case a personal interest will of course disqualify on the principles discussed above. However, the policy goals of the decision maker or conflicting interests built into the administrative structure by statute do not invalidate the decision unless the decision maker acts unfairly by closing his mind to relevant factors (e.g. *R v Frankland Prison Visitors ex parte Lewis* (1986): prison visitors having judicial and investigatory roles; *R v Secretary of State for the Environment ex parte Kirkstall Valley Campaign Ltd* (1996): local authority had interest in developing land for which it also had to decide whether to grant planning permission). This approach has been held to satisfy the European Convention on Human Rights (below). A decision may also be upheld if there is no unbiased decision maker available (see *R v Barnsley Licencing Justices* (1960): all justices members of the local Co-Op).

### 15.2.4 Reasons for Decisions

There is no general duty to give reasons for decisions, although many statutes impose such a duty (see *R* v *Criminal Injuries Compensation board ex parte Moore* (1999); *Stefan* v *GMC* (1999); Tribunals and Inquiries Act 1992 s.10). This has been justified on the grounds of cost, excessive formality, the difficulties of expressing subjective reasons, and because, in the case of collective decisions, it may be impossible to identify specific reasons (see *McInnes* v *Onslow-Fane* (1978); *R* v *Higher Education Funding Council* (1994); *Stefan* v *GMC* (1999)). However, these concerns do not meet the main justification for the giving of reasons and treat the recipients of decisions as objects. The primary justification for the giving of reasons is respect for human dignity and equality, so that those who purport to exercise power must be accountable. Even an admission that a decision is based on subjective judgement fulfils this requirement. The giving of reasons also strengthens public confidence in the decision-making process, strengthens the rationality of the process itself and helps challenge decisions, a factor regarded as essential by the European Convention on Human Rights. However, the ECHR has confined itself to holding that courts, as the citizen's last protection, must give reasons for their decisions (*Van de Hurk* v *Netherlands* (1984)). The ECHR has also held that reasons need not be detailed and comprehensive provided that they enable the parties to understand the basis of the decision (*Helle* v *Finland* (1998) see *South Bucks DC* v *Porter* (2004)).

However, the courts have required reasons to be given in a range of cases, drawing upon the general principle of fairness which allows the court to take all the circumstances into account. In *R* v *Secretary of State for the Home Department ex parte Doody* (1993) 3 All ER 92 at 107, Lord Mustill referred to 'a perceptible trend towards an insistence upon greater openness in the making of administrative decisions'. The dominant view seems to be that a duty to give reasons must either be expressed or implied in the relevant statute or there must be some special justification for giving reasons. In *R* v *Higher Education Funding Council* (above), Sedley J held that arguments which applied to all cases were not sufficient, for example the difficulty of challenging a decision in the absence of reasons. Examples of cases where there is a duty to give reasons include the following:

▶ Judicial decisions analogous to those of a court (*R* v *Minister of Defence ex parte Murray* (1998).
▶ Cases which involve very important interests, where, if reasons were not given, the individual would be at a disadvantage (e.g. *Doody* (above): fixing of minimum sentence for life prisoner; *Stefan* (above): risk of loss of livelihood, unrepresented defendant).

▶ Cases where the particular decision is unusual or where a severe penalty is involved (e.g. *R v Civil Service Appeals Board ex parte Cunningham* (1991): compensation award out of line with that given in analogous cases by industrial tribunal; *R v DPP ex parte Manning* (2000): decision not to prosecute after coroner's finding of unlawful killing).

▶ A legitimate expectation might also generate a duty to give reasons for overriding the expectation (*R v Secretary of State for Transport ex parte Richmond BC (No. 4)* (1996)).

▶ If an appeal is provided this may point to a duty to give reasons where the appeal would otherwise be pointless (*Stefan* (above)). On the other hand, a comprehensive appeal that reopens the whole case may point against a duty to give reasons at first instance.

▶ In *Padfield v Minister of Agriculture* (1968), the House of Lords suggested that if a minister refuses to give reasons the court can infer that he has no proper reasons for his decision. However in *Lonrho v Secretary of State for Trade and Industry* (1989), the House took the view that a failure to give reasons does not in itself justify the drawing of an adverse inference but is, at most, supportive of other evidence that the decision is improper.

A duty to give reasons arises after the decision is made and should be distinguished from failing before the decision is made to disclose *grounds* in the sense of allegations against the applicant. Failure to disclose such grounds would normally be unfair as a breach of the right to a hearing. There is also the 'cards on the table' doctrine. Once an applicant has obtained leave to apply for judicial review, the authority must then assist the court by disclosing the reasons for its decision but only in as far as the reasons relate to the particular ground of challenge (*R v Lancashire County Council ex parte Huddlestone* (1986)).

### 15.2.5    Natural Justice and the European Convention on Human Rights

The common law is re-enforced by the Human Rights Act 1998 s.6 which states that it is unlawful for a public authority to act in a way that is incompatible with a 'Convention Right' incorporated into the Act unless the language of a statute requires them to do so, in which case the Court can make a 'Declaration of Incompatibility '(s.4). This does not invalidate the government action but invites the government to change the law. The Human Rights Act will be discussed generally in Chapter 17.

As regards the right to a hearing and the bias rule, Article 6 of the European Convention on Human Rights states that 'in the determination of his civil rights and obligations or of any criminal charge against him, everyone is entitled to a fair and public hearing within a reasonable time by an independent and impartial tribunal established by law'. As we saw in Chapter 14, although the European Court takes a broad approach, not every decision of a public authority affects civil rights and obligations. The decision must impact either on the private law rights of the individual such as personal freedom or property or on some right specifically recognised by the Convention such as the right to home and family life (Art. 8), or the individual must have some specific entitlement against the state such as a claim to a payment. Non-binding actions such as advisory reports or the refusal of discretionary benefits may not qualify. For example in *R (M) v Secretary of State for Constitutional Affairs* (2004) it was held that a District Judge could make an interim Anti-Social Behaviour Order against certain youths suspected of drug dealing without notice or a hearing. Because the order only had temporary effect and was subject to review and confirmation at a later hearing, it did not affect civil rights.

In *R (Alconbury) v Secretary of State* (2001), Lord Hoffmann regretted the relatively broad approach taken by the jurisprudence of the European Court. He would have preferred an approach based on the separation of powers, that Art. 6 should not apply to policy decisions taken in the public interest for which the decision maker is responsible to an elected body such as land use planning decisions, even though these affect property rights but should be confined to private law adjudication, the direct purpose of which is to determine individual rights – in other words, to judicial decisions in the traditional sense.

The requirements of Article 6 cover much the same ground as the common law, although it requires particular rights in criminal cases. However, the common law does not necessarily require a public hearing (see *Bentham* v *Netherlands* (1986); *R* v *DPP ex parte Kebeline* (1999)). It is also arguable that under the Human Rights Act 1998 the right to a fair trial would require legal representation at least in the case of judicial decisions.

Apart from Art. 6, particular Convention rights may require a hearing in themselves. It has been held in cases involving deaths in government custody that the relatives of the victims have a right, under Art. 2 (right to life) to an open and public investigation to establish blame, a matter closely related to the rule of law (see *R (Middleton) v West Somerset Coroner* (2004), *R (Amin) v Secretary of State for the Home Department* (2002). This may also apply to Art. 3: torture and inhuman and degrading treatment).

As regards the bias rule, there is a distinction between policy decisions and judicial decisions. In *R (Alconbury) v Secretary of State* (2001) a variety of decisions made by the Secretary of State were challenged on the ground of incompatibility with Art. 6. These included decisions to 'call in' planning appeals which would otherwise be decided by independent inspectors and to confirm compulsory purchase orders relating to road and rail schemes in which the government had an interest. It was common ground that the Secretary of State was not an independent and impartial tribunal and, apart from the Human Rights Act, the arrangement could not be challenged because it was authorised by statute. The House of Lords held that, in order to satisfy the test of impartiality, the process as a whole should be examined including the protection given by judicial review. Overruling the lower courts, the Lords held unanimously that the process satisfied Art. 6. They held that the jurisprudence of the European Convention supported a fundamental democratic distinction between policy or political decisions, for which the minister is answerable to Parliament, and judicial decisions made by courts and similar bodies. Provided that there is judicial review in relation to the legality of the decision, 'a government minister can be both a policy maker and hear appeals without violating Art. 6, (per Lord Hutton [2001] 2 All ER 929 at 1018). The position is otherwise where a decision turns on findings of law or disputed facts as opposed to policy, where further safeguards such as independent fact-finding might be necessary (see Chapter 14, and Lord Hoffmann at 992). Thus the House of Lords endorsed the traditional English approach against a stricter application of the separation of powers.

# Summary

▶ The doctrine of *Wednesbury* unreasonableness comes near to interfering with the merits of a decision. The threshold of unreasonableness varies with the context on a sliding scale determined by the impact of the decision on the individual and whether the decision involves political factors with which a court should not interfere. At one extreme a bare 'rationality' test is applied. At the other extreme, where the Human Rights Act 1998 applies, the court itself may weight the competing considerations, exercising what is effectively an appeal function. Between these extremes the test appears to be whether the outcome is within the range of reasonable responses to the particular context. In effect the court is drawing upon widely shared social and moral values.

▶ The principle of proportionality is applied in the human rights context and may extend to other contexts. This requires the court to weigh the competing factors on the basis that the interference with the right must be no greater than is necessary to achieve a legitimate objective (in the case of some rights protected by the European Convention on Human Rights, 'a pressing social need').

▶ Natural justice or fairness requires that a person adversely affected by a decision be entitled to a hearing. The requirements of a hearing are flexible and depend on the circumstances. In order to respect the interests of government efficiency, fairness is regarded as the minimum necessary to do justice. The courts are increasingly requiring reasons to be given for decisions.

## Summary cont'd

▶ A decision maker must also be free from the appearance of illegitimate bias. This too depends on the circumstances. A direct financial interest automatically disqualifies the decision maker as perhaps does membership of an organisation which is a party to the case. Apart from that the test is whether a hypothetical reasonably informed observer would consider there to be real danger of bias.

▶ The rules of natural justice or procedural fairness are underpinned by the Human Rights Act 1998 although what amounts to a fair trial depends on the context, and in particular the extent to which the decision is a policy-orientated political decision.

# Exercises

**15.1** 'I think the day will come when it will be more widely recognised that the *Wednesbury* case was an unfortunately retrogressive decision in English administrative law' (Lord Cooke in *R* v *Secretary of State ex parte Daly* (2001). What does he mean and do you agree?

**15.2** 'The difference in practice (between *Wednesbury* unreasonableness and proportionality) is not as great as is sometimes supposed ... even without reference to the 1998 Act the time has come to recognise that this principle is part of English administrative law, not only in when judges are dealing with community acts but also when they are dealing with acts subject to domestic law' (Lord Slynn). Do you agree?

**15.3** Does the bias rule strike a reasonable balance between efficiency and justice?

**15.4** Jill is a law student. She has obtained a place at the College of Law to study for her professional qualification. She applies to Meanshire County Council for a grant for this course under a statute which requires the authority 'to have regard to the manpower needs of the community and all other material factors'. She is informed by letter that her application 'will be considered on its merits but it is the policy of the Council to award grants to law students only of exceptional ability'. Jill who has no financial resources is invited to submit a written statement, and having done so is informed that her application has been refused. No reasons are given. Jill wishes to have a personal hearing before the council to impress upon them her personal circumstances. Advise Jill.

**15.5** Sam, a pupil at a local authority sixth form college, was ordered by the head teacher to remove a tattoo across his forehead which expressed support for vegetarianism. Having refused to do so Sam was suspended. He appealed to the college governing body but his appeal was rejected. One of the members of the appeal committee was a parent governor who was a neighbour of Sam but did not vote at the governors' meeting that considered Sam's case. Another member of the committee was the manager of a local meat packing company. Advise Sam.

## Further reading

Irvine, Lord (1996) 'Judges and decision makers: the theory and practice of *Wednesbury* Review', *Public Law,* 59.

Jowell, J. (2000) 'Beyond the rule of law: towards constitutional judicial review', *Public Law,* 671.

Olowofoyeku, A. (2000) 'The Nemo Judex rule: the case against automatic disqualification', *Public Law,* 456.

Walker, P. (1995) 'What's wrong with irrationality?', *Public Law,* 556.

Wong, G. (2000) 'Towards the nutcracker principle: reconsidering the objections to proportionality', *Public Law,* 92.

# Chapter 16

## Judicial review remedies

> For this is not the liberty which we can hope, that no grievance ever should
> arise in the Commonwealth, that let no man in this world expect; but when
> complaints are freely heard, deeply considered, and speedily reformed, then
> is the outmost bound of civil liberty attained that wise men look for.
>
> (Milton, *Areopagitica*, 1644)

## Key words

▶ Protection of governmental interests
▶ Streamlining remedies
▶ Public and private rights
▶ Public and private functions
▶ Presumptions against excluding courts

## 16.1 Introduction

It could be argued that the courts provide the only open and universal
means by which the individual can challenge government action. Ministerial responsibility to Parliament is of little use to the citizen directly in that
it can be called upon only by members of Parliament who are unlikely to be
independent. The various commissions that have been established as a
result of the work of the *Committee on Standards in Public Life* play a valuable monitoring role but the citizen cannot obtain a decision from them as
a matter of right. Nor do they deliberate in public. The 'ombudsman' institution which investigates citizens complaints against government is free to
complainants and its powers of investigation into facts more extensive than
those of the courts. However, it has limited jurisdiction, concentrating on
procedural matters of maladministration, has no enforcement powers and
does not hold a public hearing (see *R* v *Local Commissioners of Administration ex parte Liverpool City Council* (2001)).

Before 1977 there was no distinctive legal process for judicial review as
such. The powers of the courts to review government action developed
historically in different courts through a variety of remedies, some of which
were general remedies applying also to private disputes. As we saw in
Chapter 5, one aspect of the 'rule of law' emphasised by Dicey was that the
common law is a single system that does not distinguish between public law
and private law but applies the same principles to government and citizen
alike so that an official is in no better position than a private individual.
However since Dicey's day, the powers of government have expanded enor-

mously and this approach has become inadequate both to protect the citizen and to reflect the public interest in the effective delivery of government policy in a democracy (a tension between liberal individualism and welfare liberalism, see Chapter 1).

Since 1977 the various remedies have been concentrated in a single section of the High Court, part of the Queen's Bench Division and now called the Administrative Court. This comprises 25 judges nominated by the Lord Chancellor but who also spend time on other kinds of case thus reflecting Dicey's objection to a specialised public law system. There is a unified procedure for all the remedies, replacing numerous technical rules which had developed over the years in relation to individual remedies. These had made challenges to government action complex and sometimes unjust, with litigants having to traverse a minefield of procedural niceties and sometimes being frustrated by choosing an inappropriate remedy in the wrong court. A Law Commission Report in 1976 (Law Com. 6407) led to the main reforms. A further Law Commission Report (No. 226, 1994), suggesting further relatively minor changes, has not yet been implemented.

The law is governed by the Supreme Court Act 1981 s.31 and the Civil Procedure Rules 1998 (CPR) Part. 54 (see *Practice Direction* [2000] 1 WLR 1654). A claim for judicial review means a claim to review the lawfulness of (i) an enactment; or (ii) a decision, action or failure to act in relation to the exercise of a public function (CPR 54.1). This allows the court to choose the most appropriate remedy from the whole range (below). It also embodies principles concerned with the special nature of disputes between government and citizen. These are of three kinds and the procedure as a whole is characterised by wide discretionary powers.

1. The remedies are designed to set aside unlawful government action and to remit the matter to the decision maker or to restrain an unlawful act but not, normally, to allow the court to make a new decision itself, thus complying with the separation of powers. However, the court might exceptionally correct a drafting mistake made, for example in a statutory instrument, where it is plain that the mistake was inadvertent and when the purpose of the instrument is clear, (*R (Confederation of Passenger Transport UK) v Humber Bridge Board* (2004)).

   There is no guarantee that any victory in the courts will be lasting since the government might subsequently change the law to suit its own interests. For example, Parliament swiftly validated regulations which, in *R v Secretary of State for Social Services ex parte Joint Council for the Welfare of Immigrants* (1996) (Chapter 5), the Court of Appeal had condemned on rule of law grounds (Asylum and Immigration Act 1996 s.11).

2.  The procedure also reflects the limited role of the courts. In particular witness and cross-examination are used only exceptionally, 'where the justice of the case so demands' reflecting that review of questions of fact is limited (Chapter 14; CPR 54. 16.(1); *Cullen v Chief Constable of the RUC* [2004] 2 All ER 237, [39]).

3.  The judicial review procedure contains safeguards designed to represent the public interest in protecting government against improper challenges (below). To a certain extent judicial review could be regarded as part of the political process since it provides a public platform for grievances against the government so that, to a well-funded partisan, even unsuccessful litigation might be attractive as a means of publicising a cause. On the other hand, any restriction on the right to go to court might be seen as an affront to the rule of law. However, in cases where a person's ordinary private rights are at stake, for example if a public authority interferes with private property, an action or defence can be brought in any court, thus reflecting the traditional idea of the rule of law.

## 16.2 The Range of Remedies

Historically there are two groups of remedies suitable for judicial review. Firstly, from the seventeenth century the courts developed the 'prerogative orders' (called so because in theory they issue on the application of the Crown). These were *mandamus, prohibition* and *certiorari*. They enabled the High Court to police the powers and duties of 'inferior bodies', that is lower courts and government officials. *Mandamus* ordered a body to perform its duty. *Prohibition* was issued in advance to prevent a body from exceeding its jurisdiction. *Certiorari* summoned up the record of an inferior body to be examined by the court and the decision to be quashed if it was invalid. These orders remain the basis of the modern law of judicial review but are now called, *mandatory orders, prohibiting orders* and *quashing orders* respectively (CPR 54.1). The judicial review procedure must be used when applying for the above remedies (CPR 54.2). In relation to a quashing order the court can also send the matter back to the decision maker to decide again. However, where it considers there is no purpose to be served in sending it back, it can take the decision itself (CPR 54.19). This would apply in the rare case where there is only one possible decision that could lawfully be made.

The second group of remedies, which are regarded as supplementary to the prerogative orders, comprises declarations, injunctions and damages (Supreme Court Act 1981 s.31 (2)). These are also available in other courts, a matter which causes problems (below). A claimant may apply for these in a claim for judicial review and must do so if he or she is seeking these remedies in addition to a prerogative order (CPR 54.3). A declaration is a statement of the legal position which declares the rights of parties – for example 'X is entitled to a tax repayment'. Declarations are not enforceable but a public authority is unlikely to disobey one. Indeed, a declaration is useful where an enforceable order would be undesirable, for example a draft government order before it is considered by Parliament or an advisory government opinion. The former prerogative orders do not lie against the Crown as such, but the declaration does. However, this is relatively unimportant because most statutory powers are conferred on ministers and the prerogative orders lie against individual ministers.

An injunction restrains a person from breaking the law or orders a person to undo something done unlawfully (a mandatory injunction). An interim injunction can restrain government action pending a full trial. In *M* v *Home Office* (1993) the House of Lords held that an injunction can be enforced against a minister of the Crown (see also *R* v *Minister of Agriculture ex parte Monsanto Plc* (1998)). This overturns a long tradition that the Crown and its servants cannot be the subject of enforceable orders (see Crown Proceedings Act 1947, s.21 which still applies to ordinary civil law actions involving contract, tort or property issues). However, it was stressed that injunctions should be granted against ministers only as a last resort. Injunctions cannot be granted against the Crown itself.

Claimants often apply for more than one of the remedies which may well overlap. For example, a quashing order has the same effect as a declaration that the offending decision is void. The court can issue any of the remedies in any combination and is not limited to those for which the claimant has applied (Supreme Court Act 1981 s.31 (5)). Other financial remedies, such as restitution of money paid as a result of an unlawful demand, are not available in judicial review proceedings but can be sought in an ordinary civil action (*Woolwich Building Society* v *IRC (No. 2)* (1993)). A mandatory order in judicial proceedings to return the money might also be available.

Claims for damages are rare in judicial review proceedings. A claimant cannot seek damages alone in judicial review proceedings but must attach it to a claim for at least one of the other remedies (CPR 54.3(2)). Damages cannot be awarded in respect of unlawful government action as such but can be awarded only in respect of conduct and losses which are not authorised by statute and which would be actionable in an ordinary civil action (Supreme Court Act 1981 s.31 (4)). Where there is a misuse of power or maladministration, Administrative Court proceedings are appropriate but in other cases, for example damage caused by a failure to comply with a statutory duty, an ordinary claim is more appropriate (see e.g. *Marcic* v *Thames Water* (2004)); *Anufrijeva* v *Southwark LBC* (2004): maladministration).

The law relating to the civil liability of public authorities is complex and cannot usefully be discussed without prior knowledge of the law of tort. We will not attempt to discuss the matter here other than to remark that the courts are reluctant to impose liability in damages upon government bodies on the basis of failure of duty alone (see e.g. *X (Minors)* v *Bedfordshire CC* (1995); *Marcic* v *Thames Water* (2004); *Cullen* v *Chief Constable of the RUC* (2004)). This is because the risk of paying damages might inhibit the decision maker from exercising its powers independently.

In three kinds of case, however, damages may be awarded on the basis of unlawful government action independently of the ordinary civil law:

1.  Under the *Francovich* principle in EC law (above, Chapter 8).
2.  The tort of 'misfeasance in public office' where an authority is motivated by a specific intention to injure or knowingly acts outside its powers being reckless as to the consequences (see *Dunlop* v *Woollahra City Council* (1982); *Calverley* v *Merseyside Chief Constable* (1989); *Racz* v *Home Office* (1994); *Three Rivers District Council* v *Bank of England (No. 3)* (2003). Where a 'fundamental constitutional right' (Chapters 1, 5) has been violated the claimant can recover damages even if he has suffered no loss (*Watkins* v *Secretary of State* (2004)).
3.  Where a right conferred by the European Convention on Human Rights is infringed (Chapter 17).

Finally there is also the ancient prerogative writ of *habeas corpus* ('produce the body'). *Habeas corpus* is not part of the judicial review procedure although the grounds for issuing it are probably the same as those of judicial review. It requires anyone detaining a person to bring the prisoner immediately before a judge to justify the detention. However, judicial review can also provide a speedy way of challenging unlawful detention. According to Dicey (1959, Introduction to the *Study of the Law of the Constitution*, 10th edn. p. 199), *habeas corpus* is 'worth a hundred constitutional articles guaranteeing civil liberty'. However *habeas corpus* may be of little practical importance today. Indeed because of its limited scope, and in particular because it cannot be used to challenge facts, *habeas corpus* has been held not to provide an effective remedy under the European Convention on Human Rights Art. 5: right to liberty (*X* v *UK* (1982)). (See Le Sueur, 'Should We Abolish the Writ of Habeas Corpus?', 1992, *Public Law* 13; Shrimpton, 'In Defence of Habeas Corpus', 1993, *Public Law* 24).

## 16.3 The Judicial Review Procedure

As we saw above an important feature of the judicial review process is that it contains mechanisms designed to protect the public interest against improper challenges. In attempting to do this it is vulnerable to objections relating the right of access to the courts and the right to a fair trial under the European Convention on Human Rights Art. 6. As so often, a balance between competing values must be struck and the court, itself vulnerable to rule of law objections, has a wide discretion. The judicial review process must also be set in the wider context of the 'Woolf' reforms in civil procedure introduced in 1999 (Woolf, *Access to Justice: a final report to the Lord Chancellor*, 1996). These reforms include the following general aspirations in respect of which the parties are under an obligation to assist the court (CPR. 1.1):

(a) ensuring that the parties are on an equal footing
(b) saving expense
(c) dealing with the case in ways which are proportionate
    (i)   to the amount of money involved
    (ii)  to the importance of the case
    (iii) to the complexity of the issues
    (iv) to the financial position of each party
(d) ensuring that it is dealt with expeditiously and fairly
(e) allocating to it an appropriate share of the court's resources while taking into account the need to allot the resources to other cases.

The main distinctive features of the judicial review procedure are as follows:

▶ Permission to apply is required from a judge before proceedings can be commenced in or transferred to the Administrative Court (Supreme Court Act 1981 s.31 (3), CPR 54.4). The procedure is *ex parte*, that is, the government side need not appear although it must be given the opportunity to do so. At this stage the applicant merely shows that he has a chance of success, so as to discourage spurious challenges and to help the court manage an ever increasing caseload by filtering out hopeless cases. Given the emphasis of the Woolf reforms on financial efficiency, the filter mechanism might lead to the impression that expediency is being put before justice. There are however further safeguards. There is a right to renew the application for permission before another judge in open court, and in the case of a refusal in open court, before the Court of Appeal then with leave to the House of Lords. After permission has been granted, interim relief preventing the implementation of the government action in question can be granted pending the full trial either by injunction (above) or under Supreme Court Act 1981 s.31.

▶ At the full hearing the court has a discretion in relation to procedural matters. The case is normally decided on the basis of affidavits (sworn written statements), but the court may order discovery of documents, witnesses and cross-examination if this is needed to do justice (above, see *O'Reilly* v *Mackman* (1982)). In practice such orders are made only exceptionally. With the agreement of the parties the court can decide the whole matter without a hearing (CPR 54.18). It is arguable that, in view of the broad policy issues that may arise in judicial review cases, particularly under the Human Rights Act, it would be desirable for a more expansive process be used, at least in cases of major importance. One suggestion has been to appoint an Advocate General or Director of Civil Proceedings with the duty of representing the public interest before the court (see Jacob, 1982, *Civil Justice Quarterly* 316–19).

▶ There is a shorter time limit than the periods of three or six years applicable to other civil litigation. The claim must be filed (a) promptly; and (b) not later than three months after the ground to make the claim first arose. In the case of a quashing order this means the date of the decision (CPR 54.5(1)(b)). The time limit cannot be extended by agreement and is subject to any shorter time limit in a particular statute (CPR 54.6). The time limit can however be extended by the court. Nevertheless, even within three months the court may refuse leave to make the application or refuse to give a remedy if 'undue delay' results in 'substantial hardship to any person, substantial prejudice to the rights of any person, or would be detrimental to good administration' (Supreme Court Act 1981, s.31 (6)(7)). In practice these considerations are usually examined at the full hearing stage. The present provision seems to cure the apparent conflict between competing rules that previously existed (see *Caswell* v *Dairy Produce Quota Tribunal* (1990)).

▶ The court can refuse to grant a remedy in its discretion even when a decision is *ultra vires* and strictly speaking void. By contrast in ordinary litigation an *ultra vires* decision is treated as a nullity (*Credit Suisse* v *Allerdale BC* (1996)). The court will not set aside a decision where for example no injustice has been done, or where the interests of third parties would be prejudiced or where intervention would cause serious public disruption (e.g. *R* v *Secretary of State for the Home Dept ex parte Swati* (1986); *R* v *Secretary of State for the Environment ex parte Association of Metropolitan Authorities* (1986)); *Coney* v *Choyce* (1975)). The court might also prefer a declaration to an enforceable order where enforcement might be impracticable or hinder the governmental process (see e.g. *R* v *Panel on Takeovers and Mergers* (1987); *Chief Constable North Wales Police* v *Evans* (1982); *R* v *Boundary Commission ex parte Foot* [1983] 1 All ER 1099,1116). The court will also take into account whether the claimant has made full disclosure of all relevant circumstances (*R* v *Lancashire County Council ex parte Huddleston* (1986)).

▶ A particularly important aspect of the court's discretionary power is that judicial review is intended as a remedy of last resort so that the court will not normally permit judicial review if there is another remedy which is at least equally appropriate (see e.g. *R v Chief Constable of the Merseyside Police ex parte Calverley* (1986); *R v Birmingham City Council ex parte Ferrero Ltd* (1993); *R (G) v Immigration Appeal Tribunal* (2004).

## 16.4 ▶ Standing *(Locus Standi)*

The applicant must show that he has 'sufficient interest' in the matter to which the application relates (Supreme Court Act 1981, s.31 (3)). The question of standing must be considered not only at the threshold stage of permission to apply, where it is used to remove obvious busybodies, but also at the full hearing when it is examined in depth in relation to the particular issues in the case and could be regarded as an aspect of the court's discretion to withhold a remedy (see *Inland Revenue Commissioners v National Federation of Self-Employed and Small Businesses Ltd* (1982); *R v Dept of Transport ex parte Presvac Engineering Ltd* (1992)).

The courts take a broad approach to standing which is not confined to persons whose legal rights are in issue. They have for example given standing to pressure groups, at least where they have a specific involvement with the matter as representatives of people directly affected by the decision or where they have showed serious involvement by investing money or expertise (*R v Inspectorate of Pollution ex parte Greenpeace (No. 2)* (1994)). Groups and individuals representing the general public interest have also been given standing at least where there is no other way of challenging the decision (*R v HM Treasury ex parte Smedley* (1985); *R v Foreign Secretary ex parte World Development Movement* (1995); *R v Secretary of State for Foreign and Commonwealth Affairs ex parte Rees-Mogg* (1994)). Indeed the contribution of pressure groups has been welcomed as adding a valuable dimension to judicial review (*R v Secretary of State ex parte Greenpeace* (1998)). Moreover it has been suggested that anyone who is not a mere busybody with no connection with the issues should have standing in relation to matters of public importance (*R v North Somerset DC ex parte Dixon* (1998): environmental issue, but contrast *R v Somerset CC ex parte Garnett* (1998)). A person who is genuinely affected by a decision can have standing on behalf of a wider group, such as public consultees, even though that person is chosen on the basis of eligibility for public funding, provided that there is no abuse of the public funding system (*R (Edwards) v Environment Agency* (2004); compare *R v Legal Aid Board ex parte Bateman* (1992)).

On the other hand in *R v Secretary of State for the Environment ex parte Rose Theatre Trust Ltd* (1990), a case that has been much criticised, it was held that a campaigning interest in protecting the site of the Shakespearian Rose Theatre was not sufficient in itself. It was also emphasised that individuals cannot give themselves standing merely by forming a group. Perhaps this could be contested on the basis that group involvement is a manifestation of democratic legitimacy? A restrictive approach was also taken in *R (Bulger)* v *Secretary of State* (2001) where it was held that the father of a baby murdered by two boys in horrific circumstances did not have standing to challenge the Lord Chief Justice's recommendation to the Home Secretary on the length of the punishment element of their sentence. The court stressed that there was no need for a third party to intervene since the Crown and the boys could both challenge the decision and raise all the relevant issues. According to Rose LJ a low threshold of standing can often be justified because of the importance to the rule of law that someone should be able to call decision makers to account, but this was not the case here.

The particular remedy is also a factor. For example in *R v Felixstowe Justices ex parte Leigh* (1987), a newspaper editor had standing for a declaration that magistrates should not hide behind anonymity, but not *mandamus* to reveal the identity of magistrates in a particular case.

At the permission stage, standing is likely to be generous, so as to filter out only hopeless cases. At the full hearing, those whose legal rights are in issue would always have standing, while in other cases the court will balance the extent of the applicant's interest against the public importance of the issues involved and the particular remedy sought. However in many cases, including *Bulger* and *Rose Theatre*, even where the claimant lacks standing the court considers the substantive issues albeit without granting any remedy. It seems therefore that the court has a broad discretion. Moreover, even where a person has no standing in their own right, the court has a discretion to hear any person, thereby broadening the scope of the process and allowing interest groups to have a say (CPR 54.17).

## 16.5 Choice of Procedure: Public and Private Law

The special features of the application for judicial review raise two questions: (i) When is the procedure available? (ii) When must it be used in place of other methods of approaching the courts? Before the judicial review procedure was created in 1977, the prerogative orders were available only in the Divisional Court of the Queen's Bench Division and are now only available in the Administrative Court. The other remedies – declaration, injunction and damages – were, and still are, available in any court. Neither the Supreme Court Act 1981 nor the Civil Procedure Rules expressly require a person to use the Administrative Court.

Until the 1980s it was accepted that the citizen, as a matter of fundamental right, could apply to any court for a declaration or injunction and could raise the invalidity of a government decision in any relevant legal proceedings (see *Pyx Granite Co. v Ministry of Housing and Local Government* [1960] AC 260). Indeed, the right to contest government action wherever and however it arises is a basic aspect of the rule of law. Nevertheless in *O'Reilly v Mackman* (1982), the House of Lords held that, other than in exceptional cases, a 'public law' matter must be brought in the Administrative Court since this ensures that safeguards designed to protect the government, and therefore the public, against improper challenges are in place. Two distinct questions must be separated: firstly, what is a public law matter? If a matter is not one of public law then the Administrative Court procedure is irrelevant; secondly, the 'exclusivity' question, namely what 'exceptional' public law cases fall outside the special procedure.

### 16.5.1 Public Law Matters: Scope of the Judicial Review Procedure

The judicial review procedure applies only to 'public functions', (CPR 54.1). This implies that not all activities of government bodies are necessarily public functions and opens the possibility that some functions carried on by bodies outside government might nevertheless be public functions. Indeed, contemporary political fashion favours using private bodies to deliver public services. It seems anomalous that a body carrying out functions on behalf of government should not be subject to judicial review. There is no clear definition of 'public'. Indeed, it is often suggested that judicial review is about controlling any concentration of power rather than government as such.

The courts have taken a relatively flexible if cautious approach. It is relevant but not enough that the function in question is exercised in the public interest nor that the body is important nor that the decision has serious consequences for those affected by it. The courts have refused to apply a single test but have indicated a number of factors which make a function 'public'.

▷ Firstly, where a power exercisable for public purposes is conferred directly by statute, or royal prerogative, it will normally be regarded as a public function (see *R v Panel on Takeovers and Mergers ex parte Datafin plc* (1987); *Scott v National Trust* (1998)). However, the fact that a body which exercises commercial functions such as an insurance company is created by statute, usually a private Act, and has statutory powers does not in itself make its functions public functions (*R (West) v Lloyds of London* (2004)).

▷ Secondly, a function which is intermeshed with or 'underpinned' by government may be public in the sense that government bodies have control over its exercise or participate in its activities. How much government involvement is required is a matter of degree in the particular circumstances, making this approach highly uncertain. In *R v Panel on Takeovers and Mergers ex parte Datafin plc* (above), it was held that the Takeover Panel, a self-regulating voluntary body which acted as a city 'watchdog', was exercising public law functions. This was because it was set up in the public interest, it reported to the government, and although not having statutory powers itself, was supported by the statutory powers of the Department of Trade. In *Hampshire County Council* v *Beer* (2003), the Court of Appeal held that a farmers' market run by a farmers' cooperative was nevertheless exercising public functions. This was for two reasons, each of which alone would have apparently sufficed. Firstly, it had control over a public space; secondly, it had previously been run by the local authority which had now handed it over to the cooperative (see also *R* v *Advertising Standards Authority* (1993)). At the other end of the scale, the fact that a body is supervised by government or receives government finance or exercises functions such as housing tenants at the request of a public authority does not suffice in itself (*R (Heather)* v *Leonard Cheshire Foundation* (2002)).

▶ It has also been held, sometimes reluctantly, that a power which is based exclusively on contract or other agreement to submit to the jurisdiction, for example the disciplinary power exercised by sport or professional associations, is a private law power (see *R* v *Disciplinary Committee of the Jockey Club ex parte the Aga Khan* (1993); *R* v *Football Association ex parte Football League* (1993); *R (Heather)* v *Leonard Cheshire Foundation* (2002): retirement home owned by Charity, *R (West)* v *Lloyds* (2004): insurance company). This seems artificial since many such bodies exercise their powers for the purpose of protecting the public in much the same way as the Takeover Panel. In such cases, for example the Jockey Club (above), the reality is that that the individual has no choice but to submit to the jurisdiction since the alternative is to be excluded from an area of public life. However, the contract test is not conclusive. Where there is an additional element of statute or governmental policy, or if the decision affects persons beyond the contractual relationship, the court may treat the matter as one of public law (*McLaren* v *Home Office* (1990). Compare *R* v *East Berkshire Health-Authority ex parte Walsh* (1985) – nurse employed under contract – with *R* v *Secretary of State for the Home Department ex parte Benwell* (1985): prison officer employed directly under statute).

▶ Another possible test is whether, if the body in question did not exist, the government would have to intervene (see *R* v *Advertising Standards Authority* (1993); *R* v *Chief Rabbi ex parte Wachman* (1993)). However, this is not reliable nor conclusive since there is no agreement on what functions are necessary in this sense (see e.g. *Aga Khan* (above)).

▶ Finally there are dicta that the scope of judicial review should take into account the practical question of the court's case load (e.g. *R* v *Football*

*Association* (above). This raises a separation of powers concern in that it invites the executive to reduce the number of judges.

### 16.5.2 Exclusivity

Assuming that a decision is one of public law, must the judicial review procedure always be used? Because the judicial review procedure is more restrictive than an ordinary action, there is a school of thought that the rule of law is threatened by forcing people to use it. As against this, the judicial review procedure is geared to the special concerns of challenging government action and in many cases is clearly appropriate in view of the remedies available and the relative speediness of the proceedings.

In *O'Reilly* v. *Mackman* (1982), prisoners sought to challenge a decision not to give them remission for good behaviour. They were outside time for judicial review and attempted to bring an ordinary civil action for a declaration. The House of Lords struck out their claim as an abuse of the court's process. Lord Diplock said that the judicial review procedure should normally be used because of its safeguards which protected the government against 'groundless, unmeritorious or tardy harassment'. Lord Diplock emphasied that a prisoner has no legal right to remission, which was an 'indulgence' from the government but at most a legitimate expectation that his case would be considered fairly. In *Cocks* v *Thanet District Council* (1983), the House of Lords applied *O'Reilly* to hold that a claimant under homelessness legislation must use judicial review rather than a more convenient action in a local county court. This was because the legislation gave him no absolute rights but required a discretionary government decision before a claimant became entitled to housing.

In *O'Reilly*, Lord Diplock suggested that there should be exceptions to the exclusivity principle but did not fully identify them He did however suggest that judicial review procedure would not be exclusive in cases of 'collateral' challenge, where the validity of government action arises incidentally in litigation, for example where a local authority resists a claim to pay a debt by arguing that the decision to incur the debt was *ultra vires* (*Credit Suisse* v *Allerdale BC* (1996)). Similarly a citizen can raise a defence in any relevant proceedings against an unlawful government claim (*Wandsworth BC* v *Winder* (1985); *Boddington* v *British Transport Police* (1998)). An ordinary civil action might also be appropriate if the issues are mainly factual or where the public law aspects are peripheral (*Mercury Communications* v *Director General of Telecommunications* (1996).

Indeed the courts have subsequently backed away from a strict application of *O'Reilly*. They have emphasised that the matter is one of discretion and that unless the procedure chosen is clearly inappropriate they will not disturb it. The most fundamental exception to the *O'Reilly* principle is where the existing private law rights of an individual are in issue. This was not the case in *O' Reilly* itself. In *Roy* v *Kensington, Chelsea and Westminster Family Practititioner Committee* (1992), a doctor was seeking a discretionary 'practice allowance' from the National Health Service. He had established entitlement to some kind of allowance, but not as to how much. The House of Lords suggested that whenever a litigant was protecting a 'private law right' he or she need not use the judicial review procedure. A private law right includes any right arising in contract or tort or property that can be protected by damages (e.g. *Clark* v *University of Lincoln* (2000). It also includes a case where a person can establish a definite entitlement against the government. For example in *Cocks* (above), had the claimant been allocated accommodation, a private right would have arisen (see also *Trustees of the Dennis Rye Pension Fund* v *Sheffield City Council* (1997); *British Steel* v *Customs and Excise Commissioners* (1997) illustrating that this may turn on complex questions of statutory interpretation).

These cases seem to leave *O'Reilly* v *Mackman* little to bite on, because in the absence of a 'private law right', judicial review with its flexible standing requirement would in any event be the only possible procedure. Examples of cases where there are no private rights include claims arising out of a refusal by government to grant benefits or permissions, including many immigration, prison and homelessness claims, and challenges to government investigations or inquiries that do not in themselves produce legal consequences. However, sometimes there may be a circular element where the existence of a private law right is influenced by the court's view as to whether judicial review would provide an adequate remedy, for example where it has to be decided whether the breach of a duty imposed on a public authority by statute gives rise to a claim for damages (e.g. *Cullen* v *Chief Constable of the RUC* (2004): failure to give prisoner access to a lawyer).

The tendency to relax the O'Reilly principle has been encouraged by Woolf reforms (above) which have narrowed the gap between judicial review and other civil actions by giving the courts wider powers to control the civil process by requiring the parties to cooperate with the court in expediting proceedings. Although permission to apply is not required in an ordinary civil action, Part 24 of the Civil Procedure Rules empowers the court to strike out a civil action at an early stage if the defendant can show that it has no reasonable chance of success. In judicial review proceedings however, the *claimant* must establish a reasonable chance of success. In *Clark* v *University of Lincolnshire and Humberside* (2000), a student brought an ordinary action for breach of contract against a decision by the University to fail her. It was argued that she should have brought a judicial review claim within the three months' time limit. The Court of Appeal held that she was entitled to bring a civil action. Even if judicial review were appropriate, as was the case here because the university also had statutory powers, the court would not strike out a claim merely because of the procedure that had been adopted unless the court's processes were being misused or the procedure chosen was unsuitable. Moreover, cases can be transferred between the Administrative Court and other courts at any stage.

## 16.6 The Exclusion of Judicial Review

Sometimes a statute attempts to exclude judicial review. The courts are reluctant to accept this and construe such statutes narrowly. For example, a provision stating that a decision shall be 'final' does not exclude review but merely prevents the decision maker from reopening the matter and excludes any right of appeal that might otherwise apply (*R v Medical Appeal Tribunal ex parte Gilmore* (1957)). Even a provision stating that a 'determination of the tribunal shall not be questioned in any court of law' is ineffective to prevent review where the tribunal exceeds its 'jurisdiction' (powers). This is because the tribunal's act is a nullity and so not a 'determination'. Given that a government body exceeds its jurisdiction whenever it makes an error of law (Chapter 14) this neatly sidesteps the 'ouster clause' (*Anisminic v. Foreign Compensation Commission* (1969)).

However, given Parliament's ultimate supremacy, a sufficiently tightly drafted 'ouster clauses' would surmount *Anisminic*. A clause often found in statutes relating to land-use planning and compulsory purchase allows challenge within six weeks and then provides that the decision 'shall not be questioned in any court of law'. The courts have interpreted this provision literally, on the ground that review is not completely excluded and that the policy of the statute is to enable development of land to be started quickly (see *R v Cornwall CC ex parte Huntingdon* (1994)).

The Anti-Terrorism, Crime and Security Act 2001 s.101 also illustrates that the court will take the policy of the Act into account. This allows an asylum seeker to appeal to the Immigration Appeal Tribunal against a decision of an adjudicator but only with the permission of the Tribunal. A decision to refuse permission to appeal can be challenged by a 'paper review' by a High Court judge, which is significantly more limited than the normal judicial review. It was held in (*R (G) v Immigration Appeal Tribunal* (2004)) that in the absence of express words in a statute, judicial review could not completely be excluded. However, given the intention of Parliament to deal with the serious problem of delays arising from the processing of asylum cases, the court would permit judicial review only in exceptional cases. A similar position might be taken under the Anti-Terrorism, Crime and Security Act 2001 where there is a right of appeal to the Special Immigration Appeals Commissioners (which includes a High Court judge) against a decision of the Home Secretary to certify that a person is an 'international terrorist'. The proceedings of the commissioners are in private and evidence is sometimes not revealed to the complainant. The Act provides that any action taken by the Home Secretary in connection with or in reliance on the certificate may be questioned in legal proceedings only by this method (s.30) (see Chapter 19).

A provision stating that a particular act, such as entry on a register or a certificate, shall be 'conclusive evidence' of compliance with the Act and of the matters stated in the certificate may also be effective since it does not exclude review as such but makes it impossible to prove invalidity. However, this may leave open the possibility of review for unfairness or unreasonableness (see *R* v *Registrar of Companies* (1985)).

Statutes dealing with the surveillance and the security services feature a clause stating that a decision cannot be challenged even on jurisdictional grounds (e.g. Security Services Act 1989 s.5 (4); Regulation of Investigatory Powers Act 2000 s.67 (8)). These may exclude judicial review completely although they do provide a right to complain to special commissioners (Chapter 19).

Where judicial review is completely excluded, Art. 6 of the ECHR may be invoked on the ground that the ouster clause prevents a fair trial in relation to a person's 'civil rights and obligations' (Chapter 17). However, if the proceedings are in themselves fair and independent, Art. 6 does not require judicial review. Moreover, it is arguable that the limited rights of challenge conferred by legislation dealing with security matters would be regarded as a proportionate response, since 'fairness' is a flexible concept. Moreover, the European Court has held that Art. 6 does not apply to decisions to remove aliens from the country since they have no civil rights and obligations in this respect (*R (G)* v *Immigration Appeal Tribunal* (2004)).

## Summary

▶ There is a special procedure for challenging decisions of public bodies. This is called the Application for Judicial Review and is highly discretionary. The procedure provides the citizen with a range of remedies including damages, but also provides machinery for protecting government against improper or trivial challenges. Leave to apply is required and judicial review will be refused where there is an equally convenient alternative remedy.

▶ Standing is flexible and increasingly liberal although a third party may not be given standing where others are in a better position to challenge the decision.

▶ The AJR applies only to public law functions which usually include powers exercised by a wide range of bodies connected to the government or exercising statutory powers but do not usually exclude powers derived exclusively from contract or consent. In some cases the citizen may challenge public law powers outside the judicial review procedure on the basis of the

## Summary cont'd

rule of law principle that, where private rights are at stake, unlawful government action can be ignored.

▷ The remedies and procedure for judicial review are discretionary so that even though an unlawful government decision is strictly speaking a nullity, the court may refuse to intervene. Delay, misbehaviour, the impact on third parties and the absence of injustice may be reasons for not interfering. Public inconvenience or administrative disruption are probably not enough in themselves but they might be relevant to the court's discretion, coupled with another factor such as delay.

▷ Sometimes statutes attempt to exclude judicial review. The courts are reluctant to see their powers taken away and interpret such provisions strictly. The Human Rights Act 1998 reinforces this.

# Exercises

(Note: material in Chapters 14 and 15 may also be relevant to some of these questions).

**16.1** What are the advantages and disadvantages of the judicial review procedure from the point of view of the citizen? When may government action be challenged in the courts by means of an ordinary action?

**16.2** 'The expressions "private law" and "public law" have recently been imported into the law of England from countries which unlike our own, have separate systems concerning public law and private law. No doubt they are convenient expressions for descriptive purposes. In this country they must be used with caution for typically, English law fastens, not upon principles but upon remedies' Lord Wilberforce in *Davy* v *Spelthorne BC* [1984] AC 262, 276. Discuss.

**16.3** '*O'Reilly* v *Mackman* is effectively a dead letter'. Discuss.

**16.4** Snobville District Council has statutory power to acquire within its area, land which in its opinion it 'is desirable to set aside as a public park'. The Council makes a compulsory purchase order in respect of a row of houses owned by Fred, who lets them at a low rent and who has frequently been prosecuted by the Council under public health legislation for offences involving overcrowding in the houses. The governing statute provides that a compulsory purchase order may be challenged in the High Court within six weeks of its confirmation by the minister on the ground of *ultra vires*, but 'thereafter a Compulsory Purchase Order shall not be questioned in any court of law'. Fred does not challenge the order, but, nine months after its confirmation by the minister, John, one of the residents in Fred's houses, learns that the Council had agreed with another landowner, X, to acquire Fred's land rather than X's on the ground that 'since Fred's houses were unhealthy this would kill two birds with one stone'. John also believes that there is already adequate provision for public parks in Snobville. Advise John.

**16.5** Forever Open Housing Association provides sheltered accommodation for vulnerable people. It is a charity and is funded and regulated by the Housing Corporation, a government agency. Mary lives in a residential home owned by Forever Open, her accommodation being paid for by the local authority under its statutory obligation to arrange for care provision for the elderly. When Mary took up residence, Forever Open told her that she 'now has a home for life'. Forever Open now proposes to close the home in order to concentrate its resources upon housing teenage drug addicts as advised by the Housing Corporation. Advise Mary whether and how she can challenge this proposal in the courts.

**16.6** By statute (fictitious) the NHS is required to provide 'an effective health care service for all UK citizens'. The statute also provides that 'the actions of any NHS hospital in relation to the provision of any service to the public shall not be questioned in any court on any ground whatsoever'. St Tony's hospital is short of money and trained staff because of government financial cuts. The Secretary of State has issued a circular to all hospitals stating, among other things, that no further patients be admitted for sex-change operations, and that hip-replacement operations should normally be performed only on patients who play an active part in the economic life of the community.

**(a)** The Holby Transsexual Rights Society, a local pressure group, objects to the circular. They discover its contents six months after it came into effect. Advise the Society as to its chances of success in the courts.

**(b)** Frank, who is an unemployed resident in a hostel for the homeless, is refused a hip-replacement operation. He wishes to bring an action in his local county court. Advise St Tony's Hospital.

## Further reading

Cane, P. (1995) 'Standing Up for the Public', *Public Law*, 276.

Craig, P. (2004) 'The Common Law, Shared Power and Judicial Review', *Oxford Journal of Legal Studies*, **24**: 129.

Fredman, S. and Morris, G. (1995) 'The Costs of Exclusivity: Public and Private Re-examined', *Public Law*, 68.

Halliday, S. (2004) *Judicial Review and Compliance with Administrative Law*, Oxford, Oxford University Press.

Harlow, C. (2000) 'Export, Import: the Ebb and Flow of English Public Law', *Public Law*, 240.

**Further reading cont'd**

Le Sueur, A. (1992) 'Applications for Judicial Review: The Requirement of Leave', *Public Law*, 102.

Richardson, G. and Genn, H. (eds) (1994) *Administrative Law and Government Action*, Oxford, Oxford University Press, Part 1.

Richardson, G. and Sunkin, M. (1996) 'Judicial Review: Questions of Impact', *Public Law*, 79.

Taggart, M. (ed.) (1997) *The Province of Administrative Law*, Oxford, Hart Publishing, Chapters 1,2,10.

Woolf, Sir H. (1995) 'Droit Publique, English Style', *Public Law*, 57.

# Chapter 17

# Human rights and civil liberties

Right is better than law. (Menander, 342–c.292 BC)

## Key words

- ▶ Law and democracy
- ▶ Interest balancing
- ▶ Individual and community
- ▶ Indeterminacy: expansive and narrow judicial attitudes
- ▶ The limits of interpretation
- ▶ Public and private
- ▶ Separation of powers

## 17.1 Introduction: The Bill of Rights Debate

Human rights disputes are significantly different from those that the courts traditionally deal with which require them to apply an existing rule contained in legislation or in precedent. Human rights cases, by contrast, require the judge to assess the validity of a legal rule or government decision against a vague concept such as freedom of expression and to decide the extent to which a right should be sacrificed to some important public goal, for example personal freedom against the suppression of terrorism. The concept of human rights derives from the individualistic ideas of the seventeenth century which came to political fruition in the eighteenth century American and French revolutions. Human rights did not become a prominent legal issue in the UK until the aftermath of the Second World War which produced a world-wide reaction against the atrocities of the Nazis.

There are three interrelated issues. The first is what counts as a fundamental right. Are these anything other than political claims on behalf of particular interests? The classic enlightenment writers, notably Locke (Chapter 1) thought that there were certain basic rights, given by God, which it is the state's duty to protect. In his case these were life, health, liberty and property. For Hobbes, by contrast, natural rights are based on the universal human interests of gain, safety and reputation and are essentially rational reasons for action rather than rights as such (Chapter 1). They include primarily self-defence, 'do-as-you-would-be-done-by', and the honouring of promises. For Hobbes there are no rights other than those created and enforced by law. Similarly, Bentham regarded the notion of a right as nonsense except in the sense of interests protected by particular laws (Chapter 1).

There is no agreement as to how we identify and justify human rights. Some claim that they are revealed by God, others that they are based upon the idea that humans have a special 'dignity', others that they are simply self-evident. For example the UN's *Universal Declaration on Human Rights* (1948) is founded on the 'inherent dignity of all members of the human family', equality, rationality and 'brotherhood' and invokes the rule of law as a means of avoiding the need for rebellion against tyranny (Preamble Art. 1). However, in the absence of a religious belief it is difficult to see where this 'dignity' comes from. Some, for example Hume (Chapter 1), claim that human rights are driven by biological species sympathy and that we can instinctively recognise them as conventions underpinning particular ways of life which we desire to preserve. Others, following Kant, derive them from apparently self-evident truths such as 'equality' or 'autonomy'. For example Dworkin (*Freedom's Law*, 1996, OUP), argues that certain interests, such as freedom of expression, and the right to a fair trial are non-negotiable conditions of a democratic society because they underpin equality, this being the nearest we can get to a bedrock principle (see also Laws, 'The Constitution, Morals and Right', 1996, *Public Law* 622, favouring autonomy). As we saw in Chapter 1, these ideas are vague and may be contradictory. Behind such assertions is the belief, most famously promoted by Kant, that reason is the ultimate source of value. However, given that humans are not fully rational and reason might point in different directions, this might permit those in power to impose their personalities on others badged as 'reason' (Chapter 1).

Such grandiose assertions also face the difficulty that any charter of rights may be too vague to be directly applied to a concrete case. Indeed, politicians and officials of the kind that draft treaties and laws might take refuge in vagueness as a way of producing agreement while leaving the hard questions to be decided by others such as the courts. Indeed, this was the case with the ECHR (see Harris, 2004, pp. 430–1; Marston, G. 'The UK's Part in the Preparation of the ECHR', 1993, *International and Corporate Law Quarterly*, **42**: 796). Moreover, claims to universality face the problem that some rights, for example private property, may not be recognised in every culture.

This leads to the second issue. What is the legal basis for a statement of fundamental rights? The UK relies on the European Convention on Human Rights. This came into force in 1953 as an international treaty under the auspices of the Council of Europe which was established in 1949 and has 41 members. The European Convention derives from the United Nations' *Universal Declaration of Human Rights* (1948; Cmd 7226). As a response to the atrocities of the Second World War, the European Convention on Human Rights concentrates upon the protection of individual freedom against state interference rather than what are known as second and third generation rights, these being respectively social claims such as housing, and community claims such as environmental quality. As an international agreement, the Convention is something of a bland compromise with many exceptions and vague language (below).

The third issue is who should have the last word in disputes relating to fundamental rights. In particular should a bill of rights be protected against being overridden by the democratic lawmaker? Even if we accept that the concept of human rights is meaningful and should be embedded in the law, nothing follows automatically from this as to what is the best mechanism for protecting them. The ultimate decision maker might for example be a court as in the USA, an elected lawmaker as is still the case in the UK or a special body, such as an ombudsman, a parliamentary committee or a commission, possibly including non-governmental organisations (NGOs).

It is often claimed that the courts are most likely to produce the 'best' outcome being independent, open and guided by intense rational analysis as a forum for public debate. However, arguments about what is the best outcome merely repeat the disagreement. Unless we agree as to what counts as a best outcome we could not agree what mechanism is most likely to produce it. For example, a court is obviously attractive to those who wish to impose philosophical master principles on others but less attractive to those who rely on a pragmatic accommodation between many competing interests. A court is limited by the circumstances and parties in a particular case and the legal process is not comfortable with wide-ranging debate. The appropriate question is therefore what mechanism can most appropriately manage disagreement, irrespective of outcomes. Arguably this should be a democratic assembly in which the whole community can participate on equal terms (see Waldron, 1999). Thus, according to William Cobbett (ibid., p. 232),

> (t)he great right of every man, the right of rights, is the right of having a share in the making of the laws to which the good of the whole makes it his duty to submit.

The favourite liberal argument is that 'democracy' is more than just the will of the majority, that it must be supported by certain basic rights of equality and freedom which must be protected by independent courts against the volatility, corruption or foolishness of the majority (see Laws, 1995 and Lord Bingham in *A* v *Secretary of State* (2004): 'a rights-based democracy'). It is therefore argued that handing over power to a court is not anti-democratic but a prudent 'pre-commitment' of a majority anxious to guard against its own weaknesses, for example a panic overreaction to a supposed threat such as that of terrorism. Just as Ulysses ordered the crew to bind him to the mast and ignore his subsequent pleas to unbind him so that he would not give way to the temptations of the Sirens or a smoker may ask a trusted friend to hide the cigarettes, by removing fundamental rights from its control the majority lessens the risk that it will misuse its power. In particular a court can protect unpopular minorities.

However, according to Waldron (1999, Chapter 11), the Ulysses and cigarette analogies are misplaced. Ulysses and the smoker voluntarily submit to external *impersonal* constraints to meet a specific problem about which there is no disagreement, whereas in the human rights context, we are surrendering our power to decide controversial matters to the personal judgement of an unaccountable and unrepresentative elite group. Waldron draws on the republican argument (Chapter 1, this volume) that we sacrifice dignity and equality by letting courts decide whether laws are valid. He relies on the old idea of positive freedom (Chapter 1, this volume) that freedom consists of obeying laws that we make ourselves Despite its risks and weaknesses, representative democracy is the nearest we can get to equal participation.

While judges may be good at interpreting and applying laws, conflicts between fundamental rights and other important interests go beyond legal rules into territory where judges have no special expertise requiring them to be political philosophers or politicians. For example in *R.J.R. MacDonald v Canada* (1995), the Canadian Supreme Court was divided as to whether the undoubted public interest in combating ill-health justified overriding freedom of expression by banning tobacco advertising. It is difficult to see why a judge is better placed than a democratic assembly to decide such an issue. Indeed, in many cases the courts recognise this and defer to the views of the democratic decision maker (below). Moreover such disputes often raise wide issues that may not be brought before the court which must concentrate on the particular parties' dispute (see e.g. *DPP v Jones* (1999) Lord Hope).

Judges are not directly accountable for their actions, a fact which might tempt the legislature to be irresponsible and to shuffle hard choices to the judges. There is no reliable way of discovering what are the values of the community. A judge might be forced to rely on his personal opinions or be swayed by the circumstances of the case before him. Politicians might appoint judges whose views reflect those of the very politicians whom the judges are supposed to protect us against. There are certainly flaws in our democracy but it seems bizarre to deal with these by an even less democratic method.

The Human Rights Act 1998 recognises this irreducible disagreement by trying to accommodate both sides (below). It uses the advantages of the courts in applying the law even to the extent of scrutinising statutes for compatibility with the Convention. On the other hand, the Act upholds democracy by leaving the final word with Parliament while empowering the courts to put pressure on Parliament thereby creating an accommodation in accordance with the separation of powers.

## 17.2 The Common Law

English lawyers have traditionally used the negative terminology of civil liberties rather than the more positive language of rights. This is because the common law embodies the liberal perspective that everyone is free to do whatever the law does not specifically prohibit. In Hobbes's language, 'freedom lies in the silence of the laws' (Chapter 1). However, in a constitution such as that of the UK, in which competing political parties continuously generate new laws, the problem lies in ensuring that the laws are indeed silent. Moreover, the notion of negative freedom assumes that all freedoms are of equal value. For example Dicey 1915, p. 500), may appear complacent:

> English law no more favours and provides for the holding of public meetings than for the giving of public concerts ... A man has a right to hear an orator as he has a right to hear a band or eat a bun.

The common law's residual or negative approach therefore depends on trusting the lawmaker, the executive and the police not to enact or enforce intrusive laws and on trusting the courts to interpret laws in a way sympathetic to individual liberty. This violates republican ideas by treating us as 'happy slaves' content with a kind master (Chapter 1). We have already met the presumption of statutory interpretation, known as the 'principle of legality', that clear language or necessary implication is required to override fundamental rights (Chapter 5, see *R* v *Secretary of State ex parte Pierson* (1997) per Lord Steyn and Lord Browne-Wilkinson; *R* v *Secretary of State ex parte Simms* [1999] 3 All ER 400 at 411, 412). However, the common law approach might overlook the creeping erosion of liberty by the accumulation of statutes which, taken individually, are relatively innocuous but which add up to a formidable armoury of state powers. For example, over 200 statutory provisions authorise officials other than the police to enter private property so that the residual freedom promoted in *Entick* v *Carrington* (1765) is somewhat frail (see *R* v *IRC ex parte Rossminster* (1980)). Moreover, it is widely recognised that legislation enacted to deal with a particular urgent problem is rarely repealed but remains in force to be used in other contexts.

It is also claimed that the common law being open to any argument and treating all parties as equals is especially suitable for a liberal society (Allan, T. 2001, *Constitutional Justice*, OUP; c.f. Poole, 2002, *Modern Law Review*, 65: 463). The courts' record has been mixed. In some contexts, notably personal liberty (see *A* v *Secretary of State* (2004)), they have been relatively libertarian. In other contexts, notably political dissent, they have been less protective and deferred to government claims based on confidentiality, national security and public order (see e.g. *R* v *Shaylor* (2002)). However, in recent years there has been a trend in favour of interpreting the law in the light of international obligations. This is of great importance in relation to treaties such as those concerning genocide, terrorism, the environment and the rights of the child that have not been formally incorporated into the law.

Even before the Human Rights Act, the courts had begun to place greater emphasis on fundamental rights, notably in relation to access to the courts, prisoners and press freedom (e.g. *R* v *Lord Chancellor ex parte Witham* (1997); *Derbyshire County Council* v *Times Newspapers* (1993); *R* v *Secretary of State ex parte Pierson* (1997); *R* v *Secretary of State ex parte Simms* (1999). Indeed, judges sometimes claim that the ECHR reflects the common law. For example, in *R* v *Secretary of State ex parte Brind* [1990] 1 All ER 469 at 477, Lord Donaldson said that

> you have to look long and hard before you can detect any difference between the English common law and the principles set out in the convention at least if you view the convention through English judicial eyes.

It is also claimed that the reasoning methods in UK law are essentially the same as those of the ECHR in that in both cases freedom can be overridden only in specified circumstances. In *A-G* v *Guardian Newspapers (No. 2)* [1998] 3 All ER 545 at 660, Lord Goff, said:

> I can see no inconsistency between English law (freedom of expression) and (the ECHR). This is scarcely surprising, since we may pride ourselves on the fact that freedom of speech has existed in this country perhaps as long if not longer than anywhere else in the world. The only difference is that [the Convention] ... proceeds to state a fundamental right and then to qualify it, we in this country (where everyone is free to do anything subject only to the provisions of the law) proceed rather on an assumption of freedom of speech, and turn to our law to discover the established exceptions to it.

The two approaches are different in important respects. Firstly, the European Convention requires special justification to override a right, whereas in the common law any sufficiently clearly worded statute will do. Secondly, the common law, sometimes described as unprincipled, is multi-factoral in the sense that it depends on accumulating factors pointing to or against a particular conclusion, without necessarily organising these within a formal hierarchy of principles. These factors include deference to Parliament (*Re McKerr* (2004)), logical coherence, social policy, and morality. On the other hand, the reasoning process under the ECHR is similar since its governing concepts are vague and open-ended. Indeed, in *Wainwright* v *Home Office* [2003] 4 All ER 969,979, Lord Hoffmann suggested that a concept such as privacy cannot be regarded as a principle of law in itself but indicates a value or sense of direction that directs the development of the law.

## 17.3 The Standards to be Applied: The European Convention on Human Rights

The ECHR as such is not part of English law. However its main provisions were incorporated into UK law by the Human Rights Act 1998. Before then the UK had resisted incorporation on the basis that the common law provided equivalent protection (cf. *Re McKerr* (2004)). The Convention claims to combine respect for individual rights with the collective rights of the community, a point frequently made by UK judges who have emphasised that the courts should respect decisions by democratic bodies (see e.g. *Brown* v *Stott* [2001] 2 All ER 97, 114, 118; *R (Alconbury)* v *Secretary of State* [2001] 2 All ER 929, 980–1). For this reason, both liberals and communitarians (Chapter 1) endorse grandiose aspirations.

A few of the rights embodied in the Convention are absolute rights but most are 'qualified' in the sense that they can be overridden in certain circumstances. Moreover, it is frequently asserted that a principle of 'fair balance' runs through the whole Convention so that even where a right appears absolute, the courts might interpret it in the light of competing considerations. Vague words such as 'fair' or 'reasonable' invite them to do so. In *Sporrong* v *Sweden* [1982] 5 EHRR 35, 52 for example it was said that:

> the Court must determine whether a fair balance was struck between the demands of the general interests of the community and the requirement of the protection of the individual's fundamental rights ... the search for the balance is inherent in the whole Convention.

Having exhausted domestic remedies an individual or company can petition the European Court of Human Rights in Strasburg. However, as an international court its decisions are not binding in UK law. The UK has long accepted the right of individuals to take proceedings in the Strasburg Court, but although the UK was an original signatory and indeed its lawyers were largely responsible for drafting the Convention, it did not incorporate the Convention into its domestic law until 1998. One result of this was that the UK was one of the most persistent defaulters in the European Court since we had no domestic remedies.

The following provisions are incorporated (Human Rights Act 1998 s.1).

▶ *Art. 2: Right to life;* except for capital punishment following criminal conviction, defence against unlawful violence, lawful arrest or prevention of unlawful escape, lawful action for quelling riot or insurrection. The right to life has been interpreted narrowly to require the state not to take life but not to authorise voluntary euthanasia. In this context the court emphasised that the Convention is not meant to intervene in controversial moral issues around which there is no consensus but is concerned to protect widely shared values (*R (Pretty)* v *DPP* (2002):

assisted euthanasia not protected). This is one way in which the court deals with the problem that it lacks democratic legitimacy.

▶ *Art. 3: Torture or inhuman or degrading treatment or punishment.* This cannot be overridden (see *Tyrer* v *UK* (1978); *Costello-Roberts* v *UK* (1993) – corporal punishment; *Soering* v *UK* (1989) – extradition to USA with risk of long delays on death row; *Ireland* v *UK* (1978) – interrogation of suspected terrorists). Art. 3 has been interpreted broadly to include, for example, government decisions to withdraw support for asylum seekers where to do so would leave them destitute (see *R (Limbuela)* v *Secretary of State for Social Security* (2004)).

▶ *Art. 4: Slavery, forced or compulsory labour.* Exceptions are prison or parole, military service, emergency or calamity, and 'normal civic obligations'.

▶ *Art. 5: Liberty and security of person.* The main exceptions are criminal convictions, disobedience to a court order, control of children, infection, mental health, alcoholism, drug addiction or vagrancy and in order to prevent illegal immigration or with a view to deportation or extradition. There are safeguards to ensure a speedy trial and adequate remedies against unlawful detention. A person arrested must be informed promptly of the reasons for the arrest and be brought promptly before a court (see *Brogan* (below, Chapter 19)). The court proceedings must be fair, and reasonably speedy.

▶ *Art. 6:* 'In relation to civil rights and obligations (see Chapters 14, 15), and the determination of any criminal charges against him there is a right to a fair trial in public before an independent and impartial tribunal established by law.' In a criminal case there must be further safeguards. These include a right 'to be informed promptly and in a language he understands and in detail, of the nature and cause of the accusation', adequate time and facilities to prepare a defence, a right to choose a lawyer and free legal assistance 'when the interests of justice so require', a right to call witnesses and to examine opposing witnesses on equal terms, and a right to an interpreter. However 'charged with a criminal offence' has been defined narrowly to exclude matters relating to sentencing and bail. These are protected by the general provisions of Arts 5 and 6 (*Phillips* v *United Kingdom* (2001), *R (DPP)* v *Havering Magistrates Court* (2001)).

Judgement shall be pronounced publicly. The press and public may be excluded from all or any part of the proceedings in the interests of morals, public order, national security in a democratic society, where the interests of juveniles or the protection of the private lives of the parties so require, or the extent strictly necessary in the opinion of the court in special circumstances where publicity would prejudice the interests of justice (see *R* v *Bow County Court ex parte Pelling* (1999)).

The right to a fair trial as such is not subject to exceptions and cannot be overridden by public interest concerns. However, its *individual ingredients* such as a right to see information held by the other side can be overridden. This is because the notion of a 'fair balance' between the public interest and the rights of the individual runs through the Convention as a whole. For example in *Brown* v *Stott* (2001), the Privy Council held that the requirement of the Road Traffic Act 1998 s.172 (2) to disclose the name of the driver was not in breach of the right against self-incrimination. The reason for this was the clear public interest in reducing the high rate of death and injury on the roads. Nevertheless, the trial overall must be fair so that any shortfall in one respect must be compensated by scrupulous fairness in others. Where a decision maker is not itself independent and impartial, as in the case of administrative policy decisions, judicial review may provide a sufficient safeguard (see *R (Alconbury)* v *Secretary of State* (2001) and Chapters 14, 15).

▶ *Art. 7: No retrospective criminal laws* except in respect of acts which were criminal when committed according to the general principles of law recognised by civilised nations.

▶ *Art. 8: Respect for privacy, family life, home and correspondence.* This is especially wide ranging. Respect, privacy, and family life are vague concepts so that, in addition to concerns with state and media surveillance and intrusion (Chapter 19), Art. 8 includes sexual and lifestyle matters, housing, and the welfare of children (e.g. *R (G)* v *Barnet LBC* [69]; *R (Razgar)* v *Secretary of State for the Home Department* (2004)). The notion of respect could impose a positive obligation on the state to protect the individual rather than merely a negative obligation not to interfere (see Lord Hope in *Harrow LBC* v *Qazi* (2003)). Privacy concerns dignity and the right to control information about oneself in relation to the esteem and respect of others (*Campbell* v *MGN* (2004): drug rehabilitation treatment; *Wainright* v *Home Office* (2003): strip searches; *Pretty* v *UK* (2002) 35 EHRR 1 para. 61: intolerable disability). Art. 8 does not apparently apply to the retention of fingerprints and DNA samples lawfully taken by the police from innocent suspects. The (not entirely convincing) reason for this appears to be that the interference with privacy is minor and the data concerned can be accessed only by specialists (see *R (S)* v *Chief Constable of South Yorkshire* (2004), Baroness Hale dissenting). An alternative rationale is that Art. 8 applies but is overridden by the public interest in investigating crime (ibid).

Art. 8 does not normally confer a right to be provided with a home but only a right to be protected in one's existing home, thus illustrating that the Convention is concerned primarily with traditional negative freedoms (*Chapman* v *UK* (2001) 10 BHRC 48, 72; *Ghaidan* v *Mendoza* (2004)). However, in extreme circumstances, Art. 8 might impose a positive obligation on the state to provide shelter to ensure that the individual has the basic requirements of a life: 'those features which are integral to a person's identity or ability to function socially as a person,' (Lord Bingham in *R (Razgar)* v *Secretary of State* (2004): removal of asylum seeker). Such a duty may arise in respect of vulnerable groups (for example *Chapman* (above): gypsies; *R (Bernard)* v *Enfield London Borough Council* (2002): disabled with children); *Anufrijeya* v *Southwark London Borough Council* (2004): asylum seekers. However, there must be culpability in the sense of a deliberate or negligent failure to act which has foreseeably serious consequences (*Anufrijeya* (above)).

Art. 8 also applies to nuisances and environmental pollution, although the courts are likely to give considerable weight to the competing demands on public authorities in this context (see *Lopes Ostra* v *Spain* (1994); *Hatton* v *UK* (2003); *Marcic* v *Thames Water* (2004)).

▷ *Art. 9: Freedom of thought, conscience and religion* (Chapter 18)

▷ *Art. 10: Freedom of expression.* This is given an especially high level of protection particularly in respect of the media (Chapter 18).

▷ *Art. 11: Freedom of assembly and association* (Chapter 18). This should also be given high protection being closely related to freedom of expression. However, public order and terrorism issues are also related to freedom of association, in respect of which the executive is often conceded a wide discretion (below).

▷ *Art. 12: The right to marry and found a family* according to national laws governing the exercise of the right. This has been narrowly interpreted as referring only to traditional marriages between biological men and women (*Rees* v *UK* (1987): transsexuals), leaving it to individual states to determine policy on this sensitive issue.

▷ *Art. 14:* 'The rights under the Convention must be secured without discrimination on the grounds of sex, race, colour, language, religion, opinion, national or social origin, association with a national minority, property, birth or other status.' However, Art. 14 has no independent life of its own, there being no general right against discrimination (*Abdulaziz* v *UK* (1985)). It applies only where discrimination takes place in relation to one of the other convention rights, although no such right need actually have been violated and even a tenuous link with another right may suffice (left open in *Ghaidan* v *Mendoza* [2004] 3 All ER 411 [11][12]: discrimination against gay partner in relation to succession to a home, although no right to be provided with a home. Art. 14 extends to grounds other than those expressly mentioned (e.g. *Ghaidan* v *Mendoza* (2004): sexual orientation; *R (Douglas)* v *North Tyneside DC*

(2004): age; *Wandsworth LBC* v *Michalack* (2002): family membership; *R (Clift)* v *Secretary of State* (2004): categories of prisoner). However, in *R (S)* v *Chief Constable of South Yorkshire* (above), the House of Lords took the view that the discrimination must relate to a 'personal characteristic' shared by the disadvantaged group. It was held that Art. 14 was not engaged by a policy of retaining DNA samples taken lawfully from suspects who were later found to be innocent.

The approach to Art. 14 suggested by Grosz, Beatson and Duffy (*Human Rights: The 1998 Act and the European Convention*, 2000) has been followed by the courts (see *Wandsworth LBC* v *Michalak* (above); *R (Clift)* v *Secretary of State* (above); *R (S)* v *Chief Constable of South Yorkshire* (above)). It prompts the following four questions (which may overlap):

1. Do the facts fall within the ambit of one or more of the substantive convention provisions?
2. If so, was there differential treatment as respects that right between the complainant on the one hand and the other persons put forward for comparison (the chosen comparators) on the other? In this connection there are two forms of discrimination. In the case of 'direct' discrimination, the group claiming disadvantage is specifically singled out in the legislation or decision. In the more difficult case of 'indirect' discrimination, the claimant is arguing that, although not specifically singled out, he or she is a member of a group which is especially disadvantaged by an apparently neutral provision, for example a claim that the procedures for selecting students for entry to the legal profession disadvantages ethnic minorities. In this kind of case the choice of a pool of comparators is crucial. It must be a representative group of those advantaged by the provision complained of.
3. Were the chosen comparators in an analogous position to the complainant's situation?
4. If so, did the difference in treatment have an objective and reasonable justification? Discrimination means arbitrary discrimination, so that singling out some characteristic might sometimes be justifiable in the public interest, for example the provision of housing for particular ethnic groups.

▶ *Art. 15:* States can derogate or reserve from most of the Convention in times of war or other public emergency threatening 'the life of the nation' (Chapter 19).
▶ *Art. 16:* Arts 10, 11 and 14 shall not prevent a state from imposing restrictions on the political activities of aliens.

▶ *Art. 17: Abuse of rights.*

> Nothing in this Convention may be interpreted as implying for any State, group or person any right to engage in any activity or perform any act aimed at the destruction of any of the rights and freedoms set forth herein or at their limitation to greater extent than is provided for in the Convention.

This is intended to prevent, for example, racist groups from exploiting convention rights such as freedom of expression or association in order to damage other rights such as religious freedom or privacy (see *Lawless* v *Ireland (No. 3) (1961)*).

▶ *Protocol 1, Art. 1:*

> Every natural or legal person is entitled to the peaceful enjoyment of his possessions. No one shall be deprived of his possessions except in the public interest and subject to the conditions provided for by law and by the general principles of international law. The preceding provisions shall not, however, in any way impair the right of a State to enforce such laws as it deems necessary to control the use of property in accordance with the general interest or to secure the payment of taxes and or other contributions or penalties.

This protects property rights against confiscation without compensation, including the right to dispose of property, but does not confer a positive right to acquire property (see *Marckx* v *Belgium* (1979)). Restrictions on the *use* of property imposed in the public interest, for example environmental and rent controls, are valid without compensation although the line between use and confiscation may be difficult to draw (*Mellacher* v *Austria* (1989); *Fredin* v *Sweden* (1991)). Moreover, the courts are not willing to use the Convention in cases where a property right is restricted by the exercise of other property rights (see *Aston Cantlow Parish Council* v *Wallbank* (2003): charge to repair church roof taking effect as a common law right).

▶ *Protocol 1, Art. 2:* Education – including parental choice in relation to religious and philosophical convictions. The UK has made a reservation in respect of this:

> only so far as compatible with 'the provision of efficient instruction and training and the avoidance of unreasonable public expenditure'.

This is a limited right. It means only a right whatever education the state chooses to provide (*A* v *Head Teacher and Governors of Lord Grey School* (2004). The right to education does not include a right to state funding (see *R (Douglas)* v *North Tyneside DC* (2004)).

▶ *Protocol 1, Art. 3:* Free elections to the legislature at reasonable intervals by secret ballot.

▶ *Protocol 13:* Abolishes the death penalty in all circumstances (Human Rights Act 1998 (Amendment Order) 2004 SI 2004/1574). The Human Rights Act 1998 s.21 (5) abolished the last remaining death penalty provisions in the UK.

## 17.4 The Structure of the Human Rights Act 1998

The Human Rights Act does not incorporate the European Convention on Human Rights as such into UK law but, by virtue of s.1, gives the rights outlined above the status of 'Convention rights' having specific consequences in UK law. Decisions and opinions of the European Court of Human Rights are not binding on the court although they must be taken into account (s.2 (1)). Convention rights do not include rights from which the UK has derogated or reserved (s.14). The Act has not incorporated Art.1: duty to secure to everyone within the jurisdiction the rights and freedoms under the convention, nor Art. 13 which requires effective domestic remedies for breach of the convention it being argued that the Act itself achieves these aims even though convention rights must give way to Acts of Parliament.

It is unclear how far the Act applies in respect of actions outside UK territory. The European Convention on Human Rights imposes a duty on states to secure the rights in respect of everyone 'within their jurisdiction'. While 'jurisdiction' certainly includes UK territory, it is unclear whether the Act applies to, for example, the actions of the army overseas (Chapter 12) or actions of the government that might expose a person to ill-treatment overseas. There is an argument that international relations might be destabilised if the courts interfere with matters occurring abroad. In *R (Ullah)* v *Special Adjudicator* (2004), the House of Lords held that the Convention applies to a decision to expel a person to a country where he is likely to be the victim of torture or inhuman or degrading treatment contrary to Art. 3. Other provisions of the Convention are more culturally variable, notably Art. 8 (privacy etc.). In these cases there must be a 'real risk of flagrant violation' of the Convention (Lord Steyn [50]. In *R (Al-Skeini)* v *Secretary of State* (2004) the High Court held that Art. 2 (right to life) applied to the treatment of prisoners in territory that was in fact under the control of the British Army.

The Act is vague and leaves considerable room for manoeuvre as to how radically it might change the law. Is the European Convention on Human Rights a floor from which we can build our own version of human rights or a ceiling which constrains us? A conservative approach has been predominant. In *R (S)* v *Chief Constable of South Yorkshire* (2004) (above), the House of Lords held that application of Art. 8 of the ECHR should be decided on a uniform basis throughout member states. This rejected the approach taken in the Court of Appeal that English law might develop its own higher standard of human rights in favour of treating the European jurisprudence as the normal guide.

A middle position might be that the decisions of the European court are taken as the primary guidance unless there is some special feature of our constitutional arrangements, legislation or case law that requires us to differ (see *R* v *Togher* [2001] 3 All ER 463, 472 per Lord Woolf; *R (Alconbury)* v *Secretary of State* [2001] 2 All ER 929, 969, Lord Slynn; *R (Ullah)* v *Special Adjudicator* (2004), Lord Bingham [20]). Judges have emphasised that the purpose of the Act is to comply with international obligations under the Convention rather than to develop our own expanded concept of human rights (e.g. *Aston Cantlow Parochial Church Council* v *Wallbank* (2003); *Harrow LBC* v *Qazi* (2003); see also Lord Hobhouse in *Wilson* v *First County Trust* (2003); *R (Pretty)* v *DPP* (2002)). However, this creates the danger of a 'race to the bottom' because international human rights jurisprudence tends towards bland compromise.

There is also a debate as to how far the Convention should override established *domestic* law. On the one hand, there is the possibility of making a fresh start: what Lord Steyn has called a 'new legal landscape' (2000, *European Human Rights Law Review* 549). In *R* v *DPP ex parte Kebeline* (2000), Lord Hope emphasised that a generous approach should be taken to the scope of fundamental rights and freedoms and in *R* v *Lambert* [2001] 3 All ER 577 at 581, Lord Slynn remarked:

> it is clear that the 1998 Act must be given its full import and that long or well entrenched ideas may have to be put aside, sacred calves culled.

In *Harrow LBC* v *Qazi* (2003) there was disagreement between the majority (Lords Hope, Millett and Scott), which took a conservative view, and Lords Bingham and Steyn. The question was whether the right to home life under Art. 8 was overridden by a landlord's property right to evict a person whose wife had terminated their joint tenancy. The majority held that property rights, unless restricted by statute, always overrode the more nebulous right to a home. However, Lord Steyn (dissenting) remarked [27]:

> It would be surprising if the views of the majority ... withstood European scrutiny ... The basic fallacy in the approach is that it allows domestic notions of title, legal and equitable rights and interests, to colour the interpretation of Art. 8 (1). The decision of today does not fit into the new landscape created by the 1998 Act.

On the other hand, supported by the belief that UK law already substantially complied with the European Convention on Human Rights, the Act could be applied conservatively so as not to disturb existing arrangements. For example, according to Lord Hoffmann (*R* v *Secretary of State ex parte Simms* [1999] 3 All ER 400 at 412, 413 ), the Act has three aims. These are firstly to provide a specific text, much of it, in his view, reflecting existing common law principles, secondly to enact the existing 'principle of legality' (Chapter 5) according to which fundamental rights can be overridden only by explicit statutory language or necessary implication, and thirdly to force Parliament to face squarely what it is doing.

Lord Hoffmann's approach is therefore relatively cautious. In *R* v *Secretary of State for Health ex parte C* (2000), he remarked that the Act 'was no doubt intended to strengthen the rule of law but not to inaugurate the rule of lawyers.' (See also his speech in *R (Alconbury)* v *Secretary of State* (2001) emphasising a desire to relate the Act to the characteristics of UK government with its principle of accountability to Parliament. Similarly in *R* v *Lambert* [2001] 3 All ER 577 at 603 Lord Hope emphasised 'the need (a) to respect the will of the legislature so far as this remains appropriate and (b) to preserve the integrity of our statute law so far as this is possible.'

The Act is sometimes described as a 'partnership' between the three branches of government. It respects the separation of powers (Chapter 6) by making provisions concerning the relationship between the three branches (see Lord Hobhouse in *Wilson* v *First County Trust* (2003)). Firstly, as regards the legislature, the court cannot override an Act of Parliament (s.3 (2)b) thereby preserving parliamentary supremacy. If an Act of Parliament violates a convention right the court must enforce it but can make a 'declaration of incompatibility' (s.4) which invites Parliament or the executive to change the law (below). Secondly, the executive, as a 'public authority', is liable in the courts for failing to comply with a convention right unless this is required by a statute or other primary legislation (ss 6, 7). Thirdly, the courts are required to interpret all legislation if it 'is possible to do so' so as to comply with convention rights (s.3) and must themselves comply with convention rights.

## 17.5 The Interpretive Obligation

At the heart of the Act is the requirement that:

> so far as is possible to do so, primary legislation and subordinate legislation must be read and given effect in a way which is compatible with Convention rights (s.3 (1)).

For this purpose primary legislation includes not only statutes but also Prerogative Orders in Council, Measures of the Church Assembly and the General Synod of the Church of England, and delegated legislation which brings into force or amends primary legislation. Subordinate legislation includes other delegated legislation and Acts of the Scottish Parliament and Northern Ireland Assembly (s.21). The court can set aside subordinate legislation that is incompatible with the Convention just as it can do so on ordinary judicial review grounds.

The limits of the s.3 obligation to interpret in line with the Convention are not precise and depend primarily on the judges' attitude to the constitutional limits on their function. The court has to keep to the right side of the border between interpretation and legislation. The government did not introduce a strong formula of the kind used in Canada under which a statute must expressly state that it overrides the Bill of Rights (Cmnd 3782, 2.10). Nevertheless s.3(1) was apparently intended to be a strong provision. The court is not confined to cases where the provision is ambiguous (*R* v *A*

(2001)). Section 3(1) is comparable with the *Marleasing* principle in EC law which requires domestic law to be interpreted where possible in line with EC law (Chapter 8) (see Cmd 3782, 2.7, 8).

In *Wilson* v *First County Trust* (2003), the House of Lords emphasised that the normal assumption of statutory interpretation, namely that the court is seeking the intention of Parliament, does not apply and that it is for the court to make an independent judgement as to whether the language of the statute can be read in a way to make it compatible with the Convention. Nor does the court apply the normal principle that the ordinary meaning of the statute must prevail. In *Harrow LBC* v *Qasi* (2003), Lord Bingham said [23]:

> The court has to arrive at a judicial choice between two possibilities, a choice which transcends the business of finding out what the legislation's words mean.

In *Ghaidan* v *Mendoza* (2004) a statutory provision entitled a person who had lived with a tenant 'as husband and wife' to succeed to the tenancy on the tenant's death. A majority of the House of Lords held that a homosexual relationship fell within the phrase 'living as husband and wife', which they made convention compatible by inserting the words 'if they were' after 'as'. The House held that even if the ordinary meaning of the statute is clear, the court could still distort its language or read in additional wording in order to achieve a meaning that complied with the Convention. The court should take a broad purposive approach. The boundary of the court's power depended on two factors. Firstly, the interpretation must not go against the grain of the legislation in the sense of contradicting its underlying purpose. The courts must look beyond the language itself and consider the policy context and legislative history of the statute in order to identify the essential features of the statutory scheme in question which they must not violate. Secondly, the courts must not make decisions for which they are not equipped in the sense of producing an interpretation that raises social or economic issues that are best left to Parliament.

The language of the statute is however a side-constraint. The courts can strain, supplement but not contradict the statutory language and have been warned to refrain from 'judicial vandalism' (*R (Anderson)* v *Secretary of State* [2002] 4 All ER 1089, 1102,3: power given to Home Secretary to interfere with sentencing process could not be circumvented). In *Ghaidan* Lord Millett gave the example of the word 'cat' in a statute [72]. In some circumstances 'cat' might be read to include 'dog', for example where the care of pets was the underlying concern. However if the legislation had originally stated 'Siamese cats' and later been amended to 'cats' this route would not be possible.

The following are examples (see also Table provided by Lord Steyn in *Ghaidan* (above)) and *Secretary of State for Work and Pensions* v *M* (2004):

▶ *R* v *Lambert* (2001). Under s.28 of the Misuse of Drugs Act 1971 it is a defence to a charge of possessing drugs for the accused to 'prove' that he neither knew of nor suspected nor had reason to suspect some fact alleged by the prosecution. This conflicts with the presumption of innocence (Art. 6(2)). The House of Lords gave the phrase 'to prove' the unusual meaning of 'to give sufficient evidence'. Thus the prosecution still has the general burden of disproving the accused's claim. Lord Hope emphasised (at 604) that great care must be taken to make the revised meaning blend in with the language and structure of the statute. 'Amendment' seems to be possible as long as it does not make the statute unintelligible or unworkable (compare [80] and [81]. See also *R (H)* v *Mental Health Review Tribunal* (2001): reverse burden of proof but no room for manoeuvre).

▶ *R* v *A* (2001) (perhaps the most radical example). The Youth Justice and Criminal Evidence Act 1999 s.41 (1) prohibited evidence in rape cases of the alleged victim's previous sexual experience without the court's consent, which could be given only in specified circumstances. It was held that the court could construe the Act so as to permit evidence necessary to make the trial fair since that was the general object of the Act. Thus additional provisions, 'subject to the right to a fair trial', could be implied into unambiguous language beyond the normal limits of statutory interpretation even if this strained the normal meaning (see Lord Steyn's speech). However, the court cannot override provisions that specifically contradict convention rights.

▶ *S (children) (care plan)* (2002): power of court to intervene in local authority care proceedings could not be added to Children Act 1989 s.38: court cannot depart substantially from fundamental feature of a statutory scheme particularly if it has practical consequences which the court cannot evaluate. Similarly *Poplar HARCA* v *Donoghue* (2001): the term 'reasonable' could not be inserted into a statute which gave a landlord an absolute right to evict a tenant.

As was pointed out in *Ghaidan* (above) the courts are still feeling their way and the limits of interpretation remain flexible. Moreover, interpretation is a two-way process and it is possible sometimes to interpret the Convention 'down' to fit existing English law thus avoiding the need to wrestle with interpreting the statute (e.g. *R (Alconbury)* v *Secretary of State* (2001), Chapter 15).

## 17.6 Declaration of Incompatibility

Where it is not possible to interpret primary legislation in line with a convention right, a higher court (High Court and above) may, but is not required to, make a 'declaration of incompatibility' (s.4). This is at the heart of the accommodation between law and democracy. A declaration of incompatibility has no effect on the validity of the law in question and is not binding on the parties (s.4 (6)). A declaration of incompatibility invites Parliament to consider whether to change the law. Its only legal consequences are to make available a 'fast track' procedure which enables a minister, by statutory instrument subject to the approval of Parliament, to make such amendments as he considers necessary to remove the incompatibility. A declaration of incompatibility is a last resort (*R* v *A* (above) [108] and should not be used in order to avoid the task of interpreting the statute to comply with the Convention (*Ghaidan* (above) per Lord Steyn [39]).

The fast-track procedure can be used where a declaration of incompatibility has been made and any available appeal rights have been used. It can also be used where an incompatibility arises because of a ruling by the European Court of Human Rights and a minister considers that there are 'compelling reasons' for proceeding (s.10). It does not apply to Measures of the Church of England. Also, subordinate legislation which conflicts with a convention right can be quashed by the court and reinstated in amended form under this procedure. Ministers are not bound to obey a declaration of incompatibility and judicial review may not lie in respect of a refusal to do so (below).

## 17.7 Statement of Compatibility

Under s.19, a minister of the Crown in charge of a bill in either House of Parliament must, before the second reading of the bill (a) make a statement to the effect that in his view the provisions of the Bill are compatible with the convention rights (a 'statement of compatibility'); or (b) make a statement to the effect that although he is unable to make a statement of compatibility the government nevertheless wishes the House to proceed with the bill. The statement must be in writing and published in such manner as the minister making it considers appropriate.

Apart from putting political pressure on the government it is not clear what is the effect of a statement of compatibility. As a statement of the opinion of the executive, the courts should not defer to it when interpreting the legislation in question. Indeed, a statement of compatibility means little where the statute in question confers a wide discretion on the executive or the police. Moreover, because the statement applies only to the second reading, it does not cover amendments that might be included at later stages. There is a Joint Parliamentary Committee on Human Rights which considers all bills having human rights implications and this might give some reinforcement to s.19. The government is considering whether to introduce a Commissioner to monitor the working of the Act such as exists in Northern Ireland.

## 17.8 Remedies

By virtue of s.6 (1), 'it is unlawful for a public authority to act in a way which is incompatible with a convention right' except where: (a) 'as a result of one or more provisions of primary legislation, the authority could not have acted differently'; or (b) 'in the case of one or more provisions of, or made under, primary legislation which cannot be read or given effect in a way which is compatible with the Convention rights, the authority was acting so as to give effect to or enforce those provisions'. For this purpose an 'act' includes a failure to act but does not include a failure to introduce or lay before Parliament a proposal for legislation nor make any primary legislation or remedial order (s.6 (6)).

Section 7 entitles a 'victim' to bring proceedings in respect of an act which is unlawful under s.6, and also to rely on convention rights in the appropriate court or tribunal or in any legal proceedings such as defence against a criminal charge or administrative action or an appeal. However, the Secretary of State can make rules designating an appropriate court or tribunal for particular purposes (s.7 (1)a, s.9 (1)c). The Secretary of State has exercised this power principally in relation to special tribunals concerning immigration, asylum and other cases involving national security matters (Chapter 19). Reflecting the concerns of judicial independence, in relation to the judicial functions of a court or tribunal, proceedings must be by appeal or judicial review or otherwise as provided for by rules made by the Lord Chancellor or Secretary of State.

'Victim' has the same meaning as in cases brought before the ECHR (s.7 (7)). The claimant or a close relative must be directly affected, or at least very likely to be affected, by the action complained of (see *Klass* v *Germany* (1979); *Open Door* v *Ireland* (1992)). There is no standing for NGOs representing the collective or public interests (*Director General of Fair Trading* v *Proprietary Association of Great Britain* (2001)). In a judicial review case an NGO would be able to challenge a decision only on domestic grounds while a victim could join the same proceedings on human rights grounds (s.7 (3)). It appears that a public authority cannot be a victim against another public authority (see *Aston Cantlow Parochial Church Council* v *Wallbank* (2003)). However, this is questionable in the UK context since we have no unitary concept of the state (Chapter 4).

Under s.8 the court can award any of the remedies normally available to it 'as it considers just and appropriate'. Damages can be awarded only by a court which has power to award damages or order compensation in civil proceedings (for example not by criminal courts and other specialist courts) and then only if the court is satisfied that 'the award is necessary to afford just satisfaction to the person in whose favour it is made' (s.8 (4)). The phrase 'just satisfaction' is part of the jurisprudence of the ECHR and the court must take into account the principles applied by the ECHR in awarding compensation (ibid.) (see Mowbray, [1997], *Public Law* 647). However, apart from insisting that there must be substantial loss or injury, these do not give clear guidance and the court has considerable discretion which goes beyond domestic law (see Z v UK (2001), *Damages Under the Human Rights Act 1998*, Law Com No. 266; Cullen v *Chief Constable RUC* [2004] 2 All ER 237, 262). In order to safeguard judicial independence, where an action for damages is brought in respect of a judicial act, meaning in this context an act of a court, there is no liability in respect of an act in good faith except for an unlawful arrest or detention. The action must be brought against the Crown with the judge concerned being made a party (HRA 1998 s.9 (3)(4)).

## 17.9 ▶ Public Authorities

The European Convention on Human Rights applies to states and their agencies. Similarly the Human Rights Act can be directly enforced only against a public authority (s.6 (1)). For the purposes of the Act, 'public authority' includes a court or tribunal (s.6 (3)). A public authority also includes any body 'certain of whose functions are functions of a public nature' (ibid). However Parliament, or a person exercising functions in connection with proceedings in Parliament, is not a public authority except the House of Lords in its judicial capacity (s.6 (4)).

There are therefore two kinds of public authority. Firstly, there are bodies such as central and local government and the police which are inherently public and are known as 'core' public authorities. All the activities of these bodies fall within the Act. This can be contrasted with the approach taken in domestic judicial review law which is primarily functional (Chapter 16). Secondly, there are 'functional' public authorities. These are more difficult to identify. Functional public authorities may perform some functions on behalf of government but also perform private functions. The 'private acts' of bodies of this kind do not fall within the Act (s.6 (5)). The issue is particularly important given the current popularity of various forms of privatisation. On the one hand, it has been argued that a broad view should be taken so as to subject a wide range of powerful bodies to the Act. This was recently endorsed by the Joint Committee on Human Rights (*7th Report*, 2003–04, HL 39, HC 382). On the other hand, it has been suggested that private bodies should be subject to less onerous obligations than public bodies narrowly defined (see Oliver, 2004; cf. Sunkin 2004, *Public Law* 643).

The European Court of Human Rights has not addressed the question directly of what is a public authority or a public function. Its approach seems to be based on whether the particular act is carried out under the control of the government or on behalf of the government (see *Sigurjónnson* v *Iceland* (1993)). The UK courts have broadly followed this approach. They have also been influenced by the belief that a body which is a public authority cannot itself claim human rights against another branch of the government. This is particularly significant in relation, for example, to religious bodies and charities which protect vulnerable minorities.

In *Aston Cantlow Parochial Church Council* v *Wallbank* (2003), the House of Lords held, overruling the Court of Appeal, that a parochial church council of the Church of England is not a core public authority even though the Church of England has a close connection with the state and has many special legal powers and privileges. A core public authority must be 'governmental' in the sense that its activities are for the benefit of the general public interest whereas the Church of England primarily benefits its own members. However, some aspects of the Church of England might fall into the category of *functional* public authority, for example functions in connection with marriages and funerals since these involve public rights. The case itself concerned the statutory right of a parochial church council to enforce an obligation to pay for the repair of a church roof, against a houseowner. A majority, emphasising the European Court's approach, held that this was a private function, being the enforcement of a property right for the primary benefit of churchgoers. Lord Scott, dissenting, thought that this was a 'public' function in that it involved historic conservation for the benefit of the community enforced by special powers. *Wallbank* therefore illustrates the artificiality and uncertainty of attempting to distinguish between the public and the private and that the matter depends on a combination of factors. These include, in particular, public benefit and the connection between the body in question and another acknowledged public authority.

*Poplar Housing Association* v *Donoghue* (2001) is the other main authority. This concerned whether a charitable housing association set up by a local authority was a public authority. The Court of Appeal held that the matter depends on accumulation of factors, no single one being conclusive, which impose a public stamp on the activities of the body in question. These include, in particular, statutory authority and the intermeshing of the body in question with government proper. Lord Woolf emphasised that it was not sufficient that the body was a charity carrying out functions in the public interest, nor that it was publicly funded, nor that it was subject to regulation by the government although these matters might be relevant. He pointed out that, although the test is not necessarily the same as that for judicial review, there was a close analogy with judicial review cases (Chapter 16) and that a broad view should be taken, the matter being one of fact and degree in the particular context. The association was exercising a public function in relation to its tenants because its activities were significantly influenced by local authority policy and there were local authority representatives on its governing board. The Court of Appeal held that it was exercising a public function. On the other hand, some of its activities such as raising money on the markets might be regarded as private. An individual can be a public authority (*A* v *Head Teacher and Governors of Lord Grey School* [2004] 4 All ER 587).

### 17.9.1 Horizontal Effect

Even though the primary liability under the Act is that of a public authority the Act has substantial 'horizontal effect' in the sense that private persons as well as public bodies may be required to respect human rights. It is arguable that human rights should pervade all law. Even private legal relationships are created and defined by the state, which could therefore be regarded as responsible for ensuring that the law meets the minimum standards appropriate to a democratic society. For example, it would be anomalous if there were a right of privacy against an NHS hospital and not a private hospital. On the other hand, the purpose of the Human Rights Act is to give effect to the European Convention on Human Rights, which is enforceable only against a state (Art. 34). It can therefore be argued that in their nature, convention rights are directed only against the state (Buxton (2000)). Moreover, the Act does not include Art. 1 of the ECHR which requires states to 'secure to everyone within their jurisdiction' the rights and freedoms conferred by the Convention.

The main arguments in favour of horizontal effect are as follows:

▶ All legislation must be interpreted according to the Convention even that applying to private relationships. In *Ghaidan* v *Mendoza* (2004) the House of Lords applied Art. 14 (discrimination) to legislation which discriminated against homosexual couples occupying property owned by private landlords (see also *Wilson* v *First County Trust* (2003)).

▶ By virtue of s.6, the courts are public authorities. Wade (2000) therefore suggests that a court would act 'unlawfully' if it did not apply convention rights in every case before it even between private persons. The victim's right would be against the court itself not directly against the other private party. The courts do not seem to have accepted this broad view.

▶ A less extreme view is that, while s.6 prevents a new cause of action against a private body, it requires the court to apply convention rights in the context of *existing causes of action* or in respect of the court's own powers to make orders and grant remedies (Hunt, 1998, and see *Wilson* v *First County Trust* [2003] 4 All ER 97 [174]; *Campbell* v *MGN* (2004) [133] per Baroness Hale). The matter would therefore have to arise in the course of other legal proceedings into which a human rights dimension could be implied. Thus a private person might be denied the assistance of the court in enforcing a claim contrary to a convention right and a court enforcement order might be opposed on human rights grounds. For example, a court might be entitled to refuse to give a possession order to a private landlord who attempted to evict a tenant from her home (*R (McLellan* v *Bracknell Forest BC* [2002] 1 All ER 899, [42]). The weakness of this approach seems to be that it is random, in that it depends on the matter falling into an existing category of UK law.

▶ Particular convention rights may include a positive obligation on the state to require private persons to respect the right in question (see *Kroon* v *Netherlands* (1994)). The ECHR has applied this particularly to Art. 8 (privacy), even though this is expressly limited to the acts of public authorities (see e.g. *X and Y* v *Netherlands* (1985): child abuse; *A* v *UK* (1998): parental chastisement).

▶ The courts might develop the common law by analogy with the European Convention on Human Rights (as was beginning to happen before the Human Rights Act (above)). In *Campbell* v *MGN Ltd* (2004), the House of Lords used Arts. 8 and 10 as a guide in determining the ambit of the common law of breach of confidence in relation to press freedom but the majority did not seem to think that the matter strictly fell within the Human Rights Act (see [17] [18] [19] [49]).

## 17.10 Retrospective Effect

The Act applies to legislation made both before and after it came into force (s.3 (2) a). However, the Act is not in general retrospective. In the case of a defence to 'proceedings brought by a public authority', it applies whenever the Act in question took place but otherwise applies only where the particular Act complained of took place or is continued after the Act came into force (s.22 (4)). The Act therefore cannot change rights established before that date. For example in *Wilson* v *First County Trust* (2003), the House of Lords held that the Act did not apply to a contract that was unenforceable when it was made before the Act came into force even though the court order to enforce it was made after that date. (See also *Re McKerr* (2004)).

## 17.11 Overriding Protected Rights

Any workable code of fundamental rights must be expressed in general language and with sufficient exceptions to permit governments to act in the public interest or to resolve conflicts with other rights. Several methods are available to accommodate competing concerns and to adjust the law to changing circumstances. The Convention has been described as a 'living instrument', meaning that the rights themselves and their ranking against other factors change with the times (e.g. *Soering* v *UK* (1989): present day attitudes to death penalty mean that extradition to death row in USA would violate Art. 3; *Ghaidan* v *Mendoza* (2004): homosexual partners). Although these two examples would command support from many liberals, it is not self-evident that courts are especially well equipped to make this kind of judgement.

It is tempting to seek an overarching principle that would combine the human right with the competing interest under some overall concept of common good or to find a 'balance' – a concept which itself presupposes some overriding objective measure.

However it is doubtful whether, given the complexities and contradictions of human nature, any overriding principle is possible. Indeed in *R (S)* v *South Yorkshire Chief Constable* (2004), Sedley LJ in the Court of Appeal pointed out that the notion of 'balancing' individual rights against the public interest means that the latter will always prevail (see also Lord Steyn in *Brown* v *Stott* [2001] 2 All ER 97 at 118).

Moreover, there are competing approaches as to what human rights are about. On one view, that of liberal individualists, human rights concern a zone of individual freedom which might exceptionally be overridden in the public interest but recognising the sacrifice involved. On the other hand, communitarians and republicans, favouring 'positive freedom', might argue that human rights in themselves are valuable only by virtue of their contribution to some greater good (see Klug, 2000). For example in *Gough* v *Chief Constable of Derbyshire* [2001] 4 All ER 289 at 321, Laws LJ said:

> rights are divisive, harmful, ultimately worthless, unless their possession is conditional upon the public good.

and

> it is inherent in the nature of the right itself that that the individual who claims its benefit may have to give way to the supervening weight of other claims ... the right's practical utility rests upon the fact that there can be no tranquillity within the state without a plethora of unruly individual freedoms. (320)

From this perspective, accommodating human rights and the public interest would be less difficult since rights would be conditional upon conforming to whatever happens to be the particular preference as to what constitutes society's 'good', thus raising Isiaah Berlin's worries about authoritarianism (Chapter 1).

As regards the mechanisms available for interest-balancing under the Human Rights Act; firstly some rights are 'absolute'. These include the prohibitions on torture and inhuman and degrading treatment (Art. 3), slavery (Art. 4.1), the right to a fair trial (Art. 6), and discrimination (Art. 14). Any accommodation with other interests must found by exploiting the meaning of the right. For example, what counts as 'torture' might be redefined according to changing sensibilities, and 'fairness' and 'discrimination' embody the notion of a reasonable balance between competing concerns.

Secondly, other rights are qualified, being limited in ways specified in the particular article sometimes to the point of having little meaning (for example Art. 12, right to marry in accordance with the laws of the particular state). In some cases there is no question of balancing the right against another interest since the qualification of the right itself is built into its definition (for example Art. 4, 'forced labour', does not include military service).

Thirdly, the court may be required to balance the right against a specified override which might be another right or a more general public concern. Arts 8 to 11 provide characteristic examples. The overrides vary with the particular article but in all cases include public safety, public order, the prevention and detection of serious crime, the protection of health and morals and the protection of the rights of others. The overrides have been strictly interpreted and the onus is on the state to establish them (*Sunday Times* v *United Kingdom* (1979)).

Before applying an override there are certain threshold requirements. Firstly, the restrictions must be 'prescribed by law' or 'in accordance with the law', terms which apparently mean the same (*Malone* v *UK* (1984)). This imports traditional rule of law ideas (Chapter 5). Thus the restrictions must be clear (for example the vague terms used in UK public order legislation (Chapter 18) may be vulnerable), must not involve wide discretion and must be made in accordance with a regular and accessible lawmaking process (see *Sunday Times* v *UK* (1979); *Klass* v *Germany* (1979)). Taking into consideration the circumstances of the domestic law, the applicant must be able reasonably to foresee that the conduct in question would be unlawful and there must be adequate safeguards including independent and accessible courts (see *Open Door* v *Ireland* (1992); *Kruslin* v *France* (1990); *Bentham* v *Netherlands* (1986); *Leander* v *Sweden* (1987); *Airey* v *Ireland* (1979); *Brogan* v *UK* (1989)).

Secondly, the restrictions must be 'necessary in a democratic society' (this overlaps with proportionality, below). The concept of 'necessary in a democratic society' is vague and invites the judge to impose his or her personal views. It does not mean absolute necessity but means a 'pressing social need' which is more than merely 'useful', 'reasonable' or desirable' (*Handyside* v *UK* (1976); *Fayed* v *UK* (1994); see *Brown* v *Stott* (2001): combating drunk driving; *Gough* v *Chief Constable of Derbyshire* [2001] 4 All ER 289, 321: public order and police resources). The court has power to hear any person and takes into account evidence, for example from government departments and voluntary bodies. As we shall see the court often defers to the government on the matter (below).

In *R (Samaroo)* v *Secretary of State* (2001), Dyson LJ listed factors that are taken into account in the 'balancing' exercise. They include the following:

▶ Is the right absolute or subject to overrides? 'Absolute' rights have a higher status but, by implication, even these might sometimes be compromised.

▶ The extent to which economic, social or political factors are involved that would require the court to defer to the government on democratic grounds.

▶ The extent to which the court has special expertise, for example in relation to criminal matters.

▶ Whether the right claimed is of special importance, requiring a high level of protection. This applies to torture, a fair trial, discrimination and also probably personal liberty, but not to the more nebulous rights to home and family life.

### 17.11.1  Proportionality

The concept of proportionality gives some guidance as to how the 'fair balance' is struck. It also applies where the state has a positive duty to secure a right (*R (Pretty)* v *DPP* (2002) [90]. Proportionality asks whether the legislative purpose is sufficiently important to override the right in question and whether it can be achieved by less intrusive means. It is of general application and not limited to cases where the Convention specifically requires that the restriction be 'necessary in a democratic society'. Proportionality was summarised by Laws LJ in *Gough* v *Chief Constable of Derbyshire* [2001] 4 All ER 289 at 321 as follows:

> the right in question is not to be interfered with save on substantial and objective grounds of public interest and that the state, if it decides that the right must be interfered with, has to choose a means judged to constitute the least interference consistent with the policy aim in view.

In *Gough* it was held that the serious threat of football hooliganism justified bans on suspected troublemakers from travelling abroad in view of the limited resources available to the police which prevented them from taking more selective measures.

The court will ask firstly whether the restriction is imposed for a proper and practicable purpose; secondly whether the breach is 'necessary' to meet a pressing social need (above); thirdly whether less restrictive means could have been employed; fourthly whether there are safeguards to protect the individual (see *R* v *Shaylor* [2002] Chapter 19). For example in *McVeigh* v *UK* (1983), the European Court held that an emergency restriction on personal freedom, while necessary to meet a pressing social need, did not justify a refusal to let the claimants contact their wives. Proportionality also requires that the restrictions must not be discriminatory in the sense that like cases must be treated alike (*Marckx* v *Belgium* (1979)).

Proportionality might require restricting the right, but not destroying it completely. For example, an important aspect of freedom of expression is whether there are alternative outlets for what the claimant wishes to communicate (Chapter 18), *R (Szluk)* v *Governor of Full Sutton Prison* (2004). The social need might also be compromised. For example in *R.J.R. Macdonald* v *Canada* (1995), the Canadian Supreme Court was divided over the extent to which tobacco advertising should be restricted in order to meet the public interest in health (see also *R (British American Tobacco UK Ltd)* v *Secretary of State for Health* (2004)). Why should anything less than a total ban be proportionate and how is a court, from the narrow perspective of the individual case, in a position to make this kind of judgement?

It has been held that in dealing with legislation concerning matters of general social or economic policy, the question of proportionality should be decided at the macro-level of the legislation in general and, other than in exceptional circumstances, not the micro-level of the facts of the individual case (*Wandsworth London Borough Council* v *Michalak* (2002); *Harrow LBC* v *Qazi* (2003); *Wilson* v *First County Trust* (2003) [74] [75][76]). It might well be thought that judgements at this level are best made by the legislature which can seek a practical accommodation based on public opinion.

Sometimes the competition is between two individual protected rights, for example privacy and freedom of expression. In *Campbell* v *MGN* (2004), the *Daily Mirror* had published information and photographs about the treatment for drug addiction undergone by a famous fashion model. The newspaper's and indirectly the public's right to freedom of expression was balanced against the claimant's right to privacy. The House of Lords regarded these rights as of equal importance and looked closely at all the circumstances with the aim of producing the least harmful outcome, thus taking a utilitarian approach (Chapter 1). It was held firstly that the fact the claimant had been a drug addict was not protected since she had repeatedly told the media that she was not on drugs, thus putting the matter into the public domain. However, it was also held that the information about the details of her treatment should not have been published since this was inherently confidential in nature. Importantly, there were no political or democratic values in issue of a kind which supported press freedom. Lords Nicholls and Hoffmann dissented, taking a wider view of press freedom, that a newspaper should be able to add colour and detail to its reporting and that journalists should be entitled to some latitude in the wider interests of a healthy press. A restrictive approach might inhibit the press and so hamper democracy. Thus in the end, proportionality is a subjective judgement raising the question whether the courts are in the best position to make it.

Margin of Appreciation/Discretion

This concept of the margin of appreciation, sometimes called the discretionary area of judgement, was developed by the European Court of

Human Rights in order to accommodate national differences in political, religious or moral values or practices. When asking whether state action is proportionate the ECHR will not substitute its views for those of the state but ask itself only whether the national authorities were reasonably entitled to think that the interference complained of was justifiable, see *Handyside* v *UK* (1976); *Open Door and Dublin Well Woman* v *Ireland* (1992); *Buckley* v *United Kingdom* (1997)). This is another important aspect of incommensurability (above, Chapter 1). Different communities may have different but justifiable blends of values and attitudes and if an international tribunal intervened it might forfeit respect.

It is arguable therefore that the doctrine of margin of appreciation as such should play no part in domestic cases. However, by whatever name, the courts are leaving a discretionary area of judgement to ministers. In *R* v *DPP ex parte Kebeline* [1999] 3 WLR 972, 974 Lord Hope spoke of an

> area of judgement within which the judiciary will defer, on democratic grounds, to the considered opinion of the elected body or person whose act or decision is said to be incompatible with the Convention ... It will be easier for such an area of judgement to be recognised when the Convention itself requires a balance to be struck, much less so when the right is stated in terms that are unqualified. It will be easier for it to be recognised where the issue involves questions of social and economic policy, much less so where the rights are of high constitutional importance or are of a kind where the courts are especially well placed to assess the need for protection.

In other words the margin of discretion is an application of the flexible judicial review standard of unreasonableness (Chapter 15). In *R (Mahmood)* v *Secretary of State* (2001), Lord Phillips MR emphasised that, even where human rights are at stake, the role of the court is supervisory or secondary. The court would only intervene when the decision fell outside the range of responses open to a reasonable decision maker:

> The court will bear in mind that, just as individual states enjoy a margin of appreciation which permits them to respond, within the law, in a manner that is not uniform, so there will often be an area of discretion permitted to the executive of a country before a response can be demonstrated to infringe the Convention... The court will ask the question, applying an objective test, whether the decision maker could reasonably have concluded that that the interference was necessary to achieve one or more of the legitimate aims recognised by the Convention.

In *Blessing Edore* v *Secretary of State* (2003) the Court of Appeal explained the margin of discretion as describing 'no more than an area within which two reasonable albeit opposite views may fairly be reached.'

The margin of discretion does not apply to the initial question of whether the convention right in question applies at all. It comes into its own in connection with the question whether the government is entitled to override the right (*R (S)* v *Chief Constable of South Yorkshire* (2004) [27] [64]). To some extent, it meets the common criticism of the courts that they are unduly narrow and formalistic, have limited information and may ignore wider questions of the public interest, giving spurious certainty to matters where there is legitimate disagreement. Its width varies according to the importance of the right, the importance of the public interest in question and the democratic content of the decision. In *Gough* (above) it was said [78] that the margin of discretion is greater, perhaps akin to the *Wednesbury* test, when the decision maker is the primary legislator. In *Poplar HARCA v Donoghue* (2001) the Court of Appeal refused to condemn s.21 (4) of the Housing Act 1988 which gave social landlords an automatic right to possession of a dwelling house in certain circumstances. Lord Woolf LCJ remarked [69] that:

> the economic and other implications of any policy in this area are extremely complex and far reaching. This is an area where in our judgement the courts must treat the decisions of Parliament as to what is in the public interest with particular deference.

And in *R (S) v Chief Constable of Yorkshire Police* (2004) [16] Lord Woolf said:

> I regard it as being fundamental that the court keeps at the forefront of its consideration its lack of any democratic credentials.

In *R (Pro Life) Alliance v BBC* (2003), Lord Hoffmann criticised the use of the language of deference to describe the margin of discretion. He pointed out that the concept reflected the separation of powers' distinction between the role of the courts and those of the other branches of government. According to Lord Hoffmann, the courts are deferring to no one but are upholding those roles, which is their constitutional function (also Lord Bingham, *A v Secretary of State* (2004)).

The margin is particularly strong in security and anti-terrorism matters and areas involving controversial political discretions with limited legal content (*R (Farrakhan) v Secretary of State* (2002); *A v Secretary of State* (2004)). It is also strong in relation to legislation intended to meet general social and economic goals such as the provision of social housing, particularly where these conflict with broad, nebulous rights such as the right to a home or child welfare under Art. 8 (*Poplar HARCA* (above); *R (G) v Barnet LBC* (2004) [69]) and in public order, defence and immigration matters (*International Transport Roth GmbH v Secretary of State for the Home Department* (2002)). The European Court has emphasised that the margin may depend upon whether the matter has been subject to considered democratic deliberation as opposed to 'unquestioning and passive adherence to a historic tradition' (*Hirst v UK* (2004), Chapter 10). If this were to apply in domestic law it would strengthen the position of the legislature.

Some matters are so fundamental as to fall outside any possible margin of discretion. Prominent among these is the case of discrimination on the grounds of race, gender, ethnicity and sexuality (see Baroness Hales's speech in *Ghaidan* v *Mendoza* (2004)). Other examples are the right to a fair trial and matters involving personal liberty (*Youssef* v *Home Office* (2004)), serious restrictions on freedom of political expression (Chapter 18) or access to the courts (see Laws LJ in *Mahmood* (above); Lord Bingham in *R* v *Secretary of State ex parte Daly* (2001), above 16.5; *R* v *A* [2001] 3 All ER 1,14). Moreover, even where there is a margin of discretion, the government must provide some factual basis for its actions (*Gough* v *Chief Constable of Derbyshire* (2001), *Matthews* v *Ministry of Defence* (2003)).

## Summary

▶ The human rights debate involves attempts to accommodate competing and incommensurable values without any coherent overarching principle to enable a choice to be made. It is therefore arguable that an elected body rather than a court should have the last word. The Human Rights Act 1998 has attempted a compromise by leaving Parliament the last word but giving the court power to influence Parliament.

▶ Freedom in the common law is residual in the sense that one can do anything unless there is a specific law to the contrary. I suggested that this is an inadequate method of safeguarding important liberties. There is a debate as to the extent to which the common law embodies the principles of the ECHR and it is suggested that there are important differences in the approaches of the two systems.

▶ The ECHR as such is not strictly binding upon English courts but can be taken into account where the law is unclear or where a judge has discretionary powers.

▶ The Human Rights Act 1998, while not incorporating the convention as such, has given the main rights created by the ECHR effect in domestic law. UK legislation must be interpreted to be compatible with convention rights, and public bodies other than Parliament must comply with convention rights. The courts must take decisions of the ECHR into account but are not bound by them. It is unlawful for a public authority to act in a way that is incompatible with a convention right. Victims have can bring proceedings under the Act against a public authority and rely on convention rights in any legal proceedings.

▶ The Act can be directly enforced only against public authorities and by a 'victim' defined in accordance with the case law of the European Court. 'Public authority' includes all the activities of government bodies proper and courts and tribunals, but in relation to bodies that have a mixture of public and private functions (for example social landlords) only to their public 'acts'. The courts seem to be taking a similar approach to the question of what is public function as in judicial review cases.

▶ 'Horizontal effect' may be direct, where the court is required to enforce a right against a private person, or indirect, where the state is required to protect against violations by private persons. It is not clear how far the Act has horizontal effect although there are several devices that might enable it to do so.

## Summary cont'd

▶ Parliamentary supremacy is preserved in that convention rights must give way where they are incompatible with a statute. The courts have taken a moderate approach in relation to the obligation to interpret statutes, 'so far as it is possible to do so', to be compatible with convention rights. However, there are differences of emphasis between judges as to the assumptions on which interpretation should be approached, in particular the extent to which established English law should be respected.

▶ Where primary legislation is incompatible, the court can draw attention to violations by making a declaration of incompatibility. There is a 'fast track' procedure available in special circumstances to enable amendments to legislation to be made. The government must be explicit as to any intention to override convention rights.

▶ Some convention rights can be overridden by prescribed public interest concerns or other rights, and a principle of fair balance runs through the convention as a whole. The courts are guided to some extent by the concept of proportionality. While these devices help to structure and rationalise decision making, they do not remove the need for the court to make a subjective political judgement.

▶ The courts have applied the notion of 'margin of appreciation' or margin of discretion in the context of decisions made by elected officials. The width of the margin of appreciation depends on various factors, chief among which are the importance and extent of the particular right that is violated in relation to the seriousness of the public harm if the right were not overridden, and the extent to which the matter involves controversial political, social or economic choices.

# Exercises

**17.1** 'This is the trouble with fundamental values. Whichever one you take with you as a guide, another one is waiting round the corner with a sock full of sand' Sedley.
Explain and discuss.

**17.2** 'The (Human Rights) Bill is a key component of our drive to modernise our society and refresh our democracy in a way that will strengthen representative and democratic government' Jack Straw.
Do you agree?

**17.3** To what extent does Section 3 of the Human Rights Act 1998 empower the courts to override democracy?

**17.4** 'My impression is that two factors are contributing to a misunderstanding of the remedial scheme of the 1998 Act. First there is the constant refrain that a judicial reading down or reading in would flout the will of Parliament. The second factor may be an excessive concentration on linguistic factors of the particular statute' Lord Steyn in *Ghaidan* v *Mendoza* (2004) [40][41]. Explain and critically evaluate this statement.

17.5 'The court will bear in mind that, just as individual states enjoy a margin of appreciation which permits them to respond, within the law, in a manner that is not uniform, so there will often be an area of discretion permitted to the executive of a country before a response can be demonstrated to infringe the Convention' Phillips LJ in *R (Mahmood)* v *Secretary of State* (2001). Explain and discuss critically.

17.6 Explain the mechanics and constitutional significance of the Declaration of Incompatibility.

17.7 The 'Flashers (Zero Tolerance) Act 2004' (imaginary) provides that a constable may arrest any person found wandering in woodlands whom he suspects is likely to cause offence to any person. The defendant is guilty unless he can prove that he was not intending to cause offence. Widmerpool was discovered by a constable dancing naked in a woodland at midnight. He was arrested and convicted of an offence under the 1999 Act. Advise Widmerpool who claims that his activities were part of a religious festival.

17.8 The Vicar of Dabley arranges a special service for all families with children who have lived together in Dabley for at least 15 years. Gill and Heather are a gay couple who have two adopted children. Even though they have lived together in Dabley for more than 15 years, the Vicar refuses to let Gill and Heather participate in the service. Advise them as to any rights they might have under the Human Rights Act 1998.

## Further reading

Allan, T. (1996) 'Bills of Rights and Judicial Power: A Liberal's Quandary', *Oxford Journal of Legal Studies*, **16**: 337.

Buxton, R. (2000) 'The Human Rights Act and Private Law', *Law Quarterly Review*, **116**: 48.

Campbell, T., Ewing, K.D. and Tomkins, A. (eds) (2001), *Sceptical Essays on Human Rights*, Oxford, Oxford University Press, Chapters 2, 3, 5, 6.

Ewing, K.D. (1999) 'The Human Rights Act and Parliamentary Democracy', *Modern Law Review*, **62**: 79.

Feldman, D. (1999) 'The Human Rights Act and Constitutional Principles', *Legal Studies*, **19**: 165.

Harris, D.J. (2004) 'Human Rights and Mythical Beasts', *Law Quarterly Review*, **120**: 428.

Hoffman, Lord (1999) 'Human Rights and the House of Lords', *Modern Law Review*, **62**: 159.

## Further reading cont'd

Hunt, M. (1998) 'The "Horizontal Effect" of the Human Rights Act', *Public Law*, 423.

Irvine, Lord D. (2003) 'The Impact of the Human Rights Act: Parliament, the Courts and the Executive', *Public Law*, 308.

Jowell, J. and Cooper, J. (eds) (2003) *Delivering Rights: How the Human Rights Act is Working*, Oxford, Hart Publishing.

Klug, F. (2000) *Values for a Godless Age*, Penguin Books.

Laws, J. (1995) 'Law and Democracy', *Public Law*, 72.

Laws, Sir J.(1998) 'The Limitation of Human Rights', *Public Law*, 254.

Leigh, I. (2002) 'Taking Rights Proportionately,' *Public Law*, 265.

Morgan, J. (2002) 'Law's British Empire', *Oxford Journal of Legal Studies*, **22**: 729.

Oliver, D. (2000) 'The Frontiers of the State: Public Authorities and Public Functions under the Human Rights Act 1998' *Public Law*, 476.

Oliver, D. (2004) 'Functions of a Public Nature and the Human Rights Act', *Public Law*, 329.

Wade, Sir W. (2000), 'Horizons of Horizontality', *Law Quarterly Review*, **116**: 217.

Waldron, J. (1993) 'A Rights Based Critique of Constitutional Rights', *Oxford Journal of Legal Studies*, **13**: 132.

Waldron, J. (1999) *Law and Disagreement*, Part III, Oxford, Oxford University Press.

## Chapter 18
# Freedom of expression and assembly

A free press is not a privilege but an organic necessity in a great society... without criticism and reliable and intelligent reporting, the government cannot govern. (Walter Lippmann, 1889–1974, Journalist)

## Key words

▶ Freedom of expression and democracy
▶ Freedom of expression and reputation
▶ Freedom of expression and privacy
▶ Freedom of expression and property rights
▶ Right to disagree
▶ Harm and offence
▶ Vaguely defined offences
▶ Police discretion: is peaceful protest protected?

### 18.1 Introduction: Justifications for Freedom of Expression

Freedom of expression, particularly freedom of the press, has long been identified as important by judges, politicians and commentators on the constitution. Blackstone in the eighteenth century and Dicey in the nineteenth saw a free press as essential to a free state, and contemporary judges claim that freedom of expression has especially high priority (see e.g. *Derbyshire County Council* v *Times Newspapers Ltd* (1993); *R* v *Secretary of State for the Home Department ex parte Simms* [1999] 3 All ER 400, 407–8, Lord Steyn: 'the primary freedom'; *McCartan-Turkington Breen* v *Times Newspapers Ltd* [2001] 2 AC 277, 296–7, Lord Bingham; (*R (Pro Life Alliance)* v *BBC* [2003] 2 All ER 977, 982, Lord Nicholls).

A range of arguments can be advanced in support of freedom of expression (e.g. Greenawalt, 'Free Speech Justifications', 1989, *Columbia Law Review* **89**(1): 119). The arguments have been placed into two broad groups (Dworkin, *Freedom's Law*, 1996, OUP, pp. 199–200). Arguments in the first group identify freedom of expression as intrinsically valuable, meaning valuable as an end in itself as a defining characteristic of a human being (for example Lord Steyn in *Simms* (above)). Dworkin (above, p. 201) argues that freedom of expression is valuable in itself because it is an essential and 'constitutive' feature of a just political society that government treat all its members, except those who are incompetent, as responsible moral agents.

In other words, those upon whom the right to freedom of expression is conferred are regarded as capable of 'making up their own minds about what is good or bad in life or in politics, or what is true and false in matters of justice and faith' and are properly entitled to 'participate in politics' and to 'contribute to the formation of [their] moral or aesthetic climate'. Like Kant who uses 'reason' in much the same way, Dworkin seems to regard freedom of speech as a badge of moral worth (see also Freeden, *Rights*, OUP, 1991, pp. 8–59).

This might be regarded as merely a recital of liberal faith (Chapter 1) and easily rejected, for example from a religious perspective. It is moreover an uncomfortable notion for those whom Dworkin regards as incompetent. We are perhaps on stronger ground with the second group of justifications. This regards freedom of expression as instrumentally valuable: that is, valuable as a means by which to pursue some other valuable end. The ends in question were identified by Mill (Chapter 1) as democracy, self-fulfillment and the testing of truth.

As regards democracy, Lord Steyn in *Simms* (above) emphasised the democratic purposes of freedom of speech in informing debate, as a safety valve to encourage consent, and as a brake on the abuse of power. Democracy can only flourish in circumstances where a free press can offer comment concerning matters of public significance and the public has a right to receive such information and comment. Indeed from a republican perspective (Chapter 1), freedom of expression can be regarded not only as a right but as a duty (c.f. *R (Pro Life Alliance) v BBC* (below)).

Lord Steyn also emphasised that freedom of speech was not absolute and that not all aspects of it are equally important. This leads to the danger, identified by Berlin (Chapter 1), of freedom of speech being regarded as a 'positive freedom' conditional upon those in power assessing its worthiness. In *Simms* a prisoner was held entitled to have access to a journalist in order to publicise his claim that he was wrongly convicted. Lord Steyn thought that he would not have had such access to indulge in pornography or even in a political or economic debate. In *R (British American Tobacco UK Ltd v Secretary of State for Health* (2004) it was held that 'commercial speech', that is, advertising has a relatively low value.

The argument that freedom of expression provides a means to the end of self-actualisation has been advanced by, *inter alia*, J.S. Mill and Thomas Emerson. Its starting point is the proposition that the proper end of humanity is the realisation of individual character and potentialities which cannot flourish without freedom of expression. Mill in particular was concerned that people should be free to experiment with different lifestyles without censorship by authority, provided only that they did not harm others. In this argument, we hear echoes of the Romantic movement. According to the

Romantics, 'we find truth within us' and come to understand it in the course of giving expression to our 'inner voice' (Taylor, *Sources of the Self: The Making of the Modern Identity*, CUP, 1989, Chapter 21). A variation on this theme has been advanced by Joseph Raz. He argues that freedom of expression provides a means by which the styles of life we adopt can, through public portrayals and representations, be validated (Raz, 'Free Expression and Personal Identification', 1991, *Oxford Journal of Legal Studies* **11**(3): 303).

The argument that freedom of expression facilitates the pursuit of truth and the acquisition of knowledge suppressed by official orthodoxy has a long history. It was expressed in the seventeenth century by John Milton in his *Areopagitica*. In the early twentieth century, it was advanced by many American judges, notably Holmes in his dissenting judgement in *Abrams* v *United States* (1919, p. 630):

> the best test of truth is the power of a [given] thought to get itself accepted in the competition of the market [place of ideas].

Holmes's point is that where different arguments are advanced, the stronger can be expected, other things being equal, to drive out the weaker. Thus, according to the philosopher of science Karl Popper, critical discussion provides a means by which to eliminate errors in our thinking and thus to move towards ever more plausible working hypotheses, but never incontrovertible truths (*The Open Society and its Enemies*, 1996). More confusingly and less modestly in *Whitney* v *California* (1927), 357, 375 Brandeis J wrote that:

> freedom to think as you will and to speak as you will are means indispensable to the discovery and spread of political truth.

Brandeis J does not offer a definition of 'political truth'. Indeed, his assertion implies that once 'truth' is discovered and spread there is no further need for freedom of speech. In the political sphere, at least from a liberal perspective, the point of freedom of speech is arguably to keep diversity and disagreement alive. Moreover, in the marketplace of ideas is there any reason to suppose that truth rather than the loudest and best paid voice will prevail?

Bollinger has argued that freedom of expression facilitates 'the development of [a] capacity for tolerance' (Bollinger, 'The Tolerant Society: a Response to Critics', 1990, *Columbia Law Review*, **90**(1): 979). A capacity for tolerance weakens 'a general bias against receiving or acknowledging new ideas' (ibid.). Secondly, it is particularly valuable in large and complex societies containing people with varied beliefs and interests. Thirdly, in circumstances where people are willing to tolerate views other than their own, they may be more ready than would otherwise be the case to tolerate activities that they regard as objectionable.

Freedom of speech has inevitable costs and is unlikely to be considered as an absolute right in that it is bound to upset someone and in extreme cases is a threat to security. The cost of freedom of speech may be felt in risks to security and public order, offence to religious and cultural susceptibilities, and intrusions into the private lives of politicians and other public figures which may violate the basic human needs of reputation, self-respect and personal privacy. These needs are difficult to define. The issue is whether it is possible to protect them without inhibiting the public interest that the press should investigate whether those who govern are fit to do so. Vaguely defined limits to freedom of expression might have a 'chilling' effect on the press by discouraging bold investigations. A utilitarian argument (Chapter 1) also sometimes presented (for example by Lord Hutton in *R* v *Shaylor*, Chapter 19) is that freedom of speech might weaken confidence in those who govern us.

The protection of free expression against state intrusion has its dangers. In the political context it could be argued that freedom of expression without constraint allows the loudest voice to prevail, thus risking the 'tyranny of the majority' (Chapter 1). For example in the USA, it is unconstitutional for the law to restrict expenditure on election campaigns whereas in UK law there are substantial restrictions on campaign expenses (Chapter 10). Some argue that these dangers have been realised in the USA, where considerable reverence is attached to the First Amendment of the Constitution as a protection against the state (e.g. *Brandenburg* v *Ohio* (1969)). It has been suggested that protection against state interference encourages indirect censorship by commercial and social forces which are intolerant of minority opinions. A free press is necessarily influenced by commercial concerns: the need to sell newspapers or advertising space. This leads to the press including trivial or sensational personal stories to attract customers or to publish material that suits the prejudices of the majority. According to this view, society is polarised between a deeply conformist majority and marginalized dissenters, and the protection of minorities might be improved through greater state intervention (see Paton, 'Respecting Freedom of Speech', 1995, *Oxford Journal of Legal Studies* 15(4)).

## 18.2 The Legal Status of Freedom of Expression

Freedom of expression is therefore not an absolute good. It might give way to another interest, most obviously the Hobbesian value of security. More vaguely Mill's 'harm' principle might be invoked (Chapter 1). This claims that freedom of speech should be restricted when it causes 'harm' to others but not where it merely causes 'offence'. However, we may not agree as to what counts as harm: for example, is an attack on religious beliefs or aesthetic feelings harmful or merely offensive? Is harm confined to physical injury? The law has not provided answers to these questions. In view of the vagueness of the concepts involved, there is a suspicion that governments may equate 'harm' with objections to their political interests.

The European Convention on Human Rights accommodates freedom of speech with other concerns by providing a list of overrides to that freedom. Art. 10 confers the right of freedom of expression, subject to 'duties and responsibilities'. These duties and responsibilities entitle the state to limit freedom of expression in a manner 'prescribed by law' and 'necessary in a democratic society' for the following purposes:

- national security;
- territorial integrity or public safety;
- prevention of disorder or crime;
- protection of health or morals;
- protection of the reputation or rights of others. In particular, freedom of expression may have to be compromised by the right to a fair trial (Art. 6), privacy (Art. 8, below Chapter 19), and freedom of religion (Art. 9);
- preventing the disclosure of information received in confidence;
- maintaining the authority and impartiality of the judiciary.

Among the rights protected by the European Convention on Human Rights, some judges have claimed that freedom of expression has an especially high status (e.g. Laws LJ in *R (Mahmood)* v *Secretary of State* (2001); Lord Nicholls in *R (Pro Life Alliance)* v *BBC* (above [6]). Indeed in *R* v *Central Independent Television plc* [1994] 3 All ER 641 at 652, Hoffmann LJ said that 'freedom of speech is a trump card that always wins'. However, as Sedley LJ pointed out in *Douglas and Zeta-Jones* v *Hello! Ltd* [2001] 2 All ER 289 at 323-4, Lord Hoffmann was speaking in a context where there was no competition with the overrides in the ECHR. Indeed in *Campbell* v *MGN* [2004] 2 All ER 995, 1011), Lord Hoffmann said that neither freedom of the press nor personal privacy has any automatic priority over the other.

> The question is rather to what extent is it *necessary* to qualify the one right in order to protect the underlying value which is protected by the other.

There are other related rights. Art. 9 confers a right to freedom of thought, conscience and religion with overrides on the same basis for public safety, public order, health or morals, or the protection of the rights and freedoms of others. Art. 11 confers a right to freedom of assembly and association with the same overrides plus the prevention of disorder or crime.

Where these freedoms conflict with an override, the court must apply the principle of proportionality (Chapter 17) to decide which should prevail and to what extent. There is no overriding master principle. Proportionality provides guidance to the extent that freedom of speech must be restricted to the least degree necessary to protect the competing interest and tells us that the competing interest must be important. Beyond that the judge must make a subjective choice. This could be a moral choice or an attempt to do a utilitarian calculation of the least harmful outcome.

*R (Pro Life Alliance) v BBC* (2003) provides a representative illustration of the kind of disagreement that pervades the judiciary. The House of Lords was asked to decide whether an obligation imposed on the BBC under a royal charter (treated here as analogous to the statutory obligation imposed on other broadcasters), to ensure that its programmes do not offend 'good taste and decency', overrode the right to freedom of expression of the Alliance who wished to include in an election broadcast vivid but accurate and unsensationalised images of the process of abortion.

A majority of the House refused to intervene on the ground that this judgement was not appropriate to a court and that the BBC has a margin of discretion which it had exercised reasonably. By taking this line the court accepted the principle that free speech could be restricted on the ground of taste. Indeed, Lord Hoffmann emphasised the pervasive influence of television with the implication that protective measures are especially justified. A distinction was drawn between banning someone altogether from what he or she wished to say and restricting a particular form of access to the media. Just as no one has a right to have his work published by a particular publisher, no one has a right to appear on TV. This analogy may seem unreal given the importance of television as a medium of political communication and the fact that access to it is regulated by the state.

This line of reasoning overruled that of Laws ʟᴊ in the Court of Appeal who had argued that free speech should never be outweighed by considerations of taste and decency and that it was for the court to 'decide for itself whether censorship was justified'. The majority in the Lords avoided talking this issue directly on the ground that to do so would involve challenging the mechanism provided by Parliament itself and the parties had not argued for this.

Lord Scott, apparently from a republican perspective (Chapter 1) dissented on the ground that the restriction was unreasonable. The difference between his approach and that of the majority was that he gave greater weight to the democratic importance of an election broadcast. Far from wishing to protect the public against offence, he thought that 'the public in a mature democracy are not entitled to be offended by the broadcasting of such a programme' and that a ban would be 'positively inimical to the values of a democratic society to which values it must be assumed that the public adheres' [98]. His lordship also remarked in the context of 'voter apathy' that:

(a) broadcaster's mindset that rejects a party election television programme on the ground that large numbers of the voting public would find the programme 'offensive' denigrates the voting public, treats them like children who need to be protected from the unpleasant realities of life, seriously undervalues their political maturity and can only promote (voter apathy).[99]

## 18.3 Press Freedom and Censorship

Political speech is widely regarded as especially important so that attacks on the government are subject to restriction only in extreme cases (see *Castells* v *Spain* (1992)). Therefore the press enjoys a high level of protection because the press (including for this purpose the broadcast media) is a watchdog over government on behalf of the public (see *Jersild* v *Denmark* (1994); *Lingens* v *Austria* (1986)). In *Hector* v *A-G of Antigua and Bermuda* [1990] 2 All ER 103 at 106, Lord Bridge said that:

> in a free democratic society ... those who hold office in government must always be open to criticism. Any attempt to stifle or fetter such criticism amounts to political censorship of the most insidious and objectionable kind.

In *Attorney General* v *Punch* (2003), Lord Nicholls asserted [27] that: 'restrictions on the freedom of the press call for particularly rigorous scrutiny' (although in that case the restriction survived judicial scrutiny (below).

In the eighteenth century Blackstone promoted the distinction between censorship of speech in advance by requiring government approval, and punishing the speaker after the event (*Commentaries*, 1765, III, 17). Prior restraint is regarded as an especially serious violation of freedom of expression because it removes from the public sphere the possibility of assessing the matter, whereas punishment may be regarded as a legitimate compromise between competing goods. Prior restraint should therefore be resorted to only as a last resort. Since the abolition in 1695 of state licensing of printing presses, English law has no general censorship powers over the printed word although, in characteristically British fashion, there are voluntary mechanisms presided over by committees of insiders for the purpose of encouraging self-censorship (the 'D' Notice Committee) and remedying intrusive practices (the Press Complaints Commission). There is, however, state censorship over broadcasting and the cinema (Communications Act 2003; Wireless Telegraphy Act 1949: BBC licence agreement; Cinemas Act 1985: local authority licensing). The ECHR subjects prior restraint to a high level of scrutiny, particularly in the case of news 'which is a perishable commodity' (see *Observer and Guardian Newspapers* v *UK* (1992)). Indeed in *Open Door and Dublin Well Woman* v *Ireland* (1992), five judges thought that prior restraint should never be tolerated.

The European Court has held that that the public has a right to receive information, ideas and opinions, so that the state has a corresponding duty to safeguard the free-flow even of undesirable information and opinion. For example *Jersild* v *Denmark* (1994) concerned a television interview with representatives of an extremist political group. The interview was edited to highlight abusive remarks made about ethnic groups within Denmark. The TV interviewer, who did not challenge the racist remarks, was charged with aiding and abetting the offence of 'threatening, insulting or degrading a group of persons on account of their race, colour, national or ethnic origin or belief'. The court held, with seven dissenters, that the interview was protected by Art. 10 because of the duty of the press to report controversial opinions in its role of public watchdog, and the corresponding right of the public to be informed. It was not for the court to decide how journalists presented their material provided that, taken in its whole context, the broadcast did not support the views put forward. In these circumstances restricting the press was not necessary in a democratic society as required by Art. 10 (see also *Castells v Spain* (1992) para. 43; *Lingens v Austria* (1986) para. 41; *Goodwin v UK* (1996)).

The press is particularly at risk in connection with the courts' prior restraint powers in the form of an injunction, disobedience to which attracts imprisonment for contempt of court. The Attorney-General can seek an injunction in the name of the public interest, most notably in the case of publications that risk prejudicing legal proceedings such as newspaper comments on matters related to pending litigation (contempt of court) and in the interests of national security (Chapter 19). A temporary injunction pending a full trial can sometimes be granted since once material is published there is no turning back (see *A-G v Guardian Newspapers Ltd* (1987)). A temporary injunction prevents anyone, whether a party or not, publishing the material with the intention to impede the court's purpose in granting the injunction (*A-G v Observer Ltd* (1988); *A-G v Times Newspapers Ltd* (1991)).

However an injunction will be granted only if it serves a useful purpose. Once material becomes public, even if unlawfully, the press has a duty to disseminate it, and to comment on it and further restraint cannot be justified (see *Observer and Guardian Newspapers v UK* (1992)).

Before the Human Rights Act 1998, UK law violated the European Convention on Human Rights because the power to grant an injunction has been used in a manner disproportionate to the risk of harm. In *A-G v Times Newspapers Ltd* (1974), the House of Lords held that it was a contempt for a newspaper to comment on the merits of civil litigation concerning the victims of thalidomide, for the reason that 'trial by newspaper' was undesirable in itself, irrespective of whether the publication might influence the outcome of the trial. However in *Sunday Times v UK* (1979), the ECHR held that contempt law could inhibit freedom of expression only where this was necessary, in this case to ensure a fair trial.

However the meaning of 'necessary' is flexible. In *Attorney General v Punch* (2003) the House of Lords upheld a wide injunction. A magazine published a series of articles by Derek Shaylor, a former member of the security services against whom a prosecution under the Official Secrets Act was pending for disclosing information about intelligence operations (Chapter

19). The injunction prevented publication of any material obtained by Mr Shaylor in the course of or as a result of his employment in the security services. The House of Lords was critical of this wide restriction pointing out that the press should not be restricted more than is necessary to achieve the purpose of the injunction, which in this case was to safeguard material that might be relevant to the trial. Lord Nicholls emphasised the chilling effect on freedom of speech of restrictions that are not precisely targeted [61]–[63]. Nevertheless, reversing the Court of Appeal, the House rejected the editor's argument that he did not intend to damage national security on the ground that this was irrelevant to the court's purpose in granting the injunction, and the editor should have realised this. Moreover, again contrary to the view of the Court of Appeal, this was not censorship by the Attorney-General who, under the terms of the injunction, could clear publication since the matter was in the control of the courts.

The importance of freedom of expression in relation to the press was reinforced by s.12 of the Human Rights Act 1998 (which was introduced after press lobbying). Section 12 provides firstly that a court order limiting the 'Convention right of freedom of expression' cannot normally be granted in the absence of the respondent. This affects interim injunctions which might be sought as an emergency measure against the media. Secondly s.12 prevents an interim order being made unless the applicant is likely to establish that publication should not be allowed. Thirdly, s.12 requires the court to have particular regard to freedom of expression and, 'where the proceedings relate to material which the respondent claims or which appears to the court to be journalistic, literary or artistic material (or to conduct connected with such material), to (a) the extent to which (i) the material has, or is about to, become available to the public; or (ii) it is, or would be, in the public interest for the material to be published; and (b) any relevant privacy code' (for example that made by the Press Complaints Commission).

It is sometimes argued that s.12 has the effect of privileging freedom of expression above other convention rights. However, in *Douglas and Zeta-Jones* v *Hello! Ltd* (2001), the Court of Appeal held that s.12 does not have this effect. According to the Court of Appeal, s.12 ensures that the competing rights in question are taken into account even at the interim stage. Traditionally an injunction has been granted merely where there is a serious issue to be tried (see *American Cyanamid* v *Ethicon* (1975)). In *Cream Holdings* v *Banerjee* (2004) the House of Lords held that, where s.12 applies, the normal threshold is that the applicant would 'more likely than not' succeed at the trial. However, the approach must be flexible so that, for example, if publication would cause serious harm a lower threshold would be justified. The House refused an injunction preventing the press from publishing allegations of corruption by a former employee.

Press Confidentiality

It is important that the confidentiality of those who supply information to the press is protected. In *R v Central Criminal Court ex parte Bright, Alton and Rusbridger* (2001), the Court of Appeal quashed a production order sought by the Crown against the editors of the Guardian and the Observer to disclose information received from Derek Shaylor, a former MI5 agent, whom the government were seeking to prosecute under the Official Secrets Act. It was held that disclosure would inhibit press freedom without there being a compelling reason for the disclosure. The press also has statutory protection in relation to contempt of court. Section 10 of the Contempt of Court Act 1981 protects the anonymity of a publisher's sources of information except where the court thinks that disclosure is necessary on the grounds of the interests of justice, national security or the prevention of crime and disorder.

Section 10 does not automatically require disclosure but permits the court to exercise a discretion between the competing concerns. Before the Human Rights Act the courts interpreted the exceptions broadly against the press, influenced by the common law idea that the press should have no special privileges. For example in *X v Morgan Grampian* (1991), the House of Lords held that a commercial interest in discovering the source of a leak outweighed press freedom. This was condemned by the European Court in *Goodwin v UK* (1996) on the ground that limitations on journalistic confidentiality require 'the most careful scrutiny'. The UK courts have also held that 'necessary' does not mean essential but only 'important' (*Re an Inquiry under the Companies Securities (Insider Dealing) Act 1985* (1988)) and that, where national security or wrongdoing is involved, the court will usually order disclosure (*X v Morgan Grampian* (1991); *Ashworth Hospital v MGN Ltd* (2001)). However in *John v Express Newpapers Ltd* (2000), which concerned the leaking of draft advice from a barrister, it was held that a confidential source should be publicly disclosed only as a last resort.

In the rest of this chapter we shall discuss particular areas of law which affect political freedom, emphasising press freedom and also the right of individuals and groups to demonstrate in public.

## 18.4 Reputation and Press Freedom: Defamation

Defamation concerns the protection of reputation which is an aspect of the human need for self-esteem (see *Reynolds v Times Newspapers Ltd* (2001) 201, per Lord Nicholls: '[r]eputation [as] an integral and important part of the dignity of the individual'). However, freedom of expression is also part of individual dignity but to the extent that we protect freedom of expression,we reduce the protection given to reputational interests and vice versa.

Moreover, both interests secure autonomy by providing protection against arbitrary interference. Hence, those who have the task of accommodating these values within the law must make agonising and politically controversial choices.

Material is defamatory if it:

(i) reflects on the claimant's reputation so as to lower him or her in the estimation of right-thinking members of society generally (*Sim* v *Stretch* (1936)); or

(ii) would tend to cause the claimant to be shunned or avoided (*Youssoupoff* v *Metro-Goldwyn-Mayer Pictures Ltd* (1934)); or

(iii) would bring the claimant into ridicule or contempt (*Dunlop Rubber Co. Ltd* v *Dunlop* (1921)).

A claimant must prove that the relevant material is (i) defamatory, (ii) has been published and (iii) refers to him or her. Publication means merely communication to another person. Thus everyone in the distribution chain of a newspaper from the reporter to the delivery boy publishes a defamation contained in the paper. Defamatory publications take one of two forms: namely, libel and slander. Material is libellous if it is published in a permanent form, for example writing or another recorded media. It is slanderous if it takes a less than permanent form, for example word of mouth.

Defamation law recognises the importance of freedom of expression. To this end, there are various defences. These include:

(i) *Truth* (or justification): Subject to an exception under the Rehabilitation of Offenders Act 1974 s.8., this defence can be pleaded even in circumstances where a defendant has been actuated by malice (i.e., spite or ill-will).

(ii) *Absolute privilege:* liability for defamation cannot be imposed in the course of:
   (a) parliamentary proceedings (Chapter 9)
   (b) judicial proceedings
   (c) official communications (as between, for example, ministers of the Crown (*Chatterton* v *Secretary of State for India* (1895)).

(iii) *Qualified privilege:* this defence applies where a defendant who honestly believes what he or she says to be true meets the following two requirements (see *Reynolds* v *Times Newspapers Ltd* (2001) 194–5 and 200, per Lord Nicholls):
   (a) the defendant has an interest or a duty (legal, social, or moral) to communicate the relevant material to another or others
   (b) the recipient of the material must have a corresponding interest or duty to receive it.

This important defence is discussed further below.

(iv) *Fair comment:* this defence protects honest expressions of opinion on matters of public interest. Judges sometimes identify it as a bulwark of free expression (see, for example, *Slim* v *Daily Telegraph Ltd* (1968), 170, per Lord Denning MR). While fair comment protects expressions of opinion, defendants have to establish that their views were based on a substratum of fact that was true at the time of publication (*Cohen* v *Daily Telegraph Ltd* (1968)). This defence has been identified as protecting comment on the behaviour of public institutions and officials, the behaviour of public figures, and items submitted for public criticism (including books, public exhibitions and theatrical performances). As with qualified privilege, a plea of fair comment can be defeated by a showing that the defendant was actuated by malice.

Just as the defences described above are supposed to protect freedom of expression, so too are two further features of the law. First, the institution of the jury and, second, the limited availability of the remedy of an injunction. Defamation actions (which are heard in the High Court) are usually tried with a jury which is regarded as providing a safeguard against official repression (see Fox's Libel Act 1792). However, in *Grobbelaar* v *News Group Newspapers Ltd* (2001) the Court of Appeal took the (apparently) ground-breaking step of overturning a jury's findings of fact on the ground that they were perverse and unreasonable.

The judiciary has long exhibited, in the defamation context, considerable reluctance to grant injunctions. This is because it fears introducing censorship. Hence, this remedy will not be granted unless the plaintiff can satisfy a number of exacting conditions. He or she will, for example, have to show that there is no real ground for supposing that the defendant may avoid liability by pleading the defences of truth, privilege or fair comment (*Bonnard* v *Perryman* (1891)). Further, judges are particularly grudging in their readiness to grant interim (or interlocutory) injunctions which restrain the offending speech pending a full trial (ibid.). Such injunctions are only granted where (i) a court is satisfied that publication will result in immediate and irreparable injury and (ii) damages would not provide an adequate remedy (see *Monson* v *Tussauds Ltd* (1894), see also Human Rights Act 1998 s.12 (above)).

In recent years, three features of defamation law have been modified by the judiciary with a view to establishing a balance between press freedom and reputational interests compatible with the European Convention on Human Rights. These concern public bodies, damages and qualified privilege.

Public Bodies and Political Parties

In *Derbyshire County Council* v *Times Newspapers Ltd* (1993) the House of Lords, upholding the Court of Appeal, held that a local authority and other public bodies cannot sue in defamation. The Council sued following the publication in *The Sunday Times* of an allegation of impropriety vis-à-vis the management of pension funds. Lord Keith explained their Lordships' decision by stating that: '[i]t is of the *highest public importance* that a democratically elected body … should be open to *uninhibited public criticism*' (p. 1017, emphasis added). Hence, the law could not be allowed to exert a 'chilling effect' on expressive activity. Such an effect manifests itself in circumstances where liability rules encourage writers and other commentators to censor themselves rather than risk the (potentially negative) consequences of litigation, see Gibbons, 'Defamation Reconsidered', 1996, *Oxford Journal of Legal Studies* **16**(4): 587; Wright, *Tort Law and Human Rights*, Oxford, Hart Publishing, 2001, p. 161). The House of Lords did not base its decision on the ECHR but the found support in 'the common law of England'. Lord Keith did, however, conclude that English common law was 'consistent' with the ECHR's requirements. He also followed US cases (*City of Chicago* v *Tribune Co.* (1923) and *New York Times* v *Sullivan* (1964)).

The importance attached by Lord Keith in *Derbyshire* to 'uninhibited public criticism' of local authorities suggests a strong commitment to democracy. But two other features of the case suggest that their Lordships' commitment to freedom of expression is rather half-hearted. First, the House held that councils can maintain actions in the tort of injurious falsehood (which provides a remedy vis-à-vis false statements that are made maliciously and prove to be harmful). Second, Lord Keith indicated (*obiter*) that *individual* public officials can sue in defamation on the same basis as private individuals.

The House of Lords has been criticised for failing to follow the US Supreme Court's lead in *New York Times* v *Sullivan* (above) by introducing the 'actual malice' rule into UK defamation law in relation to individuals (see Loveland 'The Constitutionalisation of Political Libels in English Common Law', 1998, *Public Law*, 633, 634). This rule protects statements against both public institutions and individual public officials made in the absence of malice with knowledge that they are false. As the Supreme Court recognised in *Sullivan*, the introduction of this rule would have helped to protect politically significant expression. It would also have brought the law of defamation into closer alignment with the jurisprudence of the European Court of Human Rights. The European Court has read Article 10 of the ECHR as requiring three distinctions, namely political figures should receive less protection from defamation law than private individuals, and governmental bodies (and political parties) should receive even less protection from the law than political figures ((see *Lingens* v *Austria* (1986); *Castells* v *Spain* (1992); *Oberschlick* v *Austria* (1995)).

*Derbyshire* was extended to political parties in *Goldsmith* v *Bhoyrul* (1997). This case concerned a newspaper article that appeared in *Sunday Business*. In the article it was stated that the plaintiff's political party was preparing, due to unpopularity, to withdraw many of its candidates from the 1997 General Election so as to avoid humiliation at the polls. Buckley J held that political parties could not maintain defamation claims. He justified his decision by reference to the public interest in uninhibited expression concerning matters of political significance. However, Buckley J also stated that 'any individual candidate, official or other person connected with the party who was sufficiently identified could sue' (p. 271).

## 18.4.2 Defamation Law and Damages

Damages are the principal remedy for defamation. Plaintiffs are entitled to damages for both reputational and economic injury (for example, loss of employment). Ceilings have never been placed, either at common law or by statute, on the amount of damages that can be recovered in defamation actions. Juries determine the amount and, until recently, they were not furnished with clear guidance as to the appropriate sum to award. This sometimes led to very large awards. Such awards are open to objection on at least two grounds. First, they are a disproportionate response to a defendant's wrongdoing. Second, the prospect of having to pay such a sum may exert a powerful 'chilling effect' on expressive activity.

Objections such as these have prompted change in the law. Under the Courts and Legal Services Act 1990 Section 8 the Court of Appeal has the power, where a jury has awarded 'excessive' compensation, to substitute a lower sum. This power was first exercised by the Appeal Court in *Rantzen* v *Mirror Group Newspapers* (1994), where the Court substituted an award of £110,000 for the jury's award of £250,000. While the Court of Appeal based its decision on the Act, it also justified it by reference to Article 10 of the ECHR. Neill LJ stated that the Convention required that damages should not exceed the level 'necessary to compensate the plaintiff and re-establish his reputation' (p. 994). See also *Tolstoy Miloslavsky* v *UK* (1995); *John* v *Mirror Group Newspapers Ltd* (1996)).

In the *John* case (above), the Court of Appeal also restricted the range of circumstances in which a plaintiff can recover exemplary or punitive damages. The Court stated that awards of this sort could only be recovered where the plaintiff offers 'clear' proof of the two following things (p. 58, per Lord Bingham): first, the defendant knowingly or recklessly published untruths; second, the defendant proceeded to publish the relevant untruths having cynically calculated that the profit accruing from the publication would be likely to exceed any damages award made against him or her. The Court buttressed its decision by reference to Art. 10, which according to Lord Bingham requires that '[f]reedom of expression should not be restricted by awards of exemplary damages save to the extent shown to be strictly necessary for the protection of reputations' (ibid).

### 18.4.3 Qualified Privilege and Public Bodies

In our earlier discussion of qualified privilege, we noted that defendants must be able to prove that they stand in a relationship of reciprocity, meaning (a) that they had an interest or duty (legal, social or moral) to communicate the material and (b) that the recipient(s) of the material had a corresponding interest or duty to receive it (see *Adam* v *Ward* (1917), p. 334, per Lord Atkinson). One class of defendants who have experienced difficulty in establishing reciprocity are newspapers vis-à-vis material communicated to the public at large. This is because the judges have been of the view that to accept such a plea would be to bestow on newspapers and other media organs an open-ended 'public interest' defence. The judicial reluctance to accept such a defence can be illustrated by reference to *Blackshaw* v *Lord* (1984). In this case, the Court of Appeal conceded that, in some circumstances, communication to the general public *may* be in the public interest but not simply because they concerned 'a matter of public interest believed by the publisher to be true in relation to which he has exercised reasonable care' (p. 327, per Stephenson LJ).

In *Reynolds* v *Times Newspapers Ltd* (2001), the House of Lords held that qualified privilege can, in some circumstances, be pleaded where political material is disseminated to the general public. However their Lordships emphasised that such material would still have to fall within the criteria for reciprocity (p. 200 and p. 204, per Lord Nicholls). Their Lordships also rejected the gloss placed on the qualified privilege defence by Lord Bingham LCJ in the Court of Appeal who stated that the press would have to satisfy an additional condition, namely what Lord Bingham termed 'the circumstantial test' (p. 909). To satisfy this test, defendants were required to show that 'the nature, status and source of the material and all the circumstances of its publication' were such that the publication should 'in the public interest' be protected (p. 912).

However their Lordships (rather equivocally) identified 'circumstances' as a highly relevant consideration. Lord Nicholls stated:

> [th]rough the cases runs the strain that, when determining whether the public at large had a right to know the particular information, *the court has regard to all the circumstances.* The Court is concerned to assess whether the information was of sufficient value to the public that, in the public interest, it should be protected by the privilege in the absence of malice. (p. 195, emphasis added).

To this his Lordship added a (non-exhaustive) list of considerations relevant to the question whether the qualified privilege defence should be available *viz*: (i) the seriousness of the allegation(s); (ii) the nature of the information, and the extent to which the matter is a matter of public concern; (iii) the source of the information; (iv) the steps taken to verify the information; (v) the status of the information; (vi) the urgency of the matter; (vii) whether comment was sought from the claimant; (viii) whether the relevant publication contained the gist of the claimant's side of the story; (ix) the tone of the article; and (x) the circumstances of the publication (p. 205).

The position staked out by the House in *Reynolds* is open to at least two criticisms. First, where judges draw on the considerations listed by Lord Nicholls, they will be defining standards of good journalistic practice. It is far from obvious that this is a task that they are well equipped to undertake. Second, the House's decision can be expected to produce uncertainty and so the chilling effect.

By contrast in *Lange* v *Atkinson and Consolidated Press NZ Ltd* (1998), the New Zealand Court of Appeal held that defendants can plead qualified privilege vis-à-vis politically significant material communicated to the public. As well as expanding the qualified privilege defence, the Court also sought to forestall the danger of chilling effects. To this end, it stated that plaintiffs must, in order to defeat a plea of qualified privilege, prove that the defendant lacked an honest belief in the truth of his or her statements. Further, the New Zealand Court found support for the position it adopted in Article 10 of the ECHR. The New Zealand Court of Appeal's decision in *Lange* was subsequently appealed to the Privy Council. The Privy Council remitted the case to New Zealand for rehearing, thus affording the New Zealand Appeal Court the opportunity to consider the House of Lords' decision (*Lange* v *Atkinson* (2000)). While prepared to 'amplify' its earlier decision, the New Zealand Appeal Court declined to follow the House's approach in *Reynolds*. One of the reasons it gave for this decision was the greater readiness of the New Zealand press, as compared with the British press, to behave responsibly (p. 398)).

### 18.5 Privacy and Confidentiality

Privacy relates to the human need for dignity, independence and self-respect. Confidentiality concerns wrongful disclosure of true information and relates to a range of concerns some being matters of efficiency, for example commercial and professional confidentiality, others relating to dignity. Art. 8 of the ECHR states that 'everyone has a right to respect for his family and private life' (Chapter 17). This is extremely vague. Indeed, English law has no right to privacy as such, regarding privacy as a general value that influences specific causes of action such as breach of confidence (see *Wainright* v *Home Office* (2003); see also *Kaye* v *Robertson* (1991)). In constitutional law the most important aspect of confidentiality is the claim that some government information must be secret in the interests of effective government, the most obvious examples being security and intelligence matters. This will be discussed in Chapter 19. In this chapter we shall briefly consider the general question of privacy from the perspective of press freedom.

The cause of action for breach of confidence that has been fashioned by the judiciary protects secrets and personal information. A plaintiff can secure a remedy (damages and/or injunctive relief) for breaches of confidence in circumstances where the following three conditions (which were approved by the House of Lords in *Attorney-General* v *Guardian Newspapers (No. 2)* (1990)) can be satisfied:

1. The information is confidential in character: that is, it must not be public knowledge.
2. The information must have been imparted in circumstances imposing an obligation of confidence: for example, it was imparted for a limited purpose. Earlier cases requiring a specific confidential relationship such as family or employment no longer apply (*Campbell* v *MGN* (2004). Thus confidentiality is more strongly linked to privacy as a value in itself and the courts have acknowledged the influence of Art. 8 of the European Convention on Human Rights (above). The claimant must however establish that the relevant information was acquired in circumstances where a reasonable person would have realised that it was confidential. For example in *HRH Princess of Wales* v *MGN Newspapers Ltd and Others* (1993), information acquired by the press (i.e., photographs of the plaintiff exercising in a semi-public gymnasium) was held to be subject to a duty of confidentiality. This was because it would have been obvious to a reasonable person that the plaintiff did not wish the information to be obtained.
3. There must be an unauthorised use of the relevant information by the confidant or a third party with knowledge of the confidence such as a newspaper: for example, use of the information by the confidant for a purpose other than that for which it was imparted.

In order to accommodate the competing concern of freedom of expression there is the defence that disclosure of the relevant material was (a) in the public interest and (b) that this outweighs the interest in preserving confidentiality. Thus where freedom of expression and confidentiality conflict, a third value, some particular public interest, must be used as a tie breaker. Moreover, we must go behind freedom of speech and confidentiality to ask what are their underlying rationales in the particular context and how strongly they apply, taking all circumstances into account. As usual the judges must make a subjective choice between competing goods. The uncertainty generated by this risks inhibiting freedom of expression.

For example in *Campbell* v *MGN* (2004), concerning press reports relating to drug dependency therapy undergone by a famous model, a majority of the House of Lords held that the reports breached the claimant's right to privacy. This was because the information had no public importance. The minority (Lords Nicholls and Hoffmann) thought that freedom of the press should prevail. The dissenters favoured some journalistic licence in support of a free press particularly as their Lordships did not consider that the material published adversely affected matters of dignity and self-respect. All agreed however that the bare fact that the claimant was drug dependent could be published. The claimant had courted publicity, specifically by public denials that she was on drugs, and so had put herself into the public domain and to that extent given up her privacy. Importantly however it was not suggested that she forfeited her privacy completely.

In relation to government information greater weight is placed on freedom of expression. Where the government is relying on the public interest, the onus is on the government to prove a public interest in confidentiality (Chapter 19). Where a private person (even if a public figure) is the claimant, a public interest in disclosure must be shown.

Breach of confidence protects privacy up to a point. Its main limitation is that the quality of confidence is lost once the material has been released into the public domain so that the claimant has no remedy in respect of publication after that time (*A-G* v *Guardian Newspapers (No. 2)* (1998). Wacks (*Privacy and Press Freedom*, London: Blackstone, 1995, p. 56) argues that breach of confidence does not deal adequately with 'the archetypal "privacy" claim because the action is largely concerned with: (a) disclosure or use rather than publicity, (b) the source rather than the nature of the information, and (c) the preservation of confidence rather than the possible harm to the plaintiff caused by the breach'.

Judges are exhibiting a readiness to develop existing private law actions in the context of the ECHR relating to invasions of privacy and press freedom although not to create a separate cause of action for privacy (*Wainwright* v *Home Office* (2003)). This can be illustrated by reference to two recent cases namely *Campbell* v *MGN* (above) and *Thompson and Venables* v *News Group Newspapers Ltd* (2001); see also *Douglas* v *Hello! Ltd* (2001) for more radical dicta by Sedley LJ). In *Thompson*, the claimants (the notorious killers of James Bulger) sought an indefinite continuation of injunctions restraining the press from disclosing their (new) identities on release from custody. Since the circumstances of the case were 'exceptional', Dame Butler-Sloss granted the injunction. While recognising that courts are under a duty to act compatibly with convention rights, she identified this duty as extending only to existing causes of action. With respect to Article 10, she stated that it will only be necessary to grant injunctive relief where it can be 'convincingly demonstrated' that the requirements of Article 10(2), as to overrides, can be satisfied.

## 18.6 'Hate Speech'

Although the expression of opinions that offend others is not itself a justification for restricting freedom of expression the position is different where the views expressed upset others to the extent of creating a risk to public safety. The narrow Hobbesian justification for law, the safety of the realm is the supreme law, requires such restrictions. The problem is particularly acute where a choice has to made between banning, for example, a political speaker or protecting the speaker by controlling opponents in the audience. The latter course of action might require substantial use of police resources. Special considerations might also apply where freedom of speech is used against vulnerable minorities. Here individualistic liberalism and group liberalism are in conflict (Chapter 1).

As usual the law must find an accommodation. One way of achieving this is by attempting to distinguish between expressing opinions, however distasteful, and actually inciting unlawful behaviour: an application of Mill's 'harm' test (above). However, in the case of particularly vulnerable groups, this line is breached and some forms of expression that are offensive to such groups are also prohibited. The law is sensitive to particular historical circumstances and is not entirely consistent. For example, there is protection in respect of racial or ethnic hate speech and to lesser extent in respect of religion but not in relation to gender or sexual hate speech as such.

### 18.6.1 Blasphemy

This is an ancient common law offence, the gist of which is an attack upon religion. Its purpose is unclear. The rationale of blasphemy has changed over the centuries in response to changing political contexts. Originally it was used to enforce loyalty to the state. By the nineteenth century it was justified on the basis of public order. Today, in accordance with liberal pluralism (Chapter 1), the emphasis is on respect for different beliefs. Nevertheless as a historical legacy, blasphemy seems to apply only to the Christian faiths. It does not require a threat to public order (*R v Chief Metropolitan Stipendiary Magistrate ex parte Choudhury* (1991); c.f. *R v Gott* (1922); *R v Gathercole* (1838)). In the interests of freedom of expression there is a high threshold of tolerance. Religious belief can be denied or questioned provided that 'the decencies of controversy are observed' (see *Bowman v Secular Society* (1917); *R v Ramsey*

& *Foot* (1883)). There must be conduct which seriously offends the ordinary Christian by 'insulting or vilifying the deity, God or Christianity' (see *R* v *Lemon* (1979); *Wingrove* v *UK* (below): poem depicting Christ as homosexual).

Reformers are divided between libertarians who would abolish blasphemy in favour of freedom of expression and pluralists who would extend it to other religions in order to reflect our multi-cultural society. Article 9 of the European Convention on Human Rights concerns freedom of religion but does not protect religions against abuse (compare Art. 8 which requires 'respect' for privacy). The European Court has left the matter to the discretion of individual states under the margin of appreciation doctrine (Chapter 17). Thus the state can protect religions against abuse but is not bound to do so. In *Otto Preminger Institut* v *Austria* (1994) the state seized a film depicting Christ and his mother as in league with the devil which offended the Roman Catholic majority in the Tyrol. The ECHR held that the seizure was lawful for the purpose of protecting the rights of others. Recognising that there are differences in religious sensibilities between states and regions, the Court conceded a wide margin of appreciation to the state:

> in the context of religious opinion and beliefs ... may legitimately be included an obligation to avoid as far as possible expressions that are gratuitously offensive to others and thus an infringement of their rights, and which therefore do not contribute to any form of public debate capable of furthering progress in human affairs.

(See also *Wingrove* v *UK* (1997): homoerotic imagery discomforting to some Christians, ban upheld but strong dissent; compare *Choudhury* v *UK* (1991): state not required to criminalise attacks on Islam).

The Human Rights Act 1998 s.13 requires courts to have particular regard in matters involving religious organisations to the importance of freedom of thought, conscience and religion. This could be read as authorising religious organisations to violate other rights such as privacy or to discriminate on religious grounds. Under the Anti-Terrorism, Crime and Security Act 2001 s.39, the penalties for the offences of 'fear or provocation of violence' and 'harassment alarm and distress' under the Public Order Act 1986 (below) are increased where there is a religious motivation.

## 18.6.2 Sedition

The old common law offence of seditious libel consists of publishing material with the intention to incite hostility towards the government or its institutions or possibly to promote hostility between different classes of 'her majesty's subjects' (*R* v *Burns* (1886)). During the eighteenth century, which was punctuated by fear of popular uprising against the landowning classes, seditious libel was used as a tool of state control in that the judges had a wide power to decide what was seditious. Under Fox's Libel Act (1792) this was made a matter for the jury, thus providing a safeguard for the individual in that judges cannot direct a jury to convict and juries do not have to give reasons for their decisions.

There is an important limiting factor in that the accused must intend to incite violence or disorder either in ordinary people or in the particular audience, for example if it includes extremists (*R* v *Burns* (1886); *R* v *Aldred* (1909)). There need not actually be violence. In *R* v *Chief Metropolitan Stipendiary Magistrate ex parte Choudhury* (1991), which concerned a novel that was offensive to Muslims, it was held that sedition applies only to incitement against the government (including, however, any person exercising public functions), and not to attacks on religious groups (c.f. *R* v *Caunt* (1947): anti-semitism). Under the European Convention on Human Rights the limits of permissible criticism are wider with regard to the government than in relation to a private citizen or even a politician (*Castells* v *Spain* (1992) para. 46). Therefore, if prosecution is limited to cases of serious disorder it is unlikely that a proportionate response would fall foul of the Human Rights Act 1998.

There are other offences related to sedition which are little used but because of their vague language remain potential threats against political dissenters. The Incitement to Disaffection Act 1934 makes it an offence maliciously and advisedly to endeavour to seduce any member of the armed forces from his duty or to aid, counsel or procure him to do so. The Police Act 1996 s.91 creates a similar offence in relation to the police and the Aliens Restrictions (Amendment) Act 1917 prohibits an alien from attempting to cause sedition or disaffection and also from promoting or interfering in an industrial dispute in an industry in which he has not been employed for at least two years immediately before the offence. It is questionable whether these provisions, particularly the latter, are Human Rights Act compliant.

### 18.6.3 Racism

Racism has been so widely condemned throughout Europe as to amount to a special case. Freedom from discrimination as such is not protected under the convention which expressly prohibits discrimination only in respect of the other protected rights (Art. 14, above). However, the International Convention on the Elimination of All Forms of Racial Discrimination (1965) (CERD) has been ratified by most members of the Council of Europe (not Ireland, Lithuania or Turkey). Article 4 of this convention requires signatories to create offences in relation to 'all dissemination of ideas based on racial supremacy or hatred, incitement to racial discrimination, as well as acts of violence or incitement to such acts against any race or group of persons of another colour or ethnic origin'. Article 4 also requires states to have 'due regard' to *(inter alia)* the right to freedom of opinion and expression.

Racist speech is not entirely outside the protection of Art. 10 but has a low level of protection, usually being outweighed by the need to protect the rights of others and to prevent disorder. In *Jersild* v *Denmark* (above) the objective reporting by the media of racist abuse was held to be protected by Art. 10. The reason for this is the role of the media as a watchdog against obnoxious elements in society. This reflects the 'search for truth' rationale of freedom of expression. In *Jersild* the court expressed the view that deliberate racist abuse would not be protected and that racism is a substantial threat to democracy. Measures to combat racism are reinforced by Art. 17 which aims at preventing reliance on a convention right in order to undermine another. It is unlikely, therefore, that UK law contravenes the ECHR.

The main anti-racism offences are contained in sections 17 to 23 of the Public Order Act 1986, which extend earlier provisions. The gist of the main offence is the use of 'threatening, abusive or insulting words or behaviour or displaying written material which is threatening, abusive or insulting if (a) he intends to stir up hatred or, (b) having regard to all the circumstances, such hatred is likely to be stirred up therby' (s.18). Race includes colour, race, nationality, ethnic or national origins (s.17). An ethnic group can be defined by cultural as well as physical characteristics (see *Mandla* v *Dowell-Lee* (1983): Sikhs; *Commission for Racial Equality* v *Dutton* (1989): gypsies but not other travellers).

The offence can be committed in public or private places except exclusively within a dwelling (s.18 (2) (4)). Thus the offence applies even to activities within a private club or other association. Public disorder is not required nor is the presence at the time of any member of the targeted racial group. For example, the offence could apply to an academic paper read to an audience in a university with which the whole audience agrees. The accused is not guilty if he did not intend to stir up racial hatred and did not intend his words or behaviour to be, and was not aware that it might be threatening, abusive or insulting (s.18 (2) (5)). It is also an offence to publish or distribute written material in the same circumstances (s.17) and to possess racially inflammatory material (s.23). The police have wide powers of entry and search (s.24).

Similar provisions apply to a public performance of a play (s.20), to distributing, showing or playing recordings, and to broadcasting or cable services, except from the BBC and ITC (ss22 (7)), 23(4)). Broadcasts by the BBC and ITC are governed by their own internal systems of regulation and the Home Secretary has power to ban any broadcast.

Under the Crime and Disorder Act 1998 ss. 28, 31, the penalties for the offences of 'fear or provocation of violence' and 'harassment, alarm and distress' under the Public Order Act 1986 (below) are increased where there is a racial motivation.

## 18.7 Public Order: Demonstrations and Meetings

Public demonstrations and meetings are an important expression of democracy. However, there are many statutory restrictions imposed for the purpose of public order and the police have wide discretionary powers. It is sometimes said that modern methods of communicating, such as mass circulation newspapers, broadcasting and the internet, make it less important to worry about public space than was the case 50 years ago. Nevertheless, public meetings, demonstrations or processions in the open air remain the only means by which people without money or influence can express their views.

The law has developed as a series of pragmatic responses to particular problems and political agendas. This illustrates the weakness of the traditional residual approach to liberty under which, according to Dicey, the right to hold a public procession is in principle no different from the right to eat a bun. Under the European Convention on Human Rights, however, interference on public order grounds with the Art. 10 right of freedom of speech and the Art. 11 right of freedom of assembly must be proportionate. A particular problem arises where rival groups, each claiming these freedoms, clash in the streets. In these circumstances the margin of discretion given to the police is crucial. In *Plattform 'Arzte fur das Leben' v Austria* (1988), it was held that the state should take positive measures to protect freedom of expression, by policing arrangements at public meetings. However, this was under Art. 13 (duty to provide adequate remedies), which is not incorporated by the Human Rights Act.

The notion that everything is permitted unless forbidden is particularly ironic in the case of public meetings. All meetings and processions take place on land. All land, even a public highway, is owned by someone, whether a private body, a local authority, the Crown or a government department. Holding a meeting without the consent of the owner may be a trespass (see *Harrison v Duke of Rutland* (1893)). Trespass as such is not a criminal offence. However, the offences of 'aggravated trespass' and 'trespassory assembly' (below) put a powerful weapon into the hands of the police to remove trespassers from land.

The essential question is what are the public's rights in relation to the highway (which includes roads and their verges, footpaths, bridleways and waters over which there is a public right of navigation)? The traditional view has been that the public has a right only to 'pass or repass' on a highway (that is, to travel) and also to stop on the highway for purposes which are reasonably incidental such as 'reasonable rest and refreshment' (*Hickman v Maisey* (1900)). In *Hubbard v Pitt* (1976), for example, a majority of the Court of Appeal held that peaceful picketing by a protest group who distributed leaflets and questionnaires was not a lawful use of the highway.

Dicey thought that a procession, but not a static meeting, would usually be lawful because processions comprise a large number of individuals exercising their right to travel at the same time. However, the procession could be unlawful if it paused to allow a speech to be made.

However in *DPP* v *Jones* (1999), a majority of the House of Lords upheld the right of peaceful demonstration in a public place although the limits of this are not clear. The defendant was part of a group of environmentalists who were arrested during a demonstration at Stonehenge. The demonstration was peaceful, and nobody was obstructed. Lord Irvine LC held that the law should now recognise that the public should have a right to enjoy the highway for any reasonable purpose whether the land was public or private, provided that the activities did not constitute a nuisance and did not obstruct other people's freedom of movement. Lords Hutton and Clyde agreed, but took a narrower approach emphasising that not every nonobtrusive and peaceful use of the highway is necessarily lawful. Lord Hutton said:

> the common law recognises that there is a right for members of the public to assemble together to express views on matters of public concern and I consider that that the common law should now recognise that this right, which is one of the fundamental rights of citizens in this country, is unduly restricted unless it can be exercised in some circumstances on the public highway.

Lords Hope and Slynn dissented, Lord Hope because of the effect of such a right on property owners who were not before the court to defend their interests, Lord Slynn because of a reluctance to unsettle established law.

The law of trespass might be used to restrict political activity in premises such as shopping malls. Although the public has access to these places they are not in law public places and are privately owned, often by commercial companies. The owner can therefore require anyone to obey whatever restrictions the owner wishes to impose and can exclude anyone from the premises. Whether the Human Rights Act applies to protect freedom of speech in such places is questionable. It might be argued that the Act has 'horizontal effect' (Chapter 17) and is engaged because the owner has invited the public to visit the premises on a basis similar to the traditional idea of a public marketplace. In *Appelby* v *UK* (2003) the European Court held that the owner of a shopping mall could prevent environmental campaigners from setting up a stall and distributing leaflets. However, the court stressed that they had other means of communicating their concerns. Moreover, restrictions must have a rational justification.

### 18.7.1   Police Powers

The police have wide powers to regulate public meetings and processions. These are supplemented by powers relating to particular places (e.g. Seditious

Meetings Act 1817 s.3: meetings of 50 or more people in the vicinity of Westminster when Parliament is sitting). There are also common law powers to prevent a breach of the peace. The main general police powers are as follows:

▶ The 'organiser' of a public procession intended (i) to demonstrate support for or opposition to the views or actions of any person or body of persons; (ii) to publicise a campaign or cause; and (iii) to mark or commemorate an event must give advance notice to the police. There are certain exceptions. These include (i) processions commonly or customarily held in the area; (ii) funeral processions organised by a funeral director in the normal course of his business; and (iii) cases where it is not reasonably practicable to give advance notice (for example a spontaneous march) (Public Order Act s.11).

▶ If a 'senior police officer' reasonably believes (a) that any public procession may result in serious public disorder, serious damage to property, or serious disruption to the life of the community, or (b) that the purpose of the organisers is to intimidate people into doing something they have a right not to do, or not doing something they have a right to do, he can impose such conditions as appear to him to be necessary to prevent such disorder, damage, disruption or intimidation, including conditions as to the route of the procession or prohibit it from entering any public place specified in the directions (ibid s.12). A senior police officer is either the chief constable, Metropolitan police commissioner, or the senior officer present on the scene (s.12 (2)). Intimidation requires more than merely causing discomfort and must contain an element of compulsion.

▶ All public processions, or any class of public procession, can be banned if the chief constable or Metropolitan police commissioner reasonably believes that the power to impose conditions is not adequate in the circumstances (ibid s.13). The decision is for the local authority, with the consent of a Secretary of State (in practice the Home Secretary).

▶ There are powers to impose conditions upon public meetings for the same purposes as in the case of processions (ibid s.14). For this purpose a public assembly is an assembly of 20 or more people in a public place which is wholly or partly open to the air (s.16). Unlike processions, the police have no general power to ban a lawful assembly but can control its location, timing and the numbers attending.

▶ The Criminal Justice and Public Order Act 1994 s.70 (inserting ss. 14 A, B, C into the Public Order Act 1986) confers power on a local authority with the consent of the Secretary of State to impose a blanket ban upon certain assemblies in a place to which the public has no right of access or only a limited right of access. This includes private land and buildings where the public is invited, for example ancient monuments such as Stonehenge, meeting rooms, shops, sports and entertainment centres and libraries. The chief constable must reasonably believe that an assembly is (a) a trespassory assembly (below), being likely to be held without the permission of the occupier or to exceed the limits of his permission or of the public's rights of access, and (b) may result in serious disruption to the life of the community or, where the land or a building or monument on it is of historical, architectural or scientific importance, may result in significant damage to the land, building or monument. A ban can last for up to four days within an area of up to five miles. The ban covers all trespassory assemblies and cannot be confined to particular assemblies.

▶ The Terrorism Act 2000 imposes further wide restrictions on political meetings because of its broad definition of terrorism (Chapter 19).

▶ Where a breach of the peace is taking place or is reasonably anticipated, the police have a summary power to arrest anyone who refuses to obey their reasonable requirements. A charge of obstructing the police is also possible (Police Act 1996 ss 8, 9(1)). The meaning of breach of the peace may be confined to violence or the likelihood of violence (see *R* v *Howell* (1982)). However, in *R* v *Chief Constable of Devon and Cornwall* [1981] 3 All ER 826 at 832, Lord Denning MR thought that there is a breach of the peace 'wherever a person who is lawfully carrying out his work is unlawfully and physically prevented by another from doing it' (protesters lying in front of a drilling machine). Thus passive resistance might be a breach of the peace. Lord Denning also thought that in deciding whether to intervene the police did not need to go into the rights and wrongs of the matter and could clear the site irrespective of who is to blame.

The power to prevent a breach of the peace includes a right of entry to private premises (*Thomas* v *Sawkins* (1935)), a right to control the number of pickets on a picket line (*Piddington* v *Bates* (1960)) and even a right to prevent people from travelling to a demonstration held several miles away (*Moss* v *McLachlan* (1985)). It is not clear how 'imminent' or likely a breach of the peace must be. In *Moss*, the court emphasised that the matter is for the judgement of the policeman on the spot, who must consider on the basis of some evidence that there is a 'real risk' of a breach of peace 'in the sense that it is in close proximity both in space and time'.

▶ *Anti-Social Behaviour.* Under s.30 of the Anti-Social Behaviour Act 2003 a police officer of the rank of superintendent and above can make an order valid for up to six months within an area defined in the order. An order can be made where the officer has reasonable grounds to believe that the presence or behaviour of any persons is likely to result in any member of the public being intimidated, harassed, abused or distressed where there have previously been complaints of such behaviour. An ASBO empowers a constable to disperse any group of two or more people where the constable has reasonable grounds to believe that the behaviour of those persons is likely to result in any member of the public being intimidated, harassed abused or distressed. There are exceptions for lawful picketing under trade union legislation and for lawful processions under s.11 of the Public Order Act 1986 (above). This power is mainly directed at hooligans but has also been used against political protestors. Indeed, under current Home Office proposals, a new offence is proposed of protesting outside homes in a way that causes harassment, alarm and distress to residents.

A general issue arises in relation to these powers. Where there is a protest, itself peaceful but which becomes the focus of disturbances among its audience which may include people such as government supporters objecting to the protest, what action should the police take? Should the police protect freedom of expression by attempting to control the audience or can they put public order first by taking what may well be the most efficient course of action and breaking up the meeting? The old case of *Beatty* v *Gillbanks* (1882) is often cited as an endorsement of freedom of assembly. A temperance march by the Salvation Army was disrupted by a gang, known as the Skeleton Army, sponsored by brewery interests. The organisers of the march were held not be guilty of the offence of unlawful assembly (replaced by Public Order Act 1986, below) on the ground that their behaviour was in itself lawful. However, the issue was essentially that of causation and the more general question of the powers of the police to prevent a breach of the peace was not raised. Nevertheless, the Human Rights Act 1998 may embody a similar principle in order to show that the response is proportionate. We saw earlier that the ECHR has held that the state has a positive duty to attempt to protect freedom of expression and assembly. Moreover, because it is indefinite, the police common law power may fall foul of the principle that a violation of convention rights must be 'prescribed by law'.

However, the courts are reluctant to interfere with police discretion. Before the Human Rights Act they applied the minimal *'Wednesbury'* test of unreasonableness, according to which they will interfere only where the police decision is irrational (Chapter 15). The main consideration seems to be that of efficiency in giving the police the power to control the disturbance as they see fit within the resources available to them (see *R* v

*Chief Constable of Devon and Cornwall* (1981); *R v Chief Constable of Sussex ex parte International Traders Ferry Ltd* (1999)). Therefore, even where a peaceful and lawful meeting is disrupted by hooligans or political opponents, the police may prevent a likely breach of the peace by ordering the speaker to stop in preference to controlling the troublemakers (*Duncan v Jones* (1936)) or by removing provocative symbols from the speaker (*Humphries v Connor* (1864)).

Moreover, although the police must act even-handedly (*Harris v Sheffield United Football Club* [1988] QB 77 at 95) there is a risk that they will exercise their discretion in favour of interests supported by the government or at least supported by majoritarian opinion. For example, during the miners' strike of 1983 the police restricted the activities of demonstrators in order to protect the 'right to work' of non-strikers, going as far as to escort non-strikers to work and spending vast sums of money on police reinforcements A cheaper and less provocative policy would have been to restrain the non-strikers (see also *R v Coventry City Council ex parte Phoenix Aviation* (1995) duty to protect business interests).

It is arguable that, under the Human Rights Act, the police may be required to give higher priority to freedom of expression. In *Plattform 'Arzte fur das Leben' v Austria* (1988) the ECHR held, in the context of an anti-abortion demonstration, that a peaceful demonstration should be protected even though it may annoy or give offence to persons opposed to the ideas and claims which it is seeking to promote. However in *R v Chief Constable of Sussex* (1999), Lord Hoffmann said that there is no difference in the wide margin of appreciation that is required in domestic law and under the 'superimposed' ECHR. The case concerned a police ban on lorries entering a port at times when the police had insufficient resources to provide security against disruption caused by animal rights demonstrators. The ban was upheld on the basis that the matter is one of police discretion. *Beatty v Gillbanks* (above) was distinguished on the basis that police discretion was not involved in that case. In *R (Laporte) v Chief Constable of Gloucestershire* (2004), the court upheld a police decision to turn back coaches heading for a demonstration at a local airfield. It was held that the police were not required to distinguish between activists and others. However, the police were not entitled to detain anyone longer than was required to keep the peace nor could they force anyone back onto the coach to London.

### 18.7.2  Public Order Offences

There are a number of specific public order offences. Even minor punishments or disciplinary measures might be condemned under the ECHR as disproportionate or uncertain and so 'chilling' the right of assembly (*Ezelin* v *France* (1992)). The offences strike primarily at people who intentionally cause violence, but sometimes go beyond that. Moreover, the offences overlap, allowing police discretion in relation to the penalties.

The development of this subject is an example of creeping erosion of civil liberties of a kind that Dicey did not anticipate, illustrating the problem of a pragmatic approach based on statutes which respond to particular perceived threats. Taken individually each provision may be desirable but taken together they amount to a range of restrictions which, being loosely drafted, could be used for purposes other than those for which they were originally intended. The Public Order Act 1936 was a response to fears of fascism and communism. Much of it has been replaced by the Public Order Act 1986 which was provoked by race riots. Further legislation has been aimed at miscellaneous targets of the government of the day. These included anti-nuclear weapon, environmental and animal rights activists, hunt saboteurs, travellers, anti-social behaviour in residential areas, 'stalkers' and football hooligans (see Criminal Justice and Public Order Act 1994; Protection from Harassment Act 1997; Crime and Disorder Act 1998; Football (Offences and Disorder) Act 1999; Football (Disorder) Act 2000). Whether or not all of these are legitimate causes for concern, the legislation may be drafted loosely enough to include wider political activities, thereby attracting human rights arguments based on uncertainty, proportionality and discrimination.

The main offences are as follows:

1.  Under the Highways Act 1980 s.137, it is an offence to obstruct the highway. It is not necessary that the highway be completely blocked or even that people are inconvenienced. The accused's intentions are also irrelevant (*Arrowsmith* v *Jenkins* (1963); *Homer* v *Cadman* (1886); *Hirst and Agu* v *West Yorkshire Chief Constable* (1986)). However, as a result of *DPP* v *Jones* (above) a reasonable peaceful demonstration would probably not be unlawful. There are also numerous local statutes and bylaws regulating public meetings in particular places.

2.  The Public Order Act 1986 creates several offences, replacing a clutch of ancient and ill-defined common law offences (rout, riot, affray and unlawful assembly). They are as follows (in descending order of seriousness):
    ▶ *Riot* (s.1). Where 12 or more people act in concert and use or threaten unlawful violence for a common purpose, each person using violence is guilty of the offence.
    ▶ *Violent disorder* (s.2). At least three people acting in concert and using or threatening unlawful violence.

▶ *Affray* (s.3). One person suffices. Using or threatening unlawful violence is sufficient, but threats by words alone do not count.

All three offences may be committed in public or in private and the conduct must be such 'as would cause a person of reasonable firmness present at the scene to fear for his personal safety'. No such person need actually be on the scene. The defendant must either intend to threaten or use violence or be aware that his conduct may be violent or threaten violence (s.6). 'Violence' is broadly defined to include violent conduct to property and persons and is not restricted to conduct intended to cause injury or damage (s.8).

▶ *Fear or provocation of violence* (s.4). This offence is somewhat wider and places a political speaker at the mercy of the susceptibilities of the audience. A person is guilty who uses towards another person 'threatening, abusive or insulting words or behaviour or distributes or displays any writing, sign or visible representation that is threatening, abusive or insulting'. The offence can be committed in a public or a private place except exclusively within a dwelling or between dwellings (s.8). The meaning of threatening, abusive or insulting is left to the jury (see *Brutus* v *Cozens* (1973)) but the accused must be aware that his words are threatening, abusive or insulting (s.6 (3)). The act must be aimed at another person with the intention either to cause that person to believe that immediate unlawful violence will be used or to provoke that person into immediate unlawful violence. Alternatively the accused's conduct must be likely to have that effect even though he does not so intend. In *R* v *Horseferry Road Magistrate Court ex parte Siadatan* (1991), Penguin books were prosecuted under s.4 in relation to the publication of Salman Rushdie's book *Satanic Verses*. It was alleged that the book was likely to provoke future violence because it was offensive to Muslims. It was held that the violence must be likely within a short time of the behaviour in question. However, whether the other person's reaction is reasonable is irrelevant, so that the principle that a speaker 'takes his audience as he finds it' seems to apply. Thus, provoking a hostile or extremist audience, as in *Beatty* (above) would be an offence, provided that the words used or act performed is, to the knowledge of the accused, threatening, abusive or insulting to that particular audience (*Jordan* v *Burgoyne* (1963)).

▶ *Threatening, abusive or insulting behaviour* or disorderly behaviour with intent to cause harassment, alarm and distress where harassment, alarm or distress is actually caused (s.4A) (inserted by the Criminal Justice and Public Order Act 1994). Violence is not involved.

▶ *Harassment, alarm, or distress* (s.5). This is the widest offence and applies not only to threatening, abusive or insulting words or behaviour but also to 'disorderly behaviour', an expression which is not defined. Section 5 does not require an intent to cause harassment etc., but only that a person who actually sees or hears the conduct must be likely to be caused 'harassment, alarm or distress'. The defendant has the defences (i) that he had no reason to believe that any such person was present; (ii) that he did not intend or know that his words or actions were threatening, abusive or insulting, or disorderly, as the case may be; (iii) that his conduct was 'reasonable'. For example in *DPP* v *Clarke* (1992), the accused was protesting against abortion outside an abortion clinic by displaying upsetting images. It was held that although her conduct was threatening, abusive or insulting and was not reasonable and she was aware that her conduct was likely to cause distress, she was nevertheless not guilty because she did not subjectively believe that her actions were threatening, abusive or insulting. This is a safeguard of a kind, but may not suffice to meet the concerns of freedom of expression (c.f. *DPP* v *Fidler* (1992)).

The police have a summary power of arrest in relation to all the above offences but under s.5 must first warn the accused to stop. The conduct before and after the warning need not be the same.

It is unlikely that the offences under sections 1 to 4 are contrary to the ECHR in that they aim at preventing violence. Sections 4A and 5 are more vulnerable. In addition to 'threatening' behaviour, they target abusive, insulting and disorderly behaviour which leads to no more than distress. This arguably runs counter to the view of the European Court that conduct which shocks and offends is a price to be paid for democracy (*Handyside* v *UK* (1976), see Geddes [2004] *Public Law* 853).

3. Section 1 of the Public Order Act 1936 prohibits the wearing of political uniforms in any public place or public meeting without police consent, which can be obtained for special occasions. 'Uniform' includes any garment which has political significance, for example a black beret (*O'Moran* v *DPP* (1975)). Political significance can be identified from any of the circumstances, or from historical evidence.

4. *Aggravated trespass.* Trespass is not in itself an offence. However, under s.68 of the Criminal Justice and Public Order Act 1994, the offence of aggravated trespass occurs where a person who trespasses on land in the open air does anything (such as shouting threats, blowing a horn or erecting barricades) which, in relation to any lawful activity that persons are engaging or about to engage in on that land or on adjoining

land, is intended to have the effect (a) of intimidating those persons or any one of them so as to deter them or any one of them from engaging in that lawful activity; (b) of obstructing that activity; or (c) of disrupting that activity. For this purpose a lawful activity is any activity that is not a criminal offence or a trespass (s.68 (2)).

There is no defence of reasonableness and violence is not an ingredient. The police have a power of arrest. Moreover, the police can order a person committing or who has committed or who intends to commit an offence to leave the land (s.69). The police can also order two or more people who are present with the common purpose of committing the offence to leave the land. In both cases it is an offence to return within three months. Section 68 is aimed at anti-hunting protesters. It would not seem to cover passive protests such as refusing to move, although it would cover the forming of a human barricade. It is unclear whether the act of assembling on land in order to demonstrate would be an aggravated trespass.

5. *Harassment.* Under s.1 (2) of the Protection from Harassment Act 1997 a course of conduct (meaning conduct on at least two occasions) 'which amounts to the harassment of another and which the perpetrator knows or ought to know amounts to the harassment of another' is an offence. The test is whether a reasonable person in possession of the same information as the accused would think the conduct likely to cause harassment (s.1 (2). Harassment includes alarm and distress (s.7 (2)) and can also include 'collective' harassment by a group (Criminal Justice and Police Act 2001, s.44). There are defences of preventing or detecting crime, and acting under lawful authority. There is a broad defence of 'reasonableness' (s.1 (3)c). This would allow the press to claim that its duty to inform the public overrides the victim's right of privacy.

# Summary

▶ We first examined the justifications for freedom of expression and its general problems. These justifications concern the advancement of truth, the protection of democracy and the rule of law and also personal dignity. Press freedom is particularly important in a democracy. Freedom of expression involves the state not only abstaining from interference but in some cases, particularly in relation to the press, taking positive steps to protect freedom of expression.

▶ Freedom of expression may conflict with other rights, notably religious freedom and privacy. It may also be overridden by public interest concerns.

## Summary cont'd

▶ We distinguished between prior restraint (censorship) and punishments after the event. UK law has some direct censorship by the executive in relation to the broadcast and film media. More general powers of censorship are available by applying to the courts for injunction. We discussed the courts' wide powers of censorship by granting injunctions and in relation to s.10 of the Contempt of Court Act 1981. These may be too broad in the light of the Human Rights Act 1998.

▶ We discussed defamation which protects a person's interest in reputation, emphasising that public bodies are not protected by the law of defamation although, perhaps unjustifiably, individual public officials are. The protection of qualified privilege is available to the press although its scope is uncertain.

▶ English law has no distinct right of privacy which protects interests in self-esteem, dignity and autonomy. Breach of confidence covers some but not all of the ground. Protection for press freedom is based on establishing a public interest in disclosure. A governmental body must establish that secrecy is in the public interest.

▶ We discussed 'hate speech', including blasphemy, sedition and racism, pointing out that even in these cases there must be some tolerance of freedom of expression. In relation to blasphemy, English law is anomalous in privileging Christianity.

▶ We discussed the law relating to public meetings and processions. This sets freedom of expression and assembly against public order. This is characterised by broad police discretion, which does not require freedom of expression to be given special weight. This has not yet been tested against the Human Rights Act. A range of statutes responding to perceived threats has created various offences that restrict freedom of expression and give the police extensive powers to regulate public gatherings, and protests and lobbying by individuals and groups. The police also have wide common law powers to prevent breaches of the peace.

# Exercises

18.1 'Freedom of speech is a trump card that always wins' Lord Hoffmann. Does this reflect the present state of the law?

18.2 'In the context of religious opinion and beliefs may legitimately be included an obligation to avoid as far as possible expressions that are gratuitously offensive to others and thus an infringement of their rights, and which therefore do not contribute to any form of public debate capable of furthering progress in human affairs' *Otto Preminger Institut* v *Austria* (1994). Discuss the implications of this for freedom of expression.

18.3 'The common law recognises that there is a right for members of the public

to assemble together to express views on matters of public concern and I consider that the common law should now recognise this right which is one of the fundamental rights of citizens in this country is unduly restricted unless it can be exercised in some circumstances on the public highway' (Lord Hutton in *DPP* v *Jones* (1999)).
Discuss whether there is such a right and what are its limits.

18.4 To what extent do 'prior restraint' powers enable the courts to censor the media?

18.5 'A function of free speech is to invite dispute. It may indeed best serve its purpose when it induces a condition of unrest, creates dissatisfaction with conditions as they are and even stirs people to anger' (Mr Justice Douglas in *Terminiello* v *Chicago* 337 US 1 (1949)).
To what extent does English law protect 'hate speech'?

18.6 Freda, the leader of the Families for Freedom Council organises a procession followed by a meeting at a hall in the local university, hired for the occasion, to be addressed by the Prime Minister's spouse. The police learn that the Gay Rights Group plan to disrupt the event.

(i) Advise the local chief constable.

(ii) The meeting takes place and the Prime Minister's spouse praises the Families for Freedom Council as means of combating 'deviance'. The address is constantly interrupted by members of the Gay Rights Group. Joe, a policeman, hearing the commotion, enters the hall despite the protests of the doorman. The speaker refuses to obey Joe's order to leave and is arrested by Joe for 'obstruction'. Discuss what offences have been committed, if any, and by whom.

18.7 Newcottage Debating Society proposes to hold a public meeting in its premises addressed by a speaker from the Anti-Religion Syndicate. The address is to include a video screening illustrating a series of atrocities alleged to have been carried out by the Catholic Church. The local Catholic bishop wishes to stop the lecture taking place. Advise him.

18.8 Animal rights protesters are holding a continuous vigil in the road outside Tynbury docks. They threaten to prevent any vehicle carrying live animals from entering the docks. The local chief constable announces on television that his force has insufficient resources to police the docks and that any animal rights protester who approaches within one mile of the docks will be required to return home. Discuss the legal implications of this announcement.

18.9 The Socialist Workers Party distributes leaflets in a shopping mall in Westchester every Saturday morning. They include appeals to the armed forces to refuse to fight in Iraq, and to civil servants to strike against public spending cuts. One of the distributors of the leaflets is Jan, a US citizen. Last week security guards employed by the owners of the mall, an insurance company, ordered the leaflet distributors, including Jan, to leave and when they refused to do so removed them by force. Discuss the legality of these events.

18.10 The *Daily Rag* has prepared an article based upon interviews with a civil servant which accuses a government minister of taking bribes from city institutions. The ministers serves a writ for libel upon the publishers of the *Rag*. The minister requests the court to order the *Rag* to disclose the name of its informant, and also seeks an injunction preventing publication of the article on the ground that it will prejudice his proposed legal action. Advise the *Rag*.

# Further reading

Ghandi, S. and James, J. (1998) 'The English Law of Blasphemy and the European Convention on Human Rights,' *European Human Rights Law Review*, 430.

Lester, A. (1993) 'Freedom of expression', in MacDonald, R., Matscher, F. and Petzold, H. (eds) *The European System for the Protection of Human Rights,* Dordrecht, Nijhoff.

Loveland, I. (2003) *Constitutional Law, Administrative Law and Human Rights: a Critical Introduction*, 3rd edn, London, Butterworths, Chapters 18, 582–98.

Loveland, I. (1998) *Importing the First Amendment*, Oxford, Hart Publishing.

McCrudden, C. and Chambers, G. (1998) *Individual Rights and the Law in Britain*, Oxford, Clarendon Press, Chapters 2, 5, 8.

Nicolson, D. and Reid, K. (1996) 'Arrest for breach of the peace and the ECHR', *Criminal Law Review*, 764.

Whitty, N., Murphy, T. and Livingstone, S. (2001) *Civil Liberties Law: The Human Rights Act Era*, London, Butterworths, Chapters 2, 7, 8.

Williams, D.G.T. (1987) 'Processions, assemblies and the freedom of the individual', *Criminal Law Review*, 167.

# Chapter 19

# Exceptional powers: National security, state secrecy and emergencies

The words 'national security' have acquired over the years an almost mystical significance and the mere incantation of the phrase of itself instantly discourages the court from satisfactorily fulfilling its normal role of deciding where the balance of public interest lies. (Sir Simon Brown, 1994)

## Key words

▶ Minimum standards and safeguards
▶ Reduced role of courts
▶ Vague powers
▶ Domination of executive
▶ Reduced role of Parliament
▶ Fair trial

## 19.1 Introduction

The ideal of the rule of law requires that government powers be defined by clear laws and that there should be safeguards for individual freedom. Liberal democracy requires that laws be made by means of a democratic debate and that citizens should be fully informed as to what government is doing. As against this, the Hobbesian minimum duty of the state is to safeguard human life by keeping order. This may involve facing unpredictable events, working in secrecy and surrendering legal rights in favour of executive discretion. Political pressures may encourage a government to be perceived as taking decisive action to protect the people, thereby creating the incoherent claim that illiberal methods must be used to protect liberalism itself. Moreover, history tells us that governments may use the excuse of an emergency as a means of reinforcing their own positions.

Emergency laws risk violating the normal standards of the rule of law and democracy in several respects. For example:

▶ parliamentary scrutiny of legislation may be rushed or truncated
▶ vaguely defined powers such as the targeting of ill-defined groups because the needs of an emergency might favour flexibility. The judicial review doctrines that powers must be used reasonably and for

proper purposes may be frustrated by the wide terms in which the powers are conferred

▷ safeguards such as judicial review might be restricted in the interests of speed and certainty (Chapter 16)

▷ extreme measures may be taken for reasons of political propaganda (see e.g. *Brind* v *Secretary of State* (1991))

▷ requirements of secrecy in court proceedings

▷ disclosure of evidence in legal proceedings may be restricted, for example by allowing evidence taken by oppressive means, uncorroborated statements by anonymous informers or altering the burden of proof

▷ jury trial has been removed in some cases (Northern Ireland (Emergency Provisions) Act 1978)

▷ random stop and search powers

▷ intrusive surveillance

▷ extended powers of detention without going before a court

▷ minorities might be targeted on the basis that those who do not support majority 'liberal' values are a security risk. For example Lord Rooker, a Home Office minster, stated that:

> in a tolerant liberal society, if we are not guarded we will find that those who do not seek to be part of our society will use our tolerance and liberalism to destroy that society. (HL Deb. Nov. 27 2001, col. 143)

▷ measures originally introduced to meet an emergency becoming permanent.

The rhetoric of human rights that there must be a 'proportionate response' (Chapter 17) expresses a benevolent aspiration but does not rule out any particular violation of individual rights. The rhetoric of 'balancing' the interests of security and the rights of the individual is of limited assistance since there is no objective measure to tell us where the balance should be struck. This has led to famous judicial disagreements (e.g. *Liversidge* v *Anderson* (below)). See also Marshal J in *Skinner* v *Railway Labor Executives' Association* 489 US 602, 635-6) (1989):

> When we allow fundamental freedoms to be sacrificed in the name of real or perceived exigency, we invariably come to regret it.

A state can derogate or reserve from most of the European Convention on Human Rights in times of war or other public emergency threatening 'the life of the nation' (Art. 15). Article 2, right to life, cannot be derogated from except in respect of deaths resulting from lawful acts of war, nor can Arts 3 (torture and inhuman and degrading treatment), 4 (1) (slavery), or Art. 7 (retrospective punishment). However, the concepts of torture and inhuman and degrading treatment are vague and do not in themselves tell us where the limits of acceptable behaviour lie.

The state must show firstly that the threat is current or imminent, secondly that the threat must affect the whole population, involving a breakdown in the social fabric, thirdly that the measures do not go beyond a necessary response to the emergency, fourthly that other international obligations are not violated. There must also be the safeguard of judicial review by an independent court (*Chahal* v *UK* (1996)). However, protection ultimately depends on the extent to which the Court is prepared to accept the government's word as to the needs of the situation. The UK has partly derogated from the Convention (Art. 5, liberty and security) in order to enable it to imprison non-citizens suspected of terrorism without trial. In *A* v *Secretary of State* (2004), Lord Hoffmann held that fear of terrorist attack did not threaten the social fabric. The majority deferred to the government on this point but held that the derogation was discriminatory (below).

## 19.2 National Security and the Courts

The courts have traditionally been reluctant to interfere with national security matters. On the one hand, the European Court has emphasised the need for safeguards against abuse, as being necessary in a democratic society but, on the other hand, has given a wide margin of discretion and been reluctant to attribute improper motives to a government (see *Lawless* v *Ireland* (1961); *Klass* v *Germany* (1979); (*Malone* v *UK* (1984); *Aksoy* v *Turkey* (1996); *Brogan* v *UK* (1989)).

The high water mark is represented by the majority of the House of Lords in the wartime case of *Liversidge and Anderson* (1942). They held that the Home Secretary need not objectively justify a decision to intern an alien even though the statute required him to have 'reasonable cause'. Lord Atkin famously dissented, deploring judges

> who when face to face with claims involving the liberty of the subject show themselves more executive minded than the executive.

Lord Atkin was subsequently ostracised by his colleagues but is now widely recognised as having been right (*see* Lord Diplock in *R* v *IRC ex parte Rossminster* [1980] AC 952, 1011 and *M* v *Secretary of State* (below)). Nevertheless, review in national security cases is still restrained. In *CCSU* v *Minister for the Civil Service* (1985) the House of Lords held that the court can require evidence that the matter is genuinely one of national security but, subject to that, according to Lord Diplock, national security:

> is *par excellence* a non-justiciable question. The judicial process is totally inept to deal with the type of problems which it involves.

(See also *R* v *Secretary of State ex parte Hosenball* (1977); *R* v *Secretary of State ex parte McQuillan* (1995); *R* v *Secretary of State ex parte Adams* (1995); *Secretary of State* v *Rehman* (2002), emphasising the global dimension of national security).

The court could also interfere on the ground of perversity or bad faith although these would be difficult to establish (see *R* v *Secretary of State ex parte Cheblak* (1991)). In *R* v *Shaylor* (2002) the House of Lords emphasised that the courts would carefully scrutinise the proportionality of government restrictions on the freedom of expression of a member of the security services but nevertheless were willing to trust internal safeguards; Lord Hutton emphasised that good faith on the part of officials must be assumed (below).

In deciding whether an exceptional interference with a convention right is justified, the courts are particularly concerned with safeguards to prevent an abuse of power. These include clearly defined limits on the power, access to independent courts and a fair trial including legal advice, provision for special powers to expire within a limited time and proper supervision of the use of those powers. Any limits on democratic scrutiny must be temporary and should end automatically when the emergency is over. There is no commission to monitor human rights in Great Britain (unlike Northern Ireland) although proposals are currently being considered to introduce one. Recent illustrations of the attempt to strike a balance in a national security context are provided by *R (Gillam)* v *Metropolitan Police Commissioner* (below) and *M* v *Secretary of State* (below).

## 19.3 State Secrecy

Secrecy is justified under the European Convention on Human Rights particularly on the grounds of national security and the prevention of crime but subject to the existence of independent safeguards and the test of proportionality (see *Klass* v *Germany* (1979); *Kruslin* v *France* (1990)). The Convention gives states a wide margin of appreciation in relation to security matters and confidentiality has been held to be to be a legitimate state interest in that it advances the proper working of government (see *Ireland* v *UK* (1978); *Leander* v *Sweden* (1987); *Observer and Guardian Newspapers* v *UK* (1992). On the other hand in *McQuillan* (above), Sedley J pointed out that the English approach ignores the fact that not all national security considerations are necessarily of the same weight and importance.

The principle of open government might also be compromised in cases which go beyond emergencies. At one extreme, some necessary governmental functions, in particular police and intelligence work, and some negotiations with foreign governments could not be carried on without secrecy. In some circumstances economic information, such as possible policy changes, should not be prematurely disclosed so as not to distort the market. More questionable is the argument that publicity inhibits officials from communicating freely and frankly with each other. In cases where information cannot be disclosed, there should again be safeguards in the form of an element of independent adjudication and, where legal proceedings are involved, additional measures to ensure a fair trial.

There are two aspects to state secrecy. The first concerns a public right of access to information held by government. Our private law traditions mean that the basic position is that no such right exists. The state is the Crown not the people (Chapter 4) and just like a private person can control its own information. For example, ministers and senior civil servants agree to subject any memoirs they propose to publish to vetting by the Cabinet Office:

> All information obtained by virtue of office is regarded as held for the State and not for the benefit of the office holder or the interested reader. (Cmnd 6386, 1986, para. 62)

Apart from cases where the principles of natural justice apply (Chapter 15), the common law gives no right to information. Indeed in *Burmah Oil* v *Bank of England* [1980] AC 1090 at 1112, Lord Wilberforce did not believe that the courts should support open government. There are however certain statutory rights to information of which the Freedom of Information Act 2000 is the most general. This came into force in 2005. On the other hand there are also particular doctrines such as public interest immunity in litigation and the absence of a general duty to give reasons for government action (Chapter 15) that reinforce state secrecy.

The second aspect of secrecy concerns claims by the state to suppress information held by others such as the media. Here the state is interfering with common law rights and also the right of freedom of expression under Art. 10 of the European Convention on Human Rights. The onus is therefore on the state to justify its intervention. In relation to government information, secrecy is re-enforced by statutes, notably the Official Secrets Act 1989, forbidding disclosure of certain information, by the civil law of breach of confidence, and by employment contracts. There is also a culture of voluntary secrecy generated by the priority of efficiency over accountability and partly perhaps by the psychological condition of persons holding public office who may be disposed towards self-importance and tribalism. Contemporary policies of privatisation and encouraging public bodies to follow commercial practices, including 'commercial confidentiality', also militate against openness in favour of a protective, defensive culture.

Access to government information as such is not protected by the ECHR. Article 10 has been said to protect people who wish to disclose information and does not force anyone to do so (see *Leander* v *Sweden* (1987)). However, this takes no account of the democratic interest in the free flow of information which the ECHR has recognised in the context of press freedom (above, Chapter 18). There may however be a right to information, under Art. 6 (right to a fair trial) and Art. 8 (respect for family life; see *Gaskin* v *UK* (1990) – adoption records; applied restrictively in *Gunn-Russo* v *Nugent Care Housing Society* (2001)).

In addition to general concerns about freedom, arguments in favour of 'open government' include the following:

▶ *Democracy:* officials should be accountable to a well-informed public opinion.
▶ *Autonomy:* people should be able to exercise informed choice in relation to their own affairs.
▶ *Justice:* in being able to correct false information.
▶ *Direct public participation:* in decision making as an end in itself.
▶ *Public confidence:* in government.

Arguments in favour of government secrecy are primarily efficiency based and include the following:

▶ Release of certain kinds of information might cause serious harm, for example national security, crime prevention, child care and some economic information.
▶ Expense and delay, bearing in mind that seekers of information may be cranks, enemies or maniacs.
▶ Freedom of information could weaken ministerial responsibility to Parliament.
▶ Frankness within government, for example the danger of policy making being inhibited by premature criticism or the quality of debate being diluted by the temptation to play to the gallery.
▶ Public panic if disclosures are misunderstood.
▶ Vanity and self–protection by public officials without which it might be more difficult to make public appointments.
▶ The mystique of government emphasised by Bagehot as a source of stability (see Chapter 3).

### 19.3.1  The Freedom of Information Act 2000

Subject to many exemptions, the Act requires public authorities to disclose information on request and also to confirm or deny whether the information exists (s.1). This is supervised and enforced by an Information Commissioner who also has advisory and promotional functions. The Information Commissioner will also supervise a Code of Practice on Access to Government Information and approve publication schemes. The Act does not prevent an authority from disclosing any information (s.78).

The scope of the Act is potentially wide. Under Sched. 1, central government departments (but not the Cabinet, the royal household or the security services), Parliament, the Welsh Assembly (but not the Scottish government), local authorities, the police, the armed forces, state educational bodies and NHS bodies are automatically public authorities as is a long list of other specified bodies including companies which are wholly owned by these bodies (s.6). The Secretary of State may also designate other bodies, office holders or persons as public authorities which appear to him to be exercising 'functions of a public nature' or who provide services under a contract with a public authority, the functions of which include the provision of that service (s.3 (1)). This might include for example a voluntary body acting on behalf of a government agency. The Secretary of State can however limit the kind of information that the listed bodies can disclose (s.7).

The Act gives a right to any person to request in writing (s.8), information held by the authority on its own behalf or held by another on behalf of the authority (s.3 (2)). The person making the request is entitled to be told whether or not the authority possesses the information (duty to confirm or deny) and to have the information communicated to him (s.1 (1)). Reasons do not normally have to be given for the request. However, disclosure can be refused if the applicant has not provided such further information as the authority reasonably requires to enable the requested information to be found (s.1), although the authority must provide reasonable advice and assistance (s.16). A request can also be refused if the cost of compliance exceeds a limit set by the Secretary of State or where the request is vexatious or repetitive (s.14). A fee regulated by the Secretary of State can be charged (s.9). The authority must respond promptly and within 20 working days (s.10). However, if the matter might involve an exemption there is no time limit other than a 'reasonable' time to make a decision. Thus the right is far from absolute and there is considerable scope for bureaucratic obfuscation.

The Information Commissioner can require the authority to disclose information either on his own initiative (enforcement notice, s.52), or on the application of a complainant whose request has been refused (decision notice, s.50). Reasons must be given for a refusal and the Commissioner can, where appropriate, inspect the information in question and also require further information. An authority can refuse to disclose to the Commissioner any information which might expose it to criminal proceedings other than proceedings under the Act itself. Both sides may appeal to the Information Tribunal on the merits, with a further appeal to the High Court on a point of law (s.57). The right to information can be enforced by the courts through the law of contempt but no civil action is possible (s.56).

The right to information under the Act is subject to many exemptions contained in Part II. These apply both to the information itself and usually to the duty to confirm or deny. Most are blanket exemptions for whole classes of information. Some require a 'prejudice' test relating to the particular document. However, this is less onerous for the government than the 'substantial prejudice' that was originally envisaged (White Paper, 1997).

Some exemptions are absolute, those that are not absolute are subject to a public interest test (below). The absolute exemptions are as follows:

▶ information which is already reasonably accessible to the public even if payment is required (s.21);
▶ information supplied by or relating to the intelligence and security services (s.23). A minister's certificate is conclusive subject to an appeal to the Tribunal by the Commissioner or the applicant, which in respect of the reasonableness of the decision is limited to the judicial review grounds (s.60);
▶ information contained in court records widely defined (s.32);
▶ information protected by parliamentary privilege (s.34);
▶ information that would prejudice the conduct of public affairs in the House of Commons or the House of Lords (s.36);
▶ certain personal information, although some of this is available under the Data Protection Act 1998 (s.40 (1)(2));
▶ information the disclosure of which would be an actionable breach of confidence (s.41);
▶ information protected by legal obligations such as legal professional privilege or European Law (s.44).

In other cases the exemption applies only where it appears to the authority that 'the public interest in maintaining the secrecy of the information outweighs the public interest in disclosure' (s.2 (1)b). The balance is therefore tipped in favour of disclosure. However, because this test is subjective, the Commissioner's powers may be limited to the grounds of judicial review. The main exemptions of this kind are as follows:

▶ information which is held at the time of request with a view to be published in the future (s.22). No particular time for publication need be set although it must be reasonable that the information be withheld;
▶ information required for the purpose of safeguarding national security. There is provision for a minister's certificate as under s.23 (above);
▶ information held at any time for the purposes of criminal proceedings or investigations which may lead to criminal proceedings or relate to information provided by confidential sources (s.30). This would include many inquiries into matters of public concern;
▶ information the disclosure of which would or would be likely to prejudice defence, foreign relations, relations between the UK devolved govern-

ments, the House of Commons or the House of Lords, law enforcement widely defined to include many official inquiries, the commercial interests of any person including the public authority holding the information, or the economic interests of the UK. Nor does the duty to conform or deny arise in these circumstances (ss. 26, 27, 28, 29, 31);

- audit functions;
- communications with the royal family;
- health and safety matters;
- environmental information (this is subject to special provisions (below);
- information concerning the 'formulation or development' of government policy (s.35). This also includes all communications between ministers, cabinet proceedings, advice from the law officers and the operation of any ministerial private office. It also seems to include advice from civil servants. However, once a decision has been taken statistical background can be released;
- information held by government departments, and the Welsh Assembly not covered by s.35 above and information held by any other public authority which 'in the reasonable opinion of a qualified person' would or would be likely to prejudice collective ministerial responsibility or which would or would be likely to inhibit 'free and frank' provision of advice or exchange of views or 'would otherwise prejudice or be likely to prejudice the effective conduct of public affairs' (s.36). This would again ensure that civil service advice remains secret. A 'qualified person' is the minister or other official in charge of the department. Because the test is subjective it appears that the Commissioner would have no power to intervene except where the qualified person's decision was 'unreasonable'. A question here would be whether the minimal *Wednesbury* version of unreasonableness would apply.

Ministers also have power to veto the Commission's enforcement powers. In the case of information held by the central government, the Welsh Assembly and other bodies designated by the Secretary of State, an 'accountable person' (a cabinet minister, or the Attorney-General or their equivalents in Scotland and Northern Ireland) can serve a certificate on the Commissioner 'stating that he has on reasonable grounds formed the opinion' that there was no failure to comply with the duty to disclose the information (s.53). Reasons must be given and the certificate must be laid before Parliament. The certificate would also be subject to judicial review.

### 19.3.2    Other Statutory Rights to Information

There are certain statutory rights to information held by the government. They are characterised by broad exceptions and weak or non-existent enforcement mechanisms. None of them gives access to the contemporary inner workings of the central government. The most important of them are as follows:

▶ Historical records (see Cm 853, 1991). These are, subject to exceptions, made available after 30 years (Public Records Acts 1958, 1967, 1975). The 1993 White Paper on open government (Cm 2290) proposed that records be withheld beyond 30 years only where actual damage to national security, economic interests or law and order can be shown, or if disclosure would be a breach of confidence or cause substantial distress or danger. At present many records are subject to blanket exclusion. The Freedom of Information Act 2000 removes exemptions for communications within UK government departments, court records, decision making and policy formation, legal professional privilege and trade secrets contained in historical records. Information relating to honours is to be protected for 75 years and law enforcement matters for 100 years.

▶ Personal information held on computer or in structured manual records (Data Protection Act 1998). However, the Act exempts much government data including national security matters, law and tax enforcement matters and data 'relating to the exercise of statutory functions'.

▶ Local government information. The Local Government (Access to Information) Act 1985 gives a public right to attend local authority meetings including those of committees and sub-committees and to see background papers, agendas, reports and minutes. There are large exemptions which include decisions taken by officers, confidential information, information from central government, personal matters excluded by the relevant committee, and 'the financial or business affairs of any person'. The Act appears to be easy to evade by using officers or informal groups to make decisions. It is not clear what counts as a background paper.

▶ The Public Bodies (Admission to Meetings) Act 1960 gives a right to attend meetings of parish councils and certain other public bodies. The public can be excluded on the grounds of public interest (see *R* v *Brent Health Authority ex parte Francis* (1985)).

▶ The Access to Personal Files Act 1987 authorises access to local authority housing and social work records by the subject of the records and in accordance with regulations made by the Secretary of State (see also Housing Act 1985 s.106 (5)).

▶ The Environmental Information Regulations 1992 (SI 1992 no. 320) implementing EC Directive (90/313) require public authorities to disclose certain information about environmental standards and measures. The information must be made available on request, but there are no specific requirements as to how this is to be done. A charge can be made. Requests can be refused on grounds including manifest unreasonableness or a too-general request (how does a citizen know what to ask for?), confidentiality, increasing the likelihood of environmental damage, information voluntarily supplied unless the supplier consents, international relations, and national security. Under the Aarhus Convention, *Access to Information, Public Participation and in Decision Making and Access to Justice in Environmental Matters* (1998, Cm 4736) the government is required to make regulations giving a general right to environmental information subject to exceptions on public interest grounds. These will replace the present regulations and be integrated into the machinery of the Freedom of Information Act 2000 under s.74 of that Act (see also HL 9 1996–97, *Freedom of Access to Information on the Environment*).

## 19.4 Unlawful Disclosure of Government Information

### 19.4.1 The Official Secrets Act 1989: Criminal Law

The Official Secrets Act 1989 protects certain kinds of government information from unauthorised disclosure. It was enacted in response to long-standing and widespread criticism of the Official Secrets Act 1911 s.2 which covered all information, however innocuous, concerning the central government (see Franks Committee Report, Cmnd 6104, 1972). A series of controversial prosecutions culminated in the *Ponting* trial in 1995 where a civil servant who gave information to an MP concerning alleged governmental malpractice during the Falklands war was acquitted by a jury against the judge's summing up. Section 2 required the Crown to show that the disclosure was not made under a duty to the 'state'. The judge emphasised that civil servants owed absolute loyalty to ministers and held that the 'state' meant the government of the day (see Chapter 4), thus making it clear the 'public interest' could not justify disclosure. However, Ponting's acquittal meant that the government could no longer resist reform.

Section 1 of the 1911 Act, which concerns spying activities remains in force but section 2 has been repealed. The Official Secrets Act 1989 is narrower but more sharply focused. It identifies four protected areas of government activity and provides defences which vary with each area. The aim is to make enforcement more effective in respect of the more sensitive areas of government. In each case it is an offence to disclose information without 'lawful authority'. In the case of a Crown servant or 'notified person' (above) this means 'in accordance with his official duty' (s.7). In the case of a government contractor, lawful authority means either with official authorisation, or disclosure for the purpose of his functions as such, for example giving information to a sub-contractor. In the case of other persons who may fall foul of the Act, for example a former civil servant, lawful authority means disclosure to a Crown servant for the purpose of his functions as such (s.7 (3)a, s.12 (1)), for example to a minister, the Metropolitan Police Commissioner, or the Director of Public Prosecutions but not a Member of Parliament since these are not Crown servants. Alternatively, lawful authority means in accordance with an official authorisation presumably by the head of the relevant department (ss7 (3)b, 7 (5)). The protected areas are as follows:

1. *Security and intelligence* (s.1). This applies (i) to a member or former member of the security and intelligence services; (ii) to anyone else who is 'notified' by a minister that he is within this provision; (iii) to any existing or former Crown servant or government contractor. In the cases of (i) and (ii) any disclosure is an offence unless the accused did not know and had no reasonable cause to believe that the information related to security or intelligence. The nature of the information is irrelevant. In the case of (iii) the disclosure must be 'damaging' or where the the information or document is of a kind where disclosure is likely to be damaging (s.1 (4)). However, 'damaging' does not concern the public interest generally but means only damaging to 'the work of the security and intelligence services'. This might include, for example, informing MPs that security agents are breaking the law. It is a defence that the accused did not know and had no reasonable cause to believe that the disclosure would be damaging.

In *R v Shaylor* (2002) the House of Lords held that Section 1 did not violate the right to freedom of expression. The accused, a former member of the security services, had handed over documents to journalists which, according to him, revealed criminal behaviour by members of the service, including a plot to assassinate President Gadiffi of Libya. His motive was to have MI5 reformed in order to remove a public danger. The House of Lords held that the interference with the right to freedom of expression was proportionate. The main reason for this was that the restriction was not absolute. It allowed information to be released with 'lawful authority' (above), thereby inviting the claimant to approach a range of 'senior and responsible crown servants' such as the Metropolitan Police Commissioner and the Security and Intelligence Commission [103]. The consent of the Attorney-General is required for a prosecution although, again, it is questionable whether this provides independence (Chapter 6).

Lord Hutton [99]–[101] went further than the others in emphasising that the need to protect the secrecy of intelligence and military operations was justified as a 'pressing social need' even where the disclosure was not itself harmful to the public interest (c.f. Lord Scott [120]). This was to protect confidence in the security services both among its own members and those who dealt with them. Moreover, an individual whistleblower may not be sufficiently informed of the consequences of his actions. Lord Hutton [105–106] also rejected the argument that senior officials or politicians might be reluctant to investigate complaints of wrongdoing, holding that the court must assume that the relevant legislation is being applied properly. By contrast Lord Hope asserted [70] that 'institutions tend to protect their own and to resist criticism from wherever it may come'.

Their Lordships also emphasised the safeguard of judicial review and that a reviewing court would apply a strong proportionality test to a refusal to authorise disclosure. Lord Bingham emphasised [34] that he could not envisage circumstances where disclosure would be refused to a qualified lawyer on a claimant's behalf even where this had to be limited to a special counsel appointed by the court (see also Lord Hope [73], Lord Hutton [108]–[116]). However, the courts have always given a wide margin of discretion in security matters (Chapter 14).

The Court of Appeal had left open the possibility that a defence of necessity might apply to the Official Secrets Act 1989. This would apply only in extreme circumstances where disclosure was needed to avert an immediate threat to life or perhaps property. The House of Lords did not comment on this issue.

2. *Defence* (s.2). This applies to any present or former Crown servant or government contractor. In all cases the disclosure must be damaging. Here damaging means hampering the armed forces, leading to death or injury of military personnel, or leading to serious damage to military equipment or installations. A similar defence of ignorance applies as in (1).

3. *International relations* (s.3). Again this applies to any present or former Crown servant or government contractor. Two kinds of information are covered: (i) any information concerning international relations; (ii) any confidential information obtained from a foreign state or an international organisation. The disclosure must again be damaging. Damaging here refers to endangering the interest of the UK abroad or endangering the safety of British citizens abroad. The fact that information in this class is confidential in its 'nature or contents' may be sufficient in itself to establish that the disclosure is damaging (s. 3(3)). There is a defence of ignorance on the same basis as in (1) (s. 3(4)).

4. *Crime and special investigation powers* (s.4). This applies to present or former Crown servants or contractors and covers information relating

to the commission of offences, escapes from custody, crime prevention, detection or prosecution work. 'Special investigations' include telephone tapping under a warrant from the Home Secretary, and entering on private property in accordance with a warrant under the Security Services Act 1989 (see below). Section 4 does not require that the information be damaging as such because damage is implicit in its nature. There is however a defence of 'ignorance of the nature' of the information (s.4 (4)(5)).

Section 5 makes it an offence to pass on protected information, for example by the press. Protected information is information falling within the above provisions which has come into a person's possession as a result of (i) having been 'disclosed' (whether to him or another) by a Crown servant or government contractor without lawful authority; or (ii) entrusted to him in confidence; or (iii) disclosed to him by a person to whom it was entrusted in confidence. This does not seem to cover someone who receives information from a *former* Crown servant or government contractor. If this is so, the publisher of the memoirs of a retired civil servant may be safe although the retired civil servant himself will not (but see *Lord Advocate* v *Scotsman Publications* (1990) where s.5 was applied). Nor does the section seem to apply to a person who accidentally finds protected information (for example a civil servant leaves his briefcase in a restaurant). Could this be regarded as a 'disclosure'? It is an offence for a Crown servant or government contractor not to look after the protected information and for anyone to fail to hand it back if officially required to do so (s.8).

The Crown must prove that the accused knew or had reasonable cause to believe that the information was protected under the Act and that it came into his possession contrary to the Act. In the case of information in categories 1, 2 and 3 (above) the Crown must also show that disclosure is 'damaging' and that he knew or had reasonable cause to believe that this was so.

### 19.4.2 Civil Liability: Breach of Confidence

As we saw in Chapter 18, information given in confidence can be prevented from publication by means of an injunction. As a legal person the Crown is free to take advantage of this. However, a public authority must show positively that secrecy is in the public interest, which the court will balance against any countervailing public interest in disclosure. Conversely a public authority can rely on a public interest in disclosure in order to override private confidentiality even where the information has been given only for a specific purpose (see *Hellewell* v *Chief Constable of Derbyshire* (1995); *Woolgar* v *Chief Constable of Sussex* (1999).

An action for breach of confidence may be attractive to governments since it avoids a jury trial, can be very speedy and requires a lower standard of proof than in a criminal case. Indeed under the common law, a temporary injunction, which against the press may destroy a topical story, could be obtained from a judge at any time on the basis merely of an arguable case (*A-G v Guardian Newspapers* (1987)). However s.12 of the Human Rights Act 1998 (see Chapter 18) may have shifted the balance.

In *A-G v Guardian Newspapers Ltd (No. 2)* (1990) (*Spycatcher*), the House of Lords in principle supported the interests of government secrecy. Peter Wright, a retired member of the security service, had published his memoirs abroad revealing possible malpractice within the service. Their Lordships refused to grant a permanent injunction but only because the memoirs were no longer secret, having become freely available in Britain. It was held that, in principle, publication was unlawful and that the Crown could probably obtain compensation from Wright and from newspapers in respect of publication in the UK before the memoirs had been published abroad. This was confirmed by the ECHR as proportionate. In *Observer and Guardian v UK* (1992)) the ECHR, with a strong dissent from Morenilla J, held that in the area of national security an injunction is justifiable to protect confidential information even where the content of the particular information is not in itself harmful (see also *Sunday Times (No. 2) v UK* (1992); *AG v Jonathan Cape* (1975)).

*Spycatcher* also confirmed that members of the security services have a 'lifelong duty of confidence'. In *AG v Blake* (1998), a former civil servant had been convicted of spying but escaped to Moscow where he published his memoirs. The House of Lords held that, even though the content of the memoirs created no danger to national security and were no longer confidential, Blake was liable to account for his royalties to the government on the ground that he should not be permitted to profit from his wrong.

The exposure of 'iniquity' (serious wrongdoing or crime) by government officers can justify disclosure (see e.g. *Lion Laboratories v Evans* (1985)). In *Spycatcher*, serious iniquity was not established and it remains to be seen whether 'iniquity' overrides national security. The method of disclosure must be reasonable and the discloser must probably complain internally before going public (*Francombe v Mirror Group Newspapers* (1984)). This suggests that a high standard of evidence is required given that *Spycatcher* involved allegations of criminal activity against security service members including a plot to destabilise the Labour government.

It is often suspected that a common response by UK officials to those who disclose official wrongdoing is to punish the whistleblower rather than condemn the wrongdoer (see Committee on Standards in Public Life, consultation paper, 2003, *Getting the Balance Right*). For example Steve

Moxon, a civil servant who had revealed irregularities in the processing of immigration visas to the press leading to the resignation of the responsible minister, was dismissed for 'an irretrievable breakdown in trust' (*Independent* 2 August 2004).

The Public Interest Disclosure Act 1998 (Employment Rights Act 1996 Part 4A) protects employees against unfair dismissal in certain cases. 'Qualifying disclosures' are those which the whistleblower reasonably believes relate to the commission or likelihood of commission of any of the following: criminal offences, breaches of legal duties, miscarriages of justice, danger to health and safety or danger to the environment. Internal disclosure in good faith to an employer or responsible superior is protected and also disclosure to a minister or to a person prescribed by a minister. However, there is no protection where the disclosure is an offence, for example under the Official Secrets Act 1989 (above), and employees working in national security areas can be excluded (s.11). Exceptionally, an employee can make a disclosure to another person or even to the press. However this must be 'reasonable' and applies only where either the matter is exceptionally serious or the discloser reasonably believes either that s/he will be victimised or that evidence will be concealed, or there is no prescribed person or the matter has already been disclosed to the employer. In the public sector the Act has mainly been used by National Health Service employees of whom in the first three years of the Act some 25% reported reprisals.

### 19.4.3 Public Interest Immunity

An important aspect of government secrecy concerns the doctrine once called 'Crown privilege' and now known as 'public interest, immunity' (PII). A party to a legal action is normally required to disclose relevant documents and other evidence in his possession, but where public interest immunity applies, documents and the information in them need not be disclosed. In deciding whether to accept a claim of public interest immunity the court is required to 'balance' the public interest in the administration of justice against the public interest in confidentiality. At one time the courts would always accept the government's word that disclosure should be prohibited. However, as a result of *Conway* v *Rimmer* (1968) the court itself does the balancing exercise.

Public interest immunity applies both to civil and criminal proceedings (see Criminal Procedure and Investigations Act 1996 ss3 (6), 7 (5)). Any person can raise a claim of public interest immunity. Claims are often made by ministers following a well-established procedure involving advice from the Attorney-General, ostensibly acting independently of the government. It appears that a minister is not under a duty to make a claim even if he believes that there is a public interest at stake but must personally do an initial balancing exercise. In *R* v *Brown* (1993) the court emphasised that it was objectionable for a minister automatically to accept the Attorney's advice. Other persons are probably required to put forward the claim to the court or to hand the matter to a minister (see *R* v *West Midlands Chief Constable ex parte Wiley* (1994)).

Where a PII certificate is issued the person seeking disclosure must first satisfy the court that the document is likely to be necessary for fairly disposing of the case, or in a criminal case, of assisting the defence, a less difficult burden (see *Air Canada* v *Secretary of State* (1983); *Goodridge* v *Hampshire Chief Constable* (1999); Criminal Procedure and Investigations Act 1996 s.3). The court can inspect the documents at this stage but is reluctant to do so in order to discourage 'fishing expeditions' (see *Burmah Oil Co. Ltd* v *Bank of England* (1980)).

The court will then 'balance' the competing public interests involved, at this stage inspecting the documents. Grounds for refusing disclosure include national security, the protection of anonymous informers or covert surveillance operations (*Rogers* v *Home Secretary* (1973); *D.* v *NSPCC* (1978)); financially or commercially sensitive material, in particular communications between the government and the Bank of England and between the bank and private businesses (*Burmah Oil Co. Ltd* v *Bank of England* (1980)), the protection of children, and relationships with foreign governments. It has also been said that preventing 'ill-informed or premature criticism of the government' is in the public interest (*Conway* v *Rimmer* [1968] AC 910 at 952). There is no automatic immunity for high level documents such as cabinet minutes but a specially strong case would have to be made for their disclosure (see *Burmah Oil* v *Bank of England* (1980) and *Air Canada* v *Secretary of State* (1983)).

The desire to protect candour and frankness within the public service is probably not a sufficient justification (*Conway* v *Rimmer* (above) at 957, 976, 993–4, 995); *R* v *West Midlands Chief Constable* (above); *Williams* v *Home Office* (No. 2) [1981] 1 All ER 1151 at 1155; *Science Research Council* v *Nasse* [1980] AC 1028 at 1970, 108: candour a 'private' interest; but see *Burmah Oil* v *Bank of England* [1980] AC 1090 at 1132). The courts also consider the purpose for which the information was given. Information given in confidence for a particular purpose will not be disclosed for another purpose unless the donor consents in circumstances where disclosure would not be harmful to the public interest (*R* v *West Midlands Chief Constable* (1994); *Lonrho* v *Fayed* (No. 4) (1994); c.f. *Peach* v *Metropolitan Police Commissioner* (1986): nothing to lose).

A distinction is often made between 'class claims' and 'contents' claims. Under a class claim, even if the contents of a document are innocuous, it should still be protected because it is a member of a class of document of which disclosure would prevent the efficient working of government, such as policy advice given by civil servants or diplomatic communications. In *R v West Midlands Chief Constable* (above) it was claimed that evidence given to the police complaints authority was protected by class immunity. The House of Lords rejected this blanket claim, holding that immunity depended on whether the contents of the particular document raised a public interest, which on the facts they did not. It is not clear whether the notion of a class claim as such survives this decision since their Lordships rejected the claim only in relation to that particular class of document. However, Lord Templeman remarked (at 424) that the distinction between a class and a contents claim loses 'much of its significance'.

A successful public interest immunity claim means that there is unfairness to the individual which is outweighed by other more important concerns. Moreover, before the Human Rights Act, at least in civil cases, the court did not give special weight to the interests of justice but applied a balance of probabilities test. In both respects, therefore, public interest immunity may violate the right to a fair trial in Art. 6 of the ECHR, (see *Borgers* v *Belgium* (1991)). Article 6 contains no overrides except to the extent that the press or public may in certain circumstances be excluded from a trial. Indeed in *R v DPP ex parte Kebeline* (2000), Lord Bingham, remarked that 'I can conceive of no circumstances in which, having concluded that that feature rendered the trial unfair, the court would not go on to find a violation of Art. 6'. In *Kostovski v The Netherlands* (1989), the European Court of Human Rights refused to allow the state to protect the anonymity of witnesses. It applied a test of whether the exclusion placed the accused at a substantial disadvantage. The Court emphasised that the right to a fair trial 'cannot be sacrificed to expediency'.

Nevertheless public interest immunity has been held not to violate the Convention provided that the trial overall is 'fair' (*Edwards* v *UK* (2003); *Rowe* v *UK* (2001); *Jasper* v *UK* (2000); *Fitt* v *UK* (2000)). In *R v H and C* (2004), Lord Bingham asserted that PII must 'never imperil the overall fairness of the trial'. However, unless the information to be protected is trivial or irrelevant, it is difficult to see how PII can be anything other than a departure from fairness.

In *R v H and C* (above) the House of Lords specified principles that must be applied, at least in a criminal case, to minimise unfairness. The government must show a pressing social need which cannot be met by less intrusive means. The parties must be given an opportunity to argue the reasons for the claim in open court and also for the procedure to be adopted. However, this may not be possible without revealing the information itself. *As a last resort* the court can appoint a special advocate who acts on the accused's behalf and might see the material without disclosing it to the parties. However, this device creates serious ethical problems relating to the confidence inherent in the lawyer client relationship. As much as possible of the material must be disclosed although there may be extreme cases where it cannot be revealed even that a PII application is being made. Where a criminal conviction is likely to be unsafe as a result of PII the trial must probably be discontinued. Lord Bingham remarked that it is axiomatic that if a person charged with a criminal offence cannot receive a fair trial he should not be tried at all.

## 19.5 Security and Covert Surveillance

Although privacy as such may not be a specific right in English law, privacy is protected by Art. 8 of the ECHR (see *Wainright* v *Home Office* (2003); *R* v *Khan* (1996)). Public authorities exercising statutory powers must therefore weigh privacy against the overrides contained in Art. 8 according to the proportionality principle. The overrides to Art. 8 are wide. They include national security, public safety or the economic well-being of the country, the prevention of disorder or crime, the protection of health or morals and the protection of the rights and freedoms of others. Moreover, both national security and public order attract a wide margin of discretion (Chapter 17).

### 19.5.1 The Security and Intelligence Services

The 'secret services' comprise the security services, the intelligence services and the government communications centre, GCHQ. Traditionally they have operated under the general law without special powers other than the possibility of royal prerogative power. They were in principle accountable to ministers, ultimately to the Prime Minister, but there was no formal mechanism for parliamentary accountability. Their role has been primarily that of information gathering. Where powers of arrest or interference with property were required, the assistance of the police was requested. However the 'Spycatcher' litigation (above) brought to a head recurrent concerns that security agents were out of control and unaccountable and they have now been placed within a statutory framework. This relies heavily on the discretionary powers of ministers but contains certain safeguards, albeit judicial review is restricted.

The security services (formerly MI6) deal with internal security (Security Services Act 1989, 1996). They report to the Prime Minister. Their responsibilities include 'the protection of national security and, in particular, its protection against threats from espionage, terrorism and sabotage, from the activities of agents of foreign powers, and from actions intended to overthrow or undermine parliamentary democracy by political or violent means' (s.1). Section 1(3) includes the safeguarding of 'the economic well-being of the UK against threats posed by the actions or intentions of persons outside the British Islands'. This is extremely wide and could extend for example to the lawful activities of environmental NGOs. The Security Services Act 1996 extends the functions of the security services to include assisting the police in the prevention and detection of serious crime. This includes the use of violence, crimes resulting in substantial financial gain, or conduct by a large number of persons in pursuit of a common purpose or crimes carrying a sentence of three years or more. This is wide enough to include political public order offences and industrial disputes and may violate ECHR notions of clarity and proportionality.

The intelligence services (formerly MI5 and GCHQ, Intelligence Services Act 1994) deal with threats from outside the UK. They are under the control of the Foreign Office but also report to the Prime Minister. Their functions 'to obtain and provide information relating to the actions and intentions of persons outside the British Islands' and 'to perform other tasks relating to the actions and intentions of such persons'. Reflecting the European Convention on Human Rights their powers are limited to national security, with particular reference to defence and foreign policies, the economic well-being of the UK in relation to the actions and intentions of persons outside the British islands and the prevention and detection of serious crime (ss. 1(2), 3(2)). GCHQ monitors electronic communications and 'other emissions' and can provide advice and information to the armed forces and other organisations specified by the Prime Minister.

### 19.5.2 Covert Surveillance

This involves Art. 8 of the European Convention on Human Rights (privacy). The problem of the state amassing information about its citizens is of increasing concern because of computer technology which enables large amounts of information to be stored, collated, speedily accessed and transferred without apparent safeguards. Thus proposals innocuous in themselves, such as the introduction of identity cards, are viewed with suspicion, not only because of the risk of abuse of power but also because of the risk of errors and accidents.

Under the common law there was no right to privacy and therefore, provided that no trespass occurred, telephone tapping and other covert listening devices were lawful (*Malone* v *Metropolitan Police Commissioner* (1979)). However, the European Court of Human Rights held that although covert surveillance was not unlawful in itself, there must be safeguards. These must include clearly defined limits on the power and supervision by an independent court (*Malone* v *UK* (1984); *Khan* v *UK* (2001)).

The Interception of Communications Act 1985, now largely incorporated into the Regulation of Investigatory Powers Act 2000 (RIPA), attempted to respond to the European Convention on Human Rights. RIPA includes telephone tapping, and intercepting electronic data such as emails and websites. It also creates significant new powers of surveillance by making clear that certain forms of interception and uses of information are lawful, including bugging devices. It also regulates covert human intelligence such as undercover agents and imposes duties on communication providers, such as internet service providers, to cooperate with the authorities.

The circumstances in which these powers can be exercised reflect the European Convention on Human Rights, in particular the concept of proportionality and the overrides affecting the right to privacy (see e.g. ss 5, 15, 32, 49, 74). These include national security, the prevention and detection of serious crime, the safeguarding of the economic well-being of the country and, in the case of conduct other than interception, the safeguarding of public health, public safety, tax collection, emergencies protecting life and health and 'other purposes specified by the Secretary of State' (s.22).

Without lawful authority (below) and subject to certain exceptions, it is an offence at any place in the UK to intercept any communication intentionally in the course of its transmission by a public postal service or a public telecommunications system (s.1 (1)). It is also an offence to intercept a private telecommunication system, for example the internet, without the consent of the controller of the system (s.1 (2)(6)). However, in this case there may be civil liability to both the sender and the recipient of a message if it is intercepted without lawful authority (below) (s.1 (3)).

'Lawful authority' (s.1 (5)) means:

(i)   the consent of both sender and recipient of the message or reasonable grounds for belief in such consent (s.3 (1))
(ii)  either the sender or the recipient has consented in relation to a secret surveillance operation authorised under Part II of the Act (below), for example intercepting a kidnapper telephoning the relatives of a hostage (s.3 (2))
(iii) interceptions for the purposes of monitoring of postal or telecommunications services by their provider (s.3 (3))
(iv)  interceptions in connection with lawful interceptions overseas in accordance with regulations made by the Secretary of State (s.4 (1))
(v)   interceptions in accordance with regulations made by the Secretary of State concerning business practices (s.4 (2)) and under other regulations relating to prisons and high security mental hospitals
(vi)  interceptions under a warrant issued by the Secretary of State (s.5).

As regards the Secretary of State's warrant, unlike ordinary search warrants, no prior judicial authority is required. The heads of the security and intelligence services, the national criminal intelligence service, defence intelligence, chief constables and the commissioners of Customs and Excise can apply for warrants (s.6). The power is subject to restrictions and safeguards based on the European Convention on Human Rights. The Secretary State must believe that the warrant is necessary on prescribed grounds (national security, the prevention and detection of serious crime (s.81 (3)). He must apply a proportionality test, and 'consider the possibility' that the information could reasonably be obtained by other means (s.5 (4)) He must ensure that the information is exposed and used as little as possible and destroyed once it has been used (s.15).

In addition, under ss 5 and 6 of the Intelligence Services Act 1994 and the Security Services Act 1996 s.2 (2), 'no entry on or interference with property or wireless telegraphy shall be unlawful' if authorised by a warrant from the Secretary of State, usually in person. A warrant can be issued to the security service relating to property inside and outside the UK if the Secretary of State thinks it necessary to take the proposed action in order to obtain information because (i) it is likely to be of substantial value in assisting the service to discharge any of its functions; and (ii) there is no reasonable alternative. The Secretary of State must also be satisfied that satisfactory arrangements are in force to prevent use of the information except for the authorised purposes of the Acts.

The obtaining and use of 'communications data' can be authorised by a wide range of police and other public officials (RIPA Part 1, Chapter 2)). Communications data does not include the content of a message as such but includes 'traffic information' such as billing data and the source and destination. The Anti-terrorism, Crime and Security Act 2001 Part II extends this power in order to require communications providers, such as internet service providers, to make archived communications data available which can be trawled through at leisure.

Controversially, RIPA empowers anyone in lawful possession of intercepted information to require the disclosure of the key to protected (encryptified) data on the grounds of national security, serious crime and, more dubiously, that it is necessary for the performance of a public function (s.49). The UK is the only leading democracy to allow this. A disclosure notice must be authorised by a circuit judge who must be satisfied that there is no other means of obtaining the required information and that the direction is proportionate to what is sought to be achieved. In the case of a company the notice must be served on a senior officer or employee (s.49 (5)) and the Secretary of State must contribute to the cost of compliance (s.51). A disclosure notice requested by the police, the security services or the customs and excise commissioners can also contain 'tipping-off' provisions imposing a life-long secrecy requirement as to the existence of the notice (s.54).

In general English law permits unlawfully obtained evidence to be admitted in court subject to a test of reliability, (Police and Criminal Evidence Act 1984 s.78; *Schenk* v *Switzerland* (1988); *R* v *Sang* (1979)). However, evidence cannot normally be given suggesting that there has been telephone tapping, lawful or otherwise (RIPA ss17, 18). In *R* v *Preston* [1993] 4 All ER 638, 670, Lord Mustill recognised that 'Parliament has grasped the nettle and put secrecy first'. Information obtained by telephone tapping cannot therefore be used as evidence in court (ibid., see also *Morgans* v *DPP* (2000)). However, the Act only applies to telephone tapping in the UK and information obtained from overseas surveillance can be used (*R* v *P* (2001)). It has also been held that information obtained from telephone tapping can be used in police interviews and presumably by the executive for other purposes (*R* v *Sargent* (2003)).

Information obtained by bugging devices, CCTV and undercover agents can however be used in court (*R* v *Khan* (1996)). In *J.H. Ltd* v *UK* (2001) the European Court held that bugging in a police station, although not contrary to internal UK law, without safeguards was a violation of the right to privacy (see also *Halford* v *UK* (1997)): employer; *Khan* v *UK* (2001): police suspect). Part II of RIPA 2000 extends authorisation provisions to the customs and excise, security, intelligence and military services. It also provides for the authorisation of covert surveillance by human agents such as informants or undercover agents. Surveillance by human agents (covert human intelligence sources) is not unlawful as such, although without authorisation it is vulnerable to challenge under the Human Rights Act 1998 because of the absence of safeguards.

Under RIPA 'directed surveillance' and the use of covert human intelligence sources can be authorised by the numerous public officials on a wide range of grounds subject to proportionality (s.28, s.29). 'Directed surveillance' does not involve the presence of the agent on residential premises, hotel bedrooms or in a private vehicle or the use of a bugging device. 'Intrusive surveillance' does involve these features. In the case of the police and the customs, intrusive surveillance can be authorised only by heads of the relevant services on the grounds of national security, the prevention and detection of serious crime and the economic well-being of the UK subject to proportionality (s.32). The consent of a surveillance commissioner (below) is required (s.36). In the case of the intelligence services, the Ministry of Defence and the armed forces, authorisation is by the Home Secretary with no further consents. It appears therefore that bugging devices can be used without authorisation only in public places or non-residential establishments.

The use of covert surveillance devices by the police is also regulated by the Police Act 1997 and the two regimes overlap. Authorisations to interfere with property by planting and removing bugging devices can be given by a chief of a police force or other equivalent officials (s.93) where the investigation concerns serious crime, and the action proposed is proportionate (ss 91, 93). Authorisation by a surveillance commissioner is required in the case of residences, hotel bedrooms, legal privilege, specified personal information and journalistic information (s.97).

### 19.5.3 Safeguards

The ordinary courts are largely excluded. There are limited independent safeguards in relation to the use of the above powers. The Director General of the relevant service is responsible as both poacher and gamekeeper for the efficiency of the service, and for making 'arrangements' for securing that information is neither obtained or disclosed 'except in so far as is necessary for the proper discharge of its functions' or, in the case of disclosure, for the prevention or detection of serious crime. The services must not take action to further the interests of any political party (Security Service Act 1989 52 (2), Intelligence Services Act 1994 s.2 (3)).

Independent scrutiny takes the form of commissioners for intelligence services, interception of communications, and surveillance who review the exercise of the various powers of investigation and use of material under the legislation (Regulation of Investigatory Powers Act 2000, ss 57, 59, Police Act 1997). The commissioners, who must be senior judges, can report to the Prime Minister at any time. The Prime Minister must lay their annual reports before Parliament.

There is also an Intelligence and Security Committee, composed of backbench members of Parliament, which examines the spending, administration and policy of the intelligence services (Intelligence Services Act 1994 s.11). However, this is appointed by and reports to the Prime Minister and is not strictly speaking a committee of Parliament with a duty to Parliament itself. Its annual report is laid before Parliament but can be censored by the Prime Minister after consultation with the committee. Its members are subject to the Official Secrets Act 1989 as 'notified persons' (above).

RIPA also creates a unified Investigatory Powers Tribunal to hear allegations of misuse of power by the security and intelligence services and also in relation to the interference with property, interception of communications, covert surveillance or misuse of information by the police and other bodies (s.65). The tribunal is also concerned with claims based on human rights for which it is made the only forum for actions against a public body under section 7 of the Human Rights Act 1998. The tribunal may award compensation, and make other orders including quashing warrants or authorisations and ordering records to be destroyed (ibid.). The tribunal is required to apply judicial review principles (s.67). In view of the wide powers involved, this affords only a low level of review although it probably satisfies the ECHR. However, decisions of the tribunal and the commissioners (above) cannot be questioned in the courts even on jurisdictional grounds (Intelligence Services Act 1994 s.5 (4); RIPA s.67 (8)), a provision that might violate the European Convention on Human Rights (see Chapter 16).

The tribunal must refer a complaint about interference with property to a commissioner who must then investigate. If a warrant has been issued, the commissioner is banned from probing any deeper than would a court applying judicial review principles (ibid.). The commissioner reports back to the tribunal (Schedule 1(4)(2)). In the case of the intelligence services, the tribunal may, where it does not decide in favour of the complainant, refer a matter to the commissioner where it thinks it appropriate for there to be an investigation into 'whether the service has in any other respect acted unreasonably in relation to the complainant or his property'. The commissioner may then report to the Secretary of State who can make an award of compensation (Schedule 1(7)).

## 19.6 Emergency Powers

There is a range of exceptional powers that can be triggered in an emergency. In some countries this device has been used in order to justify military or other authoritarian rule. Emergencies may involve a breakdown of public order or essential services or a grave external threat. An emergency might be caused by, for example, a general strike, a natural disaster or a terrorist threat but the measures to be taken to safeguard life and health may not comply with normal expectations of fair procedures nor make nuanced moral distinctions possible.

Public order has high priority as one of the underlying values of English law. As we saw in Chapter 18 the police have a general power to prevent a breach of the peace. There is no legal obstacle to the armed forces being used in support of this provided that the force used is no more than is reasonable in the circumstances for self-defence or the defence of others (see Criminal Law Act 1967 s.3). Indeed, everyone has a right and perhaps a duty to aid the civil power in quelling a disturbance (*Charge to the Bristol Grand Jury* (1832)). Under the royal prerogative the armed forces can be deployed at the discretion of the Crown and the Crown can also arm the police (Chapter 12). The Crown may also enter private property in an emergency but must pay compensation for any damage caused other than in wartime (War Damage Act 1965; *Saltpetre Case* (1607); *Attorney-General* v *De Keyser's Royal Hotel* (1920)). The Secretary of State for Defence is politically accountable to Parliament for the use of these powers.

In law an individual policeman or soldier is liable for the excessive use of force, thus illustrating the strict application of the rule of law. In deciding what is reasonable the court will take into account the pressure of the circumstances (see *Attorney-General for Northern Ireland's Reference (No.1)* (1975); *McCann* v *UK* (1995)). However obedience to orders as such is probably not a defence (*Keighley* v *Bell* (1866)).

Beyond this there is the possibility that, where there is such a serious disruption to public order that the courts cannot function, the military may assume control under a state of martial law. However Dicey denied that martial law is part of English law (1915, Chapter 8) although the concept has been used and indeed extended to a case where the courts were still sitting in relation to colonial territories (*Marais* v *General Officer Commanding* (1902)). Martial law was declared in Ireland in 1920 and the House of Lords accepted the possibility that the courts could in principle control the activities of the military under martial law (*Re Clifford and O' Sullivan* (1921)). It is arguable that the principle of martial law is no more than an application of the broad doctrine of necessity which justifies the deployment of the armed forces. The courts are unlikely to interfere with the such decisions (*Chandler* v *DPP* (1964); Chapter 14).

The executive also has statutory powers in an emergency (Civil Contingencies Act 2004). An emergency means:

> an event or situation which threatens serious damage to human welfare or the environment in the United Kingdom or in a Part or region, or war or terrorism which threatens serious damage to the security of the United Kingdom, (s.19 (1))

These threats are widely drawn. Human welfare includes loss of life, illness or injury, homelessness, property damage, disruption of supplies of money, food, water, energy and fuel, disruption of a communication system, facilities for transport or health services. Environmental damage is limited to biological chemical or radioactive contamination or disruption to or destruction of plant or animal life (s.19 (2) (3)).

Regulations can be made by Order in Council (or, if this would cause serious delay, by a senior minister) if the relevant person is satisfied that an emergency exists or is imminent, that there is an urgent need to deal with it and that existing legislation is inadequate for the purpose (ss 20, 21). Parliament must meet within five days and the regulations lapse unless approved by Parliament within seven days. They lapse in any event after 30 days but in both cases can be renewed (ss 26, 27).

Intended to modernise the law, the Act allows ministers to alter statutes and it confers wider powers to interfere with individuals, including the power to deploy the armed forces, to require people to perform unpaid functions and to provide information, the power to ban travel and assemblies and the power to take property without compensation (s.22). There are safeguards based on the principles underlying the European Convention on Human Rights. These include tests of proportionality and compliance with Convention rights. The powers can be used only for the specific purpose of dealing with the threats created by the emergency. There can be no military conscription nor outlawing industrial action. No offence can be created except one triable summarily by magistrates or the Sheriff's Court in Scotland nor punishable with more than three months' imprisonment. Criminal procedure cannot be altered nor the Human Rights Act 1998 (s.23). Judicial review is not specifically presented but 'regard' must be had to its importance (s.22 (5)).

## 19.7 Anti-terrorism Measures

The UK's anti-terrorism laws originated as an emergency response to the conflict in Northern Ireland (Northern Ireland (Emergency Provisions) Act 1978 and the Prevention of Terrorism (Temporary Provisions) Act 1974). These Acts created new offences and wider police powers to investigate terrorist activity associated with Northern Irish paramilitary organisations. These were additions to ordinary criminal law but they could only be used in cases involving terrorism and no other forms of crime. Two sets of legislation created inconsistency and there were extra powers and provisions for Northern Ireland which did not exist in the rest of the UK. These included additional powers of search, arrest and detention, the introduction of trial by a judge alone and powers to detain without trial. Between 1973 and 2000 the Acts were repeatedly extended and modified, and in 1984 the Prevention of Terrorism Act was extended to include international terrorism. With the advent of the peace process in Northern Ireland, a review was undertaken to reconsider the powers required to counter terrorism in the 21st century. The 1996 Lloyd Report (Cm 3420) recommended wide-ranging changes, including the harmonisation of counter-terrorism laws across the UK, the expansion of these powers to all domestic and international terrorism, and a new definition of terrorism. Many of these recommendations were enacted in the Terrorism Act 2000 (TA). This new legislative regime was expanded upon in the Anti-terrorism, Crime and Security Act (ATCS) 2001 passed in the wake of September 11th. The ATCS is highly controversial and limits human rights and civil liberties in a number of ways, most notably in the wide discretion it confers with only limited duties to justify action, thus challenging basic assumptions of liberalism and the rule of law. The hasty and panic-fuelled manner in which the ATCS came into being exemplifies the single most important theme to emerge from the UK's anti-terrorism legislation: the prioritisation of government discretion over human rights, civil liberties and other liberal freedoms. On the other hand, in keeping with one of the fundamental safeguards against misuse of emergency powers, the Act contains 'sunset provisions' under which its measures expire automatically after a prescribed time (see e.g. s.29: 15 months).

### 19.7.1 Legal Definition of Terrorism

In the UK's anti-terrorism laws there are very wide additional police powers to investigate, arrest, and detain (below). They depend upon the criminal acts being investigated falling within the definition of terrorism. In addition it is an offence in itself to belong to or to support a proscribed organisation (Terrorism Act 2000 ss11, 12). Proscribed organisations are listed in the Terrorism Act 2000 or have the same name as one listed. They mainly include Irish and Islamic organisations but also include Basque separatists, the Tamil Tigers, the International Sikh Youth Federation and the Kurdistan Workers Party. The Secretary of State can add to the list any other organisation which he believes is 'concerned in terrorism' (Terrorism Act 2000 s.3). He does not apparently have to show reasonable grounds for his belief. There is a right of appeal to the Proscribed Organisations Appeal Tribunal against a refusal by the Secretary of State to remove an organisation from the list, but this is limited to the grounds of judicial review (s.5). There is a further appeal but only with permission to the Court of Appeal (s.6). The tribunal is appointed by the Lord Chancellor and includes an appellate court judge. The Lord Chancellor can make rules permitting its proceedings to be in secret and of evidence to be withheld from the parties and their representatives (Sched. 3).

Apart from other forms of support such as funding (s.15) a person supports terrorism who addresses a meeting with the purpose of encouraging support for a proscribed organisation or furthering its activities or who arranges or helps to arrange a meeting (of three or more persons) which he knows supports or furthers the activities of a proscribed organisation or which is addressed by a person who belongs to or professes to belong to a proscribed organisation, irrespective apparently of the subject of the meeting (s.12). In the case of a *private* meeting there is a defence that the person has no reasonable cause to believe that the address would support a proscribed organisation or further its activities. There are therefore serious restrictions on freedom of expression.

There is a duty to inform the police of suspicions that a person has committed any of these offences. This applies to information which has come to the informer's attention in a business, trade, professional or employment context but excludes profession legal privilege (s.19).

The definition of terrorism in section 1 of the Terrorism Act 2000 is complex and, 'sweepingly broad and extraordinarily vague' (per Richards J in R

*(Kurdistan Workers Party)* v *Secretary of State for the Home Department* (2002) EWHC 644). It has three constituent elements. Firstly, there must be an act or the threat of an action that falls into one of five categories: (i) serious violence against a person; (ii) serious violence against property; (iii) endangers life; (iv) creates a serious risk to the health or safety of the public or a section of the public; (v) seriously disrupts or interferes with an electronic system. The threat of these actions is sufficient to classify an act as terrorism and violence is only a necessary component in categories (i) and (ii). Secondly, the action must be intended to advance a political, religious or ideological cause. Thirdly, the action must be designed to influence the government, or coerce the public or a section of it. This includes the use or threat for the purpose of advancing a political, religious or ideological cause of action which involves serious violence against persons or property. Vague concepts such as 'threat,' 'ideological', 'violence' and 'safety' mean that terrorism might include campaigning organisations such as parents' groups. Moreover it is not necessary for the action to be carried out on UK soil, against a UK citizen or property owned by a UK citizen. The openness of this definition means that attacks or threats against any government anywhere in the world can be investigated by British police. Moreover, people resident in the UK who are active political agitators against other states can fall within the terrorism legislation. Thus, it is possible that the TA could be used to police international politics, raising grave questions of traditional liberties.

The breadth of the definition has led to criticism because it could potentially be applied to situations where the low threat of violence does not justify the use of specialised powers and offences (see Walker, C. *Terrorism and Political Violence*, 2000 **12**(2): 1–36, 11–12). During the Terrorism Bill's passage through Parliament Jack Straw, the Home Secretary, conceded that the definition allowed a large area of discretion to the enforcement agencies and the courts over which individuals, activities and organisations could be proceeded against (HC Deb. 1999–2000 vol. 341 col. 162). Similarly the Home Office stated that it would be up to the courts to decide the limits of the new definition (Standing Committee D 18.01.2000 col. 22). Hence, the implementers of the legislation, the police and the courts, establish the legislation's boundaries rather than Parliament. Given the breadth of the definition, the police will have a very significant role in deciding who is or is not a terrorist.

## 19.7.2  Powers of Search, Arrest and Detention

The problems that the wide definition of terrorism raises for human rights are demonstrated well by the use of search, arrest and detention powers under the Terrorism Act 2000:

▶ Under ss 44 and 45 of the Terrorism Act 2000, a policeman can stop and search at random within a designated area for articles of a kind that could be used in connection with terrorism. Reasonable ground need not be shown. By contrast, except after an arrest, search powers normally require a warrant specifying the nature of the material to be searched for (see Police and Criminal Evidence Act 1984 Part II). In *R (Gillam)* v *Metropolitan Police Commissioner* (2004) a policeman used this power against a student demonstrating against an arms sale fair supported by the government. The Court of Appeal held that, in view of the exceptional threat to the public from terrorists, this power satisfied Art. 8 of the European Convention on Human Rights. However, the court emphasised that this was so only because the Act provided safeguards against abuse. These include a requirement that a senior officer designate the area in question, a requirement for confirmation by the Home Secretary and a provision that the order has a limited life of 28 days. Moreover, the police must use the power circumspectly and only in relation to terrorism. The police were unable to satisfy the court that this was so.

▶ A constable may arrest without warrant a person whom he reasonably suspects to be a terrorist (s.41). This is a very wide power because, unlike ordinary powers of arrest, it does not tie the arrest powers to the suspicion of a specific offence (*R* v *Officer in Charge of Police Office Castlereagh Belfast ex parte Lynch* (1980)). Moreover, and significant in the context of liberal values of human dignity, the officer does not need to disclose to the arrestee all of the grounds for his suspicions (*Oscar* v *Chief Constable RUC* (1992)). Once the person has been arrested he or she can be detained for questioning without charge for up to two weeks (Sched. 8 as amended by Criminal Justice Act 2003 s.306). To detain a person for longer than 48 hours, permission must be granted by a magistrate if the police believe detention is necessary to obtain or preserve evidence and the investigation is being conducted diligently and expeditiously (ibid.), but again the police investigation does not need to be tied to a specific crime.

The power to detain without charge originated in the Prevention of Terrorism (Temporary Provisions) Act 1989 s.14 under which police could detain a suspect for up to seven days with permission from the Home Secretary. In *Brogan* v *UK* (1989) the European Court of Human Rights held this power to be in breach of the Convention because seven days was too long a period to detain without charge. The court decided that a suspect should be brought before a judicial authority within a maximum of four days of arrest. The UK then derogated from the European Convention on Human Rights. The Terrorism Act was intended to end this difficulty. Accordingly, the new detention power requires a suspect to be presented before a judicial authority within the specified four-day period and is therefore in accordance with a strict legal interpretation of the judgement. However, the continued ability to detain a suspect for up to seven days flouts the intention of the ruling. This narrow interpretation of the European Court of Human Rights' ruling reveals the state's ambivalence towards protecting terrorist suspects' human rights.

There is also indefinite detention without trial. After the attack in America on 11 September 2001 the Home Secretary introduced a large number of new anti-terrorism provisions in the Anti-terrorism, Crime and Security Act 2001. The most controversial of these has been the new power in s.21 and s.23 to indefinitely detain without charge a person whom the Home Secretary certifies as being a 'suspected international terrorist'. This means a foreign national whose presence in the UK the Home Secretary reasonably believes is a risk to national security and whom he reasonably suspects is a terrorist (in this context 'terrorist' means a person who 'is or has been concerned in the commission, preparation or instigation of acts of international terrorism') or whom he believes to be a member of an international terrorism organisation or to have links with such an organisation (s.21). When the Secretary of State issues a certificate, that person can be detained pending deportation, even if their deportation is prevented by legal or practical considerations (s.23).

There is a right of appeal (s.25) to the Special Immigration Appeals Commission (SIAC). This three-person tribunal includes a senior judge, a senior immigration adjudicator and a person with experience of national security matters (Special Immigration Appeals Commission Act 1997). It can sit in private and can withhold evidence from the appellant and his or her lawyers. There is a further appeal to the Court of Appeal on a point of law but the Act purports to exclude other judicial review (s.30, Chapter 16).

To introduce this power the UK has had once again (on the basis that there is an emergency) to derogate from its obligations under the European Convention on Human Rights (Human Rights Act 1998 (Designated Derogation) Order 2001, (S.I. 2001/3644). However in *A v Secretary of State* (2004) the House of Lords held by an 8 to 1 majority that the derogation was too wide to be proportionate to the emergency, this being the threat from *Al-Quaeda*, and also that it was discriminatory in singling out foreign nationals. The House quashed the derogation order and issued a declaration of incompatibility in relation to sections 21 and 23. It is not clear at the time of writing what action Parliament proposes to take. The government claims that these powers are necessary because of *Chahal v UK* (1996) in which the European Court held that a non-national could not be deported to a country where there was a real threat that he or she would be subject to torture, inhuman or degrading treatment. The UK's position was that *Chahal* had made it impossible to deal with suspects who were too dangerous to be at large, but yet against whom no criminal charges were brought.

In *M* v *Secretary of State for the Home Department* (2004) the Court of Appeal required the Secretary of State to show that he has properly considered all relevant factors. The appellant was a Libyan asylum seeker, a member of an organisation devoted to opposing the regime of Colonel Gaddafi. There was evidence that some members of the appellant's organisation might be involved with *Al Qaidar*, a proscribed organisation, but none linking the appellant himself with *Al Qaidar*. The Court of Appeal held that the SIAC was justified in overturning the Home Secretary's certificate. It was not enough to show suspicious circumstances. The Home Secretary had to take a broad overall view based on all the circumstances and supported by evidence. However, the court endorsed the process itself. Lord Woolf remarked ([2004] 2 All ER 863 at 868) that the undoubted unfairness involved in this secretive procedure can be necessary because of the interests of national security but that so far as possible the disadvantage must be avoided or, if it cannot be avoided, minimised. In particular, the claimant's interests might be represented by a special advocate appointed by the court who can test and object to evidence and to the need for secrecy. However, the special advocate has no duty to give information to the claimant nor to take instructions from the claimant.

The courts accept that the Home Secretary is entitled to entirely rely upon 'closed' evidence, that the defendant is prohibited from seeing on the basis of national security (*A* v *Secretary of State* (above)). If closed material is under consideration the Commission will sit as a closed court. This does not sit comfortably with the earlier case of *Murray* v *United Kingdom* (1994) which held that Secretary of State must not use 'closed material' as the only source for suspicion.

The quality of the evidence is less than that required in a criminal court. In *A* v *Secretary of State for the Home Department* (2004) the Court of Appeal (Neuberger LJ dissenting) held that the Home Secretary does not have to investigate the validity of every statement he relies upon in order to assess whether it was made in circumstances that would amount to torture, degrading or inhuman treatment. The court thought that, given the broad judgements which had to be made, it would be unrealistic for the Secretary of State to investigate every statement and undesirable to investigate the conduct of other friendly governments. It is not clear, however, whether the Secretary of State can take into account evidence which he knows has been obtained by torture. In an ordinary criminal court, statements made under torture, or degrading and inhuman treatment are strictly inadmissible, and it was situations like this that led to famous miscarriages of justice, such as the convictions of the Guildford Four and Birmingham Six. Indeed, a recent review of the implementation of the legislation suggests that the government is overplaying the threat to the suspects if deported in order to detain them (see *Anti-terrorism, Crime and Security Act 2001, Part IV Review by Lord Carlile of Berriew*, February 2003).

### 19.7.3  Parliament's Hierarchy of Human Rights

Parliamentarians who maintain that counter-terrorism legislation in the UK is necessary have had to reconcile the harshness of the legislation with the principles of democratic freedom. There seems to be no objective way of 'balancing' these competing concerns other than by public opinion. A major aim of the Lloyd Review in 1996 (above) was to create a balance between individual rights and the public interests in developing security needs and anti-terrorism measures. However, during the debates the Government stated that it believed that some rights ought to be accorded more protection than others. According to Lord Bassam, HL Deb. 1999–2000 vol. 611 col. 1482):

> In bringing forward permanent UK-wide legislation, the government recognise a responsibility to achieve the balance between protecting the human rights of individual citizens and protecting the public against terrorism ... Terrorism is a fundamental threat to human rights. In seeking to use violence and fear instead of democratic means, it strikes at the heart of the foundations of government. In taking care to guard the rights of the individual to a fair trial, to freedom of association and expression, and so on, it is important to us to remember at all times the need to guard the rights of the public to go about their everyday, lawful lives free from the fear of terrorist attack or the paralysing hold that terrorist groups can have over communities.

The British government's argument proposes that human rights and liberal freedoms must be understood in a hierarchy of rights, with some rights being accorded more worth than others. In *A* v *Secretary of State* (2004), Lord Hoffmann in particular regarded personal freedom as fundamental. Freedom of property and privacy might be regarded as less important. The right to a fair trial is particularly difficult since it has been whittled away without making clear what its irreducible minimum might comprise. Access to independent courts and to independent legal advice might be so regarded but these rights may be futile if evidence can be withheld. Proportionality indicates that infringements of human rights are acceptable as long as the extent of the threat justifies those infringements (Lloyd Report para. 3.1) but this is no more than rhetoric.

The argument that anti-terrorism legislation necessitates a hierarchy of rights has also found support amongst academic commentators (see Hogan, G. & Walker, C., *Political Violence and the Law in Ireland*, Manchester University Press, 1989, pp. 171–2; Robertson, K.G., 'Intelligence, Terrorism and Civil

Liberties', *Conflict Quarterly*, 7, pp. 43–62; Wilkinson, P., *The International Library of Terrorism, vol. 1. Terrorism: British Perspectives*, Dartmouth, 1993, pp. 303–22). For example, Hogan and Walker (op. cit. pp. 95–6) argued that the legislative response ought to be graduated. They concluded that even the power to intern without trial ought to be retained but that it should:

> be used most sparingly because it entails the grossest infringement of procedural rights and liberty as well as special status for those held. Therefore, the device should be a last resort – special policing powers and lesser executive measures [exclusion] should take priority. Even then, internment should be treated as a short-term palliative, to be taken only while the security forces are strengthened.

Donohue notes that this treatment of human rights as a hierarchy of more important and lesser rights is one reason why this nominally emergency and temporary legislation has become embedded in British law (*Counter-Terrorist Law and Emergency Powers in the United Kingdom 1922–2000*, Irish Academic Press, 2001, pp. 331–40). She also notes that it may partly be because the legislation adheres to the trappings of parliamentary processes and legal forms that it has slowly become accepted. The widely framed arrest powers, the associated detention powers and indefinite detention without trial of non-nationals began their lives being regarded as draconian and distasteful yet have come to be seen as necessary.

The most common criticism of the anti-terrorism legislation is that it is too wide and capable of including non-violent persons whose activities are disliked by the government. It may inflame the conditions that it is intended to alleviate. Indeed it has been widely recognised that:

> situations involving mass and flagrant violations of human rights and fundamental freedoms ... may give rise to international terrorism and may endanger international peace and security. (UN General Assembly Resolution, A/RES/40/61, (1985), 9 December 1985, para. 9)

From the Hobbesian perspective, the state's overriding and primary duty is to ensure security even at the cost of liberal freedoms, but the UK's security-driven response to terrorism and to other special powers might be part of the disease it is attempting to cure.

# Summary

▶ The courts give the executive a wide margin of discretion in relation to security matters. Under the European Convention on Human Rights there is also a wide margin and states can derogate from some of its provisions in the event of an emergency. However, the courts protect fundamental rights by requiring safeguards, in particular independent judicial supervision.

▶ There is no general right to the disclosure of governmental information. There is a voluntary code subject to many exceptions, and the government proposes

## Summary cont'd

to introduce a freedom of information bill where information must be disclosed unless to do so would be harmful. Again there are exceptions.

▶ There are certain statutory rights to the disclosure of specified information, but these are outnumbered by many statutes prohibiting the disclosure of particular information.

▶ The Freedom of Information Act 2000 confers a right to 'request' the disclosure of documents held by public authorities. However, this can often be overridden by the government and is subject to many exceptions, particularly in relation to central government policy. The Act is not yet in force.

▶ Under the Official Secrets Act 1989 certain categories of information are protected by criminal penalties. Except in the case of national security, the information must be damaging. There is also a defence of ignorance.

▶ The law of confidence requires the court to balance the public interest in 'openness' against the public interest in effective government. The balance is struck differently according to context. The courts have endorsed the importance of freedom of expression and a public body is required to show a public interest in secrecy. The main remedy is an injunction. Third parties such as the press are not directly bound by an injunction but might be liable for contempt of court if they knowingly frustrate its purpose.

▶ Public interest immunity allows the government to withhold evidence. The court makes the decision on the basis of balancing the public interest in the administration of justice against the public interest in effective government. The courts' approach to public interest immunity is affected by the Human Rights Act 1998 which requires that any claim satisfies the proportionality principle and preserves the essentials of the right to a fair trial.

▶ The security and intelligence services are subject to a certain degree of control, largely outside the ordinary courts.

▶ There is regulation of electronic and other forms of surveillance by the police and other law enforcement agencies, also outside the ordinary courts. The overlapping regimes of the Police Act 1997 and the Regulation of Investigatory Powers Act 2000 give the government wide powers of interception and surveillance, subject to procedural safeguards and to limits derived from the European Convention on Human Rights as to permissible purposes and proportionality.

▶ In an emergency the police, supported by the armed forces may take action to keep the peace and can use reasonable force in self-defence and the defence of others. It is questionable whether martial law as such is part of English law. There are statutory provisions giving the executive wide powers to deal with an emergency. These are subject to limitations concerned with basic rights and to control by Parliament. The Civil Contingencies Bill increases the scope of emergency powers, subject to safeguards based on the European Convention on Human Rights.

# Exercises

**19.1** To what extent is the law relating to government secrecy affected by the Human Rights Act 1998?

**19.2** 'We have moved from a discretionary open government regime under a voluntary Code of Practice to a statutory open government regime in which the power to decide what is to be disclosed lies within the discretion of government and is denied to independent bodies' Nigel Johnson (2001), *New Law Journal* 151, p. 1031).
Explain and discuss critically.

**19.3** Tony, a United States citizen, and Gordon, a UK citizen, are arrested by the police on suspicion of being associated with an international terrorist group. The police discover that certain incriminating information which they received from the United States was probably extracted from Tony by torture. Gordon is released but Tony is detained under a certificate issued by the Home Secretary stating that he is suspected of being a terrorist. Tony demands to see the evidence against him and also claims that it cannot be used against him. He also asks for a lawyer but the request is refused.
Discuss.

**19.4** Derek, a civil servant in the Department of Health, believes that the cabinet minister in charge of his department has been ordering government statisticians to alter the latest National Health Service performance figures in order to show that government policies are bearing fruit. Derek gives this information to the editor of the *Daily Whinge* who contacts the relevant minister for his comments. The Attorney-General immediately applies for a temporary injunction and commences an action for breach of confidence against Derek. Derek requests the production of letters between civil servants and the minister (the existence of which he learned from an anonymous email) which he claims would support his version of events. The government issues a PII certificate on the ground that the information is in a category the disclosure of which would inhibit free and frank discussion within the Cabinet. The minister who signed the certificate did not examine the information personally but relied on advice from the Attorney-General that the 'certificate will cover us for all cabinet level documents'.

(i) Advise Derek.

(ii) Advise the Attorney-General whether he should prosecute Derek under the Official Secrets Act.

**19.5** 'Terrorist threats and actions test the Executive's commitment to the rule of law and good governance. Because of the extreme powers given by such extraordinary legislation, there is an incumbent requirement to provide limits to its terms, scope and life span.' Thomas 'Emergency and Anti-Terrorist Powers 9/11: USA and UK', 2003, *Fordham International Law Journal*, **26**(4): 1993)'. Does the current law meet these requirements?

## Further reading

*Counter Terrorist Powers: Reconciling Security and Liberty in an Open Society* (2004) Cm 6147.

Leigh, I. and Lustgarten, L. (1991) 'The Security Commission: Constitutional Achievement or Curiosity?', *Public Law*, pp. 215–32.

Newton Committee of Privy Counsellors, *Anti-Terrorism Crime and Security Act 2001 Review* (2003 HC 100).

Oliver, D. (1998) 'Freedom of Information and Ministerial Accountability', *Public Law*, 171.

Palmer, S. (1990) 'Tightening Secrecy Law', *Public Law*, 243.

Scott, Sir R. (1996) 'The Acceptable and Unacceptable Uses of Public Interest Immunity', *Public Law*, 427.

Simon Brown, L.J. (1994) 'Public Interest Immunity', *Public Law*, 579.

Uglow, S. (1999) 'Surveillance and the European Convention on Human Rights', *Criminal Law Review*, 287.

White Paper, (1997) *Your Right to Know: Freedom of Information*, Cm 3818.

Whitty, N. Murphy, T. and Livingstone, S. *Civil Liberties Law: The Human Rights Act Era*, London, Butterworth, Chapters 3, 7.

# Index